ROUTLEDGE
STUDENT STATUTES

Family Law Statutes

2011–2012

'Focused content, layout and price – Routledge competes and wins in relation to all of these factors' – *Craig Lind, University of Sussex, UK*

'The best value and best format books on the market' – *Ed Bates, Southampton University, UK*

Routledge Student Statutes present all the legislation students need in one easy-to-use volume. Developed in response to feedback from lecturers and students, this book offers a fully up-to-date, comprehensive, and clearly presented collection of legislation – ideal for LLB and GDL course and exam use.

Routledge Student Statutes are:

- **Exam Friendly:** un-annotated and conforming to exam regulations
- **Tailored to fit your course:** 80% of lecturers we surveyed agree that *Routledge Student Statutes* match their course and cover the relevant legislation
- **Trustworthy:** *Routledge Student Statutes* are compiled by subject experts, updated annually and have been developed to meet student needs through extensive market research
- **Easy to use:** a clear text design, comprehensive table of contents, multiple indexes and highlighted amendments to the law make these books the more student-friendly Statutes on the market
- **Competitively Priced:** *Routledge Student Statutes* offer content and usability rated as good or better than our major competitor, but at a more competitive price
- **Supported by a Companion Website:** presenting scenario questions for interpreting Statutes, annotated web links, and multiple-choice questions, these resources are designed to help students to be confident and prepared.

Phil Bates is Lecturer in Law at The Open University, where he is the module team chair for the new course 'W224: Relationships, Families and the Law'. He has taught Family Law and Child Law at the University of Reading, King's College London, and the University of Buckingham.

ROUTLEDGE STUDENT STATUTES

Titles in the series:

Company Law Statutes 2011–2012
MARC MOORE

Contract, Tort and Restitution Statutes 2011–2012
JAMES DEVENNEY AND HOWARD JOHNSON

Criminal Law Statutes 2011–2012
JONATHAN HERRING

Employment Law Statutes 2011–2012
JANICE NAIRNS

European Union Legislation 2011–2012
JEFFREY KENNER

Evidence Statutes 2011–2012
CLAIRE MCGOURLAY

Family Law Statutes 2011–2012
PHIL BATES

International Trade Law Statutes and Conventions 2011–2013
INDIRA CARR AND MIRIAM GOLDBY

Property Law Statutes 2011–2012
RUSSELL HEWITSON

Public Law and Human Rights 2011–2012
PHILIP JONES

http://cw.routledge.com/textbooks/statutes

Praise for Routledge Student Statutes

'The best value and best format books on the market' – Ed Bates, University of Southampton, UK

'Focused content, layout and price – Routledge competes and wins in relation to all of these factors' – Craig Lind, University of Sussex, UK

'comprehensive and reliable' – Andromachi Georgosouli, University of Leicester, UK

'user friendly and sensibly laid out' – John Stanton, Kingston University, UK

'An exciting and valuable selection of the key legislative material' – David Radlett, University of Kent, UK

'I prefer the layout of the Routledge statute book to other statute books that I have seen' – Nicola Haralambous, University of Hertfordshire, UK

'Well-presented and has thorough content [. . .] clearly a good competitor' – Brian Coggon, University of Lincoln, UK

'. . . given the addition of the useful web resource and the easy to read section headings, I would be more inclined to recommend this book than other statute texts' – Emma Warner-Reed, Leeds Metropolitan University, UK

'excellent and relevant' – Sarwan Singh, City University London, UK

'I personally prefer the Routledge series as it is better laid out and more accessible' – Jonathan Doak, University of Nottingham, UK

'Routledge Student Statutes are practical and carefully designed for the needs of the students' – Stelios Andreadakis, Oxford Brookes University, UK

'an excellent statute text' – Fang Ma, University of Hertfordshire, UK

'Other statute books are not as attractive in look or feel, not as easy to navigate, more expensive and amendments are less clear' – Jason Lowther, University of Plymouth, UK

'Gives good coverage and certainly includes all elements addressed on our current syllabus. I personally think this statute is more clearly set out than other statute books and is more user friendly for it' – Samantha Pegg, Nottingham Trent University, UK

'This statute book is a student friendly material. Index features as well as the overall content make this book a valuable contribution to student reading lists' – Orkun Akseli, Newcastle University, UK

'A very welcome publication' – Simon Barnett, University of Hertfordshire, UK

'I am sticking with Routledge Student Statutes' – Francis Tansinda, Manchester Metropolitan University, UK

ROUTLEDGE
STUDENT STATUTES

Family Law Statutes

2011–2012

PHIL BATES
Lecturer in Law at The Open University

Routledge
Taylor & Francis Group
LONDON AND NEW YORK

First published 2012
by Routledge
2 Park Square, Milton Park, Abingdon, Oxon OX14 4RN

Simultaneously published in the USA and Canada
by Routledge
711 Third Avenue, New York, NY 10017

Routledge is an imprint of the Taylor & Francis Group, an informa business

British Library Cataloguing in Publication Data
A catalogue record for this book is available from the British Library

Library of Congress Cataloging in Publication Data
A catalog record for this book has been requested

ISBN: 978-0-415-68461-3 (pbk)

Typeset in Sabon
by RefineCatch Limited, Bungay, Suffolk

MIX
Paper from responsible sources
FSC® C004839

Printed and bound in Great Britain by
TJ International Ltd, Padstow, Cornwall

Contents

Preface

Even if family law legislation makes it through the Parliamentary process, this does not guarantee that it will be implemented quickly, or ever. Amendments to the Matrimonial Causes Act 1973 and the Civil Parnership Act 2004 made by the Pensions Act 2008 are now in force, allowing courts to make pension compensation sharing orders in certain cases. The Children and Young Persons Act 2008 made amendments to the Children Act 1989, including substituting sections 22A–22G for the original section 23. These provisions were implemented this year in England, but they are not yet in force in Wales. New provisions for domestic violence protection included in the Crime and Security Act 2010 are being brought into force on 30 June 2011 for a 12 month period in certain regions, as part of a Pilot Scheme. With this one exception, the statutes in this book appear in the from that was in force on 1st June 2011. The divorce reform provisions in Part II of the Family Law Act 1996 have never been brought into force, but they remain a useful reference point for considering 'what might have been'. These unimplemented provisions are included as an appendix.

I would like to thank my own family, Jennifer, Griffin and Zoë for their love and support.

Phil Bates
June 2011

Guide to the Companion Website

http://cw.routledge.com/textbooks/statutes/

Visit the Companion Website for Routledge Student Statutes in order to:

- Understand how to use a statute book in tutorials and exams;
- Learn how to interpret statutes and other legislation to maximum effect;
- Gain essential practice in statute interpretation prior to your exams, through unique problem-based scenarios;
- Test your understanding of statutes through a set of Multiple Choice Questions for revision or to check your own progress;
- Understand how the law is developing with updates, additional information and links to useful websites.

Alphabetical Index

Chronological Index

International Instruments

Primary Legislation

Wills Act 1837

(7 Will 4 & 1 Vict c 26)

1 MEANING OF CERTAIN WORDS IN THIS ACT

The words and expressions herein-after mentioned, which in their ordinary signification have a more confined or a different meaning, shall in this Act, except where the nature of the provisions or the context of the Act shall exclude such construction, be interpreted as follows; (that is to say,) the word "will" shall extend to a testament, and to a codicil, and to an appointment by will or by writing in the nature of a will in exercise of a power, and also to an appointment by will of a guardian of a child, and also to an appointment by will of a representative under section 4 of the Human Tissue Act 2004, and to any other testamentary disposition; . . .

. . .

18 WILL TO BE REVOKED BY MARRIAGE

(1) Subject to subsections (2) to (4) below, a will shall be revoked by the testator's marriage.

(2) A disposition in a will in exercise of a power of appointment shall take effect notwithstanding the testator's subsequent marriage unless the property so appointed would in default of appointment pass to his personal representatives.

(3) Where it appears from a will that at the time it was made the testator was expecting to be married to a particular person and that he intended that the will should not be revoked by the marriage, the will shall not be revoked by his marriage to that person.

(4) Where it appears from a will that at the time it was made the testator was expecting to be married to a particular person and that he intended that a disposition in the will should not be revoked by his marriage to that person,—
(a) that disposition shall take effect notwithstanding the marriage; and
(b) any other disposition in the will shall take effect also,
unless it appears from the will that the testator intended the disposition to be revoked by the marriage.

18A EFFECT OF DISSOLUTION OR ANNULMENT OF MARRIAGE ON WILLS

(1) Where, after a testator has made a will, a decree of a court of civil jurisdiction in England and Wales dissolves or annuls his marriages or his marriage is dissolved or annulled and the divorce or annulment is entitled to recognition in England and Wales by virtue of Part II of the Family Law Act 1986—

(a) provisions of the will appointing executors or trustees or conferring a power of appointment, if they appoint or confer the power on the former spouse, shall take effect as if the former spouse had died on the date on which the marriage is dissolved or annulled, and
(b) any property which, or an interest in which, is devised or bequeathed to the former spouse shall pass as if the former spouse had died on that date,

except in so far as a contrary intention appears by the will.

(2) Subsection (1)(b) above is without prejudice to any right of the former spouse to apply for financial provision under the Inheritance (Provision for Family and Dependants) Act 1975.

18B WILL TO BE REVOKED BY CIVIL PARTNERSHIP

(1) Subject to subsections (2) to (6), a will is revoked by the formation of a civil partnership between the testator and another person.

(2) A disposition in a will in exercise of a power of appointment takes effect despite the formation of a subsequent civil partnership between the testator and another person unless the property so appointed would in default of appointment pass to the testator's personal representatives.

(3) If it appears from a will—
(a) that at the time it was made the testator was expecting to form a civil partnership with a particular person, and
(b) that he intended that the will should not be revoked by the formation of the civil partnership,

the will is not revoked by its formation.

(4) Subsections (5) and (6) apply if it appears from a will—
(a) that at the time it was made the testator was expecting to form a civil partnership with a particular person, and
(b) that he intended that a disposition in the will should not be revoked by the formation of the civil partnership.

(5) The disposition takes effect despite the formation of the civil partnership.

(6) Any other disposition in the will also takes effect, unless it appears from the will that the testator intended the disposition to be revoked by the formation of the civil partnership.

18C EFFECT OF DISSOLUTION OR ANNULMENT OF CIVIL PARTNERSHIP ON WILLS

(1) This section applies if, after a testator has made a will—
(a) a court of civil jurisdiction in England and Wales dissolves his civil partnership or makes a nullity order in respect of it, or
(b) his civil partnership is dissolved or annulled and the dissolution or annulment is entitled to recognition in England and Wales by virtue of Chapter 3 of Part 5 of the Civil Partnership Act 2004.

(2) Except in so far as a contrary intention appears by the will—
(a) provisions of the will appointing executors or trustees or conferring a power of appointment, if they appoint or confer the power on the former civil partner, take effect as if the former civil partner had died on the date on which the civil partnership is dissolved or annulled, and
(b) any property which, or an interest in which, is devised or bequeathed to the former civil partner shall pass as if the former civil partner had died on that date.

(3) Subsection (2)(b) does not affect any right of the former civil partner to apply for financial provision under the Inheritance (Provision for Family and Dependants) Act 1975.

As amended by: Statute Law Revision Act 1893, s 1, Schedule; Statute Law (Repeals) Act 1969, s 1, Schedule, Pt III; Administration of Justice Act 1982, s 18; Family Law Act 1986, s 53; Children Act 1989, s 108(5), (6), Sch 13, Sch 14; Law Reform (Succession) Act 1995, ss 3, 5, Schedule; Trusts of Land and Appointment of Trustees 1996, s 25(2), Sch 4; Human Tissue Act 2004, s 56, Sch 6; Civil Partnership Act 2004, s 71, Sch 4.

Married Women's Property Act 1882

(45 & 46 Vict c 75)

17 QUESTIONS BETWEEN HUSBAND AND WIFE AS TO PROPERTY TO BE DECIDED IN A SUMMARY WAY

In any question between husband and wife as to the title to or possession of property, either party, may apply by summons or otherwise in a summary way to the High Court or such county court as may be prescribed and the court may, on such an application (which may be heard in private), make such order with respect to the property as it thinks fit.

In this section "prescribed" means prescribed by rules of court and rules made for the purposes of this section may confer jurisdiction on county courts whatever the situation or value of the property in dispute.

As amended by: Statute Law (Repeals) Act 1969; Matrimonial and Family Proceedings Act 1984, s 43.

Law of Property Act 1925

(15 & 16 Geo 5 c 20)

37 RIGHTS OF HUSBAND AND WIFE

A husband and wife shall, for all purposes of acquisition of any interest in property, under a disposition made or coming into operation after the commencement of this Act, be treated as two persons.

. . .

53 INSTRUMENTS REQUIRED TO BE IN WRITING

(1) Subject to the provisions hereinafter contained with respect to the creation of interests in land by parol—
  (a) no interest in land can be created or disposed of except by writing signed by the person creating or conveying the same, or by his agent thereunto lawfully authorised in writing, or by will, or by operation of law;
  (b) a declaration of trust respecting any land or any interest therein must be manifested and proved by some writing signed by some person who is able to declare such trust or by his will;

(c) a disposition of an equitable interest or trust subsisting at the time of the disposition, must be in writing signed by the person disposing of the same, or by his agent thereunto lawfully authorised in writing or by will.

(2) This section does not affect the creation or operation of resulting, implied or constructive trusts.

...

184 PRESUMPTION OF SURVIVORSHIP IN REGARD TO CLAIMS TO PROPERTY

In all cases where, after the commencement of this Act, two or more persons have died in circumstances rendering it uncertain which of them survived the other or others, such deaths shall (subject to any order of the court), for all purposes affecting the title of property, be presumed to have occurred in order of seniority, and accordingly the younger shall be deemed to have survived the elder.

Children and Young Persons Act 1933

(23 & 24 Geo 5 c 12)

1 CRUELTY TO PERSONS UNDER SIXTEEN

(1) If any person who has attained the age of sixteen years and has responsibility for any child or young person under that age, wilfully assaults, ill-treats, neglects, abandons, or exposes him, or causes or procures him to be assaulted, ill-treated, neglected, abandoned, or exposed, in a manner likely to cause him unnecessary suffering or injury to health (including injury to or loss of sight, or hearing, or limb, or organ of the body, and any mental derangement), that person shall be guilty of a misdemeanour, and shall be liable—

(a) on conviction on indictment, to a fine, or alternatively, or in addition thereto, to imprisonment for any term not exceeding ten years;

(b) on summary conviction, to a fine not exceeding the prescribed sum or alternatively, or in addition thereto, to imprisonment for any term not exceeding six months.

(2) For the purposes of this section—

(a) a parent or other person legally liable to maintain a child or young person, or the legal guardian of a child or young person, shall be deemed to have neglected him in a manner likely to cause injury to his health if he has failed to provide adequate food, clothing, medical aid or lodging for him, or if, having been unable otherwise to provide such food, clothing, medical aid or lodging, he has failed to take steps to procure it to be provided under the enactments applicable in that behalf;

(b) where it is proved that the death of an infant under three years of age was caused by suffocation (not being suffocation caused by disease or the presence of any foreign body in the throat or air passages of the infant) while the infant was in bed with some other person who has attained the age of sixteen years, that other person shall, if he was, when he went to bed, under the influence of drink, be deemed to have neglected the infant in a manner likely to cause injury to its health.

(3) A person may be convicted of an offence under this section—

(a) notwithstanding that actual suffering or injury to health, or the likelihood of actual suffering or injury to health, was obviated by the action of another person;

(b) notwithstanding the death of the child or young person in question.

...

Principles to be observed by all Courts in dealing with Children and Young Persons

44 GENERAL CONSIDERATIONS

(1) Every court in dealing with a child or young person who is brought before it, either as an offender or otherwise, shall have regard to the welfare of the child or young person and shall in a proper case take steps for removing him from undesirable surroundings, and for securing that proper provision is made for his education and training.

. . .

107 INTERPRETATION

(1) In this Act, unless the context otherwise requires, the following expressions have the meanings hereby respectively assigned to them, that is to say—

. . .

"Child" means a person under the age of fourteen years;

"Guardian", in relation to a child or young person, includes any person who, in the opinion of the court having cognisance of any case in relation to the child or young person or in which the child or young person is concerned, has for the time being the care of the child or young person;

"legal guardian", in relation to a child or young person, means a guardian of a child as defined in the Children Act 1989;

. . .

"Young person" means a person who has attained the age of fourteen and is under the age of eighteen years.

As amended by: National Assistance (Adaptation of Enactments) Regulations 1950, SI 1951/174; Children and Young Persons Act 1963, s 64(1), (3), Sch 3, para 1, Sch 5; Criminal Law Act 1967, s 10, Sch 2, para 13(1), Sch 3, Part III; Children and Young Persons Act 1969, s 72(3), (4), Sch 5, para 12(3), Sch 6; Children Act 1975, s 108(1)(b), Sch 4, Part III; Magistrates' Courts Act 1980, s 32(2); Criminal Justice Act 1988, ss 45, 170(2), Sch 16; Children Act 1989, s 108, Sch 12, Sch 13, Sch 15; Criminal Justice Act 1991, s 68, Sch 8; Children Act 2004, ss 58(5), 64, Sch 5, Pt 5.

Marriage Act 1949

(12 & 13 Geo 6 c 76)

Part I RESTRICTIONS ON MARRIAGE

1 MARRIAGES WITHIN PROHIBITED DEGREES

(1) A marriage solemnized between a person and any person mentioned in the list in Part 1 of Schedule 1 shall be void.

(2) Subject to subsection (3) of this section, a marriage solemnized between a person and any person mentioned in the list in Part 2 of Schedule 1 shall be void.

(3) Any such marriage as is mentioned in subsection (2) of this section shall not be void by reason only of affinity if both the parties to the marriage have attained the age of twenty-one at the time of the marriage and the younger party has not at any time before attaining the age of eighteen been a child of the family in relation to the other party.

2 MARRIAGES OF PERSONS UNDER SIXTEEN

A marriage solemnized between persons either of whom is under the age of sixteen shall be void.

3 MARRIAGES OF PERSONS UNDER EIGHTEEN

(1) Where the marriage of a child, not being a widower or widow, is intended to be solemnized on the authority of certificates issued by a superintendent registrar under Part III of this Act, the consent of the appropriate persons shall be required:
Provided that—

(a) if the superintendent registrar is satisfied that the consent of any person whose consent is so required cannot be obtained by reason of absence or inaccessibility or by reason of his being under any disability, the necessity for the consent of that person shall be dispensed with, if there is any other person whose consent is also required; and if the consent of no other person is required, the Registrar General may dispense with the necessity of obtaining any consent, or the court may, on application being made, consent to the marriage, and the consent of the court so given shall have the same effect as if it had been given by the person whose consent cannot be so obtained;

(b) if any person whose consent is required refuses his consent, the court may, on application being made, consent to the marriage, and the consent of the court so given shall have the same effect as if it had been given by the person whose consent is refused.

(1A) The appropriate persons are—

(a) if none of paragraphs (b) to (h) apply, each of the following—
  (i) any parent of the child who has parental responsibility for him; and
  (ii) any guardian of the child;

(b) where a special guardianship order is in force with respect to a child, each of the child's special guardians, unless any of paragraphs (c) to (g) applies;

(c) where a care order has effect with respect to the child, the local authority designated in the order, and each parent, guardian or special guardian (in so far as their parental responsibility has not been restricted under section 33(3) of the Children Act 1989), unless paragraph (e) applies;

(d) where a residence order has effect with respect to the child, the persons with whom the child lives, or is to live, as a result of the order, unless paragraph (e) applies;

(e) where an adoption agency is authorised to place the child for adoption under section 19 of the Adoption and Children Act 2002, that agency or, where a care order has effect with respect to the child, the local authority designated in the order;

(f) where a placement order is in force with respect to the child, the appropriate local authority;

(g) where a child has been placed for adoption with prospective adopters, the prospective adopters (in so far as their parental responsibility has not been restricted under section 25(4) of the Adoption and Children Act 2002), in addition to those persons specified in paragraph (e) or (f);

(h) where none of paragraphs (b) to (g) apply but a residence order was in force with respect to the child immediately before he reached the age of sixteen, the persons with whom he lived, or was to live, as a result of the order.

(1B) In this section—

"guardian of a child", "parental responsibility", "residence order", "special guardian", "special guardianship order" and "care order" have the same meaning as in the Children Act 1989;

"adoption agency", "placed for adoption", "placement order" and "local authority" have the same meaning as in the Adoption and Children Act 2002;

"appropriate local authority" means the local authority authorised by the placement order to place the child for adoption.

(2) Subsection (1) shall apply to marriages intended to be solemnized on the authority of a common licence, with the substitution of references to the ecclesiastical authority by whom the licence was granted for references to the superintendent registrar, and with the substitution of a reference to the Master of the Faculties for the reference to the Registrar General.

(3) Where the marriage of a child, not being a widower or widow, is intended to be solemnized after the publication of banns of matrimony then, if any person whose consent to the marriage would have been required under this section in the case of a marriage intended to be solemnized otherwise than after the publication of the banns, openly and publicly declares or causes to be declared, in the church or chapel in which the banns are published, at the time of the publication, his dissent from the intended marriage, the publication of banns shall be void.

(4) A clergyman shall not be liable to ecclesiastical censure for solemnizing the marriage of a child after the publication of banns without the consent of the parents or guardians of the child unless he had notice of the dissent of any person who is entitled to give notice of dissent under the last foregoing subsection.

(5) For the purposes of this section, "the court" means the High Court, the county court of the district in which any applicant or respondent resides or a court of summary jurisdiction (acting in the local justice area in which any applicant or respondent resides and rules of court may be made for enabling applications under this section—

(a) if made to the High Court, to be heard in chambers;

(b) if made to the county court, to be heard and determined by the registrar subject to appeal to the judge;

(c) if made to a court of summary jurisdiction, to be heard and determined otherwise than in open court,

and shall provide that, where an application is made in consequence of a refusal to give consent, notice of the application shall be served on the person who has refused consent.

(6) Nothing in this section shall dispense with the necessity of obtaining the consent of the High Court to the marriage of a ward of court.

4 HOURS FOR SOLEMNIZATION OF MARRIAGES

A marriage may be solemnized at any time between the hours of eight in the forenoon and six in the afternoon.

Part II MARRIAGE ACCORDING TO RITES OF THE CHURCH OF ENGLAND

Preliminary

5 METHODS OF AUTHORISING MARRIAGES

A marriage according to the rites of the Church of England may be solemnized—

(a) after the publication of banns of matrimony;

(b) on the authority of a special licence of marriage granted by the Archbishop of Canterbury or any other person by virtue of the Ecclesiastical Licences Act 1533 (in this Act referred to as a "special licence");

(c) on the authority of a licence of marriage (other than a special licence) granted by an ecclesiastical authority having power to grant such a licence (in this Act referred to as a "common licence"); or

(d) on the authority of certificates issued by a superintendent registrar under Part III of this Act;

except that paragraph (a) of this section shall not apply in relation to the solemnization of any marriage mentioned in subsection (2) of section 1 of this Act.

5A MARRIAGES BETWEEN CERTAIN PERSONS RELATED BY AFFINITY

No clergyman shall be obliged—

(a) to solemnize a marriage which, apart from the Marriage (Prohibited Degrees of Relationship) Act 1986 or the Marriage Act 1949 (Remedial) Order 2007, would have been void by reason of the relationship of the persons to be married; or

(b) to permit such a marriage to be solemnized in the church or chapel of which he is the minister.

5B MARRIAGES INVOLVING PERSON OF ACQUIRED GENDER

(1) A clergyman is not obliged to solemnise the marriage of a person if the clergyman reasonably believes that the person's gender has become the acquired gender under the Gender Recognition Act 2004.

(2) A clerk in Holy Orders of the Church in Wales is not obliged to permit the marriage of a person to be solemnised in the church or chapel of which the clerk is the minister if the clerk reasonably believes that the person's gender has become the acquired gender under that Act.

. . .

Miscellaneous Provisions

22 WITNESSES

All marriages solemnized according to the rites of the Church of England shall be solemnized in the presence of two or more witnesses in addition to the clergyman by whom the marriage is solemnized.

. . .

24 PROOF OF RESIDENCE NOT NECESSARY TO VALIDITY OF MARRIAGE BY BANNS OR COMMON LICENCE

(1) Where any marriage has been solemnized after the publication of banns of matrimony, it shall not be necessary in support of the marriage to give any proof of the residence of the

parties or either of them in any parish or other ecclesiastical district in which the banns were published, and no evidence shall be given to prove the contrary in any proceedings touching the validity of the marriage.

(2) Where any marriage has been solemnized on the authority of a common licence, it shall not be necessary in support of the marriage to give any proof that the usual place of residence of one of the parties was for fifteen days immediately before the grant of the licence in the parish or other ecclesiastical district in which the marriage was solemnized, and no evidence shall be given to prove the contrary in any proceedings touching the validity of the marriage.

25 VOID MARRIAGES

If any persons knowingly and wilfully intermarry according to the rites of the Church of England (otherwise than by special licence)—

(a) except in the case of a marriage in pursuance of section 26(1)(dd) of this Act in any place other than a church or other building in which banns may be published;

(b) without banns having been duly published, a common licence having been obtained, or certificates having been duly issued under Part III of this Act by a superintendent registrar to whom due notice of marriage has been given; or

(c) on the authority of a publication of banns which is void by virtue of subsection (3) of section three or subsection (2) of section twelve of this Act, on the authority of a common licence which is void by virtue of subsection (3) of section sixteen of this Act, or on the authority of certificates of a superintendent registrar which are void by virtue of subsection (2) of section thirty-three of this Act;

(d) in the case of a marriage on the authority of certificates of a superintendent registrar, in any place other than the church building or other place specified in the notices of marriage and certificates as the place where the marriage is to be solemnized;

or if they knowingly and wilfully consent to or acquiesce in the solemnization of the marriage by any person who is not in Holy Orders, the marriage shall be void.

Part III MARRIAGE UNDER SUPERINTENDENT REGISTRAR'S CERTIFICATE

Issue of certificates

26 MARRIAGES WHICH MAY BE SOLEMNIZED ON AUTHORITY OF SUPERINTENDENT REGISTRAR'S CERTIFICATE

(1) Subject to the provisions of this Part of this Act, the following marriages may be solemnized on the authority of two certificates of a superintendent registrar—
   (a) a marriage in a registered building according to such form and ceremony as the persons to be married see fit to adopt;
   (b) a marriage in the office of a superintendent registrar;
   (bb) a marriage on approved premises;
   (c) a marriage according to the usages of the Society of Friends (commonly called Quakers);
   (d) a marriage between two persons professing the Jewish religion according to the usages of the Jews;
   (dd) the marriage (other than a marriage in pursuance of paragraph (c) or (d) above) of a person who is house-bound or is a detained person at the place where he or she usually resides;
   (e) a marriage according to the rites of the Church of England in any church or chapel in which banns of matrimony may be published.

. . .

Marriages in registered buildings

41 REGISTRATION OF BUILDINGS

(1) Any proprietor or trustee of a building, which has been certified as required by law as a place of religious worship may apply to the superintendent registrar of the registration district in which the building is situated for the building to be registered for the solemnization of marriages therein.

(2) Any person making such an application as aforesaid shall deliver to the superintendent registrar a certificate, signed in duplicate by at least twenty householders and dated not earlier than one month before the making of the application, stating that the building is being used by them as their usual place of public religious worship and that they desire that the building should be registered as aforesaid, and both certificates shall be countersigned by the proprietor or trustee by whom they are delivered.

(3) The superintendent registrar shall send both certificates delivered to him under the last foregoing subsection to the Registrar General who shall register the building in a book to be kept for that purpose in the General Register Office.

. . .

(7) A building may be registered for the solemnization of marriages under this section whether it is a separate building or forms part of another building.

. . .

43 APPOINTMENT OF AUTHORISED PERSONS

(1) For the purpose of enabling marriages to be solemnized in a registered building without the presence of a registrar, the trustees or governing body of that building may authorise a person to be present at the solemnization of marriages in that building and, where a person is so authorised in respect of any registered building, the trustees or governing body of that building shall, within the prescribed time and in the prescribed manner, certify the name and address of the person so authorised to the Registrar General and to the superintendent registrar of the registration district in which the building is situated.

Provided that in relation to a building which becomes registered after the thirty-first day of December, nineteen hundred and fifty-eight, the power conferred by this subsection to authorise a person to be present as aforesaid shall not be exercisable before the expiration of one year from the date of registration of the building or, where the congregation on whose behalf the building is registered previously used for the purpose of public religious worship another building of which the registration has been cancelled not earlier than one month before the date of registration aforesaid, one year from the date of registration of that other building.

(2) Any person whose name and address have been certified as aforesaid is in this Act referred to as an "authorised person".

(3) Nothing in this section shall be taken to relate or have any reference to marriages solemnized according to the usages of the Society of Friends or of persons professing the Jewish religion.

44 SOLEMNIZATION OF MARRIAGE IN REGISTERED BUILDING

(1) Subject to the provisions of this section, where the notices of marriage and certificates issued by a superintendent registrar state that a marriage between the persons named therein is

intended to be solemnized in a registered building, the marriage may be solemnized in that building according to such form and ceremony as those persons may see fit to adopt:

Provided that no marriage shall be solemnized in any registered building without the consent of the minister or of one of the trustees, owners, deacons or managers thereof, or in the case of a registered building of the Roman Catholic Church, without the consent of the officiating minister thereof.

(2) Subject to the provisions of this section, a marriage solemnized in a registered building shall be solemnized with open doors in the presence of two or more witnesses and in the presence of either—
(a) a registrar of the registration district in which the registered building is situated, or
(b) an authorised person whose name and address have been certified in accordance with the last foregoing section by the trustees or governing body of that registered building or of some other registered building in the same registration district.

(3) Where a marriage is solemnized in a registered building each of the persons contracting the marriage shall, in some part of the ceremony and in the presence of the witnesses and the registrar or authorised person, make the following declaration:—

"I do solemnly declare that I know not of any lawful impediment why I, *AB*, may not be joined in matrimony to *CD*"

and each of them shall say to the other:—

"I call upon these persons here present to witness that I, *AB*, do take thee, *CD*, to be my lawful wedded wife (*or* husband)".

(3A) As an alternative to the declaration set out in subsection (3) of this section the persons contracting the marriage may make the requisite declaration either—
(a) by saying "I declare that I know of no legal reason why I (*name*) may not be joined in marriage to (*name*)"; or
(b) by replying "I am" to the question put to them successively "Are you (*name*) free lawfully to marry (*name*)?";
and as an alternative to the words of contract set out in that subsection the persons to be married may say to each other "I (*name*) take you (*or* thee) (*name*) to be my wedded wife (*or* husband)".

(4) A marriage shall not be solemnized in a registered building without the presence of a registrar until duplicate marriage register books have been supplied by the Registrar General under Part IV of this Act to the authorised person or to the trustees or governing body of the building.

(5) If the Registrar General is not satisfied with respect to any building registered or proposed to be registered for the solemnization of marriages therein that sufficient security exists for the due registration of marriages by an authorised person under Part IV of this Act and for the safe custody of marriage register books, he may in his discretion attach to the continuance of the registration, or to the registration, of the building a condition that no marriage may be solemnized therein without the presence of a registrar.

Marriages in register offices

45 SOLEMNIZATION OF MARRIAGE IN REGISTER OFFICE

(1) Where a marriage is intended to be solemnized on the authority of certificates of a superintendent registrar, the persons to be married may state in the notices of marriage that they wish to be married in the office of the superintendent registrar or one of the

superintendent registrars, as the case may be, to whom notice of marriage is given, and where any such notices have been given and the certificates have been issued accordingly, the marriage may be solemnized in the said office, with open doors, in the presence of the superintendent registrar and a registrar of the registration district of that superintendent registrar and in the presence of two witnesses, and the persons to be married shall make the declarations and use the form of words set out in subsection (3) or (3A) of the last foregoing section in the case of marriages in registered buildings.

(2) No religious service shall be used at any marriage solemnized in the office of a superintendent registrar.

45A SOLEMNIZATION OF CERTAIN MARRIAGES

(1) This section applies to marriages solemnized, otherwise than according to the rites of the Church of England, in pursuance of section 26(1)(dd) of this Act at the place where a person usually resides.

(2) The marriage may be solemnized according to a relevant form, rite or ceremony in the presence of a registrar of the registration district in which the place where the marriage is solemnized is situated and of two witnesses and each of the persons contracting the marriage shall make the declaration and use the form of words set out in subsection (3) or (3A) of section 44 of this Act in the case of marriages in registered buildings.

(3) Where the marriage is not solemnized in pursuance of subsection (2) of this section it shall be solemnized in the presence of the superintendent registrar and a registrar of the registration district in which the place where the marriage is solemnized is situated and in the presence of two witnesses, and the persons to be married shall make the declarations and use the form of words set out in subsection (3) or (3A) of section 44 of this Act in the case of marriages in registered buildings.

(4) No religious service shall be used at any marriage solemnized in the presence of a superintendent registrar.

(5) In subsection (2) of this section a "relevant form, rite or ceremony" means a form, rite or ceremony of a body of persons who meet for religious worship in any registered building being a form, rite or ceremony in accordance with which members of that body are married in any such registered building.

46 REGISTER OFFICE MARRIAGE FOLLOWED BY RELIGIOUS CEREMONY

(1) If the parties to a marriage solemnised in the presence of a superintendent registrar desire to add the religious ceremony ordained or used by the church or persuasion of which they are members, they may present themselves, after giving notice of their intention so to do, to the clergyman or minister of the church or persuasion of which they are members, and the clergyman or minister, upon the production of a certificate of their marriage before the superintendent registrar and upon the payment of the customary fees (if any), may, if he sees fit, read or celebrate in the church or chapel of which he is the regular minister the marriage service of the church or persuasion to which he belongs or nominate some other minister to do so.

(2) Nothing in the reading or celebration of a marriage service under this section shall supersede or invalidate any marriage previously solemnised in the presence of a superintendent registrar, and the reading or celebration shall not be entered as a marriage in any marriage register book kept under Part IV of this Act.

(3) No person who is not entitled to solemnize marriages according to the rites of the Church of England shall by virtue of this section be entitled to read or celebrate the marriage service in any church or chapel of the Church of England.

Marriages on approved premises

46A APPROVAL OF PREMISES

(1) The Secretary of State may by regulations make provision for and in connection with the approval by local authorities of premises for the solemnization of marriages in pursuance of section 26(1)(bb) of this Act.

(2) The matters dealt with by the regulations may include—

(a) the kinds of premises in respect of which approvals may be granted;
(b) the procedure to be followed in relation to applications for approval;
(c) the considerations to be taken into account by a local authority in determining whether to approve any premises;
(d) the duration and renewal of approvals;
(e) the conditions that must or may be imposed by a local authority on granting or renewing an approval;
(f) the determination and charging by local authorities of fees in respect of applications for the approval of premises and in respect of the renewal of approvals;
(g) the circumstances in which a local authority must or may revoke an approval;
(h) the review of any decision to refuse an approval or the renewal of an approval, to impose conditions on granting or renewing an approval or to revoke an approval;
(i) the notification to the Registrar General of all approvals granted, renewed or revoked;
(j) the keeping by local authorities of registers of approved premises;
(k) the issue by the Registrar General of guidance supplementing the provision made by the regulations.

. . .

46B SOLEMNIZATION OF MARRIAGE ON APPROVED PREMISES

(1) Any marriage on approved premises in on pursuance of section 26(1)(bb) of this Act shall be solemnized in the presence of—

(a) two witnesses, and
(b) the superintendent registrar and a registrar of the registration district in which the premises are situated.

(2) Without prejudice to the width of section 46A(2)(e) of this Act, the Secretary of State shall exercise his power to provide for the imposition of conditions as there mentioned so as to secure that members of the public are permitted to attend any marriage solemnized on approved premises in pursuance of section 26(1)(bb) of this Act.

(3) Each of the persons contracting such a marriage shall make the declaration and use the form of words set out in section 44(3) or (3A) of this Act in the case of marriages in registered buildings.

(4) No religious service shall be used at a marriage on approved premises in pursuance of section 26(1)(bb) of this Act.

Marriages according to usages of Society of Friends

47 MARRIAGES ACCORDING TO USAGES OF SOCIETY OF FRIENDS

(1) No person who is not a member of the Society of Friends shall be married according to the usages of that Society unless he or she is authorised to be so married under or in pursuance of a general rule of the said Society in England.

(2) A marriage solemnized according to the said usages shall not be valid unless either—
   (a) each person giving notice of marriage declares, either verbally or, if so required, in writing, that each of the parties to the marriage is either a member of the Society of Friends or is in profession with or of the persuasion of that Society; or
   (b) there is produced to the superintendent registrar, at the time when notice of marriage is given, a certificate purporting to be signed by a registering officer of the Society of Friends in England to the effect that any party to the marriage who is not a member of the Society of Friends or in profession with or of the persuasion of that Society, is authorised to be married according to the said usages under or in pursuance of a general rule of the said Society in England.

(3) Any such certificate as aforesaid shall be for all purposes conclusive evidence that any person to whom it relates is authorised to be married according to the usages of the said Society, and the entry of the marriage in a marriage register book under Part IV of this Act, or a certified copy thereof made under the said Part IV, shall be conclusive evidence of the production of such a certificate.

(4) A copy of any general rule of the Society of Friends purporting to be signed by the recording clerk for the time being of the said Society in London shall be admitted as evidence of the general rule in all proceedings touching the validity of any marriage solemnized according to the usages of the said Society.

Miscellaneous Provisions

48 PROOF OF CERTAIN MATTERS NOT NECESSARY TO VALIDITY OF MARRIAGES

(1) Where any marriage has been solemnized under the provisions of this Part of this Act, it shall not be necessary in support of the marriage to give any proof—
   (a) that before the marriage either of the parties thereto resided, or resided for any period, in the registration district stated in the notices of marriage to be that of his or her place of residence;
   (b) that any person whose consent to the marriage was required by section three of this Act had given his consent;
   (c) that the registered building in which the marriage was solemnized had been certified as required by law as a place of religious worship;
   (d) that that building was the usual place of worship of either of the parties to the marriage; or
   (e) that the facts stated in a declaration made under subsection (1) of section thirty-five of this Act were correct;

nor shall any evidence be given to prove the contrary in any proceedings touching the validity of the marriage.

(2) A marriage solemnized in accordance with the provisions of this Part of this Act in a registered building which has not been certified as required by law as a place of religious worship shall be as valid as if the building had been so certified.

49 VOID MARRIAGES

If any persons knowingly and wilfully intermarry under the provisions of this Part of this Act—

(a) without having given due notice of marriage to the superintendent registrar;

(b) without a certificate for marriage having been duly issued, in respect of each of the persons to be married, by the superintendent registrar to whom notice of marriage was given;

(d) on the authority of certificates which are void by virtue of subsection (2) of section thirty-three of this Act;

(e) in any place other than the church, chapel, registered building, office or other place specified in the notices of marriage and certificates of the superintendent registrar;

(ee) in the case of a marriage purporting to be in pursuance of section 26(1)(bb) of this Act, on any premises that at the time the marriage is solemnized are not approved premises;

(f) in the case of a marriage in a registered building (not being a marriage in the presence of an authorised person), in the absence of a registrar of the registration district in which the registered building is situated;

(g) in the case of a marriage in the office of a superintendent registrar, in the absence of the superintendent registrar or of a registrar of the registration district of that superintendent registrar;

(gg) in the case of a marriage on approved premises, in the absence of the superintendent registrar of the registration district in which the premises are situated or in the absence of a registrar of that district; or

(h) in the case of a marriage to which section 45A of this Act applies, in the absence of any superintendent registrar or registrar whose presence at that marriage is required by that section;

the marriage shall be void.

. . .

Part VI GENERAL

. . .

78 INTERPRETATION

(1) In this Act, except where the context otherwise requires, the following expressions have the meanings hereby respectively assigned to them, that is to say—

"approved premises" means premises approved in accordance with regulations under section 46A of this Act as premises on which marriages may be solemnized in pursuance of section 26(1)(bb) of this Act;

"authorised chapel" means—

(a) in relation to a chapelry, a chapel of the chapelry in which banns of matrimony could lawfully be published immediately before the passing of the Marriage Act 1823, or in which banns may be published and marriages may be solemnized by virtue of section two of the Marriages Confirmation Act 1825, or of an authorisation given under section three of the Marriage Act 1823;

(b) in relation to an extra-parochial place, a church or chapel of that place in which banns may be published and marriages may be solemnized by virtue of section two of the Marriages Confirmation Act 1825, or of an authorisation given under section three of the Marriage Act 1823, or section twenty-one of this Act;

(c) in relation to a district specified in a licence granted under section twenty of this Act, the chapel in which banns may be published and marriages may be solemnized by virtue of that licence;

"authorised person" has the meaning assigned to it by section forty-three of this Act;

"brother" includes a brother of the half blood;

"child", except where used to express a relationship, means a person under the age of eighteen;

"child of the family", in relation to any person, means a child who has lived in the same household as that person and been treated by that person as a child of his family;

"clergyman" means a clerk in Holy Orders of the Church of England;

"common licence" has the meaning assigned to it by section five of this Act;

"ecclesiastical district," in relation to a district other than a parish, means a district specified in a licence granted under section twenty of this Act, a chapelry or an extra-parochial place;

"marriage notice book" has the meaning assigned to it by section twenty-seven of this Act;

"parish" means an ecclesiastical parish and includes a district constituted under the Church Building Acts 1818 to 1884 notwithstanding that the district has not become a new parish by virtue of section fourteen of the New Parishes Act 1856, or section five of the New Parishes Measure 1943, being a district to which Acts of Parliament relating to the publication of banns of matrimony and the solemnization of marriages were applied by the said Church Building Acts as if the district had been an ancient parish, and the expression "parish church" shall be construed accordingly;

"prescribed" means prescribed by regulations made under section seventy-four of this Act;

"registered building" means a building registered under Part III of this Act;

"registrar" means a registrar of marriages;

"Registrar General" means the Registrar General of Births, Deaths and Marriages in England;

"registration district" means the district of a superintendent registrar;

"sister" includes a sister of the half blood;

"special licence" has the meaning assigned to it by section five of this Act;

"superintendent registrar" means a superintendent registrar of births, deaths and marriages;

"trustees or governing body," in relation to Roman Catholic registered buildings, includes a bishop or vicar general of the diocese.

(2) Any reference in this Act to the Church of England shall, unless the context otherwise requires, be construed as including a reference to the Church in Wales.

(3) For the purposes of this Act a person is house-bound if—

(a) each notice of his or her marriage given in accordance with section 27 of this Act is accompanied by a medical statement (within the meaning of section 27A(7) of this Act) made, not more than fourteen days before the date on which that notice was given, in relation to that person; and

(b) he or she is not a detained person.

(4) For the purposes of this Act a person is a detained person if he or she is for the time being detained—

(a) otherwise than by virtue of section 2, 4, 5, 35, 36 or 136 of the Mental Health Act 1983 (short term detentions), as a patient in a hospital; or

(b) in a prison or other place to which the Prison Act 1952 applies, and in paragraph (a) above "patient" and "hospital" have the same meanings as in Part II of the Mental Health Act 1983.

(5) For the purposes of this Act a person who is house-bound or is a detained person shall be taken, if he or she would not otherwise be, to be resident and usually resident at the place where he or she is for the time being.

. . .

SCHEDULE 1 KINDRED AND AFFINITY

Part 1 PROHIBITED DEGREES: KINDRED

1. (1) The list referred to in section 1(1) is—

Adoptive child
Adoptive parent
Child
Former adoptive child
Former adoptive parent
Grandparent
Grandchild
Parent
Parent's sibling
Sibling
Sibling's child

(2) In the list "sibling" means a brother, sister, half-brother or halfsister.

Part 2 DEGREES OF AFFINITY REFERRED TO IN SECTION 1(2) AND (3)

2. The list referred to in section 1(2) is as follows—

Child of former civil partner
Child of former spouse
Former civil partner of grandparent
Former civil partner of parent
Former spouse of grandparent
Former spouse of parent
Grandchild of former civil partner
Grandchild of former spouse.

As amended by: Marriage Act 1949 (Amendment) Act 1954, ss 1, 2; Marriage Acts Amendment Act 1958, s 1; Marriage (Enabling) Act 1960, s 1(4), Schedule; Registration of Births, Deaths and Marriages (Fees) Order 1968, SI 1968/1242, art 4(1), Sch 2; Family Law Reform Act 1969, s 2(2); Statute Law (Repeals) Act 1975; Domestic Proceedings and Magistrates' Courts Act 1978, s 89(2), Sch 2; Marriage Act 1983, s 1(7), Sch 1; Marriage (Prohibited Degrees of Relationship) Act 1986, ss 1, 3, Sch 1; Family Law Reform Act 1987, s 33(1), Sch 2; Children Act 1989, s 108(4), (7), Sch 12, Sch 15; Marriage (Registration of Buildings) Act 1990, s 1(1); Marriage Act 1994, ss 1, 2, Schedule; City of London (Approved Premises for Marriage) Act 1996, s 3(2); Marriage Ceremony (Prescribed Words) Act 1996, s 1; Access to Justice Act 1999, s 106, Sch 15, Pt V; Immigration and Asylum Act 1999, ss 160=N163, 169, Sch 14, Sch 16; Adoption and Children Act 2002, s 139(1), Sch 3; Courts Act 2003, s 109(1), Sch 8; Gender Recognition Act 2004, s 11, Sch 4; Civil Partnership Act 2004, s 261(1), Sch 27; Civil Partnership Act 2004 (Overseas Relationships and Consequential, etc. Amendments) Order 2005, SI 2005/3129, art 4(2), Sch 2; Marriage Act 1949 (Remedial) Order 2007, SI 2007/438, arts 2, 3; Transfer of Functions (Registration) Order 2008, SI 2008/678, arts 3, 5, Sch 1, Sch 2.

Matrimonial Causes (Property and Maintenance) Act 1958

(6 & 7 Eliz 2 c 35)

7 EXTENSION OF S 17 OF MARRIED WOMEN'S PROPERTY ACT 1882

(1) Any right of a wife, under section seventeen of the Married Women's Property Act 1882 to apply to a judge of the High Court or of a county court, in any question between husband and wife as to the title to or possession of property, shall include the right to make such an application where it is claimed by the wife that her husband has had in his possession or under his control—

(a) money to which, or to a share of which, she was beneficially entitled (whether by reason that it represented the proceeds of property to which, or to an interest in which, she was beneficially entitled, or for any other reason), or

(b) property (other than money) to which, or to an interest in which, she was beneficially entitled, and that either that money or other property has ceased to be in his possession or under his control or that she does not know whether it is still in his possession or under his control.

(2) Where, on an application made to a judge of the High Court or of a county court under the said section seventeen, as extended by the preceding subsection, the judge is satisfied—

(a) that the husband has had in his possession or under his control money or other property as mentioned in paragraph (a) or paragraph (b) of the preceding subsection, and

(b) that he has not made to the wife, in respect of that money or other property, such payment or disposition as would have been appropriate in the circumstances, the power to make orders under that section shall be extended in accordance with the next following subsection.

(3) Where the last preceding subsection applies, the power to make orders under the said section seventeen shall include power for the judge to order the husband to pay to the wife—

(a) in a case falling within paragraph (a) of subsection (1) of this section, such sum in respect of the money to which the application relates, or the wife's share thereof, as the case may be, or

(b) in a case falling within paragraph (b) of the said subsection (1), such sum in respect of the value of the property to which the application relates, or the wife's interest therein, as the case may be,

as the judge may consider appropriate.

(4) Where on an application under the said section seventeen as extended by this section it appears to the judge that there is any property which—

(a) represents the whole or part of the money or property in question, and

(b) is property in respect of which an order could have been made under that section if an application had been made by the wife thereunder in a question as to the title to or possession of that property,

the judge (either in substitution for or in addition to the making of an order in accordance with the last preceding subsection) may make any order under that section in respect of that property which he could have made on such an application as is mentioned in paragraph (b) of this subsection.

(5) The preceding provisions of this section shall have effect in relation to a husband as they have effect in relation to a wife, as if any reference to the husband were a reference to the wife and any reference to the wife were a reference to the husband.

(6) Any power of a judge which is exercisable on an application under the said section seventeen shall be exercisable in relation to an application made under that section as extended by this section.

(7) For the avoidance of doubt it is hereby declared that any power conferred by the said section seventeen to make orders with respect to any property includes power to order a sale of the property.

As amended by: Matrimonial and Family Proceedings Act 1984, s 46(1), Sch 1.

Marriage (Enabling) Act 1960

(8 & 9 Eliz c 29)

1 CERTAIN MARRIAGES NOT TO BE VOID

(1) No marriage hereafter contracted (whether in or out of Great Britain) between a man and a woman who is the sister, aunt or niece of a former wife of his (whether living or not), or was formerly the wife of his brother, uncle or nephew (whether living or not), shall by reason of that relationship be void or voidable under any enactment or rule of law applying in Great Britain as a marriage between persons within the prohibited degrees of affinity.

(2) In the foregoing subsection words of kinship apply equally to kin of the whole and of the half blood.

(3) This section does not validate a marriage, if either party to it is at the time of the marriage domiciled in a country outside Great Britain, and under the law of that country there cannot be a valid marriage between the parties.

As amended by: Statute Law (Repeals) Act 1974.

Married Women's Property Act 1964

(1964 c 19)

1 MONEY AND PROPERTY DERIVED FROM HOUSEKEEPING ALLOWANCE

If any question arises as to the right of a husband or wife to money derived from any allowance made by the husband for the expenses of the matrimonial home or for similar purposes, or to any property acquired out of such money, the money or property shall, in the absence of any agreement between them to the contrary, be treated as belonging to the husband and the wife in equal shares.

Forthcoming amendment: Equality Act 2010, s 200(1)(a).

Civil Evidence Act 1968

(1968 c 64)

12 FINDINGS OF ADULTERY AND PATERNITY AS EVIDENCE IN CIVIL PROCEEDINGS

(1) In any civil proceedings—

(a) the fact that a person has been found guilty of adultery in any matrimonial proceedings; and

(b) the fact that a person has been found to be the father of a child in relevant proceedings before any court in England and Wales or Northern Ireland or has been adjudged to be the father of a child in affiliation proceedings before any court in the United Kingdom;

shall (subject to subsection (3) below) be admissible in evidence for the purpose of proving, where to do so is relevant to any issue in those civil proceedings, that he committed the adultery to which the finding relates or, as the case may be, is (or was) the father of that child, whether or not he offered any defence to the allegation of adultery or paternity and whether or not he is a party to the civil proceedings; but no finding or adjudication other than a subsisting one shall be admissible in evidence by virtue of this section.

(2) In any civil proceedings in which by virtue of this section a person is proved to have been found guilty of adultery as mentioned in subsection (1)(a) above or to have been found or adjudged to be the father of a child as mentioned in subsection (1)(b) above—

(a) he shall be taken to have committed the adultery to which the finding relates or, as the case may be, to be (or have been) the father of that child, unless the contrary is proved; and

(b) without prejudice to the reception of any other admissible evidence for the purpose of identifying the facts on which the finding or adjudication was based, the contents of any document which was before the court, or which contains any pronouncement of the court, in the other proceedings in question shall be admissible in evidence for that purpose.

(3) Nothing in this section shall prejudice the operation of any enactment whereby a finding of fact in any matrimonial or affiliation proceedings is for the purposes of any other proceedings made conclusive evidence of any fact.

(4) Subsection (4) of section 11 of this Act shall apply for the purposes of this section as if the reference to subsection (2) were a reference to subsection (2) of this section.

(5) In this section—

"matrimonial proceedings" means any matrimonial cause in the High Court or a county court in England and Wales or in the High Court in Northern Ireland, any consistorial action in Scotland, or any appeal arising out of any such cause or action;

"relevant proceedings" means—

(a) proceedings on a complaint under section 42 of the National Assistance Act 1948 or section 26 of the Social Security Act 1986;

(b) proceedings under the Children Act 1989;

(c) proceedings which would have been relevant proceedings for the purposes of this section in the form in which it was in force before the passing of the Children Act 1989; . . .

. . .

Privilege

14 PRIVILEGE AGAINST INCRIMINATION OF SELF OR SPOUSE OR CIVIL PARTNER

(1) The right of a person in any legal proceedings other than criminal proceedings to refuse to answer any question or produce any document or thing if to do so would tend to expose that person to proceedings for an offence or for the recovery of a penalty—
  (a) shall apply only as regards criminal offences under the law of any part of the United Kingdom and penalties provided for by such law; and
  (b) shall include a like right to refuse to answer any question or produce any document or thing if to do so would tend to expose the spouse or civil partner of that person to proceedings for any such criminal offence or for the recovery of any such penalty.

(2) In so far as any existing enactment conferring (in whatever words) powers of inspection or investigation confers on a person (in whatever words) any right otherwise than in criminal proceedings to refuse to answer any question or give any evidence tending to incriminate that person, subsection (1) above shall apply to that right as it applies to the right described in that subsection; and every such existing enactment shall be construed accordingly.

(3) In so far as any existing enactment provides (in whatever words) that in any proceedings other than criminal proceedings a person shall not be excused from answering any question or giving any evidence on the ground that to do so may incriminate that person, that enactment shall be construed as providing also that in such proceedings a person shall not be excused from answering any question or giving any evidence on the ground that to do so may incriminate the husband or wife of that person.

(4) Where any existing enactment (however worded) that—
  (a) confers powers of inspection or investigation; or
  (b) provides as mentioned in subsection (3) above,

further provides (in whatever words) that any answer or evidence given by a person shall not be admissible in evidence against that person in any proceedings or class of proceedings (however described, and whether criminal or not), that enactment shall be construed as providing also that any answer or evidence given by that person shall not be admissible in evidence against the husband or wife of that person in the proceedings or class of proceedings in question.

(5) In this section "existing enactment" means any enactment passed before this Act; and the references to giving evidence are references to giving evidence in any manner, whether by furnishing information, making discovery, producing documents or otherwise.

As amended by: Family Law Reform Act 1987, s 29; Courts and Legal Services Act 1990, s 116, Sch 16; Child Support Act 1991, s 27(5); Children (Northern Ireland Consequential Amendments) Order 1995, SI 1995/756, art 6'; Child Support, Pensions and Social Security Act 2000, s 85, Sch 9; Civil Partnership Act 2004, s 261(1), Sch 27.

Family Law Reform Act 1969

(1969 c 46)

Part I REDUCTION OF AGE OF MAJORITY AND RELATED PROVISIONS

1 REDUCTION OF AGE OF MAJORITY FROM 21 TO 18

(1) As from the date on which this section comes into force a person shall attain full age on attaining the age of eighteen instead of on attaining the age of twenty-one; and a person shall attain full age on that date if he has then already attained the age of eighteen but not the age of twenty-one.

(2) The foregoing subsection applies for the purposes of any rule of law, and, in the absence of a definition or of any indication of a contrary intention, for the construction of "full age", "infant", "infancy", "minor", "minority" and similar expressions in—
- (a) any statutory provision, whether passed or made before, on or after the date on which this section comes into force; and
- (b) any deed, will or other instrument of whatever nature (not being a statutory provision) made on or after that date. . . .

8 CONSENT BY PERSONS OVER 16 TO SURGICAL, MEDICAL AND DENTAL TREATMENT

(1) The consent of a minor who has attained the age of sixteen years to any surgical, medical or dental treatment which, in the absence of consent, would constitute a trespass to his person, shall be as effective as it would be if he were of full age; and where a minor has by virtue of this section given an effective consent to any treatment it shall not be necessary to obtain any consent for it from his parent or guardian.

(2) In this section "surgical, medical or dental treatment" includes any procedure undertaken for the purposes of diagnosis, and this section applies to any procedure (including, in particular, the administration of an anaesthetic) which is ancillary to any treatment as it applies to that treatment.

(3) Nothing in this section shall be construed as making ineffective any consent which would have been effective if this section had not been enacted.

9 TIME AT WHICH A PERSON ATTAINS A PARTICULAR AGE

(1) The time at which a person attains a particular age expressed in years shall be the commencement of the relevant anniversary of the date of his birth.

(2) This section applies only where the relevant anniversary falls on a date after that on which this section comes into force, and, in relation to any enactment, deed, will or other instrument, has effect subject to any provision therein.

. . .

12 PERSONS UNDER FULL AGE MAY BE DESCRIBED AS MINORS INSTEAD OF INFANTS

A person who is not of full age may be described as a minor instead of as an infant, and accordingly in this Act "minor" means such a person as aforesaid.

. . .

Part III PROVISIONS FOR USE OF SCIENTIFIC TESTS IN DETERMINING PARENTAGE

20 POWER OF COURT TO REQUIRE USE OF SCIENTIFIC TESTS

(1) In any civil proceedings in which the parentage of any person falls to be determined, the court may, either of its own motion or on an application by any party to the proceedings, give a direction—
  (a) for the use of scientific tests to ascertain whether such tests show that a party to the proceedings is or is not the father or mother of that person; and
  (b) for the taking, within a period specified in the direction, of bodily samples from all or any of the following, namely, that person, any party who is alleged to be the father or mother of that person and any other party to the proceedings;

and the court may at any time revoke or vary a direction previously given by it under this subsection.

(1A) Tests required by a direction under this section may only be carried out by a body which has been accredited for the purposes of this section by—
  (a) the Lord Chancellor, or
  (b) a body appointed by him for the purpose.

(2) The individual carrying out scientific tests in pursuance of a direction under subsection (1) above shall make to the court a report in which he shall state—
  (a) the results of the tests;
  (b) whether any party to whom the report relates is or is not excluded by the results from being the father or mother of the person whose parentage is to be determined; and
  (c) in relation to any party who is not so excluded, the value, if any, of the results in determining whether that party is the father or mother of that person;

and the report shall be received by the court as evidence in the proceedings of the matters stated in it.

(2A) Where the proceedings in which the parentage of any person falls to be determined are proceedings on an application under section 55A or 56 of the Family Law Act 1986, any reference in subsection (1) or (2) of this section to any party to the proceedings shall include a reference to any person named in the application.

(3) A report under subsection (2) of this section shall be in the form prescribed by regulations made under section 22 of this Act.

(4) Where a report has been made to a court under subsection (2) of this section, any party may, with the leave of the court, or shall, if the court so directs, obtain from the tester a written statement explaining or amplifying any statement made in the report, and that statement shall be deemed for the purposes of this section (except subsection (3) thereof) to form part of the report made to the court . . . .

21 CONSENTS, ETC, REQUIRED FOR TAKING OF BODILY SAMPLES

(1) Subject to the provisions of subsections (3) and (4) of this section, a bodily sample which is required to be taken from any person for the purpose of giving effect to a direction under section 20 of this Act shall not be taken from that person except with his consent.

(2) The consent of a minor who has attained the age of sixteen years to the taking from himself of a bodily sample shall be as effective as it would be if he were of full age; and where a minor has by virtue of this subsection given an effective consent to the taking of a bodily sample it shall not be necessary to obtain any consent for it from any other person.

(3) A bodily sample may be taken from a person under the age of sixteen years, not being such a person as is referred to in subsection (4) of this section,
(a) if the person who has the care and control of him consents; or
(b) where that person does not consent, if the court considers that it would be in his best interests for the sample to be taken.

(4) A bodily sample may be taken from a person who lacks capacity (within the meaning of the Mental Capacity Act 2005) to give his consent, if consent is given by the court giving the direction under section 20 or by—
(a) adonee of an enduring power of attorney or lasting power of attorney (within the meaning of that Act), or
(b) a deputy appointed, or any other person authorised, by the Court of Protection, with power in that respect.

(5) The foregoing provisions of this section are without prejudice to the provisions of section 23 of this Act.

. . .

23 FAILURE TO COMPLY WITH DIRECTION FOR TAKING SCIENTIFIC TESTS

(1) Where a court gives a direction under section 20 of this Act and any person fails to take any step required of him for the purpose of giving effect to the direction, the court may draw such inferences, if any, from that fact as appear proper in the circumstances.

(2) Where in any proceedings in which the parentage of any person falls to be determined by the court hearing the proceedings there is a presumption of law that that person is legitimate, then if—
(a) a direction is given under section 20 of this Act in those proceedings, and
(b) any party who is claiming any relief in the proceedings and who for the purpose of obtaining that relief is entitled to rely on the presumption fails to take any step required of him for the purpose of giving effect to the direction,

the court may adjourn the hearing for such period as it thinks fit to enable that party to take that step, and if at the end of that period he has failed without reasonable cause to take it the court may, without prejudice to subsection (1) of this section, dismiss his claim for relief notwithstanding the absence of evidence to rebut the presumption.

(3) Where any person named in a direction under section 20 of this Act fails to consent to the taking of a bodily sample from himself or from any person named in the direction of whom he has the care and control, he shall be deemed for the purposes of this section to have failed to take a step required of him for the purpose of giving effect to the direction.

. . .

25 INTERPRETATION OF PART III

In this Part of this Act the following expressions have the meanings hereby respectively assigned to them, that is to say—

"bodily sample[s]" means a sample of bodily fluid or bodily tissue taken for the purpose of scientific tests;

"excluded" means excluded subject to the occurrence of mutation to section 27 of the Family Law Reform Act 1987, to sections 27 to 29 of the Human Fertilisation and

Embryology Act 1990 and to sections 33 to 47 of the Human Fertilisation and Embryology Act 2008;

"scientific tests" means scientific tests carried out under this Act and made with the object of ascertaining the inheritable characteristics of bodily fluids or bodily tissue.

Part IV **MISCELLANEOUS AND GENERAL**

26 REBUTTAL OF PRESUMPTION AS TO LEGITIMACY AND ILLEGITIMACY

Any presumption of law as to the legitimacy or illegitimacy of any person may in any civil proceedings be rebutted by evidence which shows that it is more probable than not that that person is illegitimate or legitimate, as the case may be, and it shall not be necessary to prove that fact beyond reasonable doubt in order to rebut the presumption.

As amended by: Family Law Reform Act 1987, s 23(2), 33(1), Sch 2; Human Fertilisation and Embryology Act 1990, ss 49(5), 56, Sch 4, Sch 6; Child Support, Pensions and Social Security Act 2000, ss 82, 83, Sch 8; Mental Capacity Act 2005, s 67(1), Sch 6.

Law Reform (Miscellaneous Provisions) Act 1970

(1970 c 33)

Legal consequences of termination of contract to marry

1 ENGAGEMENTS TO MARRY NOT ENFORCEABLE AT LAW

(1) An agreement between two persons to marry one another shall not under the law of England and Wales have effect as a contract giving rise to legal rights and no action shall lie in England and Wales for breach of such an agreement, whatever the law applicable to the agreement.

(2) This section shall have effect in relation to agreements entered into before it comes into force, except that it shall not affect any action commenced before it comes into force.

2 PROPERTY OF ENGAGED COUPLES

(1) Where an agreement to marry is terminated, any rule of law relating to the rights of husbands and wives in relation to property in which either or both has or have a beneficial interest, including any such rule as explained by section 37 of the Matrimonial Proceedings and Property Act 1970, shall apply, in relation to any property in which either or both of the parties to the agreement had a beneficial interest while the agreement was in force, as it applies in relation to property in which a husband or wife has a beneficial interest.

(2) Where an agreement to marry is terminated, section 17 of the Married Women's Property Act 1882 and section 7 of the Matrimonial Causes (Property and Maintenance) Act 1958 (which sections confer power on a judge of the High Court or a county court to settle disputes between husband and wife about property) shall apply, as if the parties were married, to any dispute between, or claim by, one of them in relation to property in which

either or both had a beneficial interest while the agreement was in force; but an application made by virtue of this section to the judge under the said section 17, as originally enacted or as extended by the said section 7, shall be made within three years of the termination of the agreement.

3 GIFTS BETWEEN ENGAGED COUPLES

(1) A party to an agreement to marry who makes a gift of property to the other party to the agreement on the condition (express or implied) that it shall be returned if the agreement is terminated shall not be prevented from recovering the property by reason only of his having terminated the agreement.

(2) The gift of an engagement ring shall be presumed to be an absolute gift; this presumption may be rebutted by proving that the ring was given on the condition, express or implied, that it should be returned if the marriage did not take place for any reason.

Enticement of spouse, etc

5 ABOLITION OF ACTIONS FOR ENTICEMENT, SEDUCTION AND HARBOURING OF SPOUSE OR CHILD

No person shall be liable in tort under the law of England and Wales—

(a) to any other person on the ground only of his having induced the wife or husband of that other person to leave or remain apart from the other spouse;

(b) to a parent (or person standing in the place of a parent) on the ground only of his having deprived the parent (or other person) of the services of his or her child by raping, seducing or enticing that child; or

(c) to any other person for harbouring the wife or child of that other person, except in the case of a cause of action accruing before this Act comes into force if an action in respect thereof has been begun before this Act comes into force.

MARRIAGE (REGISTRAR GENERAL'S LICENCE) ACT 1970

(1970 c 34)

1 MARRIAGES WHICH MAY BE SOLEMNISED BY REGISTRAR GENERAL'S LICENCE

(1) Subject to the provisions of subsection (2) below, any marriage which may be solemnised on the authority of certificates of a superintendent registrar may be solemnised on the authority of the Registrar General's licence elsewhere than at a registered building, the office of a superintendent registrar or approved premises:

Provided that any such marriage shall not be solemnised according to the rites of the Church of England or the Church in Wales.

(2) The Registrar General shall not issue any licence for the solemnising of a marriage as is mentioned in subsection (1) above unless he is satisfied that one of the persons to be married is seriously ill and is not expected to recover and cannot be moved to a place at which under the provisions of the Marriage Act 1949 (hereinafter called the "principal Act") the marriage could be solemnised (disregarding for this purpose the provisions of that Act relating to marriages in pursuance of section 26(1)(dd) of that Act).

. . .

12 PROOF OF CERTAIN MATTERS NOT NECESSARY TO VALIDITY OF MARRIAGES

The provisions of section 48 of the principal Act (proof of certain matters not necessary to validity of marriages) shall apply with the appropriate modifications to a marriage solemnised under the authority of the Registrar General's licence as they apply to a marriage solemnised under the authority of a certificate of a superintendent registrar.

13 VOID MARRIAGES

The provisions of section 49 of the principal Act (void marriages) shall apply to a marriage under the authority of the Registrar General's licence—

(a) with the substitution in paragraph (b) for the words from "certificates for marriage" onwards of the words "a Registrar General's licence";

(c) with the substitution for paragraph (d) of the words "on the authority of a licence which is void by virtue of section 8(2) of the Marriage (Registrar General's Licence) Act 1970";

(d) with the substitution for paragraph (e) of the words "in any place other than the place specified in the notice of marriage and the Registrar General's licence";

(e) with the substitution for paragraphs (f) and (g) of the words "in the absence of a registrar or, where the marriage is by civil ceremony, of a superintendent registrar, except where the marriage is solemnised according to the usages of the Society of Friends or is a marriage between two persons professing the Jewish religion according to the usages of the Jews".

As amended by: Criminal Law Act 1977, s 32(1); Magistrates' Courts Act 1980, s 32(2); Children Act 1989, s 108(7), Sch 15; Marriage Act 1994, s 1(3), Schedule; Marriage Ceremony (Prescribed Words) Act 1996, s 1(2)(b); Immigration and Asylum Act 1999, s 169(1), Sch 14.

Matrimonial Proceedings and Property Act 1970

(1970 c 45)

Provisions relating to property of married persons

37 CONTRIBUTIONS BY SPOUSE IN MONEY OR MONEY'S WORTH TO THE IMPROVEMENT OF PROPERTY

It is hereby declared that where a husband or wife contributes in money or money's worth to the improvement of real or personal property in which or in the proceeds of sale of which either or both of them has or have a beneficial interest, the husband or wife so contributing shall, if the contribution is of a substantial nature and subject to any agreement between them to the contrary express or implied, be treated as having then acquired by virtue of his or her contribution a share or an enlarged share, as the case may be, in that beneficial interest of such an extent as may have been then agreed or, in default of such agreement, as may seem in all the circumstances just to any court before which the question of the existence or extent of the beneficial interest of the husband or wife arises (whether in proceedings between them or in any other proceedings).

39 EXTENSION OF S 17 OF MARRIED WOMEN'S PROPERTY ACT 1882

An application may be made to the High Court or a county court under section 17 of the Married Women's Property Act 1882 (powers of the court in disputes between husband and wife about property) (including that section as extended by section 7 of the Matrimonial Causes (Property and Maintenance) Act 1958) by either of the parties to a marriage notwithstanding that their marriage has been dissolved or annulled so long as the application is made within the period of three years beginning with the date on which the marriage was dissolved or annulled; and references in the said section 17 and the said section 7 to a husband or a wife shall be construed accordingly.

MATRIMONIAL CAUSES ACT 1973

(1973 c 18)

Part I DIVORCE, NULLITY AND OTHER MATRIMONIAL SUITS

Divorce

1 DIVORCE ON BREAKDOWN OF MARRIAGE

(1) Subject to section 3 below, a petition for divorce may be presented to the court by either party to a marriage on the ground that the marriage has broken down irretrievably.

(2) The court hearing a petition for divorce shall not hold the marriage to have broken down irretrievably unless the petitioner satisfies the court of one or more of the following facts, that is to say—

- (a) that the respondent has committed adultery and the petitioner finds it intolerable to live with the respondent;
- (b) that the respondent has behaved in such a way that the petitioner cannot reasonably be expected to live with the respondent;
- (c) that the respondent has deserted the petitioner for a continuous period of at least two years immediately preceding the presentation of the petition;
- (d) that the parties of the marriage have lived apart for a continuous period of at least two years immediately preceding the presentation of the petition (hereafter in this Act referred to as "two years' separation") and the respondent consents to a decree being granted;
- (e) that the parties to the marriage have lived apart for a continuous period of at least five years immediately preceding the presentation of the petition (hereafter in this Act referred to as "five years' separation").

(3) On a petition for divorce it shall be the duty of the court to inquire, so far as it reasonably can, into the facts alleged by the petitioner and into any facts alleged by the respondent.

(4) If the court is satisfied on the evidence of any such fact as is mentioned in subsection (2) above, then, unless it is satisfied on all the evidence that the marriage has not broken down irretrievably, it shall, subject to section 5 below, grant a decree of divorce.

(5) Every decree of divorce shall in the first instance be a decree nisi and shall not be made absolute before the expiration of six months from its grant unless the High Court by general order from time to time fixes a shorter period, or unless in any particular case the court in which the proceedings are for the time being pending from time to time by special order fixes a shorter period than the period otherwise applicable for the time being by virtue of this subsection.

2 SUPPLEMENTAL PROVISIONS AS TO FACTS RAISING PRESUMPTION OF BREAKDOWN

(1) One party to a marriage shall not be entitled to rely for the purposes of section 1(2)(a) above on adultery committed by the other if, after it became known to him that the other had committed that adultery, the parties have lived with each other for a period exceeding, or periods together exceeding, six months.

(2) Where the parties to a marriage have lived with each other after it became known to one party that the other had committed adultery, but subsection (1) above does not apply, in any proceedings for divorce in which the petitioner relies on that adultery the fact that the parties have lived with each other after that time shall be disregarded in determining for the purposes of section 1(2)(a) above whether the petitioner finds it intolerable to live with the respondent.

(3) Where in any proceedings for divorce the petitioner alleges that the respondent has behaved in such a way that the petitioner cannot reasonably be expected to live with him, but the parties to the marriage have lived with each other for a period or periods after the date of the occurrence of the final incident relied on by the petitioner and held by the court to support his allegation, that fact shall be disregarded in determining for the purposes of section 1(2)(b) above whether the petitioner cannot reasonably be expected to live with the respondent if the length of that period or of those periods together was six months or less.

(4) For the purposes of section 1(2)(c) above the court may treat a period of desertion as having continued at a time when the deserting party was incapable of continuing the necessary intention if the evidence before the court is such that, had that party not been so incapable, the court would have inferred that his desertion continued at that time.

(5) In considering for the purposes of section 1(2) above whether the period for which the respondent has deserted the petitioner or the period for which the parties to a marriage have lived apart has been continuous, no account shall be taken of any one period (not exceeding six months) or of any two or more periods (not exceeding six months in all) during which the parties resumed living with each other, but no period during which the parties lived with each other shall count as part of the period of desertion or of the period for which the parties to the marriage lived apart, as the case may be.

(6) For the purposes of section 1(2)(d) and (e) above and this section a husband and wife shall be treated as living apart unless they are living with each other in the same household, and references in this section to the parties to a marriage living with each other shall be construed as references to their living with each other in the same household.

(7) Provision shall be made by rules of court for the purpose of ensuring that where in pursuance of section 1(2)(d) above the petitioner alleges that the respondent consents to a decree being granted the respondent has been given such information as will enable him to understand the consequences to him of his consenting to a decree being granted and the steps which he must take to indicate that he consents to the grant of a decree.

3 BAR ON PETITIONS FOR DIVORCE WITHIN ONE YEAR OF MARRIAGE

(1) No petition for divorce shall be presented to the court before the expiration of the period of one year from the date of the marriage.

(2) Nothing in this section shall prohibit the presentation of a petition based on matters which occurred before the expiration of that period.

4 DIVORCE NOT PRECLUDED BY PREVIOUS JUDICIAL SEPARATION

(1) A person shall not be prevented from presenting a petition for divorce, or the court from granting a decree of divorce, by reason only that the petitioner or respondent has at any time, on the same facts or substantially the same facts as those proved in support of the petition, been granted a decree of judicial separation or an order under, or having effect as if made under, the Matrimonial Proceedings (Magistrates' Courts) Act 1960 or Part I of the Domestic Proceedings and Magistrates' Courts Act 1978 or any corresponding enactments in force in Northern Ireland, the Isle of Man or any of the Channel Islands.

(2) On a petition for divorce in such a case as is mentioned in subsection (1) above, the court may treat the decree or order as sufficient proof of any adultery, desertion or other fact by reference to which it was granted, but shall not grant a decree of divorce without receiving evidence from the petitioner.

(3) Where a petition for divorce in such a case follows a decree of judicial separation or (subject to subsection (5) below) an order containing a provision exempting one party to the marriage from the obligation to cohabit with the other, for the purposes of that petition a period of desertion immediately preceding the institution of the proceedings for the decree or order shall, if the parties have not resumed cohabitation and the decree or order has been continuously in force since it was granted, be deemed immediately to precede the presentation of the petition.

(4) For the purposes of section 1(2)(c) above the court may treat as a period during which the respondent has deserted the petitioner any of the following periods, that is to say—
- (a) any period during which there is in force an injunction granted by the High Court or a county court which excludes the respondent from the matrimonial home;
- (b) any period during which there is in force an order made by the High Court or a county court under section 1 or 9 of the Matrimonial Homes Act 1983 which prohibits the exercise by the respondent of the right to occupy a dwelling-house in which the applicant and the respondent have or at any time have had a matrimonial home;
- (c) any period during which there is in force an order made by a magistrates' court under section 16(3) of the Domestic Proceedings and Magistrates' Courts Act 1978 which requires the respondent to leave the matrimonial home or prohibits the respondent from entering the matrimonial home.

(5) Where—
- (a) a petition for divorce is presented after the date on which Part I of the Domestic Proceedings and Magistrates' Courts Act 1978 comes into force, and
- (b) an order made under the Matrimonial Proceedings (Magistrates' Courts) Act 1960 containing a provision exempting the petitioner from the obligation to cohabit with the respondent is in force on that date,

then, for the purpose of section 1(2)(c) above, the court may treat a period during which such a provision was included in that order (whether before or after that date) as a period during which the respondent has deserted the petitioner.

5 REFUSAL OF DECREE IN FIVE YEAR SEPARATION CASES ON GROUNDS OF GRAVE HARDSHIP TO RESPONDENT

(1) The respondent to a petition for divorce in which the petitioner alleges five years' separation may oppose the grant of a decree on the ground that the dissolution of the marriage will result in grave financial or other hardship to him and that it would in all the circumstances be wrong to dissolve the marriage.

(2) Where the grant of a decree is opposed by virtue of this section, then—
(a) if the court finds that the petitioner is entitled to rely in support of his petition on the fact of five years' separation and makes no such finding as to any other fact mentioned in section 1(2) above, and
(b) if apart from this section the court would grant a decree on the petition,
the court shall consider all the circumstances, including the conduct of the parties to the marriage and the interests of those parties and of any children or other persons concerned, and if of opinion that the dissolution of the marriage will result in grave financial or other hardship to the respondent and that it would in all the circumstances be wrong to dissolve the marriage it shall dismiss the petition.

(3) For the purposes of this section hardship shall include the loss of the chance of acquiring any benefit which the respondent might acquire if the marriage were not dissolved.

6 ATTEMPTS AT RECONCILIATION OF PARTIES TO MARRIAGE

(1) Provision shall be made by rules of court for requiring the legal representative acting for a petitioner for divorce to certify whether he has discussed with the petitioner the possibility of a reconciliation and given him the names and addresses of persons qualified to help effect a reconciliation between parties to a marriage who have becomes estranged.

(2) If at any stage of proceedings for divorce it appears to the court that there is a reasonable possibility of a reconciliation between the parties to the marriage, the court may adjourn the proceedings for such period as it thinks fit to enable attempts to be made to effect such a reconciliation. The power conferred by the foregoing provision is additional to any other power of the court to adjourn proceedings.

7 CONSIDERATION BY THE COURT OF CERTAIN AGREEMENTS OR ARRANGEMENTS

Provision may be made by rules of court for enabling the parties to a marriage, or either of them, on application made either before or after the presentation of a petition for divorce, to refer to the court any agreement or arrangement made or proposed to be made between them, being an agreement or arrangement which relates to, arises out of, or is connected with, the proceedings for divorce which are contemplated or, as the case may be, have begun, and for enabling the court to express an opinion, should it think it desirable to do so, as to the reasonableness of the agreement or arrangement and to give such directions, if any, in the matter as it thinks fit.

8 INTERVENTION OF QUEEN'S PROCTOR

(1) In the case of a petition for divorce—
(a) the court may, if it thinks fit, direct all necessary papers in the matter to be sent to the Queen's Proctor, who shall under the directions of the Attorney-General instruct counsel to argue before the court any question in relation to the matter which the court considers it necessary or expedient to have fully argued;

(b) any person may at any time during the progress of the proceedings or before the decree nisi is made absolute give information to the Queen's Proctor on any matter material to the due decision of the case, and the Queen's Proctor may thereupon take such steps as the Attorney-General considers necessary or expedient.

(2) Where the Queen's Proctor intervenes or shows cause against a decree nisi in any proceedings for divorce, the court may make such order as may be just as to the payment by other parties to the proceedings of the costs incurred by him in so doing or as to the payment by him of any costs incurred by any of those parties by reason of his so doing.

(3) The Queen's Proctor shall be entitled to charge as part of the expenses of his office—
(a) the costs of any proceedings under subsection (1)(a) above;
(b) where his reasonable costs of intervening or showing cause as mentioned in subsection (2) above are not fully satisfied by any order under that subsection, the amount of the difference;
(c) if the Treasury so directs, any costs which he pays to any parties under an order made under subsection (2).

9 PROCEEDINGS AFTER DECREE NISI: GENERAL POWERS OF COURT

(1) Where a decree of divorce has been granted but not made absolute, then, without prejudice to section 8 above, any person (excluding a party to the proceedings other than the Queen's Proctor) may show cause why the decree should not be made absolute by reason of material facts not having been brought before the court; and in such a case the court may—
(a) notwithstanding anything in section 1(5) above (but subject to sections 10(2) to (4) and 41 below) make the decree absolute; or
(b) rescind the decree; or
(c) require further inquiry; or
(d) otherwise deal with the case as it thinks fit.

(2) Where a decree of divorce has been granted and no application for it to be made absolute has been made by the party to whom it was granted, then, at any time after the expiration of three months from the earliest date on which that party could have made such an application, the party against whom it was granted may make an application to the court, and on that application the court may exercise any of the powers mentioned in paragraphs (a) to (d) of subsection (1) above.

10 PROCEEDINGS AFTER DECREE NISI: SPECIAL PROTECTION FOR RESPONDENT IN SEPARATION CASES

(1) Where in any case the court has granted a decree of divorce on the basis of a finding that the petitioner was entitled to rely in support of his petition on the fact of two years' separation coupled with the respondent's consent to a decree being granted and has made no such finding as to any other fact mentioned in section 1(2) above, the court may, on an application made by the respondent at any time before the decree is made absolute, rescind the decree if it is satisfied that the petitioner misled the respondent (whether intentionally or unintentionally) about any matter which the respondent took into account in deciding to give his consent.

(2) The following provisions of this section apply where—
(a) the respondent to a petition for divorce in which the petitioner alleged two years' or five years' separation coupled, in the former case, with the respondent's consent to a

decree being granted, has applied to the court for consideration under subsection (3) below of his financial position after the divorce; and
(b) the court has granted a decree on the petition on the basis of a finding that the petitioner was entitled to rely in support of his petition on the fact of two years' or five years' separation (as the case may be) and has made no such finding as to any other fact mentioned in section 1(2) above.

(3) The court hearing an application by the respondent under subsection (2) above shall consider all the circumstances, including the age, health, conduct, earning capacity, financial resources and financial obligations of each of the parties, and the financial position of the respondent as, having regard to the divorce, it is likely to be after the death of the petitioner should the petitioner die first; and, subject to subsection (4) below, the court shall not make the decree absolute unless it is satisfied—
(a) that the petitioner should not be required to make any financial provision for the respondent, or
(b) that the financial provision made by the petitioner for the respondent is reasonable and fair or the best that can be made in the circumstances.

(4) The court may if it thinks fit make the decree absolute notwithstanding the requirements of subsection (3) above if—
(a) it appears that there are circumstances making it desirable that the decree should be made absolute without delay, and
(b) the court has obtained a satisfactory undertaking from the petitioner that he will make such financial provision for the respondent as the court may approve.

10A PROCEEDINGS AFTER DECREE NISI: RELIGIOUS MARRIAGE

(1) This section applies if a decree of divorce has been granted but not made absolute and the parties to the marriage concerned—
(a) were married in accordance with—
(i) the usages of the Jews, or
(ii) any other prescribed religious usages; and
(b) must co-operate if the marriage is to be dissolved in accordance with those usages.

(2) On the application of either party, the court may order that a decree of divorce is not to be made absolute until a declaration made by both parties that they have taken such steps as are required to dissolve the marriage in accordance with those usages is produced to the court.

(3) An order under subsection (2)—
(a) may be made only if the court is satisfied that in all the circumstances of the case it is just and reasonable to do so; and
(b) may be revoked at any time.

(4) A declaration of a kind mentioned in subsection (2)—
(a) must be in a specified form;
(b) must, in specified cases, be accompanied by such documents as may be specified; and
(c) must, in specified cases, satisfy such other requirements as may be specified.

(5) The validity of a decree of divorce made by reference to such a declaration is not to be affected by any inaccuracy in that declaration.

(6) "Prescribed" means prescribed in an order made by the Lord Chancellor after consulting the Lord Chief Justice and such an order—
(a) must be made by statutory instrument;
(b) shall be subject to annulment in pursuance of a resolution of either House of Parliament.

(7) "Specified" means specified in rules of court.

(8) The Lord Chief Justice may nominate a judicial office holder (as defined in section 109(4) of the Constitutional Reform Act 2005) to exercise his functions under this section.

Nullity

11 GROUNDS ON WHICH A MARRIAGE IS VOID

A marriage celebrated after 31st July 1971 shall be void on the following grounds only, that is to say—

(a) that it is not a valid marriage under the provisions of the Marriage Acts 1949 to 1986 (that is to say where—
  (i) the parties are within the prohibited degrees of relationship;
  (ii) either party is under the age of sixteen; or
  (iii) the parties have intermarried in disregard of certain requirements as to the formation of marriage);

(b) that at the time of the marriage either party was already lawfully married or a civil partner;

(c) that the parties are not respectively male and female;

(d) in the case of a polygamous marriage entered into outside England and Wales, that either party was at the time of the marriage domiciled in England and Wales.

For the purposes of paragraph (d) of this subsection a marriage is not polygamous if at its inception neither party has any spouse additional to the other.

12 GROUNDS ON WHICH A MARRIAGE IS VOIDABLE

A marriage celebrated after 31st July 1971 shall be voidable on the following grounds only, that is to say—

(a) that the marriage has not been consummated owing to the incapacity of either party to consummate it;

(b) that the marriage has not been consummated owing to the wilful refusal of the respondent to consummate it;

(c) that either party to the marriage did not validly consent to it, whether in consequence of duress, mistake, unsoundness of mind or otherwise;

(d) that at the time of the marriage either party, though capable of giving a valid consent, was suffering (whether continuously or intermittently) from mental disorder within the meaning of the Mental Health Act 1983 of such a kind or to such an extent as to be unfitted for marriage;

(e) that at the time of the marriage the respondent was suffering from venereal disease in a communicable form;

(f) that at the time of the marriage the respondent was pregnant by some person other than the petitioner;

(g) that an interim gender recognition certificate under the Gender Recognition Act 2004 has, after the time of the marriage, been issued to either party to the marriage;

(h) that the respondent is a person whose gender at the time of the marriage had become the acquired gender under the Gender Recognition Act 2004.

13 BARS TO RELIEF WHERE MARRIAGE IS VOIDABLE

(1) The court shall not, in proceedings instituted after 31st July 1971, grant a decree of nullity on the ground that a marriage is voidable if the respondent satisfies the court—
- (a) that the petitioner, with knowledge that it was open to him to have the marriage avoided, so conducted himself in relation to the respondent as to lead the respondent reasonably to believe that he would not seek to do so; and
- (b) that it would be unjust to the respondent to grant the decree.

(2) Without prejudice to subsection (1) above, the court shall not grant a decree of nullity by virtue of section 12 above on the grounds mentioned in paragraph (c), (d), (e), (f) or (h) of that section unless—
- (a) it is satisfied that proceedings were instituted within the period of three years from the date of the marriage, or
- (b) leave for the institution of proceedings after the expiration of that period has been granted under subsection (4) below.

(2A) Without prejudice to subsection (1) above, the court shall not grant a decree of nullity by virtue of section 12 above on the ground mentioned in paragraph (g) of that section unless it is satisfied that proceedings were instituted within the period of six months from the date of issue of the interim gender recognition certificate.

(3) Without prejudice to subsections (1) and (2) above, the court shall not grant a decree of nullity by virtue of section 12 above on the grounds mentioned in paragraph (e), (f) or (h) of that section unless it is satisfied that the petitioner was at the time of the marriage ignorant of the facts alleged.

(4) In the case of proceedings for the grant of a decree of nullity by virtue of section 12 above on the grounds mentioned in paragraph (c), (d), (e), (f) or (h) of that section, a judge of the court may, on an application made to him, grant leave for the institution of proceedings after the expiration of the period of three years from the date of the marriage if—
- (a) he is satisfied that the petitioner has at some time during that period suffered from mental disorder within the meaning of the Mental Health Act 1983, and
- (b) he considers that in all the circumstances of the case it would be just to grant leave for the institution of proceedings.

(5) An application for leave under subsection (4) above may be made after the expiration of the period of three years from the date of the marriage.

14 MARRIAGES GOVERNED BY FOREIGN LAW OR CELEBRATED ABROAD UNDER ENGLISH LAW

(1) Subject to subsection (3) where, apart from this Act, any matter affecting the validity of a marriage would fall to be determined (in accordance with the rules of private international law) by reference to the law of a country outside England and Wales, nothing in section 11, 12 or 13(1) above shall—
- (a) preclude the determination of that matter as aforesaid; or
- (b) require the application to the marriage of the grounds or bar there mentioned except so far as applicable in accordance with those rules.

(2) In the case of a marriage which purports to have been celebrated under the Foreign Marriage Acts 1892 to 1947 or has taken place outside England and Wales and purports to be a marriage under common law, section 11 above is without prejudice to any ground on which the marriage may be void under those Acts or, as the case may be, by virtue of the rules governing the celebration of marriages outside England and Wales under common law.

(3) No marriage is to be treated as valid by virtue of subsection (1) if, at the time when it purports to have been celebrated, either party was already a civil partner.

15 APPLICATION OF SS 1(5), 8 AND 9 TO NULLITY PROCEEDINGS

Sections 1(5), 8 and 9 above shall apply in relation to proceedings for nullity of marriage as if for any reference in those provisions to divorce there were substituted a reference to nullity of marriage.

16 EFFECT OF DECREE OF NULLITY IN CASE OF VOIDABLE MARRIAGE

A decree of nullity granted after 31st July 1971 in respect of a voidable marriage shall operate to annul the marriage only as respects any time after the decree has been made absolute, and the marriage shall, notwithstanding the decree, be treated as if it had existed up to that time.

Other matrimonial suits

17 JUDICIAL SEPARATION

(1) A petition for judicial separation may be presented to the court by either party to a marriage on the ground that any such fact as is mentioned in section 1(2) above exists, and the provisions of section 2 above shall apply accordingly for the purposes of a petition for judicial separation alleging any such fact, as they apply in relation to a petition for divorce alleging that fact.

(2) On a petition for judicial separation it shall be the duty of the court to inquire, so far as it reasonably can, into the facts alleged by the petitioner and into any facts alleged by the respondent, but the court shall not be concerned to consider whether the marriage has broken down irretrievably, and if it is satisfied on the evidence of any such fact as is mentioned in section 1(2) above it shall, subject to section 41 below, grant a decree of judicial separation.

(3) Sections 6 and 7 above shall apply for the purpose of encouraging the reconciliation of parties to proceedings for judicial separation and of enabling the parties to a marriage to refer to the court for its opinion an agreement or arrangement relevant to actual or contemplated proceedings for judicial separation, as they apply in relation to proceedings for divorce.

18 EFFECTS OF JUDICIAL SEPARATION

(1) Where the court grants a decree of judicial separation it shall no longer be obligatory for the petitioner to cohabit with the respondent.

(2) If while a decree of judicial separation is in force and the separation is continuing either of the parties to the marriage dies intestate as respects all or any of his or her real or personal property, the property as respects which he or she died intestate shall devolve as if the other party to the marriage had then been dead.

(3) Notwithstanding anything in section 2(1)(a) of the Matrimonial Proceedings (Magistrates' Courts) Act 1960, a provision in force under an order made, or having effect as if made, under that section exempting one party to a marriage from the obligation to cohabit with the other shall not have effect as a decree of judicial separation for the purposes of subsection (2) above.

19 PRESUMPTION OF DEATH AND DISSOLUTION OF MARRIAGE

(1) Any married person who alleges that reasonable grounds exist for supposing that the other party to the marriage is dead may present a petition to the court to have it presumed that the other party is dead and to have the marriage dissolved, and the court may, if satisfied that such reasonable grounds exist, grant a decree of presumption of death and dissolution of the marriage.

(3) In any proceedings under this section the fact that for a period of seven years or more the other party to the marriage has been continually absent from the petitioner and the petitioner has no reason to believe that the other party has been living within that time shall be evidence that the other party is dead until the contrary is proved.

(4) Sections 1(5), 8 and 9 above shall apply to a petition and a decree under this section as they apply to a petition for divorce and a decree of divorce respectively.

(6) It is hereby declared that neither collusion nor any other conduct on the part of the petitioner which has at any time been a bar to relief in matrimonial proceedings constitutes a bar to the grant of a decree under this section.

General

20 RELIEF FOR RESPONDENT IN DIVORCE PROCEEDINGS

If in any proceedings for divorce the respondent alleges and proves any such fact as is mentioned in subsection (2) of section 1 above (treating the respondent as the petitioner and the petitioner as the respondent for the purposes of that subsection) the court may give to the respondent the relief to which he would have been entitled if he had presented a petition seeking that relief.

Part II FINANCIAL RELIEF FOR PARTIES TO MARRIAGE AND CHILDREN OF FAMILY

Financial provision and property adjustment orders

21 FINANCIAL PROVISION AND PROPERTY ADJUSTMENT ORDERS

(1) The financial provision orders for the purposes of this Act are the orders for periodical or lump sum provision available (subject to the provisions of this Act) under section 23 below for the purpose of adjusting the financial position of the parties to a marriage and any children of the family in connection with proceedings for divorce, nullity of marriage or judicial separation and under section 27(6) below on proof of neglect by one party to a marriage to provide, or to make a proper contribution towards, reasonable maintenance for the other or a child of the family, that is to say—

(a) any order for periodical payments in favour of a party to a marriage under section 23(1)(a) or 27(6)(a) or in favour of a child of the family under section 23(1)(d), (2) or (4) or 27(6)(d);

(b) any order for secured periodical payments in favour of a party to a marriage under section 23(1)(b) or 27(6)(b) or in favour of a child of the family under section 23(1)(e), (2) or (4) or 27(6)(e); and

(c) any order for lump sum provision in favour of a party to a marriage under section 23(1)(c) or 27(6)(c) or in favour of a child of the family under section 23(1)(f), (2) or (4) or 27(6)(f);

and references in this Act (except in paragraphs 17(1) and 23 of Schedule 1 below) to periodical payments orders, secured periodical payments orders, and orders for the payment of a lump sum are references to all or some of the financial provision orders requiring the sort of financial provision in question according as the context of each reference may require.

(2) The property adjustment orders for the purposes of this Act are the orders dealing with property rights available (subject to the provisions of this Act) under section 24 below for the purpose of adjusting the financial position of the parties to a marriage and any children of the family on or after the grant of a decree of divorce, nullity of marriage or judicial separation, that is to say—
(a) any order under subsection (1)(a) of that section for a transfer of property;
(b) any order under subsection (1)(b) of that section for a settlement of property; and
(c) any order under subsection (1)(c) or (d) of that section for a variation of settlement.

21A PENSION SHARING ORDERS

(1) For the purposes of this Act, a pension sharing order is an order which—
(a) provides that one party's—
(i) shareable rights under a specified pension arrangement, or
(ii) shareable state scheme rights, be subject to pension sharing for the benefit of the other party, and
(b) specifies the percentage value to be transferred.

(2) In subsection (1) above—
(a) the reference to shareable rights under a pension arrangement is to rights in relation to which pension sharing is available under Chapter I of Part IV of the Welfare Reform and Pensions Act 1999, or under corresponding Northern Ireland legislation,
(b) the reference to shareable state scheme rights is to rights in relation to which pension sharing is available under Chapter II of Part IV of the Welfare Reform and Pensions Act 1999, or under corresponding Northern Ireland legislation, and
(c) "party" means a party to a marriage.

21B PENSION COMPENSATION SHARING ORDERS

(1) For the purposes of this Act, a pension compensation sharing order is an order which—
(a) provides that one party's shareable rights to PPF compensation that derive from rights under a specified pension scheme are to be subject to pension compensation sharing for the benefit of the other party, and
(b) specifies the percentage value to be transferred.

(2) In subsection (1)—
(a) the reference to shareable rights to PPF compensation is to rights in relation to which pension compensation sharing is available under Chapter 1 of Part 3 of the Pensions Act 2008 . . .;
(b) "party" means a party to a marriage;
(c) "specified" means specified in the order.

21C PENSION COMPENSATION: INTERPRETATION

In this Part—

"PPF compensation" means compensation payable under the pension compensation provisions;

"the pension compensation provisions" means—

(a) Chapter 3 of Part 2 of the Pensions Act 2004 (pension protection) and any regulations or order made under it,
(b) Chapter 1 of Part 3 of the Pensions Act 2008 (pension compensation on divorce etc) and any regulations or order made under it . . .

Ancillary relief in connection with divorce proceedings, etc

22 MAINTENANCE PENDING SUIT

On a petition for divorce, nullity of marriage or judicial separation, the court may make an order for maintenance pending suit, that is to say, an order requiring either party to the marriage to make to the other such periodical payments for his or her maintenance and for such term, being a term beginning not earlier than the date of the presentation of the petition and ending with the date of the determination of the suit, as the court thinks reasonable.

23 FINANCIAL PROVISION ORDERS IN CONNECTION WITH DIVORCE PROCEEDINGS, ETC

(1) On granting a decree of divorce, a decree of nullity of marriage or a decree of judicial separation or at any time thereafter (whether, in the case of a decree of divorce or of nullity of marriage, before or after the decree is made absolute), the court may make any one or more of the following orders, that is to say—
(a) an order that either party to the marriage shall make to the other such periodical payments, for such term, as may be specified in the order;
(b) an order that either party to the marriage shall secure to the other to the satisfaction of the court such periodical payments, for such term, as may be so specified;
(c) an order that either party to the marriage shall pay to the other such lump sum or sums as may be so specified;
(d) an order that a party to the marriage shall make to such person as may be specified in the order for the benefit of a child of the family, or to such a child, such periodical payments, for such term, as may be so specified;
(e) an order that a party to the marriage shall secure to such person as may be so specified for the benefit of such a child, or to such a child, to the satisfaction of the court, such periodical payments, for such term, as may be so specified;
(f) an order that a party to the marriage shall pay to such person as may be so specified for the benefit of such a child, or to such a child, such lump sum as may be so specified;
subject, however, in the case of an order under paragraph (d), (e) or (f) above, to the restrictions imposed by section 29(1) and (3) below on the making of financial provision orders in favour of children who have attained the age of eighteen.

(2) The court may also, subject to those restrictions, make any one or more of the orders mentioned in subsection (1)(d), (e) and (f) above—
(a) in any proceedings for divorce, nullity of marriage or judicial separation, before granting a decree; and
(b) where any such proceedings are dismissed after the beginning of the trial, either forthwith or within a reasonable period after the dismissal.

(3) Without prejudice to the generality of subsection (1)(c) or (f) above—
(a) an order under this section that a party to a marriage shall pay a lump sum to the other party may be made for the purpose of enabling that other party to meet any liabilities or expenses reasonably incurred by him or her in maintaining himself or herself or any child of the family before making an application for an order under this section in his or her favour;

(b) an order under this section for the payment of a lump sum to or for the benefit of a child of the family may be made for the purpose of enabling any liabilities or expenses reasonably incurred by or for the benefit of that child before the making of an application for an order under this section in his favour to be met; and
(c) an order under this section for the payment of a lump sum may provide for the payment of that sum by instalments of such amount as may be specified in the order and may require the payment of the instalments to be secured to the satisfaction of the court.

(4) The power of the court under subsection (1) or (2)(a) above to make an order in favour of a child of the family shall be exercisable from time to time; and where the court makes an order in favour of a child under subsection (2)(b) above, it may from time to time, subject to the restrictions mentioned in subsection (1) above, make a further order in his favour of any of the kinds mentioned in subsection (1)(d), (e) or (f) above.

(5) Without prejudice to the power to give a direction under section 30 below for the settlement of an instrument by conveyancing counsel, where an order is made under subsection (1)(a), (b) or (c) above on or after granting a decree of divorce or nullity of marriage, neither the order nor any settlement made in pursuance of the order shall take effect unless the decree has been made absolute.

(6) Where the court—
(a) makes an order under this section for the payment of a lump of sum; and
(b) directs—
(i) that payment of that sum or any part of it shall be deferred; or
(ii) that that sum or any part of it shall be paid by instalments,
the court may order that the amount deferred or the instalments shall carry interest at such rate as may be specified by the order from such date, not earlier than the date of the order, as may be so specified, until the date when payment of it is due.

24 PROPERTY ADJUSTMENT ORDERS IN CONNECTION WITH DIVORCE PROCEEDINGS, ETC

(1) On granting a decree of divorce, a decree of nullity of marriage or a decree of judicial separation or at any time thereafter (whether, in the case of a decree of divorce or of nullity of marriage, before or after the decree is made absolute), the court may make any one or more of the following orders, that is to say—
(a) an order that a party to the marriage shall transfer to the other party, to any child of the family or to such person as may be specified in the order for the benefit of such a child such property as may be so specified, being property to which the first-mentioned party is entitled, either in possession or reversion;
(b) an order that a settlement of such property as may be so specified, being property to which a party to the marriage is so entitled, be made to the satisfaction of the court for the benefit of the other party to the marriage and of the children of the family or either or any of them;
(c) an order varying for the benefit of the parties to the marriage and of the children of the family or either or any of them any ante-nuptial or post-nuptial settlement (including such a settlement made by will or codicil) made on the parties to the marriage, other than one in the form of a pension arrangement (within the meaning of section 25D below);
(d) an order extinguishing or reducing the interest of either of the parties to the marriage under any such settlement, other than one in the form of a pension arrangement (within the meaning of section 25D below);

subject, however, in the case of an order under paragraph (a) above, to the restrictions imposed by section 29(1) and (3) below on the making of orders for a transfer of property in favour of children who have attained the age of eighteen.

(2) The court may make an order under subsection (1)(c) above notwithstanding that there are no children of the family.

(3) Without prejudice to the power to give a direction under section 30 below for the settlement of an instrument by conveyancing counsel, where an order is made under this section on or after granting a decree of divorce or nullity of marriage, neither the order nor any settlement made in pursuance of the order shall take effect unless the decree has been made absolute.

24A ORDERS FOR SALE OF PROPERTY

(1) Where the court makes under section 23 or 24 of this Act a secured periodical payments order, an order for the payment of a lump sum or a property adjustment order, then, on making that order or at any time thereafter, the court may make a further order for the sale of such property as may be specified in the order, being property in which or in the proceeds of sale of which either or both of the parties to the marriage has or have a beneficial interest, either in possession or reversion.

(2) Any order made under subsection (1) above may contain such consequential or supplementary provisions as the court thinks fit and, without prejudice to the generality of the foregoing provision, may include—
- (a) provision requiring the making of a payment out of the proceeds of sale of the property to which the order relates, and
- (b) provision requiring any such property to be offered for sale to a person, or class of persons, specified in the order.

(3) Where an order is made under subsection (1) above on or after the grant of a decree of divorce or nullity of marriage, the order shall not take effect unless the decree has been made absolute.

(4) Where an order is made under subsection (1) above, the court may direct that the order, or such provision thereof as the court may specify, shall not take effect until the occurrence of an event specified by the court or the expiration of a period so specified.

(5) Where an order under subsection (1) above contains a provision requiring the proceeds of sale of the property to which the order relates to be used to secure periodical payments to a party to the marriage, the order shall cease to have effect on the death or re-marriage of, or formation of a civil partnership by, that person.

(6) Where a party to a marriage has a beneficial interest in any property, or in the proceeds of sale thereof, and some other person who is not a party to the marriage also has a beneficial interest in that property or in the proceeds of sale thereof, then, before deciding whether to make an order under this section in relation to that property, it shall be the duty of the court to give that other person an opportunity to make representations with respect to the order; and any representations made by that other person shall be included among the circumstances to which the court is required to have regard under section 25(1) below.

24B PENSION SHARING ORDERS IN CONNECTION WITH DIVORCE PROCEEDINGS ETC

(1) On granting a decree of divorce or a decree of nullity of marriage or at any time thereafter (whether before or after the decree is made absolute), the court may, on an application

made under this section, make one or more pension sharing orders in relation to the marriage.

(2) A pension sharing order under this section is not to take effect unless the decree on or after which it is made has been made absolute.

(3) A pension sharing order under this section may not be made in relation to a pension arrangement which—
(a) is the subject of a pension sharing order in relation to the marriage, or
(b) has been the subject of pension sharing between the parties to the marriage.

(4) A pension sharing order under this section may not be made in relation to shareable state scheme rights if—
(a) such rights are the subject of a pension sharing order in relation to the marriage, or
(b) such rights have been the subject of pension sharing between the parties to the marriage.

(5) A pension sharing order under this section may not be made in relation to the rights of a person under a pension arrangement if there is in force a requirement imposed by virtue of section 25B or 25C below which relates to benefits or future benefits to which he is entitled under the pension arrangement.

24C PENSION SHARING ORDERS: DUTY TO STAY

(1) No pension sharing order may be made so as to take effect before the end of such period after the making of the order as may be prescribed by regulations made by the Lord Chancellor.

(2) The power to make regulations under this section shall be exercisable by statutory instrument which shall be subject to annulment in pursuance of a resolution of either House of Parliament.

24D PENSION SHARING ORDERS: APPORTIONMENT OF CHARGES

If a pension sharing order relates to rights under a pension arrangement, the court may include in the order provision about the apportionment between the parties of any charge under section 41 of the Welfare Reform and Pensions Act 1999 (charges in respect of pension sharing costs), or under corresponding Northern Ireland legislation.

24E PENSION COMPENSATION SHARING ORDERS IN CONNECTION WITH DIVORCE PROCEEDINGS

(1) On granting a decree of divorce or a decree of nullity of marriage or at any time thereafter (whether before or after the decree is made absolute), the court may, on an application made under this section, make a pension compensation sharing order in relation to the marriage.

(2) A pension compensation sharing order under this section is not to take effect unless the decree on or after which it is made has been made absolute.

(3) A pension compensation sharing order under this section may not be made in relation to rights to PPF compensation that—
(a) are the subject of pension attachment,
(b) derive from rights under a pension scheme that were the subject of pension sharing between the parties to the marriage,

(c) are the subject of pension compensation attachment, or
(d) are or have been the subject of pension compensation sharing between the parties to the marriage.

(4) For the purposes of subsection (3)(a), rights to PPF compensation "are the subject of pension attachment" if any of the following three conditions is met.

(5) The first condition is that—
(a) the rights derive from rights under a pension scheme in relation to which an order was made under section 23 imposing a requirement by virtue of section 25B(4), and
(b) that order, as modified under section 25E(3), remains in force.

(6) The second condition is that—
(a) the rights derive from rights under a pension scheme in relation to which an order was made under section 23 imposing a requirement by virtue of section 25B(7), and
(b) that order—
(i) has been complied with, or
(ii) has not been complied with and, as modified under section 25E(5), remains in force.

(7) The third condition is that—
(a) the rights derive from rights under a pension scheme in relation to which an order was made under section 23 imposing a requirement by virtue of section 25C, and
(b) that order remains in force.

(8) For the purposes of subsection (3)(b), rights under a pension scheme "were the subject of pension sharing between the parties to the marriage" if the rights were at any time the subject of a pension sharing order in relation to the marriage or a previous marriage between the same parties.

(9) For the purposes of subsection (3)(c), rights to PPF compensation "are the subject of pension compensation attachment" if there is in force a requirement imposed by virtue of section 25F relating to them.

(10) For the purposes of subsection (3)(d), rights to PPF compensation "are or have been the subject of pension compensation sharing between the parties to the marriage" if they are or have ever been the subject of a pension compensation sharing order in relation to the marriage or a previous marriage between the same parties.

24F PENSION COMPENSATION SHARING ORDERS: DUTY TO STAY

(1) No pension compensation sharing order may be made so as to take effect before the end of such period after the making of the order as may be prescribed by regulations made by the Lord Chancellor.

(2) The power to make regulations under this section shall be exercisable by statutory instrument which shall be subject to annulment in pursuance of a resolution of either House of Parliament.

24G PENSION COMPENSATION SHARING ORDERS: APPORTIONMENT OF CHARGES

The court may include in a pension compensation sharing order provision about the apportionment between the parties of any charge under section 117 of the Pensions Act 2008 (charges in respect of pension compensation sharing costs) . . .

25 MATTERS TO WHICH COURT IS TO HAVE REGARD IN DECIDING HOW TO EXERCISE ITS POWERS UNDER SS 23, 24, 24A, 24B AND 24E

(1) It shall be the duty of the court in deciding whether to exercise its powers under section 23, 24, 24A, 24B or 24E above and, if so, in what manner, to have regard to all the circumstances of the case, first consideration being given to the welfare while a minor of any child of the family who has not attained the age of eighteen.

(2) As regards the exercise of the powers of the court under section 23(1)(a), (b) or (c), 24, 24A, 24B or 24E above in relation to a party to the marriage, the court shall in particular have regard to the following matters—
- (a) the income, earning capacity, property and other financial resources which each of the parties to the marriage has or is likely to have in the foreseeable future, including in the case of earning capacity any increase in that capacity which it would in the opinion of the court be reasonable to expect a party to the marriage to take steps to acquire;
- (b) the financial needs, obligations and responsibilities which each of the parties to the marriage has or is likely to have in the foreseeable future;
- (c) the standard of living enjoyed by the family before the breakdown of the marriage;
- (d) the age of each party to the marriage and the duration of the marriage;
- (e) any physical or mental disability of either of the parties to the marriage;
- (f) the contributions which each of the parties has made or is likely in the foreseeable future to make to the welfare of the family, including any contribution by looking after the home or caring for the family;
- (g) the conduct of each of the parties, if that conduct is such that it would in the opinion of the court be inequitable to disregard it;
- (h) the value to each of the parties to the marriage of any benefit which, by reason of the dissolution or annulment of the marriage, that party will lose the chance of acquiring.

(3) As regards the exercise of the powers of the court under section 23(1)(d), (e) or (f), (2) or (4), 24 or 24A above in relation to a child of the family, the court shall in particular have regard to the following matters—
- (a) the financial needs of the child;
- (b) the income, earning capacity (if any), property and other financial resources of the child;
- (c) any physical or mental disability of the child;
- (d) the manner in which he was being and in which the parties to the marriage expected him to be educated or trained;
- (e) the considerations mentioned in relation to the parties to the marriage in paragraphs (a), (b), (c) and (e) of subsection (2) above.

(4) As regards the exercise of the powers of the court under section 23(1)(d), (e) or (f), (2) or (4), 24 or 24A above against a party to a marriage in favour of a child of the family who is not the child of that party, the court shall also have regard—
- (a) to whether that party assumed any responsibility for the child's maintenance, and, if so, to the extent to which, and the basis upon which, that party assumed such responsibility and to the length of time for which that party discharged such responsibility;
- (b) to whether in assuming and discharging such responsibility that party did so knowing that the child was not his or her own;
- (c) to the liability of any other person to maintain the child.

25A EXERCISE OF COURT'S POWERS IN FAVOUR OF PARTY TO MARRIAGE ON DECREE OF DIVORCE OR NULLITY OF MARRIAGE

(1) Where on or after the grant of a decree of divorce or nullity of marriage the court decides to exercise its powers under section 23(1)(a), (b) or (c), 24, 24A, 24B or 24E above in favour of a party to the marriage, it shall be the duty of the court to consider whether it would be appropriate so to exercise those powers that the financial obligations of each party towards the other will be terminated as soon after the grant of the decree as the court considers just and reasonable.

(2) Where the court decides in such a case to make a periodical payments or secured periodical payments order in favour of a party to the marriage, the court shall in particular consider whether it would be appropriate to require those payments to be made or secured only for such term as would in the opinion of the court be sufficient to enable the party in whose favour the order is made to adjust without undue hardship to the termination of his or her financial dependence on the other party.

(3) Where on or after the grant of a decree of divorce or nullity of marriage an application is made by a party to the marriage for a periodical payments or secured periodical payments order in his or her favour, then, if the court considers that no continuing obligation should be imposed on either party to make or secure periodical payments in favour of the other, the court may dismiss the application with a direction that the applicant shall not be entitled to make any future application in relation to that marriage for an order under section 23(1)(a) or (b) above.

25B PENSIONS

(1) The matters to which the court is to have regard under section 25(2) above include—
- (a) in the case of paragraph (a), any benefits under a pension arrangement which a party to the marriage has or is likely to have, and
- (b) in the case of paragraph (h), any benefits under a pension arrangement which, by reason of the dissolution or annulment of the marriage, a party to the marriage will lose the chance of acquiring,

and, accordingly, in relation to benefits under a pension arrangement, section 25(2)(a) above shall have effect as if "in the foreseeable future" were omitted.

(3) The following provisions apply where, having regard to any benefits under a pension arrangement, the court determines to make an order under section 23 above.

(4) To the extent to which the order is made having regard to any benefits under a pension arrangement, the order may require the person responsible for the pension arrangement in question, if at any time any payment in respect of any benefits under the arrangement becomes due to the party with pension rights, to make a payment for the benefit of the other party.

(5) The order must express the amount of any payment required to be made by virtue of subsection (4) above as a percentage of the payment which becomes due to the party with pension rights.

(6) Any such payment by the person responsible for the arrangement—
- (a) shall discharge so much of his liability to the party with pension rights as corresponds to the amount of the payment, and
- (b) shall be treated for all purposes as a payment made by the party with pension rights in or towards the discharge of his liability under the order.

(7) Where the party with pension rights has a right of commutation under the arrangement, the order may require him to exercise it to any extent; and this section applies to any payment due in consequence of commutation in pursuance of the order as it applies to other payments in respect of benefits under the arrangement.

(7A) The power conferred by subsection (7) above may not be exercised for the purpose of commuting a benefit payable to the party with pension rights to a benefit payable to the other party.

(7B) The power conferred by subsection (4) or (7) above may not be exercised in relation to a pension arrangement which—
(a) is the subject of a pension sharing order in relation to the marriage, or
(b) has been the subject of pension sharing between the parties to the marriage.

(7C) In subsection (1) above, references to benefits under a pension arrangement include any benefits by way of pension, whether under a pension arrangement or not.

25C PENSIONS: LUMP SUMS

(1) The power of the court under section 23 above to order a party to a marriage to pay a lump sum to the other party includes, where the benefits which the party with pension rights has or is likely to have under a pension arrangement include any lump sum payable in respect of his death, power to make any of the following provision by the order.

(2) The court may—
(a) if the person responsible for the pension arrangement in question has power to determine the person to whom the sum, or any part of it, is to be paid, require him to pay the whole or part of that sum, when it becomes due, to the other party,
(b) if the party with pension rights has power to nominate the person to whom the sum, or any part of it, is to be paid, require the party with pension rights to nominate the other party in respect of the whole or part of that sum,
(c) in any other case, require the person responsible for the pension arrangement in question to pay the whole or part of that sum, when it becomes due, for the benefit of the other party instead of to the person to whom, apart from the order, it would be paid.

(3) Any payment by the person responsible for the arrangement under an order made under section 23 above by virtue of this section shall discharge so much of his liability in respect of the party with pension rights as corresponds to the amount of the payment.

(4) The powers conferred by this section may not be exercised in relation to a pension arrangement which—
(a) is the subject of a pension sharing order in relation to the marriage, or
(b) has been the subject of pension sharing between the parties to the marriage.

25D PENSIONS: SUPPLEMENTARY

(1) Where—
(a) an order made under section 23 above by virtue of section 25B or 25C above imposes any requirement on the person responsible for a pension arrangement ("the first arrangement") and the party with pension rights acquires rights under another pension arrangement ("the new arrangement") which are derived (directly or indirectly) from the whole of his rights under the first arrangement, and
(b) the person responsible for the new arrangement has been given notice in accordance with regulations made by the Lord Chancellor, the order shall have effect as if it had been made instead in respect of the person responsible for the new arrangement.

(2) The Lord Chancellor may by regulations—
(a) in relation to any provision of sections 25B or 25C above which authorises the court making an order under section 23 above to require the person responsible for a pension arrangement to make a payment for the benefit of the other party, make provision as to the person to whom, and the terms on which, the payment is to be made,
(ab) make, in relation to payment under a mistaken belief as to the continuation in force of a provision included by virtue of section 25B or 25C above in an order under section 23 above, provision about the rights or liabilities of the payer, the payee or the person to whom the payment was due,
(b) require notices to be given in respect of changes of circumstances relevant to such orders which include provision made by virtue of sections 25B and 25C above,
(ba) make provision for the person responsible for a pension arrangement to be discharged in prescribed circumstances from a requirement imposed by virtue of section 25B or 25C above,
(e) make provision about calculation and verification in relation to the valuation of—
(i) benefits under a pension arrangement, or
(ii) shareable state scheme rights, for the purposes of the court's functions in connection with the exercise of any of its powers under this Part of this Act,

(2A) Regulations under subsection (2)(e) above may include—
(a) provision for calculation or verification in accordance with guidance from time to time prepared by a prescribed person, and
(b) provision by reference to regulations under section 30 or 49(4) of the Welfare Reform and Pensions Act 1999.

(2B) Regulations under subsection (2) above may make different provision for different cases.

(2C) Power to make regulations under this section shall be exercisable by statutory instrument which shall be subject to annulment in pursuance of a resolution of either House of Parliament.

(3) In this section and sections 25B and 25C above—

"occupational pension scheme" has the same meaning as in the Pension Schemes Act 1993;

"the party with pension rights" means the party to the marriage who has or is likely to have benefits under a pension arrangement and "the other party" means the other party to the marriage;

"pension arrangement" means—
(a) an occupational pension scheme,
(b) a personal pension scheme,
(c) a retirement annuity contract,
(d) an annuity or insurance policy purchased, or transferred, for the purpose of giving effect to rights under an occupational pension scheme or a personal pension scheme, and
(e) an annuity purchased, or entered into, for the purpose of discharging liability in respect of a pension credit under section 29(1)(b) of the Welfare Reform and Pensions Act 1999 or under corresponding Northern Ireland legislation;

"personal pension scheme" has the same meaning as in the Pension Schemes Act 1993;

"prescribed" means prescribed by regulations;

"retirement annuity contract" means a contract or scheme approved under Chapter III of Part XIV of the Income and Corporation Taxes Act 1988;

"shareable state scheme rights" has the same meaning as in section 21A(1) above; and

"trustees or managers", in relation to an occupational pension scheme or a personal pension scheme, means—
(a) in the case of a scheme established under a trust, the trustees of the scheme, and
(b) in any other case, the managers of the scheme.

(4) In this section and sections 25B and 25C above, references to the person responsible for a pension arrangement are—
(a) in the case of an occupational pension scheme or a personal pension scheme, to the trustees or managers of the scheme,
(b) in the case of a retirement annuity contract or an annuity falling within paragraph (d) or (e) of the definition of "pension arrangement" above, the provider of the annuity, and
(c) in the case of an insurance policy falling within paragraph (d) of the definition of that expression, the insurer.

25E THE PENSION PROTECTION FUND

(1) The matters to which the court is to have regard under section 25(2) include—
(a) in the case of paragraph (a), any PPF compensation to which a party to the marriage is or is likely to be entitled, and
(b) in the case of paragraph (h), any PPF compensation which, by reason of the dissolution or annulment of the marriage, a party to the marriage will lose the chance of acquiring entitlement to,

and, accordingly, in relation to PPF compensation, section 25(2)(a) shall have effect as if "in the foreseeable future" were omitted.

(2) Subsection (3) applies in relation to an order under section 23 so far as it includes provision made by virtue of section 25B(4) which—
(a) imposed requirements on the trustees or managers of an occupational pension scheme for which the Board has assumed responsibility in accordance with Chapter 3 of Part 2 of the Pensions Act 2004 (pension protection) or any provision in force in Northern Ireland corresponding to that Chapter, and
(b) was made before the trustees or managers of the scheme received the transfer notice in relation to the scheme.

(3) The order is to have effect from the time when the trustees or managers of the scheme receive the transfer notice—
(a) as if, except in prescribed descriptions of case—
(i) references in the order to the trustees or managers of the scheme were references to the Board, and
(ii) references in the order to any pension or lump sum to which the party with pension rights is or may become entitled under the scheme were references to any PPF compensation to which that person is or may become entitled in respect of the pension or lump sum, and
(b) subject to such other modifications as may be prescribed.

(4) Subsection (5) applies to an order under section 23 if—
(a) it includes provision made by virtue of section 25B(7) which requires the party with pension rights to exercise his right of commutation under an occupational pension scheme to any extent, and
(b) before the requirement is complied with the Board has assumed responsibility for the scheme as mentioned in subsection (2)(a).

(5) From the time the trustees or managers of the scheme receive the transfer notice, the order is to have effect with such modifications as may be prescribed.

(6) Regulations may modify section 25C as it applies in relation to an occupational pension scheme at any time when there is an assessment period in relation to the scheme.

(7) Where the court makes a pension sharing order in respect of a person's shareable rights under an occupational pension scheme, or an order which includes provision made by virtue of section 25B(4) or (7) in relation to such a scheme, the Board subsequently assuming responsibility for the scheme as mentioned in subsection (2)(a) does not affect—
(a) the powers of the court under section 31 to vary or discharge the order or to suspend or revive any provision of it, or
(b) on an appeal, the powers of the appeal court to affirm, reinstate, set aside or vary the order.

(8) Regulations may make such consequential modifications of any provision of, or made by virtue of, this Part as appear to the Lord Chancellor necessary or expedient to give effect to the provisions of this section.

(9) In this section—

"assessment period" means an assessment period within the meaning of Part 2 of the Pensions Act 2004 (pension protection) (see sections 132 and 159 of that Act) or an equivalent period under any provision in force in Northern Ireland corresponding to that Part;

"the Board" means the Board of the Pension Protection Fund;

"occupational pension scheme" has the same meaning as in the Pension Schemes Act 1993;

"prescribed" means prescribed by regulations;

"regulations" means regulations made by the Lord Chancellor;

"shareable rights" are rights in relation to which pension sharing is available under Chapter 1 of Part 4 of the Welfare Reform and Pensions Act 1999 or any provision in force in Northern Ireland corresponding to that Chapter;

"transfer notice" has the same meaning as in section 160 of the Pensions Act 2004 or any corresponding provision in force in Northern Ireland.

(10) Any power to make regulations under this section is exercisable by statutory instrument, which shall be subject to annulment in pursuance of a resolution of either House of Parliament.

. . .

26 COMMENCEMENT OF PROCEEDINGS FOR ANCILLARY RELIEF, ETC

(1) Where a petition for divorce, nullity of marriage or judicial separation has been presented, then, subject to subsection (2) below, proceedings for maintenance pending suit under section 22 above, for a financial provision order under section 23 above, or for a property adjustment order may be begun, subject to and in accordance with rules of court, at any time after the presentation of the petition.

(2) Rules of court may provide, in such cases as may be prescribed by the rules—

(a) that applications for any such relief as is mentioned in subsection (1) above shall be made in the petition or answer; and
(b) that applications for any such relief which are not so made, or are not made until after the expiration of such period following the presentation of the petition or filing of the answer as may be so prescribed, shall be made only with the leave of the court.

Financial provision in case of neglect to maintain

27 FINANCIAL PROVISION ORDERS, ETC, IN CASE OF NEGLECT BY PARTY TO MARRIAGE TO MAINTAIN OTHER PARTY OR CHILD OF THE FAMILY

(1) Either party to a marriage may apply to the court for an order under this section on the ground that the other party to the marriage (in this section referred to as the respondent)—
(a) has failed to provide reasonable maintenance for the applicant, or
(b) has failed to provide, or to make a proper contribution towards, reasonable maintenance for any child of the family.

(2) The court shall not entertain an application under this section unless—
(a) the applicant or the respondent is domiciled in England and Wales on the date of the application; or
(b) the applicant has been habitually resident there throughout the period of one year ending with that date; or
(c) the respondent is resident there on that date.

(3) Where an application under this section is made on the ground mentioned in subsection (1) (a) above, then, in deciding—
(a) whether the respondent has failed to provide reasonable maintenance for the applicant, and
(b) what order, if any, to make under this section in favour of the applicant,
the court shall have regard to all the circumstances of the case including the matters mentioned in section 25(2) above, and where an application is also made under this section in respect of a child of the family who has not attained the age of eighteen, first consideration shall be given to the welfare of the child while a minor.

(3A) Where an application under this section is made on the ground mentioned in subsection (1)(b) above then, in deciding—
(a) whether the respondent has failed to provide, or to make a proper contribution towards, reasonable maintenance for the child of the family to whom the application relates, and
(b) what order, if any, to make under this section in favour of the child,
the court shall have regard to all the circumstances of the case including the matters mentioned in section 25(3)(a) to (e) above, and where the child of the family to whom the application relates is not the child of the respondent, including also the matters mentioned in section 25(4) above.

(3B) In relation to an application under this section on the ground mentioned in subsection (1) (a) above, section 25(2)(c) above shall have effect as if for the reference therein to the breakdown of the marriage there were substituted a reference to the failure to provide reasonable maintenance for the applicant, and in relation to an application under this section on the ground mentioned in subsection (1)(b) above, section 25(2)(c) above (as it applies by virtue of section 25(3)(e) above) shall have effect as if for the reference therein to the breakdown of the marriage there were substituted a reference to the failure to provide, or to make a proper contribution towards, reasonable maintenance for the child of the family to whom the application relates.

(5) Where on an application under this section it appears to the court that the applicant or any child of the family to whom the application relates is in immediate need of financial assistance, but it is not yet possible to determine what order, if any, should be made on the application, the court may make an interim order for maintenance, that is to say, an order requiring the respondent to make to the applicant until the determination of the application such periodical payments as the court thinks reasonable.

(6) Where on an application under this section the applicant satisfies the court of any ground mentioned in subsection (1) above, the court may make any one or more of the following orders, that is to say—
  (a) an order that the respondent shall make to the applicant such periodical payments, for such term, as may be specified in the order;
  (b) an order that the respondent shall secure to the applicant, to the satisfaction of the court, such periodical payments, for such term, as may be so specified;
  (c) an order that the respondent shall pay to the applicant such lump sum as may be so specified;
  (d) an order that the respondent shall make to such person as may be specified in the order for the benefit of the child to whom the application relates, or to that child, such periodical payments, for such term, as may be so specified;
  (e) an order that the respondent shall secure to such person as may be so specified for the benefit of that child, or to that child, to the satisfaction of the court, such periodical payments, for such term, as may be so specified;
  (f) an order that the respondent shall pay to such person as may be so specified for the benefit of that child, or to that child, such lump sum as may be so specified;

subject, however, in the case of an order under paragraph (d), (e) or (f) above, to the restrictions imposed by section 29(1) and (3) below on the making of financial provision orders in favour of children who have attained the age of eighteen.

(6A) An application for the variation under section 31 of this Act of a periodical payments order or secured periodical payments order made under this section in favour of a child may, if the child has attained the age of sixteen, be made by the child himself.

(6B) Where a periodical payments order made in favour of a child under this section ceases to have effect on the date on which the child attains the age of sixteen or at any time after that date but before or on the date on which he attains the age of eighteen, then if, on an application made to the court for an order under this subsection, it appears to the court that—
  (a) the child is, will be or (if an order were made under this subsection) would be receiving instruction at an educational establishment or undergoing training for a trade, profession or vocation, whether or not he also is, will be or would be in gainful employment; or
  (b) there are special circumstances which justify the making of an order under this subsection,

the court shall have power by order to revive the first mentioned order from such date as the court may specify, not being earlier than the date of the making of the application, and to exercise its power under section 31 of this Act in relation to any order so revived.

(7) Without prejudice to the generality of subsection (6)(c) or (f) above, an order under this section for the payment of a lump sum—
  (a) may be made for the purpose of enabling any liabilities or expenses reasonably incurred in maintaining the applicant or any child of the family to whom the application relates before the making of the application to be met;
  (b) may provide for the payment of that sum by instalments of such amount as may be specified in the order and may require the payment of the instalments to be secured to the satisfaction of the court.

Additional provisions with respect to financial provision and property adjustment orders

28 DURATION OF CONTINUING FINANCIAL PROVISION ORDERS IN FAVOUR OF PARTY TO MARRIAGE, AND EFFECT OF REMARRIAGE OR FORMATION OF CIVIL PARTNERSHIP

(1) Subject in the case of an order made on or after the grant of a decree of a divorce or nullity of marriage to the provisions of sections 25A(2) above and 31(7) below, the term to be specified in a periodical payments or secured periodical payments order in favour of a party to a marriage shall be such term as the court thinks fit, except that the term shall not begin before or extend beyond the following limits, that is to say—

(a) in the case of a periodical payments order, the term shall begin not earlier than the date of the making of an application for the order, and shall be so defined as not to extend beyond the death of either of the parties to the marriage or, where the order is made on or after the grant of a decree of divorce or nullity of marriage, the remarriage of, or formation of a civil partnership by, the party in whose favour the order is made; and

(b) in the case of a secured periodical payments order, the term shall begin not earlier than the date of the making of an application for the order, and shall be so defined as not to extend beyond the death or, where the order is made on or after the grant of such a decree, the remarriage of, or formation of a civil partnership by, the party in whose favour the order is made.

(1A) Where a periodical payments or secured periodical payments order in favour of a party to a marriage is made on or after the grant of a decree of divorce or nullity of marriage, the court may direct that that party shall not be entitled to apply under section 31 below for the extension of the term specified in the order.

(2) Where a periodical payments or secured periodical payments order in favour of a party to a marriage is made otherwise than on or after the grant of a decree of divorce or nullity of marriage, and the marriage in question is subsequently dissolved or annulled but the order continues in force, the order shall, notwithstanding anything in it, cease to have effect on the remarriage of, or formation of a civil partnership by, that party, except in relation to any arrears due under it on the date of the remarriage or formation of the civil partnership.

(3) If after the grant of a decree dissolving or annulling a marriage either party to that marriage remarries whether at any time before or after the commencement of this Act or forms a civil partnership, that party shall not be entitled to apply, by reference to the grant of that decree, for a financial provision order in his or her favour, or for a property adjustment order, against the other party to that marriage.

29 DURATION OF CONTINUING FINANCIAL PROVISION ORDERS IN FAVOUR OF CHILDREN, AND AGE LIMIT ON MAKING CERTAIN ORDERS IN THEIR FAVOUR

(1) Subject to subsection (3) below, no financial provision order and no order for a transfer of property under section 24(1)(a) above shall be made in favour of a child who has attained the age of eighteen.

(2) The term to be specified in a periodical payments or secured periodical payments order in favour of a child may begin with the date of the making of an application for the order in question or any later date or a date ascertained in accordance with subsection (5) or (6) below but—

(a) shall not in the first instance extend beyond the date of the birthday of the child next following his attaining the upper limit of the compulsory school age (construed in accordance with section 8 of the Education Act 1996) unless the court considers that in the circumstances of the case the welfare of the child requires that it should extend to a later date; and
(b) shall not in any event, subject to subsection (3) below, extend beyond the date of the child's eighteenth birthday.

(3) Subsection (1) above, and paragraph (b) of subsection (2), shall not apply in the case of a child, if it appears to the court that—
(a) the child is, or will be, or if an order were made without complying with either or both of those provisions would be, receiving instruction at an educational establishment or undergoing training for a trade, profession or vocation, whether or not he is also, or will also be, in gainful employment; or
(b) there are special circumstances which justify the making of an order without complying with either or both of those provisions.

(4) Any periodical payments order in favour of a child shall, notwithstanding anything in the order, cease to have effect on the death of the person liable to make payments under the order, except in relation to any arrears due under the order on the date of the death.

(5) Where—
(a) a maintenance calculation ("the current calculation") is in force with respect to a child; and
(b) an application is made under Part II of this Act for a periodical payments or secured periodical payments order in favour of that child—
(i) in accordance with section 8 of the Child Support Act 1991, and
(ii) before the end of the period of 6 months beginning with the making of the current calculation

the term to be specified in any such order made on that application may be expressed to begin on, or at any time after, the earliest permitted date.

(6) For the purposes of subsection (5) above, "the earliest permitted date" is whichever is the later of—
(a) the date 6 months before the application is made; or
(b) the date on which the current calculation took effect or, where successive maintenance calculations have been continuously in force with respect to a child, on which the first of those calculations took effect.

(7) Where—
(a) a maintenance calculation ceases to have effect by or under any provision of the Child Support Act 1991; and
(b) an application is made, before the end of the period of 6 months beginning with the relevant date, for a periodical payments or secured periodical payments order in favour of a child with respect to whom that maintenance calculation was in force immediately before it ceased to have effect,

the term to be specified in any such order made on that application may begin with the date on which that maintenance calculation ceased to have effect, or any later date.

(8) In subsection (7)(b) above—
(a) where the maintenance calculation ceased to have effect, the relevant date is the date on which it so ceased;

. . .

Variation, discharge and enforcement of certain orders, etc

31 VARIATION, DISCHARGE, ETC, OF CERTAIN ORDERS FOR FINANCIAL RELIEF

(1) Where the court has made an order to which this section applies, then, subject to the provisions of this section and of section 28(1A) above, the court shall have power to vary or discharge the order or to suspend any provision thereof temporarily and to revive the operation of any provision so suspended.

(2) This section applies to the following orders, that is to say—
(a) any order for maintenance pending suit and any interim order for maintenance;
(b) any periodical payments order;
(c) any secured periodical payments order;
(d) any order made by virtue of section 23(3)(c) or 27(7)(b) above (provision for payment of a lump sum by instalments);
(dd) any deferred order made by virtue of section 23(1)(c) (lump sums) which includes provision made by virtue of—
(i) section 25B(4),
(ii) section 25C, or
(iii) section 25F(2),
(provision in respect of pension rights or pension compensation rights);
(e) any order for a settlement of property under section 24(1)(b) or for a variation of settlement under section 24(1)(c) or (d) above, being an order made on or after the grant of a decree of judicial separation;
(f) any order made under section 24A(1) above for the sale of property;
(g) a pension sharing order under section 24B above, or a pension compensation sharing order under section 24E above, which is made at a time before the decree has been made absolute.

(2A) Where the court has made an order referred to in subsection (2)(a), (b) or (c) above, then, subject to the provisions of this section, the court shall have power to remit the payment of any arrears due under the order or of any part thereof.

(2B) Where the court has made an order referred to in subsection (2)(dd)(ii) above, this section shall cease to apply to the order on the death of either of the parties to the marriage.

(3) The powers exercisable by the court under this section in relation to an order shall be exercisable also in relation to any instrument executed in pursuance of the order.

(4) The court shall not exercise the powers conferred by this section in relation to an order for a settlement under section 24(1)(b) or for a variation of settlement under section 24(1)(c) or (d) above except on an application made in proceedings—
(a) for the rescission of the decree of judicial separation by reference to which the order was made, or
(b) for the dissolution of the marriage in question.

(4A) In relation to an order which falls within paragraph (g) of subsection (2) above ("the subsection (2) order")—
(a) the powers conferred by this section may be exercised—
(i) only on an application made before the subsection (2) order has or, but for paragraph (b) below, would have taken effect; and
(ii) only if, at the time when the application is made, the decree has not been made absolute; and
(b) an application made in accordance with paragraph (a) above prevents the subsection (2) order from taking effect before the application has been dealt with.

(4B) No variation of a pension sharing order, or a pension compensation sharing order, shall be made so as to take effect before the decree is made absolute.

(4C) The variation of a pension sharing order, or a pension compensation sharing order, prevents the order taking effect before the end of such period after the making of the variation as may be prescribed by regulations made by the Lord Chancellor.

(5) Subject to subsections (7A) to (7G) below and without prejudice to any power exercisable by virtue of subsection (2)(d), (dd), (e) or (g) above or otherwise than by virtue of this section, no property adjustment order or pension sharing order or pension compensation sharing order shall be made on an application for the variation of a periodical payments or secured periodical payments order made (whether in favour of a party to a marriage or in favour of a child of the family) under section 23 above, and no order for the payment of a lump sum shall be made on an application for the variation of a periodical payments or secured periodical payments order in favour of a party to a marriage (whether made under section 23 or under section 27 above).

(6) Where the person liable to make payments under a secured periodical payments order has died, an application under this section relating to that order (and to any order made under section 24A(1) above which requires the proceeds of sale of property to be used for securing those payments) may be made by the person entitled to payments under the periodical payments order or by the personal representatives of the deceased person, but no such application shall, except with the permission of the court, be made after the end of the period of six months from the date on which representation in regard to the estate of that person is first taken out.

(7) In exercising the powers conferred by this section the court shall have regard to all the circumstances of the case, first consideration being given to the welfare while a minor of any child of the family who has not attained the age of eighteen, and the circumstances of the case shall include any change in any of the matters to which the court was required to have regard when making the order to which the application relates, and—
- (a) in the case of a periodical payments or secured periodical payments order made on or after the grant of a decree of divorce or nullity of marriage, the court shall consider whether in all the circumstances and after having regard to any such change it would be appropriate to vary the order so that payments under the order are required to be made or secured only for such further period as will in the opinion of the court be sufficient (in the light of any proposed exercise by the court, where the marriage has been dissolved, of its powers under subsection (7B) below) to enable the party in whose favour the order was made to adjust without undue hardship to the termination of those payments;
- (b) in a case where the party against whom the order was made has died, the circumstances of the case shall also include the changed circumstances resulting from his or her death.

(7A) Subsection (7B) below applies where, after the dissolution of a marriage, the court—
- (a) discharges a periodical payments order or secured periodical payments order made in favour of a party to the marriage; or
- (b) varies such an order so that payments under the order are required to be made or secured only for such further period as is determined by the court.

(7B) The court has power, in addition to any power it has apart from this subsection, to make supplemental provision consisting of any of—
- (a) an order for the payment of a lump sum in favour of a party to the marriage;
- (b) one or more property adjustment orders in favour of a party to the marriage;
- (ba) one or more pension sharing orders;

(bb) a pension compensation sharing order;
(c) a direction that the party in whose favour the original order discharged or varied was made is not entitled to make any further application for—
(i) a periodical payments or secured periodical payments order, or
(ii) an extension of the period to which the original order is limited by any variation made by the court.

(7C) An order for the payment of a lump sum made under subsection (7B) above may—
(a) provide for the payment of that sum by instalments of such amount as may be specified in the order; and
(b) require the payment of the instalments to be secured to the satisfaction of the court.

(7D) Section 23(6) above apply where the court makes an order for the payment of a lump sum under subsection (7B) above as they apply where it makes such an order under section 23 above.

(7E) If under subsection (7B) above the court makes more than one property adjustment order in favour of the same party to the marriage, each of those orders must fall within a different paragraph of section 21(2) above.

(7F) Sections 24A and 30 above apply where the court makes a property adjustment order under subsection (7B) above as they apply where it makes such an order under section 24 above.

(7G) Subsections (3) to (5) of section 24B above apply in relation to a pension sharing order under subsection (7B) above as they apply in relation to a pension sharing order under that section.

(7H) Subsections (3) to (10) of section 24E above apply in relation to a pension compensation sharing order under subsection (7B) above as they apply in relation to a pension compensation sharing order under that section.

(8) The personal representatives of a deceased person against whom a secured periodical payments order was made shall not be liable for having distributed any part of the estate of the deceased after the expiration of the period of six months referred to in subsection (6) above on the ground that they ought to have taken into account the possibility that the court might permit an application under this section to be made after that period by the person entitled to payments under the order; but this subsection shall not prejudice any power to recover any part of the estate so distributed arising by virtue of the making of an order in pursuance of this section.

(9) In considering for the purposes of subsection (6) above the question when representation was first taken out, a grant limited to settled land or to trust property shall be left out of account and a grant limited to real estate or to personal estate shall be left out of account unless a grant limited to the remainder of the estate has previously been made or is made at the same time.

(10) Where the court, in exercise of its powers under this section, decides to vary or discharge a periodical payments or secured periodical payments order, then, subject to section 28(1) and (2) above, the court shall have power to direct that the variation or discharge shall not take effect until the expiration of such period as may be specified in the order.

(11) Where—
(a) a periodical payments or secured periodical payments order in favour of more than one child ("the order") is in force;
(b) the order requires payments specified in it to be made to or for the benefit of more than one child without apportioning those payments between them;

(c) a maintenance calculation ("the calculation") is made with respect to one or more, but not all, of the children with respect to whom those payments are to be made; and
(d) an application is made, before the end of the period of 6 months beginning with the date on which the calculation was made, for the variation or discharge of the order,

the court may, in exercise of its powers under this section to vary or discharge the order, direct that the variation or discharge shall take effect from the date on which the calculation took effect or any later date.

(12) Where—
(a) an order ("the child order") of a kind prescribed for the purposes of section 10(1) of the Child Support Act 1991 is affected by a maintenance calculation;
(b) on the date on which the child order became so affected there was in force a periodical payments or secured periodical payments order ("the spousal order") in favour of a party to a marriage having the care of the child in whose favour the child order was made; and
(c) an application is made, before the end of the period of 6 months beginning with the date on which the maintenance calculation was made, for the spousal order to be varied or discharged,

the court may, in exercise of its powers under this section to vary or discharge the spousal order, direct that the variation or discharge shall take effect from the date on which the child order became so affected or any later date.

(13) For the purposes of subsection (12) above, an order is affected if it ceases to have effect or is modified by or under section 10 of the Child Support Act 1991.

(14) Subsections (11) and (12) above are without prejudice to any other power of the court to direct that the variation of discharge of an order under this section shall take effect from a date earlier than that on which the order for variation or discharge was made.

(15) The power to make regulations under subsection (4C) above shall be exercisable by statutory instrument which shall be subject to annulment in pursuance of a resolution of either House of Parliament.

32 PAYMENT OF CERTAIN ARREARS UNENFORCEABLE WITHOUT THE LEAVE OF THE COURT

(1) A person shall not be entitled to enforce through the High Court or any county court the payment of any arrears due under an order for maintenance pending suit, an interim order for maintenance or any financial provision order without the leave of that court if those arrears became due more than twelve months before proceedings to enforce the payment of them are begun.

(2) The court hearing an application for the grant of leave under this section may refuse leave, or may grant leave subject to such restrictions and conditions (including conditions as to the allowing of time for payment or the making of payment by instalments) as that court thinks proper, or may remit the payment of the arrears or of any part thereof.

(3) An application for the grant of leave under this section shall be made in such manner as may be prescribed by rules of court.

33 ORDERS FOR REPAYMENT IN CERTAIN CASES OF SUMS PAID UNDER CERTAIN ORDERS

(1) Where on an application made under this section in relation to an order to which this section applies it appears to the court that by reason of—

(a) a change in the circumstances of the person entitled to, or liable to make, payments under the order since the order was made, or

(b) the changed circumstances resulting from the death of the person so liable, the amount received by the person entitled to payments under the order in respect of a period after those circumstances changed or after the death of the person liable to make payments under the order, as the case may be, exceeds the amount which the person so liable or his or her personal representatives should have been required to pay,

the court may order the respondent to the application to pay to the applicant such sum, not exceeding the amount of the excess, as the court thinks just.

(2) This section applies to the following orders, that is to say—

(a) any order for maintenance pending suit and any interim order for maintenance;

(b) any periodical payments order; and

(c) any secured periodical payments order.

(3) An application under this section may be made by the person liable to make payments under an order to which this section applies or his or her personal representatives and may be made against the person entitled to payments under the order or her or his personal representatives.

(4) An application under this section may be made in proceedings in the High Court or a county court for—

(a) the variation or discharge of the order to which this section applies, or

(b) leave to enforce, or the enforcement of, the payment of arrears under that order;

but when not made in such proceedings shall be made to a county court, and accordingly references in this section to the court are references to the High Court or a county court, as the circumstances require.

(5) The jurisdiction conferred on a county court by this section shall be exercisable notwithstanding that by reason of the amount claimed in the application the jurisdiction would not but for this subsection be exercisable by a county court.

(6) An order under this section for the payment of any sum may provide for the payment of that sum by instalments of such amount as may be specified in the order.

Consent orders

33A CONSENT ORDERS FOR FINANCIAL PROVISION ON PROPERTY ADJUSTMENT

(1) Notwithstanding anything in the preceding provisions of this Part of this Act, on an application for a consent order for financial relief the court may, unless it has reason to think that there are other circumstances into which it ought to inquire, make an order in the terms agreed on the basis only of the prescribed information furnished with the application.

(2) Subsection (1) above applies to an application for a consent order varying or discharging an order for financial relief as it applies to an application for an order for financial relief.

(3) In this section—

"consent order", in relation to an application for an order, means an order in the terms applied for to which the respondent agrees;

"order for financial relief" means an order under any of sections 23, 24, 24A, 24B or 27 above; and

"prescribed" means prescribed by rules of court.

Maintenance agreements

34 VALIDITY OF MAINTENANCE AGREEMENTS

(1) If a maintenance agreement includes a provision purporting to restrict any right to apply to a court for an order containing financial arrangements, then—
   (a) that provision shall be void; but
   (b) any other financial arrangements contained in the agreement shall not thereby be rendered void or unenforceable and shall, unless they are void or unenforceable for any other reason (and subject to sections 35 and 36 below), be binding on the parties to the agreement.

(2) In this section and in section 35 below—

"maintenance agreement" means any agreement in writing made, whether before or after the commencement of this Act, between the parties to a marriage, being—
   (a) an agreement containing financial arrangements, whether made during the continuance or after the dissolution or annulment of the marriage; or
   (b) a separation agreement which contains no financial arrangements in a case where no other agreement in writing between the same parties contains such arrangements;

"financial arrangements" means provisions governing the rights and liabilities towards one another when living separately of the parties to a marriage (including a marriage which has been dissolved or annulled) in respect of the making or securing of payments or the disposition or use of any property, including such rights and liabilities with respect to the maintenance or education of any child, whether or not a child of the family.

35 ALTERATION OF AGREEMENTS BY COURT DURING LIVES OF PARTIES

(1) Where a maintenance agreement is for the time being subsisting and each of the parties to the agreement is for the time being either domiciled or resident in England and Wales, then, subject to subsection (3) below, either party may apply to the court or to a magistrates' court for an order under this section.

(2) If the court to which the application is made is satisfied either—
   (a) that by reason of a change in the circumstances in the light of which any financial arrangements contained in the agreement were made or, as the case may be, financial arrangements were omitted from it (including a change foreseen by the parties when making the agreement), the agreement should be altered so as to make different, or, as the case may be, so as to contain, financial arrangements, or
   (b) that the agreement does not contain proper financial arrangements with respect to any child of the family,

then subject to subsections (3), (4) and (5) below, that court may by order make such alterations in the agreement—
      (i) by varying or revoking any financial arrangements contained in it, or
      (ii) by inserting in it financial arrangements for the benefit of one of the parties to the agreement or of a child of the family, as may appear to that court to be just having regard to all the circumstances, including, if relevant, the matters mentioned in section 25(4) above; and the agreement shall have effect thereafter as if any alteration made by the order had been made by agreement between the parties and for valuable consideration.

(3) A magistrates' court shall not entertain an application under subsection (1) above unless both the parties to the agreement are resident in England and Wales and the court acts in, or is authorised by the Lord Chancellor to act for, a local justice area in which at least one of the parties is resident, and shall not have power to make any order on such an application except—
(a) in a case where the agreement includes no provision for periodical payments by either of the parties, an order inserting provision for the making by one of the parties of periodical payments for the maintenance of the other party or for the maintenance of any child of the family;
(b) in a case where the agreement includes provision for the making by one of the parties of periodical payments, an order increasing or reducing the rate of, or terminating, any of those payments.

(4) Where a court decides to alter, by order under this section, an agreement by inserting provision for the making or securing by one of the parties to the agreement of periodical payments for the maintenance of the other party or by increasing the rate of the periodical payments which the agreement provides shall be made by one of the parties for the maintenance of the other, the term for which the payments or, as the case may be, the additional payments attributable to the increase are to be made under the agreement as altered by the order shall be such term as the court may specify, subject to the following limits, that is to say—
(a) where the payments will not be secured, the term shall be so defined as not to extend beyond the death of either of the parties to the agreement or the remarriage of, or formation of a civil partnership by, the party to whom the payments are to be made;
(b) where the payments will be secured, the term shall be so defined as not to extend beyond the death or remarriage of, or formation of a civil partnership by, that party.

(5) Where a court decides to alter, by order under this section, an agreement by inserting provision for the making or securing by one of the parties to the agreement of periodical payments for the maintenance of a child of the family or by increasing the rate of the periodical payments which the agreement provides shall be made or secured by one of the parties for the maintenance of such a child, then, in deciding the term for which under the agreement as altered by the order the payments, or as the case may be, the additional payments attributable to the increase are to be made or secured for the benefit of the child, the court shall apply the provisions of section 29(2) and (3) above as to age limits as if the order in question were a periodical payments or secured periodical payments order in favour of the child.

(6) For the avoidance of doubt it is hereby declared that nothing in this section or in section 34 above affects any power of a court before which any proceedings between the parties to a maintenance agreement are brought under any other enactment (including a provision of this Act) to make an order containing financial arrangements or any right of either party to apply for such an order in such proceedings.

36 ALTERATION OF AGREEMENTS BY COURT AFTER DEATH OF ONE PARTY

(1) Where a maintenance agreement within the meaning of section 34 above provides for the continuation of payments under the agreement after the death of one of the parties and that party dies domiciled in England and Wales, the surviving party or the personal representatives of the deceased party may, subject to subsections (2) and (3) below, apply to the High Court or a county court for an order under section 35 above.

(2) An application under this section shall not, except with the permission of the High Court or a county court, be made after the end of the period of six months from the date on which representation in regard to the estate of the deceased is first taken out.

(3) A county court shall not entertain an application under this section, or an application for permission to make an application under this section, unless it would have jurisdiction by virtue of section 22 of the Inheritance (Provision for Family and Dependants) Act 1975 (which confers jurisdiction on county courts in proceedings under that Act if the value of the property mentioned in that section does not exceed £5,000 or such larger sum as may be fixed by order of the Lord Chancellor) to hear and determine proceedings for an order under section 2 of that Act in relation to the deceased's estate.

(4) If a maintenance agreement is altered by a court on an application made in pursuance of subsection (1) above, the like consequences shall ensue as if the alteration had been made immediately before the death by agreement between the parties and for valuable consideration.

(5) The provisions of this section shall not render the personal representatives of the deceased liable for having distributed any part of the estate of the deceased after the expiration of the period of six months referred to in subsection (2) above on the ground that they ought to have taken into account the possibility that a court might permit an application by virtue of this section to be made by the surviving party after that period; but this subsection shall not prejudice any power to recover any part of the estate so distributed arising by virtue of the making of an order in pursuance of this section.

(6) Section 31(9) above shall apply for the purposes of subsection (2) above as it applies for the purposes of subsection (6) of section 31.

(7) Subsection (3) of section 22 of the Inheritance (Provision for Family and Dependants) Act 1975 (which enables rules of court to provide for the transfer from a county court to the High Court or from the High court to a county court of proceedings for an order under section 2 of that Act) and paragraphs (a) and (b) of subsection (4) of that section (provisions relating to proceedings commenced in county court before coming into force of order of the Lord Chancellor under that section) shall apply in relation to proceedings consisting of any such application as is referred to in subsection (3) above as they apply in relation to proceedings for an order under section 2 of that Act.

Miscellaneous and supplemental

37 AVOIDANCE OF TRANSACTIONS INTENDED TO PREVENT OR REDUCE FINANCIAL RELIEF

(1) For the purposes of this section "financial relief" means relief under any of the provisions of sections 22, 23, 24, 24B, 27, 31 and 35 above, and any reference in this section to defeating a person's claim for financial relief is a reference to preventing financial relief from being granted to that person, or to that person for the benefit of a child of the family, or reducing the amount of any financial relief which might be so granted, or frustrating or impeding the enforcement of any order which might be or has been made at his instance under any of those provisions.

(2) Where proceedings for financial relief are brought by one person against another, the court may, on the application of the first-mentioned person—
- (a) if it is satisfied that the other party to the proceedings is, with the intention of defeating the claim for financial relief, about to make any disposition or to transfer out of the jurisdiction or otherwise deal with any property, make such order as it

thinks fit for restraining the other party from so doing or otherwise for protecting the claim;
(b) if it is satisfied that the other party has, with that intention, made a reviewable disposition and that if the disposition were set aside financial relief or different financial relief would be granted to the applicant, make an order setting aside the disposition;
(c) if it is satisfied, in a case where an order has been obtained under any of the provisions mentioned in subsection (1) above by the applicant against the other party, that the other party has, with that intention, made a reviewable disposition, make an order setting aside the disposition;

and an application for the purposes of paragraph (b) above shall be made in the proceedings for the financial relief in question.

(3) Where the court makes an order under subsection (2)(b) or (c) above setting aside a disposition it shall give such consequential directions as it thinks fit for giving effect to the order (including directions requiring the making of any payments or the disposal of any property).

(4) Any disposition made by the other party to the proceedings for financial relief in question (whether before or after the commencement of those proceedings) is a reviewable disposition for the purposes of subsection (2)(b) and (c) above unless it was made for valuable consideration (other than marriage) to a person who, at the time of the disposition, acted in relation to it in good faith and without notice of any intention on the part of the other party to defeat the applicant's claim for financial relief.

(5) Where an application is made under this section with respect to a disposition which took place less than three years before the date of the application or with respect to a disposition or other dealing with property which is about to take place and the court is satisfied—
(a) in a case falling within subsection (2)(a) or (b) above, that the disposition or other dealing would (apart from this section) have the consequence, or
(b) in a case falling within subsection (2)(c) above, that the disposition has had the consequence, of defeating the applicant's claim for financial relief,

it shall be presumed, unless the contrary is shown, that the person who disposed of or is about to dispose of or deal with the property did so or, as the case may be, is about to do so, with the intention of defeating the applicant's claim for financial relief.

(6) In this section "disposition" does not include any provision contained in a will or codicil but, with that exception, includes any conveyance, assurance or gift of property of any description, whether made by an instrument or otherwise.

(7) This section does not apply to a disposition made before 1st January 1968.

38 ORDERS FOR REPAYMENT IN CERTAIN CASES OF SUMS PAID AFTER CESSATION OF ORDER BY REASON OF REMARRIAGE OR FORMATION OF CIVIL PARTNERSHIP

(1) Where—
(a) a periodical payments or secured periodical payments order in favour of a party to a marriage (hereafter in this section referred to as "a payments order") has ceased to have effect by reason of the remarriage of, or formation of a civil partnership by, that party, and
(b) the person liable to make payments under the order or his or her personal representatives made payments in accordance with it in respect of a period after the

date of the remarriage or formation of the civil partnership in the mistaken belief that the order was still subsisting,

the person so liable or his or her personal representatives shall not be entitled to bring proceedings in respect of a cause of action arising out of the circumstances mentioned in paragraphs (a) and (b) above against the person entitled to payments under the order or her or his personal representatives, but may instead make an application against that person or her or his personal representatives under this section.

(2) On an application under this section the court may order the respondent to pay to the applicant a sum equal to the amount of the payments made in respect of the period mentioned in subsection (1)(b) above or, if it appears to the court that it would be unjust to make that order, it may either order the respondent to pay to the applicant such lesser sum as it thinks fit or dismiss the application.

(3) An application under this section may be made in proceedings in the High Court or a county court for leave to enforce, or the enforcement of, payment of arrears under the order in question, but when not made in such proceedings shall be made to a county court; and accordingly references in this section to the court are references to the High Court or a county court, as the circumstances require.

(4) The jurisdiction conferred on a county court by this section shall be exercisable notwithstanding that by reason of the amount claimed in the application the jurisdiction would not but for this subsection be exercisable by a county court.

(5) An order under this section for the payment of any sum may provide for the payment of that sum by instalments of such amount as may be specified in the order.

(6) The designated officer for a magistrates' court to whom any payments under a payments order are required to be made, and the collecting officer under an attachment of earnings order made to secure payments under a payments order, shall not be liable—
  (a) in the case of the designated officer, for any act done by him in pursuance of the payments order after the date on which that order ceased to have effect by reason of the remarriage of, or formation of a civil partnership by, the person entitled to payments under it, and
  (b) in the case of the collecting officer, for any act done by him after that date in accordance with any enactment or rule of court specifying how payments made to him in compliance with the attachment of earnings order are to be dealt with, if, but only if, the act was one which he would have been under a duty to do had the payments order not so ceased to have effect and the act was done before notice in writing of the fact that the person so entitled had remarried or formed a civil partnership was given to him by or on behalf of that person, the person liable to make payments under the payments order or the personal representatives of either of those persons.

(7) In this section "collecting officer", in relation to an attachment of earnings order, means the officer of the High Court, the registrar of a county court or the designated officer for a magistrates' court to whom a person makes payments in compliance with the order.

39 SETTLEMENT, ETC, MADE IN COMPLIANCE WITH A PROPERTY ADJUSTMENT ORDER MAY BE AVOIDED ON BANKRUPTCY OF SETTLOR

The fact that a settlement or transfer of property had to be made in order to comply with a property adjustment order shall not prevent that settlement or transfer from being a transaction in respect of which an order may be made under section 339 or 340 of the Insolvency Act 1986 (transfers at an undervalue and preferences).

40 PAYMENTS, ETC, UNDER ORDER MADE IN FAVOUR OF PERSON SUFFERING FROM MENTAL DISORDER

(1) Where the court makes an order under this Part of this Act requiring payments (including a lump sum payment) to be made, or property to be transferred, to a party to a marriage and the court is satisfied that the person in whose favour the order is made ("P") lacks capacity (within the meaning of the Mental Capacity Act 2005) in relation to the provisions of the order then, subject to any order, direction or authority made or given in relation to P under that Act, the court may order the payments to be made, or as the case may be, the property to be transferred, to such person ("D") as it may direct.

(2) In carrying out any functions of his in relation to an order made under subsection (1), D must act in P's best interests (within the meaning of that Act).

. . .

Part III PROTECTION, CUSTODY, ETC, OF CHILDREN

41 RESTRICTIONS ON DECREES FOR DISSOLUTION, ANNULMENT OR SEPARATION AFFECTING CHILDREN

(1) In any proceedings for a decree of divorce or nullity of marriage, or a decree of judicial separation, the court shall consider—
(a) whether there are any children of the family to whom this section applies; and
(b) where there are any such children, whether (in the light of the arrangements which have been, or are proposed to be, made for their upbringing and welfare) it should exercise any of its powers under the Children Act 1989 with respect to any of them.

(2) Where, in any case to which this section applies, it appears to the court that—
(a) the circumstances of the case require it, or are likely to require it, to exercise any of its powers under the Act of 1989 with respect to any such child;
(b) it is not in a position to exercise the power or (as the case may be) those powers without giving further consideration to the case; and
(c) there are exceptional circumstances which make it desirable in the interests of the child that the court should give a direction under this section,
it may direct that the decree of divorce or nullity is not to be made absolute, or that the decree of judicial separation is not to be granted, until the court orders otherwise.

(3) This section applies to—
(a) any child of the family who has not reached the age of sixteen at the date when the court considers the case in accordance with the requirements of this section; and
(b) any child of the family who has reached that age at that date and in relation to whom the court directs that this section shall apply.

Part IV MISCELLANEOUS AND SUPPLEMENTAL

47 MATRIMONIAL RELIEF AND DECLARATIONS OF VALIDITY IN RESPECT OF POLYGAMOUS MARRIAGES

(1) A court in England and Wales shall not be precluded from granting matrimonial relief or making a declaration concerning the validity of a marriage by reason only that either party to the marriage is, or has during the subsistence of the marriage been, married to more than one person.

(2) In this section "matrimonial relief" means—
(a) any decree under Part I of this Act;
(b) a financial provision order under section 27 above;
(c) an order under section 35 above altering a maintenance agreement;
(d) an order under any provision of this Act which confers a power exercisable in connection with, or in connection with proceedings for, such decree or order as is mentioned in paragraphs (a) to (c) above;
(dd) an order under Part III of the Matrimonial and Family Proceedings Act 1984;
(e) an order under Part I of the Domestic Proceedings and Magistrates' Courts Act 1978.

(3) In this section "a declaration concerning the validity of a marriage" means any declaration under Part III of the Family Law Act 1986 involving a determination as to the validity of a marriage.

(4) Provision may be made by rules of court—
(a) for requiring notice of proceedings brought by virtue of this section to be served on any additional spouse of a party to the marriage in question; and
(b) for conferring on any such additional spouse the right to be heard in the proceedings, in such cases as may be specified in the rules.

48 EVIDENCE

(1) The evidence of a husband or wife shall be admissible in any proceedings to prove that marital intercourse did or did not take place between them during any period.

(2) In any proceedings for nullity of marriage, evidence on the question of sexual capacity shall be heard in camera unless in any case the judge is satisfied that in the interests of justice any such evidence ought to be heard in open court.

49 PARTIES TO PROCEEDINGS UNDER THIS ACT

(1) Where in a petition for divorce or judicial separation, or in any other pleading praying for either form of relief, one party to a marriage alleges that the other has committed adultery, he or she shall make the person alleged to have committed adultery with the other party to the marriage a party to the proceedings unless excused by the court on special grounds from doing so.

(2) Rules of court may, either generally or in such cases as may be prescribed by the rules, exclude the application of subsection (1) above where the person alleged to have committed adultery with the other party to the marriage is not named in the petition or other pleading.

(3) Where in pursuance of subsection (1) above a person is made a party to proceedings for divorce or judicial separation, the court may, if after the close of the evidence on the part of the person making the allegation of adultery it is of opinion that there is not sufficient evidence against the person so made a party, dismiss him or her from the suit.

(4) Rules of court may make provision, in cases not falling within subsection (1) above, with respect to the joinder as parties to proceedings under this Act of persons involved in allegations of adultery or other improper conduct made in those proceedings, and with respect to the dismissal from such proceedings of any parties so joined; and rules of court made by virtue of this subsection may make different provision for different cases.

(5) In every case in which adultery with any party to a suit is alleged against any person not made a party to the suit or in which the court considers, in the interest of any person not

already a party to the suit, that that person should be made a party to the suit, the court may if it thinks fit allow that person to intervene upon such terms, if any, as the court thinks just.

52 INTERPRETATION

(1) In this Act—

"child", in relation to one or both of the parties to a marriage, includes an illegitimate child of that party or, as the case may be, of both parties;

"child of the family", in relation to the parties to a marriage, means—
(a) a child of both of those parties; and
(b) any other child, not being a child who is placed with those parties as foster parents by a local authority or voluntary organisation, who has been treated by both of those parties as a child of their family;

"the court" (except where the context otherwise requires) means the High Court or, where a county court has jurisdiction by virtue of Part V of the Matrimonial and Family Proceedings Act 1984, a county court;

"education" includes training.

"maintenance calculation" has the same meaning as it has in the Child Support Act 1991 by virtue of section 54 of that Act as read with any regulations in force under that section;

(2) In this Act—
(a) references to financial provision orders, periodical payments and secured periodical payments orders and orders for the payment of a lump sum, and references to property adjustment orders, shall be construed in accordance with section 21 above;
(aa) references to pension sharing orders shall be construed in accordance with section 21A above; and
(b) references to orders for maintenance pending suit and to interim orders for maintenance shall be construed respectively in accordance with section 22 and section 27(5) above.

(3) For the avoidance of doubt it is hereby declared that references in this Act to remarriage include references to a marriage which is by law void or voidable.

(3A) References in this Act to the formation of a civil partnership by a person include references to a civil partnership which is by law void or voidable.

(4) Except where the contrary intention is indicated, references in this Act to any enactment include references to that enactment as amended, extended or applied by or under any subsequent enactment, including this Act.

As amended by: Domicile and Matrimonial Proceedings Act 1973, ss 6(4), 17(2), Sch 6; Inheritance (Provision for Family and Dependants) Act 1975, s 26(1); Children Act 1975, s 108(1), Sch 4; Domestic Proceedings and Magistrates' Courts Act 1978, ss 62, 89(2)(a), Sch 2; Matrimonial Homes and Property Act 1981, s 7; Administration of Justice Act 1982, ss 5, 16; Matrimonial Homes Act 1983, s 12, Sch 2; Family Law Act 1986, s 68(1), Sch 1; Mental Health Act 1983, s 148, Sch 4; Marriage Act 1983, s 2(4); Matrimonial and Family Proceedings Act 1984, s 1 = N6, s46(1), Sch 1; Insolvency Act 1985, s 235, Sch 8; Marriage (Prohibited Degrees of Relationship) Act 1986, s 6(4); Insolvency Act 1986, s 439(2), Sch 14; Family Law Reform Act 1987, s 33(1), Sch 2; Children Act 1989, s 108(4), Sch 12; Maintenance Orders (Backdating)

Order 1993, SI 1993/623, art 2, Sch 1; Pensions Act 1995, s 166; Private International Law (Miscellaneous Provisions) Act 1995, s 8(2), Schedule; Family Law Act 1996, s 66(1), Sch 8; Education Act 1996, s 582(1), Sch 37; Family Law Act 1996 (Commencement) (No. 3) Order 1998, SI 1998/2572, art 4(a); Welfare Reform and Pensions Act 1999, ss 19, 85(4), Sch 3; Child Support, Pensions and Social Security Act 2000, ss 26, 85, Sch 3, Sch 9; Divorce (Religious Marriages) Act 2002, s 1; Courts Act 2003, s 109(1), Sch 8; Gender Recognition Act 2004, ss 4(4), 11, Sch 2, Sch 4; Civil Partnership Act 2004, s 261(1), Sch 27; Pensions Act 2004, s 319, Sch 12; Constitutional Reform Act 2005, s 15(1), Sch 4; Mental Capacity Act 2005, s 67(1), Sch 6; Legal Services Act 2007, s 208(1), Sch 21; Pensions Act 2008, s 120, Sch 6, Pt 1.

Domicile and Matrimonial Proceedings Act 1973

(1973 c 45)

Husband and wife

1 ABOLITION OF WIFE'S DEPENDENT DOMICILE

(1) Subject to subsection (2) below, the domicile of a married woman as at any time after the coming into force of this section shall, instead of being the same as her husband's by virtue only of marriage, be ascertained by reference to the same factors as in the case of any other individual capable of having an independent domicile.

(2) Where immediately before this section came into force a woman was married and then had her husband's domicile by dependence, she is to be treated as retaining that domicile (as a domicile of choice, if it is not also her domicile of origin) unless and until it is changed by acquisition or revival of another domicile either on or after the coming into force of this section.

(3) This section extends to England and Wales, Scotland and Northern Ireland.

Minors and pupils

3 AGE AT WHICH INDEPENDENT DOMICILE CAN BE ACQUIRED

(1) The time at which a person first becomes capable of having an independent domicile shall be when he attains the age of sixteen or marries under that age; and in the case of a person who immediately before 1st January 1974 was incapable of having an independent domicile, but had then attained the age of sixteen or been married, it shall be that date.

(2) This section extends to England and Wales and Northern Ireland (but not to Scotland).

4 DEPENDENT DOMICILE OF CHILD NOT LIVING WITH HIS FATHER

(1) Subsection (2) of this section shall have effect with respect to the dependent domicile of a child as at any time after the coming into force of this section when his father and mother are alive but living apart.

(2) The child's domicile as at that time shall be that of his mother if—
   (a) he then has his home with her and has no home with his father; or
   (b) he has at any time had her domicile by virtue of paragraph (a) above and has not since had a home with his father.

(3) As at any time after the coming into force of this section, the domicile of a child whose mother is dead shall be that which she last had before she died if at her death he had her domicile by virtue of subsection (2) above and he has not since had a home with his father.

(4) Nothing in this section prejudices any existing rule of law as to the cases in which a child's domicile is regarded as being, by dependence, that of his mother.

(5) In this section, "child" means a person incapable of having an independent domicile.

(6) This section extends to England and Wales, Scotland and Northern Ireland.

As amended by: Children Act 1975, s 108(1)(b), Sch 4, Part I.

INHERITANCE (PROVISION FOR FAMILY AND DEPENDANTS) ACT 1975

(1975 c 63)

1 APPLICATION FOR FINANCIAL PROVISION FROM DECEASED'S ESTATE

(1) Where after the commencement of this Act a person dies domiciled in England and Wales and is survived by any of the following persons—
- (a) the spouse or civil partner of the deceased;
- (b) a former spouse or former civil partner of the deceased, but not one who has formed a subsequent marriage or civil partnership;
- (ba) any person (not being a person included in paragraph (a) or (b) above) to whom subsection (1A) or (1B) below applies;
- (c) a child of the deceased;
- (d) any person (not being a child of the deceased) who, in the case of any marriage or civil partnership to which the deceased was at any time a party, was treated by the deceased as a child of the family in relation to that marriage or civil partnership;
- (e) any person (not being a person included in the foregoing paragraphs of this subsection) who immediately before the death of the deceased was being maintained, either wholly or partly, by the deceased;

that person may apply to the court for an order under section 2 of this Act on the ground that the disposition of the deceased's estate effected by his will or the law relating to intestacy, or the combination of his will and that law, is not such as to make reasonable financial provision for the applicant.

(1A) This subsection applies to a person if the deceased died on or after 1st January 1996 and, during the whole of the period of two years ending immediately before the date when the deceased died, the person was living—
- (a) in the same household as the deceased, and
- (b) as the husband or wife of the deceased.

(1B) This subsection applies to a person if for the whole of the period of two years ending immediately before the date when the deceased died the person was living—
- (a) in the same household as the deceased, and
- (b) as the civil partner of the deceased.

(2) In this Act "reasonable financial provision"—
(a) in the case of an application made by virtue of subsection (1)(a) above by the husband or wife of the deceased (except where the marriage with the deceased was the subject of a decree of judicial separation and at the date of death the decree was in force and the separation was continuing), means such financial provision as it would be reasonable in all the circumstances of the case for a husband or wife to receive, whether or not that provision is required for his or her maintenance;
(aa) in the case of an application made by virtue of subsection (1)(a) above by the civil partner of the deceased (except where, at the date of death, a separation order under Chapter 2 of Part 2 of the Civil Partnership Act 2004 was in force in relation to the civil partnership and the separation was continuing), means such financial provision as it would be reasonable in all the circumstances of the case for a civil partner to receive, whether or not that provision is required for his or her maintenance;
(b) in the case of any other application made by virtue of subsection (1) above, means such financial provision as it would be reasonable in all the circumstances of the case for the applicant to receive for his maintenance.

(3) For the purposes of subsection (1)(e) above, a person shall be treated as being maintained by the deceased, either wholly or partly, as the case may be, if the deceased, otherwise than for full valuable consideration, was making a substantial contribution in money or money's worth towards the reasonable needs of that person.

2 POWERS OF COURT TO MAKE ORDERS

(1) Subject to the provisions of this Act, where an application is made for an order under this section, the court may, if it is satisfied that the disposition of the deceased's estate effected by his will or the law relating to intestacy, or the combination of his will and that law, is not such as to make reasonable financial provision for the applicant, make any one or more of the following orders—
(a) an order for the making to the applicant out of the net estate of the deceased of such periodical payments and for such term as may be specified in the order;
(b) an order for the payment to the applicant out of that estate of a lump sum of such amount as may be so specified;
(c) an order for the transfer to the applicant of such property comprised in that estate as may be so specified;
(d) an order for the settlement for the benefit of the applicant of such property comprised in that estate as may be so specified;
(e) an order for the acquisition out of property comprised in that estate of such property as may be so specified and for the transfer of the property so acquired to the applicant or for the settlement thereof for his benefit;
(f) an order varying any ante-nuptial or post-nuptial settlement (including such a settlement made by will) made on the parties to a marriage to which the deceased was one of the parties, the variation being for the benefit of the surviving party to that marriage, or any child of that marriage, or any person who was treated by the deceased as a child of the family in relation to that marriage;
(g) an order varying any settlement made—
(i) during the subsistence of a civil partnership formed by the deceased, or
(ii) in anticipation of the formation of a civil partnership by the deceased,
on the civil partners (including such a settlement made by will), the variation being for the benefit of the surviving civil partner, or any child of both the civil partners, or any person who was treated by the deceased as a child of the family in relation to that civil partnership.

(2) An order under subsection (1)(a) above providing for the making out of the net estate of the deceased of periodical payments may provide for—
(a) payments of such amount as may be specified in the order,
(b) payments equal to the whole of the income of the net estate or of such portion thereof as may be so specified,
(c) payments equal to the whole of the income of such part of the net estate as the court may direct to be set aside or appropriated for the making out of the income thereof of payments under this section,
or may provide for the amount of the payments or any of them to be determined in any other way the court thinks fit.

(3) Where an order under subsection (1)(a) above provides for the making of payments of an amount specified in the order, the order may direct that such part of the net estate as may be so specified shall be set aside or appropriated for the making out of the income thereof of those payments; but no larger part of the net estate shall be so set aside or appropriated than is sufficient, at the date of the order, to produce by the income thereof the amount required for the making of those payments.

(4) An order under this section may contain such consequential and supplemental provisions as the court thinks necessary or expedient for the purpose of giving effect to the order or for the purpose of securing that the order operates fairly as between one beneficiary of the estate of the deceased and another and may, in particular, but without prejudice to the generality of this subsection—
(a) order any person who holds any property which forms part of the net estate of the deceased to make such payment or transfer such property as may be specified in the order;
(b) varying the disposition of the deceased's estate effected by the will or the law relating to intestacy, or by both the will and the law relating to intestacy, in such manner as the court thinks fair and reasonable having regard to the provisions of the order and all the circumstances of the case;
(c) confer on the trustees of any property which is the subject of an order under this section such powers as appear to the court to be necessary or expedient.

3 MATTERS TO WHICH COURT IS TO HAVE REGARD IN EXERCISING POWERS UNDER S 2

(1) Where an application is made for an order under section 2 of this Act, the court shall, in determining whether the disposition of the deceased's estate effected by his will or the law relating to intestacy, or the combination of his will and that law, is such as to make reasonable financial provision for the applicant and, if the court considers that reasonable financial provision has not been made, in determining whether and in what manner it shall exercise its powers under that section, have regard to the following matters, that is to say—
(a) the financial resources and financial needs which the applicant has or is likely to have in the foreseeable future;
(b) the financial resources and financial needs which any other applicant for an order under section 2 of this Act has or is likely to have in the foreseeable future;
(c) the financial resources and financial needs which any beneficiary of the estate of the deceased has or is likely to have in the foreseeable future;
(d) any obligations and responsibilities which the deceased had towards any applicant for an order under the said section 2 or towards any beneficiary of the estate of the deceased;
(e) the size and nature of the net estate of the deceased;

(f) any physical or mental disability of any applicant for an order under the said section 2 or any beneficiary of the estate of the deceased;
(g) any other matter, including the conduct of the applicant or any other person, which in the circumstances of the case the court may consider relevant.

(2) This subsection applies, without prejudice to the generality of paragraph (g) of subsection (1) above, where an application for an order under section 2 of this Act is made by virtue of section 1(1)(a) or (b) of this Act. The court shall, in addition to the matters specifically mentioned in paragraphs (a) to (f) of that subsection, have regard to—
(a) the age of the applicant and the duration of the marriage or civil partnership;
(b) the contribution made by the applicant to the welfare of the family of the deceased, including any contribution made by looking after the home or caring for the family.

In the case of an application by the wife or husband of the deceased, the court shall also, unless at the date of death a decree of judicial separation was in force and the separation was continuing, have regard to the provision which the applicant might reasonably have expected to receive if on the day on which the deceased died the marriage, instead of being terminated by death, had been terminated by a decree of divorce.

In the case of an application by the civil partner of the deceased, the court shall also, unless at the date of the death a separation order under Chapter 2 of Part 2 of the Civil Partnership Act 2004 was in force and the separation was continuing, have regard to the provision which the applicant might reasonably have expected to receive if on the day on which the deceased died the civil partnership, instead of being terminated by death, had been terminated by a dissolution order.

(2A) Without prejudice to the generality of paragraph (g) of subsection (1) above, where an application for an order under section 2 of this Act is made by virtue of section 1(1)(ba) of this Act, the court shall, in addition to the matters specifically mentioned in paragraphs (a) to (f) of that subsection, have regard to—
(a) the age of the applicant and the length of the period during which the applicant lived as the husband or wife or civil partner of the deceased and in the same household as the deceased;
(b) the contribution made by the applicant to the welfare of the family of the deceased, including any contribution made by looking after the home or caring for the family.

(3) Without prejudice to the generality of paragraph (g) of subsection (1) above, where an application for an order under section 2 of this Act is made by virtue of section 1(1)(c) or 1(1)(d) of this Act, the court shall, in addition to the matters specifically mentioned in paragraphs (a) to (f) of that subsection, have regard to the manner in which the applicant was being or in which he might expect to be educated or trained, and where the application is made by virtue of section 1(1)(d) the court shall also have regard—
(a) to whether the deceased had assumed any responsibility for the applicant's maintenance and, if so, to the extent to which and the basis upon which the deceased assumed that responsibility and to the length of time for which the deceased discharged that responsibility;
(b) to whether in assuming and discharging that responsibility the deceased did so knowing that the applicant was not his own child;
(c) to the liability of any other person to maintain the applicant.

(4) Without prejudice to the generality of paragraph (g) of subsection (1) above, where an application for an order under section 2 of this Act is made by virtue of section 1(1)(e) of this Act, the court shall, in addition to the matters specifically mentioned in paragraphs (a) to (f) of that subsection, have regard to the extent to which and the basis upon which the deceased assumed responsibility for the maintenance of the applicant, and to the length of time for which the deceased discharged that responsibility.

(5) In considering the matters to which the court is required to have regard under this section, the court shall take into account the facts as known to the court at the date of the hearing.

(6) In considering the financial resources of any person for the purposes of this section the court shall take into account his earning capacity and in considering the financial needs of any person for the purposes of this section the court shall take into account his financial obligations and responsibilities.

4 TIME-LIMIT FOR APPLICATIONS

An application for an order under section 2 of this Act shall not, except with the permission of the court, be made after the end of the period of six months from the date on which representation with respect to the estate of the deceased is first taken out.

. . .

6 VARIATION, DISCHARGE, ETC OF ORDERS FOR PERIODICAL PAYMENTS

(1) Subject to the provisions of this Act, where the court has made an order under section 2(1)(a) of this Act (in this section referred to as "the original order") for the making of periodical payments to any person (in this section referred to as "the original recipient"), the court, on an application under this section, shall have power by order to vary or discharge the original order or to suspend any provision of it temporarily and to revive the operation of any provision so suspended.

(2) Without prejudice to the generality of subsection (1) above, an order made on an application for the variation of the original order may—

(a) provide for the making out of any relevant property of such periodical payments and for such term as may be specified in the order to any person who has applied, or would but for section 4 of this Act be entitled to apply, for an order under section 2 of this Act (whether or not, in the case of any application, an order was made in favour of the applicant);

(b) provide for the payment out of any relevant property of a lump sum of such amount as may be so specified to the original recipient or to any such person as is mentioned in paragraph (a) above;

(c) provide for the transfer of the relevant property, or such part thereof as may be so specified, to the original recipient or to any such person as is so mentioned.

(3) Where the original order provides that any periodical payments payable thereunder to the original recipient are to cease on the occurrence of an event specified in the order (other than the formation of a subsequent marriage or civil partnership by a former spouse or former civil partner) or on the expiration of a period so specified, then, if, before the end of the period of six months from the date of the occurrence of that event or of the expiration of that period, an application is made for an order under this section, the court shall have power to make any order which it would have had power to make if the application had been made before the date (whether in favour of the original recipient or any such person as is mentioned in subsection (2)(a) above and whether having effect from that date or from such later date as the court may specify).

(4) Any reference in this section to the original order shall include a reference to an order made under this section and any reference in this section to the original recipient shall include a reference to any person to whom periodical payments are required to be made by virtue of an order under this section.

(5) An application under this section may be made by any of the following persons, that is to say—
(a) any person who by virtue of section 1(1) of this Act has applied, or would but for section 4 of this Act be entitled to apply, for an order under section 2 of this Act,
(b) the personal representatives of the deceased,
(c) the trustees of any relevant property, and
(d) any beneficiary of the estate of the deceased.

(6) An order under this section may only affect—
(a) property the income of which is at the date of the order applicable wholly or in part for the making of periodical payments to any person who has applied for an order under this Act, or
(b) in the case of an application under subsection (3) above in respect of payments which have ceased to be payable on the occurrence of an event or the expiration of a period, property the income of which was so applicable immediately before the occurrence of that event or the expiration of that period, as the case may be,
and any such property as is mentioned in paragraph (a) or (b) above is in subsections (2) and (5) above referred to as "relevant property".

(7) In exercising the powers conferred by this section the court shall have regard to all circumstances of the case, including any change in any of the matters to which the court was required to have regard when making the order to which the application relates.

(8) Where the court makes an order under this section, it may give such consequential directions as it thinks necessary or expedient having regard to the provisions of the order.

(9) No such order as is mentioned in section 2(1)(d), (e) or (f), 9, 10 or 11 of this Act shall be made on an application under this section.

(10) For the avoidance of doubt it is hereby declared that, in relation to an order which provides for the making of periodical payments which are to cease on the occurrence of an event specified in the order (other than the formation of a subsequent marriage or civil partnership by a former spouse or former civil partner) or on the expiration of a period so specified, the power to vary an order includes power to provide for the making of periodical payments after the expiration of that period or the occurrence of that event.

7 PAYMENT OF LUMP SUMS BY INSTALMENTS

(1) An order under section 2(1)(b) or 6(2)(b) of this Act for the payment of a lump sum may provide for the payment of that sum by instalments of such amount as may be specified in the order.

(2) Where an order is made by virtue of subsection (1) above, the court shall have power, on an application made by the person to whom the lump sum is payable, by the personal representatives of the deceased or by the trustees of the property out of which the lump sum is payable, to vary that order by varying the number of instalments payable, the amount of any instalment and the date on which any instalment becomes payable.

Property available for financial provision

. . .

9 PROPERTY HELD ON A JOINT TENANCY

(1) Where a deceased person was immediately before his death beneficially entitled to a joint tenancy of any property, then, if, before the end of the period of six months from the date

on which representation with respect to the estate of the deceased was first taken out, an application is made for an order under section 2 of this Act, the court for the purpose of facilitating the making of financial provision for the applicant under this Act may order that the deceased's severable share of that property, at the value thereof immediately before his death, shall, to such extent as appears to the court to be just in all the circumstances of the case, be treated for the purposes of this Act as part of the net estate of the deceased.

(2) In determining the extent to which any severable share is to be treated as part of the net estate of the deceased by virtue of an order under subsection (1) above, the court shall have regard to any inheritance tax payable in respect of that severable share.

(3) Where an order is made under subsection (1) above, the provisions of this section shall not render any person liable for anything done by him before the order was made.

(4) For the avoidance of doubt it is hereby declared that for the purposes of this section there may be a joint tenancy of a chose in action.

Powers of court in relation to transactions intended to defeat applications for financial provision

10 DISPOSITIONS INTENDED TO DEFEAT APPLICATIONS FOR FINANCIAL PROVISION

(1) Where an application is made to the court for an order under section 2 of this Act, the applicant may, in the proceedings on that application, apply to the court for an order under subsection (2) below.

(2) Where on an application under subsection (1) above the court is satisfied—
(a) that, less than six years before the date of the death of the deceased, the deceased with the intention of defeating an application for financial provision under this Act made a disposition, and
(b) that full valuable consideration for that disposition was not given by the person to whom or for the benefit of whom the disposition was made (in this section referred to as "the donee") or by any other person, and
(c) that the exercise of the powers conferred by this section would facilitate the making of financial provision for the applicant under this Act,

then, subject to the provisions of this section and of sections 12 and 13 of this Act, the court may order the donee (whether or not at the date of the order he holds any interest in the property disposed of to him or for his benefit by the deceased) to provide, for the purpose of the making of that financial provision, such sum of money or other property as may be specified in the order.

(3) Where an order is made under subsection (2) above as respects any disposition made by the deceased which consisted of the payment of money to or for the benefit of the donee, the amount of any sum of money or the value of any property ordered to be provided under that subsection shall not exceed the amount of the payment made by the deceased after deducting therefrom any inheritance tax borne by the donee in respect of that payment.

(4) Where an order is made under subsection (2) above as respects any disposition made by the deceased which consisted of the transfer of property (other than a sum of money) to or for the benefit of the donee, the amount of any sum of money or the value of any property ordered to be provided under that subsection shall not exceed the value at the date of the death of the deceased of the property disposed of by him to or for the benefit of the donee

(or if that property has been disposed of by the person to whom it was transferred by the deceased, the value at the date of that disposal thereof) after deducting therefrom any inheritance tax borne by the donee in respect of the transfer of that property by the deceased.

(5) Where an application (in this subsection referred to as "the original application") is made for an order under subsection (2) above in relation to any disposition, then, if on an application under this subsection by the donee or by any applicant for an order under section 2 of this Act the court is satisfied—
(a) that, less than six years before the date of the death of the deceased, the deceased with the intention of defeating an application for financial provision under this Act made a disposition other than the disposition which is the subject of the original application, and
(b) that full valuable consideration for that other disposition was not given by the person to whom or for the benefit of whom that other disposition was made or by any other person,
the court may exercise in relation to the person to whom or for the benefit of whom that other disposition was made the powers which the court would have had under subsection (2) above if the original application had been made in respect of that other disposition and the court had been satisfied as to the matters set out in paragraphs (a), (b) and (c) of that subsection; and where any application is made under this subsection, any reference in this section (except in subsection (2)(b)) to the donee shall include a reference to the person to whom or for the benefit of whom that other disposition was made.

(6) In determining whether and in what manner to exercise its powers under this section, the court shall have regard to the circumstances in which any disposition was made and any valuable consideration which was given therefor, the relationship, if any, of the donee to the deceased, the conduct and financial resources of the donee and all the other circumstances of the case.

(7) In this section "disposition" does not include—
(a) any provision in a will, any such nomination as is mentioned in section 8(1) of this Act or any donatio mortis causa, or
(b) any appointment of property made, otherwise than by will, in the exercise of a special power of appointment,
but, subject to these exceptions, includes any payment of money (including the payment of a premium under a policy of assurance) and any conveyance, assurance, appointment or gift of property of any description, whether made by an instrument or otherwise.

(8) The provisions of this section do not apply to any disposition made before the commencement of this Act.

11 CONTRACTS TO LEAVE PROPERTY BY WILL

(1) Where an application is made to a court for an order under section 2 of this Act, the applicant may, in the proceedings on that application, apply to the court for an order under this section.

(2) Where on an application under subsection (1) above the court is satisfied—
(a) that the deceased made a contract by which he agreed to leave by his will a sum of money or other property to any person or by which he agreed that a sum of money or other property would be paid or transferred to any person out of his estate, and
(b) that the deceased made that contract with the intention of defeating an application for financial provision under this Act, and

(c) that when the contract was made full valuable consideration for that contract was not given or promised by the person with whom or for the benefit of whom the contract was made (in this section referred to as "the donee") or by any other person, and

(d) that the exercise of the powers conferred by this section would facilitate the making of financial provision for the applicant under this Act,

then, subject to the provisions of this section and of sections 12 and 13 of this Act, the court may make any one or more of the following orders, that is to say—

(i) if any money has been paid or any other property has been transferred to or for the benefit of the donee in accordance with the contract, an order directing the donee to provide, for the purpose of the making of that financial provision, such sum of money or other property as may be specified in the order;

(ii) if the money or all the money has not been paid or the property or all the property has not been transferred in accordance with the contract, an order directing the personal representatives not to make any payment or transfer any property, or not to make any further payment or transfer any further property, as the case may be, in accordance therewith or directing the personal representatives only to make such payment or transfer such property as may be specified in the order.

(3) Notwithstanding anything in subsection (2) above, the court may exercise its powers thereunder in relation to any contract made by the deceased only to the extent that the court considers that the amount of any sum of money paid or to be paid or the value of any property transferred or to be transferred in accordance with the contract exceeds the value of any valuable consideration given or to be given for that contract, and for this purpose the court shall have regard to the value of property at the date of the hearing.

(4) In determining whether and in what manner to exercise its powers under this section, the court shall have regard to the circumstances in which the contract was made, the relationship, if any, of the donee to the deceased, the conduct and financial resources of the donee and all the other circumstances of the case.

(5) Where an order has been made under subsection (2) above in relation to any contract the rights of any person to enforce that contract or to recover damages or to obtain other relief for the breach thereof shall be subject to any adjustment made by the court under section 12(3) of this Act and shall survive to such extent only as is consistent with giving effect to the terms of that order.

(6) The provisions of this section do not apply to a contract made before the commencement of this Act.

12 PROVISIONS SUPPLEMENTARY TO SS 10 AND 11

(1) Where the exercise of any of the powers conferred by section 10 or 11 of this Act is conditional on the court being satisfied that a disposition or contract was made by a deceased person with the intention of defeating an application for financial provision under this Act, that condition shall be fulfilled if the court is of the opinion that, on a balance of probabilities, the intention of the deceased (though not necessarily his sole intention) in making the disposition or contract was to prevent an order for financial provision being made under this Act or to reduce the amount of the provision which might otherwise be granted by an order thereunder.

(2) Where an application is made under section 11 of this Act with respect to any contract made by the deceased and no valuable consideration was given or promised by any person

for that contract then, notwithstanding anything in subsection (1) above, it shall be presumed, unless the contrary is shown, that the deceased made that contract with the intention of defeating an application for financial provision under this Act. . . .

. . .

Special provisions relating to cases of divorce, separation, etc

14 PROVISION AS TO CASES WHERE NO FINANCIAL RELIEF WAS GRANTED IN DIVORCE PROCEEDINGS, ETC

(1) Where, within twelve months from the date on which a decree of divorce or nullity of marriage has been made absolute or a decree of judicial separation has been granted, a party to the marriage dies and—

(a) an application for a financial provision order under section 23 of the Matrimonial Causes Act 1973 or a property adjustment order under section 24 of that Act has not been made by the other party to that marriage, or

(b) such an application has been made but the proceedings thereon have not been determined at the time of the death of the deceased,

then, if an application for an order under section 2 of this Act is made by that other party, the court shall, notwithstanding anything in section 1 or section 3 of this Act, have power, if it thinks it just to do so, to treat that party for the purposes of that application as if the decree of divorce or nullity of marriage had not been made absolute or the decree of judicial separation had not been granted, as the case may be.

(2) This section shall not apply in relation to a decree of judicial separation unless at the date of the death of the deceased the decree was in force and the separation was continuing.

14A PROVISION AS TO CASES WHERE NO FINANCIAL RELIEF WAS GRANTED IN PROCEEDINGS FOR THE DISSOLUTION ETC OF A CIVIL PARTNERSHIP

(1) Subsection (2) below applies where—

(a) a dissolution order, nullity order, separation order or presumption of death order has been made under Chapter 2 of Part 2 of the Civil Partnership Act 2004 in relation to a civil partnership,

(b) one of the civil partners dies within twelve months from the date on which the order is made, and

(c) either—

(i) an application for a financial provision order under Part 1 of Schedule 5 to that Act or a property adjustment order under Part 2 of that Schedule has not been made by the other civil partner, or

(ii) such an application has been made but the proceedings on the application have not been determined at the time of the death of the deceased.

(2) If an application for an order under section 2 of this Act is made by the surviving civil partner, the court shall, notwithstanding anything in section 1 or section 3 of this Act, have power, if it thinks it just to do so, to treat the surviving civil partner as if the order mentioned in subsection (1)(a) above had not been made.

(3) This section shall not apply in relation to a separation order unless at the date of the death of the deceased the separation order was in force and the separation was continuing.

15 RESTRICTION IMPOSED IN DIVORCE PROCEEDINGS, ETC ON APPLICATION UNDER THIS ACT

(1) On the grant of a decree of divorce, a decree of nullity of marriage or a decree of judicial separation or at any time thereafter the court, if it considers it just to do so, may, on the application of either party to the marriage, order that the other party to the marriage shall not on the death of the applicant be entitled to apply for an order under section 2 of this Act.

In this subsection "the court" means the High Court or, where a county court has jurisdiction by virtue of Part V of the Matrimonial and Family Proceedings Act 1984, a county court.

(2) In the case of a decree of divorce or nullity of marriage an order may be made under subsection (1) above before or after the decree is made absolute, but if it is made before the decree is made absolute it shall not take effect unless the decree is made absolute.

(3) Where an order made under subsection (1) above on the grant of a decree of divorce or nullity of marriage has come into force with respect to a party to a marriage, then, on the death of the other party to that marriage, the court shall not entertain any application for an order under section 2 of this Act made by the first-mentioned party.

(4) Where an order made under subsection (1) above on the grant of a decree of judicial separation has come into force with respect to any party to a marriage, then, if the other party to that marriage dies while the decree is in force and the separation is continuing, the court shall not entertain any application for an order under section 2 of this Act made by the first-mentioned party.

15ZA RESTRICTION IMPOSED IN PROCEEDINGS FOR THE DISSOLUTION ETC OF A CIVIL PARTNERSHIP ON APPLICATION UNDER THIS ACT

(1) On making a dissolution order, nullity order, separation order or presumption of death order under Chapter 2 of Part 2 of the Civil Partnership Act 2004, or at any time after making such an order, the court, if it considers it just to do so, may, on the application of either of the civil partners, order that the other civil partner shall not on the death of the applicant be entitled to apply for an order under section 2 of this Act.

(2) In subsection (1) above "the court" means the High Court or, where a county court has jurisdiction by virtue of Part 5 of the Matrimonial and Family Proceedings Act 1984, a county court.

(3) In the case of a dissolution order, nullity order or presumption of death order ("the main order") an order may be made under subsection (1) above before (as well as after) the main order is made final, but if made before the main order is made final it shall not take effect unless the main order is made final.

(4) Where an order under subsection (1) above made in connection with a dissolution order, nullity order or presumption of death order has come into force with respect to a civil partner, then, on the death of the other civil partner, the court shall not entertain any application for an order under section 2 of this Act made by the surviving civil partner.

(5) Where an order under subsection (1) above made in connection with a separation order has come into force with respect to a civil partner, then, if the other civil partner dies while the separation order is in force and the separation is continuing, the court shall not entertain any application for an order under section 2 of this Act made by the surviving civil partner.

15A RESTRICTION IMPOSED IN PROCEEDINGS UNDER MATRIMONIAL AND FAMILY PROCEEDINGS ACT 1984 ON APPLICATION UNDER THIS ACT

(1) On making an order under section 17 of the Matrimonial and Family Proceedings Act 1984 (orders for financial provision and property adjustment following overseas divorces, etc) the court, if it considers it just to do so, may, on the application of either party to the marriage, order that the other party to the marriage shall not on the death of the applicant be entitled to apply for an order under section 2 of this Act.

In this subsection "the court" means the High Court or, where a county court has jurisdiction by virtue of Part V of the Matrimonial and Family Proceedings Act 1984, a county court.

(2) Where an order under subsection (1) above has been made with respect to a party to a marriage which has been dissolved or annulled, then, on the death of the other party to that marriage, the court shall not entertain an application under section 2 of this Act made by the firstmentioned party.

(3) Where an order under subsection (1) above has been made with respect to a party to a marriage the parties to which have been legally separated, then, if the other party to the marriage dies while the legal separation is in force, the court shall not entertain an application under section 2 of this Act made by the first-mentioned party.

15B RESTRICTION IMPOSED IN PROCEEDINGS UNDER SCHEDULE 7 TO THE CIVIL PARTNERSHIP ACT 2004 ON APPLICATION UNDER THIS ACT

(1) On making an order under paragraph 9 of Schedule 7 to the Civil Partnership Act 2004 (orders for financial provision, property adjustment and pension-sharing following overseas dissolution etc of civil partnership) the court, if it considers it just to do so, may, on the application of either of the civil partners, order that the other civil partner shall not on the death of the applicant be entitled to apply for an order under section 2 of this Act.

(2) In subsection (1) above "the court" means the High Court or, where a county court has jurisdiction by virtue of Part 5 of the Matrimonial and Family Proceedings Act 1984, a county court.

(3) Where an order under subsection (1) above has been made with respect to one of the civil partners in a case where a civil partnership has been dissolved or annulled, then, on the death of the other civil partner, the court shall not entertain an application under section 2 of this Act made by the surviving civil partner.

(4) Where an order under subsection (1) above has been made with respect to one of the civil partners in a case where civil partners have been legally separated, then, if the other civil partner dies while the legal separation is in force, the court shall not entertain an application under section 2 of this Act made by the surviving civil partner.

16 VARIATION AND DISCHARGE OF SECURED PERIODICAL PAYMENTS ORDERS MADE UNDER MATRIMONIAL CAUSES ACT 1973

(1) Where an application for an order under section 2 of this Act is made to the court by any person who was at the time of the death of the deceased entitled to payments from the deceased under a secured periodical payments order made under the Matrimonial Causes

Act 1973 or Schedule 5 to the Civil Partnership Act 2004, then, in the proceedings on that application, the court shall have power, if an application is made under this section by that person or by the personal representative of the deceased, to vary or discharge that periodical payments order or to revive the operation of any provision thereof which has been suspended under section 31 of that Act of 1973 or Part 11 of that Schedule.

(2) In exercising the powers conferred by this section the court shall have regard to all the circumstances of the case, including any order which the court proposes to make under section 2 or section 5 of this Act and any change (whether resulting from the death of the deceased or otherwise) in any of the matters to which the court was required to have regard when making the secured periodical payments order.

(3) The powers exercisable by the court under this section in relation to an order shall be exercisable also in relation to any instrument executed in pursuance of the order.

17 VARIATION AND REVOCATION OF MAINTENANCE AGREEMENTS

(1) Where an application for an order under section 2 of this Act is made to the court by any person who was at the time of the death of the deceased entitled to payments from the deceased under a maintenance agreement which provided for the continuation of payments under the agreement after the death of the deceased, then, in the proceedings on that application, the court shall have power, if an application is made under this section by that person or by the personal representative of the deceased, to vary or revoke that agreement.

(2) In exercising the powers conferred by this section the court shall have regard to all the circumstances of the case, including any order which the court proposes to make under section 2 or section 5 of this Act and any change (whether resulting from the death of the deceased or otherwise) in any of the circumstances in the light of which the agreement was made.

(3) If a maintenance agreement is varied by the court under this section the like consequences shall ensue as if the variation had been made immediately before the death of the deceased by agreement between the parties and for valuable consideration.

(4) In this section "maintenance agreement", in relation to a deceased person, means any agreement made, whether in writing or not and whether before or after the commencement of this Act, by the deceased with any person with whom he formed a marriage or civil partnership, being an agreement which contained provisions governing the rights and liabilities towards one another when living separately of the parties to that marriage or of the civil partners (whether or not the marriage or civil partnership has been dissolved or annulled) in respect of the making or securing of payments or the disposition or use of any property, including such rights and liabilities with respect to the maintenance or education of any child, whether or not a child of the deceased or a person who was treated by the deceased as a child of the family in relation to that marriage or civil partnership.

18 AVAILABILITY OF COURT'S POWERS UNDER THIS ACT IN APPLICATIONS UNDER SS 31 AND 36 OF THE MATRIMONIAL CAUSES ACT 1973

(1) Where—

(a) a person against whom a secured periodical payments order was made under the Matrimonial Causes Act 1973 has died and an application is made under section 31(6) of that Act for the variation or discharge of that order or for the revival of the operation of any provision thereof which has been suspended, or

(b) a party to a maintenance agreement within the meaning of section 34 of that Act has died, the agreement being one which provides for the continuation of payments thereunder after the death of one of the parties, and an application is made under section 36(1) of that Act for the alteration of the agreement under section 35 thereof.

the court shall have power to direct that the application made under the said section 31(6) or 36(1) shall be deemed to have been accompanied by an application for an order under section 2 of this Act.

(2) Where the court gives a direction under subsection (1) above it shall have power, in the proceedings on the application under the said section 31(6) or 36(1), to make any order which the court would have had power to make under the provisions of this Act if the application under the said section 31(6) or 36(1), as the case may be, had been made jointly with an application for an order under the said section 2; and the court shall have power to give such consequential directions as may be necessary for enabling the court to exercise any of the powers available to the court under this Act in the case of an application for an order under section 2.

(3) Where an order made under section 15(1) of this Act is in force with respect to a party to a marriage, the court shall not give a direction under subsection (1) above with respect to any application made under the said section 31(6) or 36(1) by that party on the death of the other party.

18A AVAILABILITY OF COURT'S POWERS UNDER THIS ACT IN APPLICATIONS UNDER PARAGRAPHS 60 AND 73 OF SCHEDULE 5 TO THE CIVIL PARTNERSHIP ACT 2004

(1) Where—

(a) a person against whom a secured periodical payments order was made under Schedule 5 to the Civil Partnership Act 2004 has died and an application is made under paragraph 60 of that Schedule for the variation or discharge of that order or for the revival of the operation of any suspended provision of the order, or

(b) a party to a maintenance agreement within the meaning of Part 13 of that Schedule has died, the agreement being one which provides for the continuation of payments under the agreement after the death of one of the parties, and an application is made under paragraph 73 of that Schedule for the alteration of the agreement under paragraph 69 of that Schedule,

the court shall have power to direct that the application made under paragraph 60 or 73 of that Schedule shall be deemed to have been accompanied by an application for an order under section 2 of this Act.

(2) Where the court gives a direction under subsection (1) above it shall have power, in the proceedings on the application under paragraph 60 or 73 of that Schedule, to make any order which the court would have had power to make under the provisions of this Act if the application under that paragraph had been made jointly with an application for an order under section 2 of this Act; and the court shall have power to give such consequential directions as may be necessary for enabling the court to exercise any of the powers available to the court under this Act in the case of an application for an order under section 2.

(3) Where an order made under section 15ZA(1) of this Act is in force with respect to a civil partner, the court shall not give a direction under subsection (1) above with respect to any application made under paragraph 60 or 73 of that Schedule by that civil partner on the death of the other civil partner.

Miscellaneous and supplementary provisions

19 EFFECT, DURATION AND FORM OF ORDERS

(1) Where an order is made under section 2 of this Act then for all purposes, including the purposes of the enactments relating to inheritance tax, the will or the law relating to intestacy, or both the will and the law relating to intestacy, as the case may be, shall have effect and be deemed to have had effect as from the deceased's death subject to the provisions of the order.

(2) Any order made under section 2 or 5 of this Act in favour of—
(a) an applicant who was the former spouse or former civil partner of the deceased, or
(b) an applicant who was the husband or wife of the deceased in a case where the marriage with the deceased was the subject of a decree of judicial separation and at the date of death the decree was in force and the separation was continuing, or
(c) an applicant who was the civil partner of the deceased in a case where, at the date of death, a separation order under Chapter 2 of Part 2 of the Civil Partnership Act 2004 was in force in relation to their civil partnership and the separation was continuing,
shall, in so far as it provides for the making of periodical payments, cease to have effect on the formation by the applicant of a subsequent marriage or civil partnership, except in relation to any arrears due under the order on the date of the formation of the subsequent marriage or civil partnership.

(3) A copy of every order made under this Act other than an order made under section 15(1) or 15ZA(1) of this Act shall be sent to the principal registry of the Family Division for entry and filing, and a memorandum of the order shall be endorsed on, or permanently annexed to, the probate or letters of administration under which the estate is being administered.

. . .

25 INTERPRETATION

(1) In this Act—

"beneficiary", in relation to the estate of a deceased person, means—
(a) a person who under the will of the deceased or under the law relating to intestacy is beneficially interested in the estate or would be so interested if an order had not been made under this Act, and
(b) a person who has received any sum of money or other property which by virtue of section 8(1) or 8(2) of this Act is treated as part of the net estate of the deceased or would have received that sum or other property if an order had not been made under this Act;

"child" includes an illegitimate child and a child en ventre sa mere at the death of the deceased;

"the court" unless the context otherwise requires means the High Court, or where a county court has jurisdiction by virtue of section 22 of this Act, a county court;

"former civil partner" means a person whose civil partnership with the deceased was during the lifetime of the deceased either—
(a) dissolved or annulled by an order made under the law of any part of the British Islands, or
(b) dissolved or annulled in any country or territory outside the British Islands by a dissolution or annulment which is entitled to be recognised as valid by the law of England and Wales;

"former spouse" means a person whose marriage with the deceased was during the lifetime of the deceased either—

(a) dissolved or annulled by a decree of divorce or a decree of nullity of marriage granted under the law of any part of the British Islands, or
(b) dissolved or annulled in any country or territory outside the British Islands by a divorce or annulment which is entitled to be recognised as valid by the law of England and Wales;

"net estate", in relation to a deceased person, means—

(a) all property of which the deceased had power to dispose by his will (otherwise than by virtue of a special power of appointment) less the amount of his funeral, testamentary and administration expenses, debts and liabilities, including any inheritance tax payable out of his estate on his death;
(b) any property in respect of which the deceased held a general power of appointment (not being a power exercisable by will) which has not been exercised;
(c) any sum of money or other property which is treated for the purposes of this Act as part of the net estate of the deceased by virtue of section 8(1) or (2) of this Act;
(d) any property which is treated for the purposes of this Act as part of the net estate of the deceased by virtue of an order made under section 9 of the Act;
(e) any sum of money or other property which is, by reason of a disposition or contract made by the deceased, ordered under section 10 or 11 of this Act to be provided for the purpose of the making of financial provision under this Act;

"property" includes any chose in action;

"reasonable financial provision" has the meaning assigned to it by section 1 of this Act;

"valuable consideration" does not include marriage or a promise of marriage;

"will" includes codicil.

(2) For the purposes of paragraph (a) of the definition of "net estate" in subsection (1) above a person who is not of full age and capacity shall be treated as having power to dispose by will of all property of which he would have had power to dispose by will if he had been of full age and capacity.

(3) Any reference in this Act to provision out of the net estate of a deceased person includes a reference to provision extending to the whole of that estate.

(4) For the purposes of this Act any reference to a spouse, wife or husband shall be treated as including a reference to a person who in good faith entered into a void marriage with the deceased unless either—

(a) the marriage of the deceased and that person was dissolved or annulled during the lifetime of the deceased and the dissolution or annulment is recognised by the law of England and Wales, or
(b) that person has during the lifetime of the deceased formed a subsequent marriage or civil partnership.

(4A) For the purposes of this Act any reference to a civil partner shall be treated as including a reference to a person who in good faith formed a void civil partnership with the deceased unless either—

(a) the civil partnership between the deceased and that person was dissolved or annulled during the lifetime of the deceased and the dissolution or annulment is recognised by the law of England and Wales, or
(b) that person has during the lifetime of the deceased formed a subsequent civil partnership or marriage.

(5) Any reference in this Act to the formation of, or to a person who has formed, a subsequent marriage or civil partnership includes (as the case may be) a reference to the formation of, or to a person who has formed, a marriage or civil partnership which is by law void or voidable.

(5A) The formation of a marriage or civil partnership shall be treated for the purposes of this Act as the formation of a subsequent marriage or civil partnership, in relation to either of the spouses or civil partners, notwithstanding that the previous marriage or civil partnership of that spouse or civil partner was void or voidable. . . .

As amended by: Matrimonial and Family Proceedings Act 1984, s 8, 25; Law Reform (Succession) Act 1995, s 2(4); Civil Partnership Act 2004, s 71, Sch 4.

Legitimacy Act 1976

(1976 c 31)

1 LEGITIMACY OF CHILDREN OF CERTAIN VOID MARRIAGES

(1) The child of a void marriage, whenever born, shall, subject to subsection (2) below and Schedule 1 to this Act, be treated as the legitimate child of his parents if at the time of the insemination resulting in the birth, or where there was no such insemination, the child's conception (or at the time of the celebration of the marriage if later) both or either of the parties reasonably believed that the marriage was valid.

(2) This section only applies where the father of the child was domiciled in England and Wales at the time of the birth or, if he died before the birth, was so domiciled immediately before his death.

(3) It is hereby declared for the avoidance of doubt that subsection (1) above applies notwithstanding that the belief that the marriage was valid was due to a mistake as to law.

(4) In relation to a child born after the coming into force of section 28 of the Family Law Reform Act 1987, it shall be presumed for the purposes of subsection (1) above, unless the contrary is shown, that one of the parties to the void marriage reasonably believed at the time of the insemination resulting in the birth or, where there was no such insemination, the child's conception (or at the time of the celebration of the marriage if later) that the marriage was valid.

2 LEGITIMATION BY SUBSEQUENT MARRIAGE OF PARENTS

Subject to the following provisions of this Act, where the parents of an illegitimate person marry one another, the marriage shall, if the father of the illegitimate person is at the date of marriage domiciled in England and Wales, render that person, if living, legitimate from the date of the marriage.

2A LEGITIMATION BY SUBSEQUENT CIVIL PARTNERSHIP OF PARENTS

Subject to the following provisions of this Act, where—

(a) a person ("the child") has a parent ("the female parent") by virtue of section 43 of the Human Fertilisation and Embryology Act 2008 (treatment provided to woman who agrees that second woman to be parent),

(b) at the time of the child's birth, the female parent and the child's mother are not civil partners of each other,

(c) the female parent and the child's mother subsequently enter into a civil partnership, and

(d) the female parent is at the date of the formation of the civil partnership domiciled in England and Wales, the civil partnership shall render the child, if living, legitimate from the date of the formation of the civil partnership.

3 LEGITIMATION BY EXTRANEOUS LAW

(1) Subject to the following provisions of this Act, where the parents of an illegitimate person marry one another and the father of the illegitimate person is not at the time of the marriage domiciled in England and Wales but is domiciled in a country by the law of which the illegitimate person became legitimated by virtue of such subsequent marriage, that person, if living, shall in England and Wales be recognised as having been so legitimated from the date of the marriage notwithstanding that, at the time of his birth, his father was domiciled in a country the law of which did not permit legitimation by subsequent marriage.

(2) Subject to the following provisions of this Act, where—
(a) a person ("the child") has a parent ("the female parent") by virtue of section 43 of the Human Fertilisation and Embryology Act 2008 (treatment provided to woman who agrees that second woman to be parent),
(b) at the time of the child's birth, the female parent and the child's mother are not civil partners of each other,
(c) the female parent and the child's mother subsequently enter into a civil partnership, and
(d) the female parent is not at the time of the formation of the civil partnership domiciled in England and Wales but is domiciled in a country by the law of which the child became legitimated by virtue of the civil partnership, the child, if living, shall in England and Wales be recognised as having been so legitimated from the date of the formation of the civil partnership notwithstanding that, at the time of the child's birth, the female parent was domiciled in a country the law of which did not permit legitimation by subsequent civil partnership.

4 LEGITIMATION OF ADOPTED CHILD

(1) Section 39 of the Adoption Act 1976 or section 67 of the Adoption and Children Act 2002 does not prevent an adopted child being legitimated under section 2 or 3 above if either natural parent is the sole adoptive parent.

(2) Where an adopted child (with a sole adoptive parent) is legitimated—
(a) subsection (2) of the said section 39 or subsection (3)(b) of the said section 67 shall not apply after the legitimation to the natural relationship with the other natural parent, and
(b) revocation of the adoption order in consequence of the legitimation shall not affect section 39, 41 or 42 of the Adoption Act 1976 or section 67, 68 or 69 of the Adoption and Children Act 2002 as it applies to any instrument made before the date of legitimation.

5 RIGHTS OF LEGITIMATED PERSONS AND OTHERS TO TAKE INTERESTS IN PROPERTY

(1) Subject to any contrary indication, the rules of construction contained in this section apply to any instrument other than an existing instrument, so far as the instrument contains a disposition of property.

(2) For the purposes of this section, provisions of the law of intestate succession applicable to the estate of a deceased person shall be treated as if contained in an instrument executed by him (while of full capacity) immediately before his death.

(3) A legitimated person, and any other person, shall be entitled to take any interest as if the legitimated person had been born legitimate.

(4) A disposition which depends on the date of birth of a child or children of the parent or parents shall be construed as if—
(a) a legitimated child had been born on the date of legitimation,
(b) two or more legitimated children legitimated on the same date had been born on that date in the order of their actual births, but this does not affect any reference to the age of a child.

(5) Examples of phrases in wills on which subsection (4) above can operate are—
1. Children of A "living at my death or born afterwards".
2. Children of A "living at my death or born afterwards before any one of such children for the time being in existence attains a vested interest, and who attain the age of 21 years".
3. As in example 1 or 2, but referring to grandchildren of A, instead of children of A.
4. A for life "until he has a child" and then to his child or children.

Note. Subsection (4) above will not affect the reference to the age of 21 years in example 2.

(6) If an illegitimate person or a person adopted by one of his natural parents dies, or has died before the commencement of this Act, and—
(a) after his death his parents marry or have married; and
(b) the deceased would, if living at the time of the marriage, have become a legitimated person,
this section shall apply for the construction of the instrument so far as it relates to the taking of interests by, or in succession to, his spouse, children and remoter issue as if he had been legitimated by virtue of the marriage.

(7) In this section "instrument" includes a private Act settling property, but not any other enactment.

6 DISPOSITIONS DEPENDING ON DATE OF BIRTH

(1) Where a disposition depends on the date of birth of a child who was born illegitimate and who is legitimated (or, if deceased, is treated as legitimated), section 5(4) above does not affect entitlement under Part II of the Family Law Reform Act 1969 (illegitimate children).

(2) Where a disposition depends on the date of birth of an adopted child who is legitimated (or, if deceased, is treated as legitimated) section 5(4) above does not affect entitlement by virtue of section 42(2) of the Adoption Act 1976 or section 69(2) of the Adoption and Children Act 2002.

(3) This section applies for example where—
(a) a testator dies in 1976 bequeathing a legacy to his eldest grandchild living at a specified time,

(b) a daughter has an illegitimate child in 1977 who is the first grandchild,
(c) his married son has a child in 1978,
(d) subsequently the illegitimate child is legitimated, and in all those cases the daughter's child remains the eldest grandchild of the testator throughout.

7 PROTECTION OF TRUSTEES AND PERSONAL REPRESENTATIVES

(1) A trustee or personal representative is not under a duty, by virtue of the law relating to trusts or the administration of estates, to enquire, before conveying or distributing any property, whether any person is illegitimate or has been adopted by one of his natural parents, and could be legitimated (or if deceased be treated as legitimated), if that fact could affect entitlement to the property.

(2) A trustee or personal representative shall not be liable to any person by reason of a conveyance or distribution of the property made without regard to any such fact if he has not received notice of the fact before the conveyance or distribution.

(3) This section does not prejudice the right of a person to follow the property, or any property representing it, into the hands of another person, other than a purchaser, who has received it.

8 PERSONAL RIGHTS AND OBLIGATIONS

A legitimated person shall have the same rights, and shall be under the same obligations in respect of the maintenance and support of himself or of any other person as if he had been born legitimate, and, subject to the provisions of this Act, the provisions of any Act relating to claims for damages, compensation, allowance, benefit or otherwise by or in respect of a legitimate child shall apply in like manner in the case of a legitimated person.

9 RE-REGISTRATION OF BIRTH OF LEGITIMATED PERSONS

(1) It shall be the duty of the parents of a legitimated person or, in cases where re-registration can be effected on information furnished by one parent and one of the parents is dead, of the surviving parent to furnish to the Registrar General information with a view to obtaining the re-registration of the birth of that person within 3 months after the date of the marriage or of the formation of the civil partnership by virtue of which he was legitimated.

(2) The failure of the parents of either of them to furnish information as required by subsection (1) above in respect of any legitimated person shall not affect the legitimation of that person.

(3) This section does not apply in relation to a person who was legitimated otherwise than by virtue of the subsequent marriage or civil partnership of his parents.

(4) Any parent who fails to give information as required by this section shall be liable on summary conviction to a fine not exceeding level 1 on the standard scale.

10 INTERPRETATION

(1) In this Act, except where the context otherwise requires—

"disposition" includes the conferring of a power of appointment and any other disposition of an interest in or right over property;

"existing", in relation to an instrument, means one made before 1st January 1976;

"legitimated person" means a person legitimated or recognised as legitimated—
(a) under section 2, 2A or 3 above; or
(b) under section 1 or 8 of the Legitimacy Act 1926; or
(c) except in section 8, by a legitimation (whether or not by virtue of the subsequent marriage of his parents) recognised by the law of England and Wales and effected under the law of any other country;

and cognate expressions shall be construed accordingly;

"power of appointment" includes any discretionary power to transfer a beneficial interest in property without the furnishing of valuable consideration;

"void marriage" means a marriage, not being voidable only, in respect of which the High Court has or had jurisdiction to grant a decree of nullity, or would have or would have had such jurisdiction if the parties were domiciled in England and Wales.

(2) For the purposes of this Act "legitimated person" includes, where the context admits, a person legitimated, or recognised as legitimated, before the passing of the Children Act 1975.

(3) For the purpose of this Act, except where the context otherwise requires,—
(a) the death of the testator is the date at which a will or codicil is to be regarded as made;
(b) an oral disposition of property shall be deemed to be contained in an instrument made when the disposition was made.

(5) Except in so far as the context otherwise requires, any reference in this Act to an enactment shall be construed as a reference to that enactment as amended by or under any other enactment, including this Act.

As amended by: Adoption Act 1976, s 73(2), Sch 3; Criminal Justice Act 1982, ss 37, 38, 46; Family Law Reform Act 1987, s 28(1), (2), Sch 3; Adoption and Children Act 2002, s 139(1), Sch 3; Human Fertilisation and Embryology Act 2008, s 56, Sch 6.

Adoption Act 1976

(1976 c 36)

38 MEANING OF "ADOPTION" IN PART IV

(1) In this Part "adoption" means adoption—
(a) by an adoption order;
(b) by an order made under the Children Act 1975, the Adoption Act 1958, the Adoption Act 1950 or any enactment repealed by the Adoption Act 1950;
(c) by an order made in Scotland, Northern Ireland, the Isle of Man or in any of the Channel Islands;
(cc) which is a Convention adoption;
(d) which is an overseas adoption; or
(e) which is an adoption recognised by the law of England and Wales and effected under the law of any other country, and cognate expressions shall be construed accordingly.

(2) The definition of adoption includes, where the context admits, an adoption effected before the passing of the Children Act 1975 but does not include an adoption of a kind

mentioned in paragraphs (c) to (e) of subsection (1) effected on or after the day which is the appointed day for the purposes of Chapter 4 of Part 1 of the Adoption and Children Act 2002, and the date of an adoption effected by an order is the date of the making of the order.

39 STATUS CONFERRED BY ADOPTION

(1) An adopted child shall be treated in law—
  (a) where the adopters are a married couple, as if he had been born as a child of the marriage (whether or not he was in fact born after the marriage was solemnized);
  (b) in any other case, as if he had been born to the adopter in wedlock (but not as a child of any actual marriage of the adopter).

(2) An adopted child shall, subject to subsections (3) and (3A), be treated in law as if he were not the child of any person other than the adopters or adopter.

(3) In the case of a child adopted by one of its natural parents as sole adoptive parent, subsection (2) has no effect as respects entitlement to property depending on relationship to that parent, or as respects anything else depending on that relationship.

(3A) Where, in the case of a Convention adoption, the High Court is satisfied, on an application under this subsection—
  (a) that under the law of the country in which the adoption was effected the adoption is not a full adoption;
  (b) that the consents referred to in Article 4(c) and (d) of the Convention have not been given for a full adoption, or that the United Kingdom is not the receiving State (within the meaning of Article 2 of the Convention); and
  (c) that it would be more favourable to the adopted child for a direction to be given under this subsection,

the Court may direct that subsection (2) shall not apply, or shall not apply to such extent as may be specified in the direction.

In this subsection "full adoption" means an adoption by virtue of which the adopted child falls to be treated in law as if he were not the child of any person other than the adopters or adopter.

(3B) The following provisions of the Family Law Act 1986—
  (a) section 59 (provisions relating to the Attorney General); and
  (b) section 60 (supplementary provision as to declarations),

shall apply in relation to, and to an application for, a direction under subsection (3A) as they apply in relation to, and to an application for, a declaration under Part III of that Act.

(4) It is hereby declared that this section prevents an adopted child from being illegitimate.

(5) This section has effect—
  (a) in the case of an adoption before 1st January 1976, from that date, and
  (b) in the case of any other adoption, from the date of the adoption.

(6) Subject to the provisions of this Part, this section—
  (a) applies for the construction of enactments or instruments passed or made before the adoption or later, and so applies subject to any contrary indication; and
  (b) has effect as respects things done, or events occurring, after the adoption, or after 31st December 1975, whichever is the later.

41 ADOPTIVE RELATIVES

(1) A relationship existing by virtue of section 39 may be referred to as an adoptive relationship, and—
(a) a male adopter may be referred to as the adoptive father;
(b) a female adopter may be referred to as the adoptive mother;
(c) any other relative of any degree under an adoptive relationship may be referred to as an adoptive relative of that degree,
but this section does not prevent the term "parent", or any other term not qualified by the word "adoptive" being treated as including an adoptive relative.

. . .

47 MISCELLANEOUS ENACTMENTS

(1) Section 39 does not apply for the purposes of section 1 of and Schedule 1 to the Marriage Act 1949 or Schedule 1 to the Civil Partnership Act 2004 (prohibited degrees of kindred and affinity), or sections 64 and 65 of the Sexual Offences Act 2003 (sex with an adult relative).

(2) Section 39 does not apply for the purposes of any provision of—
(a) the British Nationality Act 1981,
(b) the Immigration Act 1971,
(c) any instrument having effect under an enactment within paragraph (a) or (b), or
(d) any other provision of the law for the time being in force which determines British citizenship, British overseas territories citizenship, the status of a British National (Overseas) or British Overseas citizenship.

. . .

72 INTERPRETATION

(1) In this Act, unless the context otherwise requires—

. . .

"child", except where used to express a relationship, means a person who has not attained the age of 18 years;

"the Convention" means the Convention on Protection of Children and Co-operation in respect of Intercountry Adoption, concluded at the Hague on 29th May 1993;

. . .

"parent" means in relation to a child, any parent who has parental responsibility for the child under the Children Act 1989;

. . .

"relative" in relation to a child means a grandparent, brother, sister, uncle or aunt, whether of the full blood or half-blood or by affinity and includes, where the child is illegitimate, the father of the child and any person who would be a relative within the meaning of this definition if the child were the legitimate child of his mother and father;

As amended by: British Nationality Act 1981, s 52(6), Sch 7; Hong Kong (British Nationality) Order 1986, SI 1986/948, art 8, Schedule; Social Security Act 1986, s 86, Sch 11; Social Security

Act 1988, s 16, Sch 5. Children Act 1989, s 88, Sch 10; Adoption (Intercountry Aspects) Act 1999, ss 4, 8, 17; Adoption and Children Act 2002, s 139(1), Sch 3; British Overseas Territories Act 2002, s 2(3); Civil Partnership Act 2004 (Overseas Relationships and Consequential, etc. Amendments) Order 2005, SI 2005/3129; Criminal Justice and Immigration Act 2008, s 73(c), Sch 15;

Domestic Proceedings and Magistrates' Courts Act 1978

(1978 c 22)

Part I MATRIMONIAL PROCEEDINGS IN MAGISTRATES' COURTS

Powers of court to make orders for financial provision for parties to a marriage and children of the family

1 GROUNDS OF APPLICATION FOR FINANCIAL PROVISION

Either party to a marriage may apply to a magistrates' court for an order under section 2 of this Act on the ground that the other party to the marriage—

(a) has failed to provide reasonable maintenance for the applicant; or

(b) has failed to provide, or to make a proper contribution towards, reasonable maintenance for any child of the family; or

(c) has behaved in such a way that the applicant cannot reasonably be expected to live with the respondent; or

(d) has deserted the applicant.

2 POWERS OF COURT TO MAKE ORDERS FOR FINANCIAL PROVISION

(1) Where on an application for an order under this section the applicant satisfies the court of any ground mentioned in section 1 of this Act, the court may, subject to the provisions of this Part of this Act, make any one or more of the following orders, that is to say—
   (a) an order that the respondent shall make to the applicant such periodical payments, and for such term, as may be specified in the order;
   (b) an order that the respondent shall pay to the applicant such lump sum as may be so specified;
   (c) an order that the respondent shall make to the applicant for the benefit of a child of the family to whom the application relates, or to such a child, such periodical payments, and for such term, as may be so specified;
   (d) an order that the respondent shall pay to the applicant for the benefit of a child of the family to whom the application relates, or to such a child, such lump sum as may be so specified.

(2) Without prejudice to the generality of subsection (1)(b) or (d) above, an order under this section for the payment of a lump sum may be made for the purpose of enabling any liability or expenses reasonably incurred in maintaining the applicant, or any child of the family to whom the application relates, before the making of the order to be met.

(3) The amount of any lump sum required to be paid by an order under this section shall not exceed £500 or such larger amount as the Lord Chancellor may from time to time by order fix for the purposes of this subsection.

(4) An order made by the Lord Chancellor under this section—
(a) shall be made only after consultation with the Lord Chief Justice;
(b) shall be made by statutory instrument and be subject to annulment in pursuance of a resolution of either House of Parliament.

(5) The Lord Chief Justice may nominate a judicial office holder (as defined in section 109(4) of the Constitutional Reform Act 2005) to exercise his functions under this section.

3 MATTERS TO WHICH COURT IS TO HAVE REGARD IN EXERCISING ITS POWERS UNDER S 2

(1) Where an application is made for an order under section 2 of this Act, it shall be the duty of the court, in deciding whether to exercise its powers under that section and, if so, in what manner, to have regard to all the circumstances of the case, first consideration being given to the welfare while a minor of any child of the family who has not attained the age of eighteen.

(2) As regards the exercise of its powers under subsection (1)(a) or (b) of section 2, the court shall in particular have regard to the following matters—
(a) the income, earning capacity, property and other financial resources which each of the parties to the marriage has or is likely to have in the foreseeable future, including in the case of earning capacity any increase in that capacity which it would in the opinion of the court be reasonable to expect a party to the marriage to take steps to acquire;
(b) the financial needs, obligations and responsibilities which each of the parties to the marriage has or is likely to have in the foreseeable future;
(c) the standard of living enjoyed by the parties to the marriage before the occurrence of the conduct which is alleged as the ground of the application;
(d) the age of each party to the marriage and the duration of the marriage;
(e) any physical or mental disability of either of the parties to the marriage;
(f) the contributions which each of the parties has made or is likely in the foreseeable future to make to the welfare of the family, including any contribution by looking after the home or caring for the family;
(g) the conduct of each of the parties, if that conduct is such that it would in the opinion of the court be inequitable to disregard it.

(3) As regards the exercise of its power under subsection (1)(c) or (d) of section 2, the court shall in particular have regard to the following matters—
(a) the financial needs of the child;
(b) the income, earning capacity (if any), property and other financial resources of the child;
(c) any physical or mental disability of the child;
(d) the standard of living enjoyed by the family before the occurrence of the conduct which is alleged as the ground of the application;
(e) the manner in which the child was being and in which the parties to the marriage expected him to be educated or trained;
(f) the matters mentioned in relation to the parties to the marriage in paragraphs (a) and (b) of subsection (2) above.

(4) As regards the exercise of its power under section 2 in favour of a child of the family who is not the child of the respondent, the court shall also have regard—

(a) to whether the respondent has assumed any responsibility for the child's maintenance and, if he did, to the extent to which, and the basis on which, he assumed that responsibility and to the length of time during which he discharged that responsibility;
(b) to whether in assuming and discharging that responsibility the respondent did so knowing that the child was not his own child;
(c) to the liability of any other person to maintain the child.

4 DURATION OF ORDERS FOR FINANCIAL PROVISION FOR A PARTY TO A MARRIAGE

(1) The term to be specified in any order made under section 2(1)(a) of this Act shall be such term as the court thinks fit except that the term shall not begin earlier than the date of the making of the application for the order and shall not extend beyond the death of either of the parties to the marriage.

(2) Where an order is made under the said section 2(1)(a) and the marriage of the parties affected by the order is subsequently dissolved or annulled but the order continues in force, the order shall, notwithstanding anything in it, cease to have effect on the remarriage of, or formation of a civil partnership by, the party in whose favour it was made, except in relation to any arrears due under the order on the date of the remarriage or formation of the civil partnership.

5 AGE LIMIT ON MAKING ORDERS FOR FINANCIAL PROVISION FOR CHILDREN AND DURATION OF SUCH ORDERS

(1) Subject to subsection (3) below, no order shall be made under section 2(1)(c) or (d) of this Act in favour of a child who has attained the age of eighteen.

(2) The term to be specified in an order made under section 2(1)(c) of this Act in favour of a child may begin with the date of the making of an application for the order in question or any later date or a date ascertained in accordance with subsection (5) or (6) below but—
(a) shall not in the first instance extend beyond the date of the birthday of the child next following his attaining the upper limit of the compulsory school age (construed in accordance with section 8 of the Education Act 1996) unless the court considers that in the circumstances of the case the welfare of the child requires that it should extend to a later date; and
(b) shall not in any event, subject to subsection (3) below, extend beyond the date of the child's eighteenth birthday.

(3) The court—
(a) may make an order under section 2(1)(c) or (d) of this Act in favour of a child who has attained the age of eighteen, and
(b) may include in an order made under section 2(1)(c) of this Act in relation to a child who has not attained that age a provision for extending beyond the date when the child will attain that age the term for which by virtue of the order any payments are to be made to or for the benefit of that child, if it appears to the court—
(i) that the child is, or will be, or if such an order or provision were made would be, receiving instruction at an educational establishment or undergoing training for a trade, profession or vocation, whether or not he is also, or will also be, in gainful employment; or
(ii) that there are special circumstances which justify the making of the order or provision.

(4) Any order made under section 2(1)(c) of this Act in favour of a child shall, notwithstanding anything in the order, cease to have effect on the death of the person liable to make payments under the order.

(5) Where—
(a) a maintenance calculation ("the current calculation") is in force with respect to a child; and
(b) an application is made for an order under section 2(1)(c) of this Act—
(i) in accordance with section 8 of the Child Support Act 1991; and
(ii) before the end of the period of 6 months beginning with the making of the current calculation, the term to be specified in any such order made on that application may be expressed to begin on, or at any time after, the earliest permitted date.

(6) For the purposes of subsection (5) above, "the earliest permitted date" is whichever is the later of—
(a) the date 6 months before the application is made; or
(b) the date on which the current calculation took effect or, where successive maintenance assessments have been continuously in force with respect to a child, on which the first of those calculations took effect.

(7) Where—
(a) a maintenance calculation ceases to have effect under any provision of the Child Support Act 1991; and
(b) an application is made, before the end of the period of 6 months beginning with the relevant date, for an order under section 2(1)(c) of this Act in relation to a child with respect to whom that maintenance calculation was in force immediately before it ceased to have effect, the term to be specified in any such order, or in any interim order under section 19 of this Act, made on that application, may begin with the date on which that maintenance calculation ceased to have effect, or any later date.

(8) In subsection (7)(b) above—
(a) where the maintenance calculation ceased to have effect, the relevant date is the date on which it so ceased.

6 ORDERS FOR PAYMENTS WHICH HAVE BEEN AGREED BY THE PARTIES

(1) Either party to a marriage may apply to a magistrates' court for an order under this section on the ground that either the party making the application or the other party to the marriage has agreed to make such financial provision as may be specified in the application and, subject to subsection (3) below, the court on such an application may, if—
(a) it is satisfied that the applicant or the respondent, as the case may be, has agreed to make that provision, and
(b) it has no reason to think that it would be contrary to the interests of justice to exercise its powers hereunder, order that the applicant or the respondent, as the case may be, shall make the financial provision specified in the application.

(2) In this section "financial provision" means the provision mentioned in any one or more of the following paragraphs, that is to say—
(a) the making of periodical payments by one party to the other,
(b) the payment of a lump sum by one party to the other,
(c) the making of periodical payments by one party to a child of the family or to the other party for the benefit of such a child,

(d) the payment by one party of a lump sum to a child of the family or to the other party for the benefit of such a child, and any reference in this section to the financial provision specified in an application made under subsection (1) above or specified by the court under subsection (5) below is a reference to the type of provision specified in the application or by the court, as the case may be, to the amount so specified as the amount of any payment to be made thereunder and, in the case of periodical payments, to the term so specified as the term for which the payments are to be made.

(3) Where the financial provision specified in an application under subsection (1) above includes or consists of provision in respect of a child of the family, the court shall not make an order under that subsection unless it considers that the provision which the applicant or the respondent, as the case may be, has agreed to make in respect of that child provides for, or makes a proper contribution towards, the financial needs of the child.

(4) A party to a marriage who has applied for an order under section 2 of this Act shall not be precluded at any time before the determination of that application from applying for an order under this section; but if an order is made under this section on the application of either party and either of them has also made an application for an order under section 2 of this Act, the application made for the order under section 2 shall be treated as if it had been withdrawn.

(5) Where on an application under subsection (1) above the court decides—

(a) that it would be contrary to the interests of justice to make an order for the making of the financial provision specified in the application, or

(b) that any financial provision which the applicant or the respondent, as the case may be, has agreed to make in respect of a child of the family does not provide for, or make a proper contribution towards, the financial needs of that child,

but is of the opinion—

(i) that it would not be contrary to the interests of justice to make an order for the making of some other financial provision specified by the court, and

(ii) that, in so far as that other financial provision contains any provision for a child of the family, it provides for, or makes a proper contribution towards, the financial needs of that child,

then if both the parties agree, the court may order that the applicant or the respondent, as the case may be, shall make that other financial provision.

(6) Subject to subsection (8) below, the provisions of section 4 of this Act shall apply in relation to an order under this section which requires periodical payments to be made to a party to a marriage for his own benefit as they apply in relation to an order under section 2(1)(a) of this Act.

(7) Subject to subsection (8) below, the provisions of section 5 of this Act shall apply in relation to an order under this section for the making of financial provision in respect of a child of the family as they apply in relation to an order under section 2(1)(c) or (d) of this Act.

(8) Where the court makes an order under this section which contains provision for the making of periodical payments and, by virtue of subsection (4) above, an application for an order under section 2 of this Act is treated as if it had been withdrawn, then the term which may be specified as the term for which the payments are to be made may begin with the date of the making of the application for the order under section 2 or any later date.

(9) Where the respondent is not present or represented by counsel or solicitor at the hearing of an application for an order under subsection (1) above, the court shall not make an order under this section unless there is produced to the court such evidence as may be prescribed by rules of court of—

(a) the consent of the respondent to the making of the order,
(b) the financial resources of the respondent, and
(c) in a case where the financial provision specified in the application includes or consists of provision in respect of a child of the family to be made by the applicant to the respondent for the benefit of the child or to the child, the financial resources of the child.

7 POWERS OF COURT WHERE PARTIES ARE LIVING APART BY AGREEMENT

(1) Where the parties to a marriage have been living apart for a continuous period exceeding three months, neither party having deserted the other, and one of the parties has been making periodical payments for the benefit of the other party or of a child of the family, that other party may apply to a magistrates' court for an order under this section, and any application made under this subsection shall specify the aggregate amount of the payments so made during the period of three months immediately preceding the date of the making of the application.

(2) Where on an application for an order under this section the court is satisfied that the respondent has made the payments specified in the application, the court may, subject to the provisions of this Part of this Act, make one or both of the following orders, that is to say—
(a) an order that the respondent shall make to the applicant such periodical payments, and for such term, as may be specified in the order;
(b) an order that the respondent shall make to the applicant for the benefit of a child of the family to whom the application relates, or to such a child, such periodical payments, and for such term, as may be so specified.

(3) The court in the exercise of its powers under this section—
(a) shall not require the respondent to make payments which exceed in aggregate during any period of three months the aggregate amount paid by him for the benefit of the applicant or a child of the family during the period of three months immediately preceding the date of the making of the application;
(b) shall not require the respondent to make payments to or for the benefit of any person which exceed in amount the payments which the court considers that it would have required the respondent to make to or for the benefit of that person on an application under section 1 of this Act;
(c) shall not require payments to be made to or for the benefit of a child of the family who is not a child of the respondent unless the court considers that it would have made an order in favour of that child on an application under section 1 of this Act.

(4) Where on an application under this section the court considers that the orders which it has the power to make under this section—
(a) would not provide reasonable maintenance for the applicant, or
(b) if the application relates to a child of the family, would not provide, or make a proper contribution towards reasonable maintenance for that child,

the court shall refuse to make an order under this section, but the court may treat the application as if it were an application for an order under section 2 of this Act.

(5) The provisions of section 3 of this Act shall apply in relation to an application for an order under this section as they apply in relation to an application for an order under section 2 of this Act subject to the modification that for the reference in subsection (2)(c) of the said section 3 to the occurrence of the conduct which is alleged as the ground of the application there shall be substituted a reference to the living apart of the parties to the marriage.

(6) The provisions of section 4 of this Act shall apply in relation to an order under this section which requires periodical payments to be made to the applicant for his own benefit as they apply in relation to an order under section 2(1)(a) of this Act.

(7) The provisions of section 5 of this Act shall apply in relation to an order under this section for the making of periodical payments in respect of a child of the family as they apply in relation to an order under section 2(1)(c) of this Act.

Powers of court as to the custody etc of children

8 RESTRICTIONS ON MAKING OF ORDERS UNDER THIS ACT: WELFARE OF CHILDREN

Where an application is made by a party to a marriage for an order under section 2, 6 or 7 of this Act, then, if there is a child of the family who is under the age of eighteen, the court shall not dismiss or make a final order on the application until it has decided whether to exercise any of its powers under the Children Act 1989 with respect to the child.

Interim orders

19 INTERIM ORDERS

(1) Where an application is made for an order under section 2, 6 or 7 of this Act—
- (a) the magistrates' court at any time before making a final order on, or dismissing, the application or on refusing to make an order on the application by virtue of section 27 of this Act,
- (b) the High Court on ordering the application to be reheard by a magistrates' court after the refusal of an order under section 27 of this Act, and
- (c) a county court on ordering the application to be reheard by a magistrates' court on an appeal under section 29 of this Act,

shall, subject to the provisions of this Part of this Act, have the—
- (i) power to make an order (in this Part of this Act referred to as an "interim maintenance order") which requires the respondent to make to the applicant or to any child of the family who is under the age of eighteen, or to the applicant for the benefit of such a child, such periodical payments as the court thinks reasonable;

(3) An interim maintenance order may provide for payments to be made from such date as the court may specify, except that, subject to section 5(5) and (6) of this Act, the date shall not be earlier than the date of the making of the application for an order under section 2, 6 or 7 of this Act; and where such an order made by a county court on an appeal under section 29 of this Act provides for payments to be made from a date earlier than the date of the making of the order, the interim order may provide that payments made by the respondent under an order made by a magistrates' court shall, to such extent and in such manner as may be provided by the interim order, be treated as having been paid on account of any payment provided for by the interim order.

(3A) Where an application is made for an order under section 6 of this Act by the party to the marriage who has agreed to make the financial provision specified in the application—
- (a) subsection (1) shall apply as if the reference in paragraph (i) to the respondent were a reference to the applicant and the references to the applicant were references to the respondent; and
- (b) subsection (3) shall apply accordingly.

(5) Subject to subsection (6) below, an interim order made on an application for an order under section 2, 6 or 7 of this Act shall cease to have effect on whichever of the following dates occurs first, that is to say—
(a) the date, if any, specified for the purpose in the interim order;
(b) the date of the expiration of the period of three months beginning with the date of the making of the interim order;
(c) the date on which a magistrates' court either makes a final order on or dismisses the application.

(6) Where an interim order made under subsection (1) above would, but for this subsection, cease to have effect by virtue of subsection (5)(a) or (b) above, the magistrates' court which made the order or, in the case of an interim order made by the High Court or a county court, the magistrates' court by which the application for an order under section 2, 6 or 7 of this Act is to be reheard, shall have power by order to provide that the interim order shall continue in force for a further period, and any order continued in force under this subsection shall cease to have effect on whichever of the following dates occurs first, that is to say—
(a) the date, if any, specified for the purpose in the order made under this subsection;
(b) the date of the expiration of the period of three months beginning with the date of the making of the order under this subsection or, if more than one order has been made under this subsection with respect to the application, beginning with the date of the making of the first of those orders;
(c) the date on which the court either makes a final order on, or dismisses, the application.

(7) Not more than one interim maintenance order may be made with respect to any application for an order under section 2, 6 or 7 of this Act, but without prejudice to the powers of a court under this section on any further such application.

(8) No appeal shall lie from the making of or refusal to make, the variation of or refusal to vary, or the revocation of or refusal to revoke, an interim maintenance order.

(9) An interim order made by the High Court or a county court under this section on ordering that an application be reheard by a magistrates' court shall, for the purpose of its enforcement and for the purposes of section 20 of this Act, be treated as if it were an order of that magistrates' court and not of the High Court or a county court.

Variation, revocation and cessation of orders etc

20 VARIATION, REVIVAL AND REVOCATION OF ORDERS FOR PERIODICAL PAYMENTS

(1) Where a magistrates' court has made an order under section 2(1)(a) or (c) of this Act for the making of periodical payments the court shall have power, on an application made under this section, to vary or revoke that order and also to make an order under section 2(1)(b) or (d) of this Act.

(2) Where a magistrates' court has made an order under section 6 of this Act for the making of periodical payments by a party to a marriage the court shall have power, on an application made under this section, to vary or revoke that order and also to make an order for the payment of a lump sum by that party either—
(a) to the other party to the marriage, or
(b) to a child of the family or to that other party for the benefit of that child.

(3) Where a magistrates' court has made an order under section 7 of this Act for the making of periodical payments, the court shall have power, on an application made under this section, to vary or revoke that order.

(5) Where a magistrates' court has made an interim maintenance order under section 19 of this Act, the court, on an application made under this section, shall have power to vary or revoke that order, except that the court shall not by virtue of this subsection extend the period for which the order is in force.

(6) The power of the court under this section to vary an order for the making of periodical payments shall include power to suspend any provision thereof temporarily and to revive any provision so suspended.

(7) Where the court has power by virtue of this section to make an order for the payment of a lump sum, the amount of the lump sum shall not exceed the maximum amount that may at that time be required to be paid under section 2 (3) of this Act, but the court may make an order for the payment of a lump sum not exceeding that amount notwithstanding that the person required to pay the lump sum was required to pay a lump sum by a previous order under this Part of this Act.

(8) Where the court has power by virtue of subsection (2) above to make an order for the payment of a lump sum and the respondent or the applicant, as the case may be, has agreed to pay a lump sum of an amount exceeding the maximum amount that may at that time be required to be paid under section 2 (3) of this Act, the court may, notwithstanding anything in subsection (7) above, make an order for the payment of a lump sum of that amount.

(9) An order made by virtue of this section which varies an order for the making of periodical payments may, provide that the payments as so varied shall be made from such date as the court may specify, except that, subject to subsections (9A) and (9B) below, the date shall not be earlier than the date of the making of the application under this section.

(9A) Where—
- (a) there is in force an order ("the order")—
  - (i) under section 2(1)(c) of this Act,
  - (ii) under section 6(1) of this Act making provision of a kind mentioned in paragraph (c) of section 6(2) of this Act (regardless of whether it makes provision of any other kind mentioned in that paragraph),
  - (iii) under section 7(2)(b) of this Act, or
  - (iv) which is an interim maintenance order under which the payments are to be made to a child or to the applicant for the benefit of a child;
- (b) the order requires payments specified in it to be made to or for the benefit of more than one child without apportioning those payments between them;
- (c) a maintenance calculation ("the calculation") is made with respect to one or more, but not all, of the children with respect to whom those payments are to be made; and
- (d) an application is made, before the end of the period of 6 months beginning with the date on which the calculation was made, for the variation or revocation of the order,

the court may, in exercise of its powers under this section to vary or revoke the order, direct that the variation or revocation shall take effect from the date on which the calculation took effect or any later date.

(9B) Where—
- (a) an order ("the child order") of a kind prescribed for the purposes of section 10(1) of the Child Support Act 1991 is affected by a maintenance calculation;
- (b) on the date on which the child order became so affected there was in force an order ("the spousal order")—
  - (i) under section 2(1)(a) of this Act,
  - (ii) under section 6(1) of this Act making provision of a kind mentioned in section 6(2)(a) of this Act (regardless of whether it makes provision of any other kind mentioned in that paragraph),

(iii) under section 7(2)(a) of this Act, or
(iv) which is an interim maintenance order under which the payments are to be made to the applicant (otherwise than for the benefit of a child); and

(c) an application is made, before the end of the period of 6 months beginning with the date on which the maintenance calculation was made, for the spousal order to be varied or revoked,

the court may, in exercise of its powers under this section to vary or revoke the spousal order, direct that the variation or revocation shall take effect from the date on which the child order became so affected or any later date.

(9C) For the purposes of subsection (9B) above, an order is affected if it ceases to have effect or is modified by or under section 10 of the Child Support Act 1991.

(11) In exercising the powers conferred by this section the court shall, so far as it appears to the court just to do so, give effect to any agreement which has been reached between the parties in relation to the application and, if there is no such agreement or if the court decides not to give effect to the agreement, the court shall have regard to all the circumstances of the case, first consideration being given to the welfare while a minor of any child of the family who has not attained the age of eighteen, and the circumstances of the case shall include any change in any of the matters to which the court was required to have regard when making the order to which the application relates or, in the case of an application for the variation or revocation of an order made under section 6 of this Act or on an appeal under section 29 of this Act, to which the court would have been required to have regard if that order had been made under section 2 of this Act.

(12) An application under this section may be made—

(a) where it is for the variation or revocation of an order under section 2, 6, 7 or 19 of this Act for periodical payments, by either party to the marriage in question; and

(b) where it is for the variation of an order under section 2(1)(c), 6 or 7 of this Act for periodical payments to or in respect of a child, also by the child himself, if he has attained the age of sixteen.

20ZA VARIATION OF ORDERS FOR PERIODICAL PAYMENTS: FURTHER PROVISIONS

(1) Subject to subsections (7) and (8) below, the power of the court under section 20 of this Act to vary an order for the making of periodical payments shall include power, if the court is satisfied that payment has not been made in accordance with the order, to exercise one of its powers under paragraphs (a) to (d) of section 59(3) of the Magistrates' Courts Act 1980.

(2) In any case where—

(a) a magistrates' court has made an order under this Part of this Act for the making of periodical payments, and

(b) payments under the order are required to be made by any method of payment falling within section 59(6) of the Magistrates' Courts Act 1980 (standing order, etc),

an application may be made under this subsection to the court for the order to be varied as mentioned in subsection (3) below.

(3) Subject to subsection (5) below, where an application is made under subsection (2) above, a justices' clerk, after giving written notice (by post or otherwise) of the application to the respondent and allowing the respondent, within the period of 14 days beginning with the date of the giving of that notice, an opportunity to make written representations, may

vary the order to provide that payments under the order shall be made to the designated officer for the court.

(4) The clerk may proceed with an application under subsection (2) above notwithstanding that the respondent has not received written notice of the application.

(5) Where an application has been made under subsection (2) above, the clerk may, if he considers it inappropriate to exercise his power under subsection (3) above, refer the matter to the court which, subject to subsections (7) and (8) below, may vary the order by exercising one of its powers under paragraphs (a) to (d) of section 59(3) of the Magistrates' Courts Act 1980.

(6) Subsection (4) of section 59 of the Magistrates' Courts Act 1980 (power of court to order that account be opened) shall apply for the purposes of subsections (1) and (5) above as it applies for the purposes of that section.

(7) Before varying the order by exercising one of its powers under paragraphs (a) to (d) of section 59(3) of the Magistrates' Courts Act 1980, the court shall have regard to any representations made by the parties to the application.

(8) If the court does not propose to exercise its power under paragraph (c), (cc) or (d) of subsection (3) of section 59 of the Magistrates' Courts Act 1980, the court shall, unless upon representations expressly made in that behalf by the person to whom payments under the order are required to be made it is satisfied that it is undesirable to do so, exercise its power under paragraph (b) of that subsection.

(9) Subsection (12) of section 20 of this Act shall have effect for the purposes of applications under subsection (2) above as it has effect for the purposes of applications under that section.

(10) None of the powers of the court, or of a justices' clerk, conferred by this section shall be exercisable in relation to an order under this Part of this Act for the making of periodical payments which is not a qualifying maintenance order (within the meaning of section 59 of the Magistrates' Courts Act 1980).

20A REVIVAL OF ORDERS FOR PERIODICAL PAYMENTS

(1) Where an order made by a magistrates' court under this Part of this Act for the making of periodical payments to or in respect of a child (other than an interim maintenance order) ceases to have effect—
(a) on the date on which the child attains the age of sixteen, or
(b) at any time after that date but before or on the date on which he attains the age of eighteen,
the child may apply to the court which made the order for an order for its revival.

(2) If on such an application it appears to the court that—
(a) the child is, will be or (if an order were made under this subsection) would be receiving instruction at an educational establishment or undergoing training for a trade, profession or vocation, whether or not while in gainful employment, or
(b) there are special circumstances which justify the making of an order under this subsection,
the court shall have power by order to revive the order from such date as the court may specify, not being earlier than the date of the making of the application.

(3) Any order revived under this section may be varied or revoked under section 20 in the same way as it could have been varied or revoked had it continued in being.

22 VARIATION OF INSTALMENTS OF LUMP SUM

Where in the exercise of its powers under section 75 of the Magistrates' Courts Act 1980 a magistrates' court orders that a lump sum required to be paid under this Part of this Act shall be paid by instalments, the court, on an application made by either the person liable to pay or the person entitled to receive that sum, shall have power to vary that order by varying the number of instalments payable, the amount of any instalment payable and the date on which any instalment becomes payable.

23 SUPPLEMENTARY PROVISIONS WITH RESPECT TO VARIATION AND REVOCATION OF ORDERS

(2) The powers of a magistrates' court to revoke, revive or vary an order for the periodical payment of money and the power of the clerk of a magistrates' court to vary such an order under section 60 of the Magistrates' Courts Act 1980 and the power of a magistrates' court to suspend or rescind certain other orders under section 63 (2) of that Act shall not apply in relation to an order made under this Part of this Act.

25 EFFECT ON CERTAIN ORDERS OF PARTIES LIVING TOGETHER

(1) Where—
  (a) periodical payments are required to be made to one of the parties to a marriage (whether for his own benefit or for the benefit of a child of the family) by an order made under section 2, or 6 of this Act or by an interim maintenance order made under section 19 of this Act (otherwise than on an application under section 7 of this Act),

the order shall be enforceable notwithstanding that the parties to the marriage are living with each other at the date of the making of the order or that, although they are not living with each other at that date, they subsequently resume living with each other; but the order shall cease to have effect if after that date the parties continue to live with each other, or resume living with each other, for a continuous period exceeding six months.

(2) Where any of the following orders is made under this Part of this Act, that is to say—
  (a) an order under section 2, or 6 of this Act which requires periodical payments to be made to a child of the family, or
  (b) an interim maintenance order under section 19 of this Act (otherwise than on an application under section 7 of this Act) which requires periodical payments to be made to a child of the family,

then, unless the court otherwise directs, the order shall continue to have effect and be enforceable notwithstanding that the parties to the marriage in question are living with each other at the date of the making of the order or that, although they are not living with each other at that date, they subsequently resume living with each other.

(3) Any order made under section 7 of this Act, and any interim maintenance order made on an application for an order under that section, shall cease to have effect if the parties to the marriage resume living with each other.

(4) Where an order made under this Part of this Act ceases to have effect by virtue of subsection (1) or (3) above or by virtue of a direction given under subsection (2) above, a magistrates' court may, on an application made by either party to the marriage, make an order declaring that the first mentioned order ceased to have effect from such date as the court may specify.

Reconciliation

26 RECONCILIATION

(1) Where an application is made for an order under section 2 of this Act the court, before deciding whether to exercise its powers under that section, shall consider whether there is any possibility of reconciliation between the parties to the marriage in question; and if at any stage of the proceedings on that application it appears to the court that there is a reasonable possibility of such a reconciliation, the court may adjourn the proceedings for such period as it thinks fit to enable attempts to be made to effect a reconciliation.

(2) Where the court adjourns any proceedings under subsection (1) above, it may request an officer of the Service (within the meaning of the Criminal Justice and Court Services Act 2000), a Welsh family proceedings officer (within the meaning given by section 35 of the Children Act 2004) or any other person to attempt to effect a reconciliation between the parties to the marriage, and where any such request is made, that officer or other person shall report in writing to the court whether the attempt has been successful or not, but shall not include in that report any other information.

Provisions relating to the High Court and county court

27 REFUSAL OF ORDER IN CASE MORE SUITABLE FOR HIGH COURT

Where on hearing an application for an order under section 2 of this Act a magistrates' court is of the opinion that any of the matters in question between the parties would be more conveniently dealt with by the High Court, the magistrates' court shall refuse to make any order on the application, and no appeal shall lie from that refusal; but if in any proceedings in the High Court relating to or comprising the same subject matter as that application the High Court so orders, the application shall be reheard and determined by a magistrates' court acting in the same local justice area as the first mentioned court.

. . .

Provisions relating to procedure, jurisdiction and enforcement

. . .

32 ENFORCEMENT ETC OF ORDERS FOR PAYMENT OF MONEY

(1) An order for the payment of money made by a magistrates' court under this Part of this Act shall be enforceable as a magistrates' court maintenance order.

(2) Without prejudice to section 59 of the Magistrates' Courts Act 1980 (which relates to the power of a magistrates' court to direct periodical payments to be made through the designated officer for a magistrates' court), a magistrates' court making an order under this Part of this Act for the making of a periodical payment by one person to another may direct that it shall be made to some third party on that other person's behalf instead of directly to that other person; and, for the purposes of any order made under this Part of this Act, the said section 59 shall have effect as if, in subsection (7) thereof, for the words "the person who applied for the maintenance order" there were substituted the words "the person to whom the payments under the order fall to be made".

(3) Any person for the time being under an obligation to make payments in pursuance of any order for the payment of money made under this Part of this Act shall give notice of any change of address to such person, if any, as may be specified in the order; and any person

who without reasonable excuse fails to give such a notice shall be liable on summary conviction to a fine not exceeding level 2 on the standard scale.

(4) A person shall not be entitled to enforce through the High Court or any county court the payment of any arrears due under an order made by virtue of this Part of this Act without the leave of that court if those arrears became due more than twelve months before proceedings to enforce the payment of them are begun.

(5) The court hearing an application for the grant of leave under subsection (4) above may refuse leave, or may grant leave subject to such restrictions and conditions (including conditions as to the allowing of time for payment or the making of payment by instalments) as that court thinks proper, or may remit the payment of such arrears or any part thereof.

(6) An application for the grant of leave under subsection (4) above shall be made in such manner as may be prescribed by rules of court.

35 ORDERS FOR REPAYMENT IN CERTAIN CASES OF SUMS PAID AFTER CESSATION OF ORDER BY REASON OF REMARRIAGE OR FORMATION OF CIVIL PARTNERSHIP

(1) Where—

(a) an order made under section 2(1)(a), 6 or 7 of this Act has, by virtue of section 4(2) of this Act, ceased to have effect by reason of the remarriage of, or formation of a civil partnership by, the party in whose favour it was made, and

(b) the person liable to make payments under the order made payments in accordance with it in respect of a period after the date of that remarriage or the formation of that civil partnership in the mistaken belief that the order was still subsisting,

no proceedings in respect of a cause of action arising out of the circumstances mentioned in paragraphs (a) and (b) above shall be maintainable by the person so liable or his personal representatives against the person so entitled or his personal representatives, but on an application made under this section the court may exercise the powers conferred on it by subsection (2) below.

(2) The court may order the respondent to an application made under this section to pay to the applicant a sum equal to the amount of the payments made in respect of the period mentioned in subsection (1)(b) above or, if it appears to the court that it would be unjust to make that order, it may either order the respondent to pay to the applicant such lesser sum as it thinks fit or dismiss the application.

(3) An application under this section may be made by the person liable to make payments under the order made under section 2(1)(a), 6 or 7 of this Act or his personal representatives and may be made against the person entitled to payments under that order or his personal representatives.

(4) An application under this section shall be made to a county court, except that such an application may be made in proceedings in the High Court or a county court for leave to enforce, or the enforcement of, the payment of arrears under an order made under section 2(1)(a), 6 or 7 of this Act; and accordingly references in this section to the court are references to the High Court or a county court, as the circumstances require.

(5) An order under this section for the payment of any sum may provide for the payment of that sum by instalments of such amount as may be specified in the order.

(6) The jurisdiction conferred on a county court by this section shall be exercisable by a county court notwithstanding that by reason of the amount claimed in an application

under this section the jurisdiction would not but for this subsection be exercisable by a county court.

(7) The designated officer for a magistrates' court to whom any payments under an order made under section 2(1)(a), 6 or 7 of this Act are required to be made, and the collecting officer under an attachment of earnings order made to secure payments under the first mentioned order, shall not be liable—

(a) in the case of the designated officer, for any act done by him in pursuance of the first mentioned order after the date on which that order ceased to have effect by reason of the remarriage of, or formation of a civil partnership by, the person entitled to payments under it, and

(b) in the case of the collecting officer, for any act done by him after that date in accordance with any enactment or rule of court specifying how payments made to him in compliance with the attachment of earnings order are to be dealt with, if, but only if, the act was one which he would have been under a duty to do had the first mentioned order not ceased to have effect by reason of the remarriage or the formation of that civil partnership and the act was done before notice in writing of the fact that the person so entitled had remarried or formed a civil partnership was given to him by or on behalf of that person, the person liable to make payments under the first mentioned order or the personal representatives of either of those persons.

(8) In this section "collecting officer", in relation to an attachment of earnings order, means the officer of the High Court or the officer designated by the Lord Chancellor to whom a person makes payments in compliance with the order.

. . .

88 INTERPRETATION

(1) In this Act—

"child", in relation to one or both of the parties to a marriage, includes a child whose father and mother were not married to each other at the time of his birth;

"child of the family", in relation to the parties to a marriage, means—

(a) a child of both of those parties; and

(b) any other child, not being a child who is placed with those parties as foster parents by a local authority or voluntary organisation, who has been treated by both of those parties as a child of their family;

"family proceedings" has the meaning assigned to it by section 65 of the Magistrates' Courts Act 1980;

"local authority" means the council of a county (other than a metropolitan county), of a metropolitan district or of a London borough, or the Common Council of the City of London;

"magistrates' court maintenance order" has the same meaning as in section 150(1) of the Magistrates' Courts Act 1980;

"maintenance calculation" has the same meaning as it has in the Child Support Act 1991 by virtue of section 54 of that Act as read with any regulations in force under that section;

(2) References in this Act to the parties to a marriage living with each other shall be construed as references to their living with each other in the same household.

(3) For the avoidance of doubt it is hereby declared that references in this Act to remarriage include references to a marriage which is by law void or voidable.

. . .

As amended by: Magistrates' Courts Act 1980, s 154, Sch 7; Criminal Justice Act 1982, ss 37, 46; Matrimonial and Family Proceedings Act 1984, ss 9-11, 46(1), Sch 1; Family Law Reform Act 1987, s 33(1), (4), Sch 2, Sch 4; Children Act 1989, ss 92, 108(5), (7), Sch 11, Sch 13, Sch 15; Courts and Legal Services Act 1990, s 125(7), Sch 20; Maintenance Enforcement Act 1991, ss 5, 11(1), Sch 2; Transfer of Functions (Magistrates' Courts and Family Law) Order 1992, SI 1992/709, art 3(2), Sch 2; Maintenance Orders (Backdating) Order 1993, SI 1993/623, art 2, Sch 1; Child Support Act 1991 (Consequential Amendments) Order 1994, SI 1994/731, art 2; Child Support, Pensions and Social Security Act 2000, s 26, Sch 3; Criminal Justice and Court Services Act 2000, s 74, Sch 7; Courts Act 2003, s 109(1), Sch 8; Civil Partnership Act 2004, s 261(1), Sch 27; Constitutional Reform Act 2005, ss 15(1), 146, Sch 4, Sch 18; Access to Justice Act 1999 (Destination of Appeals) (Family Proceedings) Order 2009, SI 2009/871, art 3(1), (2)(a).

SENIOR COURTS ACT 1981

(1981 c 54)

41 WARDS OF COURT

(1) Subject to the provisions of this section, no minor shall be made a ward of court except by virtue of an order to that effect made by the High Court.

(2) Where an application is made for such an order in respect of a minor, the minor shall become a ward of court on the making of the application, but shall cease to be a ward of court at the end of such period as may be prescribed unless within that period an order has been made in accordance with the application.

(2A) Subsection (2) does not apply with respect to a child who is the subject of a care order (as defined by section 105 of the Children Act 1989).

(3) The High Court may, either upon an application in that behalf or without such an application, order that any minor who is for the time being a ward of court shall cease to be a ward of court.

As amended by: Children Act 1989, s 108(5), (6), Sch 13, para 45(2), Sch 14, para 1.

MARRIAGE ACT 1983

(1983 c 32)

Marriages in England and Wales

1 MARRIAGES OF HOUSE-BOUND AND DETAINED PERSONS IN ENGLAND AND WALES

(1) Subject to the provisions of this Act and the Marriage Act 1949, the marriage of a person who is house-bound or is a detained person may be solemnized in England and Wales, on

the authority of certificates of a superintendent registrar issued under Part III of the Marriage Act 1949, at the place where that person usually resides.

(2) For the purposes of this section a person is house-bound if—
   (a) each notice of his or her marriage given in accordance with section 27 of the Marriage Act 1949 is accompanied by a statement, made in a form prescribed under that Act by a registered medical practitioner not more than fourteen days before that notice is given, that, in his opinion—
      (i) by reason of illness or disability, he or she ought not to move or be moved from his or her home or the other place where he or she is at that time, and
      (ii) it is likely that it will be the case for at least the three months following the date on which the statement is made that by reason of the illness or disability he or she ought not to move or be moved from that place; and
   (b) he or she is not a detained person.

(3) For the purposes of this section, a person is a detained person if he or she is for the time being detained—
   (a) otherwise than by virtue of section 2, 4, 5, 35, 36 or 136 of the Mental Health Act 1983 (short term detentions), as a patient in a hospital; or
   (b) in a prison or other place to which the Prison Act 1952 applies.

(4) In subsection (3) above "hospital" and "patient" have the same meanings as in Part II of the Mental Health Act 1983.

(5) For the purposes of this section, a person who is house-bound or is a detained person shall be taken, if he or she would not otherwise be, to be usually resident at the place where he or she is for the time being.

(6) Nothing in the preceding provisions of this section shall be taken to relate or have any reference to any marriage according to the usages of the Society of Friends or any marriage between two persons professing the Jewish religion according to the usages of the Jews.

(7) Schedule 1 to this Act (amendment of the Marriage Act 1949 in consequence of this section) shall have effect.

As amended by: Immigration and Asylum Act 1999, s 169(1), Sch 14, para 77(a).

Child Abduction Act 1984

(1984 c 37)

1 OFFENCE OF ABDUCTION OF CHILD BY PARENT, ETC

(1) Subject to subsections (5) and (8) below, a person connected with a child under the age of sixteen commits an offence if he takes or sends the child out of the United Kingdom without the appropriate consent.

(2) A person is connected with a child for the purposes of this section if—
   (a) he is a parent of the child; or
   (b) in the case of a child whose parents were not married to each other at the time of his birth, there are reasonable grounds for believing that he is the father of the child; or
   (c) he is a guardian of the child; or

(ca) he is a special guardian of the child; or
(d) he is a person in whose favour a residence order is in force with respect to the child; or
(e) he has custody of the child.

(3) In this section "the appropriate consent", in relation to a child means—
(a) the consent of each of the following—
(i) the child's mother;
(ii) the child's father, if he has parental responsibility for him;
(iii) any guardian of the child;
(iiia) any special guardian of the child;
(iv) any person in whose favour a residence order is in force with respect to the child;
(v) any person who has custody of the child; or
(b) the leave of the court granted under or by virtue of any provision of Part II of the Children Act 1989; or
(c) if any person has custody of the child, the leave of the court which awarded custody to him.

(4) A person does not commit an offence under this section by taking or sending a child out of the United Kingdom without obtaining the appropriate consent if—
(a) he is a person in whose favour there is a residence order in force with respect to the child, and he takes or sends the child out of the United Kingdom for a period of less than one month; or
(b) he is a special guardian of the child and he takes or sends the child out of the United Kingdom for a period of less than three months.

(4A) Subsection (4) above does not apply if the person taking or sending the child out of the United Kingdom does so in breach of an order under Part II of the Children Act 1989.

(5) A person does not commit an offence under this section by doing anything without the consent of another person whose consent is required under the foregoing provisions if—
(a) he does it in the belief that the other person—
(i) has consented; or
(ii) would consent if he was aware of all the relevant circumstances; or
(b) he has taken all reasonable steps to communicate with the other person but has been unable to communicate with him; or
(c) the other person has unreasonably refused to consent,

(5A) Subsection (5)(c) above does not apply if—
(a) the person who refused to consent is a person—
(i) in whose favour there is a residence order in force with respect to the child;
(ia) who is a special guardian of the child; or
(ii) who has custody of the child; or
(b) the person taking or sending the child out of the United Kingdom is, by so acting, in breach of an order made by a court in the United Kingdom.

(6) Where, in proceedings for an offence under this section, there is sufficient evidence to raise an issue as to the application of subsection (5) above, it shall be for the prosecution to prove that that subsection does not apply.

(7) For the purposes of this section—
(a) "guardian of a child", "special guardian", "residence order" and "parental responsibility" have the same meaning as in the Children Act 1989; and
(b) a person shall be treated as having custody of a child if there is in force an order of a court in the United Kingdom awarding him (whether solely or jointly with another person) custody, legal custody or care and control of the child.

(8) This section shall have effect subject to the provisions of the Schedule to this Act in relation to a child who is in the care of a local authority detained in a place of safety, remanded to a local authority accommodation or the subject of proceedings or an order relating to adoption.

2 OFFENCE OF ABDUCTION OF CHILD BY OTHER PERSONS

(1) Subject to subsection (3) below, a person, other than one mentioned in subsection (2) below, commits an offence if, without lawful authority or reasonable excuse, he takes or detains a child under the age of sixteen—
  (a) so as to remove him from the lawful control of any person having lawful control of the child; or
  (b) so as to keep him out of the lawful control of any person entitled to lawful control of the child.

(2) The persons are—
  (a) where the father and mother of the child in question were married to each other at the time of his birth, the child's father and mother;
  (b) where the father and mother of the child in question were not married to each other at the time of his birth, the child's mother; and
  (c) any other person mentioned in section 1(2)(c) to (e) above.

(3) In proceedings against any person for an offence under this section, it shall be a defence for that person to prove—
  (a) where the father and mother of the child in question were not married to each other at the time of his birth—
    (i) that he is the child's father; or
    (ii) that, at the time of the alleged offence, he believed, on reasonable grounds, that he was the child's father; or
  (b) that, at the time of the alleged offence, he believed that the child had attained the age of sixteen.

3 CONSTRUCTION OF REFERENCES TO TAKING, SENDING AND DETAINING

For the purposes of this Part of this Act—

(a) a person shall be regarded as taking a child if he causes or induces the child to accompany him or any other person or causes the child to be taken;

(b) a person shall be regarded as sending a child if he causes the child to be sent;

(c) a person shall be regarded as detaining a child if he causes the child to be detained or induces the child to remain with him or any other person and

(d) references to a child's parents and to a child whose parents were (or were not) married to each other at the time of his birth shall be construed in accordance with section 1 of the Family Law Reform Act 1987 (which extends their meaning).

4 PENALTIES AND PROSECUTIONS

(1) A person guilty of an offence under this Part of this Act shall be liable—
  (a) on summary conviction, to imprisonment for a term not exceeding six months or to a fine not exceeding the statutory maximum, or to both such imprisonment and fine;
  (b) on conviction on indictment, to imprisonment for a term not exceeding seven years.

(2) No prosecution for an offence under section 1 above shall be instituted except by or with the consent of the Director of Public Prosecutions.

5 RESTRICTION ON PROSECUTIONS FOR OFFENCE OF KIDNAPPING

Except by or with the consent of the Director of Public Prosecutions no prosecution shall be instituted for an offence of kidnapping if it was committed—

(a) against a child under the age of sixteen; and

(b) by a person connected with the child, within the meaning of section 1 above.

As amended by: Statute Law (Repeals) Act 1993; Children Act 1989, s 108(4), Sch 12; Adoption and Children Act 2002, s 139(1), Sch 3.

POLICE AND CRIMINAL EVIDENCE ACT 1984

(1984 c 60)

....

80 COMPELLABILITY OF ACCUSED'S SPOUSE OR CIVIL PARTNER

(2) In any proceedings the spouse or civil partner of a person charged in the proceedings shall, subject to subsection (4) below, be compellable to give evidence on behalf of that person.

(2A) In any proceedings the spouse or civil partner of a person charged in the proceedings shall, subject to subsection (4) below, be compellable—

(a) to give evidence on behalf of any other person charged in the proceedings but only in respect of any specified offence with which that other person is charged; or

(b) to give evidence for the prosecution but only in respect of any specified offence with which any person is charged in the proceedings.

(3) In relation to the spouse or civil partner of a person charged in any proceedings, an offence is a specified offence for the purposes of subsection (2A) above if—

(a) it involves an assault on, or injury or a threat of injury to, the spouse or civil partner or a person who was at the material time under the age of 16;

(b) it is a sexual offence alleged to have been committed in respect of a person who was at the material time under that age; or

(c) it consists of attempting or conspiring to commit, or of aiding, abetting, counselling, procuring or inciting the commission of, an offence falling within paragraph (a) or (b) above.

(4) No person who is charged in any proceedings shall be compellable by virtue of subsection (2) or (2A) above to give evidence in the proceedings.

(4A) References in this section to a person charged in any proceedings do not include a person who is not, or is no longer, liable to be convicted of any offence in the proceedings (whether as a result of pleading guilty or for any other reason).

(5) In any proceedings a person who has been but is no longer married to the accused shall be compellable to give evidence as if that person and the accused had never been married.

(5A) In any proceedings a person who has been but is no longer the civil partner of the accused shall be compellable to give evidence as if that person and the accused had never been civil partners.

(6) Where in any proceedings the age of any person at any time is material for the purposes of subsection (3) above, his age at the material time shall for the purposes of that provision be deemed to be or to have been that which appears to the court to be or to have been his age at that time.

(7) In subsection (3)(b) above "sexual offence" means an offence under the Sexual Offences Act 1956, the Indecency with Children Act 1960, the Protection of Children Act 1978 or Part 1 of the Sexual Offences Act 2003.

80A RULE WHERE ACCUSED'S SPOUSE OR CIVIL PARTNER NOT COMPELLABLE

The failure of the spouse or civil partner of a person charged in any proceedings to give evidence in the proceedings shall not be made the subject of any comment by the prosecution.

As amended by: Youth Justice and Criminal Evidence Act 1999, s 67(1), (3), Sch 4, Sch 6; Sexual Offences Act 2003, s 139, 140,, Sch 6, Sch 7; Civil Partnership Act 2004, s 261(1), Sch 27;

SURROGACY ARRANGEMENTS ACT 1985

(1985 c 49)

1 MEANING OF "SURROGATE MOTHER", "SURROGACY ARRANGEMENT" AND OTHER TERMS

(1) The following provisions shall have effect for the interpretation of this Act.

(2) "Surrogate mother" means a woman who carries a child in pursuance of an arrangement—
  (a) made before she began to carry the child, and
  (b) made with a view to any child carried in pursuance of it being handed over to, and parental responsibility being met (so far as practicable) by, another person or other persons.

(3) An arrangement is a surrogacy arrangement if, were a woman to whom the arrangement relates to carry a child in pursuance of it, she would be a surrogate mother.

(4) In determining whether an arrangement is made with such a view as is mentioned in subsection (2) above regard may be had to the circumstances as a whole (and, in particular, where there is a promise or understanding that any payment will or may be made to the woman or for her benefit in respect of the carrying of any child in pursuance of the arrangement, to that promise or understanding).

(5) An arrangement may be regarded as made with such a view though subject to conditions relating to the handing over of any child.

(6) A woman who carries a child is to be treated for the purposes of subsection (2)(*a*) above as beginning to carry it at the time of the insemination or of the placing in her of an embryo, of an egg in the process of fertilisation or of sperm and eggs, as the case may be, that results in her carrying the child.

(7) "Body of persons" means a body of persons corporate or unincorporate.

(7A) "Non-profit making body" means a body of persons whose activities are not carried on for profit.

(8) "Payment" means payment in money or money's worth.

(9) This Act applies to arrangements whether or not they are lawful.

1A SURROGACY ARRANGEMENTS UNENFORCEABLE

No surrogacy arrangement is enforceable by or against any of the persons making it.

2 NEGOTIATING SURROGACY ARRANGEMENTS ON A COMMERCIAL BASIS, ETC

(1) No person shall on a commercial basis do any of the following acts in the United Kingdom, that is—
(a) initiate any negotiations with a view to the making of a surrogacy arrangement,
(aa) take part in any negotiations with a view to the making of a surrogacy arrangement,
(b) offer or agree to negotiate the making of a surrogacy arrangement, or
(c) compile any information with a view to its use in making, or negotiating the making of, surrogacy arrangements;
and no person shall in the United Kingdom knowingly cause another to do any of those acts on a commercial basis.

(2) A person who contravenes subsection (1) above is guilty of an offence; but it is not a contravention of that subsection—
(a) for a woman, with a view to becoming a surrogate mother herself, to do any act mentioned in that subsection or to cause such an act to be done, or
(b) for any person, with a view to a surrogate mother carrying a child for him, to do such an act or to cause such an act to be done.

(2A) A non-profit making body does not contravene subsection (1) merely because—
(a) the body does an act falling within subsection (1)(a) or (c) in respect of which any reasonable payment is at any time received by it or another, or
(b) it does an act falling within subsection (1)(a) or (c) with a view to any reasonable payment being received by it or another in respect of facilitating the making of any surrogacy arrangement.

(2B) A person who knowingly causes a non-profit making body to do an act falling within subsection (1)(a) or (c) does not contravene subsection (1) merely because—
(a) any reasonable payment is at any time received by the body or another in respect of the body doing the act, or
(b) the body does the act with a view to any reasonable payment being received by it or another person in respect of the body facilitating the making of any surrogacy arrangement.

(2C) Any reference in subsection (2A) or (2B) to a reasonable payment in respect of the doing of an act by a non-profit making body is a reference to a payment not exceeding the body's costs reasonably attributable to the doing of the act.

(3) For the purposes of this section, a person does an act on a commercial basis (subject to subsection (4) below) if—
(a) any payment is at any time received by himself or another in respect of it, or
(b) he does it with a view to any payment being received by himself or another in respect of making, or negotiating or facilitating the making of, any surrogacy arrangement.
In this subsection "payment" does not include payment to or for the benefit of a surrogate mother or prospective surrogate mother.

(4) In proceedings against a person for an offence under subsection (1) above, he is not to be treated as doing an act on a commercial basis by reason of any payment received by another in respect of the act if it is proved that—

(a) in a case where the payment was received before he did the act, he did not do the act knowing or having reasonable cause to suspect that any payment had been received in respect of the act; and

(b) in any case, he did not do the act with a view to any payment being received in respect of it.

(5) Where—

(a) a person acting on behalf of a body of persons takes any part in negotiating or facilitating the making of a surrogacy arrangement in the United Kingdom, and

(b) negotiating or facilitating the making of surrogacy arrangements is an activity of the body,

then, if the body at any time receives any payment made by or on behalf of—

(i) a woman who carries a child in pursuance of the arrangement,

(ii) the person or persons for whom she carries it, or

(iii) any person connected with the woman or with that person or those persons,

the body is guilty of an offence.

For the purposes of this subsection, a payment received by a person connected with a body is to be treated as received by the body.

(5A) A non-profit making body is not guilty of an offence under subsection (5), in respect of the receipt of any payment described in that subsection, merely because a person acting on behalf of the body takes part in facilitating the making of a surrogacy arrangement.

(6) In proceedings against a body for an offence under subsection (5) above, it is a defence to prove that the payment concerned was not made in respect of the arrangement mentioned in paragraph (*a*) of that subsection.

(7) A person who in the United Kingdom takes part in the management or control—

(a) of any body of persons, or

(b) of any of the activities of any body of persons,

is guilty of an offence if the activity described in subsection (8) below is an activity of the body concerned.

(8) The activity referred to in subsection (7) above is negotiating or facilitating the making of surrogacy arrangements in the United Kingdom, being—

(a) arrangements the making of which is negotiated or facilitated on a commercial basis, or

(b) arrangements in the case of which payments are received (or treated for the purposes of subsection (5) above as received) by the body concerned in

contravention of subsection (5) above.

(8A) A person is not guilty of an offence under subsection (7) if—

(a) the body of persons referred to in that subsection is a non-profit making body, and

(b) the only activity of that body which falls within subsection (8) is facilitating the making

of surrogacy arrangements in the United Kingdom.

(8B) In subsection (8A)(b) "facilitating the making of surrogacy arrangements" is to be construed in accordance with subsection (8).

(9) In proceedings against a person for an offence under subsection (7) above, it is a defence to prove that he neither knew nor had reasonable cause to suspect that the activity described in subsection (8) above was an activity of the body concerned; and for the

purposes of such proceedings any arrangement falling within subsection (8)(*b*) above shall be disregarded if it is proved that the payment concerned was not made in respect of the arrangement.

3 ADVERTISEMENTS ABOUT SURROGACY

(1) This section applies to any advertisement containing an indication (however expressed)—
 (a) that any person is or may be willing to enter into a surrogacy arrangement or to negotiate or facilitate the making of a surrogacy arrangement, or
 (b) that any person is looking for a woman willing to become a surrogate mother or for persons wanting a woman to carry a child as a surrogate mother.

(1A) This section does not apply to any advertisement placed by, or on behalf of, a non-profit making body if the advertisement relates only to the doing by the body of acts that would not contravene section 2(1) even if done on a commercial basis (within the meaning of section 2).

(2) Where a newspaper or periodical containing an advertisement to which this section applies is published in the United Kingdom, any proprietor, editor or publisher of the newspaper or periodical is guilty of an offence.

(3) Where an advertisement to which this section applies is conveyed by means of an electronic communications network so as to be seen or heard (or both) in the United Kingdom, any person who in the United Kingdom causes it to be so conveyed knowing it to contain such an indication as is mentioned in subsection (1) above is guilty of an offence.

(4) A person who publishes or causes to be published in the United Kingdom an advertisement to which this section applies (not being an advertisement contained in a newspaper or periodical or conveyed by means of [an electronic communications network]) is guilty of an offence.

(5) A person who distributes or causes to be distributed in the United Kingdom an advertisement to which this section applies (not being an advertisement contained in a newspaper or periodical published outside the United Kingdom or an advertisement conveyed by means of an electronic communications network) knowing it to contain such an indication as is mentioned in subsection (1) above is guilty of an offence.

4 OFFENCES

(1) A person guilty of an offence under this Act shall be liable on summary conviction to a fine not exceeding level 5 on the standard scale.

(2) No proceedings for an offence under this Act shall be instituted—
 (a) in England and Wales, except by or with the consent of the Director of Public Prosecutions;

 . . .

(3) Where an offence under this Act committed by a body corporate is proved to have been committed with the consent or connivance of, or to be attributable to any neglect on the part of, any director, manager, secretary or other similar officer of the body corporate or any person who was purporting to act in any such capacity, he as well as the body corporate is guilty of the offence and is liable to be proceeded against and punished accordingly.

(4) Where the affairs of a body corporate are managed by its members subsection (3) above shall apply in relation to the acts and defaults of a member in connection with his functions of management as if he were a director of the body corporate.

(5) In any proceedings for an offence under section 2 of this Act, proof of things done or of words written, spoken or published (whether or not in the presence of any party to the proceedings) by any person taking part in the management or control of a body of persons or of any of the activities of the body, or by any person doing any of the acts mentioned in subsection (1)(a) to (c) of that section on behalf of the body, shall be admissible as evidence of the activities of the body.

(6) In relation to an offence under this Act, section 127(1) of the Magistrates' Courts Act 1980 (information must be laid within six months of commission of offence) . . . shall have effect as if for the reference to six months there were substituted a reference to two years.

As amended by: Children Act 1989, s 108, Sch 13, Sch 14; Communications Act 2003, s 406, Sch 17; Criminal Justice Act 2003, s 332, Sch 37; Human Fertilisation and Embryology Act 2008, ss 36, 59, 66, Sch 8.

Housing Act 1985

(1985 c 68)

Succession on death of tenant

87 PERSONS QUALIFIED TO SUCCEED SECURE TENANT

A person is qualified to succeed the tenant under a secure tenancy if he occupies the dwelling-house as his only or principal home at the time of the tenant's death and either—

(a) he is the tenant's spouse or civil partner, or

(b) he is another member of the tenant's family and has resided with the tenant throughout the period of twelve months ending with the tenant's death;

unless, in either case, the tenant was himself a successor, as defined in section 88.

. . .

113 MEMBERS OF A PERSON'S FAMILY

(1) A person is a member of another's family within the meaning of this Part if—
  (a) he is the spouse or civil partner of that person, or he and that person live together as husband and wife or as if they were civil partners, or
  (b) he is that person's parent, grandparent, child, grandchild, brother, sister, uncle, aunt, nephew or niece.

(2) For the purpose of subsection (1)(b)—
  (a) a relationship by marriage or civil partnership shall be treated as a relationship by blood,
  (b) a relationship of the half-blood shall be treated as a relationship of the whole blood,
  (c) the stepchild of a person shall be treated as his child, and
  (d) an illegitimate child shall be treated as the legitimate child of his mother and reputed father.

As amended by: Civil Partnership Act 2004, s 81, Sch 8.

Marriage (Prohibited Degrees of Relationship) Act 1986

(1986 c 16)

1 MARRIAGE BETWEEN CERTAIN PERSONS RELATED BY AFFINITY NOT TO BE VOID

(1) A marriage solemnized after the commencement of this Act between a man and a woman who is the daughter or grand-daughter of a former spouse of his (whether the former spouse is living or not) or who is the former spouse of his father or grand-father (whether his father or grandfather is living or not) shall not be void by reason only of that relationship if both the parties have attained the age of twenty-one at the time of the marriage and the younger party has not at any time before attaining the age of eighteen been a child of the family in relation to the other party.

(2) A marriage solemnized after the commencement of this Act between a man and a woman who is the grandmother of a former spouse of his (whether the former spouse is living or not) or is a former spouse of his grandson (whether his grandson is living or not) shall not be void by reason only of that relationship.

(5) In this section "child of the family" in relation to any person, means a child who has lived in the same household as that person and been treated by that person as a child of his family.

(6) The Marriage Act 1949 shall have effect subject to the amendments specified in the Schedule to this Act, being amendments consequential on the preceding provisions of this section.

(7) Where, apart from this Act, any matter affecting the validity of a marriage would fall to be determined (in accordance with the rules of private international law) by reference to the law of a country outside England and Wales nothing in this Act shall preclude the determination of that matter in accordance with that law.

(8) Nothing in this section shall affect any marriage solemnized before the commencement of this Act.

As amended by: Marriage Act 1949 (Remedial) Order 2007, SI 2007/438, art 3(b).

Family Law Act 1986

(1986 c 55)

Part III DECLARATIONS OF STATUS

55 DECLARATIONS AS TO MARITAL STATUS

(1) Subject to the following provisions of this section, any person may apply to the High Court or a county court for one or more of the following declarations in relation to a marriage specified in the application, that is to say—
   (a) a declaration that the marriage was at its inception a valid marriage;
   (b) a declaration that the marriage subsisted on a date specified in the application;

(c) a declaration that the marriage did not subsist on a date so specified;
(d) a declaration that the validity of a divorce, annulment or legal separation obtained in any country outside England and Wales in respect of the marriage is entitled to recognition in England and Wales;
(e) a declaration that the validity of a divorce, annulment or legal separation so obtained in respect of the marriage is not entitled to recognition in England and Wales.

(2) A court shall have jurisdiction to entertain an application under subsection (1) above if, and only if, either of the parties to the marriage to which the application relates—
(a) is domiciled in England and Wales on the date of the application, or
(b) has been habitually resident in England and Wales throughout the period of one year ending with that date, or
(c) died before that date and either—
(i) was at death domiciled in England and Wales, or
(ii) had been habitually resident in England and Wales throughout the period of one year ending with the date of death.

(3) Where an application under subsection (1) above is made to a court by any person other than a party to the marriage to which the application relates, the court shall refuse to hear the application if it considers that the applicant does not have a sufficient interest in the determination of that application.

55A DECLARATIONS OF PARENTAGE

(1) Subject to the following provisions of this section, any person may apply to the High Court, a county court or a magistrates' court for a declaration as to whether or not a person named in the application is or was the parent of another person so named.

(2) A court shall have jurisdiction to entertain an application under subsection (1) above if, and only if, either of the persons named in it for the purposes of that subsection—
(a) is domiciled in England and Wales on the date of the application, or
(b) has been habitually resident in England and Wales throughout the period of one year ending with that date, or
(c) died before that date and either—
(i) was at death domiciled in England and Wales, or
(ii) had been habitually resident in England and Wales throughout the period of one year ending with the date of death.

(3) Except in a case falling within subsection (4) below, the court shall refuse to hear an application under subsection (1) above unless it considers that the applicant has a sufficient personal interest in the determination of the application (but this is subject to section 27 of the Child Support Act 1991).

(4) The excepted cases are where the declaration sought is as to whether or not—
(a) the applicant is the parent of a named person;
(b) a named person is the parent of the applicant; or
(c) a named person is the other parent of a named child of the applicant.

(5) Where an application under subsection (1) above is made and one of the persons named in it for the purposes of that subsection is a child, the court may refuse to hear the application if it considers that the determination of the application would not be in the best interests of the child.

(6) Where a court refuses to hear an application under subsection (1) above it may order that the applicant may not apply again for the same declaration without leave of the court.

(7) Where a declaration is made by a court on an application under subsection (1) above, the prescribed officer of the court shall notify the Registrar General, in such a manner and within such period as may be prescribed, of the making of that declaration.

56 DECLARATIONS OF PARENTAGE, LEGITIMACY OR LEGITIMATION

(1) Any person may apply to the High Court or a county court for a declaration—
(b) that he is the legitimate child of his parents.

(2) Any person may apply to the High Court or a county court for one (or for one or, in the alternative, the other) of the following declarations, that is to say—
(a) a declaration that he has become a legitimated person;
(b) a declaration that he has not become a legitimated person.

(3) A court shall have jurisdiction to entertain an application under this section if, the applicant—
(a) is domiciled in England and Wales on the date of the application; or
(b) has been habitually resident in England and Wales throughout the period of one year ending with that date.

(4) Where a declaration is made by a court on an application under subsection (1) above, the prescribed officer of the court shall notify the Registrar General, in such a manner and within such period as may be prescribed, of the making of that declaration.

(5) In this section "legitimated person" means a person legitimated or recognised as legitimated—
(a) under section 2, 2A or 3 of the Legitimacy Act 1976;
(b) under section 1 or 8 of the Legitimacy Act 1926; or
(c) by a legitimation (whether or not by virtue of the subsequent marriage of his parents) recognised by the law of England and Wales and effected under the law of another country.

57 DECLARATIONS AS TO ADOPTIONS EFFECTED OVERSEAS

(1) Any person whose status as an adopted child of any person depends on whether he has been adopted by that person by either—
(a) a Convention adoption, or an overseas adoption, within the meaning of the Adoption and Children Act 2002, or
(b) an adoption recognised by the law of England and Wales and effected under the law of any country outside the British Islands, may apply to the High Court or a county court for one (or for one or, in the alternative, the other) of the declarations mentioned in subsection (2) below.

(2) The said declarations are—
(a) a declaration that the applicant is for the purposes of section 39 of the Adoption Act 1976 or section 67 of the Adoption and Children Act 2002 the adopted child of that person;
(b) a declaration that the applicant is not for the purposes of that section the adopted child of that person.

(3) A court shall have jurisdiction to entertain an application under subsection (1) above if, and only if, the applicant—
(a) is domiciled in England and Wales on the date of the application, or
(b) has been habitually resident in England and Wales throughout the period of one year ending with that date.

58 GENERAL PROVISIONS AS TO THE MAKING AND EFFECT OF DECLARATIONS

(1) Where on an application to a court for a declaration under this Part the truth of the proposition to be declared is proved to the satisfaction of the court, the court shall make that declaration unless to do so would manifestly be contrary to public policy.

(2) Any declaration made under this Part shall be binding on Her Majesty and all other persons.

(3) A court, on the dismissal of an application for a declaration under this Part, shall not have power to make any declaration for which an application has not been made.

(4) No declaration which may be applied for under this Part may be made otherwise than under this Part by any court.

(5) No declaration may be made by any court, whether under this Part or otherwise—
(a) that a marriage was at its inception void;

(6) Nothing in this section shall affect the powers of any court to grant a decree of nullity of marriage.

59 PROVISIONS RELATING TO THE ATTORNEY-GENERAL

(1) On an application to a court for a declaration under this Part the court may at any stage of the proceedings, of its own motion or on the application of any party to the proceedings, direct that all necessary papers in the matter be sent to the Attorney-General.

(2) The Attorney-General, whether or not he is sent papers in relation to an application to a court for a declaration under this Part, may—
(a) intervene in the proceedings on that application in such manner as he thinks necessary or expedient, and
(b) argue before the court any question in relation to the application which the court considers it necessary to have fully argued.

(3) Where any costs are incurred by the Attorney-General in connection with any application to a court for a declaration under this Part, the court may make such order as it considers just as to the payment of those costs by parties to the proceedings.

60 SUPPLEMENTARY PROVISIONS AS TO DECLARATIONS

(1) Any declaration made under this Part, and any application for such a declaration, shall be in the form prescribed by rules of court.

(2) Rules of court may make provision—
(a) as to the information required to be given by any applicant for a declaration under this Part;
(b) as to the persons who are to be parties to proceedings on an application under this Part;
(c) requiring notice of an application under this Part to be served on the Attorney-General and on persons who may be affected by any declaration applied for.

(3) No proceedings under this Part shall affect any final judgment or decree already pronounced or made by any court of competent jurisdiction.

(4) The court hearing an application under this Part may direct that the whole or any part of the proceedings shall be heard in camera, and an application for a direction under this subsection shall be heard in camera unless the court otherwise directs.

(5) An appeal shall lie to a county court against—
(a) the making by a magistrates' court of a declaration under section 55A above,
(b) any refusal by a magistrates' court to make such a declaration, or
(c) any order under subsection (6) of that section made on such a refusal.

61 ABOLITION OF RIGHT TO PETITION FOR JACTITATION OF MARRIAGE

No person shall after the commencement of this Part be entitled to petition the High Court or a county court for jactitation of marriage.

As amended by: Family Law Reform Act 1987, ss 22, 33(1), Sch 2; Child Support, Pensions and Social Security Act 2000, ss 83, 85, Sch 8, Sch 9; Adoption and Children Act 2002, s 139(1), Sch 3; Human Fertilisation and Embryology Act 2008, s 56, Sch 6; Access to Justice Act 1999 (Destination of Appeals) (Family Proceedings) Order 2009, SI 2009/871, art 6;

Family Law Reform Act 1987

(1987 c 42)

1 GENERAL PRINCIPLE

(1) In this Act and enactments passed and instruments made after the coming into force of this section, references (however expressed) to any relationship between two persons shall, unless the contrary intention appears, be construed without regard to whether or not the father and mother of either of them, or the father and mother of any person through whom the relationship is deduced, have or had been married to each other at any time.

(2) In this Act and enactments passed after the coming into force of this section, unless the contrary intention appears—
(a) references to a person whose father and mother were married to each other at the time of his birth include; and
(b) references to a person whose father and mother were not married to each other at the time of his birth do not include, references to any person to whom subsection (3) below applies, and cognate references shall be construed accordingly.

(3) This subsection applies to any person who—
(a) is treated as legitimate by virtue of section 1 of the Legitimacy Act 1976;
(b) is a legitimated person within the meaning of section 10 of that Act;
(ba) has a parent by virtue of section 42 of the Human Fertilisation and Embryology Act 2008 (which relates to treatment provided to a woman who is at the time of treatment a party to a civil partnership or, in certain circumstances, a void civil partnership);
(bb) has a parent by virtue of section 43 of that Act (which relates to treatment provided to woman who agrees that second woman to be parent) who—
(i) is the civil partner of the child's mother at the time of the child's birth, or
(ii) was the civil partner of the child's mother at any time during the period beginning with the time mentioned in section 43(b) of that Act and ending with the child's birth;
(c) is an adopted person within the meaning of Chapter 4 of Part 1 of the Adoption and Children Act 2002; or
(d) is otherwise treated in law as legitimate.

(4) For the purpose of construing references falling within subsection (2) above, the time of a person's birth shall be taken to include any time during the period beginning with—
(a) the insemination resulting in his birth; or
(b) where there was no such insemination, his conception, and (in either case) ending with his birth.

(5) A child whose parents are parties to a void civil partnership shall, subject to subsection (6), be treated as falling within subsection (3)(bb) if at the time when the parties registered as civil partners of each other both or either of the parties reasonably believed that the civil partnership was valid.

(6) Subsection (5) applies only where the woman who is a parent by virtue of section 43 was domiciled in England and Wales at the time of the birth or, if she died before the birth, was so domiciled immediately before her death.

(7) Subsection (5) applies even though the belief that the civil partnership was valid was due to a mistake as to law.

(8) It shall be presumed for the purposes of subsection (5), unless the contrary is shown, that one of the parties to a void civil partnership reasonably believed at the time of the formation of the civil partnership that the civil partnership was valid.

Parental rights and duties: general

2 CONSTRUCTION OF ENACTMENTS RELATING TO PARENTAL RIGHTS AND DUTIES

(1) In the following enactments, namely—
(a) section 42(1) of the National Assistance Act 1948;
(b) section 6 of the Family Law Reform Act 1969;
(c) the Guardianship of Minors Act 1971 (in this Act referred to as "the 1971 Act");
(d) Part I of the Guardianship Act 1973 (in this Act referred to as "the 1973 Act");
(e) Part II of the Children Act 1975;
(f) the Child Care Act 1980 except Part I and sections 13, 24, 64 and 65;
references (however expressed) to any relationship between two persons shall be construed in accordance with section 1 above.

. . .

Miscellaneous

27 ARTIFICIAL INSEMINATION

(1) Where after the coming into force of this section a child is born in England and Wales as the result of the artificial insemination of a woman who—
(a) was at the time of the insemination a party to a marriage (being a marriage which had not at that time been dissolved or annulled); and
(b) was artificially inseminated with the semen of some person other than the other party to that marriage,
then, unless it is proved to the satisfaction of any court by which the matter has to be determined that the other party to that marriage did not consent to the insemination, the child shall be treated in law as the child of the parties to that marriage and shall not be treated as the child of any person other than the parties to that marriage.

(2) Any reference in this section to a marriage includes a reference to a void marriage if at the time of the insemination resulting in the birth of the child both or either of the parties

reasonably believed that the marriage was valid; and for the purposes of this section it shall be presumed, unless the contrary is shown, that one of the parties so believed at that time that the marriage was valid.

(3) Nothing in this section shall affect the succession to any dignity or title of honour or render any person capable of succeeding to or transmitting a right to succeed to any such dignity or title.

As amended by: Social Security (Consequential Provisions) Act 1992, s 3, Sch 1; Adoption and Children Act 2002, s 139(1); Health and Social Care Act 2008, s 166, Sch 15; Human Fertilisation and Embryology Act 2008, s 56, Sch 6;

HOUSING ACT 1988

(1988 c 50)

17 SUCCESSION TO ASSURED PERIODIC TENANCY BY SPOUSE

(1) In any case where—
(a) the sole tenant under an assured periodic tenancy dies, and
(b) immediately before the death, the tenant's spouse or civil partner was occupying the dwelling-house as his or her only or principal home, and
(c) the tenant was not himself a successor, as defined in subsection (2) or subsection (3) below,
then, on the death, the tenancy vests by virtue of this section in the spouse or civil partner (and, accordingly, does not devolve under the tenant's will or intestacy).

(2) For the purposes of this section, a tenant is a successor in relation to a tenancy if—
(a) the tenancy became vested in him either by virtue of this section or under the will or intestacy of a previous tenant; or
(b) at some time before the tenant's death the tenancy was a joint tenancy held by himself and one or more other persons and, prior to his death, he became the sole tenant by survivorship; or
(c) he became entitled to the tenancy as mentioned in section 39(5) below.

(3) For the purposes of this section, a tenant is also a successor in relation to a tenancy (in this subsection referred to as "the new tenancy") which was granted to him (alone or jointly with others) if—
(a) at some time before the grant of the new tenancy, he was, by virtue of subsection (2) above, a successor in relation to an earlier tenancy of the same or substantially the same dwelling-house as is let under the new tenancy; and
(b) at all times since he became such a successor he has been a tenant (alone or jointly with others) of the dwelling-house which is let under the new tenancy or of a dwelling-house which is substantially the same as that dwelling-house.

(4) For the purposes of this section—
(a) a person who was living with the tenant as his or her wife or husband shall be treated as the tenant's spouse, and
(b) a person who was living with the tenant as if they were civil partners shall be treated as the tenant's civil partner.

(5) If, on the death of the tenant, there is, by virtue of subsection (4) above, more than one person who fulfils the condition in subsection (1)(b) above, such one of them as may be decided by agreement or, in default of agreement, by the county court shall for the purposes of this section be treated (according to whether that one of them is of the opposite sex to, or of the same sex as, the tenant) as the tenant's spouse or the tenant's civil partner.

As amended by: Civil Partnership Act 2004, s 81, Sch 8.

Children Act 1989

(1989 c 41)

Part I INTRODUCTORY

1 WELFARE OF THE CHILD

(1) When a court determines any question with respect to—
  (a) the upbringing of a child; or
  (b) the administration of a child's property or the application of any income arising from it,

the child's welfare shall be the court's paramount consideration.

(2) In any proceedings in which any question with respect to the upbringing of a child arises, the court shall have regard to the general principle that any delay in determining the question is likely to prejudice the welfare of the child.

(3) In the circumstances mentioned in subsection (4), a court shall have regard in particular to—
  (a) the ascertainable wishes and feelings of the child concerned (considered in the light of his age and understanding);
  (b) his physical, emotional and educational needs;
  (c) the likely effect on him of any change in his circumstances;
  (d) his age, sex, background and any characteristics of his which the court considers relevant;
  (e) any harm which he has suffered or is at risk of suffering;
  (f) how capable each of his parents, and any other person in relation to whom the court considers the question to be relevant, is of meeting his needs;
  (g) the range of powers available to the court under this Act in the proceedings in question.

(4) The circumstances are that—
(a) the court is considering whether to make, vary or discharge a section 8 order, and the making, variation or discharge of the order is opposed by any party to the proceedings; or
(b) the court is considering whether to make, vary or discharge a special guardianship order or an order under Part IV.

(5) Where a court is considering whether or not to make one or more orders under this Act with respect to a child, it shall not make the order or any of the orders unless it considers that doing so would be better for the child than making no order at all.

2 PARENTAL RESPONSIBILITY FOR CHILDREN

(1) Where a child's father and mother were married to each other at the time of his birth, they shall each have parental responsibility for the child.

(1A) Where a child—
(a) has a parent by virtue of section 42 of the Human Fertilisation and Embryology Act 2008; or
(b) has a parent by virtue of section 43 of that Act and is a person to whom section 1(3) of the Family Law Reform Act 1987 applies,
the child's mother and the other parent shall each have parental responsibility for the child.

(2) Where a child's father and mother were not married to each other at the time of his birth—
(a) the mother shall have parental responsibility for the child;
(b) the father shall have parental responsibility for the child if he has acquired it (and has not ceased to have it) in accordance with the provisions of this Act.

(2A) Where a child has a parent by virtue of section 43 of the Human Fertilisation and Embryology Act 2008 and is not a person to whom section 1(3) of the Family Law Reform Act 1987 applies—
(a) the mother shall have parental responsibility for the child;
(b) the other parent shall have parental responsibility for the child if she has acquired it (and has not ceased to have it) in accordance with the provisions of this Act.

(3) References in this Act to a child whose father and mother were, or (as the case may be) were not, married to each other at the time of his birth must be read with section 1 of the Family Law Reform Act 1987 (which extends their meaning).

(4) The rule of law that a father is the natural guardian of his legitimate child is abolished.

(5) More than one person may have parental responsibility for the same child at the same time.

(6) A person who has parental responsibility for a child at any time shall not cease to have that responsibility solely because some other person subsequently acquires parental responsibility for the child.

(7) Where more than one person has parental responsibility for a child, each of them may act alone and without the other (or others) in meeting that responsibility; but nothing in this Part shall be taken to affect the operation of any enactment which requires the consent of more than one person in a matter affecting the child.

(8) The fact that a person has parental responsibility for a child shall not entitle him to act in any way which would be incompatible with any order made with respect to the child under this Act.

(9) A person who has parental responsibility for a child may not surrender or transfer any part of that responsibility to another but may arrange for some or all of it to be met by one or more persons acting on his behalf.

(10) The person with whom any such arrangement is made may himself be a person who already has parental responsibility for the child concerned.

(11) The making of any such arrangement shall not affect any liability of the person making it which may arise from any failure to meet any part of his parental responsibility for the child concerned.

3 MEANING OF "PARENTAL RESPONSIBILITY"

(1) In this Act "parental responsibility" means all the rights, duties, powers, responsibilities and authority which by law a parent of a child has in relation to the child and his property.

(2) It also includes the rights, powers and duties which a guardian of the child's estate (appointed, before the commencement of section 5, to act generally) would have had in relation to the child and his property.

(3) The rights referred to in subsection (2) include, in particular, the right of the guardian to receive or recover in his own name, for the benefit of the child, property of whatever description and wherever situated which the child is entitled to receive or recover.

(4) The fact that a person has, or does not have, parental responsibility for a child shall not affect—
- (a) any obligation which he may have in relation to the child (such as a statutory duty to maintain the child); or
- (b) any rights which, in the event of the child's death, he (or any other person) may have in relation to the child's property.

(5) A person who—
- (a) does not have parental responsibility for a particular child; but
- (b) has care of the child,

may (subject to the provisions of this Act) do what is reasonable in all the circumstances of the case for the purpose of safeguarding or promoting the child's welfare.

4 ACQUISITION OF PARENTAL RESPONSIBILITY BY FATHER

(1) Where a child's father and mother were not married to each other at the time of his birth, the father shall acquire parental responsibility for the child if—
- (a) he becomes registered as the child's father under any of the enactments specified in subsection (1A);
- (b) he and the child's mother make an agreement (a "parental responsibility agreement") providing for him to have parental responsibility for the child; or
- (c) the court, on his application, orders that he shall have parental responsibility for the child.

(1A) The enactments referred to in subsection (1)(a) are—
- (a) paragraphs (a), (b) and (c) of section 10(1) and of section 10A(1) of the Births and Deaths Registration Act 1953;
- (b) paragraphs (a), (b)(i) and (c) of section 18(1), and sections 18(2)(b) and 20(1)(a) of the Registration of Births, Deaths and Marriages (Scotland) Act 1965; and
- (c) sub-paragraphs (a), (b) and (c) of Article 14(3) of the Births and Deaths Registration (Northern Ireland) Order 1976.

(1B) The Secretary of State may by order amend subsection (1A) so as to add further enactments to the list in that subsection.

(2) No parental responsibility agreement shall have effect for the purposes of this Act unless—
(a) it is made in the form prescribed by regulations made by the Lord Chancellor; and
(b) where regulations are made by the Lord Chancellor prescribing the manner in which such agreements must be recorded, it is recorded in the prescribed manner.

(2A) A person who has acquired parental responsibility under subsection (1) shall cease to have that responsibility only if the court so orders.

(3) The court may make an order under subsection (2A) on the application—
(a) of any person who has parental responsibility for the child; or
(b) with the leave of the court, of the child himself, subject, in the case of parental responsibility acquired under subsection (1)(c), to section 12(4).

(4) The court may only grant leave under subsection (3)(b) if it is satisfied that the child has sufficient understanding to make the proposed application.

4ZA ACQUISITION OF PARENTAL RESPONSIBILITY BY SECOND FEMALE PARENT

(1) Where a child has a parent by virtue of section 43 of the Human Fertilisation and Embryology Act 2008 and is not a person to whom section 1(3) of the Family Law Reform Act 1987 applies, that parent shall acquire parental responsibility for the child if—
(a) she becomes registered as a parent of the child under any of the enactments specified in subsection (2);
(b) she and the child's mother make an agreement providing for her to have parental responsibility for the child; or
(c) the court, on her application, orders that she shall have parental responsibility for the child.

(2) The enactments referred to in subsection (1)(a) are—
(a) paragraphs (a), (b) and (c) of section 10(1B) and of section 10A(1B) of the Births and Deaths Registration Act 1953;
(b) paragraphs (a), (b) and (d) of section 18B(1) and sections 18B(3)(a) and 20(1)(a) of the Registration of Births, Deaths and Marriages (Scotland) Act 1965; and
(c) sub-paragraphs (a), (b) and (c) of Article 14ZA(3) of the Births and Deaths Registration (Northern Ireland) Order 1976.

(3) The Secretary of State may by order amend subsection (2) so as to add further enactments to the list in that subsection.

(4) An agreement under subsection (1)(b) is also a "parental responsibility agreement", and section 4(2) applies in relation to such an agreement as it applies in relation to parental responsibility agreements under section 4.

(5) A person who has acquired parental responsibility under subsection (1) shall cease to have that responsibility only if the court so orders.

(6) The court may make an order under subsection (5) on the application—
(a) of any person who has parental responsibility for the child; or
(b) with the leave of the court, of the child himself, subject, in the case of parental responsibility acquired under subsection (1)(c), to section 12(4).

(7) The court may only grant leave under subsection (6)(b) if it is satisfied that the child has sufficient understanding to make the proposed application.

4A ACQUISITION OF PARENTAL RESPONSIBILITY BY STEP-PARENT

(1) Where a child's parent ("parent A") who has parental responsibility for the child is married to, or a civil partner of, a person who is not the child's parent ("the step-parent")—
- (a) parent A or, if the other parent of the child also has parental responsibility for the child, both parents may by agreement with the step-parent provide for the step-parent to have parental responsibility for the child; or
- (b) the court may, on the application of the step-parent, order that the step-parent shall have parental responsibility for the child.

(2) An agreement under subsection (1)(a) is also a "parental responsibility agreement", and section 4(2) applies in relation to such agreements as it applies in relation to parental responsibility agreements under section 4.

(3) A parental responsibility agreement under subsection (1)(a), or an order under subsection (1)(b), may only be brought to an end by an order of the court made on the application—
- (a) of any person who has parental responsibility for the child; or
- (b) with the leave of the court, of the child himself.

(4) The court may only grant leave under subsection (3)(b) if it is satisfied that the child has sufficient understanding to make the proposed application.

5 APPOINTMENT OF GUARDIANS

(1) Where an application with respect to a child is made to the court by any individual, the court may by order appoint that individual to be the child's guardian if—
- (a) the child has no parent with parental responsibility for him; or
- (b) a residence order has been made with respect to the child in favour of a parent, guardian or special guardian of his who has died while the order was in force; or
- (c) paragraph (b) does not apply, and the child's only or last surviving special guardian dies.

(2) The power conferred by subsection (1) may also be exercised in any family proceedings if the court considers that the order should be made even though no application has been made for it.

(3) A parent who has parental responsibility for his child may appoint another individual to be the child's guardian in the event of his death.

(4) A guardian of a child may appoint another individual to take his place as the child's guardian in the event of his death; and a special guardian of a child may appoint another individual to be the child's guardian in the event of his death.

(5) An appointment under subsection (3) or (4) shall not have effect unless it is made in writing, is dated and is signed by the person making the appointment or—
- (a) in the case of an appointment made by a will which is not signed by the testator, is signed at the direction of the testator in accordance with the requirements of section 9 of the Wills Act 1837; or
- (b) in any other case, is signed at the direction of the person making the appointment, in his presence and in the presence of two witnesses who each attest the signature.

(6) A person appointed as a child's guardian under this section shall have parental responsibility for the child concerned.

(7) Where—
- (a) on the death of any person making an appointment under subsection (3) or (4), the child concerned has no parent with parental responsibility for him; or

(b) immediately before the death of any person making such an appointment, a residence order in his favour was in force with respect to the child, or he was the child's only (or last surviving) special guardian,

the appointment shall take effect on the death of that person.

(8) Where, on the death of any person making an appointment under subsection (3) or (4)—

(a) the child concerned has a parent with parental responsibility for him; and

(b) subsection (7)(b) does not apply,

the appointment shall take effect when the child no longer has a parent who has parental responsibility for him.

(9) Subsections (1) and (7) do not apply if the residence order referred to in paragraph (b) of those subsections was also made in favour of a surviving parent of the child.

(10) Nothing in this section shall be taken to prevent an appointment under subsection (3) or (4) being made by two or more persons acting jointly.

(11) Subject to any provision made by rules of court, no court shall exercise the High Court's inherent jurisdiction to appoint a guardian of the estate of any child.

(12) Where rules of court are made under subsection (11) they may prescribe the circumstances in which, and conditions subject to which, an appointment of such a guardian may be made.

(13) A guardian of a child may only be appointed in accordance with the provisions of this section.

6 GUARDIANS: REVOCATION AND DISCLAIMER

(1) An appointment under section 5(3) or (4) revokes an earlier such appointment (including one made in an unrevoked will or codicil) made by the same person in respect of the same child, unless it is clear (whether as the result of an express provision in the later appointment or by any necessary implication) that the purpose of the later appointment is to appoint an additional guardian.

(2) An appointment under section 5(3) or (4) (including one made in an unrevoked will or codicil) is revoked if the person who made the appointment revokes it by a written and dated instrument which is signed—

(a) by him; or

(b) at his direction, in his presence and in the presence of two witnesses who each attest the signature.

(3) An appointment under section 5(3) or (4) (other than one made in a will or codicil) is revoked if, with the intention of revoking the appointment, the person who made it—

(a) destroys the instrument by which it was made; or

(b) has some other person destroy that instrument in his presence.

(3A) An appointment under section 5(3) or (4) (including one made in an unrevoked will or codicil) is revoked if the person appointed is the spouse of the person who made the appointment and either—

(a) a decree of a court of civil jurisdiction in England and Wales dissolves or annuls the marriage, or

(b) the marriage is dissolved or annulled and the divorce or annulment is entitled to recognition in England and Wales by virtue of Part II of the Family Law Act 1986,

unless a contrary intention appears by the appointment.

(3B) An appointment under section 5(3) or (4) (including one made in an unrevoked will or codicil) is revoked if the person appointed is the civil partner of the person who made the appointment and either—

(a) an order of a court of civil jurisdiction in England and Wales dissolves or annuls the civil partnership, or
(b) the civil partnership is dissolved or annulled and the dissolution or annulment is entitled to recognition in England and Wales by virtue of Chapter 3 of Part 5 of the Civil Partnership Act 2004, unless a contrary intention appears by the appointment.

(4) For the avoidance of doubt, an appointment under section 5(3) or (4) made in a will or codicil is revoked if the will or codicil is revoked.

(5) A person who is appointed as a guardian under section 5(3) or (4) may disclaim his appointment by an instrument in writing signed by him and made within a reasonable time of his first knowing that the appointment has taken effect.

(6) Where regulations are made by the Lord Chancellor prescribing the manner in which such disclaimers must be recorded, no such disclaimer shall have effect unless it is recorded in the prescribed manner.

(7) Any appointment of a guardian under section 5 may be brought to an end at any time by order of the court—
(a) on the application of any person who has parental responsibility for the child;
(b) on the application of the child concerned, with leave of the court; or
(c) in any family proceedings, if the court considers that it should be brought to an end even though no application has been made.

7 WELFARE REPORTS

(1) A court considering any question with respect to a child under this Act may—
(a) ask an officer of the Service or a Welsh family proceedings officer; or
(b) ask a local authority to arrange for—
(i) an officer of the authority; or
(ii) such other person (other than an officer of the Service or a Welsh family proceedings officer) as the authority considers appropriate, to report to the court on such matters relating to the welfare of that child as are required to be dealt with in the report.

(2) The Lord Chancellor may, after consulting the Lord Chief Justice, make regulations specifying matters which, unless the court orders otherwise, must be dealt with in any report under this section.

(3) The report may be made in writing, or orally, as the court requires.

(4) Regardless of any enactment or rule of law which would otherwise prevent it from doing so, the court may take account of—
(a) any statement contained in the report; and
(b) any evidence given in respect of the matters referred to in the report, in so far as the statement or evidence is, in the opinion of the court, relevant to the question which it is considering.

(5) It shall be the duty of the authority or officer of the Service or a Welsh family proceedings officer to comply with any request for a report under this section.

(6) The Lord Chief Justice may nominate a judicial office holder (as defined in section 109(4) of the Constitutional Reform Act 2005) to exercise his functions under subsection (2).

Part II ORDERS WITH RESPECT TO CHILDREN IN FAMILY PROCEEDINGS

General

8 RESIDENCE, CONTACT AND OTHER ORDERS WITH RESPECT TO CHILDREN

(1) In this Act—

"a contact order" means an order requiring the person with whom a child lives, or is to live, to allow the child to visit or stay with the person named in the order, or for that person and the child otherwise to have contact with each other;

"a prohibited steps order" means an order that no step which could be taken by a parent in meeting his parental responsibility for a child, and which is of a kind specified in the order, shall be taken by any person without the consent of the court;

"a residence order" means an order settling the arrangements to be made as to the person with whom a child is to live; and

"a specific issue order" means an order giving directions for the purpose of determining a specific question which has arisen, or which may arise, in connection with any aspect of parental responsibility for a child.

(2) In this Act "a section 8 order" means any of the orders mentioned in subsection (1) and any order varying or discharging such an order.

(3) For the purposes of this Act "family proceedings" means any proceedings—
(a) under the inherent jurisdiction of the High Court in relation to children; and
(b) under the enactments mentioned in subsection (4),
but does not include proceedings on an application for leave under section 100(3).

(4) The enactments are—
(a) Parts I, II and IV of this Act;
(b) the Matrimonial Causes Act 1973;
(ba) Schedule 5 to the Civil Partnership Act 2004;
(d) the Adoption and Children Act 2002;
(e) the Domestic Proceedings and Magistrates' Courts Act 1978;
(ea) Schedule 6 to the Civil Partnership Act 2004;
(g) Part III of the Matrimonial and Family Proceedings Act 1984.
(h) the Family Law Act 1996.
(i) sections 11 and 12 of the Crime and Disorder Act 1998.

9 RESTRICTIONS ON MAKING SECTION 8 ORDERS

(1) No court shall make any section 8 order, other than a residence order, with respect to a child who is in the care of a local authority.

(2) No application may be made by a local authority for a residence order or contact order and no court shall make such an order in favour of a local authority.

(3) A person who is, or was at any time within the last six months, a local authority foster parent of a child may not apply for leave to apply for a section 8 order with respect to the child unless—
(a) he has the consent of the authority;
(b) he is a relative of the child; or
(c) the child has lived with him for at least one year preceding the application.

(5) No court shall exercise its powers to make a specific issue order or prohibited steps order—
(a) with a view to achieving a result which could be achieved by making a residence or contact order; or
(b) in any way which is denied to the High Court (by section 100(2)) in the exercise of its inherent jurisdiction with respect to children.

(6) No court shall make a specific issue order, contact order or prohibited steps order which is to have effect for a period which will end after the child has reached the age of sixteen unless it is satisfied that the circumstances of the case are exceptional.

(7) No court shall make any section 8 order, other than one varying or discharging such an order, with respect to a child who has reached the age of sixteen unless it is satisfied that the circumstances of the case are exceptional.

10 POWER OF COURT TO MAKE SECTION 8 ORDERS

(1) In any family proceedings in which a question arises with respect to the welfare of any child, the court may make a section 8 order with respect to the child if—
(a) an application for the order has been made by a person who—
(i) is entitled to apply for a section 8 order with respect to the child; or
(ii) has obtained the leave of the court to make the application; or
(b) the court considers that the order should be made even though no such application has been made.

(2) The court may also make a section 8 order with respect to any child on the application of a person who—
(a) is entitled to apply for a section 8 order with respect to the child; or
(b) has obtained the leave of the court to make the application.

(3) This section is subject to the restrictions imposed by section 9.

(4) The following persons are entitled to apply to the court for any section 8 order with respect to a child—
(a) any parent, guardian or special guardian of the child;
(aa) any person who by virtue of section 4A has parental responsibility for the child;
(b) any person in whose favour a residence order is in force with respect to the child.

(5) The following persons are entitled to apply for a residence or contact order with respect to a child—
(a) any party to a marriage (whether or not subsisting) in relation to whom the child is a child of the family;
(aa) any civil partner in a civil partnership (whether or not subsisting) in relation to whom the child is a child of the family;
(b) any person with whom the child has lived for a period of at least three years;
(c) any person—
(i) in any case where a residence order is in force with respect to the child, has the consent of each of the persons in whose favour the order was made;
(ii) in any case where the child is in the care of a local authority, has the consent of that authority; or
(iii) in any other case, has the consent of each of those (if any) who have parental responsibility for the child.

(5A) A local authority foster parent is entitled to apply for a residence order with respect to a child if the child has lived with him for a period of at least one year immediately preceding the application.

(5B) A relative of a child is entitled to apply for a residence order with respect to the child if the child has lived with the relative for a period of at least one year immediately preceding the application.

(6) A person who would not otherwise be entitled (under the previous provisions of this section) to apply for the variation or discharge of a section 8 order shall be entitled to do so if—
(a) the order was made on his application; or
(b) in the case of a contact order, he is named in the order.

(7) Any person who falls within a category of person prescribed by rules of court is entitled to apply for any such section 8 order as may be prescribed in relation to that category of person.

(7A) If a special guardianship order is in force with respect to a child, an application for a residence order may only be made with respect to him, if apart from this subsection the leave of the court is not required, with such leave.

(8) Where the person applying for leave to make an application for a section 8 order is the child concerned, the court may only grant leave if it is satisfied that he has sufficient understanding to make the proposed application for the section 8 order.

(9) Where the person applying for leave to make an application for a section 8 order is not the child concerned, the court shall, in deciding whether or not to grant leave, have particular regard to—
(a) the nature of the proposed application for the section 8 order;
(b) the applicant's connection with the child;
(c) any risk there might be of that proposed application disrupting the child's life to such an extent that he would be harmed by it; and
(d) where the child is being looked after by a local authority—
(i) the authority's plans for the child's future; and
(ii) the wishes and feelings of the child's parents.

(10) The period of three years mentioned in subsection (5)(b) need not be continuous but must not have begun more than five years before, or ended more than three months before, the making of the application.

11 GENERAL PRINCIPLES AND SUPPLEMENTARY PROVISIONS

(1) In proceedings in which any question of making a section 8 order, or any other question with respect to such an order, arises, the court shall (in the light of any rules made by virtue of subsection (2))—
(a) draw up a timetable with a view to determining the question without delay; and
(b) give such directions as it considers appropriate for the purpose of ensuring, so far as is reasonably practicable, that that timetable is adhered to.

(2) Rules of court may—
(a) specify periods within which specified steps must be taken in relation to proceedings in which such questions arise; and
(b) make other provision with respect to such proceedings for the purpose of ensuring, so far as is reasonably practicable, that such questions are determined without delay.

(3) Where a court has power to make a section 8 order, it may do so at any time during the course of the proceedings in question even though it is not in a position to dispose finally of those proceedings.

(4) Where a residence order is made in favour of two or more persons who do not themselves all live together, the order may specify the periods during which the child is to live in the different households concerned.

(5) Where—
(a) a residence order has been made with respect to a child; and
(b) as a result of the order the child lives, or is to live, with one of two parents who each have parental responsibility for him,
the residence order shall cease to have effect if the parents live together for a continuous period of more than six months.

(6) A contact order which requires the parent with whom a child lives to allow the child to visit, or otherwise have contact with, his other parent shall cease to have effect if the parents live together for a continuous period of more than six months.

(7) A section 8 order may—
(a) contain directions about how it is to be carried into effect;
(b) impose conditions which must be complied with by any person—
(i) in whose favour the order is made;
(ii) who is a parent of the child concerned;
(iii) who is not a parent of his but who has parental responsibility for him; or
(iv) with whom the child is living, and to whom the conditions are expressed to apply;
(c) be made to have effect for a specified period, or contain provisions which are to have effect for a specified period;
(d) make such incidental, supplemental or consequential provision as the court thinks fit.

11A CONTACT ACTIVITY DIRECTIONS

(1) This section applies in proceedings in which the court is considering whether to make provision about contact with a child by making—
(a) a contact order with respect to the child, or
(b) an order varying or discharging a contact order with respect to the child.

(2) The court may make a contact activity direction in connection with that provision about contact.

(3) A contact activity direction is a direction requiring an individual who is a party to the proceedings to take part in an activity that promotes contact with the child concerned.

(4) The direction is to specify the activity and the person providing the activity.

(5) The activities that may be so required include, in particular—
(a) programmes, classes and counselling or guidance sessions of a kind that—
(i) may assist a person as regards establishing, maintaining or improving contact with a child;
(ii) may, by addressing a person's violent behaviour, enable or facilitate contact with a child;
(b) sessions in which information or advice is given as regards making or operating arrangements for contact with a child, including making arrangements by means of mediation.

(6) No individual may be required by a contact activity direction—
(a) to undergo medical or psychiatric examination, assessment or treatment;
(b) to take part in mediation.

(7) A court may not on the same occasion—
(a) make a contact activity direction, and
(b) dispose finally of the proceedings as they relate to contact with the child concerned.

(8) Subsection (2) has effect subject to the restrictions in sections 11B and 11E.

(9) In considering whether to make a contact activity direction, the welfare of the child concerned is to be the court's paramount consideration.

11B CONTACT ACTIVITY DIRECTIONS: FURTHER PROVISION

(1) A court may not make a contact activity direction in any proceedings unless there is a dispute as regards the provision about contact that the court is considering whether to make in the proceedings.

(2) A court may not make a contact activity direction requiring an individual who is a child to take part in an activity unless the individual is a parent of the child in relation to whom the court is considering provision about contact.

(3) A court may not make a contact activity direction in connection with the making, variation or discharge of a contact order, if the contact order is, or would if made be, an excepted order.

(4) A contact order with respect to a child is an excepted order if—
(a) it is made in proceedings that include proceedings on an application for a relevant adoption order in respect of the child; or
(b) it makes provision as regards contact between the child and a person who would be a parent or relative of the child but for the child's adoption by an order falling within subsection (5).

(5) An order falls within this subsection if it is—
(a) a relevant adoption order;
(b) an adoption order, within the meaning of section 72(1) of the Adoption Act 1976, other than an order made by virtue of section 14 of that Act on the application of a married couple one of whom is the mother or the father of the child;
(c) a Scottish adoption order, within the meaning of the Adoption and Children Act 2002, other than an order made—
(i) by virtue of section 14 of the Adoption (Scotland) Act 1978 on the application of a married couple one of whom is the mother or the father of the child, or
(ii) by virtue of section 15(1)(aa) of that Act; or
(d) a Northern Irish adoption order, within the meaning of the Adoption and Children Act 2002, other than an order made by virtue of Article 14 of the Adoption (Northern Ireland) Order 1987 on the application of a married couple one of whom is the mother or the father of the child.

(6) A relevant adoption order is an adoption order, within the meaning of section 46(1) of the Adoption and Children Act 2002, other than an order made—
(a) on an application under section 50 of that Act by a couple (within the meaning of that Act) one of whom is the mother or the father of the person to be adopted, or
(b) on an application under section 51(2) of that Act.

(7) A court may not make a contact activity direction in relation to an individual unless the individual is habitually resident in England and Wales; and a direction ceases to have effect if the individual subject to the direction ceases to be habitually resident in England and Wales.

11C CONTACT ACTIVITY CONDITIONS

(1) This section applies if in any family proceedings the court makes—
(a) a contact order with respect to a child, or
(b) an order varying a contact order with respect to a child.

(2) The contact order may impose, or the contact order may be varied so as to impose, a condition (a "contact activity condition") requiring an individual falling within subsection (3) to take part in an activity that promotes contact with the child concerned.

(3) An individual falls within this subsection if he is—
(a) for the purposes of the contact order so made or varied, the person with whom the child concerned lives or is to live;
(b) the person whose contact with the child concerned is provided for in that order; or
(c) a person upon whom that order imposes a condition under section 11(7)(b).

(4) The condition is to specify the activity and the person providing the activity.

(5) Subsections (5) and (6) of section 11A have effect as regards the activities that may be required by a contact activity condition as they have effect as regards the activities that may be required by a contact activity direction.

(6) Subsection (2) has effect subject to the restrictions in sections 11D and 11E.

11D CONTACT ACTIVITY CONDITIONS: FURTHER PROVISION

(1) A contact order may not impose a contact activity condition on an individual who is a child unless the individual is a parent of the child concerned.

(2) If a contact order is an excepted order (within the meaning given by section 11B(4)), it may not impose (and it may not be varied so as to impose) a contact activity condition.

(3) A contact order may not impose a contact activity condition on an individual unless the individual is habitually resident in England and Wales; and a condition ceases to have effect if the individual subject to the condition ceases to be habitually resident in England and Wales.

11E CONTACT ACTIVITY DIRECTIONS AND CONDITIONS: MAKING

(1) Before making a contact activity direction (or imposing a contact activity condition by means of a contact order), the court must satisfy itself as to the matters falling within subsections (2) to (4).

(2) The first matter is that the activity proposed to be specified is appropriate in the circumstances of the case.

(3) The second matter is that the person proposed to be specified as the provider of the activity is suitable to provide the activity.

(4) The third matter is that the activity proposed to be specified is provided in a place to which the individual who would be subject to the direction (or the condition) can reasonably be expected to travel.

(5) Before making such a direction (or such an order), the court must obtain and consider information about the individual who would be subject to the direction (or the condition) and the likely effect of the direction (or the condition) on him.

(6) Information about the likely effect of the direction (or the condition) may, in particular, include information as to—
(a) any conflict with the individual's religious beliefs;
(b) any interference with the times (if any) at which he normally works or attends an educational establishment.

(7) The court may ask an officer of the Service or a Welsh family proceedings officer to provide the court with information as to the matters in subsections (2) to (5); and it shall be the duty of the officer of the Service or Welsh family proceedings officer to comply with any such request.

(8) In this section "specified" means specified in a contact activity direction (or in a contact activity condition).

11F CONTACT ACTIVITY DIRECTIONS AND CONDITIONS: FINANCIAL ASSISTANCE

(1) The Secretary of State may by regulations make provision authorising him to make payments to assist individuals falling within subsection (2) in paying relevant charges or fees.

(2) An individual falls within this subsection if he is required by a contact activity direction or condition to take part in an activity that promotes contact with a child, not being a child ordinarily resident in Wales.

(3) The National Assembly for Wales may by regulations make provision authorising it to make payments to assist individuals falling within subsection (4) in paying relevant charges or fees.

(4) An individual falls within this subsection if he is required by a contact activity direction or condition to take part in an activity that promotes contact with a child who is ordinarily resident in Wales.

(5) A relevant charge or fee, in relation to an activity required by a contact activity direction or condition, is a charge or fee in respect of the activity payable to the person providing the activity.

(6) Regulations under this section may provide that no assistance is available to an individual unless—
(a) the individual satisfies such conditions as regards his financial resources as may be set out in the regulations;
(b) the activity in which the individual is required by a contact activity direction or condition to take part is provided to him in England or Wales;
(c) where the activity in which the individual is required to take part is provided to him in England, it is provided by a person who is for the time being approved by the Secretary of State as a provider of activities required by a contact activity direction or condition;
(d) where the activity in which the individual is required to take part is provided to him in Wales, it is provided by a person who is for the time being approved by the National Assembly for Wales as a provider of activities required by a contact activity direction or condition.

(7) Regulations under this section may make provision—
(a) as to the maximum amount of assistance that may be paid to or in respect of an individual as regards an activity in which he is required by a contact activity direction or condition to take part;

(b) where the amount may vary according to an individual's financial resources, as to the method by which the amount is to be determined;
(c) authorising payments by way of assistance to be made directly to persons providing activities required by a contact activity direction or condition.

11G CONTACT ACTIVITY DIRECTIONS AND CONDITIONS: MONITORING

(1) This section applies if in any family proceedings the court—
(a) makes a contact activity direction in relation to an individual, or
(b) makes a contact order that imposes, or varies a contact order so as to impose, a contact activity condition on an individual.

(2) The court may on making the direction (or imposing the condition by means of a contact order) ask an officer of the Service or a Welsh family proceedings officer—
(a) to monitor, or arrange for the monitoring of, the individual's compliance with the direction (or the condition);
(b) to report to the court on any failure by the individual to comply with the direction (or the condition).

(3) It shall be the duty of the officer of the Service or Welsh family proceedings officer to comply with any request under subsection (2).

11H MONITORING CONTACT

(1) This section applies if in any family proceedings the court makes—
(a) a contact order with respect to a child in favour of a person, or
(b) an order varying such a contact order.

(2) The court may ask an officer of the Service or a Welsh family proceedings officer—
(a) to monitor whether an individual falling within subsection (3) complies with the contact order (or the contact order as varied);
(b) to report to the court on such matters relating to the individual's compliance as the court may specify in the request.

(3) An individual falls within this subsection if the contact order so made (or the contact order as so varied)—
(a) requires the individual to allow contact with the child concerned;
(b) names the individual as having contact with the child concerned; or
(c) imposes a condition under section 11(7)(b) on the individual.

(4) If the contact order (or the contact order as varied) includes a contact activity condition, a request under subsection (2) is to be treated as relating to the provisions of the order other than the contact activity condition.

(5) The court may make a request under subsection (2)—
(a) on making the contact order (or the order varying the contact order), or
(b) at any time during the subsequent course of the proceedings as they relate to contact with the child concerned.

(6) In making a request under subsection (2), the court is to specify the period for which the officer of the Service or Welsh family proceedings officer is to monitor compliance with the order;

and the period specified may not exceed twelve months.

(7) It shall be the duty of the officer of the Service or Welsh family proceedings officer to comply with any request under subsection (2).

(8) The court may order any individual falling within subsection (3) to take such steps as may be specified in the order with a view to enabling the officer of the Service or Welsh family proceedings officer to comply with the court's request under subsection (2).

(9) But the court may not make an order under subsection (8) with respect to an individual who is a child unless he is a parent of the child with respect to whom the order falling within subsection (1) was made.

(10) A court may not make a request under subsection (2) in relation to a contact order that is an excepted order (within the meaning given by section 11B(4)).

11I CONTACT ORDERS: WARNING NOTICES

Where the court makes (or varies) a contact order, it is to attach to the contact order (or the order varying the contact order) a notice warning of the consequences of failing to comply with the contact order.

11J ENFORCEMENT ORDERS

(1) This section applies if a contact order with respect to a child has been made.

(2) If the court is satisfied beyond reasonable doubt that a person has failed to comply with the contact order, it may make an order (an "enforcement order") imposing on the person an unpaid work requirement.

(3) But the court may not make an enforcement order if it is satisfied that the person had a reasonable excuse for failing to comply with the contact order.

(4) The burden of proof as to the matter mentioned in subsection (3) lies on the person claiming to have had a reasonable excuse, and the standard of proof is the balance of probabilities.

(5) The court may make an enforcement order in relation to the contact order only on the application of—
- (a) the person who is, for the purposes of the contact order, the person with whom the child concerned lives or is to live;
- (b) the person whose contact with the child concerned is provided for in the contact order;
- (c) any individual subject to a condition under section 11(7)(b) or a contact activity condition imposed by the contact order; or
- (d) the child concerned.

(6) Where the person proposing to apply for an enforcement order in relation to a contact order is the child concerned, the child must obtain the leave of the court before making such an application.

(7) The court may grant leave to the child concerned only if it is satisfied that he has sufficient understanding to make the proposed application.

(8) Subsection (2) has effect subject to the restrictions in sections 11K and 11L.

(9) The court may suspend an enforcement order for such period as it thinks fit.

(10) Nothing in this section prevents a court from making more than one enforcement order in relation to the same person on the same occasion.

(11) Proceedings in which any question of making an enforcement order, or any other question with respect to such an order, arises are to be regarded for the purposes of section 11(1) and (2) as proceedings in which a question arises with respect to a section 8 order.

(12) In Schedule A1—
(a) Part 1 makes provision as regards an unpaid work requirement;
(b) Part 2 makes provision in relation to the revocation and amendment of enforcement orders and failure to comply with such orders.

(13) This section is without prejudice to section 63(3) of the Magistrates' Courts Act 1980 as it applies in relation to contact orders.

11K ENFORCEMENT ORDERS: FURTHER PROVISION

(1) A court may not make an enforcement order against a person in respect of a failure to comply with a contact order unless it is satisfied that before the failure occurred the person had been given (in accordance with rules of court) a copy of, or otherwise informed of the terms of—
(a) in the case of a failure to comply with a contact order that was varied before the failure occurred, a notice under section 11I relating to the order varying the contact order or, where more than one such order has been made, the last order preceding the failure in question;
(b) in any other case, a notice under section 11I relating to the contact order.

(2) A court may not make an enforcement order against a person in respect of any failure to comply with a contact order occurring before the person attained the age of 18.

(3) A court may not make an enforcement order against a person in respect of a failure to comply with a contact order that is an excepted order (within the meaning given by section 11B(4)).

(4) A court may not make an enforcement order against a person unless the person is habitually resident in England and Wales; and an enforcement order ceases to have effect if the person subject to the order ceases to be habitually resident in England and Wales.

11L ENFORCEMENT ORDERS: MAKING

(1) Before making an enforcement order as regards a person in breach of a contact order, the court must be satisfied that—
(a) making the enforcement order proposed is necessary to secure the person's compliance with the contact order or any contact order that has effect in its place;
(b) the likely effect on the person of the enforcement order proposed to be made is proportionate to the seriousness of the breach of the contact order.

(2) Before making an enforcement order, the court must satisfy itself that provision for the person to work under an unpaid work requirement imposed by an enforcement order can be made in the local justice area in which the person in breach resides or will reside.

(3) Before making an enforcement order as regards a person in breach of a contact order, the court must obtain and consider information about the person and the likely effect of the enforcement order on him.

(4) Information about the likely effect of the enforcement order may, in particular, include information as to—
(a) any conflict with the person's religious beliefs;

(b) any interference with the times (if any) at which he normally works or attends an educational establishment.

(5) A court that proposes to make an enforcement order may ask an officer of the Service or a Welsh family proceedings officer to provide the court with information as to the matters in subsections (2) and (3).

(6) It shall be the duty of the officer of the Service or Welsh family proceedings officer to comply with any request under this section.

(7) In making an enforcement order in relation to a contact order, a court must take into account the welfare of the child who is the subject of the contact order.

11M ENFORCEMENT ORDERS: MONITORING

(1) On making an enforcement order in relation to a person, the court is to ask an officer of the Service or a Welsh family proceedings officer—
 (a) to monitor, or arrange for the monitoring of, the person's compliance with the unpaid work requirement imposed by the order;
 (b) to report to the court if a report under paragraph 8 of Schedule A1 is made in relation to the person;
 (c) to report to the court on such other matters relating to the person's compliance as may be specified in the request;
 (d) to report to the court if the person is, or becomes, unsuitable to perform work under the requirement.

(2) It shall be the duty of the officer of the Service or Welsh family proceedings officer to comply with any request under this section.

11N ENFORCEMENT ORDERS: WARNING NOTICES

Where the court makes an enforcement order, it is to attach to the order a notice warning of the consequences of failing to comply with the order.

11O COMPENSATION FOR FINANCIAL LOSS

(1) This section applies if a contact order with respect to a child has been made.

(2) If the court is satisfied that—
 (a) an individual has failed to comply with the contact order, and
 (b) a person falling within subsection (6) has suffered financial loss by reason of the breach,
 it may make an order requiring the individual in breach to pay the person compensation in respect of his financial loss.

(3) But the court may not make an order under subsection (2) if it is satisfied that the individual in breach had a reasonable excuse for failing to comply with the contact order.

(4) The burden of proof as to the matter mentioned in subsection (3) lies on the individual claiming to have had a reasonable excuse.

(5) An order under subsection (2) may be made only on an application by the person who claims to have suffered financial loss.

(6) A person falls within this subsection if he is—
 (a) the person who is, for the purposes of the contact order, the person with whom the child concerned lives or is to live;

(b) the person whose contact with the child concerned is provided for in the contact order;
(c) an individual subject to a condition under section 11(7)(b) or a contact activity condition imposed by the contact order; or
(d) the child concerned.

(7) Where the person proposing to apply for an order under subsection (2) is the child concerned, the child must obtain the leave of the court before making such an application.

(8) The court may grant leave to the child concerned only if it is satisfied that he has sufficient understanding to make the proposed application.

(9) The amount of compensation is to be determined by the court, but may not exceed the amount of the applicant's financial loss.

(10) In determining the amount of compensation payable by the individual in breach, the court must take into account the individual's financial circumstances.

(11) An amount ordered to be paid as compensation may be recovered by the applicant as a civil debt due to him.

(12) Subsection (2) has effect subject to the restrictions in section 11P.

(13) Proceedings in which any question of making an order under subsection (2) arises are to be regarded for the purposes of section 11(1) and (2) as proceedings in which a question arises with respect to a section 8 order.

(14) In exercising its powers under this section, a court is to take into account the welfare of the child concerned.

11P ORDERS UNDER SECTION 11O(2): FURTHER PROVISION

(1) A court may not make an order under section 11O(2) requiring an individual to pay compensation in respect of a failure by him to comply with a contact order unless it is satisfied that before the failure occurred the individual had been given (in accordance with rules of court) a copy of, or otherwise informed of the terms of—
(a) in the case of a failure to comply with a contact order that was varied before the failure occurred, a notice under section 11I relating to the order varying the contact order or, where more than one such order has been made, the last order preceding the failure in question;
(b) in any other case, a notice under section 11I relating to the contact order.

(2) A court may not make an order under section 11O(2) requiring an individual to pay compensation in respect of a failure by him to comply with a contact order where the failure occurred before the individual attained the age of 18.

(3) A court may not make an order under section 11O(2) requiring an individual to pay compensation in respect of a failure by him to comply with a contact order that is an excepted order (within the meaning given by section 11B(4)).

12 RESIDENCE ORDERS AND PARENTAL RESPONSIBILITY

(1) Where the court makes a residence order in favour of the father of a child it shall, if the father would not otherwise have parental responsibility for the child, also make an order under section 4 giving him that responsibility.

(1A) Where the court makes a residence order in favour of a woman who is a parent of a child by virtue of section 43 of the Human Fertilisation and Embryology Act 2008 it shall, if that woman would not otherwise have parental responsibility for the child, also make an order under section 4ZA giving her that responsibility.

(2) Where the court makes a residence order in favour of any person who is not the parent or guardian of the child concerned that person shall have parental responsibility for the child while the residence order remains in force.

(3) Where a person has parental responsibility for a child as a result of subsection (2), he shall not have the right—
(b) to agree, or refuse to agree, to the making of an adoption order, or an order under section 84 of the Adoption and Children Act 2002, with respect to the child; or
(c) to appoint a guardian for the child.

(4) Where subsection (1) or (1A) requires the court to make an order under section 4 or 4ZA in respect of the parent of a child, the court shall not bring that order to an end at any time while the residence order concerned remains in force.

13 CHANGE OF CHILD'S NAME OR REMOVAL FROM JURISDICTION

(1) Where a residence order is in force with respect to a child, no person may—
(a) cause the child to be known by a new surname; or
(b) remove him from the United Kingdom;
without either the written consent of every person who has parental responsibility for the child or the leave of the court.

(2) Subsection (1)(b) does not prevent the removal of a child, for a period of less than one month, by the person in whose favour the residence order is made.

(3) In making a residence order with respect to a child the court may grant the leave required by subsection (1)(b), either generally or for specified purposes.

14 ENFORCEMENT OF RESIDENCE ORDERS

(1) Where—
(a) a residence order is in force with respect to a child in favour of any person; and
(b) any other person (including one in whose favour the order is also in force) is in breach of the arrangements settled by that order,
the person mentioned in paragraph (a) may, as soon as the requirement in subsection (2) is complied with, enforce the order under section 63(3) of the Magistrates' Courts Act 1980 as if it were an order requiring the other person to produce the child to him.

(2) The requirement is that a copy of the residence order has been served on the other person.

(3) Subsection (1) is without prejudice to any other remedy open to the person in whose favour the residence order is in force.

Special guardianship

14A SPECIAL GUARDIANSHIP ORDERS

(1) A "special guardianship order" is an order appointing one or more individuals to be a child's "special guardian" (or special guardians).

(2) A special guardian—
(a) must be aged eighteen or over; and
(b) must not be a parent of the child in question, and subsections (3) to (6) are to be read in that light.

(3) The court may make a special guardianship order with respect to any child on the application of an individual who—
(a) is entitled to make such an application with respect to the child; or
(b) has obtained the leave of the court to make the application, or on the joint application of more than one such individual.

(4) Section 9(3) applies in relation to an application for leave to apply for a special guardianship order as it applies in relation to an application for leave to apply for a section 8 order.

(5) The individuals who are entitled to apply for a special guardianship order with respect to a child are—
(a) any guardian of the child;
(b) any individual in whose favour a residence order is in force with respect to the child;
(c) any individual listed in subsection (5)(b) or (c) of section 10 (as read with subsection (10) of that section);
(d) a local authority foster parent with whom the child has lived for a period of at least one year immediately preceding the application;
(e) a relative with whom the child has lived for a period of at least one year immediately preceding the application.

(6) The court may also make a special guardianship order with respect to a child in any family proceedings in which a question arises with respect to the welfare of the child if—
(a) an application for the order has been made by an individual who falls within subsection (3)(a) or (b) (or more than one such individual jointly); or
(b) the court considers that a special guardianship order should be made even though no such application has been made.

(7) No individual may make an application under subsection (3) or (6)(a) unless, before the beginning of the period of three months ending with the date of the application, he has given written notice of his intention to make the application—
(a) if the child in question is being looked after by a local authority, to that local authority, or
(b) otherwise, to the local authority in whose area the individual is ordinarily resident.

(8) On receipt of such a notice, the local authority must investigate the matter and prepare a report for the court dealing with—
(a) the suitability of the applicant to be a special guardian;
(b) such matters (if any) as may be prescribed by the Secretary of State; and
(c) any other matter which the local authority consider to be relevant.

(9) The court may itself ask a local authority to conduct such an investigation and prepare such a report, and the local authority must do so.

(10) The local authority may make such arrangements as they see fit for any person to act on their behalf in connection with conducting an investigation or preparing a report referred to in subsection (8) or (9).

(11) The court may not make a special guardianship order unless it has received a report dealing with the matters referred to in subsection (8).

(12) Subsections (8) and (9) of section 10 apply in relation to special guardianship orders as they apply in relation to section 8 orders.

(13) This section is subject to section 29(5) and (6) of the Adoption and Children Act 2002.

14B SPECIAL GUARDIANSHIP ORDERS: MAKING

(1) Before making a special guardianship order, the court must consider whether, if the order were made—
  (a) a contact order should also be made with respect to the child,
  (b) any section 8 order in force with respect to the child should be varied or discharged,
  (c) where a contact order made with respect to the child is not discharged, any enforcement order relating to that contact order should be revoked, and
  (d) where a contact activity direction has been made as regards contact with the child and is in force, that contact activity direction should be discharged.

(2) On making a special guardianship order, the court may also—
  (a) give leave for the child to be known by a new surname;
  (b) grant the leave required by section 14C(3)(b), either generally or for specified purposes.

14C SPECIAL GUARDIANSHIP ORDERS: EFFECT

(1) The effect of a special guardianship order is that while the order remains in force—
  (a) a special guardian appointed by the order has parental responsibility for the child in respect of whom it is made; and
  (b) subject to any other order in force with respect to the child under this Act, a special guardian is entitled to exercise parental responsibility to the exclusion of any other person with parental responsibility for the child (apart from another special guardian).

(2) Subsection (1) does not affect—
  (a) the operation of any enactment or rule of law which requires the consent of more than one person with parental responsibility in a matter affecting the child; or
  (b) any rights which a parent of the child has in relation to the child's adoption or placement for adoption.

(3) While a special guardianship order is in force with respect to a child, no person may—
  (a) cause the child to be known by a new surname; or
  (b) remove him from the United Kingdom,

without either the written consent of every person who has parental responsibility for the child or the leave of the court.

(4) Subsection (3)(b) does not prevent the removal of a child, for a period of less than three months, by a special guardian of his.

(5) If the child with respect to whom a special guardianship order is in force dies, his special guardian must take reasonable steps to give notice of that fact to—
  (a) each parent of the child with parental responsibility; and
  (b) each guardian of the child, but if the child has more than one special guardian, and one of them has taken such steps in relation to a particular parent or guardian, any other special guardian need not do so as respects that parent or guardian.

(6) This section is subject to section 29(7) of the Adoption and Children Act 2002.

14D SPECIAL GUARDIANSHIP ORDERS: VARIATION AND DISCHARGE

(1) The court may vary or discharge a special guardianship order on the application of—
  (a) the special guardian (or any of them, if there are more than one);
  (b) any parent or guardian of the child concerned;
  (c) any individual in whose favour a residence order is in force with respect to the child;

(d) any individual not falling within any of paragraphs (a) to (c) who has, or immediately before the making of the special guardianship order had, parental responsibility for the child;
(e) the child himself; or
(f) a local authority designated in a care order with respect to the child.

(2) In any family proceedings in which a question arises with respect to the welfare of a child with respect to whom a special guardianship order is in force, the court may also vary or discharge the special guardianship order if it considers that the order should be varied or discharged, even though no application has been made under subsection (1).

(3) The following must obtain the leave of the court before making an application under subsection (1)—
(a) the child;
(b) any parent or guardian of his;
(c) any step-parent of his who has acquired, and has not lost, parental responsibility for him by virtue of section 4A;
(d) any individual falling within subsection (1)(d) who immediately before the making of the special guardianship order had, but no longer has, parental responsibility for him.

(4) Where the person applying for leave to make an application under subsection (1) is the child, the court may only grant leave if it is satisfied that he has sufficient understanding to make the proposed application under subsection (1).

(5) The court may not grant leave to a person falling within subsection (3)(b)(c) or (d) unless it is satisfied that there has been a significant change in circumstances since the making of the special guardianship order.

14E SPECIAL GUARDIANSHIP ORDERS: SUPPLEMENTARY

(1) In proceedings in which any question of making, varying or discharging a special guardianship order arises, the court shall (in the light of any rules made by virtue of subsection (3))—
(a) draw up a timetable with a view to determining the question without delay; and
(b) give such directions as it considers appropriate for the purpose of ensuring, so far as is reasonably practicable, that the timetable is adhered to.

(2) Subsection (1) applies also in relation to proceedings in which any other question with respect to a special guardianship order arises.

(3) The power to make rules in subsection (2) of section 11 applies for the purposes of this section as it applies for the purposes of that.

(4) A special guardianship order, or an order varying one, may contain provisions which are to have effect for a specified period.

(5) Section 11(7) (apart from paragraph (c)) applies in relation to special guardianship orders and orders varying them as it applies in relation to section 8 orders.

14F SPECIAL GUARDIANSHIP SUPPORT SERVICES

(1) Each local authority must make arrangements for the provision within their area of special guardianship support services, which means—
(a) counselling, advice and information; and
(b) such other services as are prescribed, in relation to special guardianship.

(2) The power to make regulations under subsection (1)(b) is to be exercised so as to secure that local authorities provide financial support.

(3) At the request of any of the following persons—
(a) a child with respect to whom a special guardianship order is in force;
(b) a special guardian;
(c) a parent;
(d) any other person who falls within a prescribed description, a local authority may carry out an assessment of that person's needs for special guardianship support services (but, if the Secretary of State so provides in regulations, they must do so if he is a person of a prescribed description, or if his case falls within a prescribed description, or if both he and his case fall within prescribed descriptions).

(4) A local authority may, at the request of any other person, carry out an assessment of that person's needs for special guardianship support services.

(5) Where, as a result of an assessment, a local authority decide that a person has needs for special guardianship support services, they must then decide whether to provide any such services to that person.

(6) If—
(a) a local authority decide to provide any special guardianship support services to a person, and
(b) the circumstances fall within a prescribed description, the local authority must prepare a plan in accordance with which special guardianship support services are to be provided to him, and keep the plan under review.

(7) The Secretary of State may by regulations make provision about assessments, preparing and reviewing plans, the provision of special guardianship support services in accordance with plans and reviewing the provision of special guardianship support services.

(8) The regulations may in particular make provision—
(a) about the type of assessment which is to be carried out, or the way in which an assessment is to be carried out;
(b) about the way in which a plan is to be prepared;
(c) about the way in which, and the time at which, a plan or the provision of special guardianship support services is to be reviewed;
(d) about the considerations to which a local authority are to have regard in carrying out an assessment or review or preparing a plan;
(e) as to the circumstances in which a local authority may provide special guardianship support services subject to conditions (including conditions as to payment for the support or the repayment of financial support);
(f) as to the consequences of conditions imposed by virtue of paragraph (e) not being met (including the recovery of any financial support provided);
(g) as to the circumstances in which this section may apply to a local authority in respect of persons who are outside that local authority's area;
(h) as to the circumstances in which a local authority may recover from another local authority the expenses of providing special guardianship support services to any person.

(9) A local authority may provide special guardianship support services (or any part of them) by securing their provision by—
(a) another local authority; or
(b) a person within a description prescribed in regulations of persons who may provide special guardianship support services, and may also arrange with any such authority

or person for that other authority or that person to carry out the local authority's functions in relation to assessments under this section.

(10) A local authority may carry out an assessment of the needs of any person for the purposes of this section at the same time as an assessment of his needs is made under any other provision of this Act or under any other enactment.

(11) Section 27 (co-operation between authorities) applies in relation to the exercise of functions of a local authority under this section as it applies in relation to the exercise of functions of a local authority under Part 3.

Financial relief

15 ORDERS FOR FINANCIAL RELIEF WITH RESPECT TO CHILDREN

(1) Schedule 1 (which consists primarily of the re-enactment, with consequential amendments and minor modifications, of provisions of section 6 of the Family Law Reform Act 1969 the Guardianship of Minors Acts 1971 and 1973, the Children Act 1975 and of sections 15 and 16 of the Family Law Reform Act 1987) makes provision in relation to financial relief for children.

(2) The powers of a magistrates' court under section 60 of the Magistrates' Courts Act 1980 to revoke, revive or vary an order for the periodical payment of money and the power of the clerk of a magistrates' court to vary such an order shall not apply in relation to an order made under Schedule 1.

Family assistance orders

16 FAMILY ASSISTANCE ORDERS

(1) Where, in any family proceedings, the court has power to make an order under this Part with respect to any child, it may (whether or not it makes such an order) make an order requiring—
(a) an officer of the Service or a Welsh family proceedings officer to be made available; or
(b) a local authority to make an officer of the authority available, to advise, assist and (where appropriate) befriend any person named in the order.

(2) The persons who may be named in an order under this section ("a family assistance order") are—
(a) any parent, guardian or special guardian of the child;
(b) any person with whom the child is living or in whose favour a contact order is in force with respect to the child;
(c) the child himself.

(3) No court may make a family assistance order unless—
(b) it has obtained the consent of every person to be named in the order other than the child.

(4) A family assistance order may direct—
(a) the person named in the order; or
(b) such of the persons named in the order as may be specified in the order,
to take such steps as may be so specified with a view to enabling the officer concerned to be kept informed of the address of any person named in the order and to be allowed to visit any such person.

(4A) If the court makes a family assistance order with respect to a child and the order is to be in force at the same time as a contact order made with respect to the child, the family assistance order may direct the officer concerned to give advice and assistance as regards establishing, improving and maintaining contact to such of the persons named in the order as may be specified in the order.

(5) Unless it specifies a shorter period, a family assistance order shall have effect for a period of twelve months beginning with the day on which it is made.

(6) If the court makes a family assistance order with respect to a child and the order is to be in force at the same time as a section 8 order made with respect to the child, the family assistance order may direct the officer concerned to report to the court on such matters relating to the section 8 order as the court may require (including the question whether the section 8 order ought to be varied or discharged).

(7) A family assistance order shall not be made so as to require a local authority to make an officer of theirs available unless—
(a) the authority agree; or
(b) the child concerned lives or will live within their area.

16A RISK ASSESSMENTS

(1) This section applies to the following functions of officers of the Service or Welsh family proceedings officers—
(a) any function in connection with family proceedings in which the court has power to make an order under this Part with respect to a child or in which a question with respect to such an order arises;
(b) any function in connection with an order made by the court in such proceedings.

(2) If, in carrying out any function to which this section applies, an officer of the Service or a Welsh family proceedings officer is given cause to suspect that the child concerned is at risk of harm, he must—
(a) make a risk assessment in relation to the child, and
(b) provide the risk assessment to the court.

(3) A risk assessment, in relation to a child who is at risk of suffering harm of a particular sort, is an assessment of the risk of that harm being suffered by the child.

Part III LOCAL AUTHORITY SUPPORT FOR CHILDREN AND FAMILIES

Provision of services for children and their families

17 PROVISION OF SERVICES FOR CHILDREN IN NEED, THEIR FAMILIES AND OTHERS

(1) It shall be the general duty of every local authority (in addition to the other duties imposed on them by this Part)—
(a) to safeguard and promote the welfare of children within their area who are in need; and
(b) so far as is consistent with that duty, to promote the upbringing of such children by their families, by providing a range and level of services appropriate to those children's needs.

(2) For the purpose principally of facilitating the discharge of their general duty under this section, every local authority shall have the specific duties and powers set out in Part I of Schedule 2.

(3) Any service provided by an authority in the exercise of functions conferred on them by this section may be provided for the family of a particular child in need or for any member of his family, if it is provided with a view to safeguarding or promoting the child's welfare.

(4) The appropriate national authority may by order amend any provision of Part I of Schedule 2 or add any further duty or power to those for the time being mentioned there.

(4A) Before determining what (if any) services to provide for a particular child in need in the exercise of functions conferred on them by this section, a local authority shall, so far as is reasonably practicable and consistent with the child's welfare—
(a) ascertain the child's wishes and feelings regarding the provision of those services; and
(b) give due consideration (having regard to his age and understanding) to such wishes and feelings of the child as they have been able to ascertain.

(5) Every local authority—
(a) shall facilitate the provision by others (including in particular voluntary organisations) of services which it is a function of the authority to provide by virtue of this section, or section 18, 20, 22A to 22C, 23B to 23D, 24A or 24B; and
(b) may make such arrangements as they see fit for any person to act on their behalf in the provision of any such service.

(6) The services provided by a local authority in the exercise of functions conferred on them by this section may include providing accommodation and giving assistance in kind or in cash.

(7) Assistance may be unconditional or subject to conditions as to the repayment of the assistance or of its value (in whole or in part).

(8) Before giving any assistance or imposing any conditions, a local authority shall have regard to the means of the child concerned and of each of his parents.

(9) No person shall be liable to make any repayment of assistance or of its value at any time when he is in receipt of income support under Part VII of the Social Security Contributions and Benefits Act 1992, of any element of child tax credit other than the family element, of working tax credit, of an income-based jobseeker's allowance or of an income-related employment and support allowance.

(10) For the purposes of this Part a child shall be taken to be in need if—
(a) he is unlikely to achieve or maintain, or to have the opportunity of achieving or maintaining, a reasonable standard of health or development without the provision for him of services by a local authority under this Part;
(b) his health or development is likely to be significantly impaired, or further impaired, without the provision for him of such services; or
(c) he is disabled, and "family", in relation to such a child, includes any person who has parental responsibility for the child and any other person with whom he has been living.

(11) For the purposes of this Part, a child is disabled if he is blind, deaf or dumb or suffers from mental disorder of any kind or is substantially and permanently handicapped by illness, injury or congenital deformity or such other disability as may be prescribed; and in this Part—

"development" means physical, intellectual, emotional, social or behavioural development; and

"health" means physical or mental health.

(12) The Treasury may by regulations prescribe circumstances in which a person is to be treated for the purposes of this Part (or for such of those purposes as are prescribed) as in receipt of any element of child tax credit other than the family element or of working tax credit.

17A DIRECT PAYMENTS

(1) The appropriate national authority may by regulations make provision for and in connection with requiring or authorising the responsible authority in the case of a person of a prescribed description who falls within subsection (2) to make, with that person's consent, such payments to him as they may determine in accordance with the regulations in respect of his securing the provision of the service mentioned in that subsection.

(2) A person falls within this subsection if he is—
(a) a person with parental responsibility for a disabled child,
(b) a disabled person with parental responsibility for a child, or
(c) a disabled child aged 16 or 17, and a local authority ("the responsible authority") have decided for the purposes of section 17 that the child's needs (or, if he is such a disabled child, his needs) call for the provision by them of a service in exercise of functions conferred on them under that section.

(3) Subsections (3) to (5) and (7) of section 57 of the 2001 Act shall apply, with any necessary modifications, in relation to regulations under this section as they apply in relation to regulations under that section.

(4) Regulations under this section shall provide that, where payments are made under the regulations to a person falling within subsection (5)—
(a) the payments shall be made at the rate mentioned in subsection (4)(a) of section 57 of the 2001 Act (as applied by subsection (3)); and
(b) subsection (4)(b) of that section shall not apply.

(5) A person falls within this subsection if he is—
(a) a person falling within subsection (2)(a) or (b) and the child in question is aged 16 or 17, or
(b) a person who is in receipt of income support under Part 7 of the Social Security Contributions and Benefits Act 1992 (c 4), of any element of child tax credit other than the family element, of working tax credit, of an income-based jobseeker's allowance or of an income-related employment and support allowance.

(6) In this section—

"the 2001 Act" means the Health and Social Care Act 2001;

"disabled" in relation to an adult has the same meaning as that given by section 17(11) in relation to a child;

"prescribed" means specified in or determined in accordance with regulations under this section (and has the same meaning in the provisions of the 2001 Act mentioned in subsection (3) as they apply by virtue of that subsection).

. . .

Provision of accommodation for children

20 PROVISION OF ACCOMMODATION FOR CHILDREN: GENERAL

(1) Every local authority shall provide accommodation for any child in need within their area who appears to them to require accommodation as a result of—

(a) there being no person who has parental responsibility for him;
(b) his being lost or having been abandoned; or
(c) the person who has been caring for him being prevented (whether or not permanently, and for whatever reason) from providing him with suitable accommodation or care.

(2) Where a local authority provide accommodation under subsection (1) for a child who is ordinarily resident in the area of another local authority, that other local authority may take over the provision of accommodation for the child within—
(a) three months of being notified in writing that the child is being provided with accommodation; or
(b) such other longer period as may be prescribed.

(3) Every local authority shall provide accommodation for any child in need within their area who has reached the age of sixteen and whose welfare the authority consider is likely to be seriously prejudiced if they do not provide him with accommodation.

(4) A local authority may provide accommodation for any child within their area (even though a person who has parental responsibility for him is able to provide him with accommodation) if they consider that to do so would safeguard or promote the child's welfare.

(5) A local authority may provide accommodation for any person who has reached the age of sixteen but is under twenty-one in any community home which takes children who have reached the age of sixteen if they consider that to do so would safeguard or promote his welfare.

(6) Before providing accommodation under this section, a local authority shall, so far as is reasonably practicable and consistent with the child's welfare—
(a) ascertain the child's wishes and feelings regarding the provision of accommodation; and
(b) give due consideration (having regard to his age and understanding) to such wishes and feelings of the child as they have been able to ascertain.

(7) A local authority may not provide accommodation under this section for any child if any person who—
(a) has parental responsibility for him; and
(b) is willing and able to—
  (i) provide accommodation for him; or
  (ii) arrange for accommodation to be provided for him, objects.

(8) Any person who has parental responsibility for a child may at any time remove the child from accommodation provided by or on behalf of the local authority under this section.

(9) Subsections (7) and (8) do not apply while any person—
(a) in whose favour a residence order is in force with respect to the child;
(aa) who is a special guardian of the child; or
(b) who has care of the child by virtue of an order made in the exercise of the High Court's inherent jurisdiction with respect to children,
agrees to the child being looked after in accommodation provided by or on behalf of the local authority.

(10) Where there is more than one such person as is mentioned in subsection (9), all of them must agree.

(11) Subsections (7) and (8) do not apply where a child who has reached the age of sixteen agrees to being provided with accommodation under this section.

21 PROVISION FOR ACCOMMODATION FOR CHILDREN IN POLICE PROTECTION OR DETENTION OR ON REMAND, ETC

(1) Every local authority shall make provision for the reception and accommodation of children who are removed or kept away from home under Part V.

(2) Every local authority shall receive, and provide accommodation for, children—
(a) in police protection whom they are requested to receive under section 46(3)(f);
(b) whom they are requested to receive under section 38(6) of the Police and Criminal Evidence Act 1984;
(c) who are—
(i) on remand under section 23(1) of the Children and Young Persons Act 1969;
(ia) remanded to accommodation provided by or on behalf of a local authority by virtue of paragraph 4 of Schedule 1 or paragraph 6 of Schedule 8 to the Powers of Criminal Courts (Sentencing) Act 2000 (breach etc of referral orders and reparation orders);
(ii) remanded to accommodation provided by or on behalf of a local authority by virtue of paragraph 21 of Schedule 2 to the Criminal Justice an Immigration Act 2008 (breach etc of youth rehabilitation orders); or
(iii) the subject of a youth rehabilitation order imposing a local authority residence requirement or a youth rehabilitation order with fostering,
and with respect to whom they are the designated authority.

(2A) In subsection (2)(c)(iii), the following terms have the same meanings as in Part 1 of the Criminal Justice and Immigration Act 2008 (see section 7 of that Act)—

"local authority residence requirement";

"youth rehabilitation order";

"youth rehabilitation order with fostering".

(3) Where a child has been—
(a) removed under Part V; or
(b) detained under section 38 of the Police and Criminal Evidence Act 1984,
and he is not being provided with accommodation by a local authority or in a hospital vested in the Secretary of State, the Welsh Ministers or a Primary Care Trust, or otherwise made available pursuant to arrangements made by a Local Health Board or a Primary Care Trust, any reasonable expenses of accommodating him shall be recoverable from the local authority in whose area he is ordinarily resident.

Duties of local authorities in relation to children looked after by them

22 GENERAL DUTY OF LOCAL AUTHORITY IN RELATION TO CHILDREN LOOKED AFTER BY THEM

(1) In this Act, any reference to a child who is looked after by a local authority is a reference to a child who is—
(a) in their care; or
(b) provided with accommodation by the authority in the exercise of any functions (in particular those under this Act) which are social services functions within the meaning of the Local Authority Social Services Act 1970, apart from functions under sections 17, 23B and 24B.

(2) In subsection (1) "accommodation" means accommodation which is provided for a continuous period of more than 24 hours.

(3) It shall be the duty of a local authority looking after any child—
(a) to safeguard and promote his welfare; and
(b) to make such use of services available for children cared for by their own parents as appears to the authority reasonable in his case.

(3A) The duty of a local authority under subsection (3)(a) to safeguard and promote the welfare of a child looked after by them includes in particular a duty to promote the child's educational achievement.

(4) Before making any decision with respect to a child whom they are looking after, or proposing to look after, a local authority shall, so far as is reasonably practicable, ascertain the wishes and feelings of—
(a) the child;
(b) his parents;
(c) any person who is not a parent of his but who has parental responsibility for him; and
(d) any other person whose wishes and feelings the authority consider to be relevant, regarding the matter to be decided.

(5) In making any such decision a local authority shall give due consideration—
(a) having regard to his age and understanding, to such wishes and feelings of the child as they have been able to ascertain;
(b) to such wishes and feelings of any person mentioned in subsection (4)(b) to (d) as they have been able to ascertain; and
(c) to the child's religious persuasion, racial origin and cultural and linguistic background.

(6) If it appears to a local authority that it is necessary, for the purpose of protecting members of the public from serious injury, to exercise their powers with respect to a child whom they are looking after in a manner which may not be consistent with their duties under this section, they may do so.

(7) If the appropriate national authority considers it necessary, for the purpose of protecting members of the public from serious injury, to give directions to a local authority with respect to the exercise of their powers with respect to a child whom they are looking after, the appropriate national authority may give such directions to the local authority.

(8) Where any such directions are given to an authority they shall comply with them even though doing so is inconsistent with their duties under this section.

22A PROVISION OF ACCOMMODATION FOR CHILDREN IN CARE

When a child is in the care of a local authority, it is their duty to provide the child with accommodation.

22B MAINTENANCE OF LOOKED AFTER CHILDREN

It is the duty of a local authority to maintain a child they are looking after in other respects apart from the provision of accommodation.

22C WAYS IN WHICH LOOKED AFTER CHILDREN ARE TO BE ACCOMMODATED AND MAINTAINED

(1) This section applies where a local authority are looking after a child ("C").

(2) The local authority must make arrangements for C to live with a person who falls within subsection (3) (but subject to subsection (4)).

(3) A person ("P") falls within this subsection if—
(a) P is a parent of C;
(b) P is not a parent of C but has parental responsibility for C; or
(c) in a case where C is in the care of the local authority and there was a residence order in force with respect to C immediately before the care order was made, P was a person in whose favour the residence order was made.

(4) Subsection (2) does not require the local authority to make arrangements of the kind mentioned in that subsection if doing so—
(a) would not be consistent with C's welfare; or
(b) would not be reasonably practicable.

(5) If the local authority are unable to make arrangements under subsection (2), they must place C in the placement which is, in their opinion, the most appropriate placement available.

(6) In subsection (5) "placement" means—
(a) placement with an individual who is a relative, friend or other person connected with C and who is also a local authority foster parent;
(b) placement with a local authority foster parent who does not fall within paragraph (a);
(c) placement in a children's home in respect of which a person is registered under Part 2 of the Care Standards Act 2000; or
(d) subject to section 22D, placement in accordance with other arrangements which comply with any regulations made for the purposes of this section.

(7) In determining the most appropriate placement for C, the local authority must, subject to the other provisions of this Part (in particular, to their duties under section 22)—
(a) give preference to a placement falling within paragraph (a) of subsection (6) over placements falling within the other paragraphs of that subsection;
(b) comply, so far as is reasonably practicable in all the circumstances of C's case, with the requirements of subsection (8); and
(c) comply with subsection (9) unless that is not reasonably practicable.

(8) The local authority must ensure that the placement is such that—
(a) it allows C to live near C's home;
(b) it does not disrupt C's education or training;
(c) if C has a sibling for whom the local authority are also providing accommodation, it enables C and the sibling to live together;
(d) if C is disabled, the accommodation provided is suitable to C's particular needs.

(9) The placement must be such that C is provided with accommodation within the local authority's area.

(10) The local authority may determine—
(a) the terms of any arrangements they make under subsection (2) in relation to C (including terms as to payment); and
(b) the terms on which they place C with a local authority foster parent (including terms as to payment but subject to any order made under section 49 of the Children Act 2004).

(11) The appropriate national authority may make regulations for, and in connection with, the purposes of this section.

(12) In this Act "local authority foster parent" means a person who is approved as a local authority foster parent in accordance with regulations made by virtue of paragraph 12F of Schedule 2.]

22D REVIEW OF CHILD'S CASE BEFORE MAKING ALTERNATIVE ARRANGEMENTS FOR ACCOMMODATION

(1) Where a local authority are providing accommodation for a child ("C") other than by arrangements under section 22C(6)(d), they must not make such arrangements for C unless they have decided to do so in consequence of a review of C's case carried out in accordance with regulations made under section 26.

(2) But subsection (1) does not prevent a local authority making arrangements for C under section 22C(6)(d) if they are satisfied that in order to safeguard C's welfare it is necessary—
(a) to make such arrangements; and
(b) to do so as a matter of urgency.

22E CHILDREN'S HOMES PROVIDED BY APPROPRIATE NATIONAL AUTHORITY

Where a local authority place a child they are looking after in a children's home provided, equipped and maintained by an appropriate national authority under section 82(5), they must doso on such terms as that national authority may from time to time determine.

22F REGULATIONS AS TO CHILDREN LOOKED AFTER BY LOCAL AUTHORITIES

Part 2 of Schedule 2 has effect for the purposes of making further provision as to children looked after by local authorities and in particular as to the regulations which may be made under section 22C(11).

22G GENERAL DUTY OF LOCAL AUTHORITY TO SECURE SUFFICIENT ACCOMMODATION FOR LOOKED AFTER CHILDREN

(1) It is the general duty of a local authority to take steps that secure, so far as reasonably practicable, the outcome in subsection (2).

(2) The outcome is that the local authority are able to provide the children mentioned in subsection (3) with accommodation that—
(a) is within the authority's area; and
(b) meets the needs of those children.

(3) The children referred to in subsection (2) are those—
(a) that the local authority are looking after,
(b) in respect of whom the authority are unable to make arrangements under section 22C(2), and
(c) whose circumstances are such that it would be consistent with their welfare for them to be provided with accommodation that is in the authority's area.

(4) In taking steps to secure the outcome in subsection (2), the local authority must have regard to the benefit of having—
(a) a number of accommodation providers in their area that is, in their opinion, sufficient to secure that outcome; and
(b) a range of accommodation in their area capable of meeting different needs that is, in their opinion, sufficient to secure that outcome.

(5) In this section "accommodation providers" means—
local authority foster parents; and children's homes in respect of which a person is registered under Part 2 of the Care Standards Act 2000.

. . .

Secure accommodation

25 USE OF ACCOMMODATION FOR RESTRICTING LIBERTY

(1) Subject to the following provisions of this section, a child who is being looked after by a local authority may not be placed, and, if placed, may not be kept, in accommodation provided for the purpose of restricting liberty ("secure accommodation") unless it appears—
  (a) that—
    (i) he has a history of absconding and is likely to abscond from any other description of accommodation; and
    (ii) if he absconds, he is likely to suffer significant harm; or
  (b) that if he is kept in any other description of accommodation he is likely to injure himself or other persons.

(2) The appropriate national authority may by regulations—
  (a) specify a maximum period—
    (i) beyond which a child may not be kept in secure accommodation without the authority of the court; and
    (ii) for which the court may authorise a child to be kept in secure accommodation;
  (b) empower the court from time to time to authorise a child to be kept in secure accommodation for such further period as the regulations may specify; and
  (c) provide that applications to the court under this section shall be made only by local authorities.

(3) It shall be the duty of a court hearing an application under this section to determine whether any relevant criteria for keeping a child in secure accommodation are satisfied in his case.

(4) If a court determines that any such criteria are satisfied, it shall make an order authorising the child to be kept in secure accommodation and specifying the maximum period for which he may be so kept.

(5) On any adjournment of the hearing of an application under this section, a court may make an interim order permitting the child to be kept during the period of the adjournment in secure accommodation.

(6) No court shall exercise the powers conferred by this section in respect of a child who is not legally represented in that court unless, having been informed of his right to apply for representation funded by the Legal Services Commission as part of the Community Legal Service or Criminal Defence Service and having had the opportunity to do so, he refused or failed to apply.

(7) The appropriate national authority may by regulations provide that—
  (a) this section shall or shall not apply to any description of children specified in the regulations;
  (b) this section shall have effect in relation to children of a description specified in the regulations subject to such modifications as may be so specified;
  (c) such other provisions as may be so specified shall have effect for the purpose of determining whether a child of a description specified in the regulations may be placed or kept in secure accommodation.

(8) The giving of an authorisation under this section shall not prejudice any power of any court in England and Wales or Scotland to give directions relating to the child to whom the authorisation relates.

(9) This section is subject to section 20(8).

. . .

Supplemental

26 REVIEW OF CASES AND INQUIRIES INTO REPRESENTATIONS

(1) The appropriate national authority may make regulations requiring the case of each child who is being looked after by a local authority to be reviewed in accordance with the provisions of the regulations.

(2) The regulations may, in particular, make provision—
- (a) as to the manner in which each case is to be reviewed;
- (b) as to the considerations to which the local authority are to have regard in reviewing each case;
- (c) as to the time when each case is first to be reviewed and the frequency of subsequent reviews;
- (d) requiring the authority, before conducting any review, to seek the views of—
  - (i) the child;
  - (ii) his parents;
  - (iii) any person who is not a parent of his but who has parental responsibility for him; and
  - (iv) any other person whose views the authority consider to be relevant, including, in particular, the views of those persons in relation to any particular matter which is to be considered in the course of the review;
- (e) requiring the authority, in the case of a child who is in their care—
  - (i) to keep the section 31A plan for the child under review and, if they are of the opinion that some change is required, to revise the plan, or make a new plan, accordingly,
  - (ii) to consider, whether an application should be made to discharge the care order;
- (f) requiring the authority, in the case of a child in accommodation provided by the authority—
  - (i) if there is no plan for the future care of the child, to prepare one,
  - (ii) if there is such a plan for the child, to keep it under review and, if they are of the opinion that some change is required, to revise the plan or make a new plan, accordingly,
  - (iii) to consider, whether the accommodation accords with the requirements of this Part;
- (g) requiring the authority to inform the child, so far as is reasonably practicable, of any steps he may take under this Act;
- (h) requiring the authority to make arrangements, including arrangements with such other bodies providing services as it considers appropriate, to implement any decision which they propose to make in the course, or as a result, of the review;
  - (i) requiring the authority to notify details of the result of the review and of any decision taken by them in consequence of the review to—
  - (i) the child;
  - (ii) his parents;
  - (iii) any person who is not a parent of his but who has parental responsibility for him; and
  - (iv) any other person whom they consider ought to be notified;

(j) requiring the authority to monitor the arrangements which they have made with a view to ensuring that they comply with the regulations;

(3) Every local authority shall establish a procedure for considering any representations (including any complaint) made to them by—

(a) any child who is being looked after by them or who is not being looked after by them but is in need;
(b) a parent of his;
(c) any person who is not a parent of his but who has parental responsibility for him;
(d) any local authority foster parent;
(e) such other person as the authority consider has a sufficient interest in the child's welfare to warrant his representations being considered by them,

about the discharge by the authority of any of their qualifying functions in relation to the child.

(3A) The following are qualifying functions for the purposes of subsection (3)—

(a) functions under this Part,
(b) such functions under Part 4 or 5 as are specified by the appropriate national authority in regulations.

(3B) The duty under subsection (3) extends to representations (including complaints) made to the authority by—

(a) any person mentioned in section 3(1) of the Adoption and Children Act 2002 (persons for whose needs provision is made by the Adoption Service) and any other person to whom arrangements for the provision of adoption support services (within the meaning of that Act) extend,
(b) such other person as the authority consider has sufficient interest in a child who is or may be adopted to warrant his representations being considered by them, about the discharge by the authority of such functions under the Adoption and Children Act 2002 as are specified by the appropriate national authority in regulations.

(3C) The duty under subsection (3) extends to any representations (including complaints) which are made to the authority by—

(a) a child with respect to whom a special guardianship order is in force,
(b) a special guardian or a parent of such a child,
(c) any other person the authority consider has a sufficient interest in the welfare of such a child to warrant his representations being considered by them, or
(d) any person who has applied for an assessment under section 14F(3) or (4),

about the discharge by the authority of such functions under section 14F as may be specified by the appropriate national authority in regulations.

(4) The procedure shall ensure that at least one person who is not a member or officer of the authority takes part in—

(a) the consideration; and
(b) any discussions which are held by the authority about the action (if any) to be taken in relation to the child in the light of the consideration,

but this subsection is subject to subsection (5A).

(4A) Regulations may be made by the appropriate national authority imposing time limits on the making of representations under this section.

(5) In carrying out any consideration of representations under this section a local authority shall comply with any regulations made by the appropriate national authority for the purpose of regulating the procedure to be followed.

(5A) Regulations under subsection (5) may provide that subsection (4) does not apply in relation to any consideration or discussion which takes place as part of a procedure for which provision is made by the regulations for the purpose of resolving informally the matters raised in the representations.

(6) The appropriate national authority may make regulations requiring local authorities to monitor the arrangements that they have made with a view to ensuring that they comply with any regulations made for the purposes of subsection (5).

(7) Where any representation has been considered under the procedure established by a local authority under this section, the authority shall—
(a) have due regard to the findings of those considering the representation; and
(b) take such steps as are reasonably practicable to notify (in writing)—
(i) the person making the representation;
(ii) the child (if the authority consider that he has sufficient understanding); and
(iii) such other persons (if any) as appear to the authority to be likely to be affected,
of the authority's decision in the matter and their reasons for taking that decision and of any action which they have taken, or propose to take.

(8) Every local authority shall give such publicity to their procedure for considering representations under this section as they consider appropriate.

26ZB REPRESENTATIONS: FURTHER CONSIDERATION (WALES)

(1) The Welsh Ministers may by regulations make provision for the further consideration of representations which have been considered by a local authority in Wales under section 24D or section 26.

(2) The regulations may in particular make provision—
(a) for the further consideration of a representation by an independent panel established under the regulations;
(b) about the procedure to be followed on the further consideration of a representation;
(c) for the making of recommendations about the action to be taken as the result of a representation;
(d) about the making of reports about a representation;
(e) about the action to be taken by the local authority concerned as a result of the further consideration of a representation;
(f) for a representation to be referred back to the local authority concerned for reconsideration by the authority.

(3) The regulations may require—
(a) the making of a payment, in relation to the further consideration of a representation under this section, by any local authority in respect of whose functions the representation is made;
(b) any such payment to be—
(i) made to such person or body as may be specified in the regulations;
(ii) of such amount as may be specified in, or calculated or determined under, the regulations; and
(c) for an independent panel to review the amount chargeable under paragraph (a) in any particular case and, if the panel thinks fit, to substitute a lesser amount.

(4) The regulations may also—
(a) provide for different parts or aspects of a representation to be treated differently;
(b) require the production of information or documents in order to enable a representation to be properly considered;

(c) authorise the disclosure of information or documents relevant to a representation to a person or body who is further considering a representation under the regulations;

and any such disclosure may be authorised notwithstanding any rule of common law that would otherwise prohibit or restrict the disclosure.

26A ADVOCACY SERVICES

(1) Every local authority shall make arrangements for the provision of assistance to—
(a) persons who make or intend to make representations under section 24D; and
(b) children who make or intend to make representations under section 26.

(2) The assistance provided under the arrangements shall include assistance by way of representation.

(2A) The duty under subsection (1) includes a duty to make arrangements for the provision of assistance where representations under section 24D or 26 are further considered under section 26ZB.

(3) The arrangements—
(a) shall secure that a person may not provide assistance if he is a person who is prevented from doing so by regulations made by the appropriate national authority; and
(b) shall comply with any other provision made by the regulations in relation to the arrangements.

(4) The appropriate national authority may make regulations requiring local authorities to monitor the steps that they have taken with a view to ensuring that they comply with regulations made for the purposes of subsection (3).

(5) Every local authority shall give such publicity to their arrangements for the provision of assistance under this section as they consider appropriate.

. . .

30A MEANING OF APPROPRIATE NATIONAL AUTHORITY

In this Part "the appropriate national authority" means—
(a) in relation to England, the Secretary of State; and
(b) in relation to Wales, the Welsh Ministers.

Part IV CARE AND SUPERVISION

General

31 CARE AND SUPERVISION ORDERS

(1) On the application of any local authority or authorised person, the court may make an order—
(a) placing the child with respect to whom the application is made in the care of a designated local authority; or
(b) putting him under the supervision of a designated local authority.

(2) A court may only make a care order or supervision order if it is satisfied—
(a) that the child concerned is suffering, or is likely to suffer, significant harm; and
(b) that the harm, or likelihood of harm, is attributable to—
(i) the care given to the child, or likely to be given to him if the order were not made, not being what it would be reasonable to expect a parent to give to him; or
(ii) the child's being beyond parental control.

(3) No care order or supervision order may be made with respect to a child who has reached the age of seventeen (or sixteen, in the case of a child who is married).

(3A) No care order may be made with respect to a child until the court has considered a section 31A plan.

(4) An application under this section may be made on its own or in any other family proceedings.

(5) The court may—
(a) on an application for a care order, make a supervision order;
(b) on an application for a supervision order, make a care order.

(6) Where an authorised person proposes to make an application under this section he shall—
(a) if it is reasonably practicable to do so; and
(b) before making the application,
consult the local authority appearing to him to be the authority in whose area the child concerned is ordinarily resident.

(7) An application made by an authorised person shall not be entertained by the court if, at the time when it is made, the child concerned is—
(a) the subject of an earlier application for a care order, or supervision order, which has not been disposed of; or
(b) subject to—
(i) a care order or supervision order;
(ii) a youth rehabilitation order within the meaning of Part 1 of the Criminal Justice and Immigration Act 2008; . . . .

(8) The local authority designated in a care order must be—
(a) the authority within whose area the child is ordinarily resident; or
(b) where the child does not reside in the area of a local authority, the authority within whose area any circumstances arose in consequence of which the order is being made.

(9) In this section—

"authorised person" means—
(a) the National Society for the Prevention of Cruelty to Children and any of its officers; and
(b) any person authorised by order of the Secretary of State to bring proceedings under this section and any officer of a body which is so authorised;

"harm" means ill-treatment or the impairment of health or development including, for example, impairment suffered from seeing or hearing the ill-treatment of another;

"development" means physical, intellectual, emotional, social or behavioural development;

"health" means physical or mental health; and

"ill-treatment" includes sexual abuse and forms of ill-treatment which are not physical.

(10) Where the question of whether harm suffered by a child is significant turns on the child's health or development, his health or development shall be compared with that which could reasonably be expected of a similar child.

(11) In this Act—

"a care order" means (subject to section 105(1)) an order under subsection (1)(a) and (except where express provision to the contrary is made) includes an interim care order made under section 38; and "a supervision order" means an order under subsection (1)(b) and (except where express provision to the contrary is made) includes an interim supervision order made under section 38.

31A CARE ORDERS: CARE PLANS

(1) Where an application is made on which a care order might be made with respect to a child, the appropriate local authority must, within such time as the court may direct, prepare a plan ("a care plan") for the future care of the child.

(2) While the application is pending, the authority must keep any care plan prepared by them under review and, if they are of the opinion some change is required, revise the plan, or make a new plan, accordingly.

(3) A care plan must give any prescribed information and do so in the prescribed manner.

(4) For the purposes of this section, the appropriate local authority, in relation to a child in respect of whom a care order might be made, is the local authority proposed to be designated in the order.

(5) In section 31(3A) and this section, references to a care order do not include an interim care order.

(6) A plan prepared, or treated as prepared, under this section is referred to in this Act as a "section 31A plan".

32 PERIOD WITHIN WHICH APPLICATION FOR ORDER UNDER THIS PART MUST BE DISPOSED OF

(1) A court hearing an application for an order under this Part shall (in the light of any rules made by virtue of subsection (2))—
   (a) draw up a timetable with a view to disposing of the application without delay; and
   (b) give such directions as it considers appropriate for the purpose of ensuring, so far as is reasonably practicable, that that timetable is adhered to.

(2) Rules of court may—
   (a) specify periods within which specified steps must be taken in relation to such proceedings; and
   (b) make other provisions with respect to such proceedings for the purpose of ensuring, so far as is reasonably practicable, that they are disposed of without delay.

Care orders

33 EFFECT OF CARE ORDER

(1) Where a care order is made with respect to a child it shall be the duty of the local authority designated by the order to receive the child into their care and to keep him in their care while the order remains in force.

(2) Where—
   (a) a care order has been made with respect to a child on the application of an authorised person; but
   (b) the local authority designated by the order was not informed that that person proposed to make the application,

the child may be kept in the care of that person until received into the care of the authority.

(3) While a care order is in force with respect to a child, the local authority designated by the order shall—
(a) have parental responsibility for the child; and
(b) have the power (subject to the following provisions of this section) to determine the extent to which—
(i) a parent, guardian or special guardian of the child; or
(ii) a person who by virtue of section 4A has parental responsibility for the child,
may meet his parental responsibility for him.

(4) The authority may not exercise the power in subsection (3)(b) unless they are satisfied that it is necessary to do so in order to safeguard or promote the child's welfare.

(5) Nothing in subsection (3)(b) shall prevent a person mentioned in that provision who has care of the child from doing what is reasonable in all the circumstances of the case for the purpose of safeguarding or promoting his welfare.

(6) While a care order is in force with respect to a child, the local authority designated by the order shall not—
(a) cause the child to be brought up in any religious persuasion other than that in which he would have been brought up if the order had not been made; or
(b) have the right—
(ii) to agree or refuse to agree to the making of an adoption order, or an order under section 84 of the Adoption and Children Act 2002, with respect to the child; or
(iii) to appoint a guardian for the child.

(7) While a care order is in force with respect to a child, no person may—
(a) cause the child to be known by a new surname; or
(b) remove him from the United Kingdom,
without either the written consent of every person who has parental responsibility for the child or the leave of the court.

(8) Subsection (7)(b) does not—
(a) prevent the removal of such a child, for a period of less than one month, by the authority in whose care he is; or
(b) apply to arrangements for such a child to live outside England and Wales (which are governed by paragraph 19 of Schedule 2).

(9) The power in subsection (3)(b) is subject (in addition to being subject to the provisions of this section) to any right, duty, power, responsibility or authority which a person mentioned in that provision has in relation to the child and his property by virtue of any other enactment.

34 PARENTAL CONTACT ETC WITH CHILDREN IN CARE

(1) Where a child is in the care of a local authority, the authority shall (subject to the provisions of this section) allow the child reasonable contact with—
(a) his parents;
(b) any guardian or special guardian of his;
(ba) any person who by virtue of section 4A has parental responsibility for him;
(c) where there was a residence order in force with respect to the child immediately before the care order was made, the person in whose favour the order was made; and
(d) where, immediately before the care order was made a person had care of the child by virtue of an order made in the exercise of the High Court's inherent jurisdiction with respect to children, that person.

(2) On an application made by the authority or the child, the court may make such order as it considers appropriate with respect to the contact which is to be allowed between the child and any named person.

(3) On an application made by—
(a) any person mentioned in paragraphs (a) to (d) of subsection (1); or
(b) any person who has obtained the leave of the court to make the application,
the court may make such order as it considers appropriate with respect to the contact which is to be allowed between the child and that person.

(4) On an application made by the authority or the child, the court may make an order authorising the authority to refuse to allow contact between the child and any person who is mentioned in paragraphs (a) to (d) of subsection (1) and named in the order.

(5) When making a care order with respect to a child, or in any family proceedings in connection with a child who is in the care of a local authority, the court may make an order under this section, even though no application for such an order has been made with respect to the child, if it considers that the order should be made.

(6) An authority may refuse to allow the contact that would otherwise be required by virtue of subsection (1) or an order under this section if—
(a) they are satisfied that it is necessary to do so in order to safeguard or promote the child's welfare; and
(b) the refusal—
(i) is decided upon as a matter of urgency; and
(ii) does not last for more than seven days.

(7) An order under this section may impose such conditions as the court considers appropriate.

(8) The Secretary of State may by regulations make provision as to—
(a) the steps to be taken by a local authority who have exercised their powers under subsection (6);
(b) the circumstances in which, and conditions subject to which, the terms of any order under this section may be departed from by agreement between the local authority and the person in relation to whom the order is made;
(c) notification by a local authority of any variation or suspension of arrangements made (otherwise than under an order under this section) with a view to affording any person contact with a child to whom this section applies.

(9) The court may vary or discharge any order made under this section on the application of the authority, the child concerned or the person named in the order.

(10) An order under this section may be made either at the same time as the care order itself or later.

(11) Before making a care order with respect to any child the court shall—
(a) consider the arrangements which the authority have made, or propose to make, for affording any person contact with a child to whom this section applies; and
(b) invite the parties to the proceedings to comment on those arrangements.

Supervision orders

35 SUPERVISION ORDERS

(1) While a supervision order is in force it shall be the duty of the supervisor—
(a) to advise, assist and befriend the supervised child;

(b) to take such steps as are reasonably necessary to give effect to the order; and
(c) where—
(i) the order is not wholly complied with; or
(ii) the supervisor considers that the order may no longer be necessary,
to consider whether or not to apply to the court for its variation or discharge.

(2) Parts I and II of Schedule 3 make further provision with respect to supervision orders.

36 EDUCATION SUPERVISION ORDERS

(1) On the application of any local education authority, the court may make an order putting the child with respect to whom the application is made under the supervision of a designated local education authority.

(2) In this Act "an education supervision order" means an order under subsection (1).

(3) A court may only make an education supervision order if it is satisfied that the child concerned is of compulsory school age and is not being properly educated.

(4) For the purposes of this section, a child is being properly educated only if he is receiving efficient full-time education suitable to his age, ability and aptitude and any special educational needs he may have.

(5) Where a child is—
(a) the subject of a school attendance order which is in force under section 437 of the Education Act 1996 and which has not been complied with; or
(b) is not attending regularly within the meaning of section 444 of that Act—
(i) a school at which he is a registered pupil,
(ii) any place at which education is provided for him in the circumstances mentioned in subsection (1) of section 444ZA of that Act, or
(iii) any place which he is required to attend in the circumstances mentioned in subsection (2) of that section,
then, unless it is proved that he is being properly educated, it shall be assumed that he is not.

(6) An education supervision order may not be made with respect to a child who is in the care of a local authority.

(7) The local education authority designated in an education supervision order must be—
(a) the authority within whose area the child concerned is living or will live; or
(b) where—
(i) the child is a registered pupil at a school; and
(ii) the authority mentioned in paragraph (a) and the authority within whose area the school is situated agree,
the latter authority.

(8) Where a local education authority propose to make an application for an education supervision order they shall, before making the application, consult the appropriate local authority.

(9) The appropriate local authority is—
(a) in the case of a child who is being provided with accommodation by, or on behalf of, a local authority, that authority; and
(b) in any other case, the local authority within whose area the child concerned lives, or will live.

(10) Part III of Schedule 3 makes further provision with respect to education supervision orders.

Powers of court

37 POWERS OF COURT IN CERTAIN FAMILY PROCEEDINGS

(1) Where, in any family proceedings in which a question arises with respect to the welfare of any child, it appears to the court that it may be appropriate for a care or supervision order to be made with respect to him, the court may direct the appropriate authority to undertake an investigation of the child's circumstances.

(2) Where the court gives a direction under this section the local authority concerned shall, when undertaking the investigation, consider whether they should—
(a) apply for a care order or for a supervision order with respect to the child;
(b) provide services or assistance for the child or his family; or
(c) take any other action with respect to the child.

(3) Where a local authority undertake an investigation under this section, and decide not to apply for a care order or supervision order with respect to the child concerned, they shall inform the court of—
(a) their reasons for so deciding;
(b) any service or assistance which they have provided, or intend to provide, for the child and his family; and
(c) any other action which they have taken, or propose to take, with respect to the child.

(4) The information shall be given to the court before the end of the period of eight weeks beginning with the date of the direction, unless the court otherwise directs.

(5) The local authority named in a direction under subsection (1) must be—
(a) the authority in whose area the child is ordinarily resident; or
(b) where the child is not ordinarily resident in the area of a local authority, the authority within whose area any circumstances arose in consequence of which the direction is being given.

(6) If, on the conclusion of any investigation or review under this section, the authority decide not to apply for a care order or supervision order with respect to the child—
(a) they shall consider whether it would be appropriate to review the case at a later date; and
(b) if they decide that it would be, they shall determine the date on which that review is to begin.

38 INTERIM ORDERS

(1) Where—
(a) in any proceedings on an application for a care order or supervision order, the proceedings are adjourned; or
(b) the court gives a direction under section 37(1),
the court may make an interim care order or an interim supervision order with respect to the child concerned.

(2) A court shall not make an interim care order or interim supervision order under this section unless it is satisfied that there are reasonable grounds for believing that the circumstances with respect to the child are as mentioned in section 31(2).

(3) Where, in any proceedings on an application for a care order or supervision order, a court makes a residence order with respect to the child concerned, it shall also make an interim

supervision order with respect to him unless satisfied that his welfare will be satisfactorily safeguarded without an interim order being made.

(4) An interim order made under or by virtue of this section shall have effect for such period as may be specified in the order, but shall in any event cease to have effect on whichever of the following events first occurs—
 (a) the expiry of the period of eight weeks beginning with the date on which the order is made;
 (b) if the order is the second or subsequent such order made with respect to the same child in the same proceedings, the expiry of the relevant period;
 (c) in a case which falls within subsection (1)(a), the disposal of the application;
 (d) in a case which falls within subsection (1)(b), the disposal of an application for a care order or supervision order made by the authority with respect to the child;
 (e) in a case which falls within subsection (1)(b) and in which—
  (i) the court has given a direction under section 37(4), but
  (ii) no application for a care order or supervision order has been made with respect to the child, the expiry of the period fixed by that direction.

(5) In subsection (4)(b) "the relevant period" means—
 (a) the period of four weeks beginning with the date on which the order in question is made; or
 (b) the period of eight weeks beginning with the date on which the first order was made if that period ends later than the period mentioned in paragraph (a).

(6) Where the court makes an interim care order, or interim supervision order, it may give such directions (if any) as it considers appropriate with regard to the medical or psychiatric examination or other assessment of the child; but if the child is of sufficient understanding to make an informed decision he may refuse to submit to the examination or other assessment.

(7) A direction under subsection (6) may be to the effect that there is to be—
 (a) no such examination or assessment; or
 (b) no such examination or assessment unless the court directs otherwise.

(8) A direction under subsection (6) may be—
 (a) given when the interim order is made or at any time while it is in force; and
 (b) varied at any time on the application of any person falling within any class of person prescribed by rules of court for the purposes of this subsection.

(9) Paragraphs 4 and 5 of Schedule 3 shall not apply in relation to an interim supervision order.

(10) Where a court makes an order under or by virtue of this section it shall, in determining the period for which the order is to be in force, consider whether any party who was, or might have been, opposed to the making of the order was in a position to argue his case against the order in full.

38A POWER TO INCLUDE EXCLUSION REQUIREMENT IN INTERIM CARE ORDER

(1) Where—
 (a) on being satisfied that there are reasonable grounds for believing that the circumstances with respect to a child are as mentioned in section 31(2)(a) and (b)(i), the court makes an interim care order with respect to a child, and
 (b) the conditions mentioned in subsection (2) are satisfied,
the court may include an exclusion requirement in the interim care order.

(2) The conditions are—
(a) that there is reasonable cause to believe that, if a person ("the relevant person") is excluded from a dwelling-house in which the child lives, the child will cease to suffer, or cease to be likely to suffer, significant harm, and
(b) that another person living in the dwelling-house (whether a parent of the child or some other person)—
(i) is able and willing to give to the child the care which it would be reasonable to expect a parent to give him, and
(ii) consents to the inclusion of the exclusion requirement.

(3) For the purposes of this section an exclusion requirement is any one or more of the following—
(a) a provision requiring the relevant person to leave a dwelling-house in which he is living with the child,
(b) a provision prohibiting the relevant person from entering a dwelling-house in which the child lives, and
(c) a provision excluding the relevant person from a defined area in which a dwellinghouse in which the child lives is situated.

(4) The court may provide that the exclusion requirement is to have effect for a shorter period than the other provisions of the interim care order.

(5) Where the court makes an interim care order containing an exclusion requirement, the court may attach a power of arrest to the exclusion requirement.

(6) Where the court attaches a power of arrest to an exclusion requirement of an interim care order, it may provide that the power of arrest is to have effect for a shorter period than the exclusion requirement.

(7) Any period specified for the purposes of subsection (4) or (6) may be extended by the court (on one or more occasions) on an application to vary or discharge the interim care order.

(8) Where a power of arrest is attached to an exclusion requirement of an interim care order by virtue of subsection (5), a constable may arrest without warrant any person whom he has reasonable cause to believe to be in breach of the requirement.

(9) Sections 47(7), (11) and (12) and 48 of, and Schedule 5 to, the Family Law Act 1996 shall have effect in relation to a person arrested under subsection (8) of this section as they have effect in relation to a person arrested under section 47(6) of that Act.

(10) If, while an interim care order containing an exclusion requirement is in force, the local authority have removed the child from the dwelling-house from which the relevant person is excluded to other accommodation for a continuous period of more than 24 hours, the interim care order shall cease to have effect in so far as it imposes the exclusion requirement.

38B UNDERTAKINGS RELATING TO INTERIM CARE ORDERS

(1) In any case where the court has power to include an exclusion requirement in an interim care order, the court may accept an undertaking from the relevant person.

(2) No power of arrest may be attached to any undertaking given under subsection (1).

(3) An undertaking given to a court under subsection (1)—
(a) shall be enforceable as if it were an order of the court, and
(b) shall cease to have effect if, while it is in force, the local authority have removed the child from the dwelling house from which the relevant person is excluded to other accommodation for a continuous period of more than 24 hours.

(4) This section has effect without prejudice to the powers of the High Court and county court apart from this section.

(5) In this section "exclusion requirement" and "relevant person" have the same meaning as in section 38A.

39 DISCHARGE AND VARIATION ETC OF CARE ORDERS AND SUPERVISION ORDERS

(1) A care order may be discharged by the court on the application of—
  (a) any person who has parental responsibility for the child;
  (b) the child himself; or
  (c) the local authority designated by the order.

(2) A supervision order may be varied or discharged by the court on the application of—
  (a) any person who has parental responsibility for the child;
  (b) the child himself; or
  (c) the supervisor.

(3) On the application of a person who is not entitled to apply for the order to be discharged, but who is a person with whom the child is living, a supervision order may be varied by the court in so far as it imposes a requirement which affects that person.

(3A) On the application of a person who is not entitled to apply for the order to be discharged, but who is a person to whom an exclusion requirement contained in the order applies, an interim care order may be varied or discharged by the court in so far as it imposes the exclusion requirement.

(3B) Where a power of arrest has been attached to an exclusion requirement of an interim care order, the court may, on the application of any person entitled to apply for the discharge of the order so far as it imposes the exclusion requirement, vary or discharge the order in so far as it confers a power of arrest (whether or not any application has been made to vary or discharge any other provision of the order).

(4) Where a care order is in force with respect to a child the court may, on the application of any person entitled to apply for the order to be discharged, substitute a supervision order for the care order.

(5) When a court is considering whether to substitute one order for another under subsection (4) any provision of this Act which would otherwise require section 31(2) to be satisfied at the time when the proposed order is substituted or made shall be disregarded.

. . .

Representation of child

41 REPRESENTATION OF CHILD AND OF HIS INTERESTS IN CERTAIN PROCEEDINGS

(1) For the purpose of any specified proceedings, the court shall appoint an officer of the Service or a Welsh family proceedings officer for the child concerned unless satisfied that it is not necessary to do so in order to safeguard his interests.

(2) The officer of the Service or Welsh family proceedings officer shall—
  (a) be appointed in accordance with the rules of court; and
  (b) be under a duty to safeguard the interests of the child in the manner prescribed by such rules.

(3) Where—
(a) the child concerned is not represented by a solicitor; and
(b) any of the conditions mentioned in subsection (4) is satisfied,
the court may appoint a solicitor to represent him.

(4) The conditions are that—
(a) no officer of the Service or Welsh family proceedings officer has been appointed for the child;
(b) the child has sufficient understanding to instruct a solicitor and wishes to do so;
(c) it appears to the court that it would be in the child's best interests for him to be represented by a solicitor.

(5) Any solicitor appointed under or by virtue of this section shall be appointed, and shall represent the child, in accordance with rules of court.

(6) In this section "specified proceedings" means any proceedings—
(a) on an application for a care order or supervision order;
(b) in which the court has given a direction under section 37(1) and has made, or is considering whether to make, an interim care order;
(c) on an application for the discharge of a care order or the variation or discharge of a supervision order;
(d) on an application under section 39(4);
(e) in which the court is considering whether to make a residence order with respect to a child who is the subject of a care order;
(f) with respect to contact between a child who is the subject of a care order and any other person;
(g) under Part V;
(h) on an appeal against—
(i) the making of, or refusal to make, a care order, supervision order or any order under section 34;
(ii) the making of, or refusal to make, a residence order with respect to a child who is the subject of a care order; or
(iii) the variation or discharge, or refusal of an application to vary or discharge, an order of a kind mentioned in sub-paragraph (i) or (ii);
(iv) the refusal of an application under section 39(4); or
(v) the making of, or refusal to make, an order under Part V; or
(hh) on an application for the making or revocation of a placement order (within the meaning of section 21 of the Adoption and Children Act 2002);
(i) which are specified for the time being, for the purposes of this section, by rules of court.

(6A) The proceedings which may be specified under subsection (6)(i) include (for example) proceedings for the making, varying or discharging of a section 8 order.

(10) Rules of court may make provision as to—
(a) the assistance which any officer of the Service or Welsh family proceedings officer may be required by the court to give to it;
(b) the consideration to be given by any officer of the Service or Welsh family proceedings officer, where an order of a specified kind has been made in the proceedings in question, as to whether to apply for the variation or discharge of the order;
(c) the participation of officers of the Service or Welsh family proceedings officers in reviews, of a kind specified in the rules, which are conducted by the court.

(11) Regardless of any enactment or rule of law which would otherwise prevent it from doing so, the court may take account of—

(a) any statement contained in a report made by an officer of the Service or a Welsh family proceedings officer who is appointed under this section for the purpose of the proceedings in question; and
(b) any evidence given in respect of the matters referred to in the report, in so far as the statement or evidence is, in the opinion of the court, relevant to the question which the court is considering.

42 RIGHT OF OFFICER OF THE SERVICE TO HAVE ACCESS TO LOCAL AUTHORITY RECORDS

(1) Where an officer of the Service or Welsh family proceedings officer has been appointed under section 41 he shall have the right at all reasonable times to examine and take copies of—
(a) any records of, or held by, a local authority or an authorised person which were compiled in connection with the making, or proposed making, by any person of any application under this Act with respect to the child concerned;
(b) any records of, or held by, a local authority which were compiled in connection with any functions which are social services functions within the meaning of the Local Authority Social Services Act 1970, so far as those records relate to that child; or
(c) any records of, or held by, an authorised person which were compiled in connection with the activities of that person, so far as those records relate to that child.

(2) Where an officer of the Service or Welsh family proceedings officer takes a copy of any record which he is entitled to examine under this section, that copy or any part of it shall be admissible as evidence of any matter referred to in any—
(a) report which he makes to the court in the proceedings in question; or
(b) evidence which he gives in those proceedings.

(3) Subsection (2) has effect regardless of any enactment or rule of law which would otherwise prevent the record in question being admissible in evidence.

(4) In this section "authorised person" has the same meaning as in section 31.

Part V PROTECTION OF CHILDREN

43 CHILD ASSESSMENT ORDERS

(1) On the application of a local authority or authorised person for an order to be made under this section with respect to a child, the court may make the order if, but only if, it is satisfied that—
(a) the applicant has reasonable cause to suspect that the child is suffering, or is likely to suffer, significant harm;
(b) an assessment of the state of the child's health or development, or of the way in which he has been treated, is required to enable the applicant to determine whether or not the child is suffering, or is likely to suffer, significant harm; and
(c) it is unlikely that such an assessment will be made, or be satisfactory, in the absence of an order under this section.

(2) In this Act "a child assessment order" means an order under this section.

(3) A court may treat an application under this section as an application for an emergency protection order.

(4) No court shall make a child assessment order if it is satisfied—
(a) that there are grounds for making an emergency protection order with respect to the child; and
(b) that it ought to make such an order rather than a child assessment order.

(5) A child assessment order shall—
(a) specify the date by which the assessment is to begin; and
(b) have effect for such period, not exceeding 7 days beginning with that date, as may be specified in the order.

(6) Where a child assessment order is in force with respect to a child it shall be the duty of any person who is in a position to produce the child—
(a) to produce him to such person as may be named in the order; and
(b) to comply with such directions relating to the assessment of the child as the court thinks fit to specify in the order.

(7) A child assessment order authorises any person carrying out the assessment, or any part of the assessment, to do so in accordance with the terms of the order.

(8) Regardless of subsection (7), if the child is of sufficient understanding to make an informed decision he may refuse to submit to a medical or psychiatric examination or other assessment.

(9) The child may only be kept away from home—
(a) in accordance with directions specified in the order;
(b) if it is necessary for the purposes of the assessment; and
(c) for such period or periods as may be specified in the order.

(10) Where the child is to be kept away from home, the order shall contain such directions as the court thinks fit with regard to the contact that he must be allowed to have with other persons while away from home.

(11) Any person making an application for a child assessment order shall take such steps as are reasonably practicable to ensure that notice of the application is given to—
(a) the child's parents;
(b) any person who is not a parent of his but who has parental responsibility for him;
(c) any other person caring for the child;
(d) any person in whose favour a contact order is in force with respect to the child;
(e) any person who is allowed to have contact with the child by virtue of an order under section 34; and
(f) the child, before the hearing of the application.

(12) Rules of court may make provision as to the circumstances in which—
(a) any of the persons mentioned in subsection (11); or
(b) such other person as may be specified in the rules, may apply to the court for a child assessment order to be varied or discharged.

(13) In this section "authorised person" means a person who is an authorised person for the purposes of section 31.

44 ORDERS FOR EMERGENCY PROTECTION OF CHILDREN

(1) Where any person ("the applicant") applies to the court for an order to be made under this section with respect to a child, the court may make the order if, but only if, it is satisfied that—
(a) there is reasonable cause to believe that the child is likely to suffer significant harm if—
(i) he is not removed to accommodation provided by or on behalf of the applicant; or
(ii) he does not remain in the place in which he is then being accommodated;
(b) in the case of an application made by a local authority—
(i) enquiries are being made with respect to the child under section 47(1)(b); and

(ii) those enquiries are being frustrated by access to the child being unreasonably refused to a person authorised to seek access and that the applicant has reasonable cause to believe that access to the child is required as a matter of urgency; or

(c) in the case of an application made by an authorised person—

(i) the applicant has reasonable cause to suspect that a child is suffering, or is likely to suffer, significant harm;

(ii) the applicant is making enquiries with respect to the child's welfare; and

(iii) those enquiries are being frustrated by access to the child being unreasonably refused to a person authorised to seek access and the applicant has reasonable cause to believe that access to the child is required as a matter of urgency.

(2) In this section—

(a) "authorised person" means a person who is an authorised person for the purposes of section 31; and

(b) "a person authorised to seek access" means—

(i) in the case of an application by a local authority, an officer of the local authority or a person authorised by the authority to act on their behalf in connection with the enquiries; or

(ii) in the case of an application by an authorised person, that person.

(3) Any person—

(a) seeking access to a child in connection with enquiries of a kind mentioned in subsection (1); and

(b) purporting to be a person authorised to do so, shall, on being asked to do so, produce some duly authenticated document as evidence that he is such a person.

(4) While an order under this section ("an emergency protection order") is in force it—

(a) operates as a direction to any person who is in a position to do so to comply with any request to produce the child to the applicant;

(b) authorises—

(i) the removal of the child at any time to accommodation provided by or on behalf of the applicant and his being kept there; or

(ii) the prevention of the child's removal from any hospital, or other place, in which he was being accommodated immediately before the making of the order; and

(c) gives the applicant parental responsibility for the child.

(5) Where an emergency protection order is in force with respect to a child, the applicant—

(a) shall only exercise the power given by virtue of subsection (4)(b) in order to safeguard the welfare of the child;

(b) shall take, and shall only take, such action in meeting his parental responsibility for the child as is reasonably required to safeguard or promote the welfare of the child (having regard in particular to the duration of the order); and

(c) shall comply with the requirements of any regulations made by the Secretary of State for the purposes of this subsection.

(6) Where the court makes an emergency protection order, it may give such directions (if any) as it considers appropriate with respect to—

(a) the contact which is, or is not, to be allowed between the child and any named person;

(b) the medical or psychiatric examination or other assessment of the child.

(7) Where any direction is given under subsection (6)(b), the child may, if he is of sufficient understanding to make an informed decision, refuse to submit to the examination or other assessment.

(8) A direction under subsection (6)(a) may impose conditions and one under subsection (6)(b) may be to the effect that there is to be—
(a) no such examination or assessment; or
(b) no such examination or assessment unless the court directs otherwise.

(9) A direction under subsection (6) may be—
(a) given when the emergency protection order is made or at any time while it is in force; and
(b) varied at any time on the application of any person falling within any class of person prescribed by rules of court for the purposes of this subsection.

(10) Where an emergency protection order is in force with respect to a child and—
(a) the applicant has exercised the power given by subsection (4)(b)(i) but it appears to him that it is safe for the child to be returned; or
(b) the applicant has exercised the power given by subsection (4)(b)(ii) but it appears to him that it is safe for the child to be allowed to be removed from the place in question,

he shall return the child or (as the case may be) allow him to be removed.

(11) Where he is required by subsection (10) to return the child the applicant shall—
(a) return him to the care of the person from whose care he was removed; or
(b) if that is not reasonably practicable, return him to the care of—
(i) a parent of his;
(ii) any person who is not a parent of his but who has parental responsibility for him; or
(iii) such other person as the applicant (with the agreement of the court) considers appropriate.

(12) Where the applicant has been required by subsection (10) to return the child, or to allow him to be removed, he may again exercise his powers with respect to the child (at any time while the emergency protection order remains in force) if it appears to him that a change in the circumstances of the case makes it necessary for him to do so.

(13) Where an emergency protection order has been made with respect to a child, the applicant shall, subject to any direction given under subsection (6), allow the child reasonable contact with—
(a) his parents;
(b) any person who is not a parent of his but who has parental responsibility for him;
(c) any person with whom he was living immediately before the making of the order;
(d) any person in whose favour a contact order is in force with respect to him;
(e) any person who is allowed to have contact with the child by virtue of an order under section 34; and
(f) any person acting on behalf of any of those persons.

(14) Wherever it is reasonably practicable to do so, an emergency protection order shall name the child; and where it does not name him it shall describe him as clearly as possible.

(15) A person shall be guilty of an offence if he intentionally obstructs any person exercising the power under subsection (4)(b) to remove, or prevent the removal of, a child.

(16) A person guilty of an offence under subsection (15) shall be liable on summary conviction to a fine not exceeding level 3 on the standard scale.

44A POWER TO INCLUDE EXCLUSION REQUIREMENT IN EMERGENCY PROTECTION ORDER

(1) Where—
   (a) on being satisfied as mentioned in section 44(1)(a), (b) or (c), the court makes an emergency protection order with respect to a child, and
   (b) the conditions mentioned in subsection (2) are satisfied,

the court may include an exclusion requirement in the emergency protection order.

(2) The conditions are—
   (a) that there is reasonable cause to believe that, if a person ("the relevant person") is excluded from a dwelling-house in which the child lives, then—
      (i) in the case of an order made on the ground mentioned in section 44(1)(a), the child will not be likely to suffer significant harm, even though the child is not removed as mentioned in section 44(1)(a)(i) or does not remain as mentioned in section 44(1)(a)(ii), or
      (ii) in the case of an order made on the ground mentioned in paragraph (b) or (c) of section 44(1), the enquiries referred to in that paragraph will cease to be frustrated, and
   (b) that another person living in the dwelling-house (whether a parent of the child or some other person)—
      (i) is able and willing to give to the child the care which it would be reasonable to expect a parent to give him, and
      (ii) consents to the inclusion of the exclusion requirement.

(3) For the purposes of this section an exclusion requirement is any one or more of the following—
   (a) a provision requiring the relevant person to leave a dwelling-house in which he is living with the child,
   (b) a provision prohibiting the relevant person from entering a dwelling-house in which the child lives, and
   (c) a provision excluding the relevant person from a defined area in which a dwelling-house in which the child lives is situated.

(4) The court may provide that the exclusion requirement is to have effect for a shorter period than the other provisions of the order.

(5) Where the court makes an emergency protection order containing an exclusion requirement, the court may attach a power of arrest to the exclusion requirement.

(6) Where the court attaches a power of arrest to an exclusion requirement of an emergency protection order, it may provide that the power of arrest is to have effect for a shorter period than the exclusion requirement.

(7) Any period specified for the purposes of subsection (4) or (6) may be extended by the court (on one or more occasions) on an application to vary or discharge the emergency protection order.

(8) Where a power of arrest is attached to an exclusion requirement of an emergency protection order by virtue of subsection (5), a constable may arrest without warrant any person whom he has reasonable cause to believe to be in breach of the requirement.

(9) Sections 47(7), (11) and (12) and 48 of, and Schedule 5 to, the Family Law Act 1996 shall have effect in relation to a person arrested under subsection (8) of this section as they have effect in relation to a person arrested under section 47(6) of that Act.

(10) If, while an emergency protection order containing an exclusion requirement is in force, the applicant has removed the child from the dwelling-house from which the relevant person is excluded to other accommodation for a continuous period of more than 24 hours, the order shall cease to have effect in so far as it imposes the exclusion requirement.

44B UNDERTAKINGS RELATING TO EMERGENCY PROTECTION ORDERS

(1) In any case where the court has power to include an exclusion requirement in an emergency protection order, the court may accept an undertaking from the relevant person.

(2) No power of arrest may be attached to any undertaking given under subsection (1).

(3) An undertaking given to a court under subsection (1)—
(a) shall be enforceable as if it were an order of the court, and
(b) shall cease to have effect if, while it is in force, the applicant has removed the child from the dwelling-house from which the relevant person is excluded to other accommodation for a continuous period of more than 24 hours.

(4) This section has effect without prejudice to the powers of the High Court and county court apart from this section.

(5) In this section "exclusion requirement" and "relevant person" have the same meaning as in section 44A.

45 DURATION OF EMERGENCY PROTECTION ORDERS AND OTHER SUPPLEMENTAL PROVISIONS

(1) An emergency protection order shall have effect for such period, not exceeding eight days, as may be specified in the order.

(2) Where—
(a) the court making an emergency protection order would, but for this subsection, specify a period of eight days as the period for which the order is to have effect; but
(b) the last of those eight days is a public holiday (that is to say, Christmas Day, Good Friday, a bank holiday or a Sunday),

the court may specify a period which ends at noon on the first later day which is not such a holiday.

(3) Where an emergency protection order is made on an application under section 46(7), the period of eight days mentioned in subsection (1) shall begin with the first day on which the child was taken into police protection under section 46.

(4) Any person who—
(a) has parental responsibility for a child as the result of an emergency protection order; and
(b) is entitled to apply for a care order with respect to the child, may apply to the court for the period during which the emergency protection order is to have effect to be extended.

(5) On an application under subsection (4) the court may extend the period during which the order is to have effect by such period, not exceeding seven days, as it thinks fit, but may do so only if it has reasonable cause to believe that the child concerned is likely to suffer significant harm if the order is not extended.

(6) An emergency protection order may only be extended once.

(7) Regardless of any enactment or rule of law which would otherwise prevent it from doing so, a court hearing an application for, or with respect to, an emergency protection order may take account of—
(a) any statement contained in any report made to the court in the course of, or in connection with, the hearing; or
(b) any evidence given during the hearing, which is, in the opinion of the court, relevant to the application.

(8) Any of the following may apply to the court for an emergency protection order to be discharged—
(a) the child;
(b) a parent of his;
(c) any person who is not a parent of his but who has parental responsibility for him; or
(d) any person with whom he was living immediately before the making of the order.

(8A) On the application of a person who is not entitled to apply for the order to be discharged, but who is a person to whom an exclusion requirement contained in the order applies, an emergency protection order may be varied or discharged by the court in so far as it imposes the exclusion requirement.

(8B) Where a power of arrest has been attached to an exclusion requirement of an emergency protection order, the court may, on the application of any person entitled to apply for the discharge of the order so far as it imposes the exclusion requirement, vary or discharge the order in so far as it confers a power of arrest (whether or not any application has been made to vary or discharge any other provision of the order).

(10) No appeal may be made against—
(a) the making of, or refusal to make, an emergency protection order;
(b) the extension of, or refusal to extend, the period during which such an order is to have effect;
(c) the discharge of, or refusal to discharge, such an order; or
(d) the giving of, or refusal to give, any direction in connection with such an order.

(11) Subsection (8) does not apply—
(a) where the person who would otherwise be entitled to apply for the emergency protection order to be discharged—
(i) was given notice (in accordance with rules of court) of the hearing at which the order was made; and
(ii) was present at that hearing; or
(b) to any emergency protection order the effective period of which has been extended under subsection (5).

(12) A court making an emergency protection order may direct that the applicant may in exercising any powers which he has by virtue of the order, be accompanied by a registered medical practitioner, registered nurse or registered midwife, if he so chooses.

(13) The reference in subsection (12) to a registered midwife is to such a midwife who is also registered in the Specialist Community Public Health Nurses' Part of the register maintained under article 5 of the Nursing and Midwifery Order 2001.

46 REMOVAL AND ACCOMMODATION OF CHILDREN BY POLICE IN CASES OF EMERGENCY

(1) Where a constable has reasonable cause to believe that a child would otherwise be likely to suffer significant harm, he may—

(a) remove the child to suitable accommodation and keep him there; or
(b) take such steps as are reasonable to ensure that the child's removal from any hospital, or other place, in which he is then being accommodated is prevented.

(2) For the purposes of this Act, a child with respect to whom a constable has exercised his powers under this section is referred to as having been taken into police protection.

(3) As soon as is reasonably practicable after taking a child into police protection, the constable concerned shall—
(a) inform the local authority within whose area the child was found of the steps that have been, and are proposed to be, taken with respect to the child under this section and the reasons for taking them;
(b) give details to the authority within whose area the child is ordinarily resident ("the appropriate authority") of the place at which the child is being accommodated;
(c) inform the child (if he appears capable of understanding)—
(i) of the steps that have been taken with respect to him under this section and of the reasons for taking them; and
(ii) of the further steps that may be taken with respect to him under this section;
(d) take such steps as are reasonably practicable to discover the wishes and feelings of the child;
(e) secure that the case is inquired into by an officer designated for the purposes of this section by the chief officer of the police area concerned; and
(f) where the child was taken into police protection by being removed to accommodation which is not provided—
(i) by or on behalf of a local authority; or
(ii) as a refuge, in compliance with the requirements of section 51,
secure that he is moved to accommodation which is so provided.

(4) As soon as is reasonably practicable after taking a child into police protection, the constable concerned shall take such steps as are reasonably practicable to inform—
(a) the child's parents;
(b) every person who is not a parent of his but who has parental responsibility for him; and
(c) any other person with whom the child was living immediately before being taken into police protection, of the steps that he has taken under this section with respect to the child, the reasons for taking them and the further steps that may be taken with respect to him under this section.

(5) On completing any inquiry under subsection (3)(e), the officer conducting it shall release the child from police protection unless he considers that there is still reasonable cause for believing that the child would be likely to suffer significant harm if released.

(6) No child may be kept in police protection for more than 72 hours.

(7) While a child is being kept in police protection, the designated officer may apply on behalf of the appropriate authority for an emergency protection order to be made under section 44 with respect to the child.

(8) An application may be made under subsection (7) whether or not the authority know of it or agree to its being made.

(9) While a child is being kept in police protection—
(a) neither the constable concerned nor the designated officer shall have parental responsibility for him; but
(b) the designated officer shall do what is reasonable in all the circumstances of the case for the purpose of safeguarding or promoting the child's welfare (having regard in particular to the length of the period during which the child will be so protected).

(10) Where a child has been taken into police protection, the designated officer shall allow—
(a) the child's parents;
(b) any person who is not a parent of the child but who has parental responsibility for him;
(c) any person with whom the child was living immediately before he was taken into police protection;
(d) any person in whose favour a contact order is in force with respect to the child;
(e) any person who is allowed to have contact with the child by virtue of an order under section 34; and
(f) any person acting on behalf of any of those persons,
to have such contact (if any) with the child as, in the opinion of the designated officer, is both reasonable and in the child's best interests.

(11) Where a child who has been taken into police protection is in accommodation provided by, or on behalf of, the appropriate authority, subsection (10) shall have effect as if it referred to the authority rather than to the designated officer.

47 LOCAL AUTHORITY'S DUTY TO INVESTIGATE

(1) Where a local authority—
(a) are informed that a child who lives, or is found, in their area—
(i) is the subject of an emergency protection order; or
(ii) is in police protection;
(b) have reasonable cause to suspect that a child who lives, or is found, in their area is suffering, or is likely to suffer, significant harm,
the authority shall make, or cause to be made, such enquiries as they consider necessary to enable them to decide whether they should take any action to safeguard or promote the child's welfare.

(2) Where a local authority have obtained an emergency protection order with respect to a child, they shall make, or cause to be made, such enquiries as they consider necessary to enable them to decide what action they should take to safeguard or promote the child's welfare.

(3) The enquiries shall, in particular, be directed towards establishing—
(a) whether the authority should make any application to the court, or exercise any of their other powers under this Act or section 11 of the Crime and Disorder Act 1998 (child safety orders), with respect to the child;
(b) whether, in the case of a child—
(i) with respect to whom an emergency protection order has been made; and
(ii) who is not in accommodation provided by or on behalf of the authority, it would be in the child's best interests (while an emergency protection order remains in force) for him to be in such accommodation; and
(c) whether, in the case of a child who has been taken into police protection, it would be in the child's best interests for the authority to ask for an application to be made under section 46(7).

(4) Where enquiries are being made under subsection (1) with respect to a child, the local authority concerned shall (with a view to enabling them to determine what action, if any, to take with respect to him) take such steps as are reasonably practicable—
(a) to obtain access to him; or
(b) to ensure that access to him is obtained, on their behalf, by a person authorised by them for the purpose,
unless they are satisfied that they already have sufficient information with respect to him.

(5) Where, as a result of any such enquiries, it appears to the authority that there are matters connected with the child's education which should be investigated, they shall consult the relevant local education authority.

(5A) For the purposes of making a determination under this section as to the action to be taken with respect to a child, a local authority shall, so far as is reasonably practicable and consistent with the child's welfare—
(a) ascertain the child's wishes and feelings regarding the action to be taken with respect to him; and
(b) give due consideration (having regard to his age and understanding) to such wishes and feelings of the child as they have been able to ascertain.

(6) Where, in the course of enquiries made under this section—
(a) any officer of the local authority concerned; or
(b) any person authorised by the authority to act on their behalf in connection with those enquiries—
(i) is refused access to the child concerned; or
(ii) is denied information as to his whereabouts,
the authority shall apply for an emergency protection order, a child assessment order, a care order or a supervision order with respect to the child unless they are satisfied that his welfare can be satisfactorily safeguarded without their doing so.

(7) If, on the conclusion of any enquiries or review made under this section, the authority decide not to apply for an emergency protection order, a child assessment order, a care order or a supervision order they shall—
(a) consider whether it would be appropriate to review the case at a later date; and
(b) if they decide that it would be, determine the date on which that review is to begin.

(8) Where, as a result of complying with this section, a local authority conclude that they should take action to safeguard or promote the child's welfare they shall take that action (so far as it is both within their power and reasonably practicable for them to do so).

(9) Where a local authority are conducting enquiries under this section, it shall be the duty of any person mentioned in subsection (11) to assist them with those enquiries (in particular by providing relevant information and advice) if called upon by the authority to do so.

(10) Subsection (9) does not oblige any person to assist a local authority where doing so would be unreasonable in all the circumstances of the case.

(11) The persons are—
(a) any local authority;
(b) any local education authority;
(c) any local housing authority;
(d) any Local Health Board, Special Health Authority, Primary Care Trust, National Health Service trust or NHS foundation trust; and
(e) any person authorised by the Secretary of State for the purposes of this section.

(12) Where a local authority are making enquiries under this section with respect to a child who appears to them to be ordinarily resident within the area of another authority, they shall consult that other authority, who may undertake the necessary enquiries in their place.

48 POWERS TO ASSIST IN DISCOVERY OF CHILDREN WHO MAY BE IN NEED OF EMERGENCY PROTECTION

(1) Where it appears to a court making an emergency protection order that adequate information as to the child's whereabouts—

(a) is not available to the applicant for the order; but
(b) is available to another person,
it may include in the order a provision requiring that other person to disclose, if asked to do so by the applicant, any information that he may have as to the child's whereabouts.

(2) No person shall be excused from complying with such a requirement on the ground that complying might incriminate him or his spouse or civil partner of an offence; but a statement or admission made in complying shall not be admissible in evidence against either of them in proceedings for any offence other than perjury.

(3) An emergency protection order may authorise the applicant to enter premises specified by the order and search for the child with respect to whom the order is made.

(4) Where the court is satisfied that there is reasonable cause to believe that there may be another child on those premises with respect to whom an emergency protection order ought to be made, it may make an order authorising the applicant to search for that other child on those premises.

(5) Where—
(a) an order has been made under subsection (4);
(b) the child concerned has been found on the premises; and
(c) the applicant is satisfied that the grounds for making an emergency protection order exist with respect to him,
the order shall have effect as if it were an emergency protection order.

(6) Where an order has been made under subsection (4), the applicant shall notify the court of its effect.

(7) A person shall be guilty of an offence if he intentionally obstructs any person exercising the power of entry and search under subsection (3) or (4).

(8) A person guilty of an offence under subsection (7) shall be liable on summary conviction to a fine not exceeding level 3 on the standard scale.

(9) Where, on an application made by any person for a warrant under this section, it appears to the court—
(a) that a person attempting to exercise powers under an emergency protection order has been prevented from doing so by being refused entry to the premises concerned or access to the child concerned; or
(b) that any such person is likely to be so prevented from exercising any such powers,
it may issue a warrant authorising any constable to assist the person mentioned in paragraph (a) or (b) in the exercise of those powers, using reasonable force if necessary.

(10) Every warrant issued under this section shall be addressed to, and executed by, a constable who shall be accompanied by the person applying for the warrant if—
(a) that person so desires; and
(b) the court by whom the warrant is issued does not direct otherwise.

(11) A court granting an application for a warrant under this section may direct that the constable concerned may, in executing the warrant, be accompanied by a registered medical practitioner, registered nurse or registered midwife if he so chooses.

(11A) The reference in subsection (11) to a registered midwife is to such a midwife who is also registered in the Specialist Community Public Health Nurses' Part of the register maintained under article 5 of the Nursing and Midwifery Order 2001.

(12) An application for a warrant under this section shall be made in the manner and form prescribed by rules of court.

(13) Wherever it is reasonably practicable to do so, an order under subsection (4), an application for a warrant under this section and any such warrant shall name the child; and where it does not name him it shall describe him as clearly as possible.

49 ABDUCTION OF CHILDREN IN CARE ETC

(1) A person shall be guilty of an offence if, knowingly and without lawful authority or reasonable excuse, he—
(a) takes a child to whom this section applies away from the responsible person;
(b) keeps such a child away from the responsible person; or
(c) induces, assists or incites such a child to run away or stay away from the responsible person.

(2) This section applies in relation to a child who is—
(a) in care;
(b) the subject of an emergency protection order; or
(c) in police protection,
and in this section "the responsible person" means any person who for the time being has care of him by virtue of the care order, the emergency protection order, or section 46, as the case may be.

(3) A person guilty of an offence under this section shall be liable on summary conviction to imprisonment for a term not exceeding six months, or to a fine not exceeding level 5 on the standard scale, or to both.

50 RECOVERY OF ABDUCTED CHILDREN ETC

(1) Where it appears to the court that there is reason to believe that a child to whom this section applies—
(a) has been unlawfully taken away or is being unlawfully kept away from the responsible person;
(b) has run away or is staying away from the responsible person; or
(c) is missing,
the court may make an order under this section ("a recovery order").

(2) This section applies to the same children to whom section 49 applies and in this section "the responsible person" has the same meaning as in section 49.

(3) A recovery order—
(a) operates as a direction to any person who is in a position to do so to produce the child on request to any authorised person;
(b) authorises the removal of the child by any authorised person;
(c) requires any person who has information as to the child's whereabouts to disclose that information, if asked to do so, to a constable or an officer of the court;
(d) authorises a constable to enter any premises specified in the order and search for the child, using reasonable force if necessary.

(4) The court may make a recovery order only on the application of—
(a) any person who has parental responsibility for the child by virtue of a care order or emergency protection order; or
(b) where the child is in police protection, the designated officer.

(5) A recovery order shall name the child and—
(a) any person who has parental responsibility for the child by virtue of a care order or emergency protection order; or
(b) where the child is in police protection, the designated officer.

(6) Premises may only be specified under subsection (3)(d) if it appears to the court that there are reasonable grounds for believing the child to be on them.

(7) In this section—

"an authorised person" means—

(a) any person specified by the court;
(b) any constable;
(c) any person who is authorised—
  (i) after the recovery order is made; and
  (ii) by a person who has parental responsibility for the child by virtue of a care order or an emergency protection order, to exercise any power under a recovery order; and

"the designated officer" means the officer designated for the purposes of section 46.

(8) Where a person is authorised as mentioned in subsection (7)(c)—
(a) the authorisation shall identify the recovery order; and
(b) any person claiming to be so authorised shall, if asked to do so, produce some duly authenticated document showing that he is so authorised.

(9) A person shall be guilty of an offence if he intentionally obstructs an authorised person exercising the power under subsection (3)(b) to remove a child.

(10) A person guilty of an offence under this section shall be liable on summary conviction to a fine not exceeding level 3 on the standard scale.

(11) No person shall be excused from complying with any request made under subsection (3)(c) on the ground that complying with it might incriminate him or his spouse or civil partner of an offence; but a statement or admission made in complying shall not be admissible in evidence against either of them in proceedings for an offence other than perjury.

(12) Where a child is made the subject of a recovery order whilst being looked after by a local authority, any reasonable expenses incurred by an authorised person in giving effect to the order shall be recoverable from the authority. . . .

. . .

Part XII MISCELLANEOUS AND GENERAL

. . .

Effect and duration of orders etc

91 EFFECT AND DURATION OF ORDERS ETC

(1) The making of a residence order with respect to a child who is the subject of a care order discharges the care order.

(2) The making of a care order with respect to a child who is the subject of any section 8 order discharges that order.

(2A) Where a contact activity direction has been made as regards contact with a child, the making of a care order with respect to the child discharges the direction.

(3) The making of a care order with respect to a child who is the subject of a supervision order discharges that other order.

(4) The making of a care order with respect to a child who is a ward of court brings that wardship to an end.

(5) The making of a care order with respect to a child who is the subject of a school attendance order made under section 437 of the Education Act 1996 discharges the school attendance order.

(5A) The making of a special guardianship order with respect to a child who is the subject of—
(a) a care order; or
(b) an order under section 34, discharges that order.

(6) Where an emergency protection order is made with respect to a child who is in care, the care order shall have effect subject to the emergency protection order.

(7) Any order made under section 4(1), 4ZA(1), 4A(1) or 5(1) shall continue in force until the child reaches the age of eighteen, unless it is brought to an end earlier.

(8) Any—
(a) agreement under section 4, 4ZA or 4A; or
(b) appointment under section 5(3) or (4), shall continue in force until the child reaches the age of eighteen, unless it is brought to an end earlier.

(9) An order under Schedule 1 has effect as specified in that Schedule.

(10) A section 8 order other than a residence order shall, if it would otherwise still be in force, cease to have effect when the child reaches the age of sixteen, unless it is to have effect beyond that age by virtue of section 9(6).

(11) Where a section 8 order has effect with respect to a child who has reached the age of sixteen, it shall, if it would otherwise still be in force, cease to have effect when he reaches the age of eighteen.

(12) Any care order, other than an interim care order, shall continue in force until the child reaches the age of eighteen, unless it is brought to an end earlier.

(13) Any order made under any other provision of this Act in relation to a child shall, if it would otherwise still be in force, cease to have effect when he reaches the age of eighteen.

(14) On disposing of any application for an order under this Act, the court may (whether or not it makes any other order in response to the application) order that no application for an order under this Act of any specified kind may be made with respect to the child concerned by any person named in the order without leave of the court.

(15) Where an application ("the previous application") has been made for—
(a) the discharge of a care order;
(b) the discharge of a supervision order;
(c) the discharge of an education supervision order;
(d) the substitution of a supervision order for a care order; or
(e) a child assessment order,
no further application of a kind mentioned in paragraphs (a) to (e) may be made with respect to the child concerned, without leave of the court, unless the period between the disposal of the previous application and the making of the further application exceeds six months.

(16) Subsection (15) does not apply to applications made in relation to interim orders.

(17) Where—
(a) a person has made an application for an order under section 34;
(b) the application has been refused; and

(c) a period of less than six months has elapsed since the refusal,

that person may not make a further application for such an order with respect to the same child, unless he has obtained the leave of the court.

Jurisdiction and procedure etc

92 JURISDICTION OF COURTS

(1) The name "domestic proceedings", given to certain proceedings in magistrates' courts, is hereby changed to "family proceedings" and the names "domestic court" and "domestic court panel" are hereby changed to "family proceedings court" and "family panel", respectively.

(2) Proceedings under this Act shall be treated as family proceedings in relation to magistrates' courts.

(3) Subsection (2) is subject to the provisions of section 65(1) and (2) of the Magistrates' Courts Act 1980 (proceedings which may be treated as not being family proceedings), as amended by this Act.

(4) A magistrates' court shall not be competent to entertain any application, or make any order, involving the administration or application of—
   (a) any property belonging to or held in trust for a child; or
   (b) the income of any such property.

(5) The powers of a magistrates' court under section 63(2) of the Act of 1980 to suspend or rescind orders shall not apply in relation to any order made under this Act.

(6) Part I of Schedule 11 makes provision, including provision for the Lord Chancellor to make orders, with respect to the jurisdiction of courts and justices of the peace in relation to—
   (a) proceedings under this Act; and
   (b) proceedings under certain other enactments.

(7) For the purposes of this Act "the court" means the High Court, a county court or a magistrates' court.

(8) Subsection (7) is subject to the provision made by or under Part I of Schedule 11 and to any express provision as to the jurisdiction of any court made by any other provision of this Act.

(9) The Lord Chancellor may, after consulting the Lord Chief Justice, by order make provision for the principal registry of the Family Division of the High Court to be treated as if it were a county court for such purposes of this Act, or of any provision made under this Act, as may be specified in the order. . . .

. . .

94 APPEALS

(1) Subject to any express provisions to the contrary made by or under this Act, an appeal shall lie to a county court against—
   (a) the making by a magistrates' court of any order under this Act or the Adoption and Children Act 2002; or
   (b) any refusal by a magistrates' court to make such an order.

(2) Where a magistrates' court has power, in relation to any proceedings under this Act or the Adoption and Children Act 2002, to decline jurisdiction because it considers that the case

can more conveniently be dealt with by another court, no appeal shall lie against any exercise by that magistrates' court of that power.

(3) Subsection (1) does not apply in relation to an interim order for periodical payments made under Schedule 1.

(4) On an appeal under this section, a county court may make such orders as may be necessary to give effect to its determination of the appeal.

(5) Where an order is made under subsection (4) a county court may also make such incidental or consequential orders as appear to it to be just.

(6) Where an appeal from a magistrates' court relates to an order for the making of periodical payments, a county court may order that its determination of the appeal shall have effect from such date as it thinks fit to specify in the order.

(7) The date so specified must not be earlier than the earliest date allowed in accordance with rules of court made for the purposes of this section.

(8) Where, on an appeal under this section in respect of an order requiring a person to make periodical payments, a county court reduces the amount of those payments or discharges the order—
- (a) it may order the person entitled to the payments to pay to the person making them such sum in respect of payments already made as the county court thinks fit; and
- (b) if any arrears are due under the order for periodical payments,

it may remit payment of the whole, or part, of those arrears.

(9) Any order of a county court made on an appeal under this section (other than one directing that an application be re-heard by a magistrates' court) shall, for the purposes—
- (a) of the enforcement of the order; and
- (b) of any power to vary, revive or discharge orders,

be treated as if it were an order of the magistrates' court from which the appeal was brought and not an order of a county court. . . .

95 ATTENDANCE OF CHILD AT HEARING UNDER PART IV OR V

(1) In any proceedings in which a court is hearing an application for an order under Part IV or V, or is considering whether to make any such order, the court may order the child concerned to attend such stage or stages of the proceedings as may be specified in the order.

(2) The power conferred by subsection (1) shall be exercised in accordance with rules of court.

(3) Subsections (4) to (6) apply where—
- (a) an order under subsection (1) has not been complied with; or
- (b) the court has reasonable cause to believe that it will not be complied with.

(4) The court may make an order authorising a constable, or such person as may be specified in the order—
- (a) to take charge of the child and to bring him to the court; and
- (b) to enter and search any premises specified in the order if he has reasonable cause to believe that the child may be found on the premises.

(5) The court may order any person who is in a position to do so to bring the child to the court.

(6) Where the court has reason to believe that a person has information about the whereabouts of the child it may order him to disclose it to the court.

96 EVIDENCE GIVEN BY, OR WITH RESPECT TO, CHILDREN

(1) Subsection (2) applies where a child who is called as a witness in any civil proceedings does not, in the opinion of the court, understand the nature of an oath.

(2) The child's evidence may be heard by the court if, in its opinion—
(a) he understands that it is his duty to speak the truth; and
(b) he has sufficient understanding to justify his evidence being heard.

(3) The Lord Chancellor may, with the concurrence of the Lord Chief Justice, by order make provision for the admissibility of evidence which would otherwise be inadmissible under any rule of law relating to hearsay.

(4) An order under subsection (3) may only be made with respect to—
(a) civil proceedings in general or such civil proceedings, or class of civil proceedings, as may be prescribed; and
(b) evidence in connection with the upbringing, maintenance or welfare of a child.

(5) An order under subsection (3)—
(a) may, in particular, provide for the admissibility of statements which are made orally or in a prescribed form or which are recorded by any prescribed method of recording;
(b) may make different provision for different purposes and in relation to different descriptions of court; and
(c) may make such amendments and repeals in any enactment relating to evidence (other than in this Act) as the Lord Chancellor considers necessary or expedient in consequence of the provision made by the order.

(6) Subsection (5)(b) is without prejudice to section 104(4).

(7) In this section—

"civil proceedings" means civil proceedings, before any tribunal, in relation to which the strict rules of evidence apply, whether as a matter of law or by agreement of the parties, and references to "the court" shall be construed accordingly;

"prescribed" means prescribed by an order under subsection (3).

. . .

98 SELF-INCRIMINATION

(1) In any proceedings in which a court is hearing an application for an order under Part IV or V, no person shall be excused from—
(a) giving evidence on any matter; or
(b) answering any question put to him in the course of his giving evidence, on the ground that doing so might incriminate him or his spouse or civil partner of an offence.

(2) A statement or admission made in such proceedings shall not be admissible in evidence against the person making it or his spouse or civil partner in proceedings for an offence other than perjury.

100 RESTRICTIONS ON USE OF WARDSHIP JURISDICTION

(2) No court shall exercise the High Court's inherent jurisdiction with respect to children—
(a) so as to require a child to be placed in the care, or put under the supervision, of a local authority;
(b) so as to require a child to be accommodated by or on behalf of a local authority;

(c) so as to make a child who is the subject of a care order a ward of court; or
(d) for the purpose of conferring on any local authority power to determine any question which has arisen, or which may arise, in connection with any aspect of parental responsibility for a child.

(3) No application for any exercise of the court's inherent jurisdiction with respect to children may be made by a local authority unless the authority have obtained the leave of the court.

(4) The court may only grant leave if it is satisfied that—
(a) the result which the authority wish to achieve could not be achieved through the making of any order of a kind to which subsection (5) applies; and
(b) there is reasonable cause to believe that if the court's inherent jurisdiction is not exercised with respect to the child he is likely to suffer significant harm.

(5) This subsection applies to any order—
(a) made otherwise than in the exercise of the court's inherent jurisdiction; and
(b) which the local authority is entitled to apply for (assuming, in the case of any application which may only be made with leave, that leave is granted).

. . .

Search warrants

102 POWER OF CONSTABLE TO ASSIST IN EXERCISE OF CERTAIN POWERS TO SEARCH FOR CHILDREN OR INSPECT PREMISES

(1) Where, on an application made by any person for a warrant under this section, it appears to the court—
(a) that a person attempting to exercise powers under any enactment mentioned in subsection (6) has been prevented from doing so by being refused entry to the premises concerned or refused access to the child concerned; or
(b) that any such person is likely to be so prevented from exercising any such powers,
it may issue a warrant authorising any constable to assist that person in the exercise of those powers, using reasonable force if necessary.

(2) Every warrant issued under this section shall be addressed to, and executed by, a constable who shall be accompanied by the person applying for the warrant if—
(a) that person so desires; and
(b) the court by whom the warrant is issued does not direct otherwise.

(3) A court granting an application for a warrant under this section may direct that the constable concerned may, in executing the warrant, be accompanied by a registered medical practitioner, registered nurse or registered midwife if he so chooses.

(3A) The reference in subsection (3) to a registered midwife is to such a midwife who is also registered in the Specialist Community Public Health Nurses' Part of the register maintained under article 5 of the Nursing and Midwifery Order 2001.

(4) An application for a warrant under this section shall be made in the manner and form prescribed by rules of court.

(5) Where—
(a) an application for a warrant under this section relates to a particular child; and
(b) it is reasonably practicable to do so,
the application and any warrant granted on the application shall name the child; and where it does not name him it shall describe him as clearly as possible.

(6) The enactments are—
(a) sections 62, 64, 67, 76, 79U, 80, 86 and 87;
(b) paragraph 8(1)(b) and (2)(b) of Schedule 3.

. . .

105 INTERPRETATION

(1) In this Act—

"adoption agency" means a body which may be referred to as an adoption agency by virtue of section 2 of the Adoption and Children Act 2002;

"bank holiday" means a day which is a bank holiday under the Banking and Financial Dealings Act 1971;

"care home" has the same meaning as in the Care Standards Act 2000;

"care order" has the meaning given by section 31(11) and also includes any order which by or under any enactment has the effect of, or is deemed to be, a care order for the purposes of this Act; and any reference to a child who is in the care of an authority is a reference to a child who is in their care by virtue of a care order;

"child" means, subject to paragraph 16 of Schedule 1, a person under the age of eighteen;

"child assessment order" has the meaning given by section 43(2);

"child minder" has the meaning given by section 71;

"child of the family", in relation to parties to a marriage, or to two people who are civil partners of each other, means—
(a) a child of both of them, and
(b) any other child, other than a child placed with them as foster parents by a local authority or voluntary organisation, who has been treated by both of them as a child of their family;

"children's home" has the same meaning as it has for the purposes of the Care Standards Act 2000 (see section 1 of that Act);

"community home" has the meaning given by section 53;

"contact activity condition" has the meaning given by section 11C;

"contact activity direction" has the meaning given by section 11A;

"contact order" has the meaning given by section 8(1);

"day care" (except in Part XA) has the same meaning as in section 18;

"disabled", in relation to a child, has the same meaning as in section 17(11);

"domestic premises" has the meaning given by section 71('12);

dwelling-house" includes—
(a) any building or part of a building which is occupied as a dwelling;
(b) any caravan, house-boat or structure which is occupied as a dwelling;
and any yard, garden, garage or outhouse belonging to it and occupied with it;

"education supervision order" has the meaning given in section 36;

"emergency protection order" means an order under section 44;

"enforcement order" has the meaning given by section 11J;

"family assistance order" has the meaning given in section 16(2);

"family proceedings" has the meaning given by section 8(3);

"functions" includes powers and duties;

"guardian of a child" means a guardian (other than a guardian of the estate of a child) appointed in accordance with the provisions of section 5;

"harm" has the same meaning as in section 31(9) and the question of whether harm is significant shall be determined in accordance with section 31(10);

"health service hospital" means a health service hospital within the meaning given by the National Health Service Act 2006 or the National Health Service (Wales) Act 2006;

"hospital" (except in Schedule 9A) has the same meaning as in the Mental Health Act 1983, except that it does not include a hospital at which high security psychiatric services within the meaning of that Act are provided;

"ill-treatment" has the same meaning as in section 31(9);

"income-based jobseeker's allowance" has the same meaning as in the Jobseekers Act 1995;

"income-related employment and support allowance" means an income-related allowance under Part 1 of the Welfare Reform Act 2007 (employment and support allowance);

"independent hospital" has the same meaning as in the Care Standards Act 2000;

"independent school" has the same meaning as in the Education Act 1996;

"local authority" means, in relation to England, the council of a county, a metropolitan district, a London Borough or the Common Council of the City of London, in relation to Wales, the council of a county or a county borough and, in relation to Scotland, a local authority within the meaning of section 1(2) of the Social Work (Scotland) Act 1968;

"local authority foster parent" has the meaning given in section 22C(12);

"local education authority" has the same meaning as in the Education Act 1996;

"Local Health Board" means a Local Health Board established under section 11 of the National Health Service (Wales) Act 2006;

"local housing authority" has the same meaning as in the Housing Act 1985;

"officer of the Service" has the same meaning as in the Criminal Justice and Court Services Act 2000;

"parental responsibility" has the meaning given in section 3;

"parental responsibility agreement" has the meaning given in sections 4(1), 4ZA(4) and 4A(2);

"prescribed" means prescribed by regulations made under this Act;

"private children's home" means a children's home in respect of which a person is registered under Part II of the Care Standards Act 2000 which is not a community home or a voluntary home;

"Primary Care Trust" means a Primary Care Trust established under section 18 of the National Health Service Act 2006;

"privately fostered child" and "to foster a child privately" have the same meaning as in section 66;

"prohibited steps order" has the meaning given by section 8(1);

"registered pupil" has the same meaning as in the Education Act 1996;

"relative", in relation to a child, means a grandparent, brother, sister, uncle or aunt (whether of the full blood or half blood or by marriage or civil partnership) or step-parent;

"residence order" has the meaning given by section 8(1);

"responsible person", in relation to a child who is the subject of a supervision order, has the meaning given in paragraph 1 of Schedule 3;

"school" has the same meaning as in the Education Act 1996 or, in relation to Scotland, in the Education (Scotland) Act 1980;

"section 31A plan" has the meaning given by section 31A(6);

"service", in relation to any provision made under Part III, includes any facility;

"signed", in relation to any person, includes the making by that person of his mark;

"special educational needs" has the same meaning as in the Education Act 1996;

"special guardian" and "special guardianship order" have the meaning given by section 14A;

"Special Health Authority" means a Special Health Authority established under section 28 of the National Health Service Act 2006 or section 22 of the National Health Service (Wales) Act 2006;

"specific issue order" has the meaning given by section 8(1);

"Strategic Health Authority" means a Strategic Health Authority established under section 13 of the National Health Service Act 2006;

"supervision order" has the meaning given by section 31(11);

"supervised child" and "supervisor", in relation to a supervision order or an education supervision order, mean respectively the child who is (or is to be) under supervision and the person under whose supervision he is (or is to be) by virtue of the order;

"upbringing", in relation to any child, includes the care of the child but not his maintenance;

"voluntary home" has the meaning given by section 60;

"voluntary organisation" means a body (other than a public or local authority) whose activities are not carried on for profit;

"Welsh family proceedings officer" has the meaning given by section 35 of the Children Act 2004.

(2) References in this Act to a child whose father and mother were, or (as the case may be) were not, married to each other at the time of his birth must be read with section 1 of the Family Law Reform Act 1987 (which extends the meaning of such references).

(3) References in this Act to—
(a) a person with whom a child lives, or is to live, as the result of a residence order; or
(b) a person in whose favour a residence order is in force, shall be construed as references to the person named in the order as the person with whom the child is to live.

(4) References in this Act to a child who is looked after by a local authority have the same meaning as they have (by virtue of section 22) in Part III.

(5) References in this Act to accommodation provided by or on behalf of a local authority are references to accommodation so provided in the exercise of functions of that or any other local authority which are social services functions within the meaning of the Local Authority Social Services Act 1970.

. . .

(6) In determining the "ordinary residence" of a child for any purpose of this Act, there shall be disregarded any period in which he lives in any place—
(a) which is a school or other institution;
(b) in accordance with the requirements of a supervision order under this Act;
(ba) in accordance with the requirements of a youth rehabilitation order under Part 1 of the Criminal Justice and Immigration Act 2008; or
(c) while he is being provided with accommodation by or on behalf of a local authority.

(7) References in this Act to children who are in need shall be construed in accordance with section 17.

(8) Any notice or other document required under this Act to be served on any person may be served on him by being delivered personally to him, or being sent by post to him in a registered letter or by the recorded delivery service at his proper address.

(9) Any such notice or other document required to be served on a body corporate or a firm shall be duly served if it is served on the secretary or clerk of that body or a partner of that firm.

(10) For the purposes of this section, and of section 7 of the Interpretation Act 1978 in its application to this section, the proper address of a person—
(a) in the case of a secretary or clerk of a body corporate, shall be that of the registered or principal office of that body;
(b) in the case of a partner of a firm, shall be that of the principal office of the firm; and
(c) in any other case, shall be the last known address of the person to be served.

SCHEDULE 1 FINANCIAL PROVISION FOR CHILDREN

Section 15(1)

Orders for financial relief against parents

1. (1) On an application made by a parent, guardian or special guardian of a child, or by any person in whose favour a residence order is in force with respect to a child, the court may—
(a) in the case of an application to the High Court or a county court, make one or more of the orders mentioned in sub-paragraph (2);
(b) in the case of an application to a magistrates' court, make one or both of the orders mentioned in paragraphs (a) and (c) of that sub-paragraph.

(2) The orders referred to in sub-paragraph (1) are—
(a) an order requiring either or both parents of a child—
(i) to make to the applicant for the benefit of the child; or

(ii) to make to the child himself, such periodical payments, for such term, as may be specified in the order;

(b) an order requiring either or both parents of a child—

(i) to secure to the applicant for the benefit of the child; or

(ii) to secure to the child himself, such periodical payments, for such term, as may be so specified;

(c) an order requiring either or both parents of a child—

(i) to pay to the applicant for the benefit of the child; or

(ii) to pay to the child himself, such lump sum as may be so specified;

(d) an order requiring a settlement to be made for the benefit of the child, and to the satisfaction of the court, of property—

(i) to which either parent is entitled (either in possession or in reversion); and

(ii) which is specified in the order;

(e) an order requiring either or both parents of a child—

(i) to transfer to the applicant, for the benefit of the child; or

(ii) to transfer to the child himself, such property to which the parent is, or the parents are, entitled (either in possession or in reversion) as may be specified in the order.

(3) The powers conferred by this paragraph may be exercised at any time.

(4) An order under sub-paragraph (2)(a) or (b) may be varied or discharged by a subsequent order made on the application of any person by or to whom payments were required to be made under the previous order.

(5) Where a court makes an order under this paragraph—

(a) it may at any time make a further such order under sub-paragraph (2)(a), (b) or (c) with respect to the child concerned if he has not reached the age of eighteen;

(b) it may not make more than one order under sub-paragraph (2)(d) or (e) against the same person in respect of the same child.

(6) On making, varying or discharging a residence order or a special guardianship order the court may exercise any of its powers under this Schedule even though no application has been made to it under this Schedule.

(7) Where a child is a ward of court, the court may exercise any of its powers under this Schedule even though no application has been made to it.

Orders for financial relief for persons over eighteen

2. (1) If, on an application by a person who has reached the age of eighteen, it appears to the court—

(a) that the applicant is, will be or (if an order were made under this paragraph) would be receiving instruction at an educational establishment or undergoing training for a trade, profession or vocation, whether or not while in gainful employment; or

(b) that there are special circumstances which justify the making of an order under this paragraph,

the court may make one or both of the orders mentioned in sub-paragraph (2).

(2) The orders are—

(a) an order requiring either or both of the applicant's parents to pay to the applicant such periodical payments, for such term, as may be specified in the order;

(b) an order requiring either or both of the applicant's parents to pay to the applicant such lump sum as may be so specified.

(3) An application may not be made under this paragraph by any person if, immediately before he reached the age of sixteen, a periodical payments order was in force with respect to him.

(4) No order shall be made under this paragraph at a time when the parents of the applicant are living with each other in the same household.

(5) An order under sub-paragraph (2)(a) may be varied or discharged by a subsequent order made on the application of any person by or to whom payments were required to be made under the previous order.

(6) In sub-paragraph (3) "periodical payments order" means an order made under—
(a) this Schedule;
(c) section 23 or 27 of the Matrimonial Causes Act 1973;
(d) Part I of the Domestic Proceedings and Magistrates' Courts Act 1978;
(e) Part 1 or 9 of Schedule 5 to the Civil Partnership Act 2004 (financial relief in the High Court or a county court etc);
(f) Schedule 6 to the 2004 Act (financial relief in the magistrates' courts etc), for the making or securing of periodical payments.

(7) The powers conferred by this paragraph shall be exercisable at any time.

(8) Where the court makes an order under this paragraph it may from time to time while that order remains in force make a further such order.

Duration of orders for financial relief

3. (1) The term to be specified in an order for periodical payments made under paragraph 1(2)(a) or (b) in favour of a child may begin with the date of the making of an application for the order in question or any later date or a date ascertained in accordance with sub-paragraph (5) or (6) but—
(a) shall not in the first instance extend beyond the child's seventeenth birthday unless the court thinks it right in the circumstances of the case to specify a later date; and
(b) shall not in any event extend beyond the child's eighteenth birthday.

(2) Paragraph (b) of sub-paragraph (1) shall not apply in the case of a child if it appears to the court that—
(a) the child is, or will be or (if an order were made without complying with that paragraph) would be receiving instruction at an educational establishment or undergoing training for a trade, profession or vocation, whether or not while in gainful employment; or
(b) there are special circumstances which justify the making of an order without complying with that paragraph.

(3) An order for periodical payments made under paragraph 1(2)(a) or 2(2)(a) shall, notwithstanding anything in the order, cease to have effect on the death of the person liable to make payments under the order.

(4) Where an order is made under paragraph 1(2)(a) or (b) requiring periodical payments to be made or secured to the parent of a child, the order shall cease to have effect if—
(a) any parent making or securing the payments; and
(b) any parent to whom the payments are made or secured, live together for a period of more than six months.

(5) Where—
(a) a maintenance calculation ("the current calculation") is in force with respect to a child; and

(b) an application is made for an order under paragraph 1(2)(a) or (b) of this Schedule for periodical payments in favour of that child—
(i) in accordance with section 8 of the Child Support Act 1991; and
(ii) before the end of the period of 6 months beginning with the making of the current calculation,

the term to be specified in any such order made on that application may be expressed to begin on, or at any time after, the earliest permitted date.

(6) For the purposes of subsection (5) above, "the earliest permitted date" is whichever is the later of—
(a) the date 6 months before the application is made; or
(b) the date on which the current calculation took effect or, where successive maintenance calculations have been continuously in force with respect to a child, on which the first of those calculations took effect.

(7) Where—
(a) a maintenance calculation ceases to have effect under any provision of the Child Support Act 1991, and
(b) an application is made, before the end of the period of 6 months beginning with the relevant date, for an order for periodical payments under paragraph 1(2)(a) or (b) in favour of a child with respect to whom that maintenance calculation was in force immediately before it ceased to have effect,

the term to be specified in any such order, or in any interim order under paragraph 9, made on that application may begin with the date on which that maintenance calculation ceased to have effect or any later date.

(8) In sub-paragraph (7)(b)—
(a) where the maintenance calculation ceased to have effect, the relevant date is the date on which it so ceased.

Matters to which court is to have regard in making orders for financial relief

4. (1) In deciding whether to exercise its powers under paragraph 1 or 2, and if so in what manner, the court shall have regard to all the circumstances including—
(a) the income, earning capacity, property and other financial resources which each person mentioned in sub-paragraph (4) has or is likely to have in the foreseeable future;
(b) the financial needs, obligations and responsibilities which each person mentioned in sub-paragraph (4) has or is likely to have in the foreseeable future;
(c) the financial needs of the child;
(d) the income, earning capacity (if any), property and other financial resources of the child;
(e) any physical or mental disability of the child;
(f) the manner in which the child was being, or was expected to be, educated or trained.

(2) In deciding whether to exercise its powers under paragraph 1 against a person who is not the mother or father of the child, and if so in what manner, the court shall in addition have regard to—
(a) whether that person has assumed responsibility for the maintenance of the child and, if so, the extent to which and basis on which he assumed that responsibility and the length of the period during which he met that responsibility;
(b) whether he did so knowing that the child was not his child;
(c) the liability of any other person to maintain the child.

(3) Where the court makes an order under paragraph 1 against a person who is not the father of the child, it shall record in the order that the order is made on the basis that the person against whom the order is made is not the child's father.

(4) The persons mentioned in sub-paragraph (1) are—

(a) in relation to a decision whether to exercise its powers under paragraph 1, any parent of the child;
(b) in relation to a decision whether to exercise its powers under paragraph 2, the mother and father of the child;
(c) the applicant for the order;
(d) any other person in whose favour the court proposes to make the order.

(5) In the case of a child who has a parent by virtue of section 42 or 43 of the Human Fertilisation and Embryology Act 2008, any reference in sub-paragraph (2), (3) or (4) to the child's father is a reference to the woman who is a parent of the child by virtue of that section.

Provisions relating to lump sums

5. (1) Without prejudice to the generality of paragraph 1, an order under that paragraph for the payment of a lump sum may be made for the purpose of enabling any liabilities or expenses—
(a) incurred in connection with the birth of the child or in maintaining the child; and
(b) reasonably incurred before the making of the order, to be met.

(2) The amount of any lump sum required to be paid by an order made by a magistrates' court under paragraph 1 or 2 shall not exceed £1000 or such larger amount as the Lord Chancellor may, after consulting the Lord Chief Justice, from time to time by order fix for the purposes of this sub-paragraph.

(3) The power of the court under paragraph 1 or 2 to vary or discharge an order for the making or securing of periodical payments by a parent shall include power to make an order under that provision for the payment of a lump sum by that parent.

(4) The amount of any lump sum which a person may be required to pay by virtue of subparagraph

(3) shall not, in the case of an order made by a magistrates' court, exceed the maximum amount that may at the time of the making of the order be required to be paid under sub-paragraph (2), but a magistrates' court may make an order for the payment of a lump sum not exceeding that amount even though the parent was required to pay a lump sum by a previous order under this Act.

(5) An order made under paragraph 1 or 2 for the payment of a lump sum may provide for the payment of that sum by instalments.

(6) Where the court provides for the payment of a lump sum by instalments the court, on an application made either by the person liable to pay or the person entitled to receive that sum, shall have power to vary that order by varying—
(a) the number of instalments payable;
(b) the amount of any instalment payable;
(c) the date on which any instalment becomes payable.

(7) The Lord Chief Justice may nominate a judicial office holder (as defined in section 109(4) of the Constitutional Reform Act 2005) to exercise his functions under this paragraph.

Variation etc of orders for periodical payments

6. (1) In exercising its powers under paragraph 1 or 2 to vary or discharge an order for the making or securing of periodical payments the court shall have regard to all the circumstances of the case, including any change in any of the matters to which the court was required to have regard when making the order.

(2) The power of the court under paragraph 1 or 2 to vary an order for the making or securing of periodical payments shall include power to suspend any provision of the order temporarily and to revive any provision so suspended.

(3) Where on an application under paragraph 1 or 2 for the variation or discharge of an order for the making or securing of periodical payments the court varies the payments required to be made under that order, the court may provide that the payments as so varied shall be made from such date as the court may specify, except that, subject to sub-paragraph (9), the date shall not be earlier than the date of the making of the application.

(4) An application for the variation of an order made under paragraph 1 for the making or securing of periodical payments to or for the benefit of a child may, if the child has reached the age of sixteen, be made by the child himself.

(5) Where an order for the making or securing of periodical payments made under paragraph 1 ceases to have effect on the date on which the child reaches the age of sixteen, or at any time after that date but before or on the date on which he reaches the age of eighteen, the child may apply to the court which made the order for an order for its revival.

(6) If on such an application it appears to the court that—

(a) the child is, will be or (if an order were made under this sub-paragraph) would be receiving instruction at an educational establishment or undergoing training for a trade, profession or vocation, whether or not while in gainful employment; or

(b) there are special circumstances which justify the making of an order under this paragraph,

the court shall have power by order to revive the order from such date as the court may specify, not being earlier than the date of the making of the application.

(7) Any order which is revived by an order under sub-paragraph (5) may be varied or discharged under that provision, on the application of any person by whom or to whom payments are required to be made under the revived order.

(8) An order for the making or securing of periodical payments made under paragraph 1 may be varied or discharged, after the death of either parent, on the application of a guardian or special guardian of the child concerned.

(9) Where—

(a) an order under paragraph 1(2)(a) or (b) for the making or securing of periodical payments in favour of more than one child ("the order") is in force;

(b) the order requires payments specified in it to be made to or for the benefit of more than one child without apportioning those payments between them;

(c) a maintenance calculation ("the calculation") is made with respect to one or more, but not all, of the children with respect to whom those payments are to be made; and

(d) an application is made, before the end of the period of 6 months beginning with the date on which the calculation was made, for the variation or discharge of the order, the court may, in exercise of its powers under paragraph 1 to vary or discharge the order, direct that the variation or discharge shall take effect from the date on which **the assessment** the calculation took effect or any later date.

Variation of orders for periodical payments etc made by magistrates' courts

6A. (1) Subject to sub-paragraphs (7) and (8), the power of a magistrates' court—

(a) under paragraph 1 or 2 to vary an order for the making of periodical payments, or

(b) under paragraph 5(6) to vary an order for the payment of a lump sum by instalments,

shall include power, if the court is satisfied that payment has not been made in accordance with the order, to exercise one of its powers under paragraphs (a) to (d) of section 59(3) of the Magistrates' Courts Act 1980.

(2) In any case where—

(a) a magistrates' court has made an order under this Schedule for the making of periodical payments or for the payment of a lump sum by instalments, and

(b) payments under the order are required to be made by any method of payment falling within section 59(6) of the Magistrates' Courts Act 1980 (standing order, etc),

any person entitled to make an application under this Schedule for the variation of the order (in this paragraph referred to as "the applicant") may apply to a magistrates' court acting in the same local justice area as the court which made the order for the order to be varied as mentioned in sub-paragraph (3).

(3) Subject to sub-paragraph (5), where an application is made under sub-paragraph (2), a justices' clerk, after giving written notice (by post or otherwise) of the application to any interested party and allowing that party, within the period of 14 days beginning with the date of the giving of that notice, an opportunity to make written representations, may vary the order to provide that payments under the order shall be made to the designated officer for the court.

(4) The clerk may proceed with an application under sub-paragraph (2) notwithstanding that any such interested party as is referred to in sub-paragraph (3) has not received written notice of the application.

(5) Where an application has been made under sub-paragraph (2), the clerk may, if he considers it inappropriate to exercise his power under sub-paragraph (3), refer the matter to the court which, subject to sub-paragraphs (7) and (8), may vary the order by exercising one of its powers under paragraphs (a) to (d) of section 59(3) of the Magistrates' Courts Act 1980.

(6) Subsection (4) of section 59 of the Magistrates' Courts Act 1980 (power of court to order that account be opened) shall apply for the purposes of sub-paragraphs (1) and (5) as it applies for the purposes of that section.

(7) Before varying the order by exercising one of its powers under paragraphs (a) to (d) of section 59(3) of the Magistrates' Courts Act 1980, the court shall have regard to any representations made by the parties to the application.

(8) If the court does not propose to exercise its power under paragraph (c), (cc) or (d) of subsection (3) of section 59 of the Magistrates' Courts Act 1980, the court shall, unless upon representations expressly made in that behalf by the applicant for the order it is satisfied that it is undesirable to do so, exercise its power under paragraph (b) of that subsection.

(9) None of the powers of the court, or of a justices' clerk, conferred by this paragraph shall be exercisable in relation to an order under this Schedule for the making of periodical payments, or for the payment of a lump sum by instalments, which is not a qualifying maintenance order (within the meaning of section 59 of the Magistrates' Courts Act 1980).

(10) In sub-paragraphs (3) and (4) "interested party", in relation to an application made by the applicant under sub-paragraph (2), means a person who would be entitled to be a party to an application for the variation of the order made by the applicant under any other provision of this Schedule if such an application were made.

Variation of orders for secured periodical payments after death of parent

7. (1) Where the parent liable to make payments under a secured periodical payments order has died, the persons who may apply for the variation or discharge of the order shall include the personal representatives of the deceased parent.

(2) No application for the variation of the order shall, except with the permission of the court, be made after the end of the period of six months from the date on which representation in regard to the estate of that parent is first taken out.

(3) The personal representatives of a deceased person against whom a secured periodical payments order was made shall not be liable for having distributed any part of the estate of the deceased after the end of the period of six months referred to in sub-paragraph (2) on the ground that they ought to have taken into account the possibility that the court might permit an application for variation to be made after that period by the person entitled to payments under the order.

(4) Sub-paragraph (3) shall not prejudice any power to recover any part of the estate so distributed arising by virtue of the variation of an order in accordance with this paragraph.

(5) Where an application to vary a secured periodical payments order is made after the death of the parent liable to make payments under the order, the circumstances to which the court is required to have regard under paragraph 6(1) shall include the changed circumstances resulting from the death of the parent.

(6) In considering for the purposes of sub-paragraph (2) the question when representation was first taken out, a grant limited to settled land or to trust property shall be left out of account and a grant limited to real estate or to personal estate shall be left out of account unless a grant limited to the remainder of the estate has previously been made or is made at the same time.

(7) In this paragraph "secured periodical payments order" means an order for secured periodical payments under paragraph 1(2)(b).

Financial relief under other enactments

8. (1) This paragraph applies where a residence order or a special guardianship order is made with respect to a child at a time when there is in force an order ("the financial relief order") made under any enactment other than this Act and requiring a person to contribute to the child's maintenance.

(2) Where this paragraph applies, the court may, on the application of—

(a) any person required by the financial relief order to contribute to the child's maintenance; or

(b) any person in whose favour a residence order or a special guardianship order with respect to the child is in force, make an order revoking the financial relief order, or varying it by altering the amount of any sum payable under the order or by substituting the applicant for the person to whom any such sum is otherwise payable under that order.

Interim orders

9. (1) Where an application is made under paragraph 1 or 2 the court may, at any time before it disposes of the application, make an interim order—

(a) requiring either or both parents to make such periodical payments, at such times and for such term as the court thinks fit; and

(b) giving any direction which the court thinks fit.

(2) An interim order made under this paragraph may provide for payments to be made from such date as the court may specify, except that, subject to paragraph 3(5) and (6), the date shall not be earlier than the date of the making of the application under paragraph 1 or 2.

(3) An interim order made under this paragraph shall cease to have effect when the application is disposed of or, if earlier, on the date specified for the purposes of this paragraph in the interim order.

(4) An interim order in which a date has been specified for the purposes of sub-paragraph (3) may be varied by substituting a later date.

Alteration of maintenance agreements

10. (1) In this paragraph and in paragraph 11 "maintenance agreement" means any agreement in writing made with respect to a child, whether before or after the commencement of this paragraph, which—

(a) is or was made between the father and mother of the child; and

(b) contains provision with respect to the making or securing of payments, or the disposition or use of any property, for the maintenance or education of the child, and any such provisions are in this paragraph, and paragraph 11, referred to as "financial arrangements".

(2) Where a maintenance agreement is for the time being subsisting and each of the parties to the agreement is for the time being either domiciled or resident in England and Wales, then, either party may apply to the court for an order under this paragraph.

(3) If the court to which the application is made is satisfied either—

(a) that, by reason of a change in the circumstances in the light of which any financial arrangements contained in the agreement were made (including a change foreseen by the parties when making the agreement), the agreement should be altered so as to make different financial arrangements; or

(b) that the agreement does not contain proper financial arrangements with respect to the child,

then that court may by order make such alterations in the agreement by varying or revoking any financial arrangements contained in it as may appear to it to be just having regard to all the circumstances.

(4) If the maintenance agreement is altered by an order under this paragraph, the agreement shall have effect thereafter as if the alteration had been made by agreement between the parties and for valuable consideration.

(5) Where a court decides to make an order under this paragraph altering the maintenance agreement—

(a) by inserting provision for the making or securing by one of the parties to the agreement of periodical payments for the maintenance of the child; or
(b) by increasing the rate of periodical payments required to be made or secured by one of the parties for the maintenance of the child,

then, in deciding the term for which under the agreement as altered by the order the payments or (as the case may be) the additional payments attributable to the increase are to be made or secured for the benefit of the child, the court shall apply the provisions of sub-paragraphs (1) and (2) of paragraph 3 as if the order were an order under paragraph 1(2)(a) or (b).

(6) A magistrates' court shall not entertain an application under sub-paragraph (2) unless both the parties to the agreement are resident in England and Wales and the court acts in, or is authorised by the Lord Chancellor to act for, a local justice area in which at least one of the parties is resident, and shall not have power to make any order on such an application except—

(a) in a case where the agreement contains no provision for periodical payments by either of the parties, an order inserting provision for the making by one of the parties of periodical payments for the maintenance of the child;
(b) in a case where the agreement includes provision for the making by one of the parties of periodical payments, an order increasing or reducing the rate of, or terminating, any of those payments.

(7) For the avoidance of doubt it is hereby declared that nothing in this paragraph affects any power of a court before which any proceedings between the parties to a maintenance agreement are brought under any other enactment to make an order containing financial arrangements or any right of either party to apply for such an order in such proceedings.

(8) In the case of a child who has a parent by virtue of section 42 or 43 of the Human Fertilisation and Embryology Act 2008, the reference in sub-paragraph (1)(a) to the child's father is a reference to the woman who is a parent of the child by virtue of that section.

11. (1) Where a maintenance agreement provides for the continuation, after the death of one of the parties, of payments for the maintenance of a child and that party dies domiciled in England and Wales, the surviving party or the personal representatives of the deceased party may apply to the High Court or a county court for an order under paragraph 10.

(2) If a maintenance agreement is altered by a court on an application under this paragraph, the agreement shall have effect thereafter as if the alteration had been made, immediately before the death, by agreement between the parties and for valuable consideration.

(3) An application under this paragraph shall not, except with leave of the High Court or a county court, be made after the end of the period of six months beginning with the day on which representation in regard to the estate of the deceased is first taken out.

(4) In considering for the purposes of sub-paragraph (3) the question when representation was first taken out, a grant limited to settled land or to trust property shall be left out of account and a grant limited to real estate or to personal estate shall be left out of account unless a grant limited to the remainder of the estate has previously been made or is made at the same time.

(5) A county court shall not entertain an application under this paragraph, or an application for leave to make an application under this paragraph, unless it would

have jurisdiction to hear and determine proceedings for an order under section 2 of the Inheritance (Provision for Family and Dependants) Act 1975 in relation to the deceased's estate by virtue of section 25 of the County Courts Act 1984 (jurisdiction under the Act of 1975).

(6) The provisions of this paragraph shall not render the personal representatives of the deceased liable for having distributed any part of the estate of the deceased after the expiry of the period of six months referred to in sub-paragraph (3) on the ground that they ought to have taken into account the possibility that a court might grant leave for an application by virtue of this paragraph to be made by the surviving party after that period.

(7) Sub-paragraph (6) shall not prejudice any power to recover any part of the estate so distributed arising by virtue of the making of an order in pursuance of this paragraph.

Enforcement of orders for maintenance

12. (1) Any person for the time being under an obligation to make payments in pursuance of any order for the payment of money made by a magistrates' court under this Act shall give notice of any change of address to such person (if any) as may be specified in the order.

(2) Any person failing without reasonable excuse to give such a notice shall be guilty of an offence and liable on summary conviction to a fine not exceeding level 2 on the standard scale.

(3) An order for the payment of money made by a magistrates' court under this Act shall be enforceable as a magistrates' court maintenance order within the meaning of section 150(1) of the Magistrates' Courts Act 1980.

Direction for settlement of instrument by conveyancing counsel

13. Where the High Court or a county court decides to make an order under this Act for the securing of periodical payments or for the transfer or settlement of property, it may direct that the matter be referred to one of the conveyancing counsel of the court to settle a proper instrument to be executed by all necessary parties.

Financial provision for child resident in country outside England and Wales

14. (1) Where one parent of a child lives in England and Wales and the child lives outside England and Wales with—

(a) another parent of his;

(b) a guardian or special guardian of his; or

(c) a person in whose favour a residence order is in force with respect to the child,

the court shall have power, on an application made by any of the persons mentioned in paragraphs (a) to (c), to make one or both of the orders mentioned in paragraph 1(2)(a) and (b) against the parent living in England and Wales.

(2) Any reference in this Act to the powers of the court under paragraph 1(2) or to an order made under paragraph 1(2) shall include a reference to the powers which the court has by virtue of sub-paragraph (1) or (as the case may be) to an order made by virtue of sub-paragraph (1).

Local authority contribution to child's maintenance

15. (1) Where a child lives, or is to live, with a person as the result of a residence order, a local authority may make contributions to that person towards the cost of the accommodation and maintenance of the child.

(2) Sub-paragraph (1) does not apply where the person with whom the child lives, or is to live, is a parent of the child or the husband or wife or civil partner of a parent of the child.

Interpretation

16. (1) In this Schedule "child" includes, in any case where an application is made under paragraph 2 or 6 in relation to a person who has reached the age of eighteen, that person.

(2) In this Schedule, except paragraphs 2 and 15, "parent" includes—
(a) any party to a marriage (whether or not subsisting) in relation to whom the child concerned is a child of the family, and
(b) any civil partner in a civil partnership (whether or not subsisting) in relation to whom the child concerned is a child of the family;
and for this purpose any reference to either parent or both parents shall be read as a reference to any parent of his and to all of his parents.

(3) In this Schedule, "maintenance calculation" has the same meaning as it has in the Child Support Act 1991 by virtue of section 54 of that Act as read with any regulations in force under that section.

SCHEDULE 2 LOCAL AUTHORITY SUPPORT FOR CHILDREN AND FAMILIES

Sections 17, 23, 29

Part I PROVISION OF SERVICES FOR FAMILIES

Identification of children in need and provision of information

1. (1) Every local authority shall take reasonable steps to identify the extent to which there are children in need within their area.

(2) Every local authority shall—
(a) publish information—
(i) about services provided by them under sections 17, 18, 20, 23B to 23D, 24A and 24B; and
(ii) where they consider it appropriate, about the provision by others (including, in particular, voluntary organisations) of services which the authority have power to provide under those sections; and
(b) take such steps as are reasonably practicable to ensure that those who might benefit from the services receive the information relevant to them.

Maintenance of a register of disabled children

2. (1) Every local authority shall open and maintain a register of disabled children within their area.

(2) The register may be kept by means of a computer.

Assessment of children's needs

3. Where it appears to a local authority that a child within their area is in need, the authority may assess his needs for the purposes of this Act at the same time as any assessment of his needs is made under—
(a) the Chronically Sick and Disabled Persons Act 1970;
(b) Part IV of the Education Act 1996;
(c) the Disabled Persons (Services, Consultation and Representation) Act 1986; or
(d) any other enactment.

Prevention of neglect and abuse

4. (1) Every local authority shall take reasonable steps, through the provision of services under Part III of this Act, to prevent children within their area suffering ill-treatment or neglect.

(2) Where a local authority believe that a child who is at any time within their area—
(a) is likely to suffer harm; but
(b) lives or proposes to live in the area of another local authority
they shall inform that other local authority.

(3) When informing that other local authority they shall specify—
(a) the harm that they believe he is likely to suffer; and
(b) (if they can) where the child lives or proposes to live.

Provision of accommodation in order to protect child

5. (1) Where—
(a) it appears to a local authority that a child who is living on particular premises is suffering, or is likely to suffer, ill treatment at the hands of another person who is living on those premises; and
(b) that other person proposes to move from the premises, the authority may assist that other person to obtain alternative accommodation.

(2) Assistance given under this paragraph may be in cash.

(3) Subsections (7) to (9) of section 17 shall apply in relation to assistance given under this paragraph as they apply in relation to assistance given under that section.

Provision for disabled children

6. (1) Every local authority shall provide services designed—
(a) to minimise the effect on disabled children within their area of their disabilities;
(b) to give such children the opportunity to lead lives which are as normal as possible; and
(c) to assist individuals who provide care for such children to continue to do so, or to do so more effectively, by giving them breaks from caring.

(2) The duty imposed by sub-paragraph (1)(c) shall be performed in accordance with regulations made by the appropriate national authority.

Provision to reduce need for care proceedings etc

7. Every local authority shall take reasonable steps designed—
(a) to reduce the need to bring—
(i) proceedings for care or supervision orders with respect to children within their area;
(ii) criminal proceedings against such children;
(iii) any family or other proceedings with respect to such children which might lead to them being placed in the authority's care; or
(iv) proceedings under the inherent jurisdiction of the High Court with respect to children;
(b) to encourage children within their area not to commit criminal offences; and
(c) to avoid the need for children within their area to be placed in secure accommodation.

Provision for children living with their families

8. Every local authority shall make such provision as they consider appropriate for the following services to be available with respect to children in need within their area while they are living with their families—
(a) advice, guidance and counselling;

(b) occupational, social, cultural, or recreational activities;
(c) home help (which may include laundry facilities);
(d) facilities for, or assistance with, travelling to and from home for the purpose of taking advantage of any other service provided under this Act or of any similar service;
(e) assistance to enable the child concerned and his family to have a holiday.

Provision for accommodated children

8A (1) Every local authority shall make provision for such services as they consider appropriate to be available with respect to accommodated children.

(2) "Accommodated children" are those children in respect of whose accommodation the local authority have been notified under section 85 or 86.

(3) The services shall be provided with a view to promoting contact between each accommodated child and that child's family.

(4) The services may, in particular, include—
(a) advice, guidance and counselling;
(b) services necessary to enable the child to visit, or to be visited by, members of the family;
(c) assistance to enable the child and members of the family to have a holiday together.

(5) Nothing in this paragraph affects the duty imposed by paragraph 10.

Family centres

9. (1) Every local authority shall provide such family centres as they consider appropriate in relation to children within their area.

(2) "Family centre" means a centre at which any of the persons mentioned in sub-paragraph

(3) may—
(a) attend for occupational, social, cultural or recreational activities;
(b) attend for advice, guidance or counselling; or
(c) be provided with accommodation while he is receiving advice, guidance or counselling.

(3) The persons are—
(a) a child;
(b) his parents;
(c) any person who is not a parent of his but who has parental responsibility for him;
(d) any other person who is looking after him.

Maintenance of the family home

10. Every local authority shall take such steps as are reasonably practicable, where any child within their area who is in need and whom they are not looking after is living apart from his family—
(a) to enable him to live with his family; or
(b) to promote contact between him and his family, if, in their opinion, it is necessary to do so in order to safeguard or promote his welfare.

Duty to consider racial groups to which children in need belong

11. Every local authority shall, in making any arrangements—
(a) for the provision of day care within their area; or
(b) designed to encourage persons to act as local authority foster parents, have regard to the different racial groups to which children within their area who are in need belong.

Part II CHILDREN LOOKED AFTER BY LOCAL AUTHORITIES

Promotion and maintenance of contact between child and family

15. (1) Where a child is being looked after by a local authority, the authority shall, unless it is not reasonably practicable or consistent with his welfare, endeavour to promote contact between the child and—

(a) his parents;

(b) any person who is not a parent of his but who has parental responsibility for him; and

(c) any relative, friend or other person connected with him.

(2) Where a child is being looked after by a local authority—

(a) the authority shall take such steps as are reasonably practicable to secure that—

(i) his parents; and

(ii) any person who is not a parent of his but who has parental responsibility for him, are kept informed of where he is being accommodated; and

(b) every such person shall secure that the authority are kept informed of his or her address.

(3) Where a local authority ("the receiving authority") take over the provision of accommodation for a child from another local authority ("the transferring authority") under section 20(2)—

(a) the receiving authority shall (where reasonably practicable) inform—

(i) the child's parents; and

(ii) any person who is not a parent of his but who has parental responsibility for him;

(b) sub-paragraph (2)(a) shall apply to the transferring authority, as well as the receiving authority, until at least one such person has been informed of the change; and

(c) sub-paragraph (2)(b) shall not require any person to inform the receiving authority of his address until he has been so informed.

(4) Nothing in this paragraph requires a local authority to inform any person of the whereabouts of a child if—

(a) the child is in the care of the authority; and

(b) the authority has reasonable cause to believe that informing the person would prejudice the child's welfare.

(5) Any person who fails (without reasonable excuse) to comply with sub-paragraph (2)(b) shall be guilty of an offence and liable on summary conviction to a fine not exceeding level 2 on the standard scale.

(6) It shall be a defence in any proceedings under sub-paragraph (5) to prove that the defendant was residing at the same address as another person who was the child's parent or had parental responsibility for the child and had reasonable cause to believe that the other person had informed the appropriate authority that both of them were residing at that address.

Visits to or by children: expenses

16. (1) This paragraph applies where—

(a) a child is being looked after by a local authority; and

(b) the conditions mentioned in sub-paragraph (3) are satisfied.

(2) The authority may—

(a) make payments to—

(i) a parent of the child;

(ii) any person who is not a parent of his but who has parental responsibility for him; or
(iii) any relative, friend or other person connected with him, in respect of travelling, subsistence or other expenses incurred by that person in visiting the child; or

(b) make payments to the child, or to any person on his behalf, in respect of travelling, subsistence or other expenses incurred by or on behalf of the child in his visiting—
(i) a parent of his;
(ii) any person who is not a parent of his but who has parental responsibility for him; or
(iii) any relative, friend or other person connected with him.

(3) The conditions are that—
(a) it appears to the authority that the visit in question could not otherwise be made without undue financial hardship; and
(b) the circumstances warrant the making of the payments.

SCHEDULE 3 SUPERVISION ORDERS

Sections 35, 36

Part I GENERAL

Meaning of "responsible person"

1. In this Schedule, "the responsible person", in relation to a supervised child, means—
(a) any person who has parental responsibility for the child; and
(b) any other person with whom the child is living.

Power of supervisor to give directions to supervised child

2. (1) A supervision order may require the supervised child to comply with any directions given from time to time by the supervisor which require him to do all or any of the following things—
(a) to live at a place or places specified in the directions for a period or periods so specified;
(b) to present himself to a person or persons specified in the directions at a place or places and on a day or days so specified;
(c) to participate in activities specified in the directions on a day or days so specified.

(2) It shall be for the supervisor to decide whether, and to what extent, he exercises his power to give directions and to decide the form of any directions which he gives.

(3) Sub-paragraph (1) does not confer on a supervisor power to give directions in respect of any medical or psychiatric examination or treatment (which are matters dealt with in paragraphs 4 and 5).

Imposition of obligations on responsible person

3. (1) With the consent of any responsible person, a supervision order may include a requirement—
(a) that he take all reasonable steps to ensure that the supervised child complies with any direction given by the supervisor under paragraph 2;
(b) that he take all reasonable steps to ensure that the supervised child complies with any requirement included in the order under paragraph 4 or 5;
(c) that he comply with any directions given by the supervisor requiring him to attend at a place specified in the directions for the purpose of taking part in activities so specified.

(2) A direction given under sub-paragraph (1)(c) may specify the time at which the responsible person is to attend and whether or not the supervised child is required to attend with him.

(3) A supervision order may require any person who is a responsible person in relation to the supervised child to keep the supervisor informed of his address, if it differs from the child's.

Psychiatric and medical examinations

4. (1) A supervision order may require the supervised child—
(a) to submit to a medical or psychiatric examination; or
(b) to submit to any such examination from time to time as directed by the supervisor.

(2) Any such examination shall be required to be conducted—
(a) by, or under the direction of, such registered medical practitioner as may be specified in the order;
(b) at a place specified in the order and at which the supervised child is to attend as a non-resFident patient; or
(c) at—
(i) a health service hospital; or
(ii) in the case of a psychiatric examination, a hospital, independent hospital or care home, at which the child is, or is to attend as, a resident patient.

(3) A requirement of a kind mentioned in sub-paragraph (2)(c) shall not be included unless the court is satisfied, on the evidence of a registered medical practitioner, that—
(a) the child may be suffering from a physical or mental condition that requires, and may be susceptible to, treatment; and
(b) a period as a resident patient is necessary if the examination is to be carried out properly.

(4) No court shall include a requirement under this paragraph in a supervision order unless it is satisfied that—
(a) where the child has sufficient understanding to make an informed decision, he consents to its inclusion; and
(b) satisfactory arrangements have been, or can be, made for the examination.

Psychiatric and medical treatment

5. (1) Where a court which proposes to make or vary a supervision order is satisfied, on the evidence of a registered medical practitioner approved for the purposes of section 12 of the Mental Health Act 1983, that the mental condition of the supervised child—
(a) is such as requires, and may be susceptible to, treatment; but
(b) is not such as to warrant his detention in pursuance of a hospital order under Part III of that Act,

the court may include in the order a requirement that the supervised child shall, for a period specified in the order, submit to such treatment as is so specified.

(2) The treatment specified in accordance with sub-paragraph (1) must be—
(a) by, or under the direction of, such registered medical practitioner as may be specified in the order;
(b) as a non-resident patient at such a place as may be so specified; or
(c) as a resident patient in a hospital, independent hospital or care home.

(3) Where a court which proposes to make or vary a supervision order is satisfied, on the evidence of a registered medical practitioner, that the physical condition of the supervised child is such as requires, and may be susceptible to, treatment, the court

may include in the order a requirement that the supervised child shall, for a period specified in the order, submit to such treatment as is so specified.

(4) The treatment specified in accordance with sub-paragraph (3) must be—
(a) by, or under the direction of, such registered medical practitioner as may be specified in the order;
(b) as a non-resident patient at such place as may be so specified; or
(c) as a resident patient in a health service hospital.

(5) No court shall include a requirement under this paragraph in a supervision order unless it is satisfied—
(a) where the child has sufficient understanding to make an informed decision, that he consents to its inclusion; and
(b) that satisfactory arrangements have been, or can be, made for the treatment.

(6) If a medical practitioner by whom or under whose direction a supervised person is being treated in pursuance of a requirement included in a supervision order by virtue of this paragraph is unwilling to continue to treat or direct the treatment of the supervised child or is of the opinion that—
(a) the treatment should be continued beyond the period specified in the order;
(b) the supervised child needs different treatment;
(c) he is not susceptible to treatment; or
(d) he does not require further treatment, the practitioner shall make a report in writing to that effect to the supervisor.

(7) On receiving a report under this paragraph the supervisor shall refer it to the court, and on such a reference the court may make an order cancelling or varying the requirement.

Part II MISCELLANEOUS

Life of supervision order

6. (1) Subject to sub-paragraph (2) and section 91, a supervision order shall cease to have effect at the end of the period of one year beginning with the date on which it was made.

(2) A supervision order shall also cease to have effect if an event mentioned in section 25(1)(a) or (b) of the Child Abduction and Custody Act 1985 (termination of existing orders) occurs with respect to the child.

(3) Where the supervisor applies to the court to extend, or further extend, a supervision order the court may extend the order for such period as it may specify.

(4) A supervision order may not be extended so as to run beyond the end of the period of three years beginning with the date on which it was made.

Information to be given to supervisor etc

8. (1) A supervision order may require the supervised child—
(a) to keep the supervisor informed of any change in his address; and
(b) to allow the supervisor to visit him at the place where he is living.

(2) The responsible person in relation to any child with respect to whom a supervision order is made shall—
(a) if asked by the supervisor, inform him of the child's address (if it is known to him); and
(b) if he is living with the child, allow the supervisor reasonable contact with the child.

Selection of supervisor

9. (1) A supervision order shall not designate a local authority as the supervisor unless—

(a) the authority agree; or

(b) the supervised child lives or will live within their area.

Effect of supervision order on earlier orders

10. The making of a supervision order with respect to any child brings to an end any earlier care or supervision order which—

(a) was made with respect to that child; and

(b) would otherwise continue in force.

Local authority functions and expenditure

11. (1) The Secretary of State may make regulations with respect to the exercise by a local authority of their functions where a child has been placed under their supervision by a supervision order.

(2) Where a supervision order requires compliance with directions given by virtue of this section, any expenditure incurred by the supervisor for the purposes of the directions shall be defrayed by the local authority designated in the order.

Part III EDUCATION SUPERVISION ORDERS

Effect of orders

12. (1) Where an education supervision order is in force with respect to a child, it shall be the duty of the supervisor—

(a) to advise, assist and befriend, and give directions to—

(i) the supervised child; and

(ii) his parents,

in such a way as will, in the opinion of the supervisor, secure that he is properly educated;

(b) where any such directions given to—

(i) the supervised child; or

(ii) a parent of his,

have not been complied with, to consider what further steps to take in the exercise of the supervisor's powers under this Act.

(2) Before giving any directions under sub-paragraph (1) the supervisor shall, so far as is reasonably practicable, ascertain the wishes and feelings of—

(a) the child; and

(b) his parents,

including, in particular, their wishes as to the place at which the child should be educated.

(3) When settling the terms of any such directions, the supervisor shall give due consideration—

(a) having regard to the child's age and understanding, to such wishes and feelings of his as the supervisor has been able to ascertain; and

(b) to such wishes and feelings of the child's parents as he has been able to ascertain.

(4) Directions may be given under this paragraph at any time while the education supervision order is in force.

13. (1) Where an education supervision order is in force with respect to a child, the duties of the child's parents under sections 7 and 444 of the Education Act 1996 (duties to secure education of children and to secure regular attendance of registered pupils) shall be superseded by their duty to comply with any directions in force under the education supervision order.

(2) Where an education supervision order is made with respect to a child—
(a) any school attendance order—
(i) made under section 437 of the Education Act 1996 with respect to the child; and
(ii) in force immediately before the making of the education supervision order,
shall cease to have effect; and
(b) while the education supervision order remains in force, the following provisions shall not apply with respect to the child—
(i) section 437 of that Act (school attendance orders);
(ii) section 9 of that Act (pupils to be educated in accordance with wishes of their parents);
(iii) sections 411 and 423 of that Act (parental preference and appeals against admission decisions);
(c) a youth rehabilitation order made under Part 1 of the Criminal Justice and Immigration Act 2008 with respect to the child, while the education supervision order is in force, may not include an education requirement (within the meaning of that Part);
(d) any education requirement of a kind mentioned in paragraph (c), which was in force with respect to the child immediately before the making of the education supervision order, shall cease to have effect.

Effect where child also subject to supervision order

14. (1) This paragraph applies where an education supervision order and a supervision order, or youth rehabilitation order (within the meaning of Part 1 of the Criminal Justice and Immigration Act 2008), are in force at the same time with respect to the same child.

(2) Any failure to comply with a direction given by the supervisor under the education supervision order shall be disregarded if it would not have been reasonably practicable to comply with it without failing to comply with a direction or instruction given under the other order.

Duration of orders

15. (1) An education supervision order shall have effect for a period of one year, beginning with the date on which it is made.

(2) An education supervision order shall not expire if, before it would otherwise have expired, the court has (on the application of the authority in whose favour the order was made) extended the period during which it is in force.

(3) Such an application may not be made earlier than three months before the date on which the order would otherwise expire.

(4) The period during which an education supervision order is in force may be extended under sub-paragraph (2) on more than one occasion.

(5) No one extension may be for a period of more than three years.

(6) An education supervision order shall cease to have effect on—
(a) the child's ceasing to be of compulsory school age; or
(b) the making of a care order with respect to the child;
and sub-paragraphs (1) to (4) are subject to this sub-paragraph.

Information to be given to supervisor etc

16. (1) An education supervision order may require the child—

(a) to keep the supervisor informed of any change in his address; and

(b) to allow the supervisor to visit him at the place where he is living.

(2) A person who is the parent of a child with respect to whom an education supervision order has been made shall—

(a) if asked by the supervisor, inform him of the child's address (if it is known to him); and

(b) if he is living with the child, allow the supervisor reasonable contact with the child.

Discharge of orders

17. (1) The court may discharge any education supervision order on the application of—

(a) the child concerned;

(b) a parent of his; or

(c) the local education authority concerned.

(2) On discharging an education supervision order, the court may direct the local authority within whose area the child lives, or will live, to investigate the circumstances of the child.

Offences

18. (1) If a parent of a child with respect to whom an education supervision order is in force persistently fails to comply with a direction given under the order he shall be guilty of an offence.

(2) It shall be a defence for any person charged with such an offence to prove that—

(a) he took all reasonable steps to ensure that the direction was complied with;

(b) the direction was unreasonable; or

(c) he had complied with—

(i) a requirement included in a supervision order made with respect to the child; or

(ii) directions given under such a requirement, and that it was not reasonably practicable to comply both with the direction and with the requirement or directions mentioned in this paragraph.

(3) A person guilty of an offence under this paragraph shall be liable on summary conviction to a fine not exceeding level 3 on the standard scale.

Persistent failure of child to comply with directions

19. (1) Where a child with respect to whom an education supervision order is in force persistently fails to comply with any direction given under the order, the local education authority concerned shall notify the appropriate local authority.

(2) Where a local authority have been notified under sub-paragraph (1) they shall investigate the circumstances of the child.

(3) In this paragraph "the appropriate local authority" has the same meaning as in section 36.

Miscellaneous

20. The Secretary of State may by regulations make provision modifying, or displacing, the provisions of any enactment about education in relation to any child with respect to whom an education supervision order is in force to such extent as appears to the Secretary of State to be necessary or expedient in consequence of the provision made by this Act with respect to such orders.

Interpretation

21. In this Part of this Schedule "parent" has the same meaning as in the Education Act 1996.

NB On 1 June 2011, amendments made to sections 17, 26, and 105, and Sch 2, above, and substituting sections 22A–22G, above, for section 23, by the Children and Young Persons Act 2008, ss 8–10, 42, Sch 1, and Sch 4, were not in force in Wales.

As amended by: National Health Service and Community Care Act 1990, s 66(1), Sch 9; Courts and Legal Services Act 1990, ss 116, 125(7), Sch 16, Sch 20; Maintenance Enforcement Act 1991, ss 6, 11(1), Sch 2, para 10; Child Support Act 1991, s 58(14); Social Security (Consequential Provisions) Act 1992, s 4, Sch 2, para 108(a); Transfer of Functions (Magistrates' Courts and Family Law) Order 1992, SI 1992/709, art 3(2), Sch 2; Education Act 1993, s 307(1), (3), Sch 19, Sch 21; Maintenance Orders (Backdating) Order 1993, SI 1993/623, art 2, Sch 1; Local Government (Wales) Act 1994, ss 22(4), 66(8), Sch 10; Health Authorities Act 1995, ss 2(1), 5(1), Sch 1; Jobseekers Act 1995, s 41(4), Sch 2; Children (Scotland) Act 1995, s 105(4), Sch 4; Civil Evidence Act 1995, s 15(1), Sch 1; Law Reform (Succession) Act 1995, s 4; Family Law Act 1996, s 52, 66(1), (3), Sch 6, Sch 8, Sch 10; Education Act 1996, s 582(1), Sch 37; Crime and Disorder Act 1998, ss 15(4), 119, Sch 8; Access to Justice Act 1999, ss 24, 106, Sch 4, Sch 15; Health Act 1999 (Supplementary, Consequential etc. Provisions) Order 2000, SI 2000/90, arts 2(1), 3(1), Sch 1; Powers of Criminal Courts (Sentencing) Act 2000, s 165(1), Sch 9; Care Standards Act 2000, ss 116, 117(2), Sch 4, Sch 6; Child Support, Pensions and Social Security Act 2000, ss 26, 85, 86(2), Sch 3, Sch 9; Local Government Act 2000, s 107, Sch 5; Children (Leaving Care) Act 2000, s 1–5, 7; Criminal Justice and Court Services Act 2000, ss 74, 75, Sch 7, Sch 8; Health and Social Care Act 2001, s 58; Nursing and Midwifery Order 2001, SI 2002/253, art 54(3), Sch 5; Tax Credits Act 2002, ss 47, 60, Sch 3, Sch 6; Adoption and Children Act 2002, ss 100, 111–122, 139, Sch 3, Sch 5; National Health Service Reform and Health Care Professions Act 2002 (Supplementary, Consequential etc. Provisions) Regulations 2002, SI 2002/2469, reg 4, Sch 1; Health and Social Care (Community Health and Standards) Act 2003, ss 34, 116(2), (3), 117(1), Sch 4; Anti-social Behaviour Act 2003, s 88, Sch 2; Courts Act 2003, s 109(1), Sch 8; Transfer of Functions (Children, Young People and Families) Order 2003, SI 2003/3191, arts 3(a), 6, Schedule; Children Act 2004, ss 40, 49(3); 52, 53, Sch 3; Civil Partnership Act 2004, ss 75–78, 261(1), Sch 27; Health Act 1999 (Consequential Amendments) (Nursing and Midwifery) Order 2004, SI 2004/1771, art 3, Schedule; Constitutional Reform Act 2005, s 15(1); Education Act 2005, s 117, Sch 18; Children and Adoption Act 2006, ss 1–8, s 15, Sch 2, Sch 3; Childcare Act 2006, s 103, Sch 2, Sch 3; Education and Inspections Act 2006, ss 157, 184, Sch 14, Sch 18; National Health Service (Consequential Provisions) Act 2006, s 2, Sch 1; Welfare Reform Act 2007, s 28(1), Sch 3; References to Health Authorities Order 2007, SI 2007/961, art 3; Human Fertilisation and Embryology Act 2008, s 56, Sch 6; Children and Young Persons Act 2008, ss 8–10, 21(1), (2), 19, 24–25, 30, 36–39, 42, Sch 1, Sch 3, Sch 4; Criminal Justice and Immigration Act 2008, ss 6, 149, Sch 4, Sch 28; Access to Justice Act 1999 (Destination of Appeals) (Family Proceedings) Order 2009, SI 2009/871, art 7(1), (2); Policing and Crime Act 2009, s 112(2), Sch 8.

Forthcoming amendments: Education and Skills Act 2008, s 169(1), Sch 1, Pt 2, para 43; Welfare Reform Act 2009, s 56, Sch 6, Pt 2, paras 21, 22.

Human Fertilisation and Embryology Act 1990
(1990 c 37)

13 CONDITIONS OF LICENCES FOR TREATMENT

(1) The following shall be conditions of every licence under paragraph 1 of Schedule 2 to this Act.

(2) Such information shall be recorded as the Authority may specify in directions about the following—
(a) the persons for whom services are provided in pursuance of the licence,
(b) the services provided for them,
(c) the persons whose gametes are kept or used for the purposes of services provided in pursuance of the licence or whose gametes have been used in bringing about the creation of embryos so kept or used,
(d) any child appearing to the person responsible to have been born as a result of treatment in pursuance of the licence,
(e) any mixing of egg and sperm and any taking of an embryo from a woman or other acquisition of an embryo, and
(f) such other matters as the Authority may specify in directions.

(3) The records maintained in pursuance of the licence shall include any information recorded in pursuance of subsection (2) above and any consent of a person whose consent is required under Schedule 3 to this Act.

(4) No information shall be removed from any records maintained in pursuance of the licence before the expiry of such period as may be specified in directions for records of the class in question.

(5) A woman shall not be provided with treatment services unless account has been taken of the welfare of any child who may be born as a result of the treatment (including the need of that child for supportive parenting), and of any other child who may be affected by the birth.

(6) A woman shall not be provided with treatment services of a kind specified in Part 1 of Schedule 3ZA unless she and any man or woman who is to be treated together with her have been given a suitable opportunity to receive proper counselling about the implications of her being provided with treatment services of that kind, and have been provided with such relevant information as is proper.

(6A) A woman shall not be provided with treatment services after the happening of any event falling within any paragraph of Part 2 of Schedule 3ZA unless (before or after the event) she and the intended second parent have been given a suitable opportunity to receive proper counselling about the implications of the woman being provided with treatment services after the happening of that event, and have been provided with such relevant information as is proper.

(6B) The reference in subsection (6A) to the intended second parent is a reference to—
(a) any man as respects whom the agreed fatherhood conditions in section 37 of the Human Fertilisation and Embryology Act 2008 ("the 2008 Act") are for the time being satisfied in relation to treatment provided to the woman mentioned in subsection (6A), and
(b) any woman as respects whom the agreed female parenthood conditions in section 44 of the 2008 Act are for the time being satisfied in relation to treatment provided to the woman mentioned in subsection (6A).

(6C) In the case of treatment services falling within paragraph 1 of Schedule 3ZA (use of gametes of a person not receiving those services) or paragraph 3 of that Schedule (use of embryo taken from a woman not receiving those services), the information provided by virtue of subsection (6) or (6A) must include such information as is proper about—
(a) the importance of informing any resulting child at an early age that the child results from the gametes of a person who is not a parent of the child, and
(b) suitable methods of informing such a child of that fact.

(6D) Where the person responsible receives from a person ("X") notice under section 37(1)(c) or 44(1)(c) of the 2008 Act of X's withdrawal of consent to X being treated as the parent of any child resulting from the provision of treatment services to a woman ("W"), the person responsible—
(a) must notify W in writing of the receipt of the notice from X, and
(b) no person to whom the licence applies may place an embryo or sperm and eggs in W, or artificially inseminate W, until W has been so notified.

(6E) Where the person responsible receives from a woman ("W") who has previously given notice under section 37(1)(b) or 44(1)(b) of the 2008 Act that she consents to another person ("X") being treated as a parent of any child resulting from the provision of treatment services to W—
(a) notice under section 37(1)(c) or 44(1)(c) of the 2008 Act of the withdrawal of W's consent, or
(b) a notice under section 37(1)(b) or 44(1)(b) of the 2008 Act in respect of a person other than X,
the person responsible must take reasonable steps to notify X in writing of the receipt of the notice mentioned in paragraph (a) or (b).

(7) Suitable procedures shall be maintained—
(a) for determining the persons providing gametes or from whom embryos are taken for use in pursuance of the licence, and
(b) for the purpose of securing that consideration is given to the use of practices not requiring the authority of a licence as well as those requiring such authority.

(8) Subsections (9) and (10) apply in determining any of the following—
(a) the persons who are to provide gametes for use in pursuance of the licence in a case where consent is required under paragraph 5 of Schedule 3 for the use in question;
(b) the woman from whom an embryo is to be taken for use in pursuance of the licence, in a case where her consent is required under paragraph 7 of Schedule 3 for the use of the embryo;
(c) which of two or more embryos to place in a woman.

(9) Persons or embryos that are known to have a gene, chromosome or mitochondrion abnormality involving a significant risk that a person with the abnormality will have or develop—
(a) a serious physical or mental disability,
(b) a serious illness, or
(c) any other serious medical condition,
must not be preferred to those that are not known to have such an abnormality.

(10) Embryos that are known to be of a particular sex and to carry a particular risk, compared with embryos of that sex in general, that any resulting child will have or develop—
(a) a gender-related serious physical or mental disability,
(b) a gender-related serious illness, or
(c) any other gender-related serious medical condition,
must not be preferred to those that are not known to carry such a risk.

(11) For the purposes of subsection (10), a physical or mental disability, illness or other medical condition is gender-related if—
(a) it affects only one sex, or
(b) it affects one sex significantly more than the other.

(12) No embryo appropriated for the purpose mentioned in paragraph 1(1)(ca) of Schedule 2 (training in embryological techniques) shall be kept or used for the provision of treatment services.

(13) The person responsible shall comply with any requirement imposed on that person by section 31ZD.

As amended by: Human Fertilisation and Embryology (Quality and Safety) Regulations 2007, SI 2007/1522, regs 3, 14; Human Fertilisation and Embryology Act 2008, ss 14, 66, Sch 8, Pt 1.

MAINTENANCE ENFORCEMENT ACT 1991

(1991 c 17)

The High Court and county courts

1 MAINTENANCE ORDERS IN THE HIGH COURT AND COUNTY COURTS: MEANS OF PAYMENT, ATTACHMENT OF EARNINGS AND REVOCATION, VARIATION, ETC

(1) Where the High Court or a county court makes a qualifying periodical maintenance order, it may at the same time exercise either of its powers under subsection (4) below in relation to the order, whether of its own motion or on an application made under this subsection by an interested party.

(2) For the purposes of this section, a periodical maintenance order is an order—
(a) which requires money to be paid periodically by one person ("the debtor") to another ("the creditor"); and
(b) which is a maintenance order;
and such an order is a "qualifying periodical maintenance order" if, at the time it is made, the debtor is ordinarily resident in England and Wales.

(3) Where the High Court or a county court has made a qualifying periodical maintenance order, it may at any later time—
(a) on an application made under this subsection by an interested party, or
(b) of its own motion, in the course of any proceedings concerning the order,
exercise either of its powers under subsection (4) below in relation to the order.

(4) The powers mentioned in subsections (1) and (3) above are—
(a) the power to order that payments required to be made by the debtor to the creditor under the qualifying periodical maintenance order in question shall be so made by such a method of payment falling within subsection (5) below as the court may specify in the particular case; or
(b) the power, by virtue of this section, to make an attachment of earnings order under the Attachment of Earnings Act 1971 to secure payments under the qualifying periodical maintenance order in question.

(5) The methods of payment mentioned in subsection (4)(a) above are—
(a) payment by standing order; or
(b) payment by any other method which requires the debtor to give his authority for payments of a specific amount to be made from an account of his to an account of the creditor's on specific dates during the period for which the authority is in force and without the need for any further authority from the debtor.

(6) In any case where—
(a) the court proposes to exercise its power under paragraph (a) of subsection (4) above, and
(b) having given the debtor an opportunity of opening an account from which payments under the order may be made in accordance with the method of payment proposed to be ordered under that paragraph, the court is satisfied that the debtor has failed, without reasonable excuse, to open such an account,

the court in exercising its power under that paragraph may order that the debtor open such an account.

(7) Where in the exercise of its powers under subsection (1) or (3) above, the High Court or a county court has made in relation to a qualifying periodical maintenance order such an order as is mentioned in subsection (4)(a) above (a "means of payment order"), it may at any later time—
(a) on an application made under this subsection by an interested party, or
(b) of its own motion, in the course of any proceedings concerning the qualifying periodical maintenance order,

revoke, suspend, revive or vary the means of payment order.

(8) In deciding whether to exercise any of its powers under this section the court in question having (if practicable) given every interested party an opportunity to make representations shall have regard to any representations made by any such party.

(9) Nothing in this section shall be taken to prejudice—
(a) any power under the Attachment of Earnings Act 1971 which would, apart from this section, be exercisable by the High Court or a county court; or
(b) any right of any person to make any application under that Act;

and subsection (7) above is without prejudice to any other power of the High Court or a county court to revoke, suspend, revive or vary an order.

(10) For the purposes of this section—

"debtor" and "creditor" shall be construed in accordance with subsection (2) above;

"interested party" means any of the following, that is to say—
(a) the debtor;
(b) the creditor; and
(c) in a case where the person who applied for the qualifying periodical maintenance order in question is a person other than the creditor, that other person;

"maintenance order" means any order specified in Schedule 8 to the Administration of Justice Act 1970 and includes any such order which has been discharged, if any arrears are recoverable under it;

"qualifying periodical maintenance order" shall be construed in accordance with subsection (2) above, and the references to such an order in subsections (3) and (7) above are references to any such order, whether made before or after the coming into force of this section;

and the reference in subsection (2) above to an order requiring money to be paid periodically by one person to another includes a reference to an order requiring a lump sum to be paid by instalments by one person to another.

Child Support Act 1991

(1991 c 48)

The basic principles

1 THE DUTY TO MAINTAIN

(1) For the purposes of this Act, each parent of a qualifying child is responsible for maintaining him.

(2) For the purposes of this Act, a non-resident parent shall be taken to have met his responsibility to maintain any qualifying child of his by making periodical payments of maintenance with respect to the child of such amount, and at such intervals, as may be determined in accordance with the provisions of this Act.

(3) Where a maintenance calculation made under this Act requires the making of periodical payments, it shall be the duty of the non-resident parent with respect to whom the calculation was made to make those payments.

2 WELFARE OF CHILDREN: THE GENERAL PRINCIPLE

Where, in any case which falls to be dealt with under this Act, the Commission is considering the exercise of any discretionary power conferred by this Act, it shall have regard to the welfare of any child likely to be affected by its decision.

3 MEANING OF CERTAIN TERMS USED IN THIS ACT

(1) A child is a "qualifying child" if—
  (a) one of his parents is, in relation to him, a non-resident parent; or
  (b) both of his parents are, in relation to him, non-resident parents.

(2) The parent of any child is a "non-resident parent", in relation to him, if—
  (a) that parent is not living in the same household with the child; and
  (b) the child has his home with a person who is, in relation to him, a person with care.

(3) A person is a "person with care", in relation to any child, if he is a person—
  (a) with whom the child has his home;
  (b) who usually provides day to day care for the child (whether exclusively or in conjunction with any other person); and
  (c) who does not fall within a prescribed category of person.

(4) The Secretary of State shall not, under subsection (3)(c), prescribe as a category—
  (a) parents;
  (b) guardians;
  (c) persons in whose favour residence orders under section 8 of the Children Act 1989 are in force;

(5) For the purposes of this Act there may be more than one person with care in relation to the same qualifying child.

(6) Periodical payments which are required to be paid in accordance with a maintenance calculation are referred to in this Act as "child support maintenance".

(7) Expressions are defined in this section only for the purposes of this Act.

4 CHILD SUPPORT MAINTENANCE

(1) A person who is, in relation to any qualifying child or any qualifying children, either the person with care or the non-resident parent may apply to the Commission for a maintenance calculation to be made under this Act with respect to that child, or any of those children.

(2) Where a maintenance calculation has been made in response to an application under this section the Commission may, if the person with care or non-resident parent with respect to whom the calculation was made applies to it under this subsection, arrange for—
- (a) the collection of the child support maintenance payable in accordance with the calculation;
- (b) the enforcement of the obligation to pay child support maintenance in accordance with the calculation.

(3) Where an application under subsection (2) for the enforcement of the obligation mentioned in subsection (2)(b) authorises the Commission to take steps to enforce that obligation whenever it considers it necessary to do so, the Commission may act accordingly.

(4) A person who applies to the Commission under this section shall, so far as that person reasonably can, comply with such regulations as may be made by the Secretary of State with a view to the Commission being provided with the information which is required to enable—
- (a) the non-resident parent to be identified or traced (where that is necessary);
- (b) the amount of child support maintenance payable by the non-resident parent to be calculated; and
- (c) that amount to be recovered from the non-resident parent.

(5) Any person who has applied to the Commission under this section may at any time request it to cease acting under this section.

(6) It shall be the duty of the Commission to comply with any request made under subsection (5) (but subject to any regulations made under subsection (8)).

(7) The obligation to provide information which is imposed by subsection (4)—
- (a) shall not apply in such circumstances as may be prescribed; and
- (b) may, in such circumstances as may be prescribed, be waived by the Commission.

(8) The Secretary of State may by regulations make such incidental, supplemental or transitional provision as he thinks appropriate with respect to cases in which he is requested to cease to act under this section.

(10) No application may be made at any time under this section with respect to a qualifying child or any qualifying children if—
- (a) there is in force a written maintenance agreement made before 5th April 1993, or a maintenance order made before a prescribed date, in respect of that child or those children and the person who is, at that time, the non-resident parent; or
- (aa) a maintenance order made on or after the date prescribed for the purposes of paragraph (a) is in force in respect of them, but has been so for less than the period of one year beginning with the date on which it was made; . . .

5 CHILD SUPPORT MAINTENANCE: SUPPLEMENTAL PROVISIONS

(1) Where—
(a) there is more than one person with care of a qualifying child; and
(b) one or more, but not all, of them have parental responsibility for the child;
no application may be made for a maintenance calculation with respect to the child by any of those persons who do not have parental responsibility for the child.

(2) Where more than one application for a maintenance calculation is made with respect to the child concerned, only one of them may be proceeded with.

(3) The Secretary of State may by regulations make provision as to which of two or more applications for a maintenance calculation with respect to the same child is to be proceeded with.

. . .

8 ROLE OF THE COURTS WITH RESPECT TO MAINTENANCE FOR CHILDREN

(1) This subsection applies in any case where the Commission would have jurisdiction to make a maintenance calculation with respect to a qualifying child and a non-resident parent of his on an application duly made by a person entitled to apply for such a calculation with respect to that child.

(2) Subsection (1) applies even though the circumstances of the case are such that the Commission would not make a calculation if it were applied for.

(3) Except as provided in subsection (3A), in any case where subsection (1) applies, no court shall exercise any power which it would otherwise have to make, vary or revive any maintenance order in relation to the child and non-resident parent concerned.

(3A) Unless a maintenance calculation has been made with respect to the child concerned, subsection (3) does not prevent a court from varying a maintenance order in relation to that child and the non-resident parent concerned—
(a) if the maintenance order was made on or after the date prescribed for the purposes of section 4(10)(a) or 7(10)(a); or
(b) where the order was made before then, in any case in which section 4(10) or 7(10) prevents the making of an application for a maintenance calculation with respect to or by that child.

(4) Subsection (3) does not prevent a court from revoking a maintenance order.

(5) The Lord Chancellor or in relation to Scotland the Lord Advocate may by order provide that, in such circumstances as may be specified by the order, this section shall not prevent a court from exercising any power which it has to make a maintenance order in relation to a child if—
(a) a written agreement (whether or not enforceable) provides for the making, or securing, by a non-resident parent of the child of periodical payments to or for the benefit of the child; and
(b) the maintenance order which the court makes is, in all material respects, in the same terms as that agreement.

(5A) The Lord Chancellor may make an order under subsection (5) only with the concurrence of the Lord Chief Justice.

(6) This section shall not prevent a court from exercising any power which it has to make a maintenance order in relation to a child if—
(a) a maintenance calculation is in force with respect to the child;
(b) the non-resident parent's net weekly income exceeds the figure referred to in paragraph 10(3) of Schedule 1 (as it has effect from time to time pursuant to regulations made under paragraph 10A(1)(b)); and
(c) the court is satisfied that the circumstances of the case make it appropriate for the non-resident parent to make or secure the making of periodical payments under a maintenance order in addition to the child support maintenance payable by him in accordance with the maintenance calculation.

(7) This section shall not prevent a court from exercising any power which it has to make a maintenance order in relation to a child if—
(a) the child is, will be or (if the order were to be made) would be receiving instruction at an educational establishment or undergoing training for a trade, profession or vocation (whether or not while in gainful employment); and
(b) the order is made solely for the purposes of requiring the person making or securing the making of periodical payments fixed by the order to meet some or all of the expenses incurred in connection with the provision of the instruction or training.

(8) This section shall not prevent a court from exercising any power which it has to make a maintenance order in relation to a child if—
(a) a disability living allowance is paid to or in respect of him; or
(b) no such allowance is paid but he is disabled, and the order is made solely for the purpose of requiring the person making or securing the making of periodical payments fixed by the order to meet some or all of any expenses attributable to the child's disability.

(9) For the purposes of subsection (8), a child is disabled if he is blind, deaf or dumb or is substantially and permanently handicapped by illness, injury, mental disorder or congenital deformity or such other disability as may be prescribed.

(10) This section shall not prevent a court from exercising any power which it has to make a maintenance order in relation to a child if the order is made against a person with care of the child.

(11) In this Act "maintenance order", in relation to any child, means an order which requires the making or securing of periodical payments to or for the benefit of the child and which is made under—
(a) Part II of the Matrimonial Causes Act 1973;
(b) the Domestic Proceedings and Magistrates' Courts Act 1978;
(c) Part III of the Matrimonial and Family Proceedings Act 1984;
(d) the Family Law (Scotland) Act 1985;
(e) Schedule 1 to the Children Act 1989;
(ea) Schedule 5, 6 or 7 to the Civil Partnership Act 2004; or
(f) any other prescribed enactment, and includes any order varying or reviving such an order.

(12) The Lord Chief Justice may nominate a judicial office holder (as defined in section 109(4) of the Constitutional Reform Act 2005) to exercise his functions under this section.

9 AGREEMENTS ABOUT MAINTENANCE

(1) In this section "maintenance agreement" means any agreement for the making, or for securing the making, of periodical payments by way of maintenance, or in Scotland aliment, to or for the benefit of any child.

(2) Nothing in this Act shall be taken to prevent any person from entering into a maintenance agreement.

(3) Subject to section 4(10)(a) and (ab) and section 7(10), the existence of a maintenance agreement shall not prevent any party to the agreement, or any other person, from applying for a maintenance calculation with respect to any child to or for whose benefit periodical payments are to be made or secured under the agreement.

(4) Where any agreement contains a provision which purports to restrict the right of any person to apply for a maintenance calculation, that provision shall be void.

(5) Where section 8 would prevent any court from making a maintenance order in relation to a child and a non-resident parent of his, no court shall exercise any power that it has to vary any agreement so as—
(a) to insert a provision requiring that non-resident parent to make or secure the making of periodical payments by way of maintenance to or for the benefit of that child; or
(b) to increase the amount payable under such a provision.

(6) In any case in which section 4(10) or 7(10) prevents the making of an application for maintenance calculation, subsection (5) shall have effect with the omission of paragraph (b).

10 RELATIONSHIP BETWEEN MAINTENANCE CALCULATIONS AND CERTAIN COURT ORDERS AND RELATED MATTERS

(1) Where an order of a kind prescribed for the purposes of this subsection is in force with respect to any qualifying child with respect to whom a maintenance calculation is made, the order—
(a) shall, so far as it relates to the making or securing of periodical payments, cease to have effect to such extent as may be determined in accordance with regulations made by the Secretary of State; or
(b) where the regulations so provide,
shall, so far as it so relates, have effect subject to such modifications as may be so determined.

(2) Where an agreement of a kind prescribed for the purposes of this subsection is in force with respect to any qualifying child with respect to whom a maintenance calculation is made, the agreement—
(a) shall, so far as it relates to the making or securing of periodical payments, be unenforceable to such extent as may be determined in accordance with regulations made by the Secretary of State; or
(b) where the regulations so provide, shall, so far as it so relates, have effect subject to such modifications as may be so determined.

(3) Any regulations under this section may, in particular, make such provision with respect to—
(a) any case where any person with respect to whom an order or agreement of a kind prescribed for the purposes of subsection (1) or (2) has effect applies to the prescribed court, before the end of the prescribed period, for the order or agreement to be varied in the light of the maintenance calculation and of the provisions of this Act;
(b) the recovery of any arrears under the order or agreement which fell due before the coming into force of the maintenance calculation, as the Secretary of State considers appropriate and may provide that, in prescribed circumstances, an application to any court which is made with respect to an order of a prescribed kind relating to the making or securing of periodical payments to or for the benefit of a child shall be treated by the court as an application for the order to be revoked.

(4) The Secretary of State may by regulations make provision for—
(a) notification to be given by the Commission to the prescribed person in any case where it considers that the making of a maintenance calculation has affected, or is likely to affect, any order of a kind prescribed for the purposes of this subsection;
(b) notification to be given by the prescribed person to the Commission in any case where a court makes an order which it considers has affected, or is likely to affect, a maintenance calculation.

(5) Rules may be made under section 144 of the Magistrates' Courts Act 1980 (rules of procedure) requiring any person who, in prescribed circumstances, makes an application to a magistrates' court for a maintenance order to furnish the court with a statement in a prescribed form, and signed by an officer of the Commission, as to whether or not, at the time when the statement is made, there is a maintenance calculation in force with respect to that person or the child concerned.

In this subsection—

"maintenance order" means an order of a prescribed kind for the making or securing of periodical payments to or for the benefit of a child; and

"prescribed" means prescribed by the rules.

Maintenance calculations

11 MAINTENANCE CALCULATIONS

(1) An application for a maintenance calculation made to the Commission shall be dealt with by it in accordance with the provision made by or under this Act.

(2) The Commission shall (unless it decides not to make a maintenance calculation in response to the application, or makes a decision under section 12) determine the application by making a decision under this section about whether any child support maintenance is payable and, if so, how much.

(6) The amount of child support maintenance to be fixed by a maintenance calculation shall be determined in accordance with Part I of Schedule 1 unless an application for a variation has been made and agreed.

(7) If the Commission has agreed to a variation, the amount of child support maintenance to be fixed shall be determined on the basis it determines under section 28F(4).

(8) Part II of Schedule 1 makes further provision with respect to maintenance calculations.

. . .

26 DISPUTES ABOUT PARENTAGE

(1) Where a person who is alleged to be a parent of the child with respect to whom an application for a maintenance calculation has been made ("the alleged parent") denies that he is one of the child's parents, the Commission shall not make a maintenance calculation on the assumption that the alleged parent is one of the child's parents unless the case falls within one of those set out in subsection (2).

(2) The Cases are—

CASE A1

Where—
(a) the child is habitually resident in England and Wales;

(b) the Commission is satisfied that the alleged parent was married to the child's mother at some time in the period beginning with the conception and ending with the birth of the child; and
(c) the child has not been adopted.

CASE A2

Where—
(a) the child is habitually resident in England and Wales;
(b) the alleged parent has been registered as father of the child under section 10 or 10A of the Births and Deaths Registration Act 1953, or in any register kept under section 13 (register of births and still-births) or section 44 (Register of Corrections Etc) of the Registration of Births, Deaths and Marriages (Scotland) Act 1965, or under Article 14 or 18(1)(b)(ii) of the Births and Deaths Registration (Northern Ireland) Order 1976; and
(c) the child has not subsequently been adopted.

CASE A3

Where the result of a scientific test (within the meaning of section 27A) taken by the alleged parent would be relevant to determining the child's parentage, and the alleged parent—
(a) refuses to take such a test; or
(b) has submitted to such a test, and it shows that there is no reasonable doubt that the alleged parent is a parent of the child.

CASE A

Where the alleged parent is a parent of the child in question by virtue of having adopted him.

CASE B

Where the alleged parent is a parent of the child in question by virtue of an order under section 30 of the Human Fertilisation and Embryology Act 1990 or section 54 of the Human Fertilisation and Embryology Act 2008 (parental orders).

CASE B1

Where the Secretary of State is satisfied that the alleged parent is a parent of the child in question by virtue of section 27 or 28 of the Human Fertilisation and Embryology Act 1990 or any of sections 33 to 46 of the Human Fertilisation and Embryology Act 2008 (which relate to children resulting from assisted reproduction).

CASE C

Where—
(a) either—
  (i) a declaration that the alleged parent is a parent of the child in question (or a declaration which has that effect) is in force under section 55A or 56 of the Family Law Act 1986 or Article 32 of the Matrimonial and Family Proceedings (Northern Ireland) Order 1989 (declarations of parentage); or
  (ii) a declarator by a court in Scotland that the alleged parent is a parent of the child in question (or a declarator which has that effect) is in force; and
(b) the child has not subsequently been adopted.

. . .

CASE F

Where—
(a) the alleged parent has been found, or adjudged, to be the father of the child in question—
(i) in proceedings before any court in England and Wales which are relevant proceedings for the purposes of section 12 of the Civil Evidence Act 1968 or in proceedings before any court in Northern Ireland which are relevant proceedings for the purposes of section 8 of the Civil Evidence Act (Northern Ireland) 1971; or
(ii) in affiliation proceedings before any court in the United Kingdom, (whether or not he offered any defence to the allegation of paternity) and that finding or adjudication still subsists; and
(b) the child has not subsequently been adopted.

(3) In this section—

"adopted" means adopted within the meaning of Part IV of the Adoption Act 1976 or Chapter 4 of Part 1 of the Adoption and Children Act 2002 or, in relation to Scotland, Part IV of the Adoption (Scotland) Act 1978 or Chapter 3 of Part 1 of the Adoption and Children (Scotland) Act 2007 (asp 4);

. . .

27 APPLICATIONS FOR DECLARATION OF PARENTAGE UNDER FAMILY LAW ACT 1986

(1) This section applies where—
(a) an application for a maintenance calculation has been made, or a maintenance calculation is in force, with respect to a person ("the alleged parent") who denies that he is a parent of a child with respect to whom the application or calculation was made;
(b) the Commission is not satisfied that the case falls within one of those set out in section 26(2); and
(c) the Commission or the person with care makes an application for a declaration under section 55A of the Family Law Act 1986 as to whether or not the alleged parent is one of the child's parents.

(2) Where this section applies—
(a) if it is the person with care who makes the application, she shall be treated as having a sufficient personal interest for the purposes of subsection (3) of that section; and
(b) if it is the Commission who makes the application, that subsection shall not apply.

. . .

Variations

28A APPLICATION FOR VARIATION OF USUAL RULES FOR CALCULATING MAINTENANCE

(1) Where an application for a maintenance calculation is made under section 4 or 7 the person with care or the non-resident parent or (in the case of an application under section 7) either of them or the child concerned may apply to the Commission for the rules by which the calculation is made to be varied in accordance with this Act.

(2) Such an application is referred to in this Act as an "application for a variation".

(3) An application for a variation may be made at any time before the Commission has reached a decision (under section 11 or 12(1)) on the application for a maintenance calculation

(4) A person who applies for a variation—
(a) need not make the application in writing unless the Commission directs in any case that he must; and
(b) must say upon what grounds the application is made.

(5) In other respects an application for a variation is to be made in such manner as may be prescribed.

(6) Schedule 4A has effect in relation to applications for a variation.

. . .

28E MATTERS TO BE TAKEN INTO ACCOUNT

(1) In determining whether to agree to a variation, the Commission shall have regard both to the general principles set out in subsection (2) and to such other considerations as may be prescribed.

(2) The general principles are that—
(a) parents should be responsible for maintaining their children whenever they can afford to do so;
(b) where a parent has more than one child, his obligation to maintain any one of them should be no less of an obligation than his obligation to maintain any other of them.

(3) In determining whether to agree to a variation, the Commission shall take into account any representations made to it—
(a) by the person with care or non-resident parent concerned; or
(b) where the application for the current calculation was made under section 7, by either of them or the child concerned.

(4) In determining whether to agree to a variation, no account shall be taken of the fact that—
(a) any part of the income of the person with care concerned is, or would be if the Commission agreed to a variation, derived from any benefit; or
(b) some or all of any child support maintenance might be taken into account in any manner in relation to any entitlement to benefit.

(5) In this section "benefit" has such meaning as may be prescribed.

28F AGREEMENT TO A VARIATION

(1) The Commission may agree to a variation if—
(a) it is satisfied that the case is one which falls within one or more of the cases set out in Part I of Schedule 4B or in regulations made under that Part; and
(b) it is its opinion that, in all the circumstances of the case, it would be just and equitable to agree to a variation.

(2) In considering whether it would be just and equitable in any case to agree to a variation, the Commission—
(a) must have regard, in particular, to the welfare of any child likely to be affected if it did agree to a variation; and
(b) must, or as the case may be must not, take any prescribed factors into account, or must take them into account (or not) in prescribed circumstances.

(3) The Commission shall not agree to a variation (and shall proceed to make its decision on the application for a maintenance calculation without any variation) if it is satisfied that—
  (a) it has insufficient information to make a decision on the application for the maintenance calculation under section 11, and therefore that its decision would be made under section 12(1); or
  (b) other prescribed circumstances apply.

(4) Where the Commission agrees to a variation, it shall—
  (a) determine the basis on which the amount of child support maintenance is to be calculated in response to the application for a maintenance calculation; and
  (b) make a decision under section 11 on that basis.

(5) If the Commission has made an interim maintenance decision, it is to be treated as having been replaced by his decision under section 11, and except in prescribed circumstances any appeal connected with it (under section 20) shall lapse.

(6) In determining whether or not to agree to a variation, the Commission shall comply with regulations made under Part II of Schedule 4B.

. . .

Collection and enforcement

29 COLLECTION OF CHILD SUPPORT MAINTENANCE

(1) The Commission may arrange for the collection of any child support maintenance payable in accordance with a maintenance calculation where—
  (b) an application has been made to the Commission under section 4(2) or 7(3) for it to arrange for its collection.

(2) Where a maintenance calculation is made under this Act, payments of child support maintenance under the calculation shall be made in accordance with regulations made by the Secretary of State.

(3) The regulations may, in particular, make provision—
  (a) for payments of child support maintenance to be made—
    (i) to the person caring for the child or children in question;
    (ii) to, or through, the Commission; or
    (iii) to, or through, such other person as the Commission may, from time to time, specify;
  (b) as to the method by which payments of child support maintenance are to be made;
  (c) as to the intervals at which such payments are to be made;
  (d) as to the method and timing of the transmission of payments which are made, to or through the Commission or any other person, in accordance with the regulations;
  (e) empowering the Commission to direct any person liable to make payments in accordance with the calculation—
    (i) to make them by standing order or by any other method which requires one person to give his authority for payments to be made from an account of his to an account of another's on specific dates during the period for which the authority is in force and without the need for any further authority from him;
    (ii) to open an account from which payments under the calculation may be made in accordance with the method of payment which that person is obliged to adopt;
  (f) providing for the making of representations with respect to matters with which the regulations are concerned.

(4) If the regulations include provision for payment by means of deduction in accordance with an order under section 31, they must make provision—
(a) for that method of payment not to be used in any case where there is good reason not to use it; and
(b) for the person against whom the order under section 31 would be made to have a right of appeal to a magistrates' court (or, in Scotland, to the sheriff) against a decision that the exclusion required by paragraph (a) does not apply.

(5) On an appeal under regulations made under subsection (4)(b) the court or (as the case may be) the sheriff shall not question the maintenance calculation by reference to which the order under section 31 would be made.

(6) Regulations under subsection (4)(b) may include—
(a) provision with respect to the period within which a right of appeal under the regulations may be exercised;
(b) provision with respect to the powers of a magistrates' court (or, in Scotland, of the sheriff) in relation to an appeal under the regulations.

(7) If the regulations include provision for payment by means of deduction in accordance with an order under section 31, they may make provision—
(a) prescribing matters which are, or are not, to be taken into account in determining whether there is good reason not to use that method of payment;
(b) prescribing circumstances in which good reason not to use that method of payment is, or is not, to be regarded as existing.

. . .

31 DEDUCTION FROM EARNINGS ORDERS

(1) This section applies where any person ("the liable person") is liable to make payments of child support maintenance.

(2) The Commission may make an order ("a deduction from earnings order") against a liable person to secure the payment of any amount due under the maintenance calculation in question.

(3) A deduction from earnings order may be made so as to secure the payment of—
(a) arrears of child support maintenance payable under the calculation;
(b) amounts of child support maintenance which will become due under the calculation; or
(c) both such arrears and such future amounts.

(4) A deduction from earnings order—
(a) shall be expressed to be directed at a person ("the employer") who has the liable person in his employment; and
(b) shall have effect from such date as may be specified in the order.

(5) A deduction from earnings order shall operate as an instruction to the employer to—
(a) make deductions from the liable person's earnings; and
(b) pay the amounts deducted to the Commission.

(6) The Commission shall serve a copy of any deduction from earnings order which it makes under this section on—
(a) the person who appears to the Commission to have the liable person in question in his employment; and
(b) the liable person.

(7) Where—
(a) a deduction from earnings order has been made; and
(b) a copy of the order has been served on the liable person's employer,
it shall be the duty of that employer to comply with the order; but he shall not be under any liability for non-compliance before the end of the period of seven days beginning with the date on which the copy was served on him.

(8) In this section and in section 32 "earnings" has such meaning as may be prescribed.

. . .

32A ORDERS FOR REGULAR DEDUCTIONS FROM ACCOUNTS

(1) If in relation to any person it appears to the Commission—
(a) that the person has failed to pay an amount of child support maintenance; and
(b) that the person holds an account with a deposit-taker;
it may make an order against that person to secure the payment of any amount due under the maintenance calculation in question by means of regular deductions from the account.

(2) An order under this section may be made so as to secure the payment of—
(a) arrears of child support maintenance payable under the calculation;
(b) amounts of child support maintenance which will become payable under the calculation; or
(c) both such arrears and such future amounts.

(3) An order under this section may be made in respect of amounts due under a maintenance calculation which is the subject of an appeal only if it appears to the Commission—
(a) that liability for the amounts would not be affected were the appeal to succeed; or
(b) where paragraph (a) does not apply, that the making of an order under this section in respect of the amounts would nonetheless be fair in all the circumstances.

. . .

(5) An order under this section—
(a) shall specify the account in respect of which it is made;
(b) shall be expressed to be directed at the deposit-taker with which the account is held; and
(c) shall have effect from such date as may be specified in the order.

(6) An order under this section shall operate as an instruction to the deposit-taker at which it is directed to—
(a) make deductions from the amount (if any) standing to the credit of the account specified in the order; and
(b) pay the amount deducted to the Commission.

(7) The Commission shall serve a copy of any order made under this section on—
(a) the deposit-taker at which it is directed;
(b) the person against whom it is made; and
(c) if the order is made in respect of a joint account, the other account-holders.

(8) Where—
(a) an order under this section has been made; and
(b) a copy of the order has been served on the deposit-taker at which it is directed,
it shall be the duty of that deposit-taker to comply with the order; but the deposit-taker shall not be under any liability for non-compliance before the end of the period of 7 days beginning with the day on which the copy was served on the deposit-taker.

(9) Where regulations have been made under section 29(3)(a), a person liable to pay an amount of child support maintenance is to be taken for the purposes of this section to have failed to pay an amount of child support maintenance unless it is paid to or through the person specified in, or by virtue of, the regulations for the case in question.

32B ORDERS UNDER SECTION 32A: JOINT ACCOUNTS

(1) Before making an order under section 32A in respect of a joint account the Commission shall offer each of the account-holders an opportunity to make representations about—
(a) the proposal to make the order; and
(b) the amounts to be deducted under the order, if it is made.

(2) The amounts to be deducted from a joint account under such an order shall not exceed the amounts that appear to the Commission to be fair in all the circumstances.

(3) In determining those amounts the Commission shall have particular regard to—
(a) any representations made in accordance with subsection (1)(b);
(b) the amount contributed to the account by each of the account-holders; and
(c) such other matters as may be prescribed.

32C REGULATIONS ABOUT ORDERS UNDER SECTION 32A

(1) The Secretary of State may by regulations make provision with respect to orders under section 32A.

. . .

(4) The Secretary of State shall by regulations make provision for any person affected to have a right to appeal to a court—
(a) against the making of an order under section 32A;
(b) against any decision made by the Commission on an application under regulations made under subsection (2)(k).

(5) On an appeal under regulations made under subsection (4)(a), the court shall not question the maintenance calculation by reference to which the order was made.

(6) Regulations under subsection (4) may include—
(a) provision with respect to the period within which a right of appeal under the regulations may be exercised;
(b) provision with respect to the powers of the court to which the appeal under the regulations lies.

32D ORDERS UNDER SECTION 32A: OFFENCES

(1) A person who fails to comply with the requirements of—
(a) an order under section 32A, or
(b) any regulation under section 32C which is designated by the regulations for the purposes of this paragraph,
commits an offence.

(2) It shall be a defence for a person charged with an offence under subsection (1) to prove that the person took all reasonable steps to comply with the requirements in question.

(3) A person guilty of an offence under subsection (1) shall be liable on summary conviction to a fine not exceeding level two on the standard scale.

32E LUMP SUM DEDUCTIONS: INTERIM ORDERS

(1) The Commission may make an order under this section if it appears to the Commission that a person (referred to in this section and sections 32F to 32J as "the liable person") has failed to pay an amount of child support maintenance and—

(a) an amount stands to the credit of an account held by the liable person with a deposit-taker; or

(b) an amount not within paragraph (a) that is of a prescribed description is due or accruing to the liable person from another person (referred to in this section and sections 32F to 32J as the "third party").

. . .

(4) An order under this section—

(a) shall be expressed to be directed at the deposit-taker or third party in question;

(b) if made by virtue of subsection (1)(a), shall specify the account in respect of which it is made; and

(c) shall specify the amount of arrears of child support maintenance in respect of which the Commission proposes to make an order under section 32F.

(5) An order under this section may specify an amount of arrears due under a maintenance calculation which is the subject of an appeal only if it appears to the Commission—

(a) that liability for the amount would not be affected were the appeal to succeed; or

(b) where paragraph (a) does not apply, that the making of an order under section 32F in respect of the amount would nonetheless be fair in all the circumstances.

(6) The Commission shall serve a copy of any order made under this section on—

(a) the deposit-taker or third party at which it is directed;

(b) the liable person; and

(c) if the order is made in respect of a joint account, the other account-holders.

(7) An order under this section shall come into force at the time at which it is served on the deposit-taker or third party at which it is directed.

(8) An order under this section shall cease to be in force at the earliest of the following—

(a) the time at which the prescribed period ends;

(b) the time at which the order under this section lapses or is discharged; and

(c) the time at which an order under section 32F made in pursuance of the proposal specified in the order under this section is served on the deposit-taker or third party at which that order is directed.

(9) Where regulations have been made under section 29(3)(a), a person liable to pay an amount of child support maintenance is to be taken for the purposes of this section to have failed to pay the amount unless it is paid to or through the person specified in, or by virtue of, the regulations for the case in question.

32F LUMP SUM DEDUCTIONS: FINAL ORDERS

(1) The Commission may make an order under this section in pursuance of a proposal specified in an order under section 32E if—

(a) the order in which the proposal was specified ("the interim order") is in force;

(b) the period prescribed for the making of representations to the Commission in respect of the proposal specified in the interim order has expired; and

(c) the Commission has considered any representations made to it during that period.

(2) An order under this section—
(a) shall be expressed to be directed at the deposit-taker or third party at which the interim order was directed;
(b) if the interim order was made by virtue of section 32E(1)(a), shall specify the account specified in the interim order; and
(c) shall specify the amount of arrears of child support maintenance in respect of which it is made.

(3) The amount so specified—
(a) shall not exceed the amount of arrears specified in the interim order which remain unpaid at the time at which the order under this section is made; and
(b) if the order is made in respect of a joint account, shall not exceed the amount that appears to the Commission to be fair in all the circumstances.

(4) In determining the amount to be specified in an order made in respect of a joint account the Commission shall have particular regard—
(a) to the amount contributed to the account by each of the account-holders; and
(b) to such other matters as may be prescribed.

(5) An order under this section may specify an amount of arrears due under a maintenance calculation which is the subject of an appeal only if it appears to the Commission—
(a) that liability for the amount would not be affected were the appeal to succeed; or
(b) where paragraph (a) does not apply, that the making of an order under this section in respect of the amount would nonetheless be fair in all the circumstances.

(6) The Commission shall serve a copy of any order made under this section on—
(a) the deposit-taker or third party at which it is directed;
(b) the liable person; and
(c) if the order is made in respect of a joint account, the other account-holders.

32G ORDERS UNDER SECTIONS 32E AND 32F: FREEZING OF ACCOUNTS ETC

(1) During the relevant period, an order under section 32E or 32F which specifies an account held with a deposit-taker shall operate as an instruction to the deposit-taker not to do anything that would reduce the amount standing to the credit of the account below the amount specified in the order (or, if already below that amount, that would further reduce it).

(2) During the relevant period, any other order under section 32E or 32F shall operate as an instruction to the third party at which it is directed not to do anything that would reduce the amount due to the liable person below the amount specified in the order (or, if already below that amount, that would further reduce it).

(3) Subsections (1) and (2) have effect subject to regulations made under section 32I(1).

(4) In this section "the relevant period", in relation to an order under section 32E, means the period during which the order is in force.

(5) In this section and section 32H "the relevant period", in relation to an order under section 32F, means the period which—
(a) begins with the service of the order on the deposit-taker or third party at which it is directed; and
(b) (subject to subsection (6)) ends with the end of the period during which an appeal can be brought against the order by virtue of regulations under section 32J(5).

(6) If an appeal is brought by virtue of the regulations, the relevant period ends at the time at which—
(a) proceedings on the appeal (including any proceedings on a further appeal) have been concluded; and
(b) any period during which a further appeal may ordinarily be brought has ended.

(7) References in this section and sections 32H and 32J to the amount due to the liable person are to be read as references to the total of any amounts within section 32E(1)(b) that are due or accruing to the liable person from the third party in question.

32H ORDERS UNDER SECTION 32F: DEDUCTIONS AND PAYMENTS

(1) Once the relevant period has ended, an order under section 32F which specifies an account held with a deposit-taker shall operate as an instruction to the deposit-taker—
(a) if the amount standing to the credit of the account is less than the remaining amount, to pay to the Commission the amount standing to the credit of the account; and
(b) otherwise, to deduct from the account and pay to the Commission the remaining amount.

(2) If an amount of arrears specified in the order remains unpaid after any payment required by subsection (1) has been made, the order shall operate until the relevant time as an instruction to the deposit-taker—
(a) to pay to the Commission any amount (not exceeding the remaining amount) standing to the credit of the account specified in the order; and
(b) not to do anything else that would reduce the amount standing to the credit of the account.

(3) Once the relevant period has ended, any other order under section 32F shall operate as an instruction to the third party at which it is directed—
(a) if the amount due to the liable person is less than the remaining amount, to pay to the Commission the amount due to the liable person; and
(b) otherwise, to deduct from the amount due to the liable person and pay to the Commission the remaining amount.

(4) If an amount of arrears specified in the order remains unpaid after any payment required by subsection (3) has been made, the order shall operate until the relevant time as an instruction to the third party—
(a) to pay to the Commission any amount (not exceeding the remaining amount) due to the liable person; and
(b) not to do anything else that would reduce any amount due to the liable person.

(5) This section has effect subject to regulations made under sections 32I(1) and 32J(2)(c).

(6) In this section—

"the relevant time" means the earliest of the following—
(a) the time at which the remaining amount is paid;
(b) the time at which the order lapses or is discharged; and
(c) the time at which a prescribed event occurs or prescribed circumstances arise;

"the remaining amount", in relation to any time, means the amount of arrears specified in the order under section 32F which remains unpaid at that time.

. . .

32J REGULATIONS ABOUT ORDERS UNDER SECTION 32E OR 32F

(1) The Secretary of State may by regulations make provision with respect to orders under section 32E or 32F.

. . .

(5) The Secretary of State shall by regulations make provision for any person affected by an order under section 32F to have a right to appeal to a court against the making of the order.

(6) On an appeal under regulations under subsection (5), the court shall not question the maintenance calculation by reference to which the order under section 32F was made.

(7) Regulations under subsection (5) may include—
(a) provision with respect to the period within which a right of appeal under the regulations may be exercised;
(b) provision with respect to the powers of the court to which the appeal under the regulations lies.

32K LUMP SUM DEDUCTION ORDERS: OFFENCES

(1) A person who fails to comply with the requirements of—
(a) an order under section 32E or 32F; or
(b) any regulation under section 32J which is designated by the regulations for the purposes of this paragraph,
commits an offence.

(2) It shall be a defence for a person charged with an offence under subsection (1) to prove that the person took all reasonable steps to comply with the requirements in question.

(3) A person guilty of an offence under subsection (1) shall be liable on summary conviction to a fine not exceeding level two on the standard scale.

32L ORDERS PREVENTING AVOIDANCE

(1) The Commission may apply to the court, on the grounds that a person—
(a) has failed to pay an amount of child support maintenance, and
(b) with the intention of avoiding payment of child support maintenance, is about to make a disposition or to transfer out of the jurisdiction or otherwise deal with any property.
for an order restraining or, in Scotland, interdicting the person from doing so.

(2) The Commission may apply to the court, on the grounds that a person—
(a) has failed to pay an amount of child support maintenance, and
(b) with the intention of avoiding payment of child support maintenance, has at any time made a reviewable disposition,
for an order setting aside or, in Scotland, reducing the disposition.

(3) If the court is satisfied of the grounds mentioned in subsection (1) or (2) it may make an order under that subsection.

(4) Where the court makes an order under subsection (1) or (2) it may make such consequential provision by order or directions as it thinks fit for giving effect to the order (including provision requiring the making of any payments or the disposal of any property).

(5) Any disposition is a reviewable disposition for the purposes of subsection (2), unless it was made for valuable or, in Scotland, adequate consideration (other than marriage) to a person who, at the time of the disposition, acted in relation to it in good faith and without notice of an intention to avoid payment of child support maintenance.

(6) Subsection (7) applies where an application is made under this section with respect to—
(a) a disposition or other dealing with property which is about to take place, or
(b) a disposition which took place after the making of the application on which the maintenance calculation concerned was made.

(7) If the court is satisfied—
(a) in a case falling within subsection (1), that the disposition or other dealing would (apart from this section) have the consequence of making ineffective a step that has been or may be taken to recover the amount outstanding, or
(b) in a case falling within subsection (2), that the disposition has had that consequence,
it is to be presumed, unless the contrary is shown, that the person who disposed of or is about to dispose of or deal with the property did so or, as the case may be, is about to do so, with the intention of avoiding payment of child support maintenance.

(8) In this section "disposition" does not include any provision contained in a will or codicil but, with that exception, includes any conveyance, assurance or gift of property of any description, whether made by an instrument or otherwise.

(9) This section does not apply to a disposition made before the coming into force of section 24 of the Child Maintenance and Other Payments Act 2008.

(10) In this section "the court" means—
(a) in relation to England and Wales, the High Court;
(b) in relation to Scotland, the Court of Session or the sheriff.

(11) An order under this section interdicting a person—
(a) is effective for such period (including an indefinite period) as the order may specify;
(b) may, on application to the court, be varied or recalled.

. . .

33 LIABILITY ORDERS

(1) This section applies where—
(a) a person who is liable to make payments of child support maintenance ("the liable person") fails to make one or more of those payments; and
(b) it appears to the Commission that—
(i) it is inappropriate to make a deduction from earnings order against him (because, for example, he is not employed); or
(ii) although such an order has been made against him, it has proved ineffective as a means of securing that payments are made in accordance with the maintenance calculation in question.

(2) The Commission may apply to a magistrates' court for an order ("a liability order") against the liable person.

(3) Where the Commission applies for a liability order, the magistrates' court shall make the order if satisfied that the payments in question have become payable by the liable person and have not been paid.

(4) On an application under subsection (2), the court shall not question the maintenance calculation under which the payments of child support maintenance fell to be made.

(5) If the Commission designates a liability order for the purposes of this subsection it shall be treated as a judgment entered in a county court for the purposes of section 98 of the Courts Act 2003 (register of judgments and orders etc).

(6) Where regulations have been made under section 29(3)(a)—
(a) the liable person fails to make a payment (for the purposes of subsection (1)(a) of this section); and
(b) a payment is not paid (for the purposes of subsection (3)),
unless the payment is made to, or through, the person specified in or by virtue of those regulations for the case of the liable person in question.

35 ENFORCEMENT OF LIABILITY ORDERS BY DISTRESS

(1) Where a liability order has been made against a person ("the liable person"), the Commission may levy the appropriate amount by distress and sale of the liable person's goods.

. . .

39A COMMITMENT TO PRISON AND DISQUALIFICATION FROM DRIVING

(1) Where the Commission has sought—
(a) in England and Wales to levy an amount by distress under this Act; or
(b) to recover an amount by virtue of section 36 or 38,
and that amount, or any portion of it, remains unpaid it may apply to the court under this section.

(2) An application under this section is for whichever the court considers appropriate in all the circumstances of—
(a) the issue of a warrant committing the liable person to prison; or
(b) an order for him to be disqualified from holding or obtaining a driving licence.

(3) On any such application the court shall (in the presence of the liable person) inquire as to—
(a) whether he needs a driving licence to earn his living;
(b) his means; and
(c) whether there has been wilful refusal or culpable neglect on his part.

(4) The Commission may make representations to the court as to whether it thinks it more appropriate to commit the liable person to prison or to disqualify him from holding or obtaining a driving licence; and the liable person may reply to those representations.

(5) In this section and section 40B, "driving licence" means a licence to drive a motor vehicle granted under Part III of the Road Traffic Act 1988.

(6) In this section "the court" means—
(a) in England and Wales, a magistrates' court; . . .

40 COMMITMENT TO PRISON

(3) If, but only if, the court is of the opinion that there has been wilful refusal or culpable neglect on the part of the liable person it may—
(a) issue a warrant of commitment against him; or
(b) fix a term of imprisonment and postpone the issue of the warrant until such time and on such conditions (if any) as it thinks just.

(4) Any such warrant—
(a) shall be made in respect of an amount equal to the aggregate of—
(i) the amount mentioned in section 35(1) or so much of it as remains outstanding; and
(ii) an amount (determined in accordance with regulations made by the Secretary of State) in respect of the costs of commitment; and
(b) shall state that amount.

(5) No warrant may be issued under this section against a person who is under the age of 18.

(6) A warrant issued under this section shall order the liable person—
(a) to be imprisoned for a specified period; but
(b) to be released (unless he is in custody for some other reason) on payment of the amount stated in the warrant.

(7) The maximum period of imprisonment which may be imposed by virtue of subsection (6) shall be calculated in accordance with Schedule 4 to the Magistrates' Courts Act 1980 (maximum periods of imprisonment in default of payment) but shall not exceed six weeks.

(8) The Secretary of State may by regulations make provision for the period of imprisonment specified in any warrant issued under this section to be reduced where there is part payment of the amount in respect of which the warrant was issued.

(9) A warrant issued under this section may be directed to such person or persons as the court issuing it thinks fit.

(10) Section 80 of the Magistrates' Courts Act 1980 (application of money found on defaulter) shall apply in relation to a warrant issued under this section against a liable person as it applies in relation to the enforcement of a sum mentioned in subsection (1) of that section.

(11) The Secretary of State may by regulations make provision—
(a) as to the form of any warrant issued under this section;
(b) allowing an application under this section to be renewed where no warrant is issued or term of imprisonment is fixed;
(c) that a statement in writing to the effect that wages of any amount have been paid to the liable person during any period, purporting to be signed by or on behalf of his employer, shall be evidence of the facts stated;
(d) that, for the purposes of enabling an inquiry to be made as to the liable person's conduct and means, a justice of the peace may issue a summons to him to appear before a magistrates' court and (if he does not obey) may issue a warrant for his arrest;
(e) that for the purpose of enabling such an inquiry, a justice of the peace may issue a warrant for the liable person's arrest without issuing a summons;
(f) as to the execution of a warrant for arrest. . . .

. . .

Special cases

42 SPECIAL CASES

(1) The Secretary of State may by regulations provide that in prescribed circumstances a case is to be treated as a special case for the purposes of this Act.

(2) Those regulations may, for example, provide for the following to be special cases—
(a) each parent of a child is a non-resident parent in relation to the child;

(b) there is more than one person who is a person with care in relation to the same child;
(c) there is more than one qualifying child in relation to the same non-resident parent but the person who is the person with care in relation to one of those children is not the person who is the person with care in relation to all of them;
(d) a person is a non-resident parent in relation to more than one child and the other parent of each of those children is not the same person;
(e) the person with care has care of more than one qualifying child and there is more than one non-resident parent in relation to those children;
(f) a qualifying child has his home in two or more separate households;

(3) The Secretary of State may by regulations make provision with respect to special cases.

(4) Regulations made under subsection (3) may, in particular—
(a) modify any provision made by or under this Act, in its application to any special case or any special case falling within a prescribed category;
(b) make new provision for any such case; or
(c) provide for any prescribed provision made by or under this Act not to apply to any such case.

. . .

43A RECOVERY OF ARREARS FROM DECEASED'S ESTATE

(1) The Secretary of State may by regulations make provision for the recovery from the estate of a deceased person of arrears of child support maintenance for which the deceased person was liable immediately before death.

. . .

Jurisdiction

44 JURISDICTION

(1) The Commission shall have jurisdiction to make a maintenance calculation with respect to a person who is—
(a) a person with care;
(b) a non-resident parent; or
(c) a qualifying child, only if that person is habitually resident in the United Kingdom, except in the case of a non-resident parent who falls within subsection (2A).

(2) Where the person with care is not an individual, subsection (1) shall have effect as if paragraph (a) were omitted.

(2A) A non-resident parent falls within this subsection if he is not habitually resident in the United Kingdom, but is—
(a) employed in the civil service of the Crown, including Her Majesty's Diplomatic Service and Her Majesty's Overseas Civil Service;
(b) a member of the naval, military or air forces of the Crown, including any person employed by an association established for the purposes of Part XI of the Reserve Forces Act 1996;
(c) employed by a company of a prescribed description registered under the Companies Act 1985 in England and Wales or in Scotland, or under the Companies (Northern Ireland) Order 1986; or
(d) employed by a body of a prescribed description.

45 JURISDICTION OF COURTS IN CERTAIN PROCEEDINGS UNDER THIS ACT

(1) The Lord Chancellor or, in relation to Scotland, the Secretary of State may by order make such provision as he considers necessary to secure that appeals, or such class of appeals as may be specified in the order—
(a) shall be made to a court instead of being made to the First-tier Tribunal; or
(b) shall be so made in such circumstances as may be so specified.

(2) In subsection (1), "court" means—
(a) in relation to England and Wales and subject to any provision made under Schedule 11 to the Children Act 1989 (jurisdiction of courts with respect to certain proceedings relating to children) the High Court, a county court or a magistrates' court; and
(b) in relation to Scotland, the Court of Session or the sheriff.

(3) Schedule 11 to the Act of 1989 shall be amended in accordance with subsections (4) and (5).

(7) Any order under subsection (1) may make—
(a) such modifications of any provision of this Act or of any other enactment; and
(b) such transitional provision, as the Minister making the order considers appropriate in consequence of any provision made by the order.

(8) The functions of the Lord Chancellor under this section may be exercised only after consultation with the Lord Chief Justice.

(9) The Lord Chief Justice may nominate a judicial office holder (as defined in section 109(4) of the Constitutional Reform Act 2005) to exercise his functions under this section.

. . .

55 MEANING OF "CHILD"

(1) For the purposes of this Act a person is a child if—
(a) he is under the age of 16;
(b) he is under the age of 19 and receiving full-time education (which is not advanced education)—
(i) by attendance at a recognised educational establishment; or
(ii) elsewhere, if the education is recognised by the Secretary of State; or
(c) he does not fall within paragraph (a) or (b) but—
(i) he is under the age of 18, and
(ii) prescribed conditions are satisfied with respect to him.

(2) A person is not a child for the purposes of this Act if he—
(a) is or has been married or a civil partner;
(b) has celebrated a marriage, or been a party to a civil partnership, which is void; or
(c) has celebrated a marriage in respect of which a decree of nullity has been granted or has been a party to a civil partnership in respect of which a nullity order has been made.

(3) In this section—

"advanced education" means education of a prescribed description; and

"recognised educational establishment" means an establishment recognised by the Secretary of State for the purposes of this section as being, or as comparable to, a university, college or school.

(4) Where a person has reached the age of 16, the Secretary of State may recognise education provided for him otherwise than at a recognised educational establishment only if the Secretary of State is satisfied that education was being so provided for him immediately before he reached the age of 16.

(5) The Secretary of State may provide that in prescribed circumstances education is or is not to be treated for the purposes of this section as being full-time.

(6) In determining whether a person falls within subsection (1)(b), no account shall be taken of such interruptions in his education as may be prescribed.

(7) The Secretary of State may by regulations provide that a person who ceases to fall within subsection (1) shall be treated as continuing to fall within that subsection for a prescribed period.

(8) No person shall be treated as continuing to fall within subsection (1) by virtue of regulations made under subsection (7) after the end of the week in which he reaches the age of 19.

SCHEDULE 1 MAINTENANCE CALCULATIONS

Part I CALCULATION OF WEEKLY AMOUNT OF CHILD SUPPORT MAINTENANCE

General rule

1. (1) The weekly rate of child support maintenance is the basic rate unless a reduced rate, a flat rate or the nil rate applies.

(2) Unless the nil rate applies, the amount payable weekly to a person with care is—
(a) the applicable rate, if paragraph 6 does not apply; or
(b) if paragraph 6 does apply, that rate as apportioned between the persons with care in accordance with paragraph 6, as adjusted, in either case, by applying the rules about shared care in paragraph 7 or 8.

Basic rate

2. (1) The basic rate is the following percentage of the non-resident parent's net weekly income—
15% where he has one qualifying child;
20% where he has two qualifying children;
25% where he has three or more qualifying children.

(2) If the non-resident parent also has one or more relevant other children, the appropriate percentage referred to in sub-paragraph (1) is to be applied instead to his net weekly income less—
15% where he has one relevant other child;
20% where he has two relevant other children;
25% where he has three or more relevant other children.

Reduced rate

3. (1) A reduced rate is payable if—
(a) neither a flat rate nor the nil rate applies; and
(b) the non-resident parent's net weekly income is less than £200 but more than £100.

(2) The reduced rate payable shall be prescribed in, or determined in accordance with, regulations.

(3) The regulations may not prescribe, or result in, a rate of less than £5.

Flat rate

4. (1) Except in a case falling within sub-paragraph (2), a flat rate of £5 is payable if the nil rate does not apply and—
   (a) the non-resident parent's net weekly income is £100 or less; or
   (b) he receives any benefit, pension or allowance prescribed for the purposes of this paragraph of this sub-paragraph; or
   (c) he or his partner (if any) receives any benefit prescribed for the purposes of this paragraph of this sub-paragraph.

   (2) A flat rate of a prescribed amount is payable if the nil rate does not apply and—
   (a) the non-resident parent has a partner who is also a non-resident parent;
   (b) the partner is a person with respect to whom a maintenance calculation is in force; and
   (c) the non-resident parent or his partner receives any benefit prescribed under subparagraph (1)(c).

   (3) The benefits, pensions and allowances which may be prescribed for the purposes of subparagraph (1)(b) include ones paid to the non-resident parent under the law of a place outside the United Kingdom.

Nil rate

5. The rate payable is nil if the non-resident parent—
   (a) is of a prescribed description; or
   (b) has a net weekly income of below £5.

Apportionment

6. (1) If the non-resident parent has more than one qualifying child and in relation to them there is more than one person with care, the amount of child support maintenance payable is (subject to paragraph 7 or 8) to be determined by apportioning the rate between the persons with care.

   (2) The rate of maintenance liability is to be divided by the number of qualifying children, and shared among the persons with care according to the number of qualifying children in relation to whom each is a person with care.

Shared care—basic and reduced rate

7. (1) This paragraph applies only if the rate of child support maintenance payable is the basic rate or a reduced rate.

   (2) If the care of a qualifying child is shared between the non-resident parent and the person with care, so that the non-resident parent from time to time has care of the child overnight, the amount of child support maintenance which he would otherwise have been liable to pay the person with care, as calculated in accordance with the preceding paragraphs of this Part of this Schedule, is to be decreased in accordance with this paragraph.

   (3) First, there is to be a decrease according to the number of such nights which the Commission determines there to have been, or expects there to be, or both during a prescribed twelve-month period.

   (4) The amount of that decrease for one child is set out in the following Table—

Number of nights	**Fraction to subtract**
52 to 103	**One-seventh**
104 to 155	**Two-sevenths**
156 to 174	**Three-sevenths**
175 or more	One-half

(5) If the person with care is caring for more than one qualifying child of the non-resident parent, the applicable decrease is the sum of the appropriate fractions in the Table divided by the number of such qualifying children.

(6) If the applicable fraction is one-half in relation to any qualifying child in the care of the person with care, the total amount payable to the person with care is then to be further decreased by £7 for each such child.

(7) If the application of the preceding provisions of this paragraph would decrease the weekly amount of child support maintenance (or the aggregate of all such amounts) payable by the non-resident parent to the person with care (or all of them) to less than £5, he is instead liable to pay child support maintenance at the rate of £5 a week, apportioned (if appropriate) in accordance with paragraph 6.

Shared care—flat rate

8. (1) This paragraph applies only if—

(a) the rate of child support maintenance payable is a flat rate; and

(b) that rate applies because the non-resident parent falls within paragraph 4(1)(b) or (c) or 4(2).

(2) If the care of a qualifying child is shared as mentioned in paragraph 7(2) for at least 52 nights during a prescribed 12-month period, the amount of child support maintenance payable by the non-resident parent to the person with care of that child is nil.

Regulations about shared care

9. The Secretary of State may by regulations provide—

(a) for which nights are to count for the purposes of shared care under paragraphs 7 and 8, or for how it is to be determined whether a night counts;

(b) for what counts, or does not count, as "care" for those purposes; and

(c) for paragraph 7(3) or 8(2) to have effect, in prescribed circumstances, as if the period mentioned there were other than 12 months, and in such circumstances for the Table in paragraph 7(4) (or that Table as modified pursuant to regulations made under paragraph 10A(2)(a)), or the period mentioned in paragraph 8(2), to have effect with prescribed adjustments.

Net weekly income

10. (1) For the purposes of this Schedule, net weekly income is to be determined in such manner as is provided for in regulations.

(2) The regulations may, in particular, provide for the Commission to estimate any income or make an assumption as to any fact where, in his view, the information at its disposal is unreliable, insufficient, or relates to an atypical period in the life of the non-resident parent.

(3) Any amount of net weekly income (calculated as above) over £2,000 is to be ignored for the purposes of this Schedule.

Regulations about rates, figures, etc

10A. (1) The Secretary of State may by regulations provide that—

(a) paragraph 2 is to have effect as if different percentages were substituted for those set out there;

(b) paragraph 3(1) or (3), 4(1), 5, 7(7) or 10(3) is to have effect as if different amounts were substituted for those set out there.

(2) The Secretary of State may by regulations provide that—

(a) the Table in paragraph 7(4) is to have effect as if different numbers of nights were set out in the first column and different fractions were substituted for those set out in the second column;
(b) paragraph 7(6) is to have effect as if a different amount were substituted for that mentioned there, or as if the amount were an aggregate amount and not an amount for each qualifying child, or both.

Regulations about income

10B. The Secretary of State may by regulations provide that, in such circumstances and to such extent as may be prescribed—
(a) where the Commission is satisfied that a person has intentionally deprived himself of a source of income with a view to reducing the amount of his net weekly income, his net weekly income shall be taken to include income from that source of an amount estimated by the Commission;
(b) a person is to be treated as possessing income which he does not possess;
(c) income which a person does possess is to be disregarded.

References to various terms

10C. (1) References in this Part of this Schedule to "qualifying children" are to those qualifying children with respect to whom the maintenance calculation falls to be made.

(2) References in this Part of this Schedule to "relevant other children" are to—
(a) children other than qualifying children in respect of whom the non-resident parent or his partner receives child benefit under Part IX of the Social Security Contributions and Benefits Act 1992; and
(b) such other description of children as may be prescribed.

(3) In this Part of this Schedule, a person "receives" a benefit, pension, or allowance for any week if it is paid or due to be paid to him in respect of that week.

(4) In this Part of this Schedule, a person's "partner" is—
(a) if they are a couple, the other member of that couple;
(b) if the person is a husband or wife by virtue of a marriage entered into under a law which permits polygamy, another party to the marriage who is of the opposite sex and is a member of the same household.

(5) In sub-paragraph (4)(a), "couple" means—
(a) a man and a woman who are married to each other and are members of the same household,
(b) a man and a woman who are not married to each other but are living together as husband and wife,
(c) two people of the same sex who are civil partners of each other and are members of the same household, or
(d) two people of the same sex who are not civil partners of each other but are living together as if they were civil partners.

(6) For the purposes of this paragraph, two people of the same sex are to be regarded as living together as if they were civil partners if, but only if, they would be regarded as living together as husband and wife were they instead two people of the opposite sex.

. . .

SCHEDULE 4B APPLICATIONS FOR A VARIATION: THE CASES AND CONTROLS

Part I THE CASES

General

1. (1) The cases in which a variation may be agreed are those set out in this Part of this Schedule or in regulations made under this Part.

(2) In this Schedule "applicant" means the person whose application for a variation is being considered.

Special expenses

2. (1) A variation applied for by a non-resident parent may be agreed with respect to his special expenses.

(2) In this paragraph "special expenses" means the whole, or any amount above a prescribed amount, or any prescribed part, of expenses which fall within a prescribed description of expenses.

(3) In prescribing descriptions of expenses for the purposes of this paragraph, the Secretary of State may, in particular, make provision with respect to—

(a) costs incurred by a non-resident parent in maintaining contact with the child, or with any of the children, with respect to whom the application for a maintenance calculation has been made;

(b) costs attributable to a long-term illness or disability of a relevant other child (within the meaning of paragraph 10C(2) of Schedule 1);

(c) debts of a prescribed description incurred, before the non-resident parent became a non-resident parent in relation to a child with respect to whom the maintenance calculation has been applied for —

(i) for the joint benefit of both parents;

(ii) for the benefit of any such child; or

(iii) for the benefit of any other child falling within a prescribed category;

(d) boarding school fees for a child in relation to whom the application for a maintenance calculation has been made;

(e) the cost to the non-resident parent of making payments in relation to a mortgage on the home he and the person with care shared, if he no longer has an interest in it, and she and a child in relation to whom the application for a maintenance calculation has been made still live there.

(4) For the purposes of sub-paragraph (3)(b)—

(a) "disability" and "illness" have such meaning as may be prescribed; and

(b) the question whether an illness or disability is long-term shall be determined in accordance with regulations made by the Secretary of State.

(5) For the purposes of sub-paragraph (3)(d), the Secretary of State may prescribe—

(a) the meaning of "boarding school fees"; and

(b) components of such fees (whether or not itemised as such) which are, or are not, to be taken into account, and may provide for estimating any such component.

Property or capital transfers

3. (1) A variation may be agreed in the circumstances set out in sub-paragraph (2) if before 5th April 1993—

(a) a court order of a prescribed kind was in force with respect to the non-resident parent and either the person with care with respect to the application for the maintenance calculation or the child, or any of the children, with respect to whom that application was made; or

(b) an agreement of a prescribed kind between the non-resident parent and any of those persons was in force.

(2) The circumstances are that in consequence of one or more transfers of property of a prescribed kind and exceeding (singly or in aggregate) a prescribed minimum value—
(a) the amount payable by the non-resident parent by way of maintenance was less than would have been the case had that transfer or those transfers not been made; or
(b) no amount was payable by the non-resident parent by way of maintenance.

(3) For the purposes of sub-paragraph (2), "maintenance" means periodical payments of maintenance made (otherwise than under this Act) with respect to the child, or any of the children, with respect to whom the application for a maintenance calculation has been made.

Additional cases

4. (1) The Secretary of State may by regulations prescribe other cases in which a variation may be agreed.

(2) Regulations under this paragraph may, for example, make provision with respect to cases where—
(a) the non-resident parent has assets which exceed a prescribed value;
(b) a person's lifestyle is inconsistent with his income for the purposes of a calculation made under Part I of Schedule 1;
(c) a person has income which is not taken into account in such a calculation;
(d) a person has unreasonably reduced the income which is taken into account in such a calculation.

As amended by: Jobseekers Act 1995, s 41(4), Sch 2; Child Support Act 1995, ss 1(1), 5, 6(1), (2), 18, 19, 30(5), Sch 3; Children (Scotland) Act 1995, s 105(4), (5), Sch 4, Sch 5; Children (Northern Ireland Consequential Amendments) Order 1995, SI 1995/756, art 13; Social Security Act 1998, s 86(1), (2), Sch 7, Sch 8; Transfer of Functions (Lord Advocate and Secretary of State) Order 1999, SI 1999/678, art 2(1), Schedule; Child Support, Pensions and Social Security Act 2000, ss 1, 2, 5, 6(2), 15–17, 22, 25, 83(5), 85, Sch 2; Sch 3, Sch 8, Sch 9; Adoption and Children Act 2002, s 139(1), Sch 3; Civil Partnership Act 2004, ss 254(1), 261(4) Sch 24; Sch 30; Constitutional Reform Act 2005, s 15(1), Sch 4; Courts Act 2003 (Consequential Amendment) Order 2006, SI 2006/1001, art 2; Welfare Reform Act 2007, s 28(1), Sch 3; Children (Scotland) Act 2007, s 120(1), Sch 2; Child Maintenance and Other Payments Act 2008, ss 13(4), ss 22–24; 29(1); 35(1), (3); 38; 57(1), 58, Sch 3, Sch 7, Sch 8; Transfer of Tribunal Functions Order 2008, SI 2008/2833, art 9(1), Sch 3; Human Fertilisation and Embryology Act 2008, s 56, Sch 6.

Child Support Act 1995

(1995 c 34)

18 DEFERRAL OF RIGHT TO APPLY FOR MAINTENANCE ASSESSMENT

(6) Neither section 4(10) nor section 7(10) of the 1991 Act shall apply in relation to a maintenance order made in the circumstances mentioned in subsection (7) or (8) of section 8 of the 1991 Act.

(7) The Secretary of State may by regulations make provision for section 4(10), or section 7(10), of the 1991 Act not to apply in relation to such other cases as may be prescribed.

. . .

27 INTERPRETATION

(1) In this Act "the 1991 Act" means the Child Support Act 1991.

(2) Expressions in this Act which are used in the 1991 Act have the same meaning in this Act as they have in that Act.

As amended by: Child Support, Pensions and Social Security Act 2000, ss 26, 85, Sch 3, Sch 9.

FAMILY LAW ACT 1996
(1996 c 27)

Part I PRINCIPLES OF PARTS II AND III

1 THE GENERAL PRINCIPLES UNDERLYING PARTS II AND III

The court and any person, in exercising functions under or in consequence of Parts II and III, shall have regard to the following general principles—

(a) that the institution of marriage is to be supported;

(b) that the parties to a marriage which may have broken down are to be encouraged to take all practicable steps, whether by marriage counselling or otherwise, to save the marriage;

(c) that a marriage which has irretrievably broken down and is being brought to an end should be brought to an end—
  (i) with minimum distress to the parties and to the children affected;
  (ii) with questions dealt with in a manner designed to promote as good a continuing relationship between the parties and any children affected as is possible in the circumstances; and
  (iii) without costs being unreasonably incurred in connection with the procedures to be followed in bringing the marriage to an end; and

(d) that any risk to one of the parties to a marriage, and to any children, of violence from the other party should, so far as reasonably practicable, be removed or diminished.

Part II DIVORCE AND SEPARATION

Marriage support services

22 FUNDING FOR MARRIAGE SUPPORT SERVICES

(1) The Secretary of State may, with the approval of the Treasury, make grants in connection with—
  (a) the provision of marriage support services;
  (b) research into the causes of marital breakdown;
  (c) research into ways of preventing marital breakdown.

(2) Any grant under this section may be made subject to such conditions as the Secretary of State considers appropriate.

(3) In exercising his power to make grants in connection with the provision of marriage support services, the Secretary of State is to have regard, in particular, to the desirability of services of that kind being available when they are first needed.

Part IV FAMILY HOMES AND DOMESTIC VIOLENCE

Rights to occupy matrimonial or civil partnership home

30 RIGHTS CONCERNING HOME WHERE ONE SPOUSE OR CIVIL PARTNER HAS NO ESTATE, ETC

(1) This section applies if—
  (a) one spouse or civil partner ("A") is entitled to occupy a dwelling-house by virtue of—
    (i) a beneficial estate or interest or contract; or
    (ii) any enactment giving A the right to remain in occupation; and
  (b) the other spouse or civil partner ("B") is not so entitled.

(2) Subject to the provisions of this Part, B has the following rights ("home rights")—
  (a) if in occupation, a right not to be evicted or excluded from the dwelling-house or any part of it by A except with the leave of the court given by an order under section 33;
  (b) if not in occupation, a right with the leave of the court so given to enter into and occupy the dwelling-house.

(3) If B is entitled under this section to occupy a dwelling-house or any part of a dwellinghouse, any payment or tender made or other thing done by B in or towards satisfaction of any liability of A in respect of rent, mortgage payments or other outgoings affecting the dwelling-house is, whether or not it is made or done in pursuance of an order under section 40, as good as if made or done by A.

(4) B's occupation by virtue of this section—
  (a) is to be treated, for the purposes of the Rent (Agriculture) Act 1976 and the Rent Act 1977 (other than Part V and sections 103 to 106 of that Act), as occupation by A as A's residence, and
  (b) if B occupies the dwelling-house as B's only or principal home, is to be treated, for the purposes of the Housing Act 1985, Part I of the Housing Act 1988 and Chapter I of Part V of the Housing Act 1996, as occupation by A as A's only or principal home.

(5) If B—
  (a) is entitled under this section to occupy a dwelling-house or any part of a dwelling-house, and
  (b) makes any payment in or towards satisfaction of any liability of A in respect of mortgage payments affecting the dwelling-house,

the person to whom the payment is made may treat it as having been made by A, but the fact that that person has treated any such payment as having been so made does not affect any claim of B against A to an interest in the dwelling-house by virtue of the payment.

(6) If B is entitled under this section to occupy a dwelling-house or part of a dwelling-house by reason of an interest of A under a trust, all the provisions of subsections (3) to (5) apply in relation to the trustees as they apply in relation to A.

(7) This section does not apply to a dwelling-house which—
(a) in the case of spouses, has at no time been, and was at no time intended by them to be, a matrimonial home of theirs; and
(b) in the case of civil partners, has at no time been, and was at no time intended by them to be, a civil partnership home of theirs.

(8) B's home rights continue—
(a) only so long as the marriage or civil partnership subsists, except to the extent that an order under section 33(5) otherwise provides; and
(b) only so long as A is entitled as mentioned in subsection (1) to occupy the dwelling-house,
except where provision is made by section 31 for those rights to be a charge on an estate or interest in the dwelling-house.

(9) It is hereby declared that a person—
(a) who has an equitable interest in a dwelling-house or in its proceeds of sale, but
(b) is not a person in whom there is vested (whether solely or as joint tenant) a legal estate in fee simple or a legal term of years absolute in the dwelling-house, is to be treated, only for the purpose of determining whether he has home rights, as not being entitled to occupy the dwelling-house by virtue of that interest.

31 EFFECT OF HOME RIGHTS AS CHARGE ON DWELLING-HOUSE

(1) Subsections (2) and (3) apply if, at any time during a marriage or civil partnership, A is entitled to occupy a dwelling-house by virtue of a beneficial estate or interest.

(2) B's home rights are a charge on the estate or interest.

(3) The charge created by subsection (2) has the same priority as if it were an equitable interest created at whichever is the latest of the following dates—
(a) the date on which A acquires the estate or interest;
(b) the date of the marriage or of the formation of the civil partnership; and
(c) 1st January 1968 (the commencement date of the Matrimonial Homes Act 1967).

(4) Subsections (5) and (6) apply if, at any time when B's home rights are a charge on an interest of A under a trust, there are, apart from A or B, no persons, living or unborn, who are or could become beneficiaries under the trust.

(5) The rights are a charge also on the estate or interest of the trustees for A.

(6) The charge created by subsection (5) has the same priority as if it were an equitable interest created (under powers overriding the trusts) on the date when it arises.

(7) In determining for the purposes of subsection (4) whether there are any persons who are not, but could become, beneficiaries under the trust, there is to be disregarded any potential exercise of a general power of appointment exercisable by either or both of A and B alone (whether or not the exercise of it requires the consent of another person).

(8) Even though B's home rights are a charge on an estate or interest in the dwelling-house, those rights are brought to an end by—

(a) the death of A, or
(b) the termination (otherwise than by death) of the marriage or civil partnership, unless the court directs otherwise by an order made under section 33(5).

(9) If—
(a) B's home rights are a charge on an estate or interest in the dwelling-house, and
(b) that estate or interest is surrendered to merge in some other estate or interest expectant on it in such circumstances that, but for the merger, the person taking the estate or interest would be bound by the charge,

the surrender has effect subject to the charge and the persons thereafter entitled to the other estate or interest are, for so long as the estate or interest surrendered would have endured if not so surrendered, to be treated for all purposes of this Part as deriving title to the other estate or interest under A or, as the case may be, under the trustees for A, by virtue of the surrender.

(10) If the title to the legal estate by virtue of which A is entitled to occupy a dwelling-house (including any legal estate held by trustees for A) is registered under the Land Registration Act 2002 or any enactment replaced by that Act—
(a) registration of a land charge affecting the dwelling-house by virtue of this Part is to be effected by registering a notice under that Act; and
(b) B's home rights are not to be capable of falling within paragraph 2 of Schedule 1 or 3 to that Act.

(12) If—
(a) B's home rights are a charge on the estate of A or of trustees of A, and
(b) that estate is the subject of a mortgage,

then if, after the date of the creation of the mortgage ("the first mortgage"), the charge is registered under section 2 of the Land Charges Act 1972, the charge is, for the purposes of section 94 of the Law of Property Act 1925 (which regulates the rights of mortgagees to make further advances ranking in priority to subsequent mortgages), to be deemed to be a mortgage subsequent in date to the first mortgage.

(13) It is hereby declared that a charge under subsection (2) or (5) is not registrable under subsection (10) or under section 2 of the Land Charges Act 1972 unless it is a charge on a legal estate.

. . .

Occupation orders

33 OCCUPATION ORDERS WHERE APPLICANT HAS ESTATE OR INTEREST ETC OR HAS HOME RIGHTS

(1) If—
(a) a person ("the person entitled")—
(i) is entitled to occupy a dwelling-house by virtue of a beneficial estate or interest or contract or by virtue of any enactment giving him the right to remain in occupation, or
(ii) has home rights in relation to a dwelling-house, and
(b) the dwelling-house—
(i) is or at any time has been the home of the person entitled and of another person with whom he is associated, or
(ii) was at any time intended by the person entitled and any such other person to be their home, the person entitled may apply to the court for an order containing any of the provisions specified in subsections (3), (4) and (5).

(2) If an agreement to marry is terminated, no application under this section may be made by virtue of section 62(3)(e) by reference to that agreement after the end of the period of three years beginning with the day on which it is terminated.

(2A) If a civil partnership agreement (as defined by section 73 of the Civil Partnership Act 2004) is terminated, no application under this section may be made by virtue of section 62(3)(eza) by reference to that agreement after the end of the period of three years beginning with the day on which it is terminated.

(3) An order under this section may—
(a) enforce the applicant's entitlement to remain in occupation as against the other person ("the respondent");
(b) require the respondent to permit the applicant to enter and remain in the dwelling-house or part of the dwelling-house;
(c) regulate the occupation of the dwelling-house by either or both parties;
(d) if the respondent is entitled as mentioned in subsection (1)(a)(i), prohibit, suspend or restrict the exercise by him of his right to occupy the dwelling-house;
(e) if the respondent has home rights in relation to the dwelling-house and the applicant is the other spouse or civil partner, restrict or terminate those rights;
(f) require the respondent to leave the dwelling-house or part of the dwelling-house; or
(g) exclude the respondent from a defined area in which the dwelling-house is included.

(4) An order under this section may declare that the applicant is entitled as mentioned in subsection (1)(a)(i) or has home rights.

(5) If the applicant has home rights and the respondent is the other spouse or civil partner, an order under this section made during the marriage or civil partnership may provide that those rights are not brought to an end by—
(a) the death of the other spouse or civil partner; or
(b) the termination (otherwise than by death) of the marriage or civil partnership.

(6) In deciding whether to exercise its powers under subsection (3) and (if so) in what manner, the court shall have regard to all the circumstances including—
(a) the housing needs and housing resources of each of the parties and of any relevant child;
(b) the financial resources of each of the parties;
(c) the likely effect of any order, or of any decision by the court not to exercise its powers under subsection (3), on the health, safety or well-being of the parties and of any relevant child; and
(d) the conduct of the parties in relation to each other and otherwise.

(7) If it appears to the court that the applicant or any relevant child is likely to suffer significant harm attributable to conduct of the respondent if an order under this section containing one or more of the provisions mentioned in subsection (3) is not made, the court shall make the order unless it appears to it that—
(a) the respondent or any relevant child is likely to suffer significant harm if the order is made; and
(b) the harm likely to be suffered by the respondent or child in that event is as great as, or greater than, the harm attributable to conduct of the respondent which is likely to be suffered by the applicant or child if the order is not made.

(8) The court may exercise its powers under subsection (5) in any case where it considers that in all the circumstances it is just and reasonable to do so.

(9) An order under this section—
(a) may not be made after the death of either of the parties mentioned in subsection (1); and

(b) except in the case of an order made by virtue of subsection (5)(a), ceases to have effect on the death of either party.

(10) An order under this section may, in so far as it has continuing effect, be made for a specified period, until the occurrence of a specified event or until further order.

34 EFFECT OF ORDER UNDER S 33 WHERE RIGHTS ARE CHARGE ON DWELLING-HOUSE

(1) If B's home rights are a charge on the estate or interest of A or of trustees for A—
(a) an order under section 33 against A has, except so far as a contrary intention appears, the same effect against persons deriving title under A or under the trustees and affected by the charge, and
(b) sections 33(1), (3), (4) and (10) and 30(3) to (6) apply in relation to any person deriving title under A or under the trustees and affected by the charge as they apply in relation to A.

(2) The court may make an order under section 33 by virtue of subsection (1)(b) if it considers that in all the circumstances it is just and reasonable to do so.

35 ONE FORMER SPOUSE OR FORMER CIVIL PARTNER WITH NO EXISTING RIGHT TO OCCUPY

(1) This section applies if—
(a) one former spouse or former civil partner is entitled to occupy a dwelling-house by virtue of a beneficial estate or interest or contract, or by virtue of any enactment giving him the right to remain in occupation;
(b) the other former spouse or former civil partner is not so entitled; and
(c) the dwelling-house—
(i) in the case of former spouses, was at any time their matrimonial home or was at any time intended by them to be their matrimonial home, or
(ii) in the case of former civil partners, was at any time their civil partnership home or was at any time intended by them to be their civil partnership home.

(2) The former spouse or former civil partner not so entitled may apply to the court for an order under this section against the other former spouse or former civil partner ("the respondent").

(3) If the applicant is in occupation, an order under this section must contain provision—
(a) giving the applicant the right not to be evicted or excluded from the dwelling-house or any part of it by the respondent for the period specified in the order; and
(b) prohibiting the respondent from evicting or excluding the applicant during that period.

(4) If the applicant is not in occupation, an order under this section must contain provision—
(a) giving the applicant the right to enter into and occupy the dwelling-house for the period specified in the order; and
(b) requiring the respondent to permit the exercise of that right.

(5) An order under this section may also—
(a) regulate the occupation of the dwelling-house by either or both of the parties;
(b) prohibit, suspend or restrict the exercise by the respondent of his right to occupy the dwelling-house;
(c) require the respondent to leave the dwelling-house or part of the dwelling-house; or
(d) exclude the respondent from a defined area in which the dwelling-house is included.

(6) In deciding whether to make an order under this section containing provision of the kind mentioned in subsection (3) or (4) and (if so) in what manner, the court shall have regard to all the circumstances including—
(a) the housing needs and housing resources of each of the parties and of any relevant child;
(b) the financial resources of each of the parties;
(c) the likely effect of any order, or of any decision by the court not to exercise its powers under subsection (3) or (4), on the health, safety or well-being of the parties and of any relevant child;
(d) the conduct of the parties in relation to each other and otherwise;
(e) the length of time that has elapsed since the parties ceased to live together;
(f) the length of time that has elapsed since the marriage or civil partnership was dissolved or annulled; and
(g) the existence of any pending proceedings between the parties—
(i) for an order under section 23A or 24 of the Matrimonial Causes Act 1973 (property adjustment orders in connection with divorce proceedings etc);
(ia) for a property adjustment order under Part 2 of Schedule 5 to the Civil Partnership Act 2004;
(ii) for an order under paragraph 1(2)(d) or (e) of Schedule 1 to the Children Act 1989 (orders for financial relief against parents); or
(iii) relating to the legal or beneficial ownership of the dwellinghouse.

(7) In deciding whether to exercise its power to include one or more of the provisions referred to in subsection (5) ("a subsection (5) provision") and (if so) in what manner, the court shall have regard to all the circumstances including the matters mentioned in subsection (6)(a) to (e).

(8) If the court decides to make an order under this section and it appears to it that, if the order does not include a subsection (5) provision, the applicant or any relevant child is likely to suffer significant harm attributable to conduct of the respondent, the court shall include the subsection (5) provision in the order unless it appears to the court that—
(a) the respondent or any relevant child is likely to suffer significant harm if the provision is included in the order; and
(b) the harm likely to be suffered by the respondent or child in that event is as great as or greater than the harm attributable to conduct of the respondent which is likely to be suffered by the applicant or child if the provision is not included.

(9) An order under this section—
(a) may not be made after the death of either of the former spouses or former civil partners; and
(b) ceases to have effect on the death of either of them.

(10) An order under this section must be limited so as to have effect for a specified period not exceeding six months, but may be extended on one or more occasions for a further specified period not exceeding six months.

(11) A former spouse or former civil partner who has an equitable interest in the dwellinghouse or in the proceeds of sale of the dwelling-house but in whom there is not vested (whether solely or as joint tenant) a legal estate in fee simple or a legal term of years absolute in the dwelling-house is to be treated (but only for the purpose of determining whether he is eligible to apply under this section) as not being entitled to occupy the dwelling-house by virtue of that interest.

(12) Subsection (11) does not prejudice any right of such a former spouse or former civil partner to apply for an order under section 33.

(13) So long as an order under this section remains in force, subsections (3) to (6) of section 30 apply in relation to the applicant—
(a) as if he were B (the person entitled to occupy the dwelling-house by virtue of that section); and
(b) as if the respondent were A (the person entitled as mentioned in subsection (1)(a) of that section).

36 ONE COHABITANT OR FORMER COHABITANT WITH NO EXISTING RIGHT TO OCCUPY

(1) This section applies if—
(a) one cohabitant or former cohabitant is entitled to occupy a dwelling-house by virtue of a beneficial estate or interest or contract or by virtue of any enactment giving him the right to remain in occupation;
(b) the other cohabitant or former cohabitant is not so entitled; and
(c) that dwelling-house is the home in which they cohabit or a home in which they at any time cohabited or intended to cohabit.

(2) The cohabitant or former cohabitant not so entitled may apply to the court for an order under this section against the other cohabitant or former cohabitant ("the respondent").

(3) If the applicant is in occupation, an order under this section must contain provision—
(a) giving the applicant the right not to be evicted or excluded from the dwelling-house or any part of it by the respondent for the period specified in the order; and
(b) prohibiting the respondent from evicting or excluding the applicant during that period.

(4) If the applicant is not in occupation, an order under this section must contain provision—
(a) giving the applicant the right to enter into and occupy the dwelling-house for the period specified in the order; and
(b) requiring the respondent to permit the exercise of that right.

(5) An order under this section may also—
(a) regulate the occupation of the dwelling-house by either or both of the parties;
(b) prohibit, suspend or restrict the exercise by the respondent of his right to occupy the dwelling-house;
(c) require the respondent to leave the dwelling-house or part of the dwelling-house; or
(d) exclude the respondent from a defined area in which the dwelling-house is included.

(6) In deciding whether to make an order under this section containing provision of the kind mentioned in subsection (3) or (4) and (if so) in what manner, the court shall have regard to all the circumstances including—
(a) the housing needs and housing resources of each of the parties and of any relevant child;
(b) the financial resources of each of the parties;
(c) the likely effect of any order, or of any decision by the court not to exercise its powers under subsection (3) or (4), on the health, safety or well-being of the parties and of any relevant child;
(d) the conduct of the parties in relation to each other and otherwise;
(e) the nature of the parties' relationship and in particular the level of commitment involved in it;
(f) the length of time during which they have cohabited;
(g) whether there are or have been any children who are children of both parties or for whom both parties have or have had parental responsibility;
(h) the length of time that has elapsed since the parties ceased to live together; and

(i) the existence of any pending proceedings between the parties—
(i) for an order under paragraph 1 (2)(d) or (e) of Schedule to the Children Act 1989 (orders for financial relief against parents); or
(ii) relating to the legal or beneficial ownership of the dwellinghouse.

(7) In deciding whether to exercise its powers to include one or more of the provisions referred to in subsection (5) ("a subsection (5) provision") and (if so) in what manner, the court shall have regard to all the circumstances including—
(a) the matters mentioned in subsection (6)(a) to (d); and
(b) the questions mentioned in subsection (8).

(8) The questions are—
(a) whether the applicant or any relevant child is likely to suffer significant harm attributable to conduct of the respondent if the subsection (5) provision is not included in the order; and
(b) whether the harm likely to be suffered by the respondent or child if the provision is included is as great as or greater than the harm attributable to conduct of the respondent which is likely to be suffered by the applicant or child if the provision is not included.

(9) An order under this section—
(a) may not be made after the death of either of the parties; and
(b) ceases to have effect on the death of either of them.

(10) An order under this section must be limited so as to have effect for a specified period not exceeding six months, but may be extended on one occasion for a further specified period not exceeding six months.

(11) A person who has an equitable interest in the dwelling-house or in the proceeds of sale of the dwelling-house but in whom there is not vested (whether solely or as joint tenant) a legal estate in fee simple or a legal term of years absolute in the dwelling-house is to be treated (but only for the purpose of determining whether he is eligible to apply under this section) as not being entitled to occupy the dwelling-house by virtue of that interest.

(12) Subsection (11) does not prejudice any right of such a person to apply for an order under section 33.

(13) So long as the order remains in force, subsections (3) to (6) of section 30 apply in relation to the applicant—
(a) as if he were B (the person entitled to occupy the dwelling-house by virtue of that section); and
(b) as if the respondent were A (the person entitled as mentioned in subsection (1)(a) of that section).

37 NEITHER SPOUSE OR CIVIL PARTNER ENTITLED TO OCCUPY

(1) This section applies if—
(a) one spouse or former spouse and the other spouse or former spouse occupy a dwelling-house which is or was the matrimonial home; but
(b) neither of them is entitled to remain in occupation—
(i) by virtue of a beneficial estate or interest or contract; or
(ii) by virtue of any enactment giving him the right to remain in occupation.

(1A) This section also applies if—
(a) one civil partner or former civil partner and the other civil partner or former civil partner occupy a dwelling-house which is or was the civil partnership home; but

(b) neither of them is entitled to remain in occupation—
(i) by virtue of a beneficial estate or interest or contract; or
(ii) by virtue of any enactment giving him the right to remain in occupation.

(2) Either of the parties may apply to the court for an order against the other under this section.

(3) An order under this section may—
(a) require the respondent to permit the applicant to enter and remain in the dwellinghouse or part of the dwelling-house;
(b) regulate the occupation of the dwelling-house by either or both of the parties;
(c) require the respondent to leave the dwelling-house or part of the dwelling-house; or
(d) exclude the respondent from a defined area in which the dwelling-house is included.

(4) Subsections (6) and (7) of section 33 apply to the exercise by the court of its powers under this section as they apply to the exercise by the court of its powers under subsection (3) of that section.

(5) An order under this section must be limited so as to have effect for a specified period not exceeding six months, but may be extended on one or more occasions for a further specified period not exceeding six months.

38 NEITHER COHABITANT OR FORMER COHABITANT ENTITLED TO OCCUPY

(1) This section applies if—
(a) one cohabitant or former cohabitant and the other cohabitant or former cohabitant occupy a dwelling-house which is the home in which they cohabit or cohabited; but
(b) neither of them is entitled to remain in occupation—
(i) by virtue of a beneficial estate or interest or contract; or
(ii) by virtue of any enactment giving him the right to remain in occupation.

(2) Either of the parties may apply to the court for an order against the other under this section.

(3) An order under this section may—
(a) require the respondent to permit the applicant to enter and remain in the dwellinghouse or part of the dwelling-house;
(b) regulate the occupation of the dwelling-house by either or both of the parties;
(c) require the respondent to leave the dwelling-house or part of the dwelling-house; or
(d) exclude the respondent from a defined area in which the dwelling-house is included.

(4) In deciding whether to exercise its powers to include one or more of the provisions referred to in subsection (3) ("a subsection (3) provision") and (if so) in what manner, the court shall have regard to all the circumstances including—
(a) the housing needs and housing resources of each of the parties and of any relevant child;
(b) the financial resources of each of the parties;
(c) the likely effect of any order, or of any decision by the court not to exercise its powers under subsection (3), on the health, safety or well-being of the parties and of any relevant child;
(d) the conduct of the parties in relation to each other and otherwise; and
(e) the questions mentioned in subsection (5).

(5) The questions are—
(a) whether the applicant or any relevant child is likely to suffer significant harm attributable to conduct of the respondent if the subsection (3) provision is not included in the order; and

(b) whether the harm likely to be suffered by the respondent or child if the provision is included is as great as or greater than the harm attributable to conduct of the respondent which is likely to be suffered by the applicant or child if the provision is not included.

(6) An order under this section shall be limited so as to have effect for a specified period not exceeding six months, but may be extended on one occasion for a further specified period not exceeding six months.

39 SUPPLEMENTARY PROVISIONS

(1) In this Part an "occupation order" means an order under section 33, 35, 36, 37 or 38.

(2) An application for an occupation order may be made in other family proceedings or without any other family proceedings being instituted.

(3) If—
(a) an application for an occupation order is made under section 33, 35, 36, 37 or 38, and
(b) the court considers that it has no power to make the order under the section concerned, but that it has power to make an order under one of the other sections,
the court may make an order under that other section.

(4) The fact that a person has applied for an occupation order under sections 35 to 38, or that an occupation order has been made, does not affect the right of any person to claim a legal or equitable interest in any property in any subsequent proceedings (including subsequent proceedings under this Part).

40 ADDITIONAL PROVISIONS THAT MAY BE INCLUDED IN CERTAIN OCCUPATION ORDERS

(1) The court may on, or at any time after, making an occupation order under section 33, 35 or 36—
(a) impose on either party obligations as to—
(i) the repair and maintenance of the dwelling-house; or
(ii) the discharge of rent, mortgage payments or other outgoings affecting the dwelling-house;
(b) order a party occupying the dwelling-house or any part of it (including a party who is entitled to do so by virtue of a beneficial estate or interest or contract or by virtue of any enactment giving him the right to remain in occupation) to make periodical payments to the other party in respect of the accommodation, if the other party would (but for the order) be entitled to occupy the dwelling-house by virtue of a beneficial estate or interest or contract or by virtue of any such enactment;
(c) grant either party possession or use of furniture or other contents of the dwelling house;
(d) order either party to take reasonable care of any furniture or other contents of the dwelling-house;
(e) order either party to take reasonable steps to keep the dwelling-house and any furniture or other contents secure.

(2) In deciding whether and, if so, how to exercise its powers under this section, the court shall have regard to all the circumstances of the case including—
(a) the financial needs and financial resources of the parties; and
(b) the financial obligations which they have, or are likely to have in the foreseeable future, including financial obligations to each other and to any relevant child.

(3) An order under this section ceases to have effect when the occupation order to which it relates ceases to have effect.

Non-molestation orders

42 NON-MOLESTATION ORDERS

(1) In this Part a "non-molestation order" means an order containing either or both of the following provisions—
  (a) provision prohibiting a person ("the respondent") from molesting another person who is associated with the respondent;
  (b) provision prohibiting the respondent from molesting a relevant child.

(2) The court may make a non-molestation order—
  (a) if an application for the order has been made (whether in other family proceedings or without any other family proceedings being instituted) by a person who is associated with the respondent; or
  (b) if in any family proceedings to which the respondent is a party the court considers that the order should be made for the benefit of any other party to the proceedings or any relevant child even though no such application has been made.

(3) In subsection (2) "family proceedings" includes proceedings in which the court has made an emergency protection order under section 44 of the Children Act 1989 which includes an exclusion requirement (as defined in section 44A(3) of that Act).

(4) Where an agreement to marry is terminated, no application under subsection (2)(a) may be made by virtue of section 62(3)(e) by reference to that agreement after the end of the period of three years beginning with the day on which it is terminated.

(4A) A court considering whether to make an occupation order shall also consider whether to exercise the power conferred by subsection (2)(b).

(4B) In this Part "the applicant", in relation to a non-molestation order, includes (where the context permits) the person for whose benefit such an order would be or is made in exercise of the power conferred by subsection (2)(b).

(5) In deciding whether to exercise its powers under this section and, if so, in what manner, the court shall have regard to all the circumstances including the need to secure the health, safety and well-being—
  (a) of the applicant . . .; and
  (b) of any relevant child.

(6) A non-molestation order may be expressed so as to refer to molestation in general, to particular acts of molestation, or to both.

(7) A non-molestation order may be made for a specified period or until further order.

(8) A non-molestation order which is made in other family proceedings ceases to have effect if those proceedings are withdrawn or dismissed.

42A OFFENCE OF BREACHING NON-MOLESTATION ORDER

(1) A person who without reasonable excuse does anything that he is prohibited from doing by a non-molestation order is guilty of an offence.

(2) In the case of a non-molestation order made by virtue of section 45(1), a person can be guilty of an offence under this section only in respect of conduct engaged in at a time when he was aware of the existence of the order.

(3) Where a person is convicted of an offence under this section in respect of any conduct, that conduct is not punishable as a contempt of court.

(4) A person cannot be convicted of an offence under this section in respect of any conduct which has been punished as a contempt of court.

(5) A person guilty of an offence under this section is liable—
 (a) on conviction on indictment, to imprisonment for a term not exceeding five years, or a fine, or both;
 (b) on summary conviction, to imprisonment for a term not exceeding 12 months, or a fine not exceeding the statutory maximum, or both.

(6) A reference in any enactment to proceedings under this Part, or to an order under this Part, does not include a reference to proceedings for an offence under this section or to an order made in such proceedings.

"Enactment" includes an enactment contained in subordinate legislation within the meaning of the Interpretation Act 1978 (c 30).

Further provisions relating to occupation and non-molestation orders

43 LEAVE OF COURT REQUIRED FOR APPLICATIONS BY CHILDREN UNDER SIXTEEN

(1) A child under the age of sixteen may not apply for an occupation order or a non-molestation order except with the leave of the court.

(2) The court may grant leave for the purposes of subsection (1) only if it is satisfied that the child has sufficient understanding to make the proposed application for the occupation order or non-molestation order.

44 EVIDENCE OF AGREEMENT TO MARRY OR FORM A CIVIL PARTNERSHIP

(1) Subject to subsection (2), the court shall not make an order under section 33 or 42 by virtue of section 62(3)(e) unless there is produced to it evidence in writing of the existence of the agreement to marry.

(2) Subsection (1) does not apply if the court is satisfied that the agreement to marry was evidenced by—
 (a) the gift of an engagement ring by one party to the agreement to the other in contemplation of their marriage, or
 (b) a ceremony entered into by the parties in the presence of one or more other persons assembled for the purpose of witnessing the ceremony.

(3) Subject to subsection (4), the court shall not make an order under section 33 or 42 by virtue of section 62(3)(eza) unless there is produced to it evidence in writing of the existence of the civil partnership agreement (as defined by section 73 of the Civil Partnership Act 2004).

(4) Subsection (3) does not apply if the court is satisfied that the civil partnership agreement was evidenced by—
 (a) a gift by one party to the agreement to the other as a token of the agreement, or
 (b) a ceremony entered into by the parties in the presence of one or more other persons assembled for the purpose of witnessing the ceremony.

45 EX PARTE ORDERS

(1) The court may, in any case where it considers that it is just and convenient to do so, make an occupation order or a non-molestation order even though the respondent has not been given such notice of the proceedings as would otherwise be required by rules of court.

(2) In determining whether to exercise its powers under subsection (1), the court shall have regard to all the circumstances including—
   (a) any risk of significant harm to the applicant or a relevant child, attributable to conduct of the respondent, if the order is not made immediately;
   (b) whether it is likely that the applicant will be deterred or prevented from pursuing the application if an order is not made immediately; and
   (c) whether there is reason to believe that the respondent is aware of the proceedings but is deliberately evading service and that the applicant or a relevant child will be seriously prejudiced by the delay involved—
      (i) where the court is a magistrates' court, in effecting service of proceedings; or
      (ii) in any other case, in effecting substituted service.

(3) If the court makes an order by virtue of subsection (1) it must afford the respondent an opportunity to make representations relating to the order as soon as just and convenient at a full hearing.

(4) If, at a full hearing, the court makes an occupation order ("the full order"), then—
   (a) for the purposes of calculating the maximum period for which the full order may be made to have effect, the relevant section is to apply as if the period for which the full order will have effect began on the date on which the initial order first had effect; and
   (b) the provisions of section 36(10) or 38(6) as to the extension of orders are to apply as if the full order and the initial order were a single order.

(5) In this section—

"full hearing" means a hearing of which notice has been given to all the parties in accordance with rules of court;

"initial order" means an occupation order made by virtue of subsection (1); and
"relevant section" means section 33(10), 35(10), 36(10), 37(5) or 38(6).

46 UNDERTAKINGS

(1) In any case where the court has power to make an occupation order or non-molestation order, the court may accept an undertaking from any party to the proceedings.

(2) No power of arrest may be attached to any undertaking given under subsection (1).

(3) The court shall not accept an undertaking under subsection (1) instead of making an occupation order in any case where apart from this section a power of arrest would be attached to the order.

(3A) The court shall not accept an undertaking under subsection (1) instead of making a nonmolestation order in any case where it appears to the court that—
   (a) the respondent has used or threatened violence against the applicant or a relevant child; and
   (b) for the protection of the applicant or child it is necessary to make a non-molestation order so that any breach may be punishable under section 42A.

(4) An undertaking given to a court under subsection (1) is enforceable as if the court had made an occupation order or a non-molestation order in terms corresponding to those of the undertaking.

(5) This section has effect without prejudice to the powers of the High Court and the county court apart from this section.

47 ARREST FOR BREACH OF ORDER

(2) If—
(a) the court makes an occupation order; and
(b) it appears to the court that the respondent has used or threatened violence against the applicant or a relevant child, it shall attach a power of arrest to one or more provisions of the order unless satisfied that in all the circumstances of the case the applicant or child will be adequately protected without such a power of arrest.

(3) Subsection (2) does not apply in any case where the occupation order is made by virtue of section 45(1), but in such a case the court may attach a power of arrest to one or more provisions of the order if it appears to it—
(a) that the respondent has used or threatened violence against the applicant or a relevant child; and
(b) that there is a risk of significant harm to the applicant or child, attributable to conduct of the respondent, if the power of arrest is not attached to those provisions immediately.

(4) If, by virtue of subsection (3), the court attaches a power of arrest to any provisions of an occupation order, it may provide that the power of arrest is to have effect for a shorter period than the other provisions of the order.

(5) Any period specified for the purposes of subsection (4) may be extended by the court (on one or more occasions) on an application to vary or discharge the occupation order.

(6) If, by virtue of subsection (2) or (3), a power of arrest is attached to certain provisions of an order, a constable may arrest without warrant a person whom he has reasonable cause for suspecting to be in breach of any such provision.

(7) If a power of arrest is attached under subsection (2) or (3) to certain provisions of the order and the respondent is arrested under subsection (6)—
(a) he must be brought before the relevant judicial authority within the period of 24 hours beginning at the time of his arrest; and
(b) if the matter is not then disposed of forthwith, the relevant judicial authority before whom he is brought may remand him.

In reckoning for the purposes of this subsection any period of 24 hours, no account is to be taken of Christmas Day, Good Friday or any Sunday.

(8) If the court—
(a) has made a non-molestation order, or
(b) has made an occupation order but has not attached a power of arrest under subsection (2) or (3) to any provision of the order, or has attached that power only to certain provisions of the order,

then, if at any time the applicant considers that the respondent has failed to comply with the order, he may apply to the relevant judicial authority for the issue of a warrant for the arrest of the respondent.

(9) The relevant judicial authority shall not issue a warrant on an application under subsection (8) unless—
(a) the application is substantiated on oath; and
(b) the relevant judicial authority has reasonable grounds for believing that the respondent has failed to comply with the order.

(10) If a person is brought before a court by virtue of a warrant issued under subsection (9) and the court does not dispose of the matter forthwith, the court may remand him.

(11) Schedule 5 (which makes provision corresponding to that applying in magistrates' courts in civil cases under sections 128 and 129 of the Magistrates' Courts Act 1980) has effect in relation to the powers of the High Court and a county court to remand a person by virtue of this section.

(12) If a person remanded under this section is granted bail (whether in the High Court or a county court under Schedule 5 or in a magistrates' court under section 128 or 129 of the Magistrates' Courts Act 1980), he may be required by the relevant judicial authority to comply, before release on bail or later, with such requirements as appear to that authority to be necessary to secure that he does not interfere with witnesses or otherwise obstruct the course of justice.

48 REMAND FOR MEDICAL EXAMINATION AND REPORT

(1) If the relevant judicial authority has reason to consider that a medical report will be required, any power to remand a person under section 47(7)(b) or (10) may be exercised for the purpose of enabling a medical examination and report to be made.

(2) If such a power is so exercised, the adjournment must not be for more than 4 weeks at a time unless the relevant judicial authority remands the accused in custody.

(3) If the relevant judicial authority so remands the accused, the adjournment must not be for more than 3 weeks at a time.

(4) If there is reason to suspect that a person who has been arrested—
   (a) under section 47(6), or
   (b) under a warrant issued on an application made under section 47(8), is suffering from mental disorder within the meaning of the Mental Health Act 1983, the relevant judicial authority has the same power to make an order under section 35 of that Act (remand for report on accused's mental condition) as the Crown Court has under that section in the case of an accused person within the meaning of that section.

49 VARIATION AND DISCHARGE OF ORDERS

(1) An occupation order or non-molestation order may be varied or discharged by the court on an application by—
   (a) the respondent, or
   (b) the person on whose application the order was made.

(2) In the case of a non-molestation order made by virtue of section 42(2)(b), the order may be varied or discharged by the court even though no such application has been made.

(3) If B's home rights are, under section 31, are a charge on the estate or interest of the other spouse or of trustees for A, an order under section 33 against A may also be varied or discharged by the court on an application by any person deriving title under A or under the trustees and affected by the charge.

(4) If, by virtue of section 47(3), a power of arrest has been attached to certain provisions of an occupation order, the court may vary or discharge the order under subsection (1) in so far as it confers a power of arrest (whether or not any application has been made to vary or discharge any other provision of the order).

Enforcement powers of magistrates' courts

50 POWER OF MAGISTRATES' COURT TO SUSPEND EXECUTION OF COMMITTAL ORDER

(1) If, under section 63(3) of the Magistrates' Courts Act 1980, a magistrates' court has power to commit a person to custody for breach of a relevant requirement, the court may by order direct that the execution of the order of committal is to be suspended for such period or on such terms and conditions as it may specify.

(2) In subsection (1) "a relevant requirement" means—
(a) an occupation order or non-molestation order;
(b) an exclusion requirement included by virtue of section 38A of the Children Act 1989 in an interim care order made under section 38 of that Act; or
(c) an exclusion requirement included by virtue of section 44A of the Children Act 1989 in an emergency protection order under section 44 of that Act.

51 POWER OF MAGISTRATES' COURT TO ORDER HOSPITAL ADMISSION OR GUARDIANSHIP

(1) A magistrates' court has the same power to make a hospital order or guardianship order under section 37 of the Mental Health Act 1983 or an interim hospital order under section 38 of that Act in the case of a person suffering from mental disorder within the meaning of that Act who could otherwise be committed to custody for breach of a relevant requirement as a magistrates' court has under those sections in the case of a person convicted of an offence punishable on summary conviction with imprisonment.

(2) In subsection (1) "a relevant requirement" has the meaning given by section 50(2).

. . .

Transfer of tenancies

53 TRANSFER OF CERTAIN TENANCIES

Schedule 7 makes provision in relation to the transfer of certain tenancies on divorce etc or on separation of cohabitants.

Dwelling-house subject to mortgage

54 DWELLING-HOUSE SUBJECT TO MORTGAGE

(1) In determining for the purposes of this Part whether a person is entitled to occupy a dwelling-house by virtue of an estate or interest, any right to possession of the dwelling-house conferred on a mortgagee of the dwelling-house under or by virtue of his mortgage is to be disregarded.

(2) Subsection (1) applies whether or not the mortgagee is in possession.

(3) Where a person ("A") is entitled to occupy a dwelling-house by virtue of an estate or interest, a connected person does not by virtue of—
(a) any home rights conferred by section 30, or
(b) any rights conferred by an order under section 35 or 36,
have any larger right against the mortgagee to occupy the dwelling-house than A has by virtue of his estate or interest and of any contract with the mortgagee.

(4) Subsection (3) does not apply, in the case of home rights, if under section 31 those rights are a charge, affecting the mortgagee, on the estate or interest mortgaged.

(5) In this section "connected person", in relation to any person, means that person's spouse, former spouse, civil partner, former civil partner, cohabitant or former cohabitant.

55 ACTIONS BY MORTGAGEES: JOINING CONNECTED PERSONS AS PARTIES

(1) This section applies if a mortgagee of land which consists of or includes a dwelling-house brings an action in any court for the enforcement of his security.

(2) A connected person who is not already a party to the action is entitled to be made a party in the circumstances mentioned in subsection (3).

(3) The circumstances are that—
- (a) the connected person is enabled by section 30(3) or (6) (or by section 30(3) or (6) as applied by section 35(13) or 36(13)), to meet the mortgagor's liabilities under the mortgage;
- (b) he has applied to the court before the action is finally disposed of in that court; and
- (c) the court sees no special reason against his being made a party to the action and is satisfied—
  - (i) that he may be expected to make such payments or do such other things in or towards satisfaction of the mortgagor's liabilities or obligations as might affect the outcome of the proceedings; or
  - (ii) that the expectation of it should be considered under section 36 of the Administration of Justice Act 1970.

(4) In this section "connected person" has the same meaning as in section 54.

56 ACTIONS BY MORTGAGEES: SERVICE OF NOTICE ON CERTAIN PERSONS

(1) This section applies if a mortgagee of land which consists, or substantially consists, of a dwelling-house brings an action for the enforcement of his security, and at the relevant time there is—
- (a) in the case of unregistered land, a land charge of Class F registered against the person who is the estate owner at the relevant time or any person who, where the estate owner is a trustee, preceded him as trustee during the subsistence of the mortgage; or
- (b) in the case of registered land, a subsisting registration of—
  - (i) a notice under section 31(10);
  - (ii) a notice under section 2(8) of the Matrimonial Homes Act 1983; or
  - (iii) a notice or caution under section 2(7) of the Matrimonial Homes Act 1967.

(2) If the person on whose behalf—
- (a) the land charge is registered, or
- (b) the notice or caution is entered, is not a party to the action, the mortgagee must serve notice of the action on him.

(3) If—
- (a) an official search has been made on behalf of the mortgagee which would disclose any land charge of Class F, notice or caution within subsection (1)(a) or (b),
- (b) a certificate of the result of the search has been issued, and
- (c) the action is commenced within the priority period, the relevant time is the date of the certificate.

(4) In any other case the relevant time is the time when the action is commenced.

(5) The priority period is, for both registered and unregistered land, the period for which, in accordance with section 11(5) and (6) of the Land Charges Act 1972, a certificate on an official search operates in favour of a purchaser.

Jurisdiction and procedure etc

57 JURISDICTION OF COURTS

(1) For the purposes of this Part "the court" means the High Court, a county court or a magistrates' court.

(2) Subsection (1) is subject to the provision made by or under the following provisions of this section, to section 59 and to any express provision as to the jurisdiction of any court made by any other provision of this Part.

(3) The Lord Chancellor may, after consulting the Lord Chief Justice, by order specify proceedings under this Part which may only be commenced in—
(a) a specified level of court;
(b) a court which falls within a specified class of court; or
(c) a particular court determined in accordance with, or specified in, the order.

(4) The Lord Chancellor may, after consulting the Lord Chief Justice, by order specify circumstances in which specified proceedings under this Part may only be commenced in—
(a) a specified level of court;
(b) a court which falls within a specified class of court; or
(c) a particular court determined in accordance with, or specified in, the order.

(5) The Lord Chancellor may, after consulting the Lord Chief Justice, by order provide that in specified circumstances the whole, or any specified part of any specified proceedings under this Part is to be transferred to—
(a) a specified level of court;
(b) a court which falls within a specified class of court; or
(c) a particular court determined in accordance with, or specified in, the order.

(6) An order under subsection (5) may provide for the transfer to be made at any stage, or specified stage, of the proceedings and whether or not the proceedings, or any part of them, have already been transferred.

(7) An order under subsection (5) may make such provision as the Lord Chancellor thinks appropriate, after consulting the Lord Chief Justice for excluding specified proceedings from the operation of section 38 or 39 of the Matrimonial and Family Proceedings Act 1984 (transfer of family proceedings) or any other enactment which would otherwise govern the transfer of those proceedings, or any part of them.

(8) For the purposes of subsections (3), (4) and (5), there are three levels of court—
(a) the High Court;
(b) any county court; and
(c) any magistrates' court.

(9) The Lord Chancellor may, after consulting the Lord Chief Justice, by order make provision for the principal registry of the Family Division of the High Court to be treated as if it were a county court for specified purposes of this Part, or of any provision made under this Part.

(10) Any order under subsection (9) may make such provision as the Lord Chancellor thinks expedient, after consulting the Lord Chief Justice, for the purpose of applying (with or

without modifications) provisions which apply in relation to the procedure in county courts to the principal registry when it acts as if it were a county court.

(11) In this section "specified" means specified by an order under this section.

(12) The Lord Chief Justice may nominate a judicial office holder (as defined in section 109(4) of the Constitutional Reform Act 2005) to exercise his functions under this section.

58 CONTEMPT PROCEEDINGS

The powers of the court in relation to contempt of court arising out of a person's failure to comply with an order under this Part may be exercised by the relevant judicial authority.

59 MAGISTRATES' COURTS

(1) A magistrates' court shall not be competent to entertain any application, or make any order, involving any disputed question as to a party's entitlement to occupy any property by virtue of a beneficial estate or interest or contract or by virtue of any enactment giving him the right to remain in occupation, unless it is unnecessary to determine the question in order to deal with the application or make the order.

(2) A magistrates' court may decline jurisdiction in any proceedings under this Part if it considers that the case can more conveniently be dealt with by another court.

(3) The powers of a magistrates' court under section 63(2) of the Magistrates' Courts Act 1980 to suspend or rescind orders shall not apply in relation to any order made under this Part.

60 PROVISION FOR THIRD PARTIES TO ACT ON BEHALF OF VICTIMS OF DOMESTIC VIOLENCE

(1) Rules of court may provide for a prescribed person, or any person in a prescribed category, ("a representative") to act on behalf of another in relation to proceedings to which this Part applies.

(2) Rules made under this section may, in particular, authorise a representative to apply for an occupation order or for a non-molestation order for which the person on whose behalf the representative is acting could have applied.

(3) Rules made under this section may prescribe—
  (a) conditions to be satisfied before a representative may make an application to the court on behalf of another; and
  (b) considerations to be taken into account by the court in determining whether, and if so how, to exercise any of its powers under this Part when a representative is acting on behalf of another.

(4) Any rules made under this section may be made so as to have effect for a specified period and may make consequential or transitional provision with respect to the expiry of the specified period.

(5) Any such rules may be replaced by further rules made under this section.

61 APPEALS

(1) An appeal shall lie to a county court against—
  (a) the making by a magistrates' court of any order under this Part, or
  (b) any refusal by a magistrates' court to make such an order,

but no appeal shall lie against any exercise by a magistrates' court of the power conferred by section 59(2).

(2) On an appeal under this section, a county court may make such orders as may be necessary to give effect to its determination of the appeal.

(3) Where an order is made under subsection (2), a county court may also make such incidental or consequential orders as appear to it to be just.

(4) Any order of a county court made on an appeal under this section (other than one directing that an application be re-heard by a magistrates' court) shall, for the purposes—
(a) of the enforcement of the order, and
(b) of any power to vary, revive or discharge orders,
be treated as if it were an order of the magistrates' court from which the appeal was brought and not an order of a county court.

(5) The Lord Chancellor may, after consulting the Lord Chief Justice, by order make provision as to the circumstances in which appeals may be made against decisions taken by courts on questions arising in connection with the transfer, or proposed transfer, of proceedings by virtue of any order under section 57(5).

(6) Except to the extent provided for in any order made under subsection (5), no appeal may be made against any decision of a kind mentioned in that subsection.

(7) The Lord Chief Justice may nominate a judicial office holder (as defined in section 109(4) of the Constitutional Reform Act 2005) to exercise his functions under this section.

General

62 MEANING OF "COHABITANTS", "RELEVANT CHILD" AND "ASSOCIATED PERSONS"

(1) For the purposes of this Part—
(a) "cohabitants" are two persons who are neither married to each other nor civil partners of each other but are living together as husband and wife or as if they were civil partners; and
(b) "cohabit" and "former cohabitants" are to be read accordingly, but the latter expression does not include cohabitants who have subsequently married each other or become civil partners of each other.

(2) In this Part, "relevant child", in relation to any proceedings under this Part, means—
(a) any child who is living with or might reasonably be expected to live with either party to the proceedings;
(b) any child in relation to whom an order under the Adoption Act 1976, the Adoption and Children Act 2002 or the Children Act 1989 is in question in the proceedings; and
(c) any other child whose interests the court considers relevant.

(3) For the purposes of this Part, a person is associated with another person if—
(a) they are or have been married to each other;
(aa) they are or have been civil partners of each other;
(b) they are cohabitants or former cohabitants;
(c) they live or have lived in the same household, otherwise than merely by reason of one of them being the other's employee, tenant, lodger or boarder;
(d) they are relatives;
(e) they have agreed to marry one another (whether or not that agreement has been terminated);

(eza) they have entered into a civil partnership agreement (as defined by section 73 of the Civil Partnership Act 2004) (whether or not that agreement has been terminated);
(ea) they have or have had an intimate personal relationship with each other which is or was of significant duration;
(f) in relation to any child, they are both persons falling within subsection (4); or
(g) they are parties to the same family proceedings (other than proceedings under this Part).

(4) A person falls within this subsection in relation to a child if—
(a) he is a parent of the child; or
(b) he has or has had parental responsibility for the child.

(5) If a child has been adopted or falls within subsection (7), two persons are also associated with each other for the purposes of this Part if—
(a) one is a natural parent of the child or a parent of such a natural parent; and
(b) the other is the child or any person—
(i) who has become a parent of the child by virtue of an adoption order or has applied for an adoption order, or
(ii) with whom the child has at any time been placed for adoption.

(6) A body corporate and another person are not, by virtue of subsection (3)(f) or (g), to be regarded for the purposes of this Part as associated with each other.

(7) A child falls within this subsection if—
(a) an adoption agency, within the meaning of section 2 of the Adoption and Children Act 2002, has power to place him for adoption under section 19 of that Act (placing children with parental consent) or he has become the subject of an order under section 21 of that Act (placement orders), or
(b) he is freed for adoption by virtue of an order made—
(i) in England and Wales, under section 18 of the Adoption Act 1976,
(ii) in Scotland, under section 18 of the Adoption (Scotland) Act 1978, or
(iii) in Northern Ireland, under Article 17(1) or 18(1) of the Adoption (Northern Ireland) Order 1987.

63 INTERPRETATION OF PART IV

(1) In this Part—

"adoption order" means an adoption order within the meaning of section 72(1) of the Adoption Act 1976 or section 46(1) of the Adoption and Children Act 2002;

"associated", in relation to a person, is to be read with section 62(3) to (6);

"child" means a person under the age of eighteen years;

"cohabit", "cohabitant" and "former cohabitant" have the meaning given by section 62(1);

"the court" is to be read with section 57;

"development" means physical, intellectual, emotional, social or behavioural development;

"dwelling-house" includes (subject to subsection (4))—
(a) any building or part of a building which is occupied as a dwelling,
(b) any caravan, house-boat or structure which is occupied as a dwelling, and any yard, garden, garage or outhouse belonging to it and occupied with it;

"family proceedings" means any proceedings—
(a) under the inherent jurisdiction of the High Court in relation to children; or
(b) under the enactments mentioned in subsection (2);
"harm"—
(a) in relation to a person who has reached the age of eighteen years, means ill-treatment or the impairment of health; and
(b) in relation to a child, means ill-treatment or the impairment of health or development;

"health" includes physical or mental health;

"home rights" has the meaning given by section 30;

"ill-treatment" includes forms of ill-treatment which are not physical and, in relation to a child, includes sexual abuse;

"mortgage", "mortgagor" and "mortgagee" have the same meaning as in the Law of Property Act 1925;

"mortgage payments" includes any payments which, under the terms of the mortgage, the mortgagor is required to make to any person;

"non-molestation order" has the meaning given by section 42(1);

"occupation order" has the meaning given by section 39;

"parental responsibility" has the same meaning as in the Children Act 1989;

"relative", in relation to a person, means—
(a) the father, mother, stepfather, stepmother, son, daughter, stepson, stepdaughter, grandmother, grandfather, grandson or granddaughter of that person or of that person's spouse, former spouse, civil partner or former civil partner, or
(b) the brother, sister, uncle, aunt, niece, nephew or first cousin (whether of the full blood or of the half blood or by marriage or civil partnership) of that person or of that person's spouse, former spouse, civil partner or former civil partner, and includes, in relation to a person who is cohabiting or has cohabited with another person, any person who would fall within paragraph (a) or (b) if the parties were married to each other or were civil partners of each other;
"relevant child", in relation to any proceedings under this Part, has the meaning given by section 62(2);

"the relevant judicial authority", in relation to any order under this Part, means—
(a) where the order was made by the High Court, a judge of that court;
(b) where the order was made by a county court, a judge or district judge of that or any other county court; or
(c) where the order was made by a magistrates' court, any magistrates' court.

(2) The enactments referred to in the definition of "family proceedings" are—
(a) Part II;
(b) this Part;
(ba) Part 4A;
(c) the Matrimonial Causes Act 1973;
(d) the Adoption Act 1976;
(e) the Domestic Proceedings and Magistrates' Courts Act 1978;
(f) Part III of the Matrimonial and Family Proceedings Act 1984;
(g) Parts I, II and IV of the Children Act 1989;
(h) section 54 of the Human Fertilisation and Embryology Act 2008;
(i) the Adoption and Children Act 2002;
(j) Schedules 5 to 7 to the Civil Partnership Act 2004.

(3) Where the question of whether harm suffered by a child is significant turns on the child's health or development, his health or development shall be compared with that which could reasonably be expected of a similar child.

(4) For the purposes of sections 31, 32, 53 and 54 and such other provisions of this Part (if any) as may be prescribed, this Part is to have effect as if paragraph (b) of the definition of "dwelling-house" were omitted.

(5) It is hereby declared that this Part applies as between the parties to a marriage even though either of them is, or has at any time during the marriage been, married to more than one person.

Part IVA FORCED MARRIAGE

FORCED MARRIAGE PROTECTION ORDERS

63A FORCED MARRIAGE PROTECTION ORDERS

(1) The court may make an order for the purposes of protecting—
  (a) a person from being forced into a marriage or from any attempt to be forced into a marriage; or
  (b) a person who has been forced into a marriage.

(2) In deciding whether to exercise its powers under this section and, if so, in what manner, the court must have regard to all the circumstances including the need to secure the health, safety and well-being of the person to be protected.

(3) In ascertaining that person's well-being, the court must, in particular, have such regard to the person's wishes and feelings (so far as they are reasonably ascertainable) as the court considers appropriate in the light of the person's age and understanding.

(4) For the purposes of this Part a person ("A") is forced into a marriage if another person ("B") forces A to enter into a marriage (whether with B or another person) without A's free and full consent.

(5) For the purposes of subsection (4) it does not matter whether the conduct of B which forces A to enter into a marriage is directed against A, B or another person.

(6) In this Part—

"force" includes coerce by threats or other psychological means (and related expressions are to be read accordingly); and

"forced marriage protection order" means an order under this section.

63B CONTENTS OF ORDERS

(1) A forced marriage protection order may contain—
  (a) such prohibitions, restrictions or requirements; and
  (b) such other terms;
as the court considers appropriate for the purposes of the order.

(2) The terms of such orders may, in particular, relate to—
  (a) conduct outside England and Wales as well as (or instead of) conduct within England and Wales;
  (b) respondents who are, or may become, involved in other respects as well as (or instead of) respondents who force or attempt to force, or may force or attempt to force, a person to enter into a marriage;

(c) other persons who are, or may become, involved in other respects as well as respondents of any kind.

(3) For the purposes of subsection (2) examples of involvement in other respects are—
(a) aiding, abetting, counselling, procuring, encouraging or assisting another person to force, or to attempt to force, a person to enter into a marriage; or
(b) conspiring to force, or to attempt to force, a person to enter into a marriage.

63C APPLICATIONS AND OTHER OCCASIONS FOR MAKING ORDERS

(1) The court may make a forced marriage protection order—
(a) on an application being made to it; or
(b) without an application being made to it but in the circumstances mentioned in subsection (6).

(2) An application may be made by—
(a) the person who is to be protected by the order; or
(b) a relevant third party.

(3) An application may be made by any other person with the leave of the court.

(4) In deciding whether to grant leave, the court must have regard to all the circumstances including—
(a) the applicant's connection with the person to be protected;
(b) the applicant's knowledge of the circumstances of the person to be protected; and
(c) the wishes and feelings of the person to be protected so far as they are reasonably ascertainable and so far as the court considers it appropriate, in the light of the person's age and understanding, to have regard to them.

(5) An application under this section may be made in other family proceedings or without any other family proceedings being instituted.

(6) The circumstances in which the court may make an order without an application being made are where—
(a) any other family proceedings are before the court ("the current proceedings");
(b) the court considers that a forced marriage protection order should be made to protect a person (whether or not a party to the current proceedings); and
(c) a person who would be a respondent to any such proceedings for a forced marriage protection order is a party to the current proceedings.

(7) In this section—

"family proceedings" has the same meaning as in Part 4 (see section 63(1) and (2)) but also includes—
(a) proceedings under the inherent jurisdiction of the High Court in relation to adults;
(b) proceedings in which the court has made an emergency protection order under section 44 of the Children Act 1989 (c 41) which includes an exclusion requirement (as defined in section 44A(3) of that Act); and
(c) proceedings in which the court has made an order under section 50 of the Act of 1989 (recovery of abducted children etc); and
"relevant third party" means a person specified, or falling within a description of persons specified, by order of the Lord Chancellor.

(8) An order of the Lord Chancellor under subsection (7) may, in particular, specify the Secretary of State.

Further provision about orders

63D EX PARTE ORDERS: PART 4A

(1) The court may, in any case where it considers that it is just and convenient to do so, make a forced marriage protection order even though the respondent has not been given such notice of the proceedings as would otherwise be required by rules of court.

(2) In deciding whether to exercise its powers under subsection (1), the court must have regard to all the circumstances including—
  (a) any risk of significant harm to the person to be protected or another person if the order is not made immediately;
  (b) whether it is likely that an applicant will be deterred or prevented from pursuing an application if an order is not made immediately; and
  (c) whether there is reason to believe that—
    (i) the respondent is aware of the proceedings but is deliberately evading service; and
    (ii) the delay involved in effecting substituted service will cause serious prejudice to the person to be protected or (if a different person) an applicant.

(3) The court must give the respondent an opportunity to make representations about any order made by virtue of subsection (1).

(4) The opportunity must be—
  (a) as soon as just and convenient; and
  (b) at a hearing of which notice has been given to all the parties in accordance with rules of court.

63E UNDERTAKINGS INSTEAD OF ORDERS

(1) The court may, subject to subsection (3), accept an undertaking from the respondent to proceedings for a forced marriage protection order if it has power to make such an order.

(2) No power of arrest may be attached to an undertaking given under subsection (1).

(3) The court may not accept an undertaking under subsection (1) instead of making an order if a power of arrest would otherwise have been attached to the order.

(4) An undertaking given to the court under subsection (1) is enforceable as if the court had made the order in terms corresponding to those of the undertaking.

(5) This section is without prejudice to the powers of the court apart from this section.

63F DURATION OF ORDERS

A forced marriage protection order may be made for a specified period or until varied or discharged.

63G VARIATION OF ORDERS AND THEIR DISCHARGE

(1) The court may vary or discharge a forced marriage protection order on an application by—
  (a) any party to the proceedings for the order;
  (b) the person being protected by the order (if not a party to the proceedings for the order); or
  (c) any person affected by the order.

(2) In addition, the court may vary or discharge a forced marriage protection order made by virtue of section 63C(1)(b) even though no application under subsection (1) above has been made to the court.

(3) Section 63D applies to a variation of a forced marriage protection order as it applies to the making of such an order.

(4) Section 63E applies to proceedings for a variation of a forced marriage protection order as it applies to proceedings for the making of such an order.

(5) Accordingly, references in sections 63D and 63E to making a forced marriage protection order are to be read for the purposes of subsections (3) and (4) above as references to varying such an order.

(6) Subsection (7) applies if a power of arrest has been attached to provisions of a forced marriage protection order by virtue of section 63H.

(7) The court may vary or discharge the order under this section so far as it confers a power of arrest (whether or not there is a variation or discharge of any other provision of the order).

Arrest for breach of orders

63H ATTACHMENT OF POWERS OF ARREST TO ORDERS

(1) Subsection (2) applies if the court—
 (a) intends to make a forced marriage protection order otherwise than by virtue of section 63D; and
 (b) considers that the respondent has used or threatened violence against the person being protected or otherwise in connection with the matters being dealt with by the order.

(2) The court must attach a power of arrest to one or more provisions of the order unless it considers that, in all the circumstances of the case, there will be adequate protection without such a power.

(3) Subsection (4) applies if the court—
 (a) intends to make a forced marriage protection order by virtue of section 63D; and
 (b) considers that the respondent has used or threatened violence against the person being protected or otherwise in connection with the matters being dealt with by the order.

(4) The court may attach a power of arrest to one or more provisions of the order if it considers that there is a risk of significant harm to a person, attributable to conduct of the respondent, if the power of arrest is not attached to the provisions immediately.

(5) The court may provide for a power of arrest attached to any provisions of an order under subsection (4) to have effect for a shorter period than the other provisions of the order.

(6) Any period specified for the purposes of subsection (5) may be extended by the court (on one or more occasions) on an application to vary or discharge the order.

(7) In this section "respondent" includes any person who is not a respondent but to whom an order is directed.

63I ARREST UNDER ATTACHED POWERS

(1) Subsection (2) applies if a power of arrest is attached to provisions of a forced marriage protection order under section 63H.

(2) A constable may arrest without warrant a person whom the constable has reasonable cause for suspecting to be in breach of any such provision or otherwise in contempt of court in relation to the order.

(3) A person arrested under subsection (2) must be brought before the relevant judge within the period of 24 hours beginning at the time of the person's arrest.

(4) In calculating any period of 24 hours for the purposes of subsection (3), Christmas Day, Good Friday and any Sunday are to be ignored.

63J ARREST UNDER WARRANT

(1) Subsection (2) applies if the court has made a forced marriage protection order but—
 (a) no power of arrest is attached to any provision of the order under section 63H;
 (b) such a power is attached only to certain provisions of the order; or
 (c) such a power was attached for a shorter period than other provisions of the order and that period has expired.

(2) An interested party may apply to the relevant judge for the issue of a warrant for the arrest of a person if the interested party considers that the person has failed to comply with the order or is otherwise in contempt of court in relation to the order.

(3) The relevant judge must not issue a warrant on an application under subsection (2) unless—
 (a) the application is substantiated on oath; and
 (b) the relevant judge has reasonable grounds for believing that the person to be arrested has failed to comply with the order or is otherwise in contempt of court in relation to the order.

(4) In this section "interested party", in relation to a forced marriage protection order, means—
 (a) the person being protected by the order;
 (b) (if a different person) the person who applied for the order; or
 (c) any other person;
but no application may be made under subsection (2) by a person falling within paragraph (c) without the leave of the relevant judge.

63K REMAND: GENERAL

(1) The court before which an arrested person is brought under section 63I(3) or by virtue of a warrant issued under section 63J may, if the matter is not then disposed of immediately, remand the person concerned.

(2) Schedule 5 has effect in relation to the powers of the court to remand a person by virtue of this section but as if the following modifications were made to the Schedule.

(3) The modifications are that—
 (a) in paragraph 2(1) of Schedule 5, the reference to section 47 is to be read as a reference to this section; and
 (b) in paragraph 2(5)(b) of the Schedule, the reference to section 48(1) is to be read as a reference to section 63L(1).

(4) Subsection (5) applies if a person remanded under this section is granted bail under Schedule 5 as modified above.

(5) The person may be required by the relevant judge to comply, before release on bail orlater, with such requirements as appear to the relevant judge to be necessary to secure that the person does not interfere with witnesses or otherwise obstruct the course of justice.

63L REMAND: MEDICAL EXAMINATION AND REPORT

(1) Any power to remand a person under section 63K(1) may be exercised for the purpose of enabling a medical examination and report to be made if the relevant judge has reason to consider that a medical report will be required.

(2) If such a power is so exercised, the adjournment must not be for more than 4 weeks at a time unless the relevant judge remands the accused in custody.

(3) If the relevant judge remands the accused in custody, the adjournment must not be for more than 3 weeks at a time.

(4) Subsection (5) applies if there is reason to suspect that a person who has been arrested—
(a) under section 63I(2); or
(b) under a warrant issued on an application made under section 63J(2);
is suffering from mental disorder within the meaning of the Mental Health Act 1983.

(5) The relevant judge has the same power to make an order under section 35 of the Mental Health Act 1983 (c 20) (remand for report on accused's mental condition) as the Crown Court has under section 35 of that Act in the case of an accused person within the meaning of that section.

Jurisdiction and procedure

63M JURISDICTION OF COURTS: PART 4A

(1) For the purposes of this Part "the court" means the High Court or a county court.

(2) Subsection (1) is subject to any provision made by virtue of subsections (3) and (4).

(3) Section 57(3) to (12) (allocation of proceedings to courts etc) apply for the purposes of this Part as they apply for the purposes of Part 4 but as if the following modification were made.

(4) The modification is that section 57(8) is to be read as if there were substituted for it—

"(8) For the purposes of subsections (3), (4) and (5), there are two levels of court—
(a) the High Court; and
(b) any county court.

63O CONTEMPT PROCEEDINGS: PART 4A

The powers of the court in relation to contempt of court arising out of a person's failure to comply with a forced marriage protection order or otherwise in connection with such an order may be exercised by the relevant judge.

. . .

Supplementary

. . .

63R OTHER PROTECTION OR ASSISTANCE AGAINST FORCED MARRIAGE

(1) This Part does not affect any other protection or assistance available to a person who—
(a) is being, or may be, forced into a marriage or subjected to an attempt to be forced into a marriage; or
(b) has been forced into a marriage.

(2) In particular, it does not affect—
(a) the inherent jurisdiction of the High Court;
(b) any criminal liability;
(c) any civil remedies under the Protection from Harassment Act 1997 (c 40);
(d) any right to an occupation order or a non-molestation order under Part 4 of this Act;
(e) any protection or assistance under the Children Act 1989 (c 41);
(f) any claim in tort; or
(g) the law of marriage.

63S INTERPRETATION OF PART 4A

In this Part—

"the court" is to be read with section 63M;

"force" (and related expressions), in relation to a marriage, are to be read in accordance with section 63A(4) to (6);

"forced marriage protection order" has the meaning given by section 63A(6);

"marriage" means any religious or civil ceremony of marriage (whether or not legally binding); and

"the relevant judge", in relation to any order under this Part, means—
(a) where the order was made by the High Court, a judge of that court; and
(b) where the order was made by a county court, a judge or district judge of that or any other county court.

. . .

SCHEDULE 7 TRANSFER OF CERTAIN TENANCIES ON DIVORCE ETC OR ON SEPARATION OF COHABITANTS

Section 53

Part I GENERAL

Interpretation

1. In this Schedule—

"civil partner", except in paragraph 2, includes (where the context requires) former civil partner;

"cohabitant", except in paragraph 3, includes (where the context requires) former cohabitant;

"the court" does not include a magistrates' court,

"landlord" includes—
(a) any person from time to time deriving title under the original landlord; and
(b) in relation to any dwelling-house, any person other than the tenant who is, or (but for Part VII of the Rent Act 1977 or Part II of the Rent (Agriculture) Act 1976) would be, entitled to possession of the dwellinghouse;

"Part II order" means an order under Part II of this Schedule;

"a relevant tenancy" means—
(a) a protected tenancy or statutory tenancy within the meaning of the Rent Act 1977;
(b) a statutory tenancy within the meaning of the Rent (Agriculture) Act 1976;
(c) a secure tenancy within the meaning of section 79 of the Housing Act 1985;

(d) an assured tenancy or assured agricultural occupancy within the meaning of Part I of the Housing Act 1988; or
(e) an introductory tenancy within the meaning of Chapter I of Part V of the Housing Act 1996;

"spouse", except in paragraph 2, includes (where the context requires) former spouse; and

"tenancy" includes sub-tenancy.

Cases in which the court may make an order

2. (1) This paragraph applies if one spouse or civil partner is entitled, either in his own right or jointly with the other spouse or civil partner, to occupy a dwelling-house by virtue of a relevant tenancy.

(2) The court may make a Part II order—
(a) on granting a decree of divorce, a decree of nullity of marriage or a decree of judicial separation or at any time thereafter (whether, in the case of a decree of divorce or nullity of marriage, before or after the decree is made absolute), or
(b) at any time when it has power to make a property adjustment order under Part 2 of Schedule 5 to the Civil Partnership Act 2004 with respect to the civil partnership.

3. (1) This paragraph applies if one cohabitant is entitled, either in his own right or jointly with the other cohabitant, to occupy a dwelling-house by virtue of a relevant tenancy.

(2) If the cohabitants cease to cohabit, the court may make a Part II order.

4. The court shall not make a Part II order unless the dwelling-house is or was—
(a) in the case of spouses, a matrimonial home;
(aa) in the case of civil partners, a civil partnership home; or
(b) in the case of cohabitants, a home in which they cohabited.

Matters to which the court must have regard

5. In determining whether to exercise its powers under Part II of this Schedule and, if so, in what manner the court shall have regard to all the circumstances of the case including—
(a) the circumstances in which the tenancy was granted to either or both of the spouses, civil partners or cohabitants or, as the case requires, the circumstances in which either or both of them became tenant under the tenancy;
(b) the matters mentioned in section 33(6)(a), (b) and (c) and, where the parties are cohabitants and only one of them is entitled to occupy the dwelling-house by virtue of the relevant tenancy, the further matters mentioned in section 36(6)(e), (f), (g) and (h); and
(c) the suitability of the parties as tenants.

Part II ORDERS THAT MAY BE MADE

References to entitlement to occupy

6. References in this Part of this Schedule to a spouse, a civil partner or a cohabitant being entitled to occupy a dwelling-house by virtue of a relevant tenancy apply whether that entitlement is in his own right or jointly with the other spouse, civil partner or cohabitant.

Protected, secure or assured tenancy or assured agricultural occupancy

7. (1) If a spouse, civil partner or cohabitant is entitled to occupy the dwelling-house by virtue of a protected tenancy within the meaning of the Rent Act 1977, a secure tenancy within the meaning of the Housing Act 1985, an assured tenancy or assured agricultural occupancy within the meaning of Part I of the Housing Act 1988 or an

introductory tenancy within the meaning of Chapter I of Part V of the Housing Act 1996, the court may by order direct that, as from such date as may be specified in the order, there shall, by virtue of the order and without further assurance, be transferred to, and vested in, the other spouse, civil partner or cohabitant—

(a) the estate or interest which the spouse, civil partner or cohabitant so entitled had in the dwelling-house immediately before that date by virtue of the lease or agreement creating the tenancy and any assignment of that lease or agreement, with all rights, privileges and appurtenances attaching to that estate or interest but subject to all covenants, obligations, liabilities and incumbrances to which it is subject; and

(b) where the spouse, civil partner or cohabitant so entitled is an assignee of such lease or agreement, the liability of that spouse, civil partner or cohabitant under any covenant of indemnity by the assignee express or implied in the assignment of the lease or agreement to that spouse, civil partner or cohabitant.

(2) If an order is made under this paragraph, any liability or obligation to which the spouse, civil partner or cohabitant so entitled is subject under any covenant having reference to the dwelling-house in the lease or agreement, being a liability or obligation falling due to be discharged or performed on or after the date so specified, shall not be enforceable against that spouse, civil partner or cohabitant.

(3) If the spouse, civil partner or cohabitant so entitled is a successor within the meaning of Part 4 of the Housing Act 1985—

(a) his former spouse (or, in the case of judicial separation, his spouse),

(b) his former civil partner (or, if a separation order is in force, his civil partner), or

(c) his former cohabitant, is to be deemed also to be a successor within the meaning of that Part.

(3A) If the spouse, civil partner or cohabitant so entitled is a successor within the meaning of section 132 of the Housing Act 1996—

(a) his former spouse (or, in the case of judicial separation, his spouse),

(b) his former civil partner (or, if a separation order is in force, his civil partner), or

(c) his former cohabitant, is to be deemed also to be a successor within the meaning of that section.

(4) If the spouse, civil partner or cohabitant so entitled is for the purposes of section 17 of the Housing Act 1988 a successor in relation to the tenancy or occupancy—

(a) his former spouse (or, in the case of judicial separation, his spouse),

(b) his former civil partner (or, if a separation order is in force, his civil partner), or

(c) his former cohabitant, is to be deemed to be a successor in relation to the tenancy or occupancy for the purposes of that section.

(5) If the transfer under sub-paragraph (1) is of an assured agricultural occupancy, then, for the purposes of Chapter III of Part I of the Housing Act 1988—

(a) the agricultural worker condition is fulfilled with respect to the dwelling-house while the spouse, civil partner or cohabitant to whom the assured agricultural occupancy is transferred continues to be the occupier under that occupancy, and

(b) that condition is to be treated as so fulfilled by virtue of the same paragraph of Schedule 3 to the Housing Act 1988 as was applicable before the transfer.

Statutory tenancy within the meaning of the Rent Act 1977

8. (1) This paragraph applies if the spouse, civil partner or cohabitant is entitled to occupy the dwelling-house by virtue of a statutory tenancy within the meaning of the Rent Act 1977.

(2) The court may by order direct that, as from the date specified in the order—
(a) that spouse, civil partner or cohabitant is to cease to be entitled to occupy the dwelling-house; and
(b) the other spouse, civil partner or cohabitant is to be deemed to be the tenant or, as the case may be, the sole tenant under that statutory tenancy.

(3) The question whether the provisions of paragraphs 1 to 3, or (as the case may be) paragraphs 5 to 7 of Schedule 1 to the Rent Act 1977, as to the succession by the surviving spouse or surviving civil partner of a deceased tenant, or by a member of the deceased tenant's family, to the right to retain possession are capable of having effect in the event of the death of the person deemed by an order under this paragraph to be the tenant or sole tenant under the statutory tenancy is to be determined according as those provisions have or have not already had effect in relation to the statutory tenancy.

Statutory tenancy within the meaning of the Rent (Agriculture) Act 1976

9. (1) This paragraph applies if the spouse, civil partner or cohabitant is entitled to occupy the dwelling-house by virtue of a statutory tenancy within the meaning of the Rent (Agriculture) Act 1976.

(2) The court may by order direct that, as from such date as may be specified in the order—
(a) that spouse, civil partner or cohabitant is to cease to be entitled to occupy the dwelling-house; and
(b) the other spouse, civil partner or cohabitant is to be deemed to be the tenant or, as the case may be, the sole tenant under that statutory tenancy.

(3) A spouse, civil partner or cohabitant who is deemed under this paragraph to be the tenant under a statutory tenancy is (within the meaning of that Act) a statutory tenant in his own right, or a statutory tenant by succession, according as the other spouse, civil partner or cohabitant was a statutory tenant in his own right or a statutory tenant by succession.

Part III SUPPLEMENTARY PROVISIONS

Compensation

10. (1) If the court makes a Part II order, it may by the order direct the making of a payment by the spouse, civil partner or cohabitant to whom the tenancy is transferred ("the transferee") to the other spouse, civil partner or cohabitant ("the transferor").

(2) Without prejudice to that, the court may, on making an order by virtue of sub-paragraph (1) for the payment of a sum—
(a) direct that payment of that sum or any part of it is to be deferred until a specified date or until the occurrence of a specified event, or
(b) direct that that sum or any part of it is to be paid by instalments.

(3) Where an order has been made by virtue of sub-paragraph (1), the court may, on the application of the transferee or the transferor—
(a) exercise its powers under sub-paragraph (2), or
(b) vary any direction previously given under that sub-paragraph, at any time before the sum whose payment is required by the order is paid in full.

(4) In deciding whether to exercise its powers under this paragraph and, if so, in what manner, the court shall have regard to all the circumstances including—
(a) the financial loss that would otherwise be suffered by the transferor as a result of the order;

(b) the financial needs and financial resources of the parties; and
(c) the financial obligations which the parties have, or are likely to have in the foreseeable future, including financial obligations to each other and to any relevant child.

(5) The court shall not give any direction under sub-paragraph (2) unless it appears to it that immediate payment of the sum required by the order would cause the transferee financial hardship which is greater than any financial hardship that would be caused to the transferor if the direction were given.

Liabilities and obligations in respect of the dwelling-house

11. (1) If the court makes a Part II order, it may by the order direct that both spouses, civil partners or cohabitants are to be jointly and severally liable to discharge or perform any or all of the liabilities and obligations in respect of the dwelling-house (whether arising under the tenancy or otherwise) which—
(a) have at the date of the order fallen due to be discharged or performed by one only of them; or
(b) but for the direction, would before the date specified as the date on which the order is to take effect fall due to be discharged or performed by one only of them.

(2) If the court gives such a direction, it may further direct that either spouse, civil partner or cohabitant is to be liable to indemnify the other in whole or in part against any payment made or expenses incurred by the other in discharging or performing any such liability or obligation.

Date when order made between spouses or civil partners takes effect

12. The date specified in a Part II order as the date on which the order is to take effect must not be earlier than—
(a) in the case of a marriage in respect of which a decree of divorce or nullity has been granted, the date on which the decree is made absolute;
(b) in the case of a civil partnership in respect of which a dissolution or nullity order has been made, the date on which the order is made final.

Effect of remarriage or subsequent civil partnership

13. (1) If after the grant of a decree dissolving or annulling a marriage either spouse remarries or forms a civil partnership, that spouse is not entitled to apply, by reference to the grant of that decree, for a Part II order.

(2) If after the making of a dissolution or nullity order either civil partner forms a subsequent civil partnership or marries, that civil partner is not entitled to apply, by reference to the making of that order, for a Part II order.

(3) In sub-paragraphs (1) and (2)—
(a) the references to remarrying and marrying include references to cases where the marriage is by law void or voidable, and
(b) the references to forming a civil partnership include references to cases where the civil partnership is by law void or voidable.

. . .

As amended by: Housing Act 1996 (Consequential Amendments) Order 1997, SI 1997/74, art 2, Schedule; Land Registration Act 2002, ss 133, 135, Sch 11, Sch 13; Adoption and Children Act 2002, s 139(1), Sch 3; Transfer of Functions (Children, Young People and Families) Order 2003, SI 2003/3191, arts 3(b), 6, Schedule, para 2; Domestic Violence, Crime and Victims Act 2004, ss 1–4, 58(1), (2), Sch 10, Sch 11; Civil Partnership Act 2004, ss 82, 261(4), Sch 9, Sch 30; Constitutional Reform Act 2005, s 15(1), Sch 4; Mental Health Act 2007, s 1(4), Sch 1; Mental Health Act 2007 (Consequential Amendments) Order 2008, SI 2008/2828, art 5; Forced Marriage (Civil Protection) Act 2007, ss 1, 3(1), Sch 2; Human Fertilisation and Embryology Act 2008, s 56, Sch 6; Access to Justice Act 1999 (Destination of Appeals) (Family Proceedings) Order 2009, SI 2009/871, art 8.

Housing Act 1996

(1996 c 52)

Succession on death of tenant

131 PERSONS QUALIFIED TO SUCCEED TENANT

A person is qualified to succeed the tenant under an introductory tenancy if he occupies the dwelling-house as his only or principal home at the time of the tenant's death and either—

(a) he is the tenant's spouse or civil partner, or

(b) he is another member of the tenant's family and has resided with the tenant throughout the period of twelve months ending with the tenant's death;
unless, in either case, the tenant was himself a successor, as defined in section 132.

132 CASES WHERE THE TENANT IS A SUCCESSOR

(1) The tenant is himself a successor if—
  (a) the tenancy vested in him by virtue of section 133 (succession to introductory tenancy),
  (b) he was a joint tenant and has become the sole tenant,
  (c) he became the tenant on the tenancy being assigned to him (but subject to subsections (2) and (3)), or
  (d) he became the tenant on the tenancy being vested in him on the death of the previous tenant.

(2) A tenant to whom the tenancy was assigned in pursuance of an order under section 24 of the Matrimonial Causes Act 1973 (property adjustment orders in connection with matrimonial proceedings) or section 17(1) of the Matrimonial and Family Proceedings Act 1984 (property adjustment orders after overseas divorce, &c) is a successor only if the other party to the marriage was a successor.

(2A) A tenant to whom the tenancy was assigned in pursuance of an order under Part 2 of Schedule 5, or paragraph 9(2) or (3) of Schedule 7, to the Civil Partnership Act 2004 (property adjustment orders in connection with civil partnership proceedings or after overseas dissolution of civil partnership, etc) is a successor only if the other civil partner was a successor.

(3) Where within six months of the coming to an end of an introductory tenancy ("the former tenancy") the tenant becomes a tenant under another introductory tenancy, and—
  (a) the tenant was a successor in relation to the former tenancy, and
  (b) under the other tenancy either the dwelling-house or the landlord, or both, are the same as under the former tenancy,
the tenant is also a successor in relation to the other tenancy unless the agreement creating that tenancy otherwise provides.

133 SUCCESSION TO INTRODUCTORY TENANCY

(1) This section applies where a tenant under an introductory tenancy dies.

(2) Where there is a person qualified to succeed the tenant, the tenancy vests by virtue of this section in that person, or if there is more than one such person in the one to be preferred in accordance with the following rules—
- (a) the tenant's spouse or civil partner is to be preferred to another member of the tenant's family;
- (b) of two or more other members of the tenant's family such of them is to be preferred as may be agreed between them or as may, where there is no such agreement, be selected by the landlord.

(3) Where there is no person qualified to succeed the tenant, the tenancy ceases to be an introductory tenancy—
- (a) when it is vested or otherwise disposed of in the course of the administration of the tenant's estate, unless the vesting or other disposal is in pursuance of an order made under—
  - (i) section 24 of the Matrimonial Causes Act 1973 (property adjustment orders made in connection with matrimonial proceedings),
  - (ii) section 17(1) of the Matrimonial and Family Proceedings Act 1984 (property adjustment orders after overseas divorce, &c),
  - (iii) paragraph 1 of Schedule 1 to the Children Act 1989 (orders for financial relief against parents), or
  - (iv) Part 2 of Schedule 5, or paragraph 9(2) or (3) of Schedule 7, to the Civil Partnership Act 2004 (property adjustment orders in connection with civil partnership proceedings or after overseas dissolution of civil partnership, etc); or
- (b) when it is known that when the tenancy is so vested or disposed of it will not be in pursuance of such an order.

. . .

140 MEMBERS OF A PERSON'S FAMILY: CHAPTER I

(1) A person is a member of another's family within the meaning of this Chapter if—
- (a) he is the spouse or civil partner of that person, or he and that person live together as husband and wife or as if they were civil partners, or
- (b) he is that person's parent, grandparent, child, grandchild, brother, sister, uncle, aunt, nephew or niece.

(2) For the purpose of subsection (1)(b)—
- (a) a relationship by marriage or civil partnership shall be treated as a relationship by blood,
- (b) a relationship of the half-blood shall be treated as a relationship of the whole blood, and
- (c) the stepchild of a person shall be treated as his child.

As amended by: Civil Partnership Act 2004, s 81, s 261(4), Sch 8, Sch 30; Civil Partnership (Family Proceedings and Housing Consequential Amendments) Order 2005, SI 2005/3336, art 20.

EDUCATION ACT 1996

(1996 c 56)

Compulsory education

7 DUTY OF PARENTS TO SECURE EDUCATION OF CHILDREN OF COMPULSORY SCHOOL AGE

The parent of every child of compulsory school age shall cause him to receive efficient full-time education suitable—

(a) to his age, ability and aptitude, and

(b) to any special educational needs he may have,

either by regular attendance at school or otherwise.

8 COMPULSORY SCHOOL AGE

(1) Subsections (2) and (3) apply to determine for the purposes of any enactment whether a person is of compulsory school age.

(2) A person begins to be of compulsory school age—
   (a) when he attains the age of five, if he attains that age on a prescribed day, and
   (b) otherwise at the beginning of the prescribed day next following his attaining that age.

(3) A person ceases to be of compulsory school age at the end of the day which is the school leaving date for any calendar year—
   (a) if he attains the age of 16 after that day but before the beginning of the school year next following,
   (b) if he attains that age on that day, or
   (c) (unless paragraph (a) applies) if that day is the school leaving date next following his attaining that age.

(4) The Secretary of State may by order—
   (a) provide that such days in the year as are specified in the order shall be, for each calendar year, prescribed days for the purposes of subsection (2);
   (b) determine the day in any calendar year which is to be the school leaving date for that year.

Education in accordance with parental wishes

9 PUPILS TO BE EDUCATED IN ACCORDANCE WITH PARENTS' WISHES

In exercising or performing all their respective powers and duties under the Education Acts, the Secretary of State and local education authorities shall have regard to the general principle that pupils are to be educated in accordance with the wishes of their parents, so far as that is compatible with the provision of efficient instruction and training and the avoidance of unreasonable public expenditure.

As amended by: Education Act 1997, s 52(2), (3).

Protection from Harassment Act 1997

(1997 c 40)

1 PROHIBITION OF HARASSMENT

(1) A person must not pursue a course of conduct—
 (a) which amounts to harassment of another, and
 (b) which he knows or ought to know amounts to harassment of the other.

(1A) A person must not pursue a course of conduct—
 (a) which involves harassment of two or more persons, and
 (b) which he knows or ought to know involves harassment of those persons, and
 (c) by which he intends to persuade any person (whether or not one of those mentioned above)—
  (i) not to do something that he is entitled or required to do, or
  (ii) to do something that he is not under any obligation to do.

(2) For the purposes of this section, the person whose course of conduct is in question ought to know that it amounts to or involves harassment of another if a reasonable person in possession of the same information would think the course of conduct amounted to or involved harassment of the other.

(3) Subsection (1) or (1A) does not apply to a course of conduct if the person who pursued it shows—
 (a) that it was pursued for the purpose of preventing or detecting crime,
 (b) that it was pursued under any enactment or rule of law or to comply with any condition or requirement imposed by any person under any enactment, or
 (c) that in the particular circumstances the pursuit of the course of conduct was reasonable.

2 OFFENCE OF HARASSMENT

(1) A person who pursues a course of conduct in breach of section 1(1) or (1A) is guilty of an offence.

(2) A person guilty of an offence under this section is liable on summary conviction to imprisonment for a term not exceeding six months, or a fine not exceeding level 5 on the standard scale, or both.

3 CIVIL REMEDY

(1) An actual or apprehended breach of section 1(1) may be the subject of a claim in civil proceedings by the person who is or may be the victim of the course of conduct in question.

(2) On such a claim, damages may be awarded for (among other things) any anxiety caused by the harassment and any financial loss resulting from the harassment.

(3) Where—
 (a) in such proceedings the High Court or a county court grants an injunction for the purpose of restraining the defendant from pursuing any conduct which amounts to harassment, and
 (b) the plaintiff considers that the defendant has done anything which he is prohibited from doing by the injunction,

the plaintiff may apply for the issue of a warrant for the arrest of the defendant.

(4) An application under subsection (3) may be made—
(a) where the injunction was granted by the High Court, to a judge of that court, and
(b) where the injunction was granted by a county court, to a judge or district judge of that or any other county court.

(5) The judge or district judge to whom an application under subsection (3) is made may only issue a warrant if—
(a) the application is substantiated on oath, and
(b) the judge or district judge has reasonable grounds for believing that the defendant has done anything which he is prohibited from doing by the injunction.

(6) Where—
(a) the High Court or a county court grants an injunction for the purpose mentioned in subsection (3)(a), and
(b) without reasonable excuse the defendant does anything which he is prohibited from doing by the injunction,
he is guilty of an offence.

(7) Where a person is convicted of an offence under subsection (6) in respect of any conduct, that conduct is not punishable as a contempt of court.

(8) A person cannot be convicted of an offence under subsection (6) in respect of any conduct which has been punished as a contempt of court.

(9) A person guilty of an offence under subsection (6) is liable—
(a) on conviction on indictment, to imprisonment for a term not exceeding five years, or a fine, or both, or
(b) on summary conviction, to imprisonment for a term not exceeding six months, or a fine not exceeding the statutory maximum, or both.

3A INJUNCTIONS TO PROTECT PERSONS FROM HARASSMENT WITHIN SECTION 1(1A)

(1) This section applies where there is an actual or apprehended breach of section 1(1A) by any person ("the relevant person").

(2) In such a case—
(a) any person who is or may be a victim of the course of conduct in question, or
(b) any person who is or may be a person falling within section 1(1A)(c),
may apply to the High Court or a county court for an injunction restraining the relevant person from pursuing any conduct which amounts to harassment in relation to any person or persons mentioned or described in the injunction.

(3) Section 3(3) to (9) apply in relation to an injunction granted under subsection (2) above as they apply in relation to an injunction granted as mentioned in section 3(3)(a).

4 PUTTING PEOPLE IN FEAR OF VIOLENCE

(1) A person whose course of conduct causes another to fear, on at least two occasions, that violence will be used against him is guilty of an offence if he knows or ought to know that his course of conduct will cause the other so to fear on each of those occasions.

(2) For the purposes of this section, the person whose course of conduct is in question ought to know that it will cause another to fear that violence will be used against him on any occasion if a reasonable person in possession of the same information would think the course of conduct would cause the other so to fear on that occasion.

(3) It is a defence for a person charged with an offence under this section to show that—
(a) his course of conduct was pursued for the purpose of preventing or detecting crime,
(b) his course of conduct was pursued under any enactment or rule of law or to comply with any condition or requirement imposed by any person under any enactment, or
(c) the pursuit of his course of conduct was reasonable for the protection of himself or another or for the protection of his or another's property.

(4) A person guilty of an offence under this section is liable—
(a) on conviction on indictment, to imprisonment for a term not exceeding five years, or a fine, or both, or
(b) on summary conviction, to imprisonment for a term not exceeding six months, or a fine not exceeding the statutory maximum, or both.

(5) If on the trial on indictment of a person charged with an offence under this section the jury find him not guilty of the offence charged, they may find him guilty of an offence under section 2.

(6) The Crown Court has the same powers and duties in relation to a person who is by virtue of subsection (5) convicted before it of an offence under section 2 as a magistrates' court would have on convicting him of the offence.

5 RESTRAINING ORDERS ON CONVICTION

(1) A court sentencing or otherwise dealing with a person ("the defendant") convicted of an offence may (as well as sentencing him or dealing with him in any other way) make an order under this section.

(2) The order may, for the purpose of protecting the victim or victims of the offence, or any other person mentioned in the order, from conduct which—
(a) amounts to harassment, or
(b) will cause a fear of violence, prohibit the defendant from doing anything described in the order.

(3) The order may have effect for a specified period or until further order.

(3A) In proceedings under this section both the prosecution and the defence may lead, as further evidence, any evidence that would be admissible in proceedings for an injunction under section 3.

(4) The prosecutor, the defendant or any other person mentioned in the order may apply to the court which made the order for it to be varied or discharged by a further order.

(4A) Any person mentioned in the order is entitled to be heard on the hearing of an application under subsection (4).

(5) If without reasonable excuse the defendant does anything which he is prohibited from doing by an order under this section, he is guilty of an offence.

(6) A person guilty of an offence under this section is liable—
(a) on conviction on indictment, to imprisonment for a term not exceeding five years, or a fine, or both, or
(b) on summary conviction, to imprisonment for a term not exceeding six months, or a fine not exceeding the statutory maximum, or both.

(7) A court dealing with a person for an offence under this section may vary or discharge the order in question by a further order.

5A RESTRAINING ORDERS ON ACQUITTAL

(1) A court before which a person ("the defendant") is acquitted of an offence may, if it considers it necessary to do so to protect a person from harassment by the defendant, make an order prohibiting the defendant from doing anything described in the order.

(2) Subsections (3) to (7) of section 5 apply to an order under this section as they apply to an order under that one.

(3) Where the Court of Appeal allow an appeal against conviction they may remit the case to the Crown Court to consider whether to proceed under this section.

(4) Where—
(a) the Crown Court allows an appeal against conviction, or
(b) a case is remitted to the Crown Court under subsection (3),
the reference in subsection (1) to a court before which a person is acquitted of an offence is to be read as referring to that court.

(5) A person made subject to an order under this section has the same right of appeal against the order as if—
(a) he had been convicted of the offence in question before the court which made the order, and
(b) the order had been made under section 5.

. . .

7 INTERPRETATION OF THIS GROUP OF SECTIONS

(1) This section applies for the interpretation of sections 1 to 5A.

(2) References to harassing a person include alarming the person or causing the person distress.

(3) A "course of conduct" must involve—
(a) in the case of conduct in relation to a single person (see section 1(1)), conduct on at least two occasions in relation to that person, or
(b) in the case of conduct in relation to two or more persons (see section 1(1A)), conduct on at least one occasion in relation to each of those persons.

(3A) A person's conduct on any occasion shall be taken, if aided, abetted, counselled or procured by another—
(a) to be conduct on that occasion of the other (as well as conduct of the person whose conduct it is); and
(b) to be conduct in relation to which the other's knowledge and purpose, and what he ought to have known, are the same as they were in relation to what was contemplated or reasonably foreseeable at the time of the aiding, abetting, counselling or procuring.

(4) "Conduct" includes speech.

(5) References to a person, in the context of the harassment of a person, are references to a person who is an individual.

As amended by: Criminal Justice and Police Act 2001, s 44(1); Police Reform Act 2002, s 107(2), Sch 8; Domestic Violence, Crime and Victims Act 2004, ss 12, 58, Sch 10, Sch 11; Serious Organised Crime and Police Act 2005, s 125;

Human Rights Act 1998
(1998 c 42)

Introduction

1 THE CONVENTION RIGHTS

(1) In this Act "the Convention rights" means the rights and fundamental freedoms set out in—
(a) Articles 2 to 12 and 14 of the Convention,
(b) Articles 1 to 3 of the First Protocol, . . . as read with Articles 16 to 18 of the Convention.

(2) Those Articles are to have effect for the purposes of this Act subject to any designated derogation or reservation (as to which see sections 14 and 15).

(3) The Articles are set out in Schedule 1.

(4) The Secretary of State may by order make such amendments to this Act as he considers appropriate to reflect the effect, in relation to the United Kingdom, of a protocol.

(5) In subsection (4) "protocol" means a protocol to the Convention—
(a) which the United Kingdom has ratified; or
(b) which the United Kingdom has signed with a view to ratification.

(6) No amendment may be made by an order under subsection (4) so as to come into force before the protocol concerned is in force in relation to the United Kingdom.

2 INTERPRETATION OF CONVENTION RIGHTS

(1) A court or tribunal determining a question which has arisen in connection with a Convention right must take into account any—
(a) judgment, decision, declaration or advisory opinion of the European Court of Human Rights,
(b) opinion of the Commission given in a report adopted under Article 31 of the Convention,
(c) decision of the Commission in connection with Article 26 or 27(2) of the Convention, or
(d) decision of the Committee of Ministers taken under Article 46 of the Convention,
whenever made or given, so far as, in the opinion of the court or tribunal, it is relevant to the proceedings in which that question has arisen.

(2) Evidence of any judgment, decision, declaration or opinion of which account may have to be taken under this section is to be given in proceedings before any court or tribunal in such manner as may be provided by rules.

(3) In this section "rules" means rules of court or, in the case of proceedings before a tribunal, rules made for the purposes of this section—
(a) by the Lord Chancellor or the Secretary of State, . . .;

Legislation

3 INTERPRETATION OF LEGISLATION

(1) So far as it is possible to do so, primary legislation and subordinate legislation must be read and given effect in a way which is compatible with the Convention rights.

(2) This section—
  (a) applies to primary legislation and subordinate legislation whenever enacted;
  (b) does not affect the validity, continuing operation or enforcement of any incompatible primary legislation; and
  (c) does not affect the validity, continuing operation or enforcement of any incompatible subordinate legislation if (disregarding any possibility of revocation) primary legislation prevents removal of the incompatibility.

4 DECLARATION OF INCOMPATIBILITY

(1) Subsection (2) applies in any proceedings in which a court determines whether a provision of primary legislation is compatible with a Convention right.

(2) If the court is satisfied that the provision is incompatible with a Convention right, it may make a declaration of that incompatibility.

(3) Subsection (4) applies in any proceedings in which a court determines whether a provision of subordinate legislation, made in the exercise of a power conferred by primary legislation, is compatible with a Convention right.

(4) If the court is satisfied—
  (a) that the provision is incompatible with a Convention right, and
  (b) that (disregarding any possibility of revocation) the primary legislation concerned prevents removal of the incompatibility, it may make a declaration of that incompatibility.

(5) In this section "court" means—
  (a) the Supreme Court;
  (b) the Judicial Committee of the Privy Council; . . .
  (e) in England and Wales or Northern Ireland, the High Court or the Court of Appeal;
  (f) the Court of Protection, in any matter being dealt with by the President of the Family Division, the Vice-Chancellor or a puisne judge of the High Court.

(6) A declaration under this section ("a declaration of incompatibility")—
  (a) does not affect the validity, continuing operation or enforcement of the provision in respect of which it is given; and
  (b) is not binding on the parties to the proceedings in which it is made.

. . .

Public authorities

6 ACTS OF PUBLIC AUTHORITIES

(1) It is unlawful for a public authority to act in a way which is incompatible with a Convention right.

(2) Subsection (1) does not apply to an act if—
  (a) as the result of one or more provisions of primary legislation, the authority could not have acted differently; or
  (b) in the case of one or more provisions of, or made under, primary legislation which cannot be read or given effect in a way which is compatible with the Convention rights, the authority was acting so as to give effect to or enforce those provisions.

(3) In this section "public authority" includes—
  (a) a court or tribunal, and

(b) any person certain of whose functions are functions of a public nature,
but does not include either House of Parliament or a person exercising functions in connection with proceedings in Parliament.

(5) In relation to a particular act, a person is not a public authority by virtue only of subsection (3)(b) if the nature of the act is private.

(6) "An act" includes a failure to act but does not include a failure to—
(a) introduce in, or lay before, Parliament a proposal for legislation; or
(b) make any primary legislation or remedial order.

. . .

SCHEDULE 1 THE ARTICLES

Part I THE CONVENTION RIGHTS AND FREEDOMS

Article 2 Right to life

1. Everyone's right to life shall be protected by law. No one shall be deprived of his life intentionally save in the execution of a sentence of a court following his conviction of a crime for which this penalty is provided by law.

2. Deprivation of life shall not be regarded as inflicted in contravention of this Article when it results from the use of force which is no more than absolutely necessary:
(a) in defence of any person from unlawful violence;
(b) in order to effect a lawful arrest or to prevent the escape of a person lawfully detained;
(c) in action lawfully taken for the purpose of quelling a riot or insurrection.

Article 3 Prohibition of torture

No one shall be subjected to torture or to inhuman or degrading treatment or punishment.

. . .

Article 5 Right to liberty and security

1. Everyone has the right to liberty and security of person. No one shall be deprived of his liberty save in the following cases and in accordance with a procedure prescribed by law:
(a) the lawful detention of a person after conviction by a competent court;
(b) the lawful arrest or detention of a person for non-compliance with the lawful order of a court or in order to secure the fulfilment of any obligation prescribed by law;
(c) the lawful arrest or detention of a person effected for the purpose of bringing him before the competent legal authority on reasonable suspicion of having committed an offence or when it is reasonably considered necessary to prevent his committing an offence or fleeing after having done so;
(d) the detention of a minor by lawful order for the purpose of educational supervision or his lawful detention for the purpose of bringing him before the competent legal authority;
(e) the lawful detention of persons for the prevention of the spreading of infectious diseases, of persons of unsound mind, alcoholics or drug addicts or vagrants;
(f) the lawful arrest or detention of a person to prevent his effecting an unauthorised entry into the country or of a person against whom action is being taken with a view to deportation or extradition.

. . .

Article 6 Right to a fair trial

1. In the determination of his civil rights and obligations or of any criminal charge against him, everyone is entitled to a fair and public hearing within a reasonable time by an independent and impartial tribunal established by law. Judgment shall be pronounced publicly but the press and public may be excluded from all or part of the trial in the interest of morals, public order or national security in a democratic society, where the interests of juveniles or the protection of the private life of the parties so require, or to the extent strictly necessary in the opinion of the court in special circumstances where publicity would prejudice the interests of justice.

. . .

Article 8 Right to respect for private and family life

1. Everyone has the right to respect for his private and family life, his home and his correspondence.
2. There shall be no interference by a public authority with the exercise of this right except such as is in accordance with the law and is necessary in a democratic society in the interests of national security, public safety or the economic well-being of the country, for the prevention of disorder or crime, for the protection of health or morals, or for the protection of the rights and freedoms of others.

Article 9 Freedom of thought, conscience and religion

1. Everyone has the right to freedom of thought, conscience and religion; this right includes freedom to change his religion or belief and freedom, either alone or in community with others and in public or private, to manifest his religion or belief, in worship, teaching, practice and observance.
2. Freedom to manifest one's religion or beliefs shall be subject only to such limitations as are prescribed by law and are necessary in a democratic society in the interests of public safety, for the protection of public order, health or morals, or for the protection of the rights and freedoms of others.

. . .

Article 12 Right to marry

Men and women of marriageable age have the right to marry and to found a family, according to the national laws governing the exercise of this right.

Article 14 Prohibition of discrimination

The enjoyment of the rights and freedoms set forth in this Convention shall be secured without discrimination on any ground such as sex, race, colour, language, religion, political or other opinion, national or social origin, association with a national minority, property, birth or other status.

. . .

Part II THE FIRST PROTOCOL

Article 1 Protection of property

Every natural or legal person is entitled to the peaceful enjoyment of his possessions. No one shall be deprived of his possessions except in the public interest and subject to the conditions provided for by law and by the general principles of international law.

The preceding provisions shall not, however, in any way impair the right of a State to enforce such laws as it deems necessary to control the use of property in accordance with the general interest or to secure the payment of taxes or other contributions or penalties.

Article 2 Right to education
No person shall be denied the right to education. In the exercise of any functions which it assumes in relation to education and to teaching, the State shall respect the right of parents to ensure such education and teaching in conformity with their own religious and philosophical convictions.

. . .

As amended by: Human Rights Act 1998 (Amendment) Order 2004, SI 2004/1574, art 2(1); Secretary of State for Constitutional Affairs Order 2003, SI 2003/1887, art 9, Sch 2; Mental Capacity Act 2005, s 67(1), Sch 6; Transfer of Functions (Lord Chancellor and Secretary of State) Order 2005, SI 2005/3429, art 8, Schedule; Constitutional Reform Act 2005, ss 40(4), 146, Sch 9.

Immigration and Asylum Act 1999

(1999 c 33)

Reporting suspicious marriages

24 DUTY TO REPORT SUSPICIOUS MARRIAGES

(1) Subsection (3) applies if—
 (a) a superintendent registrar to whom a notice of marriage has been given under section 27 of the Marriage Act 1949,
 (b) any other person who, under section 28(2) of that Act, has attested a declaration accompanying such a notice, . . .

 has reasonable grounds for suspecting that the marriage will be a sham marriage.

(2) Subsection (3) also applies if—
 (a) a marriage is solemnized in the presence of a registrar of marriages or, in relation to Scotland, an authorised registrar (within the meaning of the Act of 1977); and
 (b) before, during or immediately after solemnization of the marriage, the registrar has reasonable grounds for suspecting that the marriage will be, or is, a sham marriage.

(3) The person concerned must report his suspicion to the Secretary of State without delay and in such form and manner as may be prescribed by regulations.

(4) The regulations are to be made—
 (a) in relation to England and Wales, by the Registrar General for England and Wales with the approval of the Secretary of State; . . .

(5) "Sham marriage" means a marriage (whether or not void)—
 (a) entered into between a person ("A") who is neither a British citizen nor a national of an EEA State other than the United Kingdom and another person (whether or not such a citizen or such a national); and
 (b) entered into by A for the purpose of avoiding the effect of one or more provisions of United Kingdom immigration law or the immigration rules.

24A DUTY TO REPORT SUSPICIOUS CIVIL PARTNERSHIPS

(1) Subsection (3) applies if—
 (a) a registration authority to whom a notice of proposed civil partnership has been given under section 8 of the Civil Partnership Act 2004,

(b) any person who, under section 8 of the 2004 Act, has attested a declaration accompanying such a notice,
(c) a district registrar to whom a notice of proposed civil partnership has been given under section 88 of the 2004 Act, or
(d) a registrar to whom a civil partnership notice has been given under section 139 of the 2004 Act,

has reasonable grounds for suspecting that the civil partnership will be a sham civil partnership.

(2) Subsection (3) also applies if—
(a) two people register as civil partners of each other under Part 2, 3 or 4 of the 2004 Act in the presence of the registrar, and
(b) before, during or immediately after they do so, the registrar has reasonable grounds for suspecting that the civil partnership will be, or is, a sham civil partnership.

(3) The person concerned must report his suspicion to the Secretary of State without delay and in such form and manner as may be prescribed by regulations.

(4) The regulations are to be made—
(a) in relation to England and Wales, by the Registrar General for England and Wales with the approval of the Secretary of State; . . .

(5) "Sham civil partnership" means a civil partnership (whether or not void)—
(a) formed between a person ("A") who is neither a British citizen nor a national of an EEA State other than the United Kingdom and another person (whether or not such a citizen or such a national), and
(b) formed by A for the purpose of avoiding the effect of one or more provisions of United Kingdom immigration law or the immigration rules.

(6) "The registrar" means—
(a) in relation to England and Wales, the civil partnership registrar acting under Part 2 of the 2004 Act;
(b) in relation to Scotland, the authorised registrar acting under Part 3 of the 2004 Act;
(c) in relation to Northern Ireland, the registrar acting under Part 4 of the 2004 Act.

As amended by: Civil Partnership Act 2004, s 261(1), Sch 27, para 162; Transfer of Functions (Registration) Order 2008, SI 2008/678, arts 3(1), 5, Sch 1, Sch 2

Care Standards Act 2000

(2000 c 14)

Part V THE CHILDREN'S COMMISSIONER FOR WALES

72 CHILDREN'S COMMISSIONER FOR WALES

(1) There shall be an office of the Children's Commissioner for Wales or Comisiynydd Plant Cymru.

(2) Schedule 2 shall have effect with respect to the Children's Commissioner for Wales (referred to in this Act as "the Commissioner").

72A PRINCIPAL AIM OF THE COMMISSIONER

The principal aim of the Commissioner in exercising his functions is to safeguard and promote the rights and welfare of children to whom this Part applies.

72B REVIEW OF EXERCISE OF FUNCTIONS OF WELSH MINISTERS AND OTHER PERSONS

(1) The Commissioner may review the effect on children to whom this Part applies of—
(a) the exercise or proposed exercise of any function of the Welsh Ministers, the First Minister for Wales or the Counsel General to the Welsh Assembly Government, including the making or proposed making of any subordinate legislation; or
(b) the exercise or proposed exercise in relation to Wales of any function of any person mentioned in Schedule 2A.

(2) The Welsh Ministers may by order amend this section or Schedule 2A by—
(a) adding any person to that Schedule;
(b) omitting any person from that Schedule;
(c) altering the description of any person mentioned in that Schedule; or
(d) making provision specifying, in respect of a person mentioned in that Schedule and specified in the order, a function of the person which although exercisable in relation to Wales is not to be treated as such for the purposes of subsection (1)(b).

(3) An order under subsection (2) may add a person to Schedule 2A only if—
(a) some or all of the person's functions are in a field in which functions are exercisable by the Welsh Ministers, the First Minister for Wales or the Counsel General to the Welsh Assembly Government;
(b) the person is established under an enactment or by virtue of Her Majesty's prerogative or is established in any other way by a Minister of the Crown or government department or by the Welsh Ministers, the First Minister for Wales, or the Counsel General to the Welsh Assembly Government; and
(c) (unless consent is given by the Secretary of State under subsection (4)), at least half of the person's expenditure on the exercise of functions in relation to Wales (or, where the person's functions relate only to a part of Wales, in relation to the part of Wales to which they relate) is met directly from payments made by the Welsh Ministers.

(4) An order under subsection (2) may add to Schedule 2A a person who does not satisfy the condition in subsection (3)(c) if the Secretary of State gives consent.

(5) An order under subsection (2) must not add to Schedule 2A a person whose sole or main activity is—
(a) the investigation of complaints by members of the public about the actions of any person; or
(b) the supervision or review of, or of steps taken following, such an investigation.

(6) The Welsh Ministers may not make an order under subsection (2) if the result would be that the Commissioner could review the effect of the exercise or proposed exercise of a person's function in a field in which no functions are exercisable by the Welsh Ministers, the First Minister for Wales or the Counsel General to the Welsh Assembly Government.

(7) In subsection (1)(a) "subordinate legislation" has the same meaning as in the Interpretation Act 1978 (c 30).

73 REVIEW AND MONITORING OF ARRANGEMENTS

(1) The Commissioner may review, and monitor the operation of, arrangements falling within subsection (2), (2A), (2B), (2C), (3) or (4) for the purpose of ascertaining whether, and to what extent, the arrangements are effective in safeguarding and promoting the rights and welfare of children—
(a) to or in respect of whom services are provided in Wales by, or on behalf of or under arrangements with, a person mentioned in Schedule 2B; or
(b) to or in respect of whom regulated children's services in Wales are provided.

(1A) The Commissioner may also assess the effect on such children of the failure of any person to make such arrangements.

(2) The arrangements falling within this subsection are the arrangements made by the providers of regulated children's services in Wales, or by the Welsh Ministers, the First Minister for Wales or the Counsel General to the Welsh Assembly Government, for dealing with complaints or representations about such services made by or on behalf of children to whom such services are provided.

(2A) The arrangements falling within this subsection are the arrangements made by a person mentioned in Schedule 2B for dealing with complaints or representations made to the person by or on behalf of a child about services provided in Wales by the person to or in respect of the child.

(2B) The arrangements falling within this subsection are the arrangements made by a person providing services in Wales on behalf of, or under arrangements with, a person mentioned in Schedule 2B for dealing with complaints or representations made to the person by or on behalf of a child about a service which is so provided to or in respect of the child.

(2C) The arrangements falling within this subsection are the arrangements made by the Welsh Ministers, the First Minister for Wales or the Counsel General to the Welsh Assembly Government for dealing with complaints or representations made by or on behalf of a child about a service which is provided in Wales to or in respect of the child by, or on behalf of or under arrangements with, a person mentioned in Schedule 2B (other than the Welsh Ministers, the First Minister for Wales or the Counsel General to the Welsh Assembly Government).

(3) The arrangements falling within this subsection are arrangements made by the providers of regulated children's services in Wales, by the Welsh Ministers, the First Minister for Wales or the Counsel General to the Welsh Assembly Government, or by another person mentioned in Schedule 2B or subsection (2B), for ensuring that proper action is taken in response to any disclosure of information which may tend to show—
(a) that a criminal offence has been committed;
(b) that a person has failed to comply with any legal obligation to which he is subject;
(c) that the health and safety of any person has been endangered; or
(d) that information tending to show that any matter falling within one of the preceding paragraphs has been deliberately concealed, in the course of or in connection with the provision of the services mentioned in subsection (3A).

(3A) The services are—
(a) in the case of a person mentioned in Schedule 2B, services provided in Wales by the person to or in respect of a child;
(b) in the case of a person mentioned in subsection (2B), services provided in Wales by the person to or in respect of a child on behalf of, or under arrangements with, a person mentioned in Schedule 2B;
(c) in the case of a provider of regulated children's services in Wales, those services.

(4) The arrangements falling within this subsection are arrangements made (whether by providers of regulated children's services in Wales, by the Welsh Ministers, the First Minister for Wales or the Counsel General to the Welsh Assembly Government or by any other person) for making persons available—
(a) to represent the views and wishes of children —
(i) to or in respect of whom services are provided in Wales by, or on behalf of or under arrangements with, a person mentioned in Schedule 2B; or
(ii) to or in respect of whom regulated children's services in Wales are provided; or
(b) to provide such children with advice and support of any prescribed kind.

(5) Regulations may confer power on the Commissioner to require prescribed persons to provide any information which the Commissioner considers it necessary or expedient to have for the purposes of his functions under this section.

. . .

74 EXAMINATION OF CASES

(1) Regulations may, in connection with the Commissioner's functions under this Part, make provision for the examination by the Commissioner of the cases of particular children to whom this Part applies.

(1A) The reference in subsection (1) to functions of the Commissioner does not include a reference to his power to consider and make representations by virtue of section 75A(1).

(2) The regulations may include provision about—
(a) the types of case which may be examined;
(b) the circumstances in which an examination may be made;
(c) the procedure for conducting an examination, including provision about the representation of parties;
(d) the publication of reports following an examination.

(3) The regulations may make provision for—
(a) requiring persons to provide the Commissioner with information; or
(b) requiring persons who hold or are accountable for information to provide the Commissioner with explanations or other assistance, for the purposes of an examination or for the purposes of determining whether any recommendation made in a report following an examination has been complied with.

(4) For the purposes mentioned in subsection (3), the Commissioner shall have the same powers as the High Court in respect of—
(a) the attendance and examination of witnesses (including the administration of oaths and affirmations and the examination of witnesses abroad); and
(b) the provision of information.

(5) No person shall be compelled for the purposes mentioned in subsection (3) to give any evidence or provide any information which he could not be compelled to give or provide in civil proceedings before the High Court.

(6) The regulations may make provision for the payment by the Commissioner of sums in respect of expenses or allowances to persons who attend or provide information for the purposes mentioned in subsection (3).

. . .

76 FURTHER FUNCTIONS

(1) Regulations may confer power on the Commissioner to assist a child to whom this Part applies—
(a) in making a complaint or representation to or in respect of a provider of regulated children's services in Wales;
(aa) in making a complaint or representation to or in respect of a person mentioned in Schedule 2B or section 73(2B); or
(b) in any prescribed proceedings, and in this subsection "proceedings" includes a procedure of any kind and any prospective proceedings.

(1A) The proceedings which may be prescribed by virtue of subsection (1)(b) are proceedings relating to—
(a) the exercise or proposed exercise of a function as mentioned in section 72B(1);
(b) the provision of services as mentioned in section 78(1)(b) or (c).

(2) For the purposes of subsection (1), assistance includes—
(a) financial assistance; and
(b) arranging for representation, or the giving of advice or assistance, by any person,
and the regulations may provide for assistance to be given on conditions, including (in the case of financial assistance) conditions requiring repayment in circumstances specified in the regulations.

(3) The Commissioner may, in connection with his functions under this Part, give advice and information to any person.

(4) Regulations may, in connection with the Commissioner's functions under this Part, confer further functions on him.

(5) The regulations may, in particular,
(a) include provision about the making of reports on any matter connected with any of his functions
(b) provide that the Commissioner may make a joint report with the Commissioner for Older People in Wales where they have discharged their respective functions under this Act and the Commissioner for Older People (Wales) Act 2006 in relation to the same matters.

(5A) The references in subsections (4) and (5) to functions of the Commissioner do not include a reference to his power to consider and make representations by virtue of section 75A(1).

(6) Apart from identifying any person investigated, a report by the Commissioner shall not—
(a) mention the name of any person; or
(b) include any particulars which, in the opinion of the Commissioner, are likely to identify any person and can be omitted without impairing the effectiveness of the report,
unless, after taking account of the public interest (as well as the interests of any person who made a complaint and other persons), the Commissioner considers it necessary for the report to mention his name or include such particulars.

(7) For the purposes of the law of defamation, the publication of any matter by the Commissioner in a report is absolutely privileged.

(8) The Commissioner or a person authorised by him may for the purposes of any function of the Commissioner under section 72B or 73 or subsection (4) of this section at any reasonable time—

(a) enter any premises, other than a private dwelling, for the purposes of interviewing any child accommodated or cared for there; and
(b) if the child consents, interview the child in private.

77 RESTRICTIONS

(1) This Part does not authorise the Commissioner to enquire into or report on any matter so far as it is the subject of legal proceedings before, or has been determined by, a court or tribunal.

(2) This Part does not authorise the Commissioner to exercise any function which by virtue of an enactment is also exercisable by a prescribed person.

78 INTERPRETATION

(1) This Part applies to a child—
(a) who is ordinarily resident in Wales;
(b) to or in respect of whom services are provided in Wales by, or on behalf of or under arrangements with, a person mentioned in Schedule 2B; or
(c) to or in respect of whom regulated children's services in Wales are provided.

(1A) Regulations may provide that, for the purposes of this Part of this Act, "child" includes a person aged 18 or over who falls within subsection (1B).

(1B) A person falls within this subsection if he is a person to or in respect of whom services are provided in Wales by, or on behalf of or under arrangements with, a county council or county borough council in Wales by virtue of—
(a) section 23C, 24, 24A or 24B of the Children Act 1989 (c 41) (which provide for the continuing duties of such councils towards young persons); or
(b) regulations made under section 23D of that Act (which may provide for the appointment of personal advisers for certain young persons).

(2) In this Part, "regulated children's services in Wales" means any of the following services for the time being provided in respect of children—
(a) services of a description provided by or in Part II undertakings, so far as provided in Wales;
(b) services provided by local authorities in Wales in the exercise of relevant adoption functions or relevant fostering functions;
(c) services of a description provided by persons registered under Part XA of the 1989 Act, so far as provided in Wales;
(d) accommodation provided by schools or by an institution within the further education sector (as defined in section 91 of the Further and Higher Education Act 1992), so far as provided in Wales.

(3) For the purposes of this Part—
(a) in the case of the services mentioned in subsection (2)(a), the person who carries on the Part II undertaking is to be treated as the provider of the services;
(b) in the case of the services mentioned in subsection (2)(d), the relevant person (as defined in section 87 of the 1989 Act) is to be treated as the provider of the services.

(4) For the purposes of this section, an establishment or agency, and an undertaking of any other description, is a Part II undertaking if the provider of the services in question is for the time being required to be registered under that Part.

(5) Where the activities of an undertaking are carried on from two or more branches, each of those branches shall be treated as a separate undertaking for the purposes of this Part.

(6) Regulations may provide for the references to a child in subsection (1) to include references to a person (including a child) who was at any time (including a time before the commencement of this Part)—
(a) a child ordinarily resident in Wales;
(b) a child to or in respect of whom services were provided in Wales by, or on behalf of or under arrangements with, a person mentioned in Schedule 2B; or
(c) a child to or in respect of whom regulated children's services in Wales were provided.

(7) In this Part—

"information" includes information recorded in any form;

"regulations" means regulations made by the Welsh Ministers.

(8) In this section, "relevant adoption functions" and "relevant fostering functions" have the same meanings as in Part III.

As amended by: Children's Commissioner for Wales Act 2001, ss 1–5; Government of Wales Act 2006, ss 46, 161(5); Government of Wales Act 2006 (Consequential Modifications and Transitional Provisions) Order 2007, SI 2007/1388, art 3, Sch 1.

Criminal Justice and Court Services Act 2000
(2000 c 43)

Chapter II CHILDREN AND FAMILY COURT ADVISORY AND SUPPORT SERVICE

11 ESTABLISHMENT OF THE SERVICE

(1) There shall be a body corporate to be known as the Children and Family Court Advisory and Support Service (referred to in this Part as the Service) which is to exercise the functions conferred on it by virtue of this Act and any other enactment.

(2) Schedule 2 (which makes provision about the constitution of the Service, its powers and other matters relating to it) is to have effect.

(3) References in this Act or any other enactment to an officer of the Service are references to—
(a) any member of the staff of the Service appointed under paragraph 5(1)(a) of that Schedule, and
(b) any other individual exercising functions of an officer of the Service by virtue of section 13(2) or (4).

12 PRINCIPAL FUNCTIONS OF THE SERVICE

(1) In respect of family proceedings in which the welfare of children other than children ordinarily resident in Wales is or may be in question, it is a function of the Service to—
(a) safeguard and promote the welfare of the children,
(b) give advice to any court about any application made to it in such proceedings,
(c) make provision for the children to be represented in such proceedings,
(d) provide information, advice and other support for the children and their families.

(2) The Service must also make provision for the performance of any functions conferred on officers of the Service by virtue of this Act or any other enactment (whether or not they are exercisable for the purposes of the functions conferred on the Service by subsection (1)).

(3) Regulations may provide for grants to be paid by the Service to any person for the purpose of furthering the performance of any of the Service's functions.

(4) The regulations may provide for the grants to be paid on conditions, including conditions—
(a) regulating the purposes for which the grant or any part of it may be used,
(b) requiring repayment to the Service in specified circumstances.

(5) In this section, "family proceedings" has the same meaning as in the Matrimonial and Family Proceedings Act 1984 and also includes any other proceedings which are family proceedings for the purposes of the Children Act 1989, but—
(a) references to family proceedings include (where the context allows) family proceedings which are proposed or have been concluded.

. . .

15 RIGHT TO CONDUCT LITIGATION AND RIGHT OF AUDIENCE

(1) The Service may authorise an officer of the Service of a prescribed description—
(a) to conduct litigation in relation to any proceedings in any court,
(b) to exercise a right of audience in any proceedings before any court, in the exercise of his functions.

(2) An officer of the Service exercising a right to conduct litigation by virtue of subsection (1)(a) who would otherwise have such a right by virtue of section 28(2)(a) of the Courts and Legal Services Act 1990 is to be treated as having acquired that right solely by virtue of this section.

(3) An officer of the Service exercising a right of audience by virtue of subsection (1)(b) who would otherwise have such a right by virtue of section 27(2)(a) of the Courts and Legal Services Act 1990 is to be treated as having acquired that right solely by virtue of this section.

(4) In this section and section 16, "right to conduct litigation" and "right of audience" have the same meanings as in section 119 of the Courts and Legal Services Act 1990.

16 CROSS-EXAMINATION OF OFFICERS OF THE SERVICE

(1) An officer of the Service may, subject to rules of court, be cross-examined in any proceedings to the same extent as any witness.

(2) But an officer of the Service may not be cross-examined merely because he is exercising a right to conduct litigation or a right of audience granted in accordance with section 15.

. . .

As amended by: Adoption and Children Act 2002, s 139(1), (3), Sch 3, Sch 5; Children Act 2004, s 40, Sch 3.

Adoption and Children Act 2002

(2002 c 38)

Part 1 ADOPTION

Chapter 1 INTRODUCTORY

1 CONSIDERATIONS APPLYING TO THE EXERCISE OF POWERS

(1) This section applies whenever a court or adoption agency is coming to a decision relating to the adoption of a child.

(2) The paramount consideration of the court or adoption agency must be the child's welfare, throughout his life.

(3) The court or adoption agency must at all times bear in mind that, in general, any delay in coming to the decision is likely to prejudice the child's welfare.

(4) The court or adoption agency must have regard to the following matters (among others)—

(a) the child's ascertainable wishes and feelings regarding the decision (considered in the light of the child's age and understanding),

(b) the child's particular needs,

(c) the likely effect on the child (throughout his life) of having ceased to be a member of the original family and become an adopted person,

(d) the child's age, sex, background and any of the child's characteristics which the court or agency considers relevant,

(e) any harm (within the meaning of the Children Act 1989 (c 41)) which the child has suffered or is at risk of suffering,

(f) the relationship which the child has with relatives, and with any other person in relation to whom the court or agency considers the relationship to be relevant, including—

(i) the likelihood of any such relationship continuing and the value to the child of its doing so,

(ii) the ability and willingness of any of the child's relatives, or of any such person, to provide the child with a secure environment in which the child can develop, and otherwise to meet the child's needs,

(iii) the wishes and feelings of any of the child's relatives, or of any such person, regarding the child.

(5) In placing the child for adoption, the adoption agency must give due consideration to the child's religious persuasion, racial origin and cultural and linguistic background.

(6) The court or adoption agency must always consider the whole range of powers available to it in the child's case (whether under this Act or the Children Act 1989); and the court must not make any order under this Act unless it considers that making the order would be better for the child than not doing so.

(7) In this section, "coming to a decision relating to the adoption of a child", in relation to a court, includes—

(a) coming to a decision in any proceedings where the orders that might be made by the court include an adoption order (or the revocation of such an order), a placement order (or the revocation of such an order) or an order under section 26 (or the revocation or variation of such an order),

(b) coming to a decision about granting leave in respect of any action (other than the initiation of proceedings in any court) which may be taken by an adoption agency or individual under this Act,

but does not include coming to a decision about granting leave in any other circumstances.

(8) For the purposes of this section—

(a) references to relationships are not confined to legal relationships,

(b) references to a relative, in relation to a child, include the child's mother and father.

Chapter 2 THE ADOPTION SERVICE

The Adoption Service

2 BASIC DEFINITIONS

(1) The services maintained by local authorities under section 3(1) may be collectively referred to as "the Adoption Service", and a local authority or registered adoption society may be referred to as an adoption agency.

(2) In this Act, "registered adoption society" means a voluntary organisation which is an adoption society registered under Part 2 of the Care Standards Act 2000 (c 14); but in relation to the provision of any facility of the Adoption Service, references to a registered adoption society or to an adoption agency do not include an adoption society which is not registered in respect of that facility.

(3) A registered adoption society is to be treated as registered in respect of any facility of the Adoption Service unless it is a condition of its registration that it does not provide that facility.

(4) No application for registration under Part 2 of the Care Standards Act 2000 may be made in respect of an adoption society which is an unincorporated body.

(5) In this Act—

"the 1989 Act" means the Children Act 1989 (c 41),

"adoption society" means a body whose functions consist of or include making arrangements for the adoption of children,

"voluntary organisation" means a body other than a public or local authority the activities of which are not carried on for profit.

(6) In this Act, "adoption support services" means—

(a) counselling, advice and information, and

(b) any other services prescribed by regulations,

in relation to adoption.

(7) The power to make regulations under subsection (6)(b) is to be exercised so as to secure that local authorities provide financial support.

(8) In this Chapter, references to adoption are to the adoption of persons, wherever they may be habitually resident, effected under the law of any country or territory, whether within or outside the British Islands.

3 MAINTENANCE OF ADOPTION SERVICE

(1) Each local authority must continue to maintain within their area a service designed to meet the needs, in relation to adoption, of—
(a) children who may be adopted, their parents and guardians,
(b) persons wishing to adopt a child, and
(c) adopted persons, their parents, natural parents and former guardians;
and for that purpose must provide the requisite facilities.

(2) Those facilities must include making, and participating in, arrangements—
(a) for the adoption of children, and
(b) for the provision of adoption support services.

(3) As part of the service, the arrangements made for the purposes of subsection (2)(b)—
(a) must extend to the provision of adoption support services to persons who are within a description prescribed by regulations,
(b) may extend to the provision of those services to other persons.

(4) A local authority may provide any of the requisite facilities by securing their provision by—
(a) registered adoption societies, or
(b) other persons who are within a description prescribed by regulations of persons who may provide the facilities in question.

(5) The facilities of the service must be provided in conjunction with the local authority's other social services and with registered adoption societies in their area, so that help may be given in a co-ordinated manner without duplication, omission or avoidable delay.

(6) The social services referred to in subsection (5) are the functions of a local authority which are social services functions within the meaning of the Local Authority Social Services Act 1970 (c 42) (which include, in particular, those functions in so far as they relate to children).

4 ASSESSMENTS ETC FOR ADOPTION SUPPORT SERVICES

(1) A local authority must at the request of—
(a) any of the persons mentioned in paragraphs (a) to (c) of section 3(1), or
(b) any other person who falls within a description prescribed by regulations (subject to subsection (7)(a)),
carry out an assessment of that person's needs for adoption support services.

(2) A local authority may, at the request of any person, carry out an assessment of that person's needs for adoption support services.

(3) A local authority may request the help of the persons mentioned in paragraph (a) or (b) of section 3(4) in carrying out an assessment.

(4) Where, as a result of an assessment, a local authority decide that a person has needs for adoption support services, they must then decide whether to provide any such services to that person.

(5) If—
(a) a local authority decide to provide any adoption support services to a person, and
(b) the circumstances fall within a description prescribed by regulations,
the local authority must prepare a plan in accordance with which adoption support services are to be provided to the person and keep the plan under review.

(6) Regulations may make provision about assessments, preparing and reviewing plans, the provision of adoption support services in accordance with plans and reviewing the provision of adoption support services.

(7) The regulations may in particular make provision—
(a) as to the circumstances in which a person mentioned in paragraph (b) of subsection(1) is to have a right to request an assessment of his needs in accordance with that subsection,
(b) about the type of assessment which, or the way in which an assessment, is to be carried out,
(c) about the way in which a plan is to be prepared,
(d) about the way in which, and time at which, a plan or the provision of adoption support services is to be reviewed,
(e) about the considerations to which a local authority are to have regard in carrying out an assessment or review or preparing a plan,
(f) as to the circumstances in which a local authority may provide adoption support services subject to conditions,
(g) as to the consequences of conditions imposed by virtue of paragraph (f) not being met (including the recovery of any financial support provided by a local authority),
(h) as to the circumstances in which this section may apply to a local authority in respect of persons who are outside that local authority's area,
(i) as to the circumstances in which a local authority may recover from another local authority the expenses of providing adoption support services to any person.

(8) A local authority may carry out an assessment of the needs of any person under this section at the same time as an assessment of his needs is made under any other enactment.

(9) If at any time during the assessment of the needs of any person under this section, it appears to a local authority that—
(a) there may be a need for the provision of services to that person by a Primary Care Trust (in Wales, a Health Authority or Local Health Board), or
(b) there may be a need for the provision to him of any services which fall within the functions of a local education authority (within the meaning of the Education Act 1996 (c 56)), the local authority must notify that Primary Care Trust, Health Authority, Local Health Board or local education authority.

(10) Where it appears to a local authority that another local authority could, by taking any specified action, help in the exercise of any of their functions under this section, they may request the help of that other local authority, specifying the action in question.

(11) A local authority whose help is so requested must comply with the request if it is consistent with the exercise of their functions.

. . .

8 ADOPTION SUPPORT AGENCIES

(1) In this Act, "adoption support agency" means an undertaking the purpose of which, or one of the purposes of which, is the provision of adoption support services; but an undertaking is not an adoption support agency—
 (a) merely because it provides information in connection with adoption other than for the purpose mentioned in section 98(1), or
 (b) if it is excepted by virtue of subsection (2).
 "Undertaking" has the same meaning as in the Care Standards Act 2000 (c 14).

(2) The following are excepted—
 (a) a registered adoption society, whether or not the society is registered in respect of the provision of adoption support services,
 (b) a local authority,
 (c) a local education authority (within the meaning of the Education Act 1996 (c 56)),
 (d) a Special Health Authority, Primary Care Trust (in Wales, a Health Authority or Local Health Board), NHS trust or NHS foundation trust,
 (e) the Registrar General,
 (f) any person, or description of persons, excepted by regulations.

(3) In section 4 of the Care Standards Act 2000 (basic definitions)—
 (a) after subsection (7) there is inserted—

 "(7A) 'Adoption support agency' has the meaning given by section 8 of the Adoption and Children Act 2002.",

 (b) in subsection (9)(a) (construction of references to descriptions of agencies), for "or a voluntary adoption agency" there is substituted "a voluntary adoption agency or an adoption support agency".

Regulations

9 GENERAL POWER TO REGULATE ADOPTION ETC AGENCIES

(1) Regulations may make provision for any purpose relating to—
 (a) the exercise by local authorities or voluntary adoption agencies of their functions in relation to adoption, or
 (b) the exercise by adoption support agencies of their functions in relation to adoption.

(2) The extent of the power to make regulations under this section is not limited by sections 10 to 12, 45, 54, 56 to 65 and 98 or by any other powers exercisable in respect of local authorities, voluntary adoption agencies or adoption support agencies.

(3) Regulations may provide that a person who contravenes or fails to comply with any provision of regulations under this section is to be guilty of an offence and liable on summary conviction to a fine not exceeding level 5 on the standard scale.

(4) In this section and section 10, "voluntary adoption agency" means a voluntary organisation which is an adoption society.

. . .

Supplemental

13 INFORMATION CONCERNING ADOPTION

(1) Each adoption agency must give to the appropriate Minister any statistical or other general information he requires about—

(a) its performance of all or any of its functions relating to adoption,
(b) the children and other persons in relation to whom it has exercised those functions.

(2) The following persons—
(a) the designated officer for each magistrates' court,
(b) the relevant officer of each county court,
(c) the relevant officer of the High Court, must give to the appropriate Minister any statistical or other general information he requires about the proceedings under this Act of the court in question.

(3) In subsection (2), "relevant officer", in relation to a county court or the High Court, means the officer of that court who is designated to act for the purposes of that subsection by a direction given by the Lord Chancellor.

(4) The information required to be given to the appropriate Minister under this section must be given at the times, and in the form, directed by him.

(5) The appropriate Minister may publish from time to time abstracts of the information given to him under this section.

. . .

15 INSPECTION OF PREMISES ETC

(1) The appropriate Minister may arrange for any premises in which—
(a) a child is living with a person with whom the child has been placed by an adoption agency, or
(b) a child in respect of whom a notice of intention to adopt has been given under section 44 is, or will be, living, to be inspected from time to time.

(2) The appropriate Minister may require an adoption agency—
(a) to give him any information, or
(b) to allow him to inspect any records (in whatever form they are held), relating to the discharge of any of its functions in relation to adoption which the appropriate Minister specifies.

(3) An inspection under this section must be conducted by a person authorised by the appropriate Minister.

(4) An officer of a local authority may only be so authorised with the consent of the authority.

(5) A person inspecting any premises under subsection (1) may—
(a) visit the child there,
(b) make any examination into the state of the premises and the treatment of the child there which he thinks fit.

(6) A person authorised to inspect any records under this section may at any reasonable time have access to, and inspect and check the operation of, any computer (and associated apparatus) which is being or has been used in connection with the records in question.

(7) A person authorised to inspect any premises or records under this section may—
(a) enter the premises for that purpose at any reasonable time,
(b) require any person to give him any reasonable assistance he may require.

(8) A person exercising a power under this section must, if required to do so, produce a duly authenticated document showing his authority.

(9) Any person who intentionally obstructs another in the exercise of a power under this section is guilty of an offence and liable on summary conviction to a fine not exceeding level 3 on the standard scale.

. . .

Chapter 3 PLACEMENT FOR ADOPTION AND ADOPTION ORDERS

Placement of children by adoption agency for adoption

18 PLACEMENT FOR ADOPTION BY AGENCIES

(1) An adoption agency may—
(a) place a child for adoption with prospective adopters, or
(b) where it has placed a child with any persons (whether under this Part or not), leave the child with them as prospective adopters,
but, except in the case of a child who is less than six weeks old, may only do so under section 19 or a placement order.

(2) An adoption agency may only place a child for adoption with prospective adopters if the agency is satisfied that the child ought to be placed for adoption.

(3) A child who is placed or authorised to be placed for adoption with prospective adopters by a local authority is looked after by the authority.

(4) If an application for an adoption order has been made by any persons in respect of a child and has not been disposed of—
(a) an adoption agency which placed the child with those persons may leave the child with them until the application is disposed of, but
(b) apart from that, the child may not be placed for adoption with any prospective adopters.
"Adoption order" includes a Scottish or Northern Irish adoption order.

(5) References in this Act (apart from this section) to an adoption agency placing a child for adoption—
(a) are to its placing a child for adoption with prospective adopters, and
(b) include, where it has placed a child with any persons (whether under this Act or not), leaving the child with them as prospective adopters;
and references in this Act (apart from this section) to a child who is placed for adoption by an adoption agency are to be interpreted accordingly.

(6) References in this Chapter to an adoption agency being, or not being, authorised to place a child for adoption are to the agency being or (as the case may be) not being authorised to do so under section 19 or a placement order.

(7) This section is subject to sections 30 to 35 (removal of children placed by adoption agencies).

19 PLACING CHILDREN WITH PARENTAL CONSENT

(1) Where an adoption agency is satisfied that each parent or guardian of a child has consented to the child—
(a) being placed for adoption with prospective adopters identified in the consent, or
(b) being placed for adoption with any prospective adopters who may be chosen by the agency, and has not withdrawn the consent,
the agency is authorised to place the child for adoption accordingly.

(2) Consent to a child being placed for adoption with prospective adopters identified in the consent may be combined with consent to the child subsequently being placed for adoption with any prospective adopters who may be chosen by the agency in circumstances where the child is removed from or returned by the identified prospective adopters.

(3) Subsection (1) does not apply where—
(a) an application has been made on which a care order might be made and the application has not been disposed of, or
(b) a care order or placement order has been made after the consent was given.

(4) References in this Act to a child placed for adoption under this section include a child who was placed under this section with prospective adopters and continues to be placed with them, whether or not consent to the placement has been withdrawn.

(5) This section is subject to section 52 (parental etc consent).

20 ADVANCE CONSENT TO ADOPTION

(1) A parent or guardian of a child who consents to the child being placed for adoption by an adoption agency under section 19 may, at the same or any subsequent time, consent to the making of a future adoption order.

(2) Consent under this section—
(a) where the parent or guardian has consented to the child being placed for adoption with prospective adopters identified in the consent, may be consent to adoption by them, or
(b) may be consent to adoption by any prospective adopters who may be chosen by the agency.

(3) A person may withdraw any consent given under this section.

(4) A person who gives consent under this section may, at the same or any subsequent time, by notice given to the adoption agency—
(a) state that he does not wish to be informed of any application for an adoption order, or
(b) withdraw such a statement.

(5) A notice under subsection (4) has effect from the time when it is received by the adoption agency but has no effect if the person concerned has withdrawn his consent.

(6) This section is subject to section 52 (parental etc consent).

21 PLACEMENT ORDERS

(1) A placement order is an order made by the court authorising a local authority to place a child for adoption with any prospective adopters who may be chosen by the authority.

(2) The court may not make a placement order in respect of a child unless—
(a) the child is subject to a care order,
(b) the court is satisfied that the conditions in section 31(2) of the 1989 Act (conditions for making a care order) are met, or
(c) the child has no parent or guardian.

(3) The court may only make a placement order if, in the case of each parent or guardian of the child, the court is satisfied—

(a) that the parent or guardian has consented to the child being placed for adoption with any prospective adopters who may be chosen by the local authority and has not withdrawn the consent, or
(b) that the parent's or guardian's consent should be dispensed with.
This subsection is subject to section 52 (parental etc consent).

(4) A placement order continues in force until—
(a) it is revoked under section 24,
(b) an adoption order is made in respect of the child, or
(c) the child marries, forms a civil partnership or attains the age of 18 years.
"Adoption order" includes a Scottish or Northern Irish adoption order.

22 APPLICATIONS FOR PLACEMENT ORDERS

(1) A local authority must apply to the court for a placement order in respect of a child if—
(a) the child is placed for adoption by them or is being provided with accommodation by them,
(b) no adoption agency is authorised to place the child for adoption,
(c) the child has no parent or guardian or the authority consider that the conditions in section 31(2) of the 1989 Act are met, and
(d) the authority are satisfied that the child ought to be placed for adoption.

(2) If—
(a) an application has been made (and has not been disposed of) on which a care order might be made in respect of a child, or
(b) a child is subject to a care order and the appropriate local authority are not authorised to place the child for adoption, the appropriate local authority must apply to the court for a placement order if they are satisfied that the child ought to be placed for adoption.

(3) If—
(a) a child is subject to a care order, and
(b) the appropriate local authority are authorised to place the child for adoption under section 19, the authority may apply to the court for a placement order.

(4) If a local authority—
(a) are under a duty to apply to the court for a placement order in respect of a child, or
(b) have applied for a placement order in respect of a child and the application has not been disposed of, the child is looked after by the authority.

(5) Subsections (1) to (3) do not apply in respect of a child—
(a) if any persons have given notice of intention to adopt, unless the period of four months beginning with the giving of the notice has expired without them applying for an adoption order or their application for such an order has been withdrawn or refused, or
(b) if an application for an adoption order has been made and has not been disposed of.
"Adoption order" includes a Scottish or Northern Irish adoption order.

(6) Where—
(a) an application for a placement order in respect of a child has been made and has not been disposed of, and
(b) no interim care order is in force,
the court may give any directions it considers appropriate for the medical or psychiatric examination or other assessment of the child; but a child who is of sufficient

understanding to make an informed decision may refuse to submit to the examination or other assessment.

(7) The appropriate local authority—
  (a) in relation to a care order, is the local authority in whose care the child is placed by the order, and
  (b) in relation to an application on which a care order might be made, is the local authority which makes the application.

23 VARYING PLACEMENT ORDERS

(1) The court may vary a placement order so as to substitute another local authority for the local authority authorised by the order to place the child for adoption.

(2) The variation may only be made on the joint application of both authorities.

24 REVOKING PLACEMENT ORDERS

(1) The court may revoke a placement order on the application of any person.

(2) But an application may not be made by a person other than the child or the local authority authorised by the order to place the child for adoption unless—
  (a) the court has given leave to apply, and
  (b) the child is not placed for adoption by the authority.

(3) The court cannot give leave under subsection (2)(a) unless satisfied that there has been a change in circumstances since the order was made.

(4) If the court determines, on an application for an adoption order, not to make the order, it may revoke any placement order in respect of the child.

(5) Where—
  (a) an application for the revocation of a placement order has been made and has not been disposed of, and
  (b) the child is not placed for adoption by the authority,

the child may not without the court's leave be placed for adoption under the order.

25 PARENTAL RESPONSIBILITY

(1) This section applies while—
  (a) a child is placed for adoption under section 19 or an adoption agency is authorised to place a child for adoption under that section, or
  (b) a placement order is in force in respect of a child.

(2) Parental responsibility for the child is given to the agency concerned.

(3) While the child is placed with prospective adopters, parental responsibility is given to them.

(4) The agency may determine that the parental responsibility of any parent or guardian, or of prospective adopters, is to be restricted to the extent specified in the determination.

26 CONTACT

(1) On an adoption agency being authorised to place a child for adoption, or placing a child for adoption who is less than six weeks old, any provision for contact under the 1989 Act

ceases to have effect and any contact activity direction relating to contact with the child is discharged.

(2) While an adoption agency is so authorised or a child is placed for adoption—
(a) no application may be made for any provision for contact under that Act, but
(b) the court may make an order under this section requiring the person with whom the child lives, or is to live, to allow the child to visit or stay with the person named in the order, or for the person named in the order and the child otherwise to have contact with each other.

(3) An application for an order under this section may be made by—
(a) the child or the agency,
(b) any parent, guardian or relative,
(c) any person in whose favour there was provision for contact under the 1989 Act which ceased to have effect by virtue of subsection (1),
(d) if a residence order was in force immediately before the adoption agency was authorised to place the child for adoption or (as the case may be) placed the child for adoption at a time when he was less than six weeks old, the person in whose favour the order was made,
(e) if a person had care of the child immediately before that time by virtue of an order made in the exercise of the High Court's inherent jurisdiction with respect to children, that person,
(f) any person who has obtained the court's leave to make the application.

(4) When making a placement order, the court may on its own initiative make an order under this section.

(5) This section does not prevent an application for a contact order under section 8 of the 1989 Act being made where the application is to be heard together with an application for an adoption order in respect of the child.

(6) In this section, "contact activity direction" has the meaning given by section 11A of the 1989 Act and "provision for contact under the 1989 Act" means a contact order under section 8 of that Act or an order under section 34 of that Act (parental contact with children in care).

27 CONTACT: SUPPLEMENTARY

(1) An order under section 26—
(a) has effect while the adoption agency is authorised to place the child for adoption or the child is placed for adoption, but
(b) may be varied or revoked by the court on an application by the child, the agency or a person named in the order.

(2) The agency may refuse to allow the contact that would otherwise be required by virtue of an order under that section if—
(a) it is satisfied that it is necessary to do so in order to safeguard or promote the child's welfare, and
(b) the refusal is decided upon as a matter of urgency and does not last for more than seven days.

(3) Regulations may make provision as to—
(a) the steps to be taken by an agency which has exercised its power under subsection (2),
(b) the circumstances in which, and conditions subject to which, the terms of any order under section 26 may be departed from by agreement between the agency and any person for whose contact with the child the order provides,

(c) notification by an agency of any variation or suspension of arrangements made (otherwise than under an order under that section) with a view to allowing any person contact with the child.

(4) Before making a placement order the court must—
(a) consider the arrangements which the adoption agency has made, or proposes to make, for allowing any person contact with the child, and
(b) invite the parties to the proceedings to comment on those arrangements.

(5) An order under section 26 may provide for contact on any conditions the court considers appropriate.

28 FURTHER CONSEQUENCES OF PLACEMENT

(1) Where a child is placed for adoption under section 19 or an adoption agency is authorised to place a child for adoption under that section—
(a) a parent or guardian of the child may not apply for a residence order unless an application for an adoption order has been made and the parent or guardian has obtained the court's leave under subsection (3) or (5) of section 47,
(b) if an application has been made for an adoption order, a guardian of the child may not apply for a special guardianship order unless he has obtained the court's leave under subsection (3) or (5) of that section.

(2) Where—
(a) a child is placed for adoption under section 19 or an adoption agency is authorised to place a child for adoption under that section, or
(b) a placement order is in force in respect of a child,
then (whether or not the child is in England and Wales) a person may not do either of the following things, unless the court gives leave or each parent or guardian of the child gives written consent.

(3) Those things are—
(a) causing the child to be known by a new surname, or
(b) removing the child from the United Kingdom.

(4) Subsection (3) does not prevent the removal of a child from the United Kingdom for a period of less than one month by a person who provides the child's home.

29 FURTHER CONSEQUENCES OF PLACEMENT ORDERS

(1) Where a placement order is made in respect of a child and either—
(a) the child is subject to a care order, or
(b) the court at the same time makes a care order in respect of the child,
the care order does not have effect at any time when the placement order is in force.

(2) On the making of a placement order in respect of a child, any order mentioned in section 8(1) of the 1989 Act, and any supervision order in respect of the child, ceases to have effect.

(3) Where a placement order is in force—
(a) no prohibited steps order, residence order or specific issue order, and
(b) no supervision order or child assessment order,
may be made in respect of the child.

(4) Subsection (3)(a) does not apply in respect of a residence order if—
(a) an application for an adoption order has been made in respect of the child, and

(b) the residence order is applied for by a parent or guardian who has obtained the court's leave under subsection (3) or (5) of section 47 or by any other person who has obtained the court's leave under this subsection.

(5) Where a placement order is in force, no special guardianship order may be made in respect of the child unless—
(a) an application has been made for an adoption order, and
(b) the person applying for the special guardianship order has obtained the court's leave under this subsection or, if he is a guardian of the child, has obtained the court's leave under section 47(5).

(6) Section 14A(7) of the 1989 Act applies in respect of an application for a special guardianship order for which leave has been given as mentioned in subsection (5)(b) with the omission of the words "the beginning of the period of three months ending with".

(7) Where a placement order is in force—
(a) section 14C(1)(b) of the 1989 Act (special guardianship: parental responsibility) has effect subject to any determination under section 25(4) of this Act,
(b) section 14C(3) and (4) of the 1989 Act (special guardianship: removal of child from UK etc) does not apply.

Removal of children who are or may be placed by adoption agencies

30 GENERAL PROHIBITIONS ON REMOVAL

(1) Where—
(a) a child is placed for adoption by an adoption agency under section 19, or
(b) a child is placed for adoption by an adoption agency and either the child is less than six weeks old or the agency has at no time been authorised to place the child for adoption,
a person (other than the agency) must not remove the child from the prospective adopters.

(2) Where—
(a) a child who is not for the time being placed for adoption is being provided with accommodation by a local authority, and
(b) the authority have applied to the court for a placement order and the application has not been disposed of,
only a person who has the court's leave (or the authority) may remove the child from the accommodation.

(3) Where subsection (2) does not apply, but—
(a) a child who is not for the time being placed for adoption is being provided with accommodation by an adoption agency, and
(b) the agency is authorised to place the child for adoption under section 19 or would be so authorised if any consent to placement under that section had not been withdrawn,
a person (other than the agency) must not remove the child from the accommodation.

(4) This section is subject to sections 31 to 33 but those sections do not apply if the child is subject to a care order.

(5) This group of sections (that is, this section and those sections) apply whether or not the child in question is in England and Wales.

(6) This group of sections does not affect the exercise by any local authority or other person of any power conferred by any enactment, other than section 20(8) of the 1989 Act (removal of children from local authority accommodation).

(7) This group of sections does not prevent the removal of a child who is arrested.

(8) A person who removes a child in contravention of this section is guilty of an offence and liable on summary conviction to imprisonment for a term not exceeding three months, or a fine not exceeding level 5 on the standard scale, or both.

31 RECOVERY BY PARENT ETC WHERE CHILD NOT PLACED OR IS A BABY

(1) Subsection (2) applies where—
  (a) a child who is not for the time being placed for adoption is being provided with accommodation by an adoption agency, and
  (b) the agency would be authorised to place the child for adoption under section 19 if consent to placement under that section had not been withdrawn.

(2) If any parent or guardian of the child informs the agency that he wishes the child to be returned to him, the agency must return the child to him within the period of seven days beginning with the request unless an application is, or has been, made for a placement order and the application has not been disposed of.

(3) Subsection (4) applies where—
  (a) a child is placed for adoption by an adoption agency and either the child is less than six weeks old or the agency has at no time been authorised to place the child for adoption, and
  (b) any parent or guardian of the child informs the agency that he wishes the child to be returned to him,

unless an application is, or has been, made for a placement order and the application has not been disposed of.

(4) The agency must give notice of the parent's or guardian's wish to the prospective adopters who must return the child to the agency within the period of seven days beginning with the day on which the notice is given.

(5) A prospective adopter who fails to comply with subsection (4) is guilty of an offence and liable on summary conviction to imprisonment for a term not exceeding three months, or a fine not exceeding level 5 on the standard scale, or both.

(6) As soon as a child is returned to an adoption agency under subsection (4), the agency must return the child to the parent or guardian in question.

32 RECOVERY BY PARENT ETC WHERE CHILD PLACED AND CONSENT WITHDRAWN

(1) This section applies where—
  (a) a child is placed for adoption by an adoption agency under section 19, and
  (b) consent to placement under that section has been withdrawn, unless an application is, or has been, made for a placement order and the application has not been disposed of.

(2) If a parent or guardian of the child informs the agency that he wishes the child to be returned to him—
  (a) the agency must give notice of the parent's or guardian's wish to the prospective adopters, and
  (b) the prospective adopters must return the child to the agency within the period of 14 days beginning with the day on which the notice is given.

(3) A prospective adopter who fails to comply with subsection (2)(b) is guilty of an offence and liable on summary conviction to imprisonment for a term not exceeding three months, or a fine not exceeding level 5 on the standard scale, or both.

(4) As soon as a child is returned to an adoption agency under this section, the agency must return the child to the parent or guardian in question.

(5) Where a notice under subsection (2) is given, but—
(a) before the notice was given, an application for an adoption order (including a Scottish or Northern Irish adoption order), special guardianship order or residence order, or for leave to apply for a special guardianship order or residence order, was made in respect of the child, and
(b) the application (and, in a case where leave is given on an application to apply for a special guardianship order or residence order, the application for the order) has not been disposed of,
the prospective adopters are not required by virtue of the notice to return the child to the agency unless the court so orders.

33 RECOVERY BY PARENT ETC WHERE CHILD PLACED AND PLACEMENT ORDER REFUSED

(1) This section applies where—
(a) a child is placed for adoption by a local authority under section 19,
(b) the authority have applied for a placement order and the application has been refused, and
(c) any parent or guardian of the child informs the authority that he wishes the child to be returned to him.

(2) The prospective adopters must return the child to the authority on a date determined by the court.

(3) A prospective adopter who fails to comply with subsection (2) is guilty of an offence and liable on summary conviction to imprisonment for a term not exceeding three months, or a fine not exceeding level 5 on the standard scale, or both.

(4) As soon as a child is returned to the authority, they must return the child to the parent or guardian in question.

34 PLACEMENT ORDERS: PROHIBITION ON REMOVAL

(1) Where a placement order in respect of a child—
(a) is in force, or
(b) has been revoked, but the child has not been returned by the prospective adopters or remains in any accommodation provided by the local authority,
a person (other than the local authority) may not remove the child from the prospective adopters or from accommodation provided by the authority.

(2) A person who removes a child in contravention of subsection (1) is guilty of an offence.

(3) Where a court revoking a placement order in respect of a child determines that the child is not to remain with any former prospective adopters with whom the child is placed, they must return the child to the local authority within the period determined by the court for the purpose; and a person who fails to do so is guilty of an offence.

(4) Where a court revoking a placement order in respect of a child determines that the child is to be returned to a parent or guardian, the local authority must return the child to the parent or guardian as soon as the child is returned to the authority or, where the child is in accommodation provided by the authority, at once.

(5) A person guilty of an offence under this section is liable on summary conviction to imprisonment for a term not exceeding three months, or a fine not exceeding level 5 on the standard scale, or both.

(6) This section does not affect the exercise by any local authority or other person of a power conferred by any enactment, other than section 20(8) of the 1989 Act.

(7) This section does not prevent the removal of a child who is arrested.

(8) This section applies whether or not the child in question is in England and Wales.

35 RETURN OF CHILD IN OTHER CASES

(1) Where a child is placed for adoption by an adoption agency and the prospective adopters give notice to the agency of their wish to return the child, the agency must—
- (a) receive the child from the prospective adopters before the end of the period of seven days beginning with the giving of the notice, and
- (b) give notice to any parent or guardian of the child of the prospective adopters' wish to return the child.

(2) Where a child is placed for adoption by an adoption agency, and the agency—
- (a) is of the opinion that the child should not remain with the prospective adopters, and
- (b) gives notice to them of its opinion,

the prospective adopters must, not later than the end of the period of seven days beginning with the giving of the notice, return the child to the agency.

(3) If the agency gives notice under subsection (2)(b), it must give notice to any parent or guardian of the child of the obligation to return the child to the agency.

(4) A prospective adopter who fails to comply with subsection (2) is guilty of an offence and liable on summary conviction to imprisonment for a term not exceeding three months, or a fine not exceeding level 5 on the standard scale, or both.

(5) Where—
- (a) an adoption agency gives notice under subsection (2) in respect of a child,
- (b) before the notice was given, an application for an adoption order (including a Scottish or Northern Irish adoption order), special guardianship order or residence order, or for leave to apply for a special guardianship order or residence order, was made in respect of the child, and
- (c) the application (and, in a case where leave is given on an application to apply for a special guardianship order or residence order, the application for the order) has not been disposed of,

prospective adopters are not required by virtue of the notice to return the child to the agency unless the court so orders.

(6) This section applies whether or not the child in question is in England and Wales.

Removal of children in non-agency cases

36 RESTRICTIONS ON REMOVAL

(1) At any time when a child's home is with any persons ("the people concerned") with whom the child is not placed by an adoption agency, but the people concerned—
(a) have applied for an adoption order in respect of the child and the application has not been disposed of,
(b) have given notice of intention to adopt, or
(c) have applied for leave to apply for an adoption order under section 42(6) and the application has not been disposed of, a person may remove the child only in accordance with the provisions of this group of sections
(that is, this section and sections 37 to 40).
The reference to a child placed by an adoption agency includes a child placed by a Scottish or Northern Irish adoption agency.

(2) For the purposes of this group of sections, a notice of intention to adopt is to be disregarded if—
(a) the period of four months beginning with the giving of the notice has expired without the people concerned applying for an adoption order, or
(b) the notice is a second or subsequent notice of intention to adopt and was given during the period of five months beginning with the giving of the preceding notice.

(3) For the purposes of this group of sections, if the people concerned apply for leave to apply for an adoption order under section 42(6) and the leave is granted, the application for leave is not to be treated as disposed of until the period of three days beginning with the granting of the leave has expired.

(4) This section does not prevent the removal of a child who is arrested.

(5) Where a parent or guardian may remove a child from the people concerned in accordance with the provisions of this group of sections, the people concerned must at the request of the parent or guardian return the child to the parent or guardian at once.

(6) A person who—
(a) fails to comply with subsection (5), or
(b) removes a child in contravention of this section, is guilty of an offence and liable on summary conviction to imprisonment for a term not exceeding three months, or a fine not exceeding level 5 on the standard scale, or both.

(7) This group of sections applies whether or not the child in question is in England and Wales.

37 APPLICANTS FOR ADOPTION

If section 36(1)(a) applies, the following persons may remove the child—
(a) a person who has the court's leave,
(b) a local authority or other person in the exercise of a power conferred by any enactment, other than section 20(8) of the 1989 Act.

38 LOCAL AUTHORITY FOSTER PARENTS

(1) This section applies if the child's home is with local authority foster parents.

(2) If—

(a) the child has had his home with the foster parents at all times during the period of five years ending with the removal and the foster parents have given notice of intention to adopt, or
(b) an application has been made for leave under section 42(6) and has not been disposed of, the following persons may remove the child.

(3) They are—
(a) a person who has the court's leave,
(b) a local authority or other person in the exercise of a power conferred by any enactment, other than section 20(8) of the 1989 Act.

(4) If subsection (2) does not apply but—
(a) the child has had his home with the foster parents at all times during the period of one year ending with the removal, and
(b) the foster parents have given notice of intention to adopt, the following persons may remove the child.

(5) They are—
(a) a person with parental responsibility for the child who is exercising the power in section 20(8) of the 1989 Act,
(b) a person who has the court's leave,
(c) a local authority or other person in the exercise of a power conferred by any enactment, other than section 20(8) of the 1989 Act.

39 PARTNERS OF PARENTS

(1) This section applies if a child's home is with a partner of a parent and the partner has given notice of intention to adopt.

(2) If the child's home has been with the partner for not less than three years (whether continuous or not) during the period of five years ending with the removal, the following persons may remove the child—
(a) a person who has the court's leave,
(b) a local authority or other person in the exercise of a power conferred by any enactment, other than section 20(8) of the 1989 Act.

(3) If subsection (2) does not apply, the following persons may remove the child—
(a) a parent or guardian,
(b) a person who has the court's leave,
(c) a local authority or other person in the exercise of a power conferred by any enactment, other than section 20(8) of the 1989 Act.

40 OTHER NON-AGENCY CASES

(1) In any case where sections 37 to 39 do not apply but—
(a) the people concerned have given notice of intention to adopt, or
(b) the people concerned have applied for leave under section 42(6) and the application has not been disposed of, the following persons may remove the child.

(2) They are—
(a) a person who has the court's leave,
(b) a local authority or other person in the exercise of a power conferred by any enactment, other than section 20(8) of the 1989 Act.

Breach of restrictions on removal

41 RECOVERY ORDERS

(1) This section applies where it appears to the court—
(a) that a child has been removed in contravention of any of the preceding provisions of this Chapter or that there are reasonable grounds for believing that a person intends to remove a child in contravention of those provisions, or
(b) that a person has failed to comply with section 31(4), 32(2), 33(2), 34(3) or 35(2).

(2) The court may, on the application of any person, by an order—
(a) direct any person who is in a position to do so to produce the child on request to any person mentioned in subsection (4),
(b) authorise the removal of the child by any person mentioned in that subsection,
(c) require any person who has information as to the child's whereabouts to disclose that information on request to any constable or officer of the court,
(d) authorise a constable to enter any premises specified in the order and search for the child, using reasonable force if necessary.

(3) Premises may only be specified under subsection (2)(d) if it appears to the court that there are reasonable grounds for believing the child to be on them.

(4) The persons referred to in subsection (2) are—
(a) any person named by the court,
(b) any constable,
(c) any person who, after the order is made under that subsection, is authorised to exercise any power under the order by an adoption agency which is authorised to place the child for adoption.

(5) A person who intentionally obstructs a person exercising a power of removal conferred by the order is guilty of an offence and liable on summary conviction to a fine not exceeding level 3 on the standard scale.

(6) A person must comply with a request to disclose information as required by the order even if the information sought might constitute evidence that he had committed an offence.

(7) But in criminal proceedings in which the person is charged with an offence (other than one mentioned in subsection (8))—
(a) no evidence relating to the information provided may be adduced, and
(b) no question relating to the information may be asked,
by or on behalf of the prosecution, unless evidence relating to it is adduced, or a question relating to it is asked, in the proceedings by or on behalf of the person.

(8) The offences excluded from subsection (7) are—
(a) an offence under section 2 or 5 of the Perjury Act 1911 (c 6) (false statements made on oath otherwise than in judicial proceedings or made otherwise than on oath),
(b) an offence under section 44(1) or (2) of the Criminal Law (Consolidation) (Scotland) Act 1995 (c 39) (false statements made on oath or otherwise than on oath).

(9) An order under this section has effect in relation to Scotland as if it were an order made by the Court of Session which that court had jurisdiction to make.

Preliminaries to adoption

42 CHILD TO LIVE WITH ADOPTERS BEFORE APPLICATION

(1) An application for an adoption order may not be made unless—
(a) if subsection (2) applies, the condition in that subsection is met,
(b) if that subsection does not apply, the condition in whichever is applicable of subsections (3) to (5) applies.

(2) If—
(a) the child was placed for adoption with the applicant or applicants by an adoption agency or in pursuance of an order of the High Court, or
(b) the applicant is a parent of the child,
the condition is that the child must have had his home with the applicant or, in the case of an application by a couple, with one or both of them at all times during the period of ten weeks preceding the application.

(3) If the applicant or one of the applicants is the partner of a parent of the child, the condition is that the child must have had his home with the applicant or, as the case may be, applicants at all times during the period of six months preceding the application.

(4) If the applicants are local authority foster parents, the condition is that the child must have had his home with the applicants at all times during the period of one year preceding the application.

(5) In any other case, the condition is that the child must have had his home with the applicant or, in the case of an application by a couple, with one or both of them for not less than three years (whether continuous or not) during the period of five years preceding the application.

(6) But subsections (4) and (5) do not prevent an application being made if the court gives leave to make it.

(7) An adoption order may not be made unless the court is satisfied that sufficient opportunities to see the child with the applicant or, in the case of an application by a couple, both of them together in the home environment have been given—
(a) where the child was placed for adoption with the applicant or applicants by an adoption agency, to that agency,
(b) in any other case, to the local authority within whose area the home is.

(8) In this section and sections 43 and 44(1)—
(a) references to an adoption agency include a Scottish or Northern Irish adoption agency,
(b) references to a child placed for adoption by an adoption agency are to be read accordingly.

43 REPORTS WHERE CHILD PLACED BY AGENCY

Where an application for an adoption order relates to a child placed for adoption by an adoption agency, the agency must—

(a) submit to the court a report on the suitability of the applicants and on any other matters relevant to the operation of section 1, and

(b) assist the court in any manner the court directs.

44 NOTICE OF INTENTION TO ADOPT

(1) This section applies where persons (referred to in this section as "proposed adopters") wish to adopt a child who is not placed for adoption with them by an adoption agency.

(2) An adoption order may not be made in respect of the child unless the proposed adopters have given notice to the appropriate local authority of their intention to apply for the adoption order (referred to in this Act as a "notice of intention to adopt").

(3) The notice must be given not more than two years, or less than three months, before the date on which the application for the adoption order is made.

(4) Where—
(a) if a person were seeking to apply for an adoption order, subsection (4) or (5) of section 42 would apply, but
(b) the condition in the subsection in question is not met,
the person may not give notice of intention to adopt unless he has the court's leave to apply for an adoption order.

(5) On receipt of a notice of intention to adopt, the local authority must arrange for the investigation of the matter and submit to the court a report of the investigation.

(6) In particular, the investigation must, so far as practicable, include the suitability of the proposed adopters and any other matters relevant to the operation of section 1 in relation to the application.

(7) If a local authority receive a notice of intention to adopt in respect of a child whom they know was (immediately before the notice was given) looked after by another local authority, they must, not more than seven days after the receipt of the notice, inform the other local authority in writing that they have received the notice.

(8) Where—
(a) a local authority have placed a child with any persons otherwise than as prospective adopters, and
(b) the persons give notice of intention to adopt,
the authority are not to be treated as leaving the child with them as prospective adopters for the purposes of section 18(1)(b).

(9) In this section, references to the appropriate local authority, in relation to any proposed adopters, are—
(a) in prescribed cases, references to the prescribed local authority,
(b) in any other case, references to the local authority for the area in which, at the time of giving the notice of intention to adopt, they have their home, and "prescribed" means prescribed by regulations.

45 SUITABILITY OF ADOPTERS

(1) Regulations under section 9 may make provision as to the matters to be taken into account by an adoption agency in determining, or making any report in respect of, the suitability of any persons to adopt a child.

(2) In particular, the regulations may make provision for the purpose of securing that, in determining the suitability of a couple to adopt a child, proper regard is had to the need for stability and permanence in their relationship.

The making of adoption orders

46 ADOPTION ORDERS

(1) An adoption order is an order made by the court on an application under section 50 or 51 giving parental responsibility for a child to the adopters or adopter.

(2) The making of an adoption order operates to extinguish—
  (a) the parental responsibility which any person other than the adopters or adopter has for the adopted child immediately before the making of the order,
  (b) any order under the 1989 Act or the Children (Northern Ireland) Order 1995 (SI 1995/755 (NI 2)),
  (c) any order under the Children (Scotland) Act 1995 (c 36) other than an excepted order, and
  (d) any duty arising by virtue of an agreement or an order of a court to make payments, so far as the payments are in respect of the adopted child's maintenance or upbringing for any period after the making of the adoption order.

"Excepted order" means an order under section 9, 11(1)(d) or 13 of the Children (Scotland) Act 1995 or an exclusion order within the meaning of section 76(1) of that Act.

(3) An adoption order—
  (a) does not affect parental responsibility so far as it relates to any period before the making of the order, and
  (b) in the case of an order made on an application under section 51(2) by the partner of a parent of the adopted child, does not affect the parental responsibility of that parent or any duties of that parent within subsection (2)(d).

(4) Subsection (2)(d) does not apply to a duty arising by virtue of an agreement—
  (a) which constitutes a trust, or
  (b) which expressly provides that the duty is not to be extinguished by the making of an adoption order.

(5) An adoption order may be made even if the child to be adopted is already an adopted child.

(6) Before making an adoption order, the court must consider whether there should be arrangements for allowing any person contact with the child; and for that purpose the court must consider any existing or proposed arrangements and obtain any views of the parties to the proceedings.

47 CONDITIONS FOR MAKING ADOPTION ORDERS

(1) An adoption order may not be made if the child has a parent or guardian unless one of the following three conditions is met; but this section is subject to section 52 (parental etc consent).

(2) The first condition is that, in the case of each parent or guardian of the child, the court is satisfied—
  (a) that the parent or guardian consents to the making of the adoption order,
  (b) that the parent or guardian has consented under section 20 (and has not withdrawn the consent) and does not oppose the making of the adoption order, or
  (c) that the parent's or guardian's consent should be dispensed with.

(3) A parent or guardian may not oppose the making of an adoption order under subsection (2)(b) without the court's leave.

(4) The second condition is that—
(a) the child has been placed for adoption by an adoption agency with the prospective adopters in whose favour the order is proposed to be made,
(b) either—
(i) the child was placed for adoption with the consent of each parent or guardian and the consent of the mother was given when the child was at least six weeks old, or
(ii) the child was placed for adoption under a placement order, and
(c) no parent or guardian opposes the making of the adoption order.

(5) A parent or guardian may not oppose the making of an adoption order under the second condition without the court's leave.

(6) The third condition is that the child is free for adoption by virtue of an order made—
(a) in Scotland, under section 18 of the Adoption (Scotland) Act 1978 (c 28), or
(b) in Northern Ireland, under Article 17(1) or 18(1) of the Adoption (Northern Ireland) Order 1987 (SI 1987/2203 (NI 22)).

(7) The court cannot give leave under subsection (3) or (5) unless satisfied that there has been a change in circumstances since the consent of the parent or guardian was given or, as the case may be, the placement order was made.

(8) An adoption order may not be made in relation to a person who is or has been married.

(8A) An adoption order may not be made in relation to a person who is or has been a civil partner.

(9) An adoption order may not be made in relation to a person who has attained the age of 19 years.

48 RESTRICTIONS ON MAKING ADOPTION ORDERS

(1) The court may not hear an application for an adoption order in relation to a child, where a previous application to which subsection (2) applies made in relation to the child by the same persons was refused by any court, unless it appears to the court that, because of a change in circumstances or for any other reason, it is proper to hear the application.

(2) This subsection applies to any application—
(a) for an adoption order or a Scottish or Northern Irish adoption order, or
(b) for an order for adoption made in the Isle of Man or any of the Channel Islands.

49 APPLICATIONS FOR ADOPTION

(1) An application for an adoption order may be made by—
(a) a couple, or
(b) one person, but only if it is made under section 50 or 51 and one of the following conditions is met.

(2) The first condition is that at least one of the couple (in the case of an application under section 50) or the applicant (in the case of an application under section 51) is domiciled in a part of the British Islands.

(3) The second condition is that both of the couple (in the case of an application under section 50) or the applicant (in the case of an application under section 51) have been habitually resident in a part of the British Islands for a period of not less than one year ending with the date of the application.

(4) An application for an adoption order may only be made if the person to be adopted has not attained the age of 18 years on the date of the application.

(5) References in this Act to a child, in connection with any proceedings (whether or not concluded) for adoption, (such as "child to be adopted" or "adopted child") include a person who has attained the age of 18 years before the proceedings are concluded.

50 ADOPTION BY COUPLE

(1) An adoption order may be made on the application of a couple where both of them have attained the age of 21 years.

(2) An adoption order may be made on the application of a couple where—
(a) one of the couple is the mother or the father of the person to be adopted and has attained the age of 18 years, and
(b) the other has attained the age of 21 years.

51 ADOPTION BY ONE PERSON

(1) An adoption order may be made on the application of one person who has attained the age of 21 years and is not married or a civil partner.

(2) An adoption order may be made on the application of one person who has attained the age of 21 years if the court is satisfied that the person is the partner of a parent of the person to be adopted.

(3) An adoption order may be made on the application of one person who has attained the age of 21 years and is married if the court is satisfied that—
(a) the person's spouse cannot be found,
(b) the spouses have separated and are living apart, and the separation is likely to be permanent, or
(c) the person's spouse is by reason of ill-health, whether physical or mental, incapable of making an application for an adoption order.

(3A) An adoption order may be made on the application of one person who has attained the age of 21 years and is a civil partner if the court is satisfied that—
(a) the person's civil partner cannot be found,
(b) the civil partners have separated and are living apart, and the separation is likely to be permanent, or
(c) the person's civil partner is by reason of ill-health, whether physical or mental, incapable of making an application for an adoption order.

(4) An adoption order may not be made on an application under this section by the mother or the father of the person to be adopted unless the court is satisfied that—
(a) the other natural parent is dead or cannot be found,
(b) by virtue of the provisions specified in subsection (5), there is no other parent, or
(c) there is some other reason justifying the child's being adopted by the applicant alone,

and, where the court makes an adoption order on such an application, the court must record that it is satisfied as to the fact mentioned in paragraph (a) or (b) or, in the case of paragraph (c), record the reason.

(5) The provisions referred to in subsection (4)(b) are—
(a) section 28 of the Human Fertilisation and Embryology Act 1990 (disregarding subsections (5A) to (5I) of that section), or

(b) sections 34 to 47 of the Human Fertilisation and Embryology Act 2008 (disregarding sections 39, 40 and 46 of that Act).

Placement and adoption: general

52 PARENTAL ETC CONSENT

(1) The court cannot dispense with the consent of any parent or guardian of a child to the child being placed for adoption or to the making of an adoption order in respect of the child unless the court is satisfied that—
(a) the parent or guardian cannot be found or lacks capacity (within the meaning of the Mental Capacity Act 2005) to give consent, or
(b) the welfare of the child requires the consent to be dispensed with.

(2) The following provisions apply to references in this Chapter to any parent or guardian of a child giving or withdrawing—
(a) consent to the placement of a child for adoption, or
(b) consent to the making of an adoption order (including a future adoption order).

(3) Any consent given by the mother to the making of an adoption order is ineffective if it is given less than six weeks after the child's birth.

(4) The withdrawal of any consent to the placement of a child for adoption, or of any consent given under section 20, is ineffective if it is given after an application for an adoption order is made.

(5) "Consent" means consent given unconditionally and with full understanding of what is involved; but a person may consent to adoption without knowing the identity of the persons in whose favour the order will be made.

(6) "Parent" (except in subsections (9) and (10) below) means a parent having parental responsibility.

(7) Consent under section 19 or 20 must be given in the form prescribed by rules, and the rules may prescribe forms in which a person giving consent under any other provision of this Part may do so (if he wishes).

(8) Consent given under section 19 or 20 must be withdrawn—
(a) in the form prescribed by rules, or
(b) by notice given to the agency.

(9) Subsection (10) applies if—
(a) an agency has placed a child for adoption under section 19 in pursuance of consent given by a parent of the child, and
(b) at a later time, the other parent of the child acquires parental responsibility for the child.

(10) The other parent is to be treated as having at that time given consent in accordance with this section in the same terms as those in which the first parent gave consent.

53 MODIFICATION OF 1989 ACT IN RELATION TO ADOPTION

(1) Where—
(a) a local authority are authorised to place a child for adoption, or
(b) a child who has been placed for adoption by a local authority is less than six weeks old, regulations may provide for the following provisions of the 1989 Act to apply with modifications, or not to apply, in relation to the child.

(2) The provisions are—
(a) section 22(4)(b), (c) and (d) and (5)(b) (duty to ascertain wishes and feelings of certain persons),
(b) paragraphs 15 and 21 of Schedule 2 (promoting contact with parents and parents' obligation to contribute towards maintenance).

(3) Where a registered adoption society is authorised to place a child for adoption or a child who has been placed for adoption by a registered adoption society is less than six weeks old, regulations may provide—
(a) for section 61 of that Act to have effect in relation to the child whether or not he is accommodated by or on behalf of the society,
(b) for subsections (2)(b) to (d) and (3)(b) of that section (duty to ascertain wishes and feelings of certain persons) to apply with modifications, or not to apply, in relation to the child.

(4) Where a child's home is with persons who have given notice of intention to adopt, no contribution is payable (whether under a contribution order or otherwise) under Part 3 of Schedule 2 to that Act (contributions towards maintenance of children looked after by local authorities) in respect of the period referred to in subsection (5).

(5) That period begins when the notice of intention to adopt is given and ends if—
(a) the period of four months beginning with the giving of the notice expires without the prospective adopters applying for an adoption order, or
(b) an application for such an order is withdrawn or refused.

(6) In this section, "notice of intention to adopt" includes notice of intention to apply for a Scottish or Northern Irish adoption order.

. . .

55 REVOCATION OF ADOPTIONS ON LEGITIMATION

(1) Where any child adopted by one natural parent as sole adoptive parent subsequently becomes a legitimated person on the marriage of the natural parents, the court by which the adoption order was made may, on the application of any of the parties concerned, revoke the order.

(2) In relation to an adoption order made by a magistrates' court, the reference in subsection(1) to the court by which the order was made includes a court acting for the same local justice area.

Disclosure of information in relation to a person's adoption

56 INFORMATION TO BE KEPT ABOUT A PERSON'S ADOPTION

(1) In relation to an adopted person, regulations may prescribe—
(a) the information which an adoption agency must keep in relation to his adoption,
(b) the form and manner in which it must keep that information.

(2) Below in this group of sections (that is, this section and sections 57 to 65), any information kept by an adoption agency by virtue of subsection (1)(a) is referred to as section 56 information.

(3) Regulations may provide for the transfer in prescribed circumstances of information held, or previously held, by an adoption agency to another adoption agency.

57 RESTRICTIONS ON DISCLOSURE OF PROTECTED ETC INFORMATION

(1) Any section 56 information kept by an adoption agency which—
  (a) is about an adopted person or any other person, and
  (b) is or includes identifying information about the person in question, may only be disclosed by the agency to a person (other than the person the information is about) in pursuance of this group of sections.

(2) Any information kept by an adoption agency—
  (a) which the agency has obtained from the Registrar General on an application under section 79(5) and any other information which would enable the adopted person to obtain a certified copy of the record of his birth, or
  (b) which is information about an entry relating to the adopted person in the Adoption Contact Register,

may only be disclosed to a person by the agency in pursuance of this group of sections.

(3) In this group of sections, information the disclosure of which to a person is restricted by virtue of subsection (1) or (2) is referred to (in relation to him) as protected information.

(4) Identifying information about a person means information which, whether taken on its own or together with other information disclosed by an adoption agency, identifies the person or enables the person to be identified.

(5) This section does not prevent the disclosure of protected information in pursuance of a prescribed agreement to which the adoption agency is a party.

(6) Regulations may authorise or require an adoption agency to disclose protected information to a person who is not an adopted person.

58 DISCLOSURE OF OTHER INFORMATION

(1) This section applies to any section 56 information other than protected information.

(2) An adoption agency may for the purposes of its functions disclose to any person in accordance with prescribed arrangements any information to which this section applies.

(3) An adoption agency must, in prescribed circumstances, disclose prescribed information to a prescribed person.

59 OFFENCE

Regulations may provide that a registered adoption society which discloses any information in contravention of section 57 is to be guilty of an offence and liable on summary conviction to a fine not exceeding level 5 on the standard scale.

60 DISCLOSING INFORMATION TO ADOPTED ADULT

(1) This section applies to an adopted person who has attained the age of 18 years.

(2) The adopted person has the right, at his request, to receive from the appropriate adoption agency—
  (a) any information which would enable him to obtain a certified copy of the record of his birth, unless the High Court orders otherwise,

(b) any prescribed information disclosed to the adopters by the agency by virtue of section 54.

(3) The High Court may make an order under subsection (2)(a), on an application by the appropriate adoption agency, if satisfied that the circumstances are exceptional.

(4) The adopted person also has the right, at his request, to receive from the court which made the adoption order a copy of any prescribed document or prescribed order relating to the adoption.

(5) Subsection (4) does not apply to a document or order so far as it contains information which is protected information.

61 DISCLOSING PROTECTED INFORMATION ABOUT ADULTS

(1) This section applies where—
(a) a person applies to the appropriate adoption agency for protected information to be disclosed to him, and
(b) none of the information is about a person who is a child at the time of the application.

(2) The agency is not required to proceed with the application unless it considers it appropriate to do so.

(3) If the agency does proceed with the application it must take all reasonable steps to obtain the views of any person the information is about as to the disclosure of the information about him.

(4) The agency may then disclose the information if it considers it appropriate to do so.

(5) In deciding whether it is appropriate to proceed with the application or disclose the information, the agency must consider—
(a) the welfare of the adopted person,
(b) any views obtained under subsection (3),
(c) any prescribed matters, and all the other circumstances of the case.

(6) This section does not apply to a request for information under section 60(2) or to a request for information which the agency is authorised or required to disclose in pursuance of regulations made by virtue of section 57(6).

62 DISCLOSING PROTECTED INFORMATION ABOUT CHILDREN

(1) This section applies where—
(a) a person applies to the appropriate adoption agency for protected information to be disclosed to him, and
(b) any of the information is about a person who is a child at the time of the application.

(2) The agency is not required to proceed with the application unless it considers it appropriate to do so.

(3) If the agency does proceed with the application, then, so far as the information is about a person who is at the time a child, the agency must take all reasonable steps to obtain—
(a) the views of any parent or guardian of the child, and
(b) the views of the child, if the agency considers it appropriate to do so having regard to his age and understanding and to all the other circumstances of the case,
as to the disclosure of the information.

(4) And, so far as the information is about a person who has at the time attained the age of 18 years, the agency must take all reasonable steps to obtain his views as to the disclosure of the information.

(5) The agency may then disclose the information if it considers it appropriate to do so.

(6) In deciding whether it is appropriate to proceed with the application, or disclose the information, where any of the information is about a person who is at the time a child—
(a) if the child is an adopted child, the child's welfare must be the paramount consideration,
(b) in the case of any other child, the agency must have particular regard to the child's welfare.

(7) And, in deciding whether it is appropriate to proceed with the application or disclose the information, the agency must consider—
(a) the welfare of the adopted person (where subsection (6)(a) does not apply),
(b) any views obtained under subsection (3) or (4),
(c) any prescribed matters, and all the other circumstances of the case.

(8) This section does not apply to a request for information under section 60(2) or to a request for information which the agency is authorised or required to disclose in pursuance of regulations made by virtue of section 57(6).

63 COUNSELLING

(1) Regulations may require adoption agencies to give information about the availability of counselling to persons—
(a) seeking information from them in pursuance of this group of sections,
(b) considering objecting or consenting to the disclosure of information by the agency in pursuance of this group of sections, or
(c) considering entering with the agency into an agreement prescribed for the purposes of section 57(5).

(2) Regulations may require adoption agencies to make arrangements to secure the provision of counselling for persons seeking information from them in prescribed circumstances in pursuance of this group of sections.

(3) The regulations may authorise adoption agencies—
(a) to disclose information which is required for the purposes of such counselling to the persons providing the counselling,
(b) where the person providing the counselling is outside the United Kingdom, to require a prescribed fee to be paid.

(4) The regulations may require any of the following persons to provide counselling for the purposes of arrangements under subsection (2)—
(a) a local authority, a council constituted under section 2 of the Local Government etc (Scotland) Act 1994 (c 39) or a Health and Social Services Board established under Article 16 of the Health and Personal Social Services (Northern Ireland) Order 1972 (SI 1972/1265 (NI 14)),
(b) a registered adoption society, an organisation within section 144(3)(b) or an adoption society which is registered under Article 4 of the Adoption (Northern Ireland) Order 1987 (SI 1987/2203 (NI 22)),
(c) an adoption support agency in respect of which a person is registered under Part 2 of the Care Standards Act 2000 (c 14).

(5) For the purposes of subsection (4), where the functions of a Health and Social Services Board are exercisable by a Health and Social Services Trust, the reference in sub-paragraph (a) to a Board is to be read as a reference to the Health and Social Services Trust.

64 OTHER PROVISION TO BE MADE BY REGULATIONS

(1) Regulations may make provision for the purposes of this group of sections, including provision as to—
- (a) the performance by adoption agencies of their functions,
- (b) the manner in which information may be received, and
- (c) the matters mentioned below in this section.

(2) Regulations may prescribe—
- (a) the manner in which agreements made by virtue of section 57(5) are to be recorded,
- (b) the information to be provided by any person on an application for the disclosure of information under this group of sections.

(3) Regulations may require adoption agencies—
- (a) to give to prescribed persons prescribed information about the rights or opportunities to obtain information, or to give their views as to its disclosure, given by this group of sections,
- (b) to seek prescribed information from, or give prescribed information to, the Registrar General in prescribed circumstances.

(4) Regulations may require the Registrar General—
- (a) to disclose to any person (including an adopted person) at his request any information which the person requires to assist him to make contact with the adoption agency which is the appropriate adoption agency in the case of an adopted person specified in the request (or, as the case may be, in the applicant's case),
- (b) to disclose to the appropriate adoption agency any information which the agency requires about any entry relating to the adopted person on the Adoption Contact Register.

(5) Regulations may provide for the payment of a prescribed fee in respect of the disclosure in prescribed circumstances of any information in pursuance of section 60, 61 or 62; but an adopted person may not be required to pay any fee in respect of any information disclosed to him in relation to any person who (but for his adoption) would be related to him by blood (including half-blood), marriage or civil partnership.

(6) Regulations may provide for the payment of a prescribed fee by an adoption agency obtaining information under subsection (4)(b).

65 SECTIONS 56 TO 65: INTERPRETATION

(1) In this group of sections—

"appropriate adoption agency", in relation to an adopted person or to information relating to his adoption, means—
- (a) if the person was placed for adoption by an adoption agency, that agency or (if different) the agency which keeps the information in relation to his adoption,
- (b) in any other case, the local authority to which notice of intention to adopt was given,

"prescribed" means prescribed by subordinate legislation,
"regulations" means regulations under section 9,

"subordinate legislation" means regulations or, in relation to information to be given by a court, rules.

Chapter 4 STATUS OF ADOPTED CHILDREN

66 MEANING OF ADOPTION IN CHAPTER 4

(1) In this Chapter "adoption" means—
(a) adoption by an adoption order or a Scottish or Northern Irish adoption order,
(b) adoption by an order made in the Isle of Man or any of the Channel Islands,
(c) an adoption effected under the law of a Convention country outside the British Islands, and certified in pursuance of Article 23(1) of the Convention (referred to in this Act as a "Convention adoption"),
(d) an overseas adoption, or
(e) an adoption recognised by the law of England and Wales and effected under the law of any other country;
and related expressions are to be interpreted accordingly.

(2) But references in this Chapter to adoption do not include an adoption effected before the day on which this Chapter comes into force (referred to in this Chapter as "the appointed day").

(3) Any reference in an enactment to an adopted person within the meaning of this Chapter includes a reference to an adopted child within the meaning of Part 4 of the Adoption Act 1976 (c 36).

67 STATUS CONFERRED BY ADOPTION

(1) An adopted person is to be treated in law as if born as the child of the adopters or adopter.

(2) An adopted person is the legitimate child of the adopters or adopter and, if adopted by—
(a) a couple, or
(b) one of a couple under section 51(2),
is to be treated as the child of the relationship of the couple in question.

(3) An adopted person—
(a) if adopted by one of a couple under section 51(2), is to be treated in law as not being the child of any person other than the adopter and the other one of the couple, and
(b) in any other case, is to be treated in law, subject to subsection (4), as not being the child of any person other than the adopters or adopter;
but this subsection does not affect any reference in this Act to a person's natural parent or to any other natural relationship.

(4) In the case of a person adopted by one of the person's natural parents as sole adoptive parent, subsection (3)(b) has no effect as respects entitlement to property depending on relationship to that parent, or as respects anything else depending on that relationship.

(5) This section has effect from the date of the adoption.

(6) Subject to the provisions of this Chapter and Schedule 4, this section—
(a) applies for the interpretation of enactments or instruments passed or made before as well as after the adoption, and so applies subject to any contrary indication, and
(b) has effect as respects things done, or events occurring, on or after the adoption.

68 ADOPTIVE RELATIVES

(1) A relationship existing by virtue of section 67 may be referred to as an adoptive relationship, and—
(a) an adopter may be referred to as an adoptive parent or (as the case may be) as an adoptive father or adoptive mother,
(b) any other relative of any degree under an adoptive relationship may be referred to as an adoptive relative of that degree.

(2) Subsection (1) does not affect the interpretation of any reference, not qualified by the word "adoptive", to a relationship.

(3) A reference (however expressed) to the adoptive mother and father of a child adopted by—
(a) a couple of the same sex, or
(b) a partner of the child's parent, where the couple are of the same sex, is to be read as a reference to the child's adoptive parents.

69 RULES OF INTERPRETATION FOR INSTRUMENTS CONCERNING PROPERTY

(1) The rules of interpretation contained in this section apply (subject to any contrary indication and to Schedule 4) to any instrument so far as it contains a disposition of property.

(2) In applying section 67(1) and (2) to a disposition which depends on the date of birth of a child or children of the adoptive parent or parents, the disposition is to be interpreted as if—
(a) the adopted person had been born on the date of adoption,
(b) two or more people adopted on the same date had been born on that date in the order of their actual births;
but this does not affect any reference to a person's age.

(3) Examples of phrases in wills on which subsection (2) can operate are—
1 Children of A "living at my death or born afterwards".
2 Children of A "living at my death or born afterwards before any one of such children for the time being in existence attains a vested interest and who attain the age of 21 years".
3 As in example 1 or 2, but referring to grandchildren of A instead of children of A.
4 A for life "until he has a child", and then to his child or children.
Note Subsection (2) will not affect the reference to the age of 21 years in example 2.

(4) Section 67(3) does not prejudice—
(a) any qualifying interest, or
(b) any interest expectant (whether immediately or not) upon a qualifying interest.
"Qualifying interest" means an interest vested in possession in the adopted person before the adoption.

(5) Where it is necessary to determine for the purposes of a disposition of property effected by an instrument whether a woman can have a child—
(a) it must be presumed that once a woman has attained the age of 55 years she will not adopt a person after execution of the instrument, and
(b) if she does so, then (in spite of section 67) that person is not to be treated as her child or (if she does so as one of a couple) as the child of the other one of the couple for the purposes of the instrument.

(6) In this section, "instrument" includes a private Act settling property, but not any other enactment.

70 DISPOSITIONS DEPENDING ON DATE OF BIRTH

(1) Where a disposition depends on the date of birth of a person who was born illegitimate and who is adopted by one of the natural parents as sole adoptive parent, section 69(2) does not affect entitlement by virtue of Part 3 of the Family Law Reform Act 1987 (c 42) (dispositions of property).

(2) Subsection (1) applies for example where—
(a) a testator dies in 2001 bequeathing a legacy to his eldest grandchild living at a specified time,
(b) his unmarried daughter has a child in 2002 who is the first grandchild,
(c) his married son has a child in 2003,
(d) subsequently his unmarried daughter adopts her child as sole adoptive parent.
In that example the status of the daughter's child as the eldest grandchild of the testator is not affected by the events described in paragraphs (c) and (d).

71 PROPERTY DEVOLVING WITH PEERAGES ETC

(1) An adoption does not affect the descent of any peerage or dignity or title of honour.

(2) An adoption does not affect the devolution of any property limited (expressly or not) to devolve (as nearly as the law permits) along with any peerage or dignity or title of honour.

(3) Subsection (2) applies only if and so far as a contrary intention is not expressed in the instrument, and has effect subject to the terms of the instrument.

72 PROTECTION OF TRUSTEES AND PERSONAL REPRESENTATIVES

(1) A trustee or personal representative is not under a duty, by virtue of the law relating to trusts or the administration of estates, to enquire, before conveying or distributing any property, whether any adoption has been effected or revoked if that fact could affect entitlement to the property.

(2) A trustee or personal representative is not liable to any person by reason of a conveyance or distribution of the property made without regard to any such fact if he has not received notice of the fact before the conveyance or distribution.

(3) This section does not prejudice the right of a person to follow the property, or any property representing it, into the hands of another person, other than a purchaser, who has received it.

73 MEANING OF DISPOSITION

(1) This section applies for the purposes of this Chapter.

(2) A disposition includes the conferring of a power of appointment and any other disposition of an interest in or right over property; and in this subsection a power of appointment includes any discretionary power to transfer a beneficial interest in property without the furnishing of valuable consideration.

(3) This Chapter applies to an oral disposition as if contained in an instrument made when the disposition was made.

(4) The date of death of a testator is the date at which a will or codicil is to be regarded as made.

(5) The provisions of the law of intestate succession applicable to the estate of a deceased person are to be treated as if contained in an instrument executed by him (while of full capacity) immediately before his death.

74 MISCELLANEOUS ENACTMENTS

(1) Section 67 does not apply for the purposes of—
(a) section 1 of and Schedule 1 to the Marriage Act 1949 or Schedule 1 to the Civil Partnership Act 2004 (prohibited degrees of kindred and affinity), or
(b) sections 64 and 65 of the Sexual Offences Act 2003 (sex with an adult relative).

(2) Section 67 does not apply for the purposes of any provision of—
(a) the British Nationality Act 1981 (c 61),
(b) the Immigration Act 1971 (c 77),
(c) any instrument having effect under an enactment within paragraph (a) or (b), or
(d) any other provision of the law for the time being in force which determines British citizenship, British overseas territories citizenship, the status of a British National (Overseas) or British Overseas citizenship.

75 PENSIONS

Section 67(3) does not affect entitlement to a pension which is payable to or for the benefit of a person and is in payment at the time of the person's adoption.

76 INSURANCE

(1) Where a child is adopted whose natural parent has effected an insurance with a friendly society or a collecting society or an industrial insurance company for the payment on the death of the child of money for funeral expenses, then—
(a) the rights and liabilities under the policy are by virtue of the adoption transferred to the adoptive parents, and
(b) for the purposes of the enactments relating to such societies and companies, the adoptive parents are to be treated as the person who took out the policy.

(2) Where the adoption is effected by an order made by virtue of section 51(2), the references in subsection (1) to the adoptive parents are to be read as references to the adopter and the other one of the couple.

Chapter 5 THE REGISTERS

Adopted Children Register etc

77 ADOPTED CHILDREN REGISTER

(1) The Registrar General must continue to maintain in the General Register Office a register, to be called the Adopted Children Register.

(2) The Adopted Children Register is not to be open to public inspection or search.

(3) No entries may be made in the Adopted Children Register other than entries—
(a) directed to be made in it by adoption orders, or
(b) required to be made under Schedule 1.

(4) A certified copy of an entry in the Adopted Children Register, if purporting to be sealed or stamped with the seal of the General Register Office, is to be received as evidence of the adoption to which it relates without further or other proof.

(5) Where an entry in the Adopted Children Register contains a record—
(a) of the date of birth of the adopted person, or
(b) of the country, or the district and sub-district, of the birth of the adopted person,
a certified copy of the entry is also to be received, without further or other proof, as evidence of that date, or country or district and sub-district, (as the case may be) in all respects as if the copy were a certified copy of an entry in the registers of live-births.

(6) Schedule 1 (registration of adoptions and the amendment of adoption orders) is to have effect.

78 SEARCHES AND COPIES

(1) The Registrar General must continue to maintain at the General Register Office an index of the Adopted Children Register.

(2) Any person may—
(a) search the index,
(b) have a certified copy of any entry in the Adopted Children Register.

(3) But a person is not entitled to have a certified copy of an entry in the Adopted Children Register relating to an adopted person who has not attained the age of 18 years unless the applicant has provided the Registrar General with the prescribed particulars.

"Prescribed" means prescribed by regulations made by the Registrar General with the approval of the Secretary of State.

(4) The terms, conditions and regulations as to payment of fees, and otherwise, applicable under the Births and Deaths Registration Act 1953 (c 20), and the Registration Service Act 1953 (c 37), in respect of—
(a) searches in the index kept in the General Register Office of certified copies of entries in the registers of live-births,
(b) the supply from that office of certified copies of entries in those certified copies,
also apply in respect of searches, and supplies of certified copies, under subsection (2).

79 CONNECTIONS BETWEEN THE REGISTER AND BIRTH RECORDS

(1) The Registrar General must make traceable the connection between any entry in the registers of live-births or other records which has been marked "Adopted" and any corresponding entry in the Adopted Children Register.

(2) Information kept by the Registrar General for the purposes of subsection (1) is not to be open to public inspection or search.

(3) Any such information, and any other information which would enable an adopted person to obtain a certified copy of the record of his birth, may only be disclosed by the Registrar General in accordance with this section.

(4) In relation to a person adopted before the appointed day the court may, in exceptional circumstances, order the Registrar General to give any information mentioned in subsection (3) to a person.

(5) On an application made in the prescribed manner by the appropriate adoption agency in respect of an adopted person a record of whose birth is kept by the Registrar General, the

Registrar General must give the agency any information relating to the adopted person which is mentioned in subsection (3).

"Appropriate adoption agency" has the same meaning as in section 65.

(6) In relation to a person adopted before the appointed day, Schedule 2 applies instead of subsection (5).

(7) On an application made in the prescribed manner by an adopted person a record of whose birth is kept by the Registrar General and who—
(a) is under the age of 18 years, and
(b) intends to be married or form a civil partnership,
the Registrar General must inform the applicant whether or not it appears from information contained in the registers of live-births or other records that the applicant and the intended spouse or civil partner may be within the prohibited degrees of relationship for the purposes of the Marriage Act 1949 (c 76) or for the purposes of the Civil Partnership Act 2004 (c 33).

(8) Before the Registrar General gives any information by virtue of this section, any prescribed fee which he has demanded must be paid.

(9) In this section—

"appointed day" means the day appointed for the commencement of sections 56 to 65,

"prescribed" means prescribed by regulations made by the Registrar General with the approval of the Secretary of State.

Adoption Contact Register

80 ADOPTION CONTACT REGISTER

(1) The Registrar General must continue to maintain at the General Register Office in accordance with regulations a register in two Parts to be called the Adoption Contact Register.

(2) Part 1 of the register is to contain the prescribed information about adopted persons who have given the prescribed notice expressing their wishes as to making contact with their relatives.

(3) The Registrar General may only make an entry in Part 1 of the register for an adopted person—
(a) a record of whose birth is kept by the Registrar General,
(b) who has attained the age of 18 years, and
(c) who the Registrar General is satisfied has such information as is necessary to enable him to obtain a certified copy of the record of his birth.

(4) Part 2 of the register is to contain the prescribed information about persons who have given the prescribed notice expressing their wishes, as relatives of adopted persons, as to making contact with those persons.

(5) The Registrar General may only make an entry in Part 2 of the register for a person—
(a) who has attained the age of 18 years, and
(b) who the Registrar General is satisfied is a relative of an adopted person and has such information as is necessary to enable him to obtain a certified copy of the record of the adopted person's birth.

(6) Regulations may provide for—

(a) the disclosure of information contained in one Part of the register to persons for whom there is an entry in the other Part,
(b) the payment of prescribed fees in respect of the making or alteration of entries in the register and the disclosure of information contained in the register.

81 ADOPTION CONTACT REGISTER: SUPPLEMENTARY

(1) The Adoption Contact Register is not to be open to public inspection or search.

(2) In section 80, "relative", in relation to an adopted person, means any person who (but for his adoption) would be related to him by blood (including half-blood), marriage or civil partnership.

(3) The Registrar General must not give any information entered in the register to any person except in accordance with subsection (6)(a) of that section or regulations made by virtue of section 64(4)(b).

(4) In section 80, "regulations" means regulations made by the Registrar General with the approval of the Secretary of State, and "prescribed" means prescribed by such regulations.

General

82 INTERPRETATION

(1) In this Chapter—

"records" includes certified copies kept by the Registrar General of entries in any register of births,

"registers of live-births" means the registers of live-births made under the Births and Deaths Registration Act 1953 (c 20).

(2) Any register, record or index maintained under this Chapter may be maintained in any form the Registrar General considers appropriate; and references (however expressed) to entries in such a register, or to their amendment, marking or cancellation, are to be read accordingly.

. . .

Chapter 7 MISCELLANEOUS

Restrictions

92 RESTRICTION ON ARRANGING ADOPTIONS ETC

(1) A person who is neither an adoption agency nor acting in pursuance of an order of the High Court must not take any of the steps mentioned in subsection (2).

(2) The steps are—
(a) asking a person other than an adoption agency to provide a child for adoption,
(b) asking a person other than an adoption agency to provide prospective adopters for a child,
(c) offering to find a child for adoption,
(d) offering a child for adoption to a person other than an adoption agency,
(e) handing over a child to any person other than an adoption agency with a view to the child's adoption by that or another person,

(f) receiving a child handed over to him in contravention of paragraph (e),
(g) entering into an agreement with any person for the adoption of a child, or for the purpose of facilitating the adoption of a child, where no adoption agency is acting on behalf of the child in the adoption,
(h) initiating or taking part in negotiations of which the purpose is the conclusion of an agreement within paragraph (g),
(i) causing another person to take any of the steps mentioned in paragraphs (a) to (h).

(3) Subsection (1) does not apply to a person taking any of the steps mentioned in paragraphs (d), (e), (g), (h) and (i) of subsection (2) if the following condition is met.

(4) The condition is that—
(a) the prospective adopters are parents, relatives or guardians of the child (or one of them is), or
(b) the prospective adopter is the partner of a parent of the child.

(5) References to an adoption agency in subsection (2) include a prescribed person outside the United Kingdom exercising functions corresponding to those of an adoption agency, if the functions are being exercised in prescribed circumstances in respect of the child in question.

(6) The Secretary of State may, after consultation with the Assembly, by order make any amendments of subsections (1) to (4), and any consequential amendments of this Act, which he considers necessary or expedient.

(7) In this section—
(a) "agreement" includes an arrangement (whether or not enforceable),
(b) "prescribed" means prescribed by regulations made by the Secretary of State after consultation with the Assembly.

93 OFFENCE OF BREACHING RESTRICTIONS UNDER SECTION 92

(1) If a person contravenes section 92(1), he is guilty of an offence; and, if that person is an adoption society, the person who manages the society is also guilty of the offence.

(2) A person is not guilty of an offence under subsection (1) of taking the step mentioned in paragraph (f) of section 92(2) unless it is proved that he knew or had reason to suspect that the child was handed over to him in contravention of paragraph (e) of that subsection.

(3) A person is not guilty of an offence under subsection (1) of causing a person to take any of the steps mentioned in paragraphs (a) to (h) of section 92(2) unless it is proved that he knew or had reason to suspect that the step taken would contravene the paragraph in question.

(4) But subsections (2) and (3) only apply if sufficient evidence is adduced to raise an issue as to whether the person had the knowledge or reason mentioned.

(5) A person guilty of an offence under this section is liable on summary conviction to imprisonment for a term not exceeding six months, or a fine not exceeding £10,000, or both.

94 RESTRICTION ON REPORTS

(1) A person who is not within a prescribed description may not, in any prescribed circumstances, prepare a report for any person about the suitability of a child for

adoption or of a person to adopt a child or about the adoption, or placement for adoption, of a child.

"Prescribed" means prescribed by regulations made by the Secretary of State after consultation with the Assembly.

(2) If a person—
(a) contravenes subsection (1), or
(b) causes a person to prepare a report, or submits to any person a report which has been prepared, in contravention of that subsection,
he is guilty of an offence.

(3) If a person who works for an adoption society—
(a) contravenes subsection (1), or
(b) causes a person to prepare a report, or submits to any person a report which has been prepared, in contravention of that subsection,
the person who manages the society is also guilty of the offence.

(4) A person is not guilty of an offence under subsection (2)(b) unless it is proved that he knew or had reason to suspect that the report would be, or had been, prepared in contravention of subsection (1).

But this subsection only applies if sufficient evidence is adduced to raise an issue as to whether the person had the knowledge or reason mentioned.

(5) A person guilty of an offence under this section is liable on summary conviction to imprisonment for a term not exceeding six months, or a fine not exceeding level 5 on the standard scale, or both.

95 PROHIBITION OF CERTAIN PAYMENTS

(1) This section applies to any payment (other than an excepted payment) which is made for or in consideration of—
(a) the adoption of a child,
(b) giving any consent required in connection with the adoption of a child,
(c) removing from the United Kingdom a child who is a Commonwealth citizen, or is habitually resident in the United Kingdom, to a place outside the British Islands for the purpose of adoption,
(d) a person (who is neither an adoption agency nor acting in pursuance of an order of the High Court) taking any step mentioned in section 92(2),
(e) preparing, causing to be prepared or submitting a report the preparation of which contravenes section 94(1).

(2) In this section and section 96, removing a child from the United Kingdom has the same meaning as in section 85.

(3) Any person who—
(a) makes any payment to which this section applies,
(b) agrees or offers to make any such payment, or
(c) receives or agrees to receive or attempts to obtain any such payment, is guilty of an offence.

(4) A person guilty of an offence under this section is liable on summary conviction to imprisonment for a term not exceeding six months, or a fine not exceeding £10,000, or both.

96 EXCEPTED PAYMENTS

(1) A payment is an excepted payment if it is made by virtue of, or in accordance with provision made by or under, this Act, the Adoption (Scotland) Act 1978 (c 28) or the Adoption (Northern Ireland) Order 1987 (SI 1987/2203 (NI 22)).

(2) A payment is an excepted payment if it is made to a registered adoption society by—
(a) a parent or guardian of a child, or
(b) a person who adopts or proposes to adopt a child,
in respect of expenses reasonably incurred by the society in connection with the adoption or proposed adoption of the child.

(3) A payment is an excepted payment if it is made in respect of any legal or medical expenses incurred or to be incurred by any person in connection with an application to a court which he has made or proposes to make for an adoption order, a placement order, or an order under section 26 or 84.

(4) A payment made as mentioned in section 95(1)(c) is an excepted payment if—
(a) the condition in section 85(2) is met, and
(b) the payment is made in respect of the travel and accommodation expenses reasonably incurred in removing the child from the United Kingdom for the purpose of adoption.

97 SECTIONS 92 TO 96: INTERPRETATION

In sections 92 to 96—
(a) "adoption agency" includes a Scottish or Northern Irish adoption agency,

(b) "payment" includes reward,

(c) references to adoption are to the adoption of persons, wherever they may be habitually resident, effected under the law of any country or territory, whether within or outside the British Islands.

Information

98 PRE-COMMENCEMENT ADOPTIONS: INFORMATION

(1) Regulations under section 9 may make provision for the purpose of—
(a) assisting persons adopted before the appointed day who have attained the age of 18 to obtain information in relation to their adoption, and
(b) facilitating contact between such persons and their relatives.

(2) For that purpose the regulations may confer functions on—
(a) registered adoption support agencies,
(b) the Registrar General,
(c) adoption agencies.

(3) For that purpose the regulations may—
(a) authorise or require any person mentioned in subsection (2) to disclose information,
(b) authorise or require the disclosure of information contained in records kept under section 8 of the Public Records Act 1958 (c 51) (court records), and may impose conditions on the disclosure of information, including conditions restricting its further disclosure.

(4) The regulations may authorise the charging of prescribed fees by any person mentioned in subsection (2) or in respect of the disclosure of information under subsection (3)(b).

(5) An authorisation or requirement to disclose information by virtue of subsection (3)(a) has effect in spite of any restriction on the disclosure of information in Chapter 5.

(6) The making of regulations by virtue of subsections (2) to (4) which relate to the Registrar General requires the approval of the Secretary of State.

(7) In this section—

"appointed day" means the day appointed for the commencement of sections 56 to 65,

"registered adoption support agency" means an adoption support agency in respect of which a person is registered under Part 2 of the Care Standards Act 2000 (c 14),

"relative", in relation to an adopted person, means any person who (but for his adoption) would be related to him by blood (including half-blood), marriage or civil partnership.

. . .

The Children and Family Court Advisory and Support Service

102 OFFICERS OF THE SERVICE

(1) For the purposes of—
- (a) any relevant application,
- (b) the signification by any person of any consent to placement or adoption, rules must provide for the appointment in prescribed cases of an officer of the Children and Family Court Advisory and Support Service ("the Service") or a Welsh family proceedings officer.

(2) The rules may provide for the appointment of such an officer in other circumstances in which it appears to the Lord Chancellor to be necessary or expedient to do so.

(3) The rules may provide for the officer—
- (a) to act on behalf of the child upon the hearing of any relevant application, with the duty of safeguarding the interests of the child in the prescribed manner,
- (b) where the court so requests, to prepare a report on matters relating to the welfare of the child in question,
- (c) to witness documents which signify consent to placement or adoption,
- (d) to perform prescribed functions.

(4) A report prepared in pursuance of the rules on matters relating to the welfare of a child must—
- (a) deal with prescribed matters (unless the court orders otherwise), and
- (b) be made in the manner required by the court.

(5) A person who—
- (a) in the case of an application for the making, varying or revocation of a placement order, is employed by the local authority which made the application,
- (b) in the case of an application for an adoption order in respect of a child who was placed for adoption, is employed by the adoption agency which placed him, or
- (c) is within a prescribed description, is not to be appointed under subsection (1) or (2).

(6) In this section, "relevant application" means an application for—
- (a) the making, varying or revocation of a placement order,
- (b) the making of an order under section 26, or the varying or revocation of such an order,
- (c) the making of an adoption order, or
- (d) the making of an order under section 84.

(7) Rules may make provision as to the assistance which the court may require an officer of the Service or a Welsh family proceedings officer to give to it.

(8) In this section and section 103 "Welsh family proceedings officer" has the meaning given by section 35 of the Children Act 2004.

103 RIGHT OF OFFICERS OF THE SERVICE TO HAVE ACCESS TO ADOPTION AGENCY RECORDS

(1) Where an officer of the Service or a Welsh family proceedings officer has been appointed to act under section 102(1), he has the right at all reasonable times to examine and take copies of any records of, or held by, an adoption agency which were compiled in connection with the making, or proposed making, by any person of any application under this Part in respect of the child concerned.

(2) Where an officer of the Service or a Welsh family proceedings officer takes a copy of any record which he is entitled to examine under this section, that copy or any part of it is admissible as evidence of any matter referred to in any—
(a) report which he makes to the court in the proceedings in question, or
(b) evidence which he gives in those proceedings.

(3) Subsection (2) has effect regardless of any enactment or rule of law which would otherwise prevent the record in question being admissible in evidence.

Evidence

104 EVIDENCE OF CONSENT

(1) If a document signifying any consent which is required by this Part to be given is witnessed in accordance with rules, it is to be admissible in evidence without further proof of the signature of the person by whom it was executed.

(2) A document signifying any such consent which purports to be witnessed in accordance with rules is to be presumed to be so witnessed, and to have been executed and witnessed on the date and at the place specified in the document, unless the contrary is proved.

. . .

General

109 AVOIDING DELAY

(1) In proceedings in which a question may arise as to whether an adoption order or placement order should be made, or any other question with respect to such an order, the court must (in the light of any rules made by virtue of subsection (2))—
(a) draw up a timetable with a view to determining such a question without delay, and
(b) give such directions as it considers appropriate for the purpose of ensuring that the timetable is adhered to.

(2) Rules may—
(a) prescribe periods within which prescribed steps must be taken in relation to such proceedings, and
(b) make other provision with respect to such proceedings for the purpose of ensuring that such questions are determined without delay.

110 SERVICE OF NOTICES ETC

Any notice or information required to be given by virtue of this Act may be given by post.

Part 2 AMENDMENTS OF THE CHILDREN ACT 1989

111 PARENTAL RESPONSIBILITY OF UNMARRIED FATHER

. . .

(7) Paragraph (a) of section 4(1) of the 1989 Act, as substituted by subsection (2) of this section, does not confer parental responsibility on a man who was registered under an enactment referred to in paragraph (a), (b) or (c) of section 4(1A) of that Act, as inserted by subsection (3) of this section, before the commencement of subsection (3) in relation to that paragraph.

. . .

Part 3 MISCELLANEOUS AND FINAL PROVISIONS

144 GENERAL INTERPRETATION ETC

(1) In this Act—

"appropriate Minister" means—
(a) in relation to England, Scotland or Northern Ireland, the Secretary of State,
(b) in relation to Wales, the Assembly, and in relation to England and Wales means the Secretary of State and the Assembly acting jointly,

"the Assembly" means the National Assembly for Wales,

. . .

"by virtue of" includes "by" and "under",

"child", except where used to express a relationship, means a person who has not attained the age of 18 years,

"the Convention" means the Convention on Protection of Children and Co-operation in respect of Intercountry Adoption, concluded at the Hague on 29th May 1993,

"Convention adoption order" means an adoption order which, by virtue of regulations under section 1 of the Adoption (Intercountry Aspects) Act 1999 (c 18) (regulations giving effect to the Convention), is made as a Convention adoption order,

"Convention country" means a country or territory in which the Convention is in force,

"court" means, subject to any provision made by virtue of Part 1 of Schedule 11 to the 1989 Act, the High Court, a county court or a magistrates' court,

"enactment" includes an enactment comprised in subordinate legislation,

"fee" includes expenses,

"guardian" has the same meaning as in the 1989 Act and includes a special guardian within the meaning of that Act,

"information" means information recorded in any form,

. . .

"relative", in relation to a child, means a grandparent, brother, sister, uncle or aunt, whether of the full blood or half-blood or by marriage or civil partnership,

. . .

(4) In this Act, a couple means—
(a) a married couple, or
(aa) two people who are civil partners of each other, or
(b) two people (whether of different sexes or the same sex) living as partners in an enduring family relationship.

(5) Subsection (4)(b) does not include two people one of whom is the other's parent, grandparent, sister, brother, aunt or uncle.

(6) References to relationships in subsection (5)—
(a) are to relationships of the full blood or half blood or, in the case of an adopted person, such of those relationships as would exist but for adoption, and
(b) include the relationship of a child with his adoptive, or former adoptive, parents, but do not include any other adoptive relationships.

(7) For the purposes of this Act, a person is the partner of a child's parent if the person and the parent are a couple but the person is not the child's parent.

As amended by: Human Fertilisation and Embryology (Deceased Fathers) Act 2003, s 2(1), Schedule; Courts Act 2003, s 109(1), Sch 8; Sexual Offences Act 2003, s 139, Sch 6, para 47; Health and Social Care (Community Health and Standards) Act 2003, s 34, Sch 4, paras 125, 126; Children Act 2004, s s40, 57, Sch 3; Civil Partnership Act 2004, s 79; Mental Capacity Act 2005, s 67(1), Sch 6; Civil Partnership Act 2004 (International Immunities and Privileges, Companies and Adoption) Order 2005, SI 2005/3542, art 4; Children and Adoption Act 2006, s 15(1), Sch 2; Children and Young Persons Act 2008, ss 34, 44; Transfer of Functions (Registration) Order 2008, SI 2008/678, arts 3(1), 5, Sch 1, Sch 2; Human Fertilisation and Embryology Act 2008, s 56, Sch 6.

Gender Recognition Act 2004

(2004 c 7)

Applications for gender recognition certificate

1 APPLICATIONS

(1) A person of either gender who is aged at least 18 may make an application for a gender recognition certificate on the basis of—
(a) living in the other gender, or
(b) having changed gender under the law of a country or territory outside the United Kingdom.

(2) In this Act "the acquired gender", in relation to a person by whom an application under subsection (1) is or has been made, means—
(a) in the case of an application under paragraph (a) of that subsection, the gender in which the person is living, or
(b) in the case of an application under paragraph (b) of that subsection, the gender to which the person has changed under the law of the country or territory concerned.

(3) An application under subsection (1) is to be determined by a Gender Recognition Panel.

(4) Schedule 1 (Gender Recognition Panels) has effect.

2 DETERMINATION OF APPLICATIONS

(1) In the case of an application under section 1(1)(a), the Panel must grant the application if satisfied that the applicant—
  (a) has or has had gender dysphoria,
  (b) has lived in the acquired gender throughout the period of two years ending with the date on which the application is made,
  (c) intends to continue to live in the acquired gender until death, and
  (d) complies with the requirements imposed by and under section 3.

(2) In the case of an application under section 1(1)(b), the Panel must grant the application if satisfied—
  (a) that the country or territory under the law of which the applicant has changed gender is an approved country or territory, and
  (b) that the applicant complies with the requirements imposed by and under section 3.

(3) The Panel must reject an application under section 1(1) if not required by subsection (1) or (2) to grant it.

(4) In this Act "approved country or territory" means a country or territory prescribed by order made by the Secretary of State after consulting the Scottish Ministers and the Department of Finance and Personnel in Northern Ireland.

3 EVIDENCE

(1) An application under section 1(1)(a) must include either—
  (a) a report made by a registered medical practitioner practising in the field of gender dysphoria and a report made by another registered medical practitioner (who may, but need not, practise in that field), or
  (b) a report made by a chartered psychologist practising in that field and a report made by a registered medical practitioner (who may, but need not, practise in that field).

(2) But subsection (1) is not complied with unless a report required by that subsection and made by—
  (a) a registered medical practitioner, or
  (b) a chartered psychologist, practising in the field of gender dysphoria includes details of the diagnosis of the applicant's gender dysphoria.

(3) And subsection (1) is not complied with in a case where—
  (a) the applicant has undergone or is undergoing treatment for the purpose of modifying sexual characteristics, or
  (b) treatment for that purpose has been prescribed or planned for the applicant, unless at least one of the reports required by that subsection includes details of it.

(4) An application under section 1(1)(a) must also include a statutory declaration by the applicant that the applicant meets the conditions in section 2(1)(b) and (c).

(5) An application under section 1(1)(b) must include evidence that the applicant has changed gender under the law of an approved country or territory.

(6) Any application under section 1(1) must include—
   (a) a statutory declaration as to whether or not the applicant is married or a civil partner,
   (b) any other information or evidence required by an order made by the Secretary of State, and
   (c) any other information or evidence which the Panel which is to determine the application may require, and may include any other information or evidence which the applicant wishes to include.

(7) The Secretary of State may not make an order under subsection (6)(b) without consulting the Scottish Ministers and the Department of Finance and Personnel in Northern Ireland.

(8) If the Panel which is to determine the application requires information or evidence under subsection (6)(c) it must give reasons for doing so.

4 SUCCESSFUL APPLICATIONS

(1) If a Gender Recognition Panel grants an application under section 1(1) it must issue a gender recognition certificate to the applicant.

(2) Unless the applicant is married or a civil partner, the certificate is to be a full gender recognition certificate.

(3) If the applicant is married or a civil partner, the certificate is to be an interim gender recognition certificate.

(4) Schedule 2 (annulment or dissolution of marriage after issue of interim gender recognition certificate) has effect.

(5) The Secretary of State may, after consulting the Scottish Ministers and the Department of Finance and Personnel in Northern Ireland, specify the content and form of gender recognition certificates.

5 ISSUE OF FULL CERTIFICATES WHERE APPLICANT HAS BEEN MARRIED

(1) A court which—
   (a) makes absolute a decree of nullity granted on the ground that an interim gender recognition certificate has been issued to a party to the marriage, or
   (b) (in Scotland) grants a decree of divorce on that ground, must, on doing so, issue a full gender recognition certificate to that party and send a copy to the Secretary of State.

(2) If an interim gender recognition certificate has been issued to a person and either—
   (a) the person's marriage is dissolved or annulled (otherwise than on the ground mentioned in subsection (1)) in proceedings instituted during the period of six months beginning with the day on which it was issued, or
   (b) the person's spouse dies within that period,

   the person may make an application for a full gender recognition certificate at any time within the period specified in subsection (3) (unless the person is again married or is a civil partner).

(3) That period is the period of six months beginning with the day on which the marriage is dissolved or annulled or the death occurs.

(4) An application under subsection (2) must include evidence of the dissolution or annulment of the marriage and the date on which proceedings for it were instituted, or of the death of the spouse and the date on which it occurred.

(5) An application under subsection (2) is to be determined by a Gender Recognition Panel.

(6) The Panel—
(a) must grant the application if satisfied that the applicant is neither married nor a civil partner, and
(b) otherwise must reject it.

(7) If the Panel grants the application it must issue a full gender recognition certificate to the applicant.

5A ISSUE OF FULL CERTIFICATES WHERE APPLICANT HAS BEEN A CIVIL PARTNER

(1) A court which—
(a) makes final a nullity order made on the ground that an interim gender recognition certificate has been issued to a civil partner, or
(b) (in Scotland) grants a decree of dissolution on that ground,
must, on doing so, issue a full gender recognition certificate to that civil partner and send a copy to the Secretary of State.

(2) If an interim gender recognition certificate has been issued to a person and either—
(a) the person's civil partnership is dissolved or annulled (otherwise than on the ground mentioned in subsection (1)) in proceedings instituted during the period of six months beginning with the day on which it was issued, or
(b) the person's civil partner dies within that period,
the person may make an application for a full gender recognition certificate at any time within the period specified in subsection (3) (unless the person is again a civil partner or is married).

(3) That period is the period of six months beginning with the day on which the civil partnership is dissolved or annulled or the death occurs.

(4) An application under subsection (2) must include evidence of the dissolution or annulment of the civil partnership and the date on which proceedings for it were instituted, or of the death of the civil partner and the date on which it occurred.

(5) An application under subsection (2) is to be determined by a Gender Recognition Panel.

(6) The Panel—
(a) must grant the application if satisfied that the applicant is neither a civil partner nor married, and
(b) otherwise must reject it.

(7) If the Panel grants the application it must issue a full gender recognition certificate to the applicant.

6 ERRORS IN CERTIFICATES

(1) Where a gender recognition certificate has been issued to a person, the person or the Secretary of State may make an application for a corrected certificate on the ground that the certificate which has been issued contains an error.

(2) If the certificate was issued by a court the application is to be determined by the court but in any other case it is to be determined by a Gender Recognition Panel.

(3) The court or Panel—
 (a) must grant the application if satisfied that the gender recognition certificate contains an error, and
 (b) otherwise must reject it.

(4) If the court or Panel grants the application it must issue a corrected gender recognition certificate to the applicant.

. . .

8 APPEALS ETC

(1) An applicant to a Gender Recognition Panel under section 1(1), 5(2), 5A(2) or 6(1) may appeal to the High Court or Court of Session on a point of law against a decision by the Panel to reject the application.

(2) An appeal under subsection (1) must be heard in private if the applicant so requests.

(3) On such an appeal the court must—
 (a) allow the appeal and issue the certificate applied for,
 (b) allow the appeal and refer the matter to the same or another Panel for reconsideration, or
 (c) dismiss the appeal.

(4) If an application under section 1(1) is rejected, the applicant may not make another application before the end of the period of six months beginning with the date on which it is rejected.

(5) If an application under section 1(1), 5(2), 5A(2) or 6(1) is granted but the Secretary of State considers that its grant was secured by fraud, the Secretary of State may refer the case to the High Court or Court of Session.

(6) On a reference under subsection (5) the court—
 (a) must either quash or confirm the decision to grant the application, and
 (b) if it quashes it, must revoke the gender recognition certificate issued on the grant of the application and may make any order which it considers appropriate in consequence of, or otherwise in connection with, doing so.

Consequences of issue of gender recognition certificate etc

9 GENERAL

(1) Where a full gender recognition certificate is issued to a person, the person's gender becomes for all purposes the acquired gender (so that, if the acquired gender is the male gender, the person's sex becomes that of a man and, if it is the female gender, the person's sex becomes that of a woman).

(2) Subsection (1) does not affect things done, or events occurring, before the certificate is issued; but it does operate for the interpretation of enactments passed, and instruments and other documents made, before the certificate is issued (as well as those passed or made afterwards).

(3) Subsection (1) is subject to provision made by this Act or any other enactment or any subordinate legislation.

10 REGISTRATION

(1) Where there is a UK birth register entry in relation to a person to whom a full gender recognition certificate is issued, the Secretary of State must send a copy of the certificate to the appropriate Registrar General.

(2) In this Act "UK birth register entry", in relation to a person to whom a full gender recognition certificate is issued, means—
(a) an entry of which a certified copy is kept by a Registrar General, or
(b) an entry in a register so kept, containing a record of the person's birth or adoption (or, if there would otherwise be more than one, the most recent).

(3) "The appropriate Registrar General" means whichever of—
(a) the Registrar General for England and Wales,
(b) the Registrar General for Scotland, or
(c) the Registrar General for Northern Ireland, keeps a certified copy of the person's UK birth register entry or the register containing that entry.

. . .

12 PARENTHOOD

The fact that a person's gender has become the acquired gender under this Act does not affect the status of the person as the father or mother of a child.

. . .

15 SUCCESSION ETC

The fact that a person's gender has become the acquired gender under this Act does not affect the disposal or devolution of property under a will or other instrument made before the appointed day.

. . .

20 GENDER-SPECIFIC OFFENCES

(1) Where (apart from this subsection) a relevant gender-specific offence could be committed or attempted only if the gender of a person to whom a full gender recognition certificate has been issued were not the acquired gender, the fact that the person's gender has become the acquired gender does not prevent the offence being committed or attempted.

(2) An offence is a "relevant gender-specific offence" if—
(a) either or both of the conditions in subsection (3) are satisfied, and
(b) the commission of the offence involves the accused engaging in sexual activity.

(3) The conditions are—
(a) that the offence may be committed only by a person of a particular gender, and
(b) that the offence may be committed only on, or in relation to, a person of a particular gender, and the references to a particular gender include a gender identified by reference to the gender of the other person involved.

21 FOREIGN GENDER CHANGE AND MARRIAGE

(1) A person's gender is not to be regarded as having changed by reason only that it has changed under the law of a country or territory outside the United Kingdom.

(2) Accordingly, a person is not to be regarded as being married by reason of having entered into a foreign post-recognition marriage.

(3) But if a full gender recognition certificate is issued to a person who has entered into a foreign post-recognition marriage, after the issue of the certificate the marriage is no longer to be regarded as being void on the ground that (at the time when it was entered into) the parties to it were not respectively male and female.

(4) However, subsection (3) does not apply to a foreign post-recognition marriage if a party to it has entered into a later (valid) marriage or civil partnership before the issue of the full gender recognition certificate.

(5) For the purposes of this section a person has entered into a foreign post-recognition marriage if (and only if)—
(a) the person has entered into a marriage in accordance with the law of a country or territory outside the United Kingdom,
(b) before the marriage was entered into the person had changed gender under the law of that or any other country or territory outside the United Kingdom,
(c) the other party to the marriage was not of the gender to which the person had changed under the law of that country or territory, and
(d) by virtue of subsection (1) the person's gender was not regarded as having changed under the law of any part of the United Kingdom.

(6) Nothing in this section prevents the exercise of any enforceable Community right.

Supplementary

. . .

25 INTERPRETATION

In this Act—

"the acquired gender" is to be construed in accordance with section 1(2),

"approved country or territory" has the meaning given by section 2(4),

"the appointed day" means the day appointed by order under section 26,

"chartered psychologist" means a person for the time being listed in the British Psychological Society's Register of Chartered Psychologists,

"enactment" includes an enactment contained in an Act of the Scottish Parliament or in any Northern Ireland legislation,

"full gender recognition certificate" and "interim gender recognition certificate" mean the certificates issued as such under section 4, 5 or 5A and "gender recognition certificate" means either of those sorts of certificate,

"gender dysphoria" means the disorder variously referred to as gender dysphoria, gender identity disorder and transsexualism,

"Gender Recognition Panel" (and "Panel") is to be construed in accordance with Schedule 1,

"subordinate legislation" means an Order in Council, an order, rules, regulations, a scheme, a warrant, bye-laws or any other instrument made under an enactment, and

"UK birth register entry" has the meaning given by section 10(2).

As amended by: Civil Partnership Act 2004, s 250.

Domestic Violence, Crime and Victims Act 2004

(2004 c 28)

Causing or allowing the death of a child or vulnerable adult

5 THE OFFENCE

(1) A person ("D") is guilty of an offence if—
 (a) a child or vulnerable adult ("V") dies as a result of the unlawful act of a person who—
  (i) was a member of the same household as V, and
  (ii) had frequent contact with him,
 (b) D was such a person at the time of that act,
 (c) at that time there was a significant risk of serious physical harm being caused to V by the unlawful act of such a person, and
 (d) either D was the person whose act caused V's death or—
  (i) D was, or ought to have been, aware of the risk mentioned in paragraph (c),
  (ii) D failed to take such steps as he could reasonably have been expected to take to protect V from the risk, and
  (iii) the act occurred in circumstances of the kind that D foresaw or ought to have foreseen.

(2) The prosecution does not have to prove whether it is the first alternative in subsection (1)(d) or the second (sub-paragraphs (i) to (iii)) that applies.

(3) If D was not the mother or father of V—
 (a) D may not be charged with an offence under this section if he was under the age of 16 at the time of the act that caused V's death;
 (b) for the purposes of subsection (1)(d)(ii) D could not have been expected to take any such step as is referred to there before attaining that age.

(4) For the purposes of this section—
 (a) a person is to be regarded as a "member" of a particular household, even if he does not live in that household, if he visits it so often and for such periods of time that it is reasonable to regard him as a member of it;
 (b) where V lived in different households at different times, "the same household as V" refers to the household in which V was living at the time of the act that caused V's death.

(5) For the purposes of this section an "unlawful" act is one that—
 (a) constitutes an offence, or
 (b) would constitute an offence but for being the act of—
  (i) a person under the age of ten, or
  (ii) a person entitled to rely on a defence of insanity.

Paragraph (b) does not apply to an act of D.

(6) In this section—

"act" includes a course of conduct and also includes omission;

"child" means a person under the age of 16;

"serious" harm means harm that amounts to grievous bodily harm for the purposes of the Offences against the Person Act 1861 (c 100);

"vulnerable adult" means a person aged 16 or over whose ability to protect himself from violence, abuse or neglect is significantly impaired through physical or mental disability or illness, through old age or otherwise.

(7) A person guilty of an offence under this section is liable on conviction on indictment to imprisonment for a term not exceeding 14 years or to a fine, or to both.

6 EVIDENCE AND PROCEDURE: ENGLAND AND WALES

(1) Subsections (2) to (4) apply where a person ("the defendant") is charged in the same proceedings with an offence of murder or manslaughter and with an offence under section 5 in respect of the same death ("the section 5 offence").

(2) Where by virtue of section 35(3) of the Criminal Justice and Public Order Act 1994 (c 33) a court or jury is permitted, in relation to the section 5 offence, to draw such inferences as appear proper from the defendant's failure to give evidence or refusal to answer a question, the court or jury may also draw such inferences in determining whether he is guilty—

(a) of murder or manslaughter, or

(b) of any other offence of which he could lawfully be convicted on the charge of murder or manslaughter,

even if there would otherwise be no case for him to answer in relation to that offence.

(3) The charge of murder or manslaughter is not to be dismissed under paragraph 2 of Schedule 3 to the Crime and Disorder Act 1998 (c 37) (unless the section 5 offence is dismissed).

(4) At the defendant's trial the question whether there is a case for the defendant to answer on the charge of murder or manslaughter is not to be considered before the close of all the evidence (or, if at some earlier time he ceases to be charged with the section 5 offence, before that earlier time). . . .

CHILDREN ACT 2004

(2004 c 31)

Part 1 CHILDREN'S COMMISSIONER

1 ESTABLISHMENT

(1) There is to be an office of Children's Commissioner.

(2) Schedule 1 has effect with respect to the Children's Commissioner.

2 GENERAL FUNCTION

(1) The Children's Commissioner has the function of promoting awareness of the views and interests of children in England.

(2) The Children's Commissioner may in particular under this section—

(a) encourage persons exercising functions or engaged in activities affecting children to take account of their views and interests;
(b) advise the Secretary of State on the views and interests of children;
(c) consider or research the operation of complaints procedures so far as relating to children;
(d) consider or research any other matter relating to the interests of children;
(e) publish a report on any matter considered or researched by him under this section.

(3) The Children's Commissioner is to be concerned in particular under this section with the views and interests of children so far as relating to the following aspects of their well-being—
(a) physical and mental health and emotional well-being;
(b) protection from harm and neglect;
(c) education, training and recreation;
(d) the contribution made by them to society;
(e) social and economic well-being.

(4) The Children's Commissioner must take reasonable steps to involve children in the discharge of his function under this section, and in particular to—
(a) ensure that children are made aware of his function and how they may communicate with him; and
(b) consult children, and organisations working with children, on the matters he proposes to consider or research under subsection (2)(c) or (d).

(5) Where the Children's Commissioner publishes a report under this section he must, if and to the extent that he considers it appropriate, also publish the report in a version which is suitable for children (or, if the report relates to a particular group of children, for those children).

(6) The Children's Commissioner must for the purposes of subsection (4) have particular regard to groups of children who do not have other adequate means by which they can make their views known.

(7) The Children's Commissioner is not under this section to conduct an investigation of the case of an individual child.

(8) The Children's Commissioner or a person authorised by him may for the purposes of his function under this section at any reasonable time—
(a) enter any premises, other than a private dwelling, for the purposes of interviewing any child accommodated or cared for there; and
(b) if the child consents, interview the child in private.

(9) Any person exercising functions under any enactment must supply the Children's Commissioner with such information in that person's possession relating to those functions as the Children's Commissioner may reasonably request for the purposes of his function under this section (provided that the information is information which that person may, apart from this subsection, lawfully disclose to him).

(10) Where the Children's Commissioner has published a report under this section containing recommendations in respect of any person exercising functions under any enactment, he may require that person to state in writing, within such period as the Children's Commissioner may reasonably require, what action the person has taken or proposes to take in response to the recommendations.

(11) In considering for the purpose of his function under this section what constitutes the interests of children (generally or so far as relating to a particular matter) the Children's Commissioner must have regard to the United Nations Convention on the Rights of the Child.

(12) In subsection (11) the reference to the United Nations Convention on the Rights of the Child is to the Convention on the Rights of the Child adopted by the General Assembly of the United Nations on 20th November 1989, subject to any reservations, objections or interpretative declarations by the United Kingdom for the time being in force.

3 INQUIRIES INITIATED BY COMMISSIONER

(1) Where the Children's Commissioner considers that the case of an individual child in England raises issues of public policy of relevance to other children, he may hold an inquiry into that case for the purpose of investigating and making recommendations about those issues.

(2) The Children's Commissioner may only conduct an inquiry under this section if he is satisfied that the inquiry would not duplicate work that is the function of another person (having consulted such persons as he considers appropriate).

(3) Before holding an inquiry under this section the Children's Commissioner must consult the Secretary of State.

(4) The Children's Commissioner may, if he thinks fit, hold an inquiry under this section, or any part of it, in private.

(5) As soon as possible after completing an inquiry under this section the Children's Commissioner must—
(a) publish a report containing his recommendations; and
(b) send a copy to the Secretary of State.

(6) The report need not identify any individual child if the Children's Commissioner considers that it would be undesirable for the identity of the child to be made public.

(7) Where the Children's Commissioner has published a report under this section containing recommendations in respect of any person exercising functions under any enactment, he may require that person to state in writing, within such period as the Children's Commissioner may reasonably require, what action the person has taken or proposes to take in response to the recommendations.

(8) Subsections (2) and (3) of section 250 of the Local Government Act 1972 (c 70) apply for the purposes of an inquiry held under this section with the substitution for references to the person appointed to hold the inquiry of references to the Children's Commissioner.

4 OTHER INQUIRIES HELD BY COMMISSIONER

(1) Where the Secretary of State considers that the case of an individual child in England raises issues of relevance to other children, he may direct the Children's Commissioner to hold an inquiry into that case.

(2) The Children's Commissioner may, if he thinks fit, hold an inquiry under this section, or any part of it, in private.

(3) The Children's Commissioner must, as soon as possible after the completion of an inquiry under this section, make a report in relation to the inquiry and send a copy to the Secretary of State.

(4) The Secretary of State must, subject to subsection (5), publish each report received by him under this section as soon as possible.

(5) Where a report made under this section identifies an individual child and the Secretary of State considers that it would be undesirable for the identity of the child to be made public—
(a) the Secretary of State may make such amendments to the report as are necessary to protect the identity of the child and publish the amended report only; or
(b) if he considers that it is not possible to publish the report without identifying the child, he need not publish the report.

(6) The Secretary of State must lay a copy of each report published by him under this section before each House of Parliament.

(7) Subsections (2) to (5) of section 250 of the Local Government Act 1972 (c 70) apply for the purposes of an inquiry held under this section.

. . .

Part 4 ADVISORY AND SUPPORT SERVICES FOR FAMILY PROCEEDINGS

CAFCASS functions in Wales

35 FUNCTIONS OF THE ASSEMBLY RELATING TO FAMILY PROCEEDINGS

(1) In respect of family proceedings in which the welfare of children ordinarily resident in Wales is or may be in question, it is a function of the Assembly to—
(a) safeguard and promote the welfare of the children;
(b) give advice to any court about any application made to it in such proceedings;
(c) make provision for the children to be represented in such proceedings;
(d) provide information, advice and other support for the children and their families.

(2) The Assembly must also make provision for the performance of the functions conferred on Welsh family proceedings officers by virtue of any enactment (whether or not they are exercisable for the purposes of subsection (1)).

(3) In subsection (1), "family proceedings" has the meaning given by section 12 of the Criminal Justice and Court Services Act 2000 (c 43).

(4) In this Part, "Welsh family proceedings officer" means—
(a) any member of the staff of the Assembly appointed to exercise the functions of a Welsh family proceedings officer; and
(b) any other individual exercising functions of a Welsh family proceedings officer by virtue of section 36(2) or (4).

. . .

37 WELSH FAMILY PROCEEDINGS OFFICERS

(1) The Assembly may authorise a Welsh family proceedings officer of a description prescribed in regulations made by the Secretary of State—
(a) to conduct litigation in relation to any proceedings in any court,
(b) to exercise a right of audience in any proceedings in any court,
in the exercise of his functions.

(2) A Welsh family proceedings officer exercising a right to conduct litigation by virtue of subsection (1)(a) who would otherwise have such a right by virtue of the fact that he is a

person who, for the purposes of the Legal Services Act 2007, is an authorised person in relation to that activity is to be treated as having acquired that right solely by virtue of this section.

(3) A Welsh family proceedings officer exercising a right of audience by virtue of subsection (1)(b) who would otherwise have such a right by virtue of the fact that he is a person who, for the purposes of the Legal Services Act 2007, is an authorised person in relation to that activity is to be treated as having acquired that right solely by virtue of this section.

(4) A Welsh family proceedings officer may, subject to rules of court, be cross-examined in any proceedings to the same extent as any witness.

(5) But a Welsh family proceedings officer may not be cross-examined merely because he is exercising a right to conduct litigation or a right of audience granted in accordance with this section.

(6) In this section, "right to conduct litigation" and "right of audience" have the same meanings as in section 119 of the Courts and Legal Services Act 1990.

. . .

Part 5 MISCELLANEOUS

. . .

58 REASONABLE PUNISHMENT

(1) In relation to any offence specified in subsection (2), battery of a child cannot be justified on the ground that it constituted reasonable punishment.

(2) The offences referred to in subsection (1) are—
- (a) an offence under section 18 or 20 of the Offences against the Person Act 1861 (c 100) (wounding and causing grievous bodily harm);
- (b) an offence under section 47 of that Act (assault occasioning actual bodily harm);
- (c) an offence under section 1 of the Children and Young Persons Act 1933 (c 12) (cruelty to persons under 16).

(3) Battery of a child causing actual bodily harm to the child cannot be justified in any civil proceedings on the ground that it constituted reasonable punishment.

(4) For the purposes of subsection (3) "actual bodily harm" has the same meaning as it has for the purposes of section 47 of the Offences against the Person Act 1861.

(5) In section 1 of the Children and Young Persons Act 1933, omit subsection (7).

As amended by: Offender Management Act 2007, s 39, Sch 3; Education and Skills Act 2008, s 169(1), Sch 1; Legal Services Act 2007, s 208(1), Sch 21.

Civil Partnership Act 2004

(2004 c 33)

Part 1 INTRODUCTION

1 CIVIL PARTNERSHIP

(1) A civil partnership is a relationship between two people of the same sex ("civil partners")—
 (a) which is formed when they register as civil partners of each other—
  (i) in England or Wales (under Part 2),
  (ii) in Scotland (under Part 3),
  (iii) in Northern Ireland (under Part 4), or
  (iv) outside the United Kingdom under an Order in Council made under Chapter 1 of Part 5 (registration at British consulates etc or by armed forces personnel), or
 (b) which they are treated under Chapter 2 of Part 5 as having formed (at the time determined under that Chapter) by virtue of having registered an overseas relationship.

(2) Subsection (1) is subject to the provisions of this Act under or by virtue of which a civil partnership is void.

(3) A civil partnership ends only on death, dissolution or annulment.

(4) The references in subsection (3) to dissolution and annulment are to dissolution and annulment having effect under or recognised in accordance with this Act.

(5) References in this Act to an overseas relationship are to be read in accordance with Chapter 2 of Part 5.

Part 2 CIVIL PARTNERSHIP: ENGLAND AND WALES

Chapter 1 REGISTRATION

Formation, eligibility and parental etc consent

2 FORMATION OF CIVIL PARTNERSHIP BY REGISTRATION

(1) For the purposes of section 1, two people are to be regarded as having registered as civil partners of each other once each of them has signed the civil partnership document—

(a) at the invitation of, and in the presence of, a civil partnership registrar, and
(b) in the presence of each other and two witnesses.

(2) Subsection (1) applies regardless of whether subsections (3) and (4) are complied with.

(3) After the civil partnership document has been signed under subsection (1), it must also be signed, in the presence of the civil partners and each other, by—
(a) each of the two witnesses, and
(b) the civil partnership registrar.

(4) After the witnesses and the civil partnership registrar have signed the civil partnership document, the relevant registration authority must ensure that—
(a) the fact that the two people have registered as civil partners of each other, and
(b) any other information prescribed by regulations, is recorded in the register as soon as is practicable.

(5) No religious service is to be used while the civil partnership registrar is officiating at the signing of a civil partnership document.

(6) "The civil partnership document" has the meaning given by section 7(1).

(7) "The relevant registration authority" means the registration authority in whose area the registration takes place.

3 ELIGIBILITY

(1) Two people are not eligible to register as civil partners of each other if—
(a) they are not of the same sex,
(b) either of them is already a civil partner or lawfully married,
(c) either of them is under 16, or
(d) they are within prohibited degrees of relationship.

(2) Part 1 of Schedule 1 contains provisions for determining when two people are within prohibited degrees of relationship.

4 PARENTAL ETC CONSENT WHERE PROPOSED CIVIL PARTNER UNDER 18

(1) The consent of the appropriate persons is required before a child and another person may register as civil partners of each other.

(2) Part 1 of Schedule 2 contains provisions for determining who are the appropriate persons for the purposes of this section.

(3) The requirement of consent under subsection (1) does not apply if the child is a surviving civil partner.

(4) Nothing in this section affects any need to obtain the consent of the High Court before a ward of court and another person may register as civil partners of each other.

(5) In this Part "child", except where used to express a relationship, means a person who is under 18.

Registration procedure: general

5 TYPES OF PRE-REGISTRATION PROCEDURE

(1) Two people may register as civil partners of each other under—
(a) the standard procedure;
(b) the procedure for house-bound persons;
(c) the procedure for detained persons;
(d) the special procedure (which is for cases where a person is seriously ill and not expected to recover).

(2) The procedures referred to in subsection (1)(a) to (c) are subject to—
(a) section 20 (modified procedures for certain non-residents);
(b) Schedule 3 (former spouses one of whom has changed sex).

(3) The procedures referred to in subsection (1) (including the procedures as modified by section 20 and Schedule 3) are subject to—
(a) Part 2 of Schedule 1 (provisions applicable in connection with prohibited degrees of relationship), and
(b) Parts 2 and 3 of Schedule 2 (provisions applicable where proposed civil partner is under 18).

(4) This section is also subject to section 249 and Schedule 23 (immigration control and formation of civil partnerships).

6 PLACE OF REGISTRATION

(1) The place at which two people may register as civil partners of each other—
(a) must be in England or Wales,
(c) must be specified in the notices, or notice, of proposed civil partnership required by this Chapter.

(3) Subsections (3A) and (3B) apply in the case of registration under the standard procedure (including that procedure modified as mentioned in section 5).

(3A) The place must be—
(a) on approved premises, or
(b) in a register office.

(3B) If it is in a register office, the place must be open to any person wishing to attend the registration.

(3C) In this Chapter "register office" means a register office provided under section 10 of the Registration Service Act 1953.

6A POWER TO APPROVE PREMISES

(1) The Secretary of State may by regulations make provision for and in connection with the approval by registration authorities of premises for the purposes of section 6(3A)(a).

. . .

7 THE CIVIL PARTNERSHIP DOCUMENT

(1) In this Part "the civil partnership document" means—
(a) in relation to the special procedure, a Registrar General's licence, and
(b) in relation to any other procedure, a civil partnership schedule.

(2) Before two people are entitled to register as civil partners of each other—
(a) the civil partnership document must be delivered to the civil partnership registrar, and
(b) the civil partnership registrar may then ask them for any information required (under section 2(4)) to be recorded in the register.

. . .

35 POWER TO ASSIMILATE PROVISIONS RELATING TO CIVIL REGISTRATION

(1) The Secretary of State may by order make—
(a) such amendments of this Act as appear to him appropriate for the purpose of assimilating any provision connected with the formation or recording of civil partnerships in England and Wales to any provision made in relation to civil marriage in England and Wales, and
(b) such amendments of other enactments and of subordinate legislation as appear to him appropriate in consequence of any amendments made under paragraph (a).

(2) "Civil marriage" means marriage solemnised otherwise than according to the rites of the Church of England or any other religious usages.

(3) "Amendment" includes repeal or revocation.

(4) "Subordinate legislation" has the same meaning as in the Interpretation Act 1978 (c 30).

. . .

Chapter 2 DISSOLUTION, NULLITY AND OTHER PROCEEDINGS

Introduction

37 POWERS TO MAKE ORDERS AND EFFECT OF ORDERS

(1) The court may, in accordance with this Chapter—
(a) make an order (a "dissolution order") which dissolves a civil partnership on the ground that it has broken down irretrievably;
(b) make an order (a "nullity order") which annuls a civil partnership which is void or voidable;
(c) make an order (a "presumption of death order") which dissolves a civil partnership on the ground that one of the civil partners is presumed to be dead;
(d) make an order (a "separation order") which provides for the separation of the civil partners.

(2) Every dissolution, nullity or presumption of death order—
(a) is, in the first instance, a conditional order, and
(b) may not be made final before the end of the prescribed period (see section 38);

and any reference in this Chapter to a conditional order is to be read accordingly.

(3) A nullity order made where a civil partnership is voidable annuls the civil partnership only as respects any time after the order has been made final, and the civil partnership is to be treated (despite the order) as if it had existed up to that time.

(4) In this Chapter, other than in sections 58 to 61, "the court" means—
(a) the High Court, or
(b) if a county court has jurisdiction by virtue of Part 5 of the Matrimonial and Family Proceedings Act 1984 (c 42), a county court.

(5) This Chapter is subject to sections 219 to 224 (jurisdiction of the court).

38 THE PERIOD BEFORE CONDITIONAL ORDERS MAY BE MADE FINAL

(1) Subject to subsections (2) to (4), the prescribed period for the purposes of section 37(2)(b) is—
   (a) 6 weeks from the making of the conditional order, or
   (b) if the 6 week period would end on a day on which the office or registry of the court dealing with the case is closed, the period of 6 weeks extended to the end of the first day on which the office or registry is next open.

(2) The Lord Chancellor may by order amend this section so as to substitute a different definition of the prescribed period for the purposes of section 37(2)(b).

(3) But the Lord Chancellor may not under subsection (2) provide for a period longer than 6 months to be the prescribed period.

(4) In a particular case the court dealing with the case may by order shorten the prescribed period.

(5) The power to make an order under subsection (2) is exercisable by statutory instrument.

(6) An instrument containing such an order is subject to annulment in pursuance of a resolution of either House of Parliament.

39 INTERVENTION OF THE QUEEN'S PROCTOR

(1) This section applies if an application has been made for a dissolution, nullity or presumption of death order.

(2) The court may, if it thinks fit, direct that all necessary papers in the matter are to be sent to the Queen's Proctor who must under the directions of the Attorney General instruct counsel to argue before the court any question in relation to the matter which the court considers it necessary or expedient to have fully argued.

(3) If any person at any time—
   (a) during the progress of the proceedings, or
   (b) before the conditional order is made final, gives information to the Queen's Proctor on any matter material to the due decision of the case, the Queen's Proctor may take such steps as the Attorney General considers necessary or expedient.

(4) If the Queen's Proctor intervenes or shows cause against the making of the conditional order in any proceedings relating to its making, the court may make such order as may be just as to—
   (a) the payment by other parties to the proceedings of the costs incurred by him in doing so, or
   (b) the payment by the Queen's Proctor of any costs incurred by any of those parties because of his doing so.

(5) The Queen's Proctor is entitled to charge as part of the expenses of his office—
   (a) the costs of any proceedings under subsection (2);
   (b) if his reasonable costs of intervening or showing cause as mentioned in subsection (4) are not fully satisfied by an order under subsection (4)(a), the amount of the difference;

(c) if the Treasury so directs, any costs which he pays to any parties under an order made under subsection (4)(b).

40 PROCEEDINGS BEFORE ORDER HAS BEEN MADE FINAL

(1) This section applies if—
(a) a conditional order has been made, and
(b) the Queen's Proctor, or any person who has not been a party to proceedings in which the order was made, shows cause why the order should not be made final on the ground that material facts have not been brought before the court.

(2) This section also applies if—
(a) a conditional order has been made,
(b) 3 months have elapsed since the earliest date on which an application could have been made for the order to be made final,
(c) no such application has been made by the civil partner who applied for the conditional order, and
(d) the other civil partner makes an application to the court under this subsection.

(3) The court may—
(a) make the order final,
(b) rescind the order,
(c) require further inquiry, or
(d) otherwise deal with the case as it thinks fit.

(4) Subsection (3)(a)—
(a) applies despite section 37(2) (period before conditional orders may be made final), but
(b) is subject to section 48(4) (protection for respondent in separation cases) and section 63 (restrictions on making of orders affecting children).

41 TIME BAR ON APPLICATIONS FOR DISSOLUTION ORDERS

(1) No application for a dissolution order may be made to the court before the end of the period of 1 year from the date of the formation of the civil partnership.

(2) Nothing in this section prevents the making of an application based on matters which occurred before the end of the 1 year period.

42 ATTEMPTS AT RECONCILIATION OF CIVIL PARTNERS

(1) This section applies in relation to cases where an application is made for a dissolution or separation order.

(2) Rules of court must make provision for requiring the solicitor acting for the applicant to certify whether he has—
(a) discussed with the applicant the possibility of a reconciliation with the other civil partner, and
(b) given the applicant the names and addresses of persons qualified to help effect a reconciliation between civil partners who have become estranged.

(3) If at any stage of proceedings for the order it appears to the court that there is a reasonable possibility of a reconciliation between the civil partners, the court may adjourn the proceedings for such period as it thinks fit to enable attempts to be made to effect a reconciliation between them.

(4) The power to adjourn under subsection (3) is additional to any other power of adjournment.

43 CONSIDERATION BY THE COURT OF CERTAIN AGREEMENTS OR ARRANGEMENTS

(1) This section applies in relation to cases where—
(a) proceedings for a dissolution or separation order are contemplated or have begun, and
(b) an agreement or arrangement is made or proposed to be made between the civil partners which relates to, arises out of, or is connected with, the proceedings.

(2) Rules of court may make provision for enabling—
(a) the civil partners, or either of them, to refer the agreement or arrangement to the court, and
(b) the court—
(i) to express an opinion, if it thinks it desirable to do so, as to the reasonableness of the agreement or arrangement, and
(ii) to give such directions, if any, in the matter as it thinks fit.

Dissolution of civil partnership

44 DISSOLUTION OF CIVIL PARTNERSHIP WHICH HAS BROKEN DOWN IRRETRIEVABLY

(1) Subject to section 41, an application for a dissolution order may be made to the court by either civil partner on the ground that the civil partnership has broken down irretrievably.

(2) On an application for a dissolution order the court must inquire, so far as it reasonably can, into—
(a) the facts alleged by the applicant, and
(b) any facts alleged by the respondent.

(3) The court hearing an application for a dissolution order must not hold that the civil partnership has broken down irretrievably unless the applicant satisfies the court of one or more of the facts described in subsection (5)(a), (b), (c) or (d).

(4) But if the court is satisfied of any of those facts, it must make a dissolution order unless it is satisfied on all the evidence that the civil partnership has not broken down irretrievably.

(5) The facts referred to in subsections (3) and (4) are—
(a) that the respondent has behaved in such a way that the applicant cannot reasonably be expected to live with the respondent;
(b) that—
(i) the applicant and the respondent have lived apart for a continuous period of at least 2 years immediately preceding the making of the application ("2 years' separation"), and
(ii) the respondent consents to a dissolution order being made;
(c) that the applicant and the respondent have lived apart for a continuous period of at least 5 years immediately preceding the making of the application ("5 years' separation");
(d) that the respondent has deserted the applicant for a continuous period of at least 2 years immediately preceding the making of the application.

45 SUPPLEMENTAL PROVISIONS AS TO FACTS RAISING PRESUMPTION OF BREAKDOWN

(1) Subsection (2) applies if—
  (a) in any proceedings for a dissolution order the applicant alleges, in reliance on section 44(5)(a), that the respondent has behaved in such a way that the applicant cannot reasonably be expected to live with the respondent, but
  (b) after the date of the occurrence of the final incident relied on by the applicant and held by the court to support his allegation, the applicant and the respondent have lived together for a period (or periods) which does not, or which taken together do not, exceed 6 months.

(2) The fact that the applicant and respondent have lived together as mentioned in subsection (1)(b) must be disregarded in determining, for the purposes of section 44(5)(a), whether the applicant cannot reasonably be expected to live with the respondent.

(3) Subsection (4) applies in relation to cases where the applicant alleges, in reliance on section 44(5)(b), that the respondent consents to a dissolution order being made.

(4) Rules of court must make provision for the purpose of ensuring that the respondent has been given such information as will enable him to understand—
  (a) the consequences to him of consenting to the making of the order, and
  (b) the steps which he must take to indicate his consent.

(5) For the purposes of section 44(5)(d) the court may treat a period of desertion as having continued at a time when the deserting civil partner was incapable of continuing the necessary intention, if the evidence before the court is such that, had he not been so incapable, the court would have inferred that the desertion continued at that time.

(6) In considering for the purposes of section 44(5) whether the period for which the civil partners have lived apart or the period for which the respondent has deserted the applicant has been continuous, no account is to be taken of—
  (a) any one period not exceeding 6 months, or
  (b) any two or more periods not exceeding 6 months in all, during which the civil partners resumed living with each other.

(7) But no period during which the civil partners have lived with each other counts as part of the period during which the civil partners have lived apart or as part of the period of desertion.

(8) For the purposes of section 44(5)(b) and (c) and this section civil partners are to be treated as living apart unless they are living with each other in the same household, and references in this section to civil partners living with each other are to be read as references to their living with each other in the same household.

46 DISSOLUTION ORDER NOT PRECLUDED BY PREVIOUS SEPARATION ORDER ETC

(1) Subsections (2) and (3) apply if any of the following orders has been made in relation to a civil partnership—
  (a) a separation order;
  (b) an order under Schedule 6 (financial relief in magistrates' courts etc);
  (c) an order under section 33 of the Family Law Act 1996 (c 27) (occupation orders);
  (d) an order under section 37 of the 1996 Act (orders where neither civil partner entitled to occupy the home).

(2) Nothing prevents—
(a) either civil partner from applying for a dissolution order, or
(b) the court from making a dissolution order,
on the same facts, or substantially the same facts, as those proved in support of the making of the order referred to in subsection (1).

(3) On the application for the dissolution order, the court—
(a) may treat the order referred to in subsection (1) as sufficient proof of any desertion or other fact by reference to which it was made, but
(b) must not make the dissolution order without receiving evidence from the applicant.

(4) If—
(a) the application for the dissolution order follows a separation order or any order requiring the civil partners to live apart,
(b) there was a period of desertion immediately preceding the institution of the proceedings for the separation order, and
(c) the civil partners have not resumed living together and the separation order has been continuously in force since it was made,
the period of desertion is to be treated for the purposes of the application for the dissolution order as if it had immediately preceded the making of the application.

(5) For the purposes of section 44(5)(d) the court may treat as a period during which the respondent has deserted the applicant any period during which there is in force—
(a) an injunction granted by the High Court or a county court which excludes the respondent from the civil partnership home, or
(b) an order under section 33 or 37 of the 1996 Act which prohibits the respondent from occupying a dwelling-house in which the applicant and the respondent have, or at any time have had, a civil partnership home.

47 REFUSAL OF DISSOLUTION IN 5 YEAR SEPARATION CASES ON GROUND OF GRAVE HARDSHIP

(1) The respondent to an application for a dissolution order in which the applicant alleges 5 years' separation may oppose the making of an order on the ground that—
(a) the dissolution of the civil partnership will result in grave financial or other hardship to him, and
(b) it would in all the circumstances be wrong to dissolve the civil partnership.

(2) Subsection (3) applies if—
(a) the making of a dissolution order is opposed under this section,
(b) the court finds that the applicant is entitled to rely in support of his application on the fact of 5 years' separation and makes no such finding as to any other fact mentioned in section 44(5), and
(c) apart from this section, the court would make a dissolution order.

(3) The court must—
(a) consider all the circumstances, including the conduct of the civil partners and the interests of the civil partners and of any children or other persons concerned, and
(b) if it is of the opinion that the ground mentioned in subsection (1) is made out, dismiss the application for the dissolution order.

(4) "Hardship" includes the loss of the chance of acquiring any benefit which the respondent might acquire if the civil partnership were not dissolved.

48 PROCEEDINGS BEFORE ORDER MADE FINAL: PROTECTION FOR RESPONDENT IN SEPARATION CASES

(1) The court may, on an application made by the respondent, rescind a conditional dissolution order if—
- (a) it made the order on the basis of a finding that the applicant was entitled to rely on the fact of 2 years' separation coupled with the respondent's consent to a dissolution order being made,
- (b) it made no such finding as to any other fact mentioned in section 44(5), and
- (c) it is satisfied that the applicant misled the respondent (whether intentionally or unintentionally) about any matter which the respondent took into account in deciding to give his consent.

(2) Subsections (3) to (5) apply if—
- (a) the respondent to an application for a dissolution order in which the applicant alleged—
  - (i) 2 years' separation coupled with the respondent's consent to a dissolution order being made, or
  - (ii) 5 years' separation, has applied to the court for consideration under subsection (3) of his financial position after the dissolution of the civil partnership, and
- (b) the court—
  - (i) has made a conditional dissolution order on the basis of a finding that the applicant was entitled to rely in support of his application on the fact of 2 years' or 5 years' separation, and
  - (ii) has made no such finding as to any other fact mentioned in section 44(5).

(3) The court hearing an application by the respondent under subsection (2) must consider all the circumstances, including—
- (a) the age, health, conduct, earning capacity, financial resources and financial obligations of each of the parties, and
- (b) the financial position of the respondent as, having regard to the dissolution, it is likely to be after the death of the applicant should the applicant die first.

(4) Subject to subsection (5), the court must not make the order final unless it is satisfied that—
- (a) the applicant should not be required to make any financial provision for the respondent, or
- (b) the financial provision made by the applicant for the respondent is—
  - (i) reasonable and fair, or
  - (ii) the best that can be made in the circumstances.

(5) The court may if it thinks fit make the order final if—
- (a) it appears that there are circumstances making it desirable that the order should be made final without delay, and
- (b) it has obtained a satisfactory undertaking from the applicant that he will make such financial provision for the respondent as it may approve.

Nullity

49 GROUNDS ON WHICH CIVIL PARTNERSHIP IS VOID

Where two people register as civil partners of each other in England and Wales, the civil partnership is void if—
- (a) at the time when they do so, they are not eligible to register as civil partners of each other under Chapter 1 (see section 3),

(b) at the time when they do so they both know—
  (i) that due notice of proposed civil partnership has not been given,
  (ii) that the civil partnership document has not been duly issued,
  (iii) that the civil partnership document is void under section 17(3) or 27(2) (registration after end of time allowed for registering),
  (iv) that the place of registration is a place other than that specified in the notices (or notice) of proposed civil partnership and the civil partnership document,
  (v) that a civil partnership registrar is not present, or
  (vi) that the place of registration is on premises that are not approved premises although the registration is purportedly in accordance with section 6(3A)(a), or

(c) the civil partnership document is void under paragraph 6(5) of Schedule 2 (civil partnership between child and another person forbidden).

50 GROUNDS ON WHICH CIVIL PARTNERSHIP IS VOIDABLE

(1) Where two people register as civil partners of each other in England and Wales, the civil partnership is voidable if—
  (a) either of them did not validly consent to its formation (whether as a result of duress, mistake, unsoundness of mind or otherwise);
  (b) at the time of its formation either of them, though capable of giving a valid consent, was suffering (whether continuously or intermittently) from mental disorder of such a kind or to such an extent as to be unfitted for civil partnership;
  (c) at the time of its formation, the respondent was pregnant by some person other than the applicant;
  (d) an interim gender recognition certificate under the Gender Recognition Act 2004 (c 7) has, after the time of its formation, been issued to either civil partner;
  (e) the respondent is a person whose gender at the time of its formation had become the acquired gender under the 2004 Act.

(2) In this section and section 51 "mental disorder" has the same meaning as in the Mental Health Act 1983 (c 20).

51 BARS TO RELIEF WHERE CIVIL PARTNERSHIP IS VOIDABLE

(1) The court must not make a nullity order on the ground that a civil partnership is voidable if the respondent satisfies the court—
  (a) that the applicant, with knowledge that it was open to him to obtain a nullity order, conducted himself in relation to the respondent in such a way as to lead the respondent reasonably to believe that he would not seek to do so, and
  (b) that it would be unjust to the respondent to make the order.

(2) Without prejudice to subsection (1), the court must not make a nullity order by virtue of section 50(1)(a), (b), (c) or (e) unless—
  (a) it is satisfied that proceedings were instituted within 3 years from the date of the formation of the civil partnership, or
  (b) leave for the institution of proceedings after the end of that 3 year period has been granted under subsection (3).

(3) A judge of the court may, on an application made to him, grant leave for the institution of proceedings if he—
  (a) is satisfied that the applicant has at some time during the 3 year period suffered from mental disorder, and

(b) considers that in all the circumstances of the case it would be just to grant leave for the institution of proceedings.

(4) An application for leave under subsection (3) may be made after the end of the 3 year period.

(5) Without prejudice to subsection (1), the court must not make a nullity order by virtue of section 50(1)(d) unless it is satisfied that proceedings were instituted within the period of 6 months from the date of issue of the interim gender recognition certificate.

(6) Without prejudice to subsections (1) and (2), the court must not make a nullity order by virtue of section 50(1)(c) or (e) unless it is satisfied that the applicant was at the time of the formation of the civil partnership ignorant of the facts alleged.

52 PROOF OF CERTAIN MATTERS NOT NECESSARY TO VALIDITY OF CIVIL PARTNERSHIP

(1) Where two people have registered as civil partners of each other in England and Wales, it is not necessary in support of the civil partnership to give any proof—
(a) that any person whose consent to the civil partnership was required by section 4 (parental etc consent) had given his consent, or
(aa) that before the registration either of the civil partners resided, or resided for any period, in the area stated in the notices of proposed civil partnership to be the area of that person's place of residence;
and no evidence is to be given to prove the contrary in any proceedings touching the validity of the civil partnership.

(2) Subsection (1)(a) is subject to section 49(c) (civil partnership void if forbidden).

53 POWER TO VALIDATE CIVIL PARTNERSHIP

(1) Where two people have registered as civil partners of each other in England and Wales, the Lord Chancellor may by order validate the civil partnership if it appears to him that it is or may be void under section 49(b).

(2) An order under subsection (1) may include provisions for relieving a person from any liability under section 31(2), 32(2) or 33(5) or (7).

(3) The draft of an order under subsection (1) must be advertised, in such manner as the Lord Chancellor thinks fit, not less than one month before the order is made.

(4) The Lord Chancellor must—
(a) consider all objections to the order sent to him in writing during that month, and
(b) if it appears to him necessary, direct a local inquiry into the validity of any such objections.

(5) An order under subsection (1) is subject to special parliamentary procedure.

54 VALIDITY OF CIVIL PARTNERSHIPS REGISTERED OUTSIDE ENGLAND AND WALES

(1) Where two people register as civil partners of each other in Scotland, the civil partnership is—
(a) void, if it would be void in Scotland under section 123, and
(b) voidable, if the circumstances fall within section 50(1)(d).

(2) Where two people register as civil partners of each other in Northern Ireland, the civil partnership is—
(a) void, if it would be void in Northern Ireland under section 173, and
(b) voidable, if the circumstances fall within any paragraph of section 50(1).

(3) Subsection (4) applies where two people register as civil partners of each other under an Order in Council under—
(a) section 210 (registration at British consulates etc), or
(b) section 211 (registration by armed forces personnel),
("the relevant section").

(4) The civil partnership is—
(a) void, if—
(i) the condition in subsection (2)(a) or (b) of the relevant section is not met, or
(ii) a requirement prescribed for the purposes of this paragraph by an Order in Council under the relevant section is not complied with, and
(b) voidable, if—
(i) the appropriate part of the United Kingdom is England and Wales or Northern Ireland and the circumstances fall within any paragraph of section 50(1), or
(ii) the appropriate part of the United Kingdom is Scotland and the circumstances fall within section 50(1)(d).

(5) The appropriate part of the United Kingdom is the part by reference to which the condition in subsection (2)(b) of the relevant section is met.

(6) Subsections (7) and (8) apply where two people have registered an apparent or alleged overseas relationship.

(7) The civil partnership is void if—
(a) the relationship is not an overseas relationship, or
(b) (even though the relationship is an overseas relationship) the parties are not treated under Chapter 2 of Part 5 as having formed a civil partnership.

(8) The civil partnership is voidable if—
(a) the overseas relationship is voidable under the relevant law,
(b) the circumstances fall within section 50(1)(d), or
(c) where either of the parties was domiciled in England and Wales or Northern Ireland at the time when the overseas relationship was registered, the circumstances fall within section 50(1)(a), (b), (c) or (e).

(9) Section 51 applies for the purposes of—
(a) subsections (1)(b), (2)(b) and (4)(b),
(b) subsection (8)(a), in so far as applicable in accordance with the relevant law, and
(c) subsection (8)(b) and (c).

(10) In subsections (8)(a) and (9)(b) "the relevant law" means the law of the country or territory where the overseas relationship was registered (including its rules of private international law).

(11) For the purposes of subsections (8) and (9)(b) and (c), references in sections 50 and 51 to the formation of the civil partnership are to be read as references to the registration of the overseas relationship.

Presumption of death orders

55 PRESUMPTION OF DEATH ORDERS

(1) The court may, on an application made by a civil partner, make a presumption of death order if it is satisfied that reasonable grounds exist for supposing that the other civil partner is dead.

(2) In any proceedings under this section the fact that—
   (a) for a period of 7 years or more the other civil partner has been continually absent from the applicant, and
   (b) the applicant has no reason to believe that the other civil partner has been living within that time,

   is evidence that the other civil partner is dead until the contrary is proved.

Separation orders

56 SEPARATION ORDERS

(1) An application for a separation order may be made to the court by either civil partner on the ground that any such fact as is mentioned in section 44(5)(a), (b), (c) or (d) exists.

(2) On an application for a separation order the court must inquire, so far as it reasonably can, into—
   (a) the facts alleged by the applicant, and
   (b) any facts alleged by the respondent, but whether the civil partnership has broken down irretrievably is irrelevant.

(3) If the court is satisfied on the evidence of any such fact as is mentioned in section 44(5)(a), (b), (c) or (d) it must, subject to section 63, make a separation order.

(4) Section 45 (supplemental provisions as to facts raising presumption of breakdown) applies for the purposes of an application for a separation order alleging any such fact as it applies in relation to an application for a dissolution order alleging that fact.

57 EFFECT OF SEPARATION ORDER

If either civil partner dies intestate as respects all or any of his or her real or personal property while—

(a) a separation order is in force, and

(b) the separation is continuing,

the property as respects which he or she died intestate devolves as if the other civil partner had then been dead.

Declarations

58 DECLARATIONS

(1) Any person may apply to the High Court or a county court for one or more of the following declarations in relation to a civil partnership specified in the application—
   (a) a declaration that the civil partnership was at its inception a valid civil partnership;
   (b) a declaration that the civil partnership subsisted on a date specified in the application;
   (c) a declaration that the civil partnership did not subsist on a date so specified;

(d) a declaration that the validity of a dissolution, annulment or legal separation obtained outside England and Wales in respect of the civil partnership is entitled to recognition in England and Wales;
(e) a declaration that the validity of a dissolution, annulment or legal separation so obtained in respect of the civil partnership is not entitled to recognition in England and Wales.

(2) Where an application under subsection (1) is made to a court by a person other than a civil partner in the civil partnership to which the application relates, the court must refuse to hear the application if it considers that the applicant does not have a sufficient interest in the determination of that application.

59 GENERAL PROVISIONS AS TO MAKING AND EFFECT OF DECLARATIONS

(1) Where on an application for a declaration under section 58 the truth of the proposition to be declared is proved to the satisfaction of the court, the court must make the declaration unless to do so would be manifestly contrary to public policy.

(2) Any declaration under section 58 binds Her Majesty and all other persons.

(3) The court, on the dismissal of an application for a declaration under section 58, may not make any declaration for which an application has not been made.

(4) No declaration which may be applied for under section 58 may be made otherwise than under section 58 by any court.

(5) No declaration may be made by any court, whether under section 58 or otherwise, that a civil partnership was at its inception void.

(6) Nothing in this section affects the powers of any court to make a nullity order in respect of a civil partnership.

. . .

General provisions

62 RELIEF FOR RESPONDENT IN DISSOLUTION PROCEEDINGS

(1) If in any proceedings for a dissolution order the respondent alleges and proves any such fact as is mentioned in section 44(5)(a), (b), (c) or (d) the court may give to the respondent the relief to which he would have been entitled if he had made an application seeking that relief.

(2) When applying subsection (1), treat—
(a) the respondent as the applicant, and
(b) the applicant as the respondent,
for the purposes of section 44(5).

63 RESTRICTIONS ON MAKING OF ORDERS AFFECTING CHILDREN

(1) In any proceedings for a dissolution, nullity or separation order, the court must consider—
(a) whether there are any children of the family to whom this section applies, and
(b) if there are any such children, whether (in the light of the arrangements which have been, or are proposed to be, made for their upbringing and welfare) it should exercise any of its powers under the Children Act 1989 (c 41) with respect to any of them.

(2) If, in the case of any child to whom this section applies, it appears to the court that—
(a) the circumstances of the case require it, or are likely to require it, to exercise any of its powers under the 1989 Act with respect to any such child,
(b) it is not in a position to exercise the power or (as the case may be) those powers without giving further consideration to the case, and
(c) there are exceptional circumstances which make it desirable in the interests of the child that the court should give a direction under this section,
it may direct that the order is not to be made final, or (in the case of a separation order) is not to be made, until the court orders otherwise.

(3) This section applies to—
(a) any child of the family who has not reached 16 at the date when the court considers the case in accordance with the requirements of this section, and
(b) any child of the family who has reached 16 at that date and in relation to whom the court directs that this section shall apply.

64 PARTIES TO PROCEEDINGS UNDER THIS CHAPTER

(1) Rules of court may make provision with respect to—
(a) the joinder as parties to proceedings under sections 37 to 56 of persons involved in allegations of improper conduct made in those proceedings,
(b) the dismissal from such proceedings of any parties so joined, and
(c) the persons who are to be parties to proceedings on an application under section 58.

(2) Rules of court made under this section may make different provision for different cases.

(3) In every case in which the court considers, in the interest of a person not already a party to the proceedings, that the person should be made a party, the court may if it thinks fit allow the person to intervene upon such terms, if any, as the court thinks just.

Chapter 3 PROPERTY AND FINANCIAL ARRANGEMENTS

65 CONTRIBUTION BY CIVIL PARTNER TO PROPERTY IMPROVEMENT

(1) This section applies if—
(a) a civil partner contributes in money or money's worth to the improvement of real or personal property in which or in the proceeds of sale of which either or both of the civil partners has or have a beneficial interest, and
(b) the contribution is of a substantial nature.

(2) The contributing partner is to be treated as having acquired by virtue of the contribution a share or an enlarged share (as the case may be) in the beneficial interest of such an extent—
(a) as may have been then agreed, or
(b) in default of such agreement, as may seem in all the circumstances just to any court before which the question of the existence or extent of the beneficial interest of either of the civil partners arises (whether in proceedings between them or in any other proceedings).

(3) Subsection (2) is subject to any agreement (express or implied) between the civil partners to the contrary.

66 DISPUTES BETWEEN CIVIL PARTNERS ABOUT PROPERTY

(1) In any question between the civil partners in a civil partnership as to title to or possession of property, either civil partner may apply to—
(a) the High Court, or
(b) such county court as may be prescribed by rules of court.

(2) On such an application, the court may make such order with respect to the property as it thinks fit (including an order for the sale of the property).

(3) Rules of court made for the purposes of this section may confer jurisdiction on county courts whatever the situation or value of the property in dispute.

67 APPLICATIONS UNDER SECTION 66 WHERE PROPERTY NOT IN POSSESSION ETC

(1) The right of a civil partner ("A") to make an application under section 66 includes the right to make such an application where A claims that the other civil partner ("B") has had in his possession or under his control—
(a) money to which, or to a share of which, A was beneficially entitled, or
(b) property (other than money) to which, or to an interest in which, A was beneficially entitled, and that either the money or other property has ceased to be in B's possession or under B's control or that A does not know whether it is still in B's possession or under B's control.

(2) For the purposes of subsection (1)(a) it does not matter whether A is beneficially entitled to the money or share—
(a) because it represents the proceeds of property to which, or to an interest in which, A was beneficially entitled, or
(b) for any other reason.

(3) Subsections (4) and (5) apply if, on such an application being made, the court is satisfied that B—
(a) has had in his possession or under his control money or other property as mentioned in subsection (1)(a) or (b), and
(b) has not made to A, in respect of that money or other property, such payment or disposition as would have been appropriate in the circumstances.

(4) The power of the court to make orders under section 66 includes power to order B to pay to A—
(a) in a case falling within subsection (1)(a), such sum in respect of the money to which the application relates, or A's s share of it, as the court considers appropriate, or
(b) in a case falling within subsection (1)(b), such sum in respect of the value of the property to which the application relates, or A's interest in it, as the court considers appropriate.

(5) If it appears to the court that there is any property which—
(a) represents the whole or part of the money or property, and
(b) is property in respect of which an order could (apart from this section) have been made under section 66,

the court may (either instead of or as well as making an order in accordance with subsection (4)) make any order which it could (apart from this section) have made under section 66.

(6) Any power of the court which is exercisable on an application under section 66 is exercisable in relation to an application made under that section as extended by this section.

68 APPLICATIONS UNDER SECTION 66 BY FORMER CIVIL PARTNERS

(1) This section applies where a civil partnership has been dissolved or annulled.

(2) Subject to subsection (3), an application may be made under section 66 (including that section as extended by section 67) by either former civil partner despite the dissolution or annulment (and references in those sections to a civil partner are to be read accordingly).

(3) The application must be made within the period of 3 years beginning with the date of the dissolution or annulment.

69 ACTIONS IN TORT BETWEEN CIVIL PARTNERS

(1) This section applies if an action in tort is brought by one civil partner against the other during the subsistence of the civil partnership.

(2) The court may stay the proceedings if it appears—
  (a) that no substantial benefit would accrue to either civil partner from the continuation of the proceedings, or
  (b) that the question or questions in issue could more conveniently be disposed of on an application under section 66.

(3) Without prejudice to subsection (2)(b), the court may in such an action—
  (a) exercise any power which could be exercised on an application under section 66, or
  (b) give such directions as it thinks fit for the disposal under that section of any question arising in the proceedings.

70 ASSURANCE POLICY BY CIVIL PARTNER FOR BENEFIT OF OTHER CIVIL PARTNER ETC

Section 11 of the Married Women's Property Act 1882 (c 75) (money payable under policy of assurance not to form part of the estate of the insured) applies in relation to a policy of assurance—
(a) effected by a civil partner on his own life, and
(b) expressed to be for the benefit of his civil partner, or of his children, or of his civil partner and children, or any of them, as it applies in relation to a policy of assurance effected by a husband and expressed to be for the benefit of his wife, or of his children, or of his wife and children, or of any of them.

71 WILLS, ADMINISTRATION OF ESTATES AND FAMILY PROVISION

Schedule 4 amends enactments relating to wills, administration of estates and family provision so that they apply in relation to civil partnerships as they apply in relation to marriage.

72 FINANCIAL RELIEF FOR CIVIL PARTNERS AND CHILDREN OF FAMILY

(1) Schedule 5 makes provision for financial relief in connection with civil partnerships that corresponds to provision made for financial relief in connection with marriages by Part 2 of the Matrimonial Causes Act 1973 (c 18).

(2) Any rule of law under which any provision of Part 2 of the 1973 Act is interpreted as applying to dissolution of a marriage on the ground of presumed death is to be treated as applying (with any necessary modifications) in relation to the corresponding provision of Schedule 5.

(3) Schedule 6 makes provision for financial relief in connection with civil partnerships that corresponds to provision made for financial relief in connection with marriages by the Domestic Proceedings and Magistrates' Courts Act 1978 (c 22).

(4) Schedule 7 makes provision for financial relief in England and Wales after a civil partnership has been dissolved or annulled, or civil partners have been legally separated, in a country outside the British Islands.

Chapter 4 CIVIL PARTNERSHIP AGREEMENTS

73 CIVIL PARTNERSHIP AGREEMENTS UNENFORCEABLE

(1) A civil partnership agreement does not under the law of England and Wales have effect as a contract giving rise to legal rights.

(2) No action lies in England and Wales for breach of a civil partnership agreement, whatever the law applicable to the agreement.

(3) In this section and section 74 "civil partnership agreement" means an agreement between two people—
- (a) to register as civil partners of each other—
  - (i) in England and Wales (under this Part),
  - (ii) in Scotland (under Part 3),
  - (iii) in Northern Ireland (under Part 4), or
  - (iv) outside the United Kingdom under an Order in Council made under Chapter 1 of Part 5 (registration at British consulates etc or by armed forces personnel), or
- (b) to enter into an overseas relationship.

(4) This section applies in relation to civil partnership agreements whether entered into before or after this section comes into force, but does not affect any action commenced before it comes into force.

74 PROPERTY WHERE CIVIL PARTNERSHIP AGREEMENT IS TERMINATED

(1) This section applies if a civil partnership agreement is terminated.

(2) Section 65 (contributions by civil partner to property improvement) applies, in relation to any property in which either or both of the parties to the agreement had a beneficial interest while the agreement was in force, as it applies in relation to property in which a civil partner has a beneficial interest.

(3) Sections 66 and 67 (disputes between civil partners about property) apply to any dispute between or claim by one of the parties in relation to property in which either or both had a beneficial interest while the agreement was in force, as if the parties were civil partners of each other.

(4) An application made under section 66 or 67 by virtue of subsection (3) must be made within 3 years of the termination of the agreement.

(5) A party to a civil partnership agreement who makes a gift of property to the other party on the condition (express or implied) that it is to be returned if the agreement is terminated is not prevented from recovering the property merely because of his having terminated the agreement.

. . .

Chapter 6 MISCELLANEOUS

82 FAMILY HOMES AND DOMESTIC VIOLENCE

Schedule 9 amends Part 4 of the Family Law Act 1996 (c 27) and related enactments so that they apply in relation to civil partnerships as they apply in relation to marriages.

. . .

84 EVIDENCE

(1) Any enactment or rule of law relating to the giving of evidence by a spouse applies in relation to a civil partner as it applies in relation to the spouse.

(2) Subsection (1) is subject to any specific amendment made by or under this Act which relates to the giving of evidence by a civil partner.

(3) For the avoidance of doubt, in any such amendment, references to a person's civil partner do not include a former civil partner.

(4) References in subsections (1) and (2) to giving evidence are to giving evidence in any way (whether by supplying information, making discovery, producing documents or otherwise).

(5) Any rule of law—
  (a) which is preserved by section 7(3) of the Civil Evidence Act 1995 (c 38) or section 118(1) of the Criminal Justice Act 2003 (c 44), and
  (b) under which in any proceedings evidence of reputation or family tradition is admissible for the purpose of proving or disproving the existence of a marriage,

is to be treated as applying in an equivalent way for the purpose of proving or disproving the existence of a civil partnership.

. . .

Part 6 RELATIONSHIPS ARISING THROUGH CIVIL PARTNERSHIP

246 INTERPRETATION OF STATUTORY REFERENCES TO STEPCHILDREN ETC

(1) In any provision to which this section applies, references to a stepchild or step-parent of a person (here, "A"), and cognate expressions, are to be read as follows—

A's stepchild includes a person who is the child of A's civil partner (but is not A's child);

A's step-parent includes a person who is the civil partner of A's parent (but is not A's parent);

A's stepdaughter includes a person who is the daughter of A's civil partner (but is not A's daughter);

A's stepson includes a person who is the son of A's civil partner (but is not A's son);

A's stepfather includes a person who is the civil partner of A's father (but is not A's parent);

A's stepmother includes a person who is the civil partner of A's mother (but is not A's parent);

A's stepbrother includes a person who is the son of the civil partner of A's parent (but is not the son of either of A's parents);

A's stepsister includes a person who is the daughter of the civil partner of A's parent (but is not the daughter of either of A's parents).

(2) For the purposes of any provision to which this section applies—

"brother-in-law" includes civil partner's brother,

"daughter-in-law" includes daughter's civil partner,

"father-in-law" includes civil partner's father,

"mother-in-law" includes civil partner's mother,

"parent-in-law" includes civil partner's parent,

"sister-in-law" includes civil partner's sister, and

"son-in-law" includes son's civil partner.

247 PROVISIONS TO WHICH SECTION 246 APPLIES: ACTS OF PARLIAMENT ETC

(1) Section 246 applies to—
- (a) any provision listed in Schedule 21 (references to stepchildren, in-laws etc in existing Acts),
- (b) except in so far as otherwise provided, any provision made by a future Act, and
- (c) except in so far as otherwise provided, any provision made by future subordinate legislation.

(2) A Minister of the Crown may by order—
- (a) amend Schedule 21 by adding to it any provision of an existing Act;
- (b) provide for section 246 to apply to prescribed provisions of existing subordinate legislation.

(3) The power conferred by subsection (2) is also exercisable—

. . .

- (c) by the National Assembly for Wales, if the order is made by virtue of subsection (2)(b) and deals with matters with respect to which functions are exercisable by the Assembly.

. . .

253 CIVIL PARTNERS TO HAVE UNLIMITED INSURABLE INTEREST IN EACH OTHER

(1) Where two people are civil partners, each of them is to be presumed for the purposes of section 1 of the Life Assurance Act 1774 (c 48) to have an interest in the life of the other.

(2) For the purposes of section 3 of the 1774 Act, there is no limit on the amount of value of the interest.

. . .

SCHEDULE 1 PROHIBITED DEGREES OF RELATIONSHIP: ENGLAND AND WALES

Sections 3(2) and 5(3)

Part 1 THE PROHIBITIONS

Absolute prohibitions

1. (1) Two people are within prohibited degrees of relationship if one falls within the list below in relation to the other.

Adoptive child
Adoptive parent
Child
Former adoptive child
Former adoptive parent
Grandparent
Grandchild
Parent
Parent's sibling
Sibling
Sibling's child

(2) In the list "sibling" means a brother, sister, half-brother or half-sister.

Qualified prohibitions

2. (1) Two people are within prohibited degrees of relationship if one of them falls within the list below in relation to the other, unless—

(a) both of them have reached 21 at the time when they register as civil partners of each other, and

(b) the younger has not at any time before reaching 18 been a child of the family in relation to the other.

Child of former civil partner
Child of former spouse
Former civil partner of grandparent
Former civil partner of parent
Former spouse of grandparent
Former spouse of parent
Grandchild of former civil partner
Grandchild of former spouse

(2) "Child of the family", in relation to another person, means a person who—

(a) has lived in the same household as that other person, and

(b) has been treated by that other person as a child of his family.

. . .

SCHEDULE 5 FINANCIAL RELIEF IN THE HIGH COURT OR A COUNTY COURT ETC

Section 72(1)

Part 1 FINANCIAL PROVISION IN CONNECTION WITH DISSOLUTION, NULLITY OR SEPARATION

Circumstances in which orders under this Part may be made

1. (1) The court may make any one or more of the orders set out in paragraph 2(1)—
   (a) on making a dissolution, nullity or separation order, or
   (b) at any time afterwards.

(2) The court may make any one or more of the orders set out in paragraph 2(1)(d), (e) and (f)—
   (a) in proceedings for a dissolution, nullity or separation order, before making the order;
   (b) if proceedings for a dissolution, nullity or separation order are dismissed after the beginning of the trial, either straightaway or within a reasonable period after the dismissal.

(3) The power of the court to make an order under sub-paragraph (1) or (2)(a) in favour of a child of the family is exercisable from time to time.

(4) If the court makes an order in favour of a child under sub-paragraph (2)(b), it may from time to time make a further order in the child's favour of any of the kinds set out in paragraph 2(1)(d), (e) or (f).

The orders: periodical and secured periodical payments and lump sums

2. (1) The orders are—
   (a) an order that either civil partner must make to the other such periodical payments for such term as may be specified;
   (b) an order that either civil partner must secure to the other, to the satisfaction of the court, such periodical payments for such term as may be specified;
   (c) an order that either civil partner must pay to the other such lump sum or sums as may be specified;
   (d) an order that one of the civil partners must make—
      (i) to such person as may be specified for the benefit of a child of the family, or
      (ii) to a child of the family, such periodical payments for such term as may be specified;
   (e) an order that one of the civil partners must secure—
      (i) to such person as may be specified for the benefit of a child of the family, or
      (ii) to a child of the family, to the satisfaction of the court, such periodical
   payments for such term as may be specified;
   (f) an order that one of the civil partners must pay such lump sum as may be specified—
      (i) to such person as may be specified for the benefit of a child of the family, or
      (ii) to a child of the family.

(2) "Specified" means specified in the order.

Particular provision that may be made by lump sum orders

3. (1) An order under this Part requiring one civil partner to pay the other a lump sum may be made for the purpose of enabling the other civil partner to meet any liabilities or expenses reasonably incurred by the other in maintaining—

(a) himself or herself, or
(b) a child of the family, before making an application for an order under this Part in his or her favour.

(2) An order under this Part requiring a lump sum to be paid to or for the benefit of a child of the family may be made for the purpose of enabling any liabilities or expenses reasonably incurred by or for the benefit of the child before making an application for an order under this Part to be met.

(3) An order under this Part for the payment of a lump sum may—
(a) provide for its payment by instalments of such amount as may be specified, and
(b) require the payment of the instalments to be secured to the satisfaction of the court.

(4) Sub-paragraphs (1) to (3) do not restrict the powers to make the orders set out in paragraph 2(1)(c) and (f).

(5) If the court—
(a) makes an order under this Part for the payment of a lump sum, and
(b) directs that—
(i) payment of the sum or any part of it is to be deferred, or
(ii) the sum or any part of it is to be paid by instalments,
it may provide for the deferred amount or the instalments to carry interest at such rate as may be specified from such date as may be specified until the date when payment of it is due.

(6) A date specified under sub-paragraph (5) must not be earlier than the date of the order.

(7) "Specified" means specified in the order.

When orders under this Part may take effect

4. (1) If an order is made under paragraph 2(1)(a), (b) or (c) on or after making a dissolution or nullity order, neither the order nor any settlement made in pursuance of it takes effect unless the dissolution or nullity order has been made final.

(2) This paragraph does not affect the power of the court to give a direction under paragraph 76 (settlement of instrument by conveyancing counsel).

Restrictions on making of orders under this Part

5. The power to make an order under paragraph 2(1)(d), (e) or (f) is subject to paragraph 49(1) and (5) (restrictions on orders in favour of children who have reached 18).

Part 2 PROPERTY ADJUSTMENT ON OR AFTER DISSOLUTION, NULLITY OR SEPARATION

Circumstances in which property adjustment orders may be made

6. (1) The court may make one or more property adjustment orders—
(a) on making a dissolution, nullity or separation order, or
(b) at any time afterwards.

(2) In this Schedule "property adjustment order" means a property adjustment order under this Part.

Property adjustment orders

7. (1) The property adjustment orders are—
(a) an order that one of the civil partners must transfer such property as may be specified, being property to which he is entitled—

(i) to the other civil partner,
(ii) to a child of the family, or
(iii) to such person as may be specified for the benefit of a child of the family;

(b) an order that a settlement of such property as may be specified, being property to which one of the civil partners is entitled, be made to the satisfaction of the court for the benefit of—
(i) the other civil partner and the children of the family, or
(ii) either or any of them;

(c) an order varying for the benefit of—
(i) the civil partners and the children of the family, or
(ii) either or any of them, a relevant settlement;

(d) an order extinguishing or reducing the interest of either of the civil partners under a relevant settlement.

(2) The court may make a property adjustment order under sub-paragraph (1)(c) even though there are no children of the family.

(3) In this paragraph—

"entitled" means entitled in possession or reversion,

"relevant settlement" means, in relation to a civil partnership, a settlement made, during its subsistence or in anticipation of its formation, on the civil partners including one made by will or codicil, but not including one in the form of a pension arrangement (within the meaning of Part 4), and

"specified" means specified in the order.

When property adjustment orders may take effect

8. (1) If a property adjustment order is made on or after making a dissolution or nullity order, neither the property adjustment order nor any settlement made under it takes effect unless the dissolution or nullity order has been made final.

(2) This paragraph does not affect the power to give a direction under paragraph 76 (settlement of instrument by conveyancing counsel).

Restrictions on making property adjustment orders

9. The power to make a property adjustment order under paragraph 7(1)(a) is subject to paragraph 49(1) and (5) (restrictions on making orders in favour of children who have reached 18).

Part 3 SALE OF PROPERTY ORDERS

Circumstances in which sale of property orders may be made

10. (1) The court may make a sale of property order—

(a) on making—
(i) under Part 1, a secured periodical payments order or an order for the payment of a lump sum, or
(ii) a property adjustment order, or

(b) at any time afterwards.

(2) In this Schedule "sale of property order" means a sale of property order under this Part.

Sale of property orders

11. (1) A sale of property order is an order for the sale of such property as may be specified, being property in which, or in the proceeds of sale of which, either or both of the civil partners has or have a beneficial interest, either in possession or reversion.

(2) A sale of property order may contain such consequential or supplementary provisions as the court thinks fit.

(3) A sale of property order may in particular include—
(a) provision requiring the making of a payment out of the proceeds of sale of the property to which the order relates, and
(b) provision requiring any property to which the order relates to be offered for sale to a specified person, or class of persons.

(4) "Specified" means specified in the order.

When sale of property orders may take effect

12. (1) If a sale of property order is made on or after the making of a dissolution or nullity order, it does not take effect unless the dissolution or nullity order has been made final.

(2) Where a sale of property order is made, the court may direct that—
(a) the order, or
(b) such provision of it as the court may specify,
is not to take effect until the occurrence of an event specified by the court or the end of a period so specified.

When sale of property orders cease to have effect

13. If a sale of property order contains a provision requiring the proceeds of sale of the property to which the order relates to be used to secure periodical payments to a civil partner, the order ceases to have effect—
(a) on the death of the civil partner, or
(b) on the formation of a subsequent civil partnership or marriage by the civil partner.

Protection of third parties

14. (1) Sub-paragraphs (2) and (3) apply if—
(a) a civil partner has a beneficial interest in any property, or in the proceeds of sale of any property, and
(b) another person ("A") who is not the other civil partner also has a beneficial interest in the property or the proceeds.

(2) Before deciding whether to make a sale of property order in relation to the property, the court must give A an opportunity to make representations with respect to the order.

(3) Any representations made by A are included among the circumstances to which the court is required to have regard under paragraph 20.

Part 4 PENSION SHARING ORDERS ON OR AFTER DISSOLUTION OR NULLITY ORDER

Circumstances in which pension sharing orders may be made

15. (1) The court may make a pension sharing order—
(a) on making a dissolution or nullity order, or
(b) at any time afterwards.

(2) In this Schedule "pension sharing order" means a pension sharing order under this Part.

Pension sharing orders

16. (1) A pension sharing order is an order which—

(a) provides that one civil partner's—

(i) shareable rights under a specified pension arrangement, or

(ii) shareable state scheme rights, are to be subject to pension sharing for the benefit of the other civil partner, and

(b) specifies the percentage value to be transferred.

(2) Shareable rights under a pension arrangement are rights in relation to which pension sharing is available under—

(a) Chapter 1 of Part 4 of the Welfare Reform and Pensions Act 1999 (c 30), or

(b) corresponding Northern Ireland legislation.

(3) Shareable state scheme rights are rights in relation to which pension sharing is available under—

(a) Chapter 2 of Part 4 of the 1999 Act, or

(b) corresponding Northern Ireland legislation.

(4) In this Part "pension arrangement" means—

(a) an occupational pension scheme,

(b) a personal pension scheme,

(c) a retirement annuity contract,

(d) an annuity or insurance policy purchased, or transferred, for the purpose of giving effect to rights under—

(i) an occupational pension scheme, or

(ii) a personal pension scheme, and

(e) an annuity purchased, or entered into, for the purpose of discharging liability in respect of a pension credit under—

(i) section 29(1)(b) of the 1999 Act, or

(ii) corresponding Northern Ireland legislation.

(5) In sub-paragraph (4)—

"occupational pension scheme" has the same meaning as in the Pension Schemes Act 1993 (c 48);

"personal pension scheme" has the same meaning as in the 1993 Act;

"retirement annuity contract" means a contract or scheme approved under Chapter 3 of Part 14 of the Income and Corporation Taxes Act 1988 (c 1).

Pension sharing orders: apportionment of charges

17. If a pension sharing order relates to rights under a pension arrangement, the court may include in the order provision about the apportionment between the civil partners of any charge under—

(a) section 41 of the 1999 Act (charges in respect of pension sharing costs), or

(b) corresponding Northern Ireland legislation.

Restrictions on making of pension sharing orders

18. (1) A pension sharing order may not be made in relation to a pension arrangement which—

(a) is the subject of a pension sharing order in relation to the civil partnership, or

(b) has been the subject of pension sharing between the civil partners.

(2) A pension sharing order may not be made in relation to shareable state scheme rights if—
(a) such rights are the subject of a pension sharing order in relation to the civil partnership, or
(b) such rights have been the subject of pension sharing between the civil partners.

(3) A pension sharing order may not be made in relation to the rights of a person under a pension arrangement if there is in force a requirement imposed by virtue of Part 6 which relates to benefits or future benefits to which that person is entitled under the pension arrangement.

When pension sharing orders may take effect

19. (1) A pension sharing order is not to take effect unless the dissolution or nullity order on or after which it is made has been made final.

(2) No pension sharing order may be made so as to take effect before the end of such period after the making of the order as may be prescribed by regulations made by the Lord Chancellor.

(3) The power to make regulations under sub-paragraph (2) is exercisable by statutory instrument which is subject to annulment in pursuance of a resolution of either House of Parliament.

Part 4A PENSION COMPENSATION SHARING ORDERS ON OR AFTER DISSOLUTION OR NULLITY ORDER

Circumstances in which pension compensation sharing orders may be made

19A (1) The court may make a pension compensation sharing order—
(a) on making a dissolution or nullity order, or
(b) at any time afterwards.

(2) In this Schedule "pension compensation sharing order" means a pension compensation sharing order under this Part.

Pension compensation sharing orders

19B (1) A pension compensation sharing order is an order which—
(a) provides that one civil partner's shareable rights to PPF compensation that derive from rights under a specified pension scheme are to be subject to pension compensation sharing for the benefit of the other civil partner, and
(b) specifies the percentage value to be transferred.

(2) Shareable rights to PPF compensation are rights in relation to which pension compensation sharing is available under—
(a) Chapter 1 of Part 3 of the Pensions Act 2008 . . .

(3) In sub-paragraph (1) "specified" means specified in the order.

Pension compensation sharing orders: apportionment of charges

19C The court may include in a pension compensation sharing order provision about the apportionment between the civil partners of any charge under—
(a) section 117 of the Pensions Act 2008 (charges in respect of pension compensation sharing costs) . . .

Restrictions on making pension compensation sharing orders

19D (1) A pension compensation sharing order may not be made in relation to rights to PPF compensation that—

(a) are the subject of pension attachment,
(b) derive from rights under a pension scheme that were the subject of pension sharing between the civil partners,
(c) are the subject of pension compensation attachment, or
(d) are or have been the subject of pension compensation sharing between the civil partners.

(2) For the purposes of sub-paragraph (1)(a), rights to PPF compensation "are the subject of pension attachment" if any of the following three conditions is met.

(3) The first condition is that—
(a) the rights derive from rights under a pension scheme in relation to which an order was made under Part 1 imposing a requirement by virtue of paragraph 25(2), and
(b) that order, as modified under paragraph 31, remains in force.

(4) The second condition is that—
(a) the rights derive from rights under a pension scheme in relation to which an order was made under Part 1 imposing a requirement by virtue of paragraph 25(5), and
(b) that order—
(i) has been complied with, or
(ii) has not been complied with and, as modified under paragraph 32, remains in force.

(5) The third condition is that—
(a) the rights derive from rights under a pension scheme in relation to which an order was made under Part 1 imposing a requirement by virtue of paragraph 26, and
(b) that order remains in force.

(6) For the purposes of sub-paragraph (1)(b), rights under a pension scheme "were the subject of pension sharing between the civil partners" if the rights were at any time the subject of a pension sharing order in relation to the civil partnership or a previous civil partnership between the same parties.

(7) For the purposes of sub-paragraph (1)(c), rights to PPF compensation "are the subject of pension compensation attachment" if there is in force a requirement imposed by virtue of Part 6 relating to them.

(8) For the purposes of sub-paragraph (1)(d), rights to PPF compensation "are or have been the subject of pension compensation sharing between the civil partners" if they are or have ever been the subject of a pension compensation sharing order in relation to the civil partnership or a previous civil partnership between the same parties.

When pension compensation sharing orders may take effect

19E (1) A pension compensation sharing order is not to take effect unless the dissolution or nullity order on or after which it is made has been made final.

(2) No pension compensation sharing order may be made so as to take effect before the end of such period after the making of the order as may be prescribed by regulations made by the Lord Chancellor.

(3) The power to make regulations under sub-paragraph (2) is exercisable by statutory instrument which is subject to annulment in pursuance of a resolution of either House of Parliament.

Interpretation

19F In this Schedule—

"PPF compensation" means compensation payable under the pension compensation provisions;

"the pension compensation provisions" means—

(a) Chapter 3 of Part 2 of the Pensions Act 2004 (pension protection) and any regulations or order made under it,

(b) Chapter 1 of Part 3 of the Pensions Act 2008 (pension compensation sharing) and any regulations or order made under it . . .

Part 5 MATTERS TO WHICH COURT IS TO HAVE REGARD UNDER PARTS 1 TO 4A

General

20. The court in deciding—

(a) whether to exercise its powers under—

(i) Part 1 (financial provision on dissolution etc),

(ii) Part 2 (property adjustment orders),

(iii) Part 3 (sale of property orders), or

(iv) any provision of Part 4 (pension sharing orders) other than paragraph 17 (apportionment of charges), or

(v) any provision of Part 4A (pension compensation sharing orders) other than paragraph 19C (apportionment of charges), and

(b) if so, in what way, must have regard to all the circumstances of the case, giving first consideration to the welfare, while under 18, of any child of the family who has not reached 18.

Particular matters to be taken into account when exercising powers in relation to civil partners

21. (1) This paragraph applies to the exercise by the court in relation to a civil partner of its powers under—

(a) Part 1 (financial provision on dissolution etc) by virtue of paragraph 2(1)(a), (b) or (c),

(b) Part 2 (property adjustment orders),

(c) Part 3 (sale of property orders),

(d) Part 4 (pension sharing orders), or

(e) Part 4A (pension compensation sharing orders).

(2) The court must in particular have regard to—

(a) the income, earning capacity, property and other financial resources which each civil partner—

(i) has, or

(ii) is likely to have in the foreseeable future, including, in the case of earning capacity, any increase in that capacity which it would in the opinion of the court be reasonable to expect a civil partner in the civil partnership to take steps to acquire;

(b) the financial needs, obligations and responsibilities which each civil partner has or is likely to have in the foreseeable future;

(c) the standard of living enjoyed by the family before the breakdown of the civil partnership;

(d) the age of each civil partner and the duration of the civil partnership;

(e) any physical or mental disability of either of the civil partners;

(f) the contributions which each civil partner has made or is likely in the foreseeable future to make to the welfare of the family, including any contribution by looking after the home or caring for the family;
(g) the conduct of each civil partner, if that conduct is such that it would in the opinion of the court be inequitable to disregard it;
(h) in the case of proceedings for a dissolution or nullity order, the value to each civil partner of any benefit which, because of the dissolution or annulment of the civil partnership, that civil partner will lose the chance of acquiring.

Particular matters to be taken into account when exercising powers in relation to children

22. (1) This paragraph applies to the exercise by the court in relation to a child of the family of its powers under—
(a) Part 1 (financial provision on dissolution etc) by virtue of paragraph 2(1)(d), (e) or (f)),
(b) Part 2 (property adjustment orders), or
(c) Part 3 (sale of property orders).

(2) The court must in particular have regard to—
(a) the financial needs of the child;
(b) the income, earning capacity (if any), property and other financial resources of the child;
(c) any physical or mental disability of the child;
(d) the way in which the child was being and in which the civil partners expected the child to be educated or trained;
(e) the considerations mentioned in relation to the civil partners in paragraph 21(2)(a), (b), (c) and (e).

(3) In relation to the exercise of any of those powers against a civil partner ("A") in favour of a child of the family who is not A's child, the court must also have regard to—
(a) whether A has assumed any responsibility for the child's maintenance;
(b) if so, the extent to which, and the basis upon which, A assumed such responsibility and the length of time for which A discharged such responsibility;
(c) whether in assuming and discharging such responsibility A did so knowing that the child was not A's child;
(d) the liability of any other person to maintain the child.

Terminating financial obligations

23. (1) Sub-paragraphs (2) and (3) apply if, on or after the making of a dissolution or nullity order, the court decides to exercise its powers under—
(a) Part 1 (financial provision on dissolution etc) by virtue of paragraph 2(1)(a), (b) or (c),
(b) Part 2 (property adjustment orders),
(c) Part 3 (sale of property orders), or
(d) Part 4 (pension sharing orders), or
(e) Part 4A (pension compensation sharing orders),
in favour of one of the civil partners.

(2) The court must consider whether it would be appropriate to exercise those powers in such a way that the financial obligations of each civil partner towards the other will be terminated as soon after the making of the dissolution or nullity order as the court considers just and reasonable.
(3) If the court decides to make—

(a) a periodical payments order, or
(b) a secured periodical payments order,
in favour of one of the civil partners ("A"), it must in particular consider whether it would be appropriate to require the payments to be made or secured only for such term as would in its opinion be sufficient to enable A to adjust without undue hardship to the termination of A's financial dependence on the other civil partner.

(4) If—
(a) on or after the making of a dissolution or nullity order, an application is made by one of the civil partners for a periodical payments or secured periodical payments order in that civil partner's favour, but
(b) the court considers that no continuing obligation should be imposed on either civil partner to make or secure periodical payments in favour of the other,

the court may dismiss the application with a direction that the applicant is not entitled to make any future application in relation to that civil partnership for an order under Part 1 by virtue of paragraph 2(1)(a) or (b).

Part 6 MAKING OF PART 1 ORDERS HAVING REGARD TO PENSION BENEFITS

Pension benefits to be included in matters to which court is to have regard

24. (1) The matters to which the court is to have regard under paragraph 21(2)(a) include any pension benefits under a pension arrangement or by way of pension which a civil partner has or is likely to have; and, accordingly, in relation to any pension benefits paragraph 21(2)(a)(ii) has effect as if "in the foreseeable future" were omitted.

(2) The matters to which the court is to have regard under paragraph 21(2)(h) include any pension benefits which, because of the making of a dissolution or nullity order, a civil partner will lose the chance of acquiring.

(3) "Pension benefits" means—
(a) benefits under a pension arrangement, or
(b) benefits by way of pension (whether under a pension arrangement or not).

Provisions applying where pension benefits taken into account in decision to make Part 1 order

25. (1) This paragraph applies if, having regard to any benefits under a pension arrangement, the court decides to make an order under Part 1.

(2) To the extent to which the Part 1 order is made having regard to any benefits under a pension arrangement, it may require the person responsible for the pension arrangement, if at any time any payment in respect of any benefits under the arrangement becomes due to the civil partner with pension rights, to make a payment for the benefit of the other civil partner.

(3) The Part 1 order must express the amount of any payment required to be made by virtue of sub-paragraph (2) as a percentage of the payment which becomes due to the civil partner with pension rights.

(4) Any such payment by the person responsible for the arrangement—
(a) discharges so much of his liability to the civil partner with pension rights as corresponds to the amount of the payment, and
(b) is to be treated for all purposes as a payment made by the civil partner with pension rights in or towards the discharge of that civil partner's liability under the order.

(5) If the civil partner with pension rights has a right of commutation under the arrangement, the Part 1 order may require that civil partner to exercise it to any extent.

(6) This paragraph applies to any payment due in consequence of commutation in pursuance of the Part 1 order as it applies to other payments in respect of benefits under the arrangement.

(7) The power conferred by sub-paragraph (5) may not be exercised for the purpose of commuting a benefit payable to the civil partner with pension rights to a benefit payable to the other civil partner.

(8) The powers conferred by sub-paragraphs (2) and (5) may not be exercised in relation to a pension arrangement which—
(a) is the subject of a pension sharing order in relation to the civil partnership, or
(b) has been the subject of pension sharing between the civil partners.

Pensions: lump sums

26. (1) This paragraph applies if the benefits which the civil partner with pension rights has or is likely to have under a pension arrangement include any lump sum payable in respect of that civil partner's death.

(2) The court's power under Part 1 to order a civil partner to pay a lump sum to the other civil partner includes the power to make by the order any provision in sub-paragraph (3) to (5).

(3) If the person responsible for the pension arrangement has power to determine the person to whom the sum, or any part of it, is to be paid, the court may require him to pay the whole or part of that sum, when it becomes due, to the other civil partner.

(4) If the civil partner with pension rights has power to nominate the person to whom the sum, or any part of it, is to be paid, the court may require the civil partner with pension rights to nominate the other civil partner in respect of the whole or part of that sum.

(5) In any other case, the court may require the person responsible for the pension arrangement in question to pay the whole or part of that sum, when it becomes due, for the benefit of the other civil partner instead of to the person to whom, apart from the order, it would be paid.

(6) Any payment by the person responsible for the arrangement under an order made under Part 1 made by virtue of this paragraph discharges so much of his liability in respect of the civil partner with pension rights as corresponds to the amount of the payment.

(7) The powers conferred by this paragraph may not be exercised in relation to a pension arrangement which—
(a) is the subject of a pension sharing order in relation to the civil partnership, or
(b) has been the subject of pension sharing between the civil partners.

Pensions: supplementary

27. If—
(a) a Part 1 order made by virtue of paragraph 25 or 26 imposes any requirement on the person responsible for a pension arrangement ("the first arrangement"),

(b) the civil partner with pension rights acquires rights under another pension arrangement ("the new arrangement") which are derived (directly or indirectly) from the whole of that civil partner's rights under the first arrangement, and

(c) the person responsible for the new arrangement has been given notice in accordance with regulations made by the Lord Chancellor,

the Part 1 order has effect as if it had been made instead in respect of the person responsible for the new arrangement.

Regulations

28. (1) The Lord Chancellor may by regulations—

(a) make provision, in relation to any provision of paragraph 25 or 26 which authorises the court making a Part 1 order to require the person responsible for a pension arrangement to make a payment for the benefit of the other civil partner, as to—

(i) the person to whom, and

(ii) the terms on which, the payment is to be made;

(b) make provision, in relation to payment under a mistaken belief as to the continuation in force of a provision included by virtue of paragraph 25 or 26 in a Part 1 order, about the rights or liabilities of the payer, the payee or the person to whom the payment was due;

(c) require notices to be given in respect of changes of circumstances relevant to Part 1 orders which include provision made by virtue of paragraphs 25 and 26;

(d) make provision for the person responsible for a pension arrangement to be discharged in prescribed circumstances from a requirement imposed by virtue of paragraph 25 or 26;

(e) make provision about calculation and verification in relation to the valuation of—

(i) benefits under a pension arrangement, or

(ii) shareable state scheme rights (within the meaning of paragraph 16(3)), for the purposes of the court's functions in connection with the exercise of any of its powers under this Schedule.

(2) Regulations under sub-paragraph (1)(e) may include—

(a) provision for calculation or verification in accordance with guidance from time to time prepared by a prescribed person, and

(b) provision by reference to regulations under section 30 or 49(4) of the 1999 Act.

(3) The power to make regulations under paragraph 27 or this paragraph is exercisable by statutory instrument which is subject to annulment in pursuance of a resolution of either House of Parliament.

(4) "Prescribed" means prescribed by regulations.

Interpretation of provisions relating to pensions

29. (1) In this Part "the civil partner with pension rights" means the civil partner who has or is likely to have benefits under a pension arrangement.

(2) In this Part "pension arrangement" has the same meaning as in Part 4.

(3) In this Part, references to the person responsible for a pension arrangement are to be read in accordance with section 26 of the Welfare Reform and Pensions Act 1999 (c 30).

Part 7 PENSION PROTECTION FUND COMPENSATION ETC

PPF compensation to be included in matters to which court is to have regard

30. (1) The matters to which a court is to have regard under paragraph 21(2)(a) include any PPF compensation to which a civil partner is or is likely to be entitled; and, accordingly, in relation to any PPF compensation paragraph 21(2)(a)(ii) has effect as if "in the foreseeable future" were omitted.

(2) The matters to which a court is to have regard under paragraph 21(2)(h) include any PPF compensation which, because of the making of a dissolution or nullity order, a civil partner will lose the chance of acquiring entitlement to.

Assumption of responsibility by PPF Board in paragraph 25(2) cases

31. (1) This paragraph applies to an order under Part 1 so far as it includes provision made by virtue of paragraph 25(2) which—

(a) imposed requirements on the trustees or managers of an occupational pension scheme for which the Board has assumed responsibility, and

(b) was made before the trustees or managers received the transfer notice.

(2) From the time the trustees or managers of the scheme receive the transfer notice, the order has effect—

(a) except in descriptions of case prescribed by regulations, with the modifications set out in sub-paragraph (3), and

(b) with such other modifications as may be prescribed by regulations.

(3) The modifications are that—

(a) references in the order to the trustees or managers of the scheme have effect as references to the Board, and

(b) references in the order to any pension or lump sum to which the civil partner with pension rights is or may become entitled under the scheme have effect as references to any PPF compensation to which that person is or may become entitled in respect of the pension or lump sum.

Assumption of responsibility by PPF Board in paragraph 25(5) cases

32. (1) This paragraph applies to an order under Part 1 if—

(a) it includes provision made by virtue of paragraph 25(5) which requires the civil partner with pension rights to exercise his right of commutation under an occupational pension scheme to any extent, and

(b) before the requirement is complied with the Board has assumed responsibility for the scheme.

(2) From the time the trustees or managers of the scheme receive the transfer notice, the order has effect with such modifications as may be prescribed by regulations.

Lump sums: power to modify paragraph 26 in respect of assessment period

33. Regulations may modify paragraph 26 in its application to an occupational pension scheme during an assessment period in relation to the scheme.

Assumption of responsibility by the Board not to affect power of court to vary order etc

34. (1) This paragraph applies where the court makes, in relation to an occupational pension scheme—

(a) a pension sharing order, or

(b) an order including provision made by virtue of paragraph 25(2) or (5).

(2) If the Board subsequently assumes responsibility for the scheme, that does not affect—

(a) the powers of the court under paragraph 51 to vary or discharge the order or to suspend or revive any provision of it;
(b) on an appeal, the powers of the appeal court to affirm, reinstate, set aside or vary the order.

. . .

Interpretation

37. (1) In this Part—

"assessment period" means—

(a) an assessment period within the meaning of Part 2 of the Pensions Act 2004 (pension protection),. . .

"the Board" means the Board of the Pension Protection Fund;

"the civil partner with compensation rights" means the civil partner who is or is likely to be entitled to PPF compensation;

"the civil partner with pension rights" has the meaning given by paragraph 29(1);

"occupational pension scheme" has the same meaning as in the Pension Schemes Act 1993 (c 48);

"prescribed" means prescribed by regulations;

"transfer notice" has the same meaning as in—

(a) Chapter 3 of Part 2 of the 2004 Act, or
(b) corresponding Northern Ireland legislation.

(2) References in this Part to the Board assuming responsibility for a scheme are to the Board assuming responsibility for the scheme in accordance with—

(a) Chapter 3 of Part 2 of the 2004 Act (pension protection), or
(b) corresponding Northern Ireland legislation.

Part 8 MAINTENANCE PENDING OUTCOME OF DISSOLUTION, NULLITY OR SEPARATION PROCEEDINGS

38. On an application for a dissolution, nullity or separation order, the court may make an order requiring either civil partner to make to the other for the other's maintenance such periodical payments for such term—

(a) beginning no earlier than the date on which the application was made, and
(b) ending with the date on which the proceedings are determined, as the court thinks reasonable.

Part 9 FAILURE TO MAINTAIN: FINANCIAL PROVISION (AND INTERIM ORDERS)

Circumstances in which orders under this Part may be made

39. (1) Either civil partner in a subsisting civil partnership may apply to the court for an order under this Part on the ground that the other civil partner ("the respondent")—

(a) has failed to provide reasonable maintenance for the applicant, or
(b) has failed to provide, or to make a proper contribution towards, reasonable maintenance for any child of the family.

(2) The court must not entertain an application under this paragraph unless—

(a) the applicant or the respondent is domiciled in England and Wales on the date of the application,

(b) the applicant has been habitually resident there throughout the period of 1 year ending with that date, or
(c) the respondent is resident there on that date.

(3) If, on an application under this paragraph, it appears to the court that—
(a) the applicant or any child of the family to whom the application relates is in immediate need of financial assistance, but
(b) it is not yet possible to determine what order, if any, should be made on the application,
the court may make an interim order.

(4) If, on an application under this paragraph, the applicant satisfies the court of a ground mentioned in sub-paragraph (1), the court may make one or more of the orders set out in paragraph 41.

Interim orders

40. An interim order is an order requiring the respondent to make to the applicant, until the determination of the application, such periodical payments as the court thinks reasonable.

Orders that may be made where failure to maintain established

41. (1) The orders are—
(a) an order that the respondent must make to the applicant such periodical payments for such term as may be specified;
(b) an order that the respondent must secure to the applicant, to the satisfaction of the court, such periodical payments for such term as may be specified;
(c) an order that the respondent must pay to the applicant such lump sum as may be specified;
(d) an order that the respondent must make such periodical payments for such term as may be specified—
(i) to such person as may be specified, for the benefit of the child to whom the application relates, or
(ii) to the child to whom the application relates;
(e) an order that the respondent must secure—
(i) to such person as may be specified for the benefit of the child to whom the application relates, or
(ii) to the child to whom the application relates, to the satisfaction of the court, such periodical payments for such term as may be specified;
(f) an order that the respondent must pay such lump sum as may be specified—
(i) to such person as may be specified for the benefit of the child to whom the application relates, or
(ii) to the child to whom the application relates.

(2) In this Part “specified” means specified in the order.

Particular provision that may be made by lump sum orders

42. (1) An order under this Part for the payment of a lump sum may be made for the purpose of enabling any liabilities or expenses reasonably incurred in maintaining the applicant or any child of the family to whom the application relates before the making of the application to be met.

(2) An order under this Part for the payment of a lump sum may—
(a) provide for its payment by instalments of such amount as may be specified, and

(b) require the payment of the instalments to be secured to the satisfaction of the court.

(3) Sub-paragraphs (1) and (2) do not restrict the power to make an order by virtue of paragraph 41(1)(c) or (f).

Matters to which the court is to have regard on application under paragraph 39(1)(a)

43. (1) This paragraph applies if an application under paragraph 39 is made on the ground mentioned in paragraph 39(1)(a).

(2) In deciding—

(a) whether the respondent has failed to provide reasonable maintenance for the applicant, and

(b) what order, if any, to make under this Part in favour of the applicant,

the court must have regard to all the circumstances of the case including the matters mentioned in paragraph 21(2).

(3) If an application is also made under paragraph 39 in respect of a child of the family who has not reached 18, the court must give first consideration to the welfare of the child while under 18.

(4) Paragraph 21(2)(c) has effect as if for the reference in it to the breakdown of the civil partnership there were substituted a reference to the failure to provide reasonable maintenance for the applicant.

Matters to which the court is to have regard on application under paragraph 39(1)(b)

44. (1) This paragraph applies if an application under paragraph 39 is made on the ground mentioned in paragraph 39(1)(b).

(2) In deciding—

(a) whether the respondent has failed to provide, or to make a proper contribution towards, reasonable maintenance for the child of the family to whom the application relates, and

(b) what order, if any, to make under this Part in favour of the child, the court must have regard to all the circumstances of the case.

(3) Those circumstances include—

(a) the matters mentioned in paragraph 22(2)(a) to (e), and

(b) if the child of the family to whom the application relates is not the child of the respondent, the matters mentioned in paragraph 22(3).

(4) Paragraph 21(2)(c) (as it applies by virtue of paragraph 22(2)(e)) has effect as if for the reference in it to the breakdown of the civil partnership there were substituted a reference to—

(a) the failure to provide, or

(b) the failure to make a proper contribution towards, reasonable maintenance for the child of the family to whom the application relates.

Restrictions on making orders under this Part

45. The power to make an order under paragraph 41(1)(d), (e) or (f) is subject to paragraph 49(1) and

(5) (restrictions on orders in favour of children who have reached 18).

Part 10 COMMENCEMENT OF CERTAIN PROCEEDINGS AND DURATION OF CERTAIN ORDERS

Commencement of proceedings for ancillary relief, etc

46. (1) Sub-paragraph (2) applies if an application for a dissolution, nullity or separation order has been made.

(2) Subject to sub-paragraph (3), proceedings for—
(a) an order under Part 1 (financial provision on dissolution etc),
(b) a property adjustment order, or
(c) an order under Part 8 (maintenance pending outcome of dissolution, nullity or separation proceedings), may be begun (subject to and in accordance with rules of court) at any time after the presentation of the application.

(3) Rules of court may provide, in such cases as may be prescribed by the rules, that—
(a) an application for any such relief as is mentioned in sub-paragraph (2) must be made in the application or response, and
(b) an application for any such relief which—
(i) is not so made, or
(ii) is not made until after the end of such period following the presentation of the application or filing of the response as may be so prescribed, may be made only with the leave of the court.

Duration of periodical and secured periodical payments orders for a civil partner

47. (1) The court may specify in a periodical payments or secured periodical payments order in favour of a civil partner such term as it thinks fit, except that the term must not—
(a) begin before the date of the making of an application for the order, or
(b) extend beyond the limits given in sub-paragraphs (2) and (3).

(2) The limits in the case of a periodical payments order are—
(a) the death of either civil partner;
(b) where the order is made on or after the making of a dissolution or nullity order, the formation of a subsequent civil partnership or marriage by the civil partner in whose favour the order is made.

(3) The limits in the case of a secured periodical payments order are—
(a) the death of the civil partner in whose favour the order is made;
(b) where the order is made on or after the making of a dissolution or nullity order, the formation of a subsequent civil partnership or marriage by the civil partner in whose favour the order is made.

(4) In the case of an order made on or after the making of a dissolution or nullity order, subparagraphs (1) to (3) are subject to paragraphs 23(3) and 59(4).

(5) If a periodical payments or secured periodical payments order in favour of a civil partner is made on or after the making of a dissolution or nullity order, the court may direct that that civil partner is not entitled to apply under paragraph 51 for the extension of the term specified in the order.

(6) If—
(a) a periodical payments or secured periodical payments order in favour of a civil partner is made otherwise than on or after the making of a dissolution or nullity order, and
(b) the civil partnership is subsequently dissolved or annulled but the order continues in force, the order ceases to have effect (regardless of anything in it) on the formation of a subsequent civil partnership or marriage by that civil partner, except in relation to any arrears due under it on the date of its formation.

Subsequent civil partnership or marriage

48. If after the making of a dissolution or nullity order one of the civil partners forms a subsequent civil partnership or marriage, that civil partner is not entitled to apply, by reference to the dissolution or nullity order, for—

(a) an order under Part 1 in that civil partner's favour, or

(b) a property adjustment order, against the other civil partner in the dissolved or annulled civil partnership.

Duration of continuing orders in favour of children, and age limit on making certain orders in their favour

49. (1) Subject to sub-paragraph (5)—

(a) no order under Part 1,

(b) no property adjustment order made by virtue of paragraph 7(1)(a) (transfer of property), and

(c) no order made under Part 9 (failure to maintain) by virtue of paragraph 41, is to be made in favour of a child who has reached 18.

(2) The term to be specified in a periodical payments or secured periodical payments order in favour of a child may begin with—

(a) the date of the making of an application for the order or a later date, or

(b) a date ascertained in accordance with sub-paragraph (7) or (8).

(3) The term to be specified in such an order—

(a) must not in the first instance extend beyond the date of the birthday of the child next following the child's reaching the upper limit of the compulsory school age unless the court considers that in the circumstances of the case the welfare of the child requires that it should extend to a later date, and

(b) must not in any event, subject to sub-paragraph (5), extend beyond the date of the child's 18th birthday.

(4) Sub-paragraph (3)(a) must be read with section 8 of the Education Act 1996 (c 56) (which applies to determine for the purposes of any enactment whether a person is of compulsory school age).

(5) Sub-paragraphs (1) and (3)(b) do not apply in the case of a child if it appears to the court that—

(a) the child is, or will be, or, if an order were made without complying with either or both of those provisions, would be—

(i) receiving instruction at an educational establishment, or

(ii) undergoing training for a trade, profession or vocation, whether or not the child also is, will be or would be in gainful employment, or

(b) there are special circumstances which justify the making of an order without complying with either or both of sub-paragraphs (1) and (3)(b).

(6) A periodical payments order in favour of a child, regardless of anything in the order, ceases to have effect on the death of the person liable to make payments under the order, except in relation to any arrears due under the order on the date of the death.

(7) If—

(a) a maintenance calculation ("the current calculation") is in force with respect to a child, and

(b) an application is made under this Schedule for a periodical payments or secured periodical payments order in favour of that child—

(i) in accordance with section 8 of the Child Support Act 1991 (c 48), and
(ii) before the end of 6 months beginning with the making of the current calculation, the term to be specified in any such order made on that application may be expressed to begin on, or at any time after, the earliest permitted date.

(8) "The earliest permitted date" is whichever is the later of—
(a) the date 6 months before the application is made, or
(b) the date on which the current calculation took effect or, where successive maintenance calculations have been continuously in force with respect to a child, on which the first of those calculations took effect.

(9) If—
(a) a maintenance calculation ceases to have effect by or under any provision of the 1991 Act, and
(b) an application is made, before the end of 6 months beginning with the relevant date, for a periodical payments or secured periodical payments order in favour of a child with respect to whom that maintenance calculation was in force immediately before it ceased to have effect, the term to be specified in any such order made on that application may begin with the date on which that maintenance calculation ceased to have effect or any later date.

(10) "The relevant date" means the date on which the maintenance calculation ceased to have effect.

(11) In this paragraph "maintenance calculation" has the same meaning as it has in the 1991 Act by virtue of section 54 of the 1991 Act as read with any regulations in force under that section.

Part 11 VARIATION, DISCHARGE ETC OF CERTAIN ORDERS FOR FINANCIAL RELIEF

Orders etc to which this Part applies

50. (1) This Part applies to the following orders—
(a) a periodical payments order under Part 1 (financial provision on dissolution etc) or Part 9 (failure to maintain);
(b) a secured periodical payments order under Part 1 or 9;
(c) an order under Part 8 (maintenance pending outcome of dissolution proceedings etc);
(d) an interim order under Part 9;
(e) an order made under Part 1 by virtue of paragraph 3(3) or under Part 9 by virtue of paragraph 42(2) (lump sum by instalments);
(f) a deferred order made under Part 1 by virtue of paragraph 2(1)(c) (lump sum for civil partner) which includes provision made by virtue of—
(i) paragraph 25(2),
(ii) paragraph 26, or
(iii) paragraph 34A(2),
(provision in respect of pension rights or pension compensation rights);
(g) a property adjustment order made on or after the making of a separation order by virtue of paragraph 7(1)(b), (c) or (d) (order for settlement or variation of settlement);
(h) a sale of property order;
(i) a pension sharing order, or a pension compensation sharing order, made before the dissolution or nullity order has been made final.

(2) If the court has made an order referred to in sub-paragraph (1)(f)(ii), this Part ceases to apply to the order on the death of either of the civil partners.

(3) The powers exercisable by the court under this Part in relation to an order are also exercisable in relation to any instrument executed in pursuance of the order.

Powers to vary, discharge, suspend or revive order

51. (1) If the court has made an order to which this Part applies, it may—
   (a) vary or discharge the order,
   (b) suspend any provision of it temporarily, or
   (c) revive the operation of any provision so suspended.

(2) Sub-paragraph (1) is subject to the provisions of this Part and paragraph 47(5).

Power to remit arrears

52. (1) If the court has made an order referred to in paragraph 50(1)(a), (b), (c) or (d), it may remit the payment of any arrears due under the order or under any part of the order.

(2) Sub-paragraph (1) is subject to the provisions of this Part.

Additional powers on discharging or varying a periodical or secured periodical payments order after dissolution of civil partnership

53. (1) Sub-paragraph (2) applies if, after the dissolution of a civil partnership, the court—
   (a) discharges a periodical payments order or secured periodical payments order made in favour of a civil partner, or
   (b) varies such an order so that payments under the order are required to be made or secured only for such further period as is determined by the court.

(2) The court may make supplemental provision consisting of any of the following—
   (a) an order for the payment of a lump sum in favour of one of the civil partners;
   (b) one or more property adjustment orders in favour of one of the civil partners;
   (c) one or more pension sharing orders;
   (ca) a pension compensation sharing order;
   (d) a direction that the civil partner in whose favour the original order discharged or varied was made is not entitled to make any further application for—
      (i) a periodical payments or secured periodical payments order, or
      (ii) an extension of the period to which the original order is limited by any variation made by the court.

(3) The power under sub-paragraph (2) is in addition to any power the court has apart from that sub-paragraph.

54. (1) An order for the payment of a lump sum under paragraph 53 may—
   (a) provide for the payment of it by instalments of such amount as may be specified, and
   (b) require the payment of the instalments to be secured to the satisfaction of the court.

(2) Sub-paragraphs (5) and (6) of paragraph 3 (interest on deferred instalments) apply where the court makes an order for the payment of a lump sum under paragraph 53 as they apply where it makes such an order under Part 1.

(3) If under paragraph 53 the court makes more than one property adjustment order in favour of the same civil partner, each of those orders must fall within a different paragraph of paragraph 7(1) (types of property adjustment orders).

(4) Part 3 (orders for the sale of property) and paragraph 76 (direction for settlement of instrument) apply where the court makes a property adjustment order under paragraph 53 as they apply where it makes any other property adjustment order.

(5) Paragraph 18 (restrictions on making of pension sharing order) applies in relation to a pension sharing order under paragraph 53 as it applies in relation to any other pension sharing order

(6) Paragraph 19D (restrictions on making pension compensation sharing orders) applies in relation to a pension compensation sharing order under paragraph 53 as it applies in relation to any other pension compensation sharing order.

Variation etc of periodical or secured periodical payments orders made in cases of failure to maintain

55. (1) An application for the variation under paragraph 51 of a periodical payments order or secured periodical payments order made under Part 9 in favour of a child may, if the child has reached 16, be made by the child himself.

(2) Sub-paragraph (3) applies if a periodical payments order made in favour of a child under Part 9 ceases to have effect—
(a) on the date on which the child reaches 16, or
(b) at any time after that date but before or on the date on which the child reaches 18.

(3) If, on an application made to the court for an order under this sub-paragraph, it appears to the court that—

(a) the child is, will be or, if an order were made under this sub-paragraph, would be—
(i) receiving instruction at an educational establishment, or
(ii) undergoing training for a trade, profession or vocation, whether or not the child also is, will be or would be in gainful employment, or
(b) there are special circumstances which justify the making of an order under this subparagraph,

the court may by order revive the order mentioned in sub-paragraph (2) from such date as it may specify.

(4) A date specified under sub-paragraph (3) must not be earlier than the date of the application under that sub-paragraph.

(5) If under sub-paragraph (3) the court revives an order it may exercise its power under paragraph 51 in relation to the revived order.

Variation etc of property adjustment, pension sharing and pension compensation orders

56. The court must not exercise the powers conferred by this Part in relation to a property adjustment order falling within paragraph 7(1)(b), (c) or (d) (order for settlement or for variation of settlement) except on an application made in proceedings—
(a) for the rescission of the separation order by reference to which the property adjustment order was made, or
(b) for a dissolution order in relation to the civil partnership.

57. (1) In relation to a pension sharing order which is made at a time before the dissolution or nullity order has been made final—
(a) the powers conferred by this Part (by virtue of paragraph 50(1)(i)) may be exercised—
(i) only on an application made before the pension sharing order or pension compensation sharing order has or, but for paragraph (b), would have taken effect, and
(ii) only if, at the time when the application is made, the dissolution or nullity order has not been made final, and
(b) an application made in accordance with paragraph (a) prevents the pension sharing order or pension compensation sharing order from taking effect before the application has been dealt with.

(2) No variation of a pension sharing order or pension compensation sharing order is to be made so as to take effect before the order is made final.

(3) The variation of a pension sharing order or pension compensation sharing order prevents the order taking effect before the end of such period after the making of the variation as may be prescribed by regulations made by the Lord Chancellor.

(4) The power to make regulations under sub-paragraph (3) is exercisable by statutory instrument which is subject to annulment in pursuance of a resolution of either House of Parliament.

58. (1) Sub-paragraphs (2) and (3)—
(a) are subject to paragraphs 53 and 54, and
(b) do not affect any power exercisable by virtue of paragraph 50(e), (f), (g) or (i) or otherwise than by virtue of this Part.

(2) No property adjustment order, pension sharing order or pension compensation sharing order may be made on an application for the variation of a periodical payments or secured periodical payments order made (whether in favour of a civil partner or in favour of a child of the family) under Part 1.

(3) No order for the payment of a lump sum may be made on an application for the variation of a periodical payments or secured periodical payments order in favour of a civil partner (whether made under Part 1 or 9).

Matters to which court is to have regard in exercising powers under this Part

59. (1) In exercising the powers conferred by this Part the court must have regard to all the circumstances of the case, giving first consideration to the welfare, while under 18, of any child of the family who has not reached 18.

(2) The circumstances of the case include, in particular, any change in any of the matters to which the court was required to have regard when making the order to which the application relates.

(3) Sub-paragraph (4) applies in the case of—
(a) a periodical payments order, or
(b) a secured periodical payments order, made on or after the making of a dissolution or nullity order.

(4) The court must consider whether in all the circumstances, and after having regard to any such change, it would be appropriate to vary the order so that payments under the order are required—
(a) to be made, or
(b) to be secured,
only for such further period as will in the opinion of the court be sufficient to enable the civil partner in whose favour the order was made to adjust without undue hardship to the termination of those payments.

(5) In considering what further period will be sufficient, the court must, if the civil partnership has been dissolved, take into account any proposed exercise by it of its powers under paragraph 53.

(6) If the civil partner against whom the order was made has died, the circumstances of the case also include the changed circumstances resulting from that civil partner's death.

Variation of secured periodical payments order where person liable has died

60. (1) This paragraph applies if the person liable to make payments under a secured periodical payments order has died.

(2) Subject to sub-paragraph (3), an application under this Part relating to the order (and to any sale of property order which requires the proceeds of sale of property to be used for securing those payments) may be made by—
(a) the person entitled to payments under the periodical payments order, or
(b) the personal representatives of the deceased person.

(3) No such application may be made without the leave of the court after the end of 6 months from the date on which representation in regard to the estate of that person is first taken out.

(4) The personal representatives of the person who has died are not liable for having distributed any part of the estate of the deceased after the end of the 6 month period on the ground that they ought to have taken into account the possibility that the court might allow an application under this paragraph to be made after that period by the person entitled to payments under the order.

(5) Sub-paragraph (4) does not affect any power to recover any part of the estate so distributed arising by virtue of the making of an order in pursuance of this paragraph.

(6) In considering for the purposes of sub-paragraph (3) the question when representation was first taken out—
(a) a grant limited to settled land or to trust property is to be disregarded, and
(b) a grant limited to real estate or to personal estate is to be disregarded unless a grant limited to the remainder of the estate has previously been made or is made at the same time.

Power to direct when variation etc is to take effect

61. (1) If the court, in exercise of its powers under this Part, decides—
(a) to vary, or
(b) to discharge, a periodical payments or secured periodical payments order, it may direct that the variation or discharge is not to take effect until the end of such period as may be specified in the order.

(2) Sub-paragraph (1) is subject to paragraph 47(1) and (6).

62. (1) If—
(a) a periodical payments or secured periodical payments order in favour of more than one child ("the order") is in force,
(b) the order requires payments specified in it to be made to or for the benefit of more than one child without apportioning those payments between them,
(c) a maintenance calculation ("the calculation") is made with respect to one or more, but not all, of the children with respect to whom those payments are to be made, and
(d) an application is made, before the end of the period of 6 months beginning with the date on which the calculation was made, for the variation or discharge of the order,

the court may, in exercise of its powers under this Part to vary or discharge the order, direct that the variation or discharge is to take effect from the date on which the calculation took effect or any later date.

(2) If—
(a) an order ("the child order") of a kind prescribed for the purposes of section 10(1) of the Child Support Act 1991 (c 48) is affected by a maintenance calculation,
(b) on the date on which the child order became so affected there was in force a periodical payments or secured periodical payments order ("the civil partner's

order") in favour of a civil partner having the care of the child in whose favour the child order was made, and

(c) an application is made, before the end of the period of 6 months beginning with the date on which the maintenance calculation was made, for the civil partner's order to be varied or discharged,

the court may, in exercise of its powers under this Part to vary or discharge the civil partner's order, direct that the variation or discharge is to take effect from the date on which the child order became so affected or any later date.

(3) For the purposes of sub-paragraph (2), an order is affected if it ceases to have effect or is modified by or under section 10 of the 1991 Act.

(4) Sub-paragraphs (1) and (2) do not affect any other power of the court to direct that the variation of discharge of an order under this Part is to take effect from a date earlier than that on which the order for variation or discharge was made.

(5) In this paragraph "maintenance calculation" has the same meaning as it has in the 1991 Act by virtue of section 54 of the 1991 Act as read with any regulations in force under that section.

. . .

Part 13 CONSENT ORDERS AND MAINTENANCE AGREEMENTS

Consent orders for financial relief

66. (1) Regardless of anything in the preceding provisions of this Schedule, on an application for a consent order for financial relief, the court may, unless it has reason to think that there are other circumstances into which it ought to inquire, make an order in the terms agreed on the basis only of such information supplied with the application as is required by rules of court.

(2) Sub-paragraph (1) applies to an application for a consent order varying or discharging an order for financial relief as it applies to an application for an order for financial relief.

(3) In this paragraph—

"consent order", in relation to an application for an order, means an order in the terms applied for to which the respondent agrees;

"order for financial relief" means an order under any of Parts 1, 2, 3, 4 and 9.

Meaning of "maintenance agreement" and "financial arrangements"

67. (1) In this Part "maintenance agreement" means any agreement in writing between the civil partners in a civil partnership which—

(a) is made during the continuance or after the dissolution or annulment of the civil partnership and contains financial arrangements, or

(b) is a separation agreement which contains no financial arrangements but is made in a case where no other agreement in writing between the civil partners contains financial arrangements.

(2) In this Part "financial arrangements" means provisions governing the rights and liabilities towards one another when living separately of the civil partners in a civil partnership (including a civil partnership which has been dissolved or annulled) in respect of—

(a) the making or securing of payments, or

(b) the disposition or use of any property, including such rights and liabilities with respect to the maintenance or education of a child

(whether or not a child of the family).

(3) "Education" includes training.

Validity of maintenance agreements

68. If a maintenance agreement includes a provision purporting to restrict any right to apply to a court for an order containing financial arrangements—

(a) that provision is void, but

(b) any other financial arrangements contained in the agreement—

(i) are not void or unenforceable as a result, and

(ii) unless void or unenforceable for any other reason, are (subject to paragraphs 69 and 73) binding on the parties to the agreement.

Alteration of agreements by court during lives of parties

69. (1) Either party to a maintenance agreement may apply to the court or, subject to subparagraph (6), to a magistrates' court for an order under this paragraph if—

(a) the maintenance agreement is for the time being subsisting, and

(b) each of the parties to the agreement is for the time being domiciled or resident in England and Wales.

(2) The court may make an order under this paragraph if it is satisfied that—

(a) because of a change in the circumstances in the light of which—

(i) any financial arrangements contained in the agreement were made, or

(ii) financial arrangements were omitted from it, the agreement should be altered so as to make different financial arrangements or so as to contain financial arrangements, or

(b) that the agreement does not contain proper financial arrangements with respect to any child of the family.

(3) In sub-paragraph (2)(a) the reference to a change in the circumstances includes a change foreseen by the parties when making the agreement.

(4) An order under this paragraph may make such alterations in the agreement—

(a) by varying or revoking any financial arrangements contained in it, or

(b) by inserting in it financial arrangements for the benefit of one of the parties to the agreement or of a child of the family, as appear to the court to be just having regard to all the circumstances, including, if relevant, the matters mentioned in paragraph 22(3).

(5) The effect of the order is that the agreement is to be treated as if any alteration made by the order had been made by agreement between the partners and for valuable consideration.

(6) The power to make an order under this paragraph is subject to paragraphs 70 and 71.

Restrictions on applications to and orders by magistrates' courts under paragraph 69

70. (1) A magistrates' court must not entertain an application under paragraph 69(1) unless—

(a) both the parties to the agreement are resident in England and Wales, and

(b) the court acts in, or is authorised by the Lord Chancellor to act for, a local justice area in which at least one of the parties is resident.

(2) A magistrates' court must not make any order on such an application other than—
(a) if the agreement includes no provision for periodical payments by either of the parties, an order inserting provision for the making by one of the parties of periodical payments for the maintenance of—
(i) the other party; or
(ii) any child of the family;
(b) if the agreement includes provision for the making by one of the parties of periodical payments, an order increasing or reducing the rate of, or terminating, any of those payments.

Provisions relating to periodical and secured periodical payments: duration

71. (1) If a court decides to make an order under paragraph 69 altering an agreement—
(a) by inserting provision for the making or securing by one of the parties to the agreement of periodical payments for the maintenance of the other party, or
(b) by increasing the rate of the periodical payments which the agreement provides shall be made by one of the parties for the maintenance of the other,
it may specify such term as it thinks fit as the term for which the payments or, as the case may be, the additional payments attributable to the increase are to be made under the altered agreement, except that the term must not extend beyond the limits in sub-paragraphs (2) and (3).

(2) The limits if the payments are not to be secured are—
(a) the death of either of the parties to the agreement, or
(b) the formation of a subsequent civil partnership or marriage by the party to whom the payments are to be made.

(3) The limits if the payments are to be secured are—
(a) the death of the party to whom the payments are to be made, or
(b) the formation of a subsequent civil partnership or marriage by that party.

(4) Sub-paragraph (5) applies if a court decides to make an order under paragraph 69 altering an agreement by—
(a) inserting provision for the making or securing by one of the parties to the agreement of periodical payments for the maintenance of a child of the family, or
(b) increasing the rate of the periodical payments which the agreement provides shall be made or secured by one of the parties for the maintenance of such a child.

(5) The court, in deciding the term for which under the agreement as altered by the order—
(a) the payments are to be made or secured for the benefit of the child, or
(b) the additional payments attributable to the increase are to be made or secured for the benefit of the child, must apply paragraph 49(2) to (5) (age limits) as if the order in question were a periodical payments or secured periodical payments order in favour of the child.

Saving

72. Nothing in paragraphs 68 to 71 affects—
(a) any power of a court before which any proceedings between the parties to a maintenance agreement are brought under any other enactment (including a provision of this Schedule) to make an order containing financial arrangements, or
(b) any right of either party to apply for such an order in such proceedings.

Alteration of agreements by court after death of one party

73. (1) This paragraph applies if—
(a) a maintenance agreement provides for the continuation of payments under the agreement after the death of one of the parties, and
(b) that party ("A") dies domiciled in England and Wales.

(2) Subject to sub-paragraph (4), the surviving party or A's personal representatives may apply to the High Court or a county court for an order under paragraph 69.

(3) If a maintenance agreement is altered by a court on an application made under subparagraph (2), the same consequences follow as if the alteration had been made immediately before the death by agreement between the parties and for valuable consideration.

(4) An application under this paragraph may not, without the leave of the High Court or a county court, be made after the end of 6 months from the date on which representation in regard to A's estate is first taken out.

(5) A's personal representatives are not liable for having distributed any part of A's estate after the end of the 6 month period on the ground that they ought to have taken into account the possibility that a court might allow an application by virtue of this paragraph to be made by the surviving party after that period.

(6) Sub-paragraph (5) does not affect any power to recover any part of the estate so distributed arising by virtue of the making of an order in pursuance of this paragraph.

(7) Paragraph 60(6) applies for the purposes of sub-paragraph (4) as it applies for the purposes of paragraph 60(3).

Part 14 MISCELLANEOUS AND SUPPLEMENTARY

Avoidance of transactions intended to prevent or reduce financial relief

74. (1) This paragraph applies if proceedings for relief ("financial relief") are brought by one person ("A") against another ("B") under Part 1, 2, 4, 8, 9, or 11 (other than paragraph 60(2)), or paragraph 69.

(2) If the court is satisfied, on an application by A, that B is, with the intention of defeating A's claim for financial relief, about to—
(a) make any disposition, or
(b) transfer out of the jurisdiction or otherwise deal with any property,
it may make such order as it thinks fit for restraining B from doing so or otherwise for protecting the claim.

(3) If the court is satisfied, on an application by A, that—
(a) B has, with the intention of defeating A's claim for financial relief, made a reviewable disposition, and
(b) if the disposition were set aside, financial relief or different financial relief would be granted to A,
it may make an order setting aside the disposition.

(4) If the court is satisfied, on an application by A in a case where an order has been obtained by A against B under any of the provisions mentioned in sub-paragraph (1), that B has, with the intention of defeating A's claim for financial relief, made a reviewable disposition,

it may make an order setting aside the disposition.

(5) An application for the purposes of sub-paragraph (3) must be made in the proceedings for the financial relief in question.

(6) If the court makes an order under sub-paragraph (3) or (4) setting aside a disposition it must give such consequential directions as it thinks fit for giving effect to the order (including directions requiring the making of any payments or the disposal of any property).

75. (1) Any reference in paragraph 74 to defeating A's claim for financial relief is to—

(a) preventing financial relief from being granted to A, or to A for the benefit of a child of the family,

(b) reducing the amount of any financial relief which might be so granted, or

(c) frustrating or impeding the enforcement of any order which might be or has been made at A's instance under any of those provisions.

(2) In paragraph 74 and this paragraph "disposition"—

(a) does not include any provision contained in a will or codicil, but

(b) subject to paragraph (a), includes any conveyance, assurance or gift of property of any description (whether made by an instrument or otherwise).

(3) Any disposition made by B (whether before or after the commencement of the proceedings for financial relief) is a reviewable disposition for the purposes of paragraphs 74(3) and (4) unless it was made—

(a) for valuable consideration (other than formation of a civil partnership), and

(b) to a person who, at the time of the disposition, acted in relation to it in good faith and without notice of any intention on B's part to defeat A's claim for financial relief.

(4) If an application is made under paragraph 74 with respect to a disposition which took place less than 3 years before the date of the application or with respect to a disposition or other dealing with property which is about to take place and the court is satisfied—

(a) in a case falling within paragraph 74(2) or (3), that the disposition or other dealing would (apart from paragraph 74) have the consequence of defeating A's claim for financial relief, or

(b) in a case falling within paragraph 74(4), that the disposition has had the consequence of defeating A's claim for financial relief, it is presumed, unless the contrary is shown, that the person who disposed of or is about to dispose of or deal with the property did so or, as the case may be, is about to do so, with the intention of defeating A's claim for financial relief.

Direction for settlement of instrument for securing payments or effecting property adjustment

76. (1) This paragraph applies if the court decides to make—

(a) an order under Part 1 or 9 requiring any payments to be secured, or

(b) a property adjustment order.

(2) The court may direct that the matter be referred to one of the conveyancing counsel of the court for him to settle a proper instrument to be executed by all necessary parties.

(3) If the order referred to in sub-paragraph (1) is to be made in proceedings for a dissolution, nullity or separation order, the court may, if it thinks fit, defer the making of the dissolution, nullity or separation order until the instrument has been duly executed.

Settlement, etc, made in compliance with a property adjustment order may be avoided on bankruptcy of settlor

77. The fact that—

(a) a settlement, or

(b) a transfer of property,

had to be made in order to comply with a property adjustment order does not prevent the settlement or transfer from being a transaction in respect of which an order may be made under section 339 or 340 of the Insolvency Act 1986 (c 45) (transfers at an undervalue and preferences).

Payments, etc, under order made in favour of person suffering from mental disorder

78. (1) This paragraph applies if—

(a) the court makes an order under this Schedule requiring—

(i) payments (including a lump sum payment) to be made, or

(ii) property to be transferred, to a civil partner, and

(b) the court is satisfied that the person in whose favour the order is made is incapable, because of mental disorder, of managing and administering his or her property and affairs.

(2) "Mental disorder" has the same meaning as in the Mental Health Act 1983 (c 20).

(3) Subject to any order, direction or authority made or given in relation to that person under Part 8 of the 1983 Act, the court may order the payments to be made or, as the case may be, the property to be transferred to such persons having charge of that person as the court may direct.

Appeals relating to pension sharing orders which have taken effect

79. (1) Sub-paragraphs (2) and (3) apply if an appeal against a pension sharing order is begun on or after the day on which the order takes effect.

(2) If the pension sharing order relates to a person's rights under a pension arrangement, the appeal court may not set aside or vary the order if the person responsible for the pension arrangement has acted to his detriment in reliance on the order taking effect.

(3) If the pension sharing order relates to a person's shareable state scheme rights, the appeal court may not set aside or vary the order if the Secretary of State has acted to his detriment in reliance on the taking effect of the order.

(4) In determining for the purposes of sub-paragraph (2) or (3) whether a person has acted to his detriment in reliance on the taking effect of the order, the appeal court may disregard any detriment which in its opinion is insignificant.

(5) Where sub-paragraph (2) or (3) applies, the appeal court may make such further orders (including one or more pension sharing orders) as it thinks fit for the purpose of putting the parties in the position it considers appropriate.

(6) Paragraph 19 only applies to a pension sharing order under this paragraph if the decision of the appeal court can itself be the subject of an appeal.

(7) In sub-paragraph (2), the reference to the person responsible for the pension arrangement is to be read in accordance with paragraph 29(3).

APPEALS RELATING TO PENSION COMPENSATION SHARING ORDERS WHICH HAVE TAKEN EFFECT

79A (1) This paragraph applies where an appeal against a pension compensation sharing order is begun on or after the day on which the order takes effect.

(2) If the Board of the Pension Protection Fund has acted to its detriment in reliance on the taking effect of the order the appeal court—
(a) may not set aside or vary the order;
(b) may make such further orders (including a pension compensation sharing order) as it thinks fit for the purpose of putting the parties in the position it considers appropriate.

(3) In determining for the purposes of sub-paragraph (2) whether the Board has acted to its detriment the appeal court may disregard any detriment which in the court's opinion is insignificant.

(4) Paragraph 19E only applies to a pension compensation sharing order under this paragraph if the decision of the appeal court can itself be the subject of an appeal.

Interpretation

80. (1) References in this Schedule to—
(a) periodical payments orders,
(b) secured periodical payments orders, and
(c) orders for the payment of a lump sum, are references to such of the orders that may be made under Parts 1 and 9 (other than interim orders) as are relevant in the context of the reference in question.

(2) In this Schedule "child of the family", in relation to two people who are civil partners of each other, means—
(a) a child of both of them, and
(b) any other child, other than a child placed with them as foster parents by a local authority or voluntary organisation, who has been treated by both the civil partners as a child of their family.

(3) In this Schedule "the court" (except where the context otherwise requires) means—
(a) the High Court, or
(b) where a county court has jurisdiction by virtue of Part 5 of the Matrimonial and Family Proceedings Act 1984 (c 42), a county court.

(4) References in this Schedule to a subsequent civil partnership include a civil partnership which is by law void or voidable.

(5) References in this Schedule to a subsequent marriage include a marriage which is by law void or voidable.

SCHEDULE 6 FINANCIAL RELIEF IN MAGISTRATES' COURTS ETC

Section 72(3)

Part 1 FAILURE TO MAINTAIN ETC: FINANCIAL PROVISION

Circumstances in which orders under this Part may be made

1. (1) On an application to it by one of the civil partners, a magistrates' court may make any one or more of the orders set out in paragraph 2 if it is satisfied that the other civil partner—

(a) has failed to provide reasonable maintenance for the applicant,
(b) has failed to provide, or to make a proper contribution towards, reasonable maintenance for any child of the family,
(c) has behaved in such a way that the applicant cannot reasonably be expected to live with the respondent, or
(d) has deserted the applicant.

(2) The power of the court under sub-paragraph (1) is subject to the following provisions of this Schedule.

The orders: periodical and secured periodical payments and lump sums

2. (1) The orders are—
(a) an order that the respondent must make to the applicant such periodical payments for such term as may be specified;
(b) an order that the respondent must pay to the applicant such lump sum as may be specified;
(c) an order that the respondent must make—
(i) to the applicant for the benefit of a child of the family to whom the application relates; or
(ii) to a child of the family to whom the application relates;
such periodical payments for such term as may be specified;
(d) an order that the respondent must pay such lump sum as may be specified—
(i) to the applicant for the benefit of a child of the family to whom the application relates; or
(ii) to such a child of the family to whom the application relates.

(2) The amount of a lump sum required to be paid under sub-paragraph (1)(b) or (d) must not exceed—
(a) £1,000, or
(b) such larger amount as the Lord Chancellor may from time to time by order fix for the purposes of this sub-paragraph.

(3) The power to make an order under sub-paragraph (2) is exercisable by statutory instrument which is subject to annulment in pursuance of a resolution of either House of Parliament.

(4) "Specified" means specified in the order.

Particular provision that may be made by lump sum orders

3. (1) An order under this Part for the payment of a lump sum may be made for the purpose of enabling any liability or expenses reasonably incurred in maintaining the applicant or any child of the family to whom the application relates before the making of the order to be met.

(2) Sub-paragraph (1) does not restrict the power to make the orders set out in paragraph 2(1)(b) and (d).

Matters to which court is to have regard in exercising its powers under this Part—general

4. If an application is made for an order under this Part, the court, in deciding—
(a) whether to exercise its powers under this Part, and
(b) if so, in what way, must have regard to all the circumstances of the case, giving first consideration to the welfare while under 18 of any child of the family who has not reached 18.

Particular matters to be taken into account when exercising powers in relation to civil partners

5. (1) This paragraph applies in relation to the exercise by the court of its power to make an order by virtue of paragraph 2(1)(a) or (b).

(2) The court must in particular have regard to—

(a) the income, earning capacity, property and other financial resources which each civil partner—

(i) has; or

(ii) is likely to have in the foreseeable future, including, in the case of earning capacity, any increase in that capacity which it would in the opinion of the court be reasonable to expect a civil partner in the civil partnership to take steps to acquire;

(b) the financial needs, obligations and responsibilities which each civil partner has or is likely to have in the foreseeable future;

(c) the standard of living enjoyed by the civil partners before the occurrence of the conduct which is alleged as the ground of the application;

(d) the age of each civil partner and the duration of the civil partnership;

(e) any physical or mental disability of either civil partner;

(f) the contributions which each civil partner has made or is likely in the foreseeable future to make to the welfare of the family, including any contribution by looking after the home or caring for the family;

(g) the conduct of each civil partner, if that conduct is such that it would in the opinion of the court be inequitable to disregard it.

Particular matters to be taken into account when exercising powers in relation to children

6. (1) This paragraph applies in relation to the exercise by the court of its power to make an order by virtue of paragraph 2(1)(c) or (d).

(2) The court must in particular have regard to—

(a) the financial needs of the child;

(b) the income, earning capacity (if any), property and other financial resources of the child;

(c) any physical or mental disability of the child;

(d) the standard of living enjoyed by the family before the occurrence of the conduct which is alleged as the ground of the application;

(e) the way in which the child was being and in which the civil partners expected the child to be educated or trained;

(f) the considerations mentioned in relation to the civil partners in paragraph 5(2)(a) and (b).

(3) In relation to the exercise of its power to make an order in favour of a child of the family who is not the respondent's child, the court must also have regard to—

(a) whether the respondent has assumed any responsibility for the child's maintenance;

(b) if so, the extent to which, and the basis on which, the respondent assumed that responsibility and the length of time during which the respondent discharged that responsibility;

(c) whether in assuming and discharging that responsibility the respondent did so knowing that the child was not the respondent's child;

(d) the liability of any other person to maintain the child.

Reconciliation

7. (1) If an application is made for an order under this Part—
   (a) the court, before deciding whether to exercise its powers under this Part, must consider whether there is any possibility of reconciliation between the civil partners, and
   (b) if at any stage of the proceedings on that application it appears to the court that there is a reasonable possibility of such a reconciliation, the court may adjourn the proceedings for such period as it thinks fit to enable attempts to be made to effect a reconciliation.

(2) If the court adjourns any proceedings under sub-paragraph (1), it may request—
   (a) an officer of the Children and Family Court Advisory and Support Service, or
   (b) any other person, to attempt to effect a reconciliation between the civil partners.

(3) If any such request is made, the officer or other person—
   (a) must report in writing to the court whether the attempt has been successful, but
   (b) must not include in the report any other information.

Refusal of order in case more suitable for High Court

8. (1) If on hearing an application for an order under this Part a magistrates' court is of the opinion that any of the matters in question between the civil partners would be more conveniently dealt with by the High Court, the magistrates' court must refuse to make any order on the application.

(2) No appeal lies from a refusal under sub-paragraph (1).

(3) But, in any proceedings in the High Court relating to or comprising the same subject matter as an application in respect of which a magistrates' court has refused to make any order, the High Court may order the application to be reheard and determined by a magistrates' court acting for the same local justice area as the court which refused to make any order.

Part 2 ORDERS FOR AGREED FINANCIAL PROVISION

Orders for payments which have been agreed by the parties

9. (1) Either civil partner may apply to a magistrates' court for an order under this Part on the ground that that civil partner or the other civil partner has agreed to make such financial provision as may be specified in the application.

(2) On such an application, the court may order that the applicant or the respondent (as the case may be) is to make the financial provision specified in the application, if—
   (a) it is satisfied that the applicant or the respondent (as the case may be) has agreed to make that provision, and
   (b) it has no reason to think that it would be contrary to the interests of justice to do so.

(3) Sub-paragraph (2) is subject to paragraph 12.

Meaning of "financial provision" and of references to specified financial provision

10. (1) In this Part "financial provision" means any one or more of the following—
   (a) the making of periodical payments by one civil partner to the other;
   (b) the payment of a lump sum by one civil partner to the other;
   (c) the making of periodical payments by one civil partner to a child of the family or to the other civil partner for the benefit of such a child;
   (d) the payment by one party of a lump sum to a child of the family or to the other civil partner for the benefit of such a child.

(2) Any reference in this Part to the financial provision specified in an application or specified by the court is a reference—
(a) to the type of provision specified in the application or by the court,
(b) to the amount so specified as the amount of any payment to be made under the application or order, and
(c) in the case of periodical payments, to the term so specified as the term for which the payments are to be made.

Evidence to be produced where respondent not present etc

11. (1) This paragraph applies if—
(a) the respondent is not present, or
(b) is not represented by counsel or a solicitor, at the hearing of an application for an order under this Part.

(2) The court must not make an order under this Part unless there is produced to it such evidence as may be prescribed by rules of court of—
(a) the consent of the respondent to the making of the order,
(b) the financial resources of the respondent, and
(c) if the financial provision specified in the application includes or consists of provision in respect of a child of the family to be made by the applicant to the respondent for the benefit of the child or to the child, the financial resources of the child.

Exercise of powers in relation to children

12. (1) This paragraph applies if the financial provision specified in an application under this Part—
(a) includes, or
(b) consists of, provision in respect of a child of the family.

(2) The court must not make an order under this Part unless it considers that the provision which the applicant or the respondent (as the case may be) has agreed to make in respect of the child provides for, or makes a proper contribution towards, the financial needs of the child.

Power to make alternative orders

13. (1) This paragraph applies if on an application under this Part the court decides—
(a) that it would be contrary to the interests of justice to make an order for the making of the financial provision specified in the application, or
(b) that any financial provision which the applicant or the respondent (as the case may be) has agreed to make in respect of a child of the family does not provide for, or make a proper contribution towards, the financial needs of that child.

(2) If the court is of the opinion—
(a) that it would not be contrary to the interests of justice to make an order for the making of some other financial provision specified by the court, and
(b) that, in so far as that other financial provision contains any provision for a child of the family, it provides for, or makes a proper contribution towards, the financial needs of that child,

then, if both the civil partners agree, the court may order that the applicant or the respondent (as the case may be) is to make that other financial provision.

Relationship between this Part and Part 1

14. (1) A civil partner who has applied for an order under Part 1 is not precluded at any time before the determination of the application from applying for an order under this Part.

(2) If—

(a) an order is made under this Part on the application of either civil partner, and

(b) either of them has also made an application for a Part 1 order, the application for the Part 1 order is to be treated as if it had been withdrawn.

Part 3 ORDERS OF COURT WHERE CIVIL PARTNERS LIVING APART BY AGREEMENT

Powers of court where civil partners are living apart by agreement

15. (1) If—

(a) the civil partners have been living apart for a continuous period exceeding 3 months, neither civil partner having deserted the other, and

(b) one of the civil partners has been making periodical payments for the benefit of the other civil partner or of a child of the family, the other civil partner may apply to a magistrates' court for an order under this Part.

(2) An application made under sub-paragraph (1) must specify the total amount of the payments made by the respondent during the period of 3 months immediately preceding the date of the making of the application.

(3) If on an application for an order under this Part the court is satisfied that the respondent has made the payments specified in the application, the court may make one or both of the orders set out in paragraph 16.

(4) Sub-paragraph (3) is subject to the provisions of this Schedule.

The orders that may be made under this Part

16. (1) The orders are—

(a) an order that the respondent is to make to the applicant such periodical payments for such term as may be specified;

(b) an order that the respondent is to make—

(i) to the applicant for the benefit of a child of the family to whom the application relates; or

(ii) to a child of the family to whom the application relates. such periodical payments for such term as may be specified.

(2) "Specified" means specified in the order.

Restrictions on orders under this Part

17. The court in the exercise of its powers under this Part must not require—

(a) the respondent to make payments whose total amount during any period of 3 months exceeds the total amount paid by him for the benefit of—

(i) the applicant; or

(ii) a child of the family, during the period of 3 months immediately preceding the date of the making of the application;

(b) the respondent to make payments to or for the benefit of any person which exceed in amount the payments which the court considers that it would have required the respondent to make to or for the benefit of that person on an application under Part 1;

(c) payments to be made to or for the benefit of a child of the family who is not the respondent's child, unless the court considers that it would have made an order in favour of that child on an application under Part 1.

Relationship with powers under Part 1

18. (1) Sub-paragraph (2) applies if on an application under this Part the court considers that the orders which it has the power to make under this Part—

(a) would not provide reasonable maintenance for the applicant, or
(b) if the application relates to a child of the family, would not provide, or make a proper contribution towards, reasonable maintenance for that child.

(2) The court—
(a) must refuse to make an order under this Part, but
(b) may treat the application as if it were an application for an order under Part 1.

Matters to be taken into consideration

19. Paragraphs 4 to 6 apply in relation to an application for an order under this Part as they apply in relation to an application for an order under Part 1, subject to the modification that for the reference in paragraph 5(2)(c) to the occurrence of the conduct which is alleged as the ground of the application substitute a reference to the living apart of the civil partners.

Part 4 INTERIM ORDERS

Circumstances in which interim orders may be made

20. (1) This paragraph applies if an application has been made for an order under Part 1, 2 or 3.

(2) A magistrates' court may make an interim order—
(a) at any time before making a final order on, or dismissing, the application, or
(b) on refusing (under paragraph 8) to make on order on the application.

(3) The High Court may make an interim order on ordering the application to be reheard by a magistrates' court (either after the refusal of an order under paragraph 8 or on an appeal made by virtue of paragraph 46).

(4) Not more than one interim order may be made with respect to an application for an order under Part 1, 2 or 3.

(5) Sub-paragraph (4) does not affect the power of a court to make an interim order on a further application under Part 1, 2 or 3.

Meaning of interim order

21. (1) An interim order is an order requiring the respondent to make such periodical payments as the court thinks reasonable—
(a) to the applicant,
(b) to any child of the family who is under 18, or
(c) to the applicant for the benefit of such a child.

(2) In relation to an interim order in respect of an application for an order under Part 2 by the civil partner who has agreed to make the financial provision specified in the application, subparagraph

(1) applies as if—
(a) the reference to the respondent were a reference to the applicant, and
(b) the references to the applicant were references to the respondent.

When interim order may start

22. (1) An interim order may provide for payments to be made from such date as the court may specify, except that the date must not be earlier than the date of the making of the application for an order under Part 1, 2 or 3.

(2) Sub-paragraph (1) is subject to paragraph 27(7) and (8).

Payments which can be treated as having been paid on account

23. (1) If an interim order made by the High Court on an appeal made by virtue of paragraph 46 provides for payments to be made from a date earlier than the date of the making of the order, the interim order may provide that payments made by the respondent under an order made by a magistrates' court are to be treated, to such extent and in such manner as may be provided by the interim order, as having been paid on account of any payment provided for by the interim order.

(2) In relation to an interim order in respect of an application for an order under Part 2 by the civil partner who has agreed to make the financial provision specified in the application, subparagraph (1) applies as if the reference to the respondent were a reference to the applicant.

When interim order ceases to have effect

24. (1) Subject to sub-paragraphs (2) and (3), an interim order made on an application for an order under Part 1, 2 or 3 ceases to have effect on the earliest of the following dates—
(a) the date, if any, specified for the purpose in the interim order;
(b) the date on which the period of 3 months beginning with the date of the making of the interim order ends;
(c) the date on which a magistrates' court either makes a final order on, or dismisses, the application.

(2) If an interim order made under this Part would, but for this sub-paragraph, cease to have effect under sub-paragraph (1)(a) or (b)—
(a) the magistrates' court which made the order, or
(b) in the case of an interim order made by the High Court, the magistrates' court by which the application for an order under Part 1, 2 or 3 is to be reheard, may by order provide that the interim order is to continue in force for a further period.

(3) An order continued in force under sub-paragraph (2) ceases to have effect on the earliest of the following dates—
(a) the date, if any, specified for the purpose in the order continuing it;
(b) the date on which ends the period of 3 months beginning with—
(i) the date of the making of the order continuing it, or
(ii) if more than one such order has been made with respect to the application, the date of the making of the first such order;
(c) the date on which the court either makes a final order on, or dismisses, the application.

Supplementary

25. (1) An interim order made by the High Court under paragraph 20(3) on ordering an application to be reheard by a magistrates' court is to be treated for the purposes of—
(a) its enforcement, and
(b) Part 6 (variation etc of orders), as if it were an order of that magistrates' court (and not of the High Court).

(2) No appeal lies from the making of or refusal to make, the variation of or refusal to vary, or the revocation of or refusal to revoke, an interim order.

Part 5 COMMENCEMENT AND DURATION OF ORDERS UNDER PARTS 1, 2 AND 3

Duration of periodical payments order for a civil partner

26. (1) The court may specify in a periodical payments order made under paragraph 2(1)(a) or Part 3 in favour of a civil partner such term as it thinks fit, except that the term must not—

(a) begin before the date of the making of the application for the order, or
(b) extend beyond the death of either of the civil partners.

(2) If—
(a) a periodical payments order is made under paragraph 2(1)(a) or Part 3 in favour of one of the civil partners, and
(b) the civil partnership is subsequently dissolved or annulled but the order continues in force,

the periodical payments order ceases to have effect (regardless of anything in it) on the formation of a subsequent civil partnership or marriage by that civil partner, except in relation to any arrears due under the order on the date of that event.

Age limit on making orders for financial provision for children and duration of such orders

27. (1) Subject to sub-paragraph (5), no order is to be made under paragraph 2(1)(c) or (d) or Part 3 in favour of a child who has reached 18.

(2) The term to be specified in a periodical payments order made under paragraph 2(1)(c) or Part 3 in favour of a child may begin with—
(a) the date of the making of an application for the order or a later date, or
(b) a date ascertained in accordance with sub-paragraph (7) or (8).

(3) The term to be specified in such an order—
(a) must not in the first instance extend beyond the date of the birthday of the child next following his reaching the upper limit of the compulsory school age unless the court considers that in the circumstances of the case the welfare of the child requires that it should extend to a later date, and
(b) must not in any event, subject to sub-paragraph (5), extend beyond the date of the child's 18th birthday.

(4) Sub-paragraph (3)(a) must be read with section 8 of the Education Act 1996 (c 56) (which applies to determine for the purposes of any enactment whether a person is of compulsory school age).

(5) Sub-paragraphs (1) and (3)(b) do not apply in the case of a child if it appears to the court that—
(a) the child is, or will be, or, if such an order were made without complying with either or both of those provisions, would be—
(i) receiving instruction at an educational establishment, or
(ii) undergoing training for a trade, profession or vocation,

whether or not also the child is, will be or would be, in gainful employment, or
(b) there are special circumstances which justify the making of the order without complying with either or both of sub-paragraphs (1) and (3)(b).

(6) Any order made under paragraph 2(1)(c) or Part 3 in favour of a child, regardless of anything in the order, ceases to have effect on the death of the person liable to make payments under the order.

(7) If—
(a) a maintenance calculation ("current calculation") is in force with respect to a child, and
(b) an application is made for an order under paragraph 2(1)(c) or Part 3—
(i) in accordance with section 8 of the Child Support Act 1991 (c 48), and
(ii) before the end of 6 months beginning with the making of the current calculation, the term to be specified in any such order made on that application may be expressed to begin on, or at any time after, the earliest permitted date.

(8) "The earliest permitted date" is whichever is the later of—
(a) the date 6 months before the application is made, or
(b) the date on which the current calculation took effect or, where successive maintenance calculations have been continuously in force with respect to a child, on which the first of those calculations took effect.

(9) If—
(a) a maintenance calculation ceases to have effect by or under any provision of the 1991 Act, and
(b) an application is made, before the end of 6 months beginning with the relevant date, for a periodical payments order under paragraph 2(1)(c) or Part 3 in favour of a child with respect to whom that maintenance calculation was in force immediately before it ceased to have effect,

the term to be specified in any such order, or in any interim order under Part 4, made on that application, may begin with the date on which that maintenance calculation ceased to have effect or any later date.

(10) "The relevant date" means the date on which the maintenance calculation ceased to have effect.

(11) In this Schedule "maintenance calculation" has the same meaning as it has in the 1991 Act by virtue of section 54 of the 1991 Act as read with any regulations in force under that section.

Application of paragraphs 26 and 27 to Part 2 orders

28. (1) Subject to sub-paragraph (3), paragraph 26 applies in relation to an order under Part 2 which requires periodical payments to be made to a civil partner for his own benefit as it applies in relation to an order under paragraph 2(1)(a).

(2) Subject to sub-paragraph (3), paragraph 27 applies in relation to an order under Part 2 for the making of financial provision in respect of a child of the family as it applies in relation to an order under paragraph 2(1)(c) or (d).

(3) If—
(a) the court makes an order under Part 2 which contains provision for the making of periodical payments, and
(b) by virtue of paragraph 14, an application for an order under Part 1 is treated as if it had been withdrawn,

the term which may be specified under Part 2 as the term for which the payments are to be made may begin with the date of the making of the application for the order under Part 1 or any later date.

Effect on certain orders of parties living together

29. (1) Sub-paragraph (2) applies if periodical payments are required to be made to a civil partner (whether for the civil partner's own benefit or for the benefit of a child of the family)—
(a) by an order made under Part 1 or 2, or
(b) by an interim order made under Part 4 (otherwise than on an application under Part 3).

(2) The order is enforceable even though—
(a) the civil partners are living with each other at the date of the making of the order, or
(b) if they are not living with each other at that date, they subsequently resume living with each other;

but the order ceases to have effect if after that date the parties continue to live with each other, or resume living with each other, for a continuous period exceeding 6 months.

(3) Sub-paragraph (4) applies if—
(a) an order is made under Part 1 or 2 which requires periodical payments to be made to a child of the family, or
(b) an interim order is made under Part 4 (otherwise than on an application under Part 3) which requires periodical payments to be made to a child of the family.

(4) Unless the court otherwise directs, the order continues to have effect and is enforceable even if—
(a) the civil partners are living with each other at the date of the making of the order, or
(b) if they are not living with each other at that date, they subsequently resume living with each other.

(5) An order made under Part 3, and any interim order made on an application for an order under that Part, ceases to have effect if the civil partners resume living with each other.

(6) If an order made under this Schedule ceases to have effect under—
(a) sub-paragraph (2) or (5), or
(b) a direction given under sub-paragraph (4), a magistrates' court may, on an application made by either civil partner, make an order declaring that the order ceased to have effect from such date as the court may specify.

Part 6 VARIATION ETC OF ORDERS

Power to vary, revoke, suspend or revive order

30. (1) If a magistrates' court has made an order for the making of periodical payments under Part 1, 2 or 3, the court may, on an application made under this Part—
(a) vary or revoke the order,
(b) suspend any provision of it temporarily, or
(c) revive any provision so suspended.

(2) If a magistrates' court has made an interim order under Part 4, the court may, on an application made under this Part—
(a) vary or revoke the order,
(b) suspend any provision of it temporarily, or
(c) revive any provision so suspended,

except that it may not by virtue of this sub-paragraph extend the period for which the order is in force.

Powers to order lump sum on variation

31. (1) If a magistrates' court has made an order under paragraph 2(1)(a) or (c) for the making of periodical payments, the court may, on an application made under this Part, make an order for the payment of a lump sum under paragraph 2(1)(b) or (d).

(2) If a magistrates' court has made an order under Part 2 for the making of periodical payments by a civil partner the court may, on an application made under this Part, make an order for the payment of a lump sum by that civil partner—

(a) to the other civil partner, or
(b) to a child of the family or to that other civil partner for the benefit of that child.

(3) Where the court has power by virtue of this paragraph to make an order for the payment of a lump sum—
(a) the amount of the lump sum must not exceed the maximum amount that may at that time be required to be paid under Part 1, but
(b) the court may make an order for the payment of a lump sum not exceeding that amount even if the person required to pay it was required to pay a lump sum by a previous order under this Schedule.

(4) Where—
(a) the court has power by virtue of this paragraph to make an order for the payment of a lump sum, and
(b) the respondent or the applicant (as the case may be) has agreed to pay a lump sum of an amount exceeding the maximum amount that may at that time be required to be paid under Part 1,
the court may, regardless of sub-paragraph (3), make an order for the payment of a lump sum of that amount.

Power to specify when order as varied is to take effect

32. An order made under this Part which varies an order for the making of periodical payments may provide that the payments as so varied are to be made from such date as the court may specify, except that, subject to paragraph 33, the date must not be earlier than the date of the making of the application under this Part.

33. (1) If—
(a) there is in force an order ("the order")—
(i) under paragraph 2(1)(c),
(ii) under Part 2 making provision of a kind set out in paragraph 10(1)(c) (regardless of whether it makes provision of any other kind mentioned in paragraph 10(1)(c)),
(iii) under paragraph 16(1)(b), or
(iv) which is an interim order under Part 4 under which the payments are to be made to a child or to the applicant for the benefit of a child,
(b) the order requires payments specified in it to be made to or for the benefit of more than one child without apportioning those payments between them,
(c) a maintenance calculation ("the calculation") is made with respect to one or more, but not all, of the children with respect to whom those payments are to be made, and
(d) an application is made, before the end of 6 months beginning with the date on which the calculation was made, for the variation or revocation of the order,
the court may, in exercise of its powers under this Part to vary or revoke the order, direct that the variation or revocation is to take effect from the date on which the calculation took effect or any later date.

(2) If—
(a) an order ("the child order") of a kind prescribed for the purposes of section 10(1) of the Child Support Act 1991 is affected by a maintenance calculation,
(b) on the date on which the child order became so affected there was in force an order ("the civil partner's order")—
(i) under paragraph 2(1)(a),
(ii) under Part 2 making provision of a kind set out in paragraph 10(1)(a) (regardless of whether it makes provision of any other kind mentioned in paragraph 10(1)(a)),

(iii) under paragraph 16(1)(a), or
(iv) which is an interim order under Part 4 under which the payments are to be made to the applicant (otherwise than for the benefit of a child), and
(c) an application is made, before the end of 6 months beginning with the date on which the maintenance calculation was made, for the civil partner's order to be varied or revoked,

the court may, in exercise of its powers under this Part to vary or revoke the civil partner's order, direct that the variation or revocation is to take effect from the date on which the child order became so affected or any later date.

(3) For the purposes of sub-paragraph (2), an order is affected if it ceases to have effect or is modified by or under section 10 of the 1991 Act.

Matters to which court is to have regard in exercising powers under this Part

34. (1) In exercising the powers conferred by this Part the court must, so far as it appears to the court just to do so, give effect to any agreement which has been reached between the civil partners in relation to the application.

(2) If—
(a) there is no such agreement, or
(b) if the court decides not to give effect to the agreement,

the court must have regard to all the circumstances of the case, giving first consideration to the welfare while under 18 of any child of the family who has not reached 18.

(3) Those circumstances include any change in any of the matters—
(a) to which the court was required to have regard when making the order to which the application relates, or
(b) in the case of an application for the variation or revocation of an order made under Part 2 or on an appeal made by virtue of paragraph 46, to which the court would have been required to have regard if that order had been made under Part 1.

Variation of orders for periodical payments: further provisions

35. (1) The power of the court under paragraphs 30 to 34 to vary an order for the making of periodical payments includes power, if the court is satisfied that payment has not been made in accordance with the order, to exercise one of its powers under section 59(3)(a) to (d) of the Magistrates' Courts Act 1980 (c 43).

(2) Sub-paragraph (1) is subject to paragraph 37.

36. (1) If—
(a) a magistrates' court has made an order under this Schedule for the making of periodical payments, and
(b) payments under the order are required to be made by any method of payment falling within section 59(6) of the 1980 Act (standing order, etc),

an application may be made under this sub-paragraph to the court for the order to be varied as mentioned in sub-paragraph (2).

(2) Subject to sub-paragraph (4), if an application is made under sub-paragraph (1), a justices' clerk, after—
(a) giving written notice (by post or otherwise) of the application to the respondent, and
(b) allowing the respondent, within the period of 14 days beginning with the date of the giving of that notice, an opportunity to make written representations,

may vary the order to provide that payments under the order are to be made to the designated officer for the court.

(3) The clerk may proceed with an application under sub-paragraph (1) even if the respondent has not received written notice of the application.

(4) If an application has been made under sub-paragraph (1), the clerk may, if he considers it inappropriate to exercise his power under sub-paragraph (2), refer the matter to the court which, subject to paragraph 37, may vary the order by exercising one of its powers under section 59(3)(a) to (d) of the 1980 Act.

37. (1) Before varying the order by exercising one of its powers under section 59(3)(a) to (d) of the 1980 Act, the court must have regard to any representations made by the parties to the application.

(2) If the court does not propose to exercise its power under section 59(3)(c), (cc) or (d) of the 1980 Act, the court must, unless upon representations expressly made in that behalf by the person to whom payments under the order are required to be made it is satisfied that it is undesirable to do so, exercise its power under section 59(3)(b).

38. (1) Section 59(4) of the 1980 Act (power of court to order that account be opened) applies for the purposes of paragraphs 35 and 36(4) as it applies for the purposes of section 59.

(2) None of the powers of the court, or of a justices' clerk, conferred by paragraphs 35 to 37 and sub-paragraph (1) is exercisable in relation to an order under this Schedule for the making of periodical payments which is not a qualifying maintenance order (within the meaning of section 59 of the 1980 Act).

Persons who may apply under this Part

39. An application under paragraph 30, 31 or 36 may be made—

(a) if it is for the variation or revocation of an order under Part 1, 2, 3 or 4 for periodical payments, by either civil partner, and

(b) if it is for the variation of an order under paragraph 2(1)(c) or Part 2 or 3 for periodical payments to or in respect of a child, also by the child himself, if he has reached 16.

Revival of orders for periodical payments

40. (1) If an order made by a magistrates' court under this Schedule for the making of periodical payments to or in respect of a child (other than an interim order) ceases to have effect—

(a) on the date on which the child reaches 16, or

(b) at any time after that date but before or on the date on which he reaches 18,

the child may apply to the court which made the order for an order for its revival.

(2) If on such an application it appears to the court that—

(a) the child is, will be or (if an order were made under this sub-paragraph) would be receiving instruction at an educational establishment or undergoing training for a trade, profession or vocation, whether or not while in gainful employment, or

(b) there are special circumstances which justify the making of an order under this subparagraph,

the court may by order revive the order from such date as the court may specify, not being earlier than the date of the making of the application.

(3) Any order revived under this paragraph may be varied or revoked under paragraphs 30 to 34 in the same way as it could have been varied or revoked had it continued in being.

Variation of instalments of lump sum

41. If in the exercise of its powers under section 75 of the 1980 Act a magistrates' court orders that a lump sum required to be paid under this Schedule is to be paid by instalments, the court, on an application made by either the person liable to pay or the person entitled to receive that sum, may vary that order by varying—
(a) the number of instalments payable,
(b) the amount of any instalment payable, and
(c) the date on which any instalment becomes payable.

Supplementary provisions with respect to variation and revocation of orders

42. None of the following powers apply in relation to an order made under this Schedule—
(a) the powers of a magistrates' court to revoke, revive or vary an order for the periodical payment of money and the power of a justices' clerk to vary such an order under section 60 of the 1980 Act;
(b) the power of a magistrates' court to suspend or rescind certain other orders under section 63(2) of the 1980 Act.

Part 7 ARREARS AND REPAYMENTS

Enforcement etc of orders for payment of money

43. Section 32 of the Domestic Proceedings and Magistrates' Courts Act 1978 (c 22) applies in relation to orders under this Schedule as it applies in relation to orders under Part 1 of that Act.

Orders for repayment after cessation of order because of subsequent civil partnership etc

44. (1) Sub-paragraphs (3) and (4) apply if—
(a) an order made under paragraph 2(1)(a) or Part 2 or 3 has, under paragraph 26(2), ceased to have effect because of the formation of a subsequent civil partnership or marriage by the party ("R") in whose favour it was made, and
(b) the person liable to make payments under the order ("P") made payments in accordance with it in respect of a relevant period in the mistaken belief that the order was still subsisting.

(2) "Relevant period" means a period after the date of the formation of the subsequent civil partnership or marriage.

(3) No proceedings in respect of a cause of action arising out of the circumstances mentioned in sub-paragraph (1)(a) and (b) is maintainable by P (or P's personal representatives) against R (or R's personal representatives).

(4) But on an application made under this paragraph by P (or P's personal representatives) against R (or R's personal representatives) the court—
(a) may order the respondent to pay to the applicant a sum equal to the amount of the payments made in respect of the relevant period, or
(b) if it appears to the court that it would be unjust to make that order, may—
(i) order the respondent to pay to the applicant such lesser sum as it thinks fit, or
(ii) dismiss the application.

(5) An order under this paragraph for the payment of any sum may provide for the payment of that sum by instalments of such amount as may be specified in the order

(6) An application under this paragraph—
(a) may be made in proceedings in the High Court or a county court for leave to enforce, or the enforcement of, the payment of arrears under an order made under paragraph 2(1)(a) or Part 2 or 3, but
(b) if not made in such proceedings, must be made to a county court, and accordingly references in this paragraph to the court are references to the High Court or a county court, as the circumstances require.

(7) The jurisdiction conferred on a county court by this paragraph is exercisable by a county court even though, because of the amount claimed in an application under this paragraph, the jurisdiction would not but for this sub-paragraph be exercisable by a county court.

(8) Subject to sub-paragraph (9)—
(a) the designated officer for a magistrates' court to whom any payments under an order made under paragraph 2(1)(a), or Part 2 or 3, are required to be made is not liable for any act done by him in pursuance of the order after the date on which that order ceased to have effect because of the formation of a subsequent civil partnership or marriage by the person entitled to payments under it, and
(b) the collecting officer under an attachment of earnings order made to secure payments under the order under paragraph 2(1)(a), or Part 2 or 3, is not liable for any act done by him after that date in accordance with any enactment or rule of court specifying how payments made to him in compliance with the attachment of earnings order are to be dealt with.

(9) Sub-paragraph (8) applies if (but only if) the act—
(a) was one which he would have been under a duty to do had the order under paragraph 2(1)(a) or Part 2 or 3 not ceased to have effect, and
(b) was done before notice in writing of the formation of the subsequent civil partnership or marriage was given to him by or on behalf of—
(i) the person entitled to payments under the order,
(ii) the person liable to make payments under it, or
(iii) the personal representatives of either of them.

(10) In this paragraph "collecting officer", in relation to an attachment of earnings order, means—
(a) the officer of the High Court, or
(b) the officer designated by the Lord Chancellor, to whom a person makes payments in compliance with the order.

Part 8 SUPPLEMENTARY

Restrictions on making of orders under this Schedule: welfare of children

45. If—
(a) an application is made by a civil partner for an order under Part 1, 2 or 3, and
(b) there is a child of the family who is under 18,
the court must not dismiss or make a final order on the application until it has decided whether to exercise any of its powers under the Children Act 1989 (c 41) with respect to the child.

Constitution of courts, powers of High Court and county court in relation to orders and appeals

46. The following provisions of the Domestic Proceedings and Magistrates' Courts Act 1978 (c 22) apply in relation to an order under this Schedule relating to a civil partnership as they apply in relation to an order under Part 1 of that Act relating to a marriage—

(a) section 28 (powers of the High Court and a county court in relation to certain orders),
(b) section 29 (appeals), and
(c) section 31 (constitution of courts).

Provisions as to jurisdiction and procedure

47. (1) Subject to section 2 of the Family Law Act 1986 (c 55) and section 70 of the Magistrates' Courts Act 1980 (c 43) and any determination of the Lord Chancellor, a magistrates' court has jurisdiction to hear an application for an order under this Schedule if it acts in, or is authorised by the Lord Chancellor to act for, a local justice area in which either the applicant or the respondent ordinarily resides at the date of the making of the application.

(2) Any jurisdiction conferred on a magistrates' court by this Schedule is exercisable even if any party to the proceedings is not domiciled in England and Wales.

(3) The Lord Chancellor may make a determination for the purposes of sub-paragraph (1) only with the concurrence of the Lord Chief Justice.

(4) The Lord Chief Justice may nominate a judicial office holder (as defined in section 109(4) of the Constitutional Reform Act 2005) to exercise his functions under this paragraph.

Meaning of "child of the family"

48. In this Schedule "child of the family", in relation to two people who are civil partners of each other, means—
(a) a child of both of them, and
(b) any other child, other than a child placed with them as foster parents by a local authority or voluntary organisation, who has been treated by both the civil partners as a child of their family.

As amended by: Civil Partnership (Amendments to Registration Provisions) Order 2005, SI 2005/2000, arts 1(3), 3, Schedule; Legislative and Regulatory Reform Act 2006, s 30(1), Schedule; Transfer of Functions (Registration) Order 2008, SI 2008/678, arts 3(1), 5, Sch 1, Sch 2; Pensions Act 2008, s 120, 148, Sch 6, Pt 3, Sch 11, Pt 4.

Welfare Reform Act 2007

(2007 c 5)

23 RECOVERY OF SUMS IN RESPECT OF MAINTENANCE

(1) Regulations may make provision for the court to have power to make a recovery order against any person where an award of income-related allowance has been made to that person's spouse or civil partner.

(2) The reference in subsection (1) to a recovery order is to an order requiring the person against whom it is made to make payments to the Secretary of State or to such other person or persons as the court may determine.

(3) Regulations under subsection (1) may include—
(a) provision as to the matters to which the court is, or is not, to have regard in determining any application under the regulations;

(b) provision as to the enforcement of orders under the regulations;
(c) provision for the transfer by the Secretary of State of the right to receive payments under, and to exercise rights in relation to, orders under the regulations.

(4) In this section, "the court" means—
(a) in relation to England and Wales, a magistrates' court;
(b) in relation to Scotland, the sheriff.

Child Maintenance and Other Payments Act 2008
(2008 c 6)

Part 1 THE CHILD MAINTENANCE AND ENFORCEMENT COMMISSION

1 THE CHILD MAINTENANCE AND ENFORCEMENT COMMISSION

(1) There shall be a body corporate to be known as the Child Maintenance and Enforcement Commission (referred to in this Act as "the Commission").

(2) Schedule 1 (which makes further provision about the Commission) has effect.

2 OBJECTIVES OF THE COMMISSION

(1) The Commission's main objective is to maximise the number of those children who live apart from one or both of their parents for whom effective maintenance arrangements are in place.

(2) The Commission's main objective is supported by the following subsidiary objectives—
(a) to encourage and support the making and keeping by parents of appropriate voluntary maintenance arrangements for their children;
(b) to support the making of applications for child support maintenance under the Child Support Act 1991 (c 48) and to secure compliance when appropriate with parental obligations under that Act.

(3) The Commission shall aim to pursue, and to have regard to, its objectives when exercising a function that is relevant to them.

3 FUNCTIONS OF THE COMMISSION: GENERAL

(1) The Commission has—
(a) the functions relating to child support transferred to it from the Secretary of State by virtue of this Act, and
(b) such other functions as are conferred by, or by virtue of, this or any other enactment.

(2) The Secretary of State may by regulations provide for the Commission to have an additional function if it appears to the Secretary of State that it is necessary or expedient for the Commission to have the function in relation to any of its objectives.

(3) The Commission must exercise its functions effectively and efficiently.

4 PROMOTION OF CHILD MAINTENANCE

The Commission must take such steps as it thinks appropriate for the purpose of raising awareness among parents of the importance of—

(a) taking responsibility for the maintenance of their children, and

(b) making appropriate arrangements for the maintenance of children of theirs who live apart from them.

5 PROVISION OF INFORMATION AND GUIDANCE

(1) The Commission must provide to parents such information and guidance as it thinks appropriate for the purpose of helping to secure the existence of effective maintenance arrangements for children who live apart from one or both of their parents.

(2) The Commission may provide information for other purposes in the course of exercising its function under subsection (1).

. . .

12 SUPPLEMENTARY PROVISIONS

(1) In this Part, "child" has the same meaning as in the Child Support Act 1991 (c 48).

(2) The Secretary of State may by regulations make provision about when a child is, or is not, to be regarded for the purposes of this Part as living apart from a parent.

. . .

Part 2 TRANSFER OF CHILD SUPPORT FUNCTIONS ETC TO THE COMMISSION

13 TRANSFER OF CHILD SUPPORT FUNCTIONS

(1) Any function under the Child Support Act 1991 which—
(a) is a function of the Secretary of State, and
(b) is not an excepted function, is by virtue of this subsection transferred to the Commission.

(2) The following functions of the Secretary of State under the Child Support Act 1991 are excepted functions for the purposes of subsection (1)—
(a) functions under sections 23A, 24 or 25 (appeals),
(b) functions under section 46 (reduced benefit decisions) or any other provision of the Act, so far as relating to such decisions,
(c) the function under section 50(7)(c) (authorisation of a person as a "responsible person" for the purposes of section 50),
(d) functions under section 58 (commencement power and power to make consequential amendments),
(e) the function under paragraph 2A of Schedule 4 (payment of expenses), and
(f) power to make regulations under any other provision of the Act.

(3) The functions of the Secretary of State under the provisions of subordinate legislation specified in Schedule 2, except so far as relating to reduced benefit decisions under section 46 of the Child Support Act 1991, are by virtue of this subsection transferred to the Commission.

Human Fertilisation and Embryology Act 2008
(2008 c 22)

Part 2 **PARENTHOOD IN CASES INVOLVING ASSISTED REPRODUCTION**

Meaning of "mother"

33 MEANING OF "MOTHER"

(1) The woman who is carrying or has carried a child as a result of the placing in her of an embryo or of sperm and eggs, and no other woman, is to be treated as the mother of the child.

(2) Subsection (1) does not apply to any child to the extent that the child is treated by virtue of adoption as not being the woman's child.

(3) Subsection (1) applies whether the woman was in the United Kingdom or elsewhere at the time of the placing in her of the embryo or the sperm and eggs.

Application of sections 35 to 47

34 APPLICATION OF SECTIONS 35 TO 47

(1) Sections 35 to 47 apply, in the case of a child who is being or has been carried by a woman (referred to in those sections as "W") as a result of the placing in her of an embryo or of sperm and eggs or her artificial insemination, to determine who is to be treated as the other parent of the child.

(2) Subsection (1) has effect subject to the provisions of sections 39, 40 and 46 limiting the purposes for which a person is treated as the child's other parent by virtue of those sections.

Meaning of "father"

35 WOMAN MARRIED AT TIME OF TREATMENT

(1) If—
   (a) at the time of the placing in her of the embryo or of the sperm and eggs or of her artificial insemination, W was a party to a marriage, and
   (b) the creation of the embryo carried by her was not brought about with the sperm of the other party to the marriage,

   then, subject to section 38(2) to (4), the other party to the marriage is to be treated as the father of the child unless it is shown that he did not consent to the placing in her of the embryo or the sperm and eggs or to her artificial insemination (as the case may be).

(2) This section applies whether W was in the United Kingdom or elsewhere at the time mentioned in subsection (1)(a).

36 TREATMENT PROVIDED TO WOMAN WHERE AGREED FATHERHOOD CONDITIONS APPLY

If no man is treated by virtue of section 35 as the father of the child and no woman is treated by virtue of section 42 as a parent of the child but—

(a) the embryo or the sperm and eggs were placed in W, or W was artificially inseminated, in the course of treatment services provided in the United Kingdom by a person to whom a licence applies,

(b) at the time when the embryo or the sperm and eggs were placed in W, or W was artificially inseminated, the agreed fatherhood conditions (as set out in section 37) were satisfied in relation to a man, in relation to treatment provided to W under the licence,

(c) the man remained alive at that time, and

(d) the creation of the embryo carried by W was not brought about with the man's sperm,

then, subject to section 38(2) to (4), the man is to be treated as the father of the child.

37 THE AGREED FATHERHOOD CONDITIONS

(1) The agreed fatherhood conditions referred to in section 36(b) are met in relation to a man ("M") in relation to treatment provided to W under a licence if, but only if,—
- (a) M has given the person responsible a notice stating that he consents to being treated as the father of any child resulting from treatment provided to W under the licence,
- (b) W has given the person responsible a notice stating that she consents to M being so treated,
- (c) neither M nor W has, since giving notice under paragraph (a) or (b), given the person responsible notice of the withdrawal of M's or W's consent to M being so treated,
- (d) W has not, since the giving of the notice under paragraph (b), given the person responsible—
  - (i) a further notice under that paragraph stating that she consents to another man being treated as the father of any resulting child, or
  - (ii) a notice under section 44(1)(b) stating that she consents to a woman being treated as a parent of any resulting child, and
- (e) W and M are not within prohibited degrees of relationship in relation to each other.

(2) A notice under subsection (1)(a), (b) or (c) must be in writing and must be signed by the person giving it.

(3) A notice under subsection (1)(a), (b) or (c) by a person ("S") who is unable to sign because of illness, injury or physical disability is to be taken to comply with the requirement of subsection (2) as to signature if it is signed at the direction of S, in the presence of S and in the presence of at least one witness who attests the signature.

38 FURTHER PROVISION RELATING TO SECTIONS 35 AND 36

(1) Where a person is to be treated as the father of the child by virtue of section 35 or 36, no other person is to be treated as the father of the child.

(2) In England and Wales and Northern Ireland, sections 35 and 36 do not affect any presumption, applying by virtue of the rules of common law, that a child is the legitimate child of the parties to a marriage.

(3) In Scotland, sections 35 and 36 do not apply in relation to any child who, by virtue of any enactment or other rule of law, is treated as the child of the parties to a marriage.

(4) Sections 35 and 36 do not apply to any child to the extent that the child is treated by virtue of adoption as not being the man's child.

39 USE OF SPERM, OR TRANSFER OF EMBRYO, AFTER DEATH OF MAN PROVIDING SPERM

(1) If—
  (a) the child has been carried by W as a result of the placing in her of an embryo or of sperm and eggs or her artificial insemination,
  (b) the creation of the embryo carried by W was brought about by using the sperm of a man after his death, or the creation of the embryo was brought about using the sperm of a man before his death but the embryo was placed in W after his death,
  (c) the man consented in writing (and did not withdraw the consent)—
    (i) to the use of his sperm after his death which brought about the creation of the embryo carried by W or (as the case may be) to the placing in W after his death of the embryo which was brought about using his sperm before his death, and
    (ii) to being treated for the purpose mentioned in subsection (3) as the father of any resulting child,
  (d) W has elected in writing not later than the end of the period of 42 days from the day on which the child was born for the man to be treated for the purpose mentioned in subsection (3) as the father of the child, and
  (e) no-one else is to be treated—
    (i) as the father of the child by virtue of section 35 or 36 or by virtue of section 38(2) or (3), or
    (ii) as a parent of the child by virtue of section 42 or 43 or by virtue of adoption,

then the man is to be treated for the purpose mentioned in subsection (3) as the father of the child.

(2) Subsection (1) applies whether W was in the United Kingdom or elsewhere at the time of the placing in her of the embryo or of the sperm and eggs or of her artificial insemination.

(3) The purpose referred to in subsection (1) is the purpose of enabling the man's particulars to be entered as the particulars of the child's father in a relevant register of births.

(4) In the application of this section to Scotland, for any reference to a period of 42 days there is substituted a reference to a period of 21 days.

40 EMBRYO TRANSFERRED AFTER DEATH OF HUSBAND ETC WHO DID NOT PROVIDE SPERM

(1) If—
  (a) the child has been carried by W as a result of the placing in her of an embryo,
  (b) the embryo was created at a time when W was a party to a marriage,
  (c) the creation of the embryo was not brought about with the sperm of the other party to the marriage,
  (d) the other party to the marriage died before the placing of the embryo in W,
  (e) the other party to the marriage consented in writing (and did not withdraw the consent)—
    (i) to the placing of the embryo in W after his death, and
    (ii) to being treated for the purpose mentioned in subsection (4) as the father of any resulting child,
  (f) W has elected in writing not later than the end of the period of 42 days from the day on which the child was born for the man to be treated for the purpose mentioned in subsection (4) as the father of the child, and
  (g) no-one else is to be treated—
    (i) as the father of the child by virtue of section 35 or 36 or by virtue of section 38(2) or (3), or

(ii) as a parent of the child by virtue of section 42 or 43 or by virtue of adoption,

then the man is to be treated for the purpose mentioned in subsection (4) as the father of the child.

(2) If—

(a) the child has been carried by W as a result of the placing in her of an embryo,

(b) the embryo was not created at a time when W was a party to a marriage or a civil partnership but was created in the course of treatment services provided to W in the United Kingdom by a person to whom a licence applies,

(c) a man consented in writing (and did not withdraw the consent)—

(i) to the placing of the embryo in W after his death, and

(ii) to being treated for the purpose mentioned in subsection (4) as the father of any resulting child,

(d) the creation of the embryo was not brought about with the sperm of that man,

(e) the man died before the placing of the embryo in W,

(f) immediately before the man's death, the agreed fatherhood conditions set out in section 37 were met in relation to the man in relation to treatment proposed to be provided to W in the United Kingdom by a person to whom a licence applies,

(g) W has elected in writing not later than the end of the period of 42 days from the day on which the child was born for the man to be treated for the purpose mentioned in subsection (4) as the father of the child, and

(h) no-one else is to be treated—

(i) as the father of the child by virtue of section 35 or 36 or by virtue of section 38(2) or (3), or

(ii) as a parent of the child by virtue of section 42 or 43 or by virtue of adoption,

then the man is to be treated for the purpose mentioned in subsection (4) as the father of the child.

(3) Subsections (1) and (2) apply whether W was in the United Kingdom or elsewhere at the time of the placing in her of the embryo.

(4) The purpose referred to in subsections (1) and (2) is the purpose of enabling the man's particulars to be entered as the particulars of the child's father in a relevant register of births.

(5) In the application of this section to Scotland, for any reference to a period of 42 days there is substituted a reference to a period of 21 days.

41 PERSONS NOT TO BE TREATED AS FATHER

(1) Where the sperm of a man who had given such consent as is required by paragraph 5 of Schedule 3 to the 1990 Act (consent to use of gametes for purposes of treatment services or nonmedical fertility services) was used for a purpose for which such consent was required, he is not to be treated as the father of the child.

(2) Where the sperm of a man, or an embryo the creation of which was brought about with his sperm, was used after his death, he is not, subject to section 39, to be treated as the father of the child.

(3) Subsection (2) applies whether W was in the United Kingdom or elsewhere at the time of the placing in her of the embryo or of the sperm and eggs or of her artificial insemination.

Cases in which woman to be other parent

42 WOMAN IN CIVIL PARTNERSHIP AT TIME OF TREATMENT

(1) If at the time of the placing in her of the embryo or the sperm and eggs or of her artificial insemination, W was a party to a civil partnership, then subject to section 45(2) to (4), the other party to the civil partnership is to be treated as a parent of the child unless it is shown that she did not consent to the placing in W of the embryo or the sperm and eggs or to her artificial insemination (as the case may be).

(2) This section applies whether W was in the United Kingdom or elsewhere at the time mentioned in subsection (1).

43 TREATMENT PROVIDED TO WOMAN WHO AGREES THAT SECOND WOMAN TO BE PARENT

If no man is treated by virtue of section 35 as the father of the child and no woman is treated by virtue of section 42 as a parent of the child but—

(a) the embryo or the sperm and eggs were placed in W, or W was artificially inseminated, in the course of treatment services provided in the United Kingdom by a person to whom a licence applies,

(b) at the time when the embryo or the sperm and eggs were placed in W, or W was artificially inseminated, the agreed female parenthood conditions (as set out in section 44) were met in relation to another woman, in relation to treatment provided to W under that licence, and

(c) the other woman remained alive at that time,

then, subject to section 45(2) to (4), the other woman is to be treated as a parent of the child.

44 THE AGREED FEMALE PARENTHOOD CONDITIONS

(1) The agreed female parenthood conditions referred to in section 43(b) are met in relation to another woman ("P") in relation to treatment provided to W under a licence if, but only if,—
  (a) P has given the person responsible a notice stating that P consents to P being treated as a parent of any child resulting from treatment provided to W under the licence,
  (b) W has given the person responsible a notice stating that W agrees to P being so treated,
  (c) neither W nor P has, since giving notice under paragraph (a) or (b), given the person responsible notice of the withdrawal of P's or W's consent to P being so treated,
  (d) W has not, since the giving of the notice under paragraph (b), given the person responsible—
    (i) a further notice under that paragraph stating that W consents to a woman other than P being treated as a parent of any resulting child, or
    (ii) a notice under section 37(1)(b) stating that W consents to a man being treated as the father of any resulting child, and
  (e) W and P are not within prohibited degrees of relationship in relation to each other.

(2) A notice under subsection (1)(a), (b) or (c) must be in writing and must be signed by the person giving it.

(3) A notice under subsection (1)(a), (b) or (c) by a person ("S") who is unable to sign because of illness, injury or physical disability is to be taken to comply with the requirement of subsection (2) as to signature if it is signed at the direction of S, in the presence of S and in the presence of at least one witness who attests the signature.

45 FURTHER PROVISION RELATING TO SECTIONS 42 AND 43

(1) Where a woman is treated by virtue of section 42 or 43 as a parent of the child, no man is to be treated as the father of the child.

(2) In England and Wales and Northern Ireland, sections 42 and 43 do not affect any presumption, applying by virtue of the rules of common law, that a child is the legitimate child of the parties to a marriage.

(3) In Scotland, sections 42 and 43 do not apply in relation to any child who, by virtue of any enactment or other rule of law, is treated as the child of the parties to a marriage.

(4) Sections 42 and 43 do not apply to any child to the extent that the child is treated by virtue of adoption as not being the woman's child.

46 EMBRYO TRANSFERRED AFTER DEATH OF CIVIL PARTNER OR INTENDED FEMALE PARENT

(1) If—
- (a) the child has been carried by W as the result of the placing in her of an embryo,
- (b) the embryo was created at a time when W was a party to a civil partnership,
- (c) the other party to the civil partnership died before the placing of the embryo in W,
- (d) the other party to the civil partnership consented in writing (and did not withdraw the consent)—
  - (i) to the placing of the embryo in W after the death of the other party, and
  - (ii) to being treated for the purpose mentioned in subsection (4) as the parent of any resulting child,
- (e) W has elected in writing not later than the end of the period of 42 days from the day on which the child was born for the other party to the civil partnership to be treated for the purpose mentioned in subsection (4) as the parent of the child, and
- (f) no one else is to be treated—
  - (i) as the father of the child by virtue of section 35 or 36 or by virtue of section 45(2) or (3), or
  - (ii) as a parent of the child by virtue of section 42 or 43 or by virtue of adoption,

then the other party to the civil partnership is to be treated for the purpose mentioned in subsection (4) as a parent of the child.

(2) If—
- (a) the child has been carried by W as the result of the placing in her of an embryo,
- (b) the embryo was not created at a time when W was a party to a marriage or a civil partnership, but was created in the course of treatment services provided to W in the United Kingdom by a person to whom a licence applies,
- (c) another woman consented in writing (and did not withdraw the consent)—
  - (i) to the placing of the embryo in W after the death of the other woman, and
  - (ii) to being treated for the purpose mentioned in subsection (4) as the parent of any resulting child,
- (d) the other woman died before the placing of the embryo in W,
- (e) immediately before the other woman's death, the agreed female parenthood conditions set out in section 44 were met in relation to the other woman in relation to

treatment proposed to be provided to W in the United Kingdom by a person to whom a licence applies,

(f) W has elected in writing not later than the end of the period of 42 days from the day on which the child was born for the other woman to be treated for the purpose mentioned in subsection (4) as the parent of the child, and

(g) no one else is to be treated—

(i) as the father of the child by virtue of section 35 or 36 or by virtue of section 45(2) or (3), or

(ii) as a parent of the child by virtue of section 42 or 43 or by virtue of adoption,

then the other woman is to be treated for the purpose mentioned in subsection (4) as a parent of the child.

(3) Subsections (1) and (2) apply whether W was in the United Kingdom or elsewhere at the time of the placing in her of the embryo.

(4) The purpose referred to in subsections (1) and (2) is the purpose of enabling the deceased woman's particulars to be entered as the particulars of the child's other parent in a relevant register of births.

(5) In the application of subsections (1) and (2) to Scotland, for any reference to a period of 42 days there is substituted a reference to a period of 21 days.

47 WOMAN NOT TO BE OTHER PARENT MERELY BECAUSE OF EGG DONATION

A woman is not to be treated as the parent of a child whom she is not carrying and has not carried, except where she is so treated—

(a) by virtue of section 42 or 43, or

(b) by virtue of section 46 (for the purpose mentioned in subsection (4) of that section), or

(c) by virtue of adoption.

Effect of sections 33 to 47

48 EFFECT OF SECTIONS 33 TO 47

(1) Where by virtue of section 33, 35, 36, 42 or 43 a person is to be treated as the mother, father or parent of a child, that person is to be treated in law as the mother, father or parent (as the case may be) of the child for all purposes.

(2) Where by virtue of section 33, 38, 41, 45 or 47 a person is not to be treated as a parent of the child, that person is to be treated in law as not being a parent of the child for any purpose.

(3) Where section 39(1) or 40(1) or (2) applies, the deceased man—

(a) is to be treated in law as the father of the child for the purpose mentioned in section 39(3) or 40(4), but

(b) is to be treated in law as not being the father of the child for any other purpose.

(4) Where section 46(1) or (2) applies, the deceased woman—

(a) is to be treated in law as a parent of the child for the purpose mentioned in section 46(4), but

(b) is to be treated in law as not being a parent of the child for any other purpose.

(5) Where any of subsections (1) to (4) has effect, references to any relationship between two people in any enactment, deed or other instrument or document (whenever passed or made) are to be read accordingly.

(6) In relation to England and Wales and Northern Ireland, a child who—
(a) has a parent by virtue of section 42, or
(b) has a parent by virtue of section 43 who is at any time during the period beginning with the time mentioned in section 43(b) and ending with the time of the child's birth a party to a civil partnership with the child's mother, is the legitimate child of the child's parents.

(7) In relation to England and Wales and Northern Ireland, nothing in the provisions of section 33(1) or sections 35 to 47, read with this section—
(a) affects the succession to any dignity or title of honour or renders any person capable of succeeding to or transmitting a right to succeed to any such dignity or title, or
(b) affects the devolution of any property limited (expressly or not) to devolve (as nearly as the law permits) along with any dignity or title of honour.

(8) In relation to Scotland—
(a) those provisions do not apply to any title, coat of arms, honour or dignity transmissible on the death of its holder or affect the succession to any such title, coat of arms or dignity or its devolution, and
(b) where the terms of any deed provide that any property or interest in property is to devolve along with a title, coat of arms, honour or dignity, nothing in those provisions is to prevent that property or interest from so devolving.

References to parties to marriage or civil partnership

49 MEANING OF REFERENCES TO PARTIES TO A MARRIAGE

(1) The references in sections 35 to 47 to the parties to a marriage at any time there referred to—
(a) are to the parties to a marriage subsisting at that time, unless a judicial separation was then in force, but
(b) include the parties to a void marriage if either or both of them reasonably believed at that time that the marriage was valid; and for the purposes of those sections it is to be presumed, unless the contrary is shown, that one of them reasonably believed at that time that the marriage was valid.

(2) In subsection (1)(a) "judicial separation" includes a legal separation obtained in a country outside the British Islands and recognised in the United Kingdom.

50 MEANING OF REFERENCES TO PARTIES TO A CIVIL PARTNERSHIP

(1) The references in sections 35 to 47 to the parties to a civil partnership at any time there referred to—
(a) are to the parties to a civil partnership subsisting at that time, unless a separation order was then in force, but
(b) include the parties to a void civil partnership if either or both of them reasonably believed at that time that the civil partnership was valid; and for the purposes of those sections it is to be presumed, unless the contrary is shown, that one of them reasonably believed at that time that the civil partnership was valid.

(2) The reference in section 48(6)(b) to a civil partnership includes a reference to a void civil partnership if either or both of the parties reasonably believed at the time when they registered as civil partners of each other that the civil partnership was valid; and for this

purpose it is to be presumed, unless the contrary is shown, that one of them reasonably believed at that time that the civil partnership was valid.

(3) In subsection (1)(a), "separation order" means—
(a) a separation order under section 37(1)(d) or 161(1)(d) of the Civil Partnership Act 2004 (c 33),
(b) a decree of separation under section 120(2) of that Act, or
(c) a legal separation obtained in a country outside the United Kingdom and recognised in the United Kingdom.

. . .

Interpretation of references to father etc where woman is other parent

53 INTERPRETATION OF REFERENCES TO FATHER ETC

(1) Subsections (2) and (3) have effect, subject to subsections (4) and (6), for the interpretation of any enactment, deed or any other instrument or document (whenever passed or made).

(2) Any reference (however expressed) to the father of a child who has a parent by virtue of section 42 or 43 is to be read as a reference to the woman who is a parent of the child by virtue of that section.

(3) Any reference (however expressed) to evidence of paternity is, in relation to a woman who is a parent by virtue of section 42 or 43, to be read as a reference to evidence of parentage.

(4) This section does not affect the interpretation of the enactments specified in subsection (5) (which make express provision for the case where a child has a parent by virtue of section 42 or 43).

(5) Those enactments are—
(a) the Legitimacy Act (Northern Ireland) 1928 (c 5 (NI)),
(b) the Schedule to the Population (Statistics) Act 1938 (c 12),
(c) the Births and Deaths Registration Act 1953 (c 20),
(d) the Registration of Births, Deaths and Marriages (Special Provisions) Act 1957 (c 58),
(e) Part 2 of the Registration of Births, Deaths and Marriages (Scotland) Act 1965 (c 49),
(f) the Congenital Disabilities (Civil Liability) Act 1976 (c 28),
(g) the Legitimacy Act 1976 (c 31),
(h) the Births and Deaths Registration (Northern Ireland) Order 1976 (SI 1976/1041 (NI 14)),
(i) the British Nationality Act 1981 (c 61),
(j) the Family Law Reform Act 1987 (c 42),
(k) Parts 1 and 2 of the Children Act 1989 (c 41),
(l) Part 1 of the Children (Scotland) Act 1995 (c 36),
(m) section 1 of the Criminal Law (Consolidation) (Scotland) Act 1995 (c 39), and
(n) Parts 2, 3 and 14 of the Children (Northern Ireland) Order 1995 (SI 1995/755 (NI 2)).

(6) This section does not affect the interpretation of references that fall to be read in accordance with section 1(2)(a) or (b) of the Family Law Reform Act 1987 or Article 155(2)(a) or (b) of the Children (Northern Ireland) Order 1995 (references to a person whose father and mother were, or were not, married to each other at the time of the person's birth).

Parental orders

54 PARENTAL ORDERS

(1) On an application made by two people ("the applicants"), the court may make an order providing for a child to be treated in law as the child of the applicants if—
(a) the child has been carried by a woman who is not one of the applicants, as a result of the placing in her of an embryo or sperm and eggs or her artificial insemination,
(b) the gametes of at least one of the applicants were used to bring about the creation of the embryo, and
(c) the conditions in subsections (2) to (8) are satisfied.

(2) The applicants must be—
(a) husband and wife,
(b) civil partners of each other, or
(c) two persons who are living as partners in an enduring family relationship and are not within prohibited degrees of relationship in relation to each other.

(3) Except in a case falling within subsection (11), the applicants must apply for the order during the period of 6 months beginning with the day on which the child is born.

(4) At the time of the application and the making of the order—
(a) the child's home must be with the applicants, and
(b) either or both of the applicants must be domiciled in the United Kingdom or in the Channel Islands or the Isle of Man.

(5) At the time of the making of the order both the applicants must have attained the age of 18.

(6) The court must be satisfied that both—
(a) the woman who carried the child, and
(b) any other person who is a parent of the child but is not one of the applicants (including any man who is the father by virtue of section 35 or 36 or any woman who is a parent by virtue of section 42 or 43),

have freely, and with full understanding of what is involved, agreed unconditionally to the making of the order.

(7) Subsection (6) does not require the agreement of a person who cannot be found or is incapable of giving agreement; and the agreement of the woman who carried the child is ineffective for the purpose of that subsection if given by her less than six weeks after the child's birth.

(8) The court must be satisfied that no money or other benefit (other than for expenses reasonably incurred) has been given or received by either of the applicants for or in consideration of—
(a) the making of the order,
(b) any agreement required by subsection (6),
(c) the handing over of the child to the applicants, or
(d) the making of arrangements with a view to the making of the order, unless authorised by the court.

(9) For the purposes of an application under this section—
(a) in relation to England and Wales, section 92(7) to (10) of, and Part 1 of Schedule 11 to, the Children Act 1989 (c 41) (jurisdiction of courts) apply for the purposes of this section to determine the meaning of "the court" as they apply for the purposes of that

Act and proceedings on the application are to be "family proceedings" for the purposes of that Act, . . .

(10) Subsection (1)(a) applies whether the woman was in the United Kingdom or elsewhere at the time of the placing in her of the embryo or the sperm and eggs or her artificial insemination.

(11) An application which—
(a) relates to a child born before the coming into force of this section, and
(b) is made by two persons who, throughout the period applicable under subsection (2) of section 30 of the 1990 Act, were not eligible to apply for an order under that section in relation to the child as husband and wife,
may be made within the period of six months beginning with the day on which this section comes into force.

55 PARENTAL ORDERS: SUPPLEMENTARY PROVISION

(1) The Secretary of State may by regulations provide—
(a) for any provision of the enactments about adoption to have effect, with such modifications (if any) as may be specified in the regulations, in relation to orders under section 54, and applications for such orders, as it has effect in relation to adoption, and applications for adoption orders, and
(b) for references in any enactment to adoption, an adopted child or an adoptive relationship to be read (respectively) as references to the effect of an order under section 54, a child to whom such an order applies and a relationship arising by virtue of the enactments about adoption, as applied by the regulations, and for similar expressions in connection with adoption to be read accordingly.

(2) The regulations may include such incidental or supplemental provision as appears to the Secretary of State to be necessary or desirable in consequence of any provision made by virtue of subsection (1)(a) or (b).

(3) In this section "the enactments about adoption" means—

. . .

(b) the Adoption and Children Act 2002 (c 38),

. . .

General

57 REPEALS AND TRANSITIONAL PROVISION RELATING TO PART 2

(1) Sections 33 to 48 have effect only in relation to children carried by women as a result of the placing in them of embryos or of sperm and eggs, or their artificial insemination (as the case may be), after the commencement of those sections.

(2) Sections 27 to 29 of the 1990 Act (which relate to status) do not have effect in relation to children carried by women as a result of the placing in them of embryos or of sperm and eggs, or their artificial insemination (as the case may be), after the commencement of sections 33 to 48.

. . .

58 INTERPRETATION OF PART 2

. . .

(2) For the purposes of this Part, two persons are within prohibited degrees of relationship if one is the other's parent, grandparent, sister, brother, aunt or uncle; and in this subsection references to relationships—
   (a) are to relationships of the full blood or half blood or, in the case of an adopted person, such of those relationships as would subsist but for adoption, and
   (b) include the relationship of a child with his adoptive, or former adoptive, parents, but do not include any other adoptive relationships.

Children and Young Persons Act 2008

(2008 c 23)

Well-being

7 WELL-BEING OF CHILDREN AND YOUNG PERSONS

(1) It is the general duty of the Secretary of State to promote the well-being of children in England.

(2) The general duty imposed by subsection (1) has effect subject to any specific duties imposed on the Secretary of State.

(3) The activities which may be undertaken or supported in the discharge of the general duty imposed by subsection (1) include activities in connection with parenting.

(4) The Secretary of State may take such action as the Secretary of State considers appropriate to promote the well-being of—
   (a) persons who are receiving services under sections 23C to 24D of the 1989 Act; and
   (b) persons under the age of 25 of a prescribed description.

(5) The Secretary of State, in discharging functions under this section, must have regard to the aspects of well-being mentioned in section 10(2)(a) to (e) of the Children Act 2004 (c 31).

(6) In this section—

"children" means persons under the age of 18; and
"prescribed" means prescribed in regulations made by the Secretary of State.

Equality Act 2010

(2010 c 15)

Part 2 EQUALITY: KEY CONCEPTS

Chapter 1 PROTECTED CHARACTERISTICS

4 THE PROTECTED CHARACTERISTICS

The following characteristics are protected characteristics—

age;
disability;
gender reassignment;

marriage and civil partnership;
pregnancy and maternity;
race;
religion or belief;
sex;
sexual orientation.

. . .

8 MARRIAGE AND CIVIL PARTNERSHIP

(1) A person has the protected characteristic of marriage and civil partnership if the person is married or is a civil partner.

(2) In relation to the protected characteristic of marriage and civil partnership—
(a) a reference to a person who has a particular protected characteristic is a reference to a person who is married or is a civil partner;
(b) a reference to persons who share a protected characteristic is a reference to persons who are married or are civil partners.

Chapter 2 PROHIBITED CONDUCT

Discrimination

13 DIRECT DISCRIMINATION

(1) A person (A) discriminates against another (B) if, because of a protected characteristic, A treats B less favourably than A treats or would treat others.

(2) If the protected characteristic is age, A does not discriminate against B if A can show A's treatment of B to be a proportionate means of achieving a legitimate aim.

(3) If the protected characteristic is disability, and B is not a disabled person, A does not discriminate against B only because A treats or would treat disabled persons more favourably than A treats B.

(4) If the protected characteristic is marriage and civil partnership, this section applies to a contravention of Part 5 (work) only if the treatment is because it is B who is married or a civil partner.

(5) If the protected characteristic is race, less favourable treatment includes segregating B from others.

(6) If the protected characteristic is sex—
(a) less favourable treatment of a woman includes less favourable treatment of her because she is breast-feeding;
(b) in a case where B is a man, no account is to be taken of special treatment afforded to a woman in connection with pregnancy or childbirth.

(7) Subsection (6)(a) does not apply for the purposes of Part 5 (work).

(8) This section is subject to sections 17(6) and 18(7).

. . .

19 INDIRECT DISCRIMINATION

(1) A person (A) discriminates against another (B) if A applies to B a provision, criterion or practice which is discriminatory in relation to a relevant protected characteristic of B's.

(2) For the purposes of subsection (1), a provision, criterion or practice is discriminatory in relation to a relevant protected characteristic of B's if—
(a) A applies, or would apply, it to persons with whom B does not share the characteristic,
(b) it puts, or would put, persons with whom B shares the characteristic at a particular disadvantage when compared with persons with whom B does not share it,
(c) it puts, or would put, B at that disadvantage, and
(d) A cannot show it to be a proportionate means of achieving a legitimate aim.

(3) The relevant protected characteristics are—
age;
disability;
gender reassignment;
marriage and civil partnership;
race;
religion or belief;
sex;
sexual orientation.

Crime and Security Act 2010

(2010 c 17)

Domestic violence

24 POWER TO ISSUE A DOMESTIC VIOLENCE PROTECTION NOTICE

(1) A member of a police force not below the rank of superintendent ("the authorising officer") may issue a domestic violence protection notice ("a DVPN") under this section.

(2) A DVPN may be issued to a person ("P") aged 18 years or over if the authorising officer has reasonable grounds for believing that—
(a) P has been violent towards, or has threatened violence towards, an associated person, and
(b) the issue of the DVPN is necessary to protect that person from violence or a threat of violence by P.

(3) Before issuing a DVPN, the authorising officer must, in particular, consider—
(a) the welfare of any person under the age of 18 whose interests the officer considers relevant to the issuing of the DVPN (whether or not that person is an associated person),
(b) the opinion of the person for whose protection the DVPN would be issued as to the issuing of the DVPN,
(c) any representations made by P as to the issuing of the DVPN, and
(d) in the case of provision included by virtue of subsection (8), the opinion of any other associated person who lives in the premises to which the provision would relate.

(4) The authorising officer must take reasonable steps to discover the opinions mentioned in subsection (3).

(5) But the authorising officer may issue a DVPN in circumstances where the person for whose protection it is issued does not consent to the issuing of the DVPN.

(6) A DVPN must contain provision to prohibit P from molesting the person for whose protection it is issued.

(7) Provision required to be included by virtue of subsection (6) may be expressed so as to refer to molestation in general, to particular acts of molestation, or to both.

(8) If P lives in premises which are also lived in by a person for whose protection the DVPN is issued, the DVPN may also contain provision—

(a) to prohibit P from evicting or excluding from the premises the person for whose protection the DVPN is issued,
(b) to prohibit P from entering the premises,
(c) to require P to leave the premises, or
(d) to prohibit P from coming within such distance of the premises as may be specified in the DVPN.

(9) An "associated person" means a person who is associated with P within the meaning of section 62 of the Family Law Act 1996.

. . .

25 CONTENTS AND SERVICE OF A DOMESTIC VIOLENCE PROTECTION NOTICE

(1) A DVPN must state—
(a) the grounds on which it has been issued,
(b) that a constable may arrest P without warrant if the constable has reasonable grounds for believing that P is in breach of the DVPN,
(c) that an application for a domestic violence protection order under section 27 will be heard within 48 hours of the time of service of the DVPN and a notice of the hearing will be given to P,
(d) that the DVPN continues in effect until that application has been determined, and
(e) the provision that a magistrates' court may include in a domestic violence protection order.

(2) A DVPN must be in writing and must be served on P personally by a constable.

(3) On serving P with a DVPN, the constable must ask P for an address for the purposes of being given the notice of the hearing of the application for the domestic violence protection order.

26 BREACH OF A DOMESTIC VIOLENCE PROTECTION NOTICE

(1) A person arrested by virtue of section 25(1)(b) for a breach of a DVPN must be held in custody and brought before the magistrates' court which will hear the application for the DVPO under section 27—
(a) before the end of the period of 24 hours beginning with the time of the arrest, or
(b) if earlier, at the hearing of that application.

(2) If the person is brought before the court by virtue of subsection (1)(a), the court may remand the person.

(3) If the court adjourns the hearing of the application by virtue of section 27(8), the court may remand the person.

(4) In calculating when the period of 24 hours mentioned in subsection (1)(a) ends, Christmas Day, Good Friday, any Sunday and any day which is a bank holiday in England and Wales under the Banking and Financial Dealings Act 1971 are to be disregarded.

27 APPLICATION FOR A DOMESTIC VIOLENCE PROTECTION ORDER

(1) If a DVPN has been issued, a constable must apply for a domestic violence protection order ("a DVPO").

(2) The application must be made by complaint to a magistrates' court.

(3) The application must be heard by the magistrates' court not later than 48 hours after the DVPN was served pursuant to section 25(2).

(4) In calculating when the period of 48 hours mentioned in subsection (3) ends, Christmas Day, Good Friday, any Sunday and any day which is a bank holiday in England and Wales under the Banking and Financial Dealings Act 1971 are to be disregarded.

(5) A notice of the hearing of the application must be given to P.

(6) The notice is deemed given if it has been left at the address given by P under section 25(3).

(7) But if the notice has not been given because no address was given by P under section 25(3), the court may hear the application for the DVPO if the court is satisfied that the constable applying for the DVPO has made reasonable efforts to give P the notice.

(8) The magistrates' court may adjourn the hearing of the application.

(9) If the court adjourns the hearing, the DVPN continues in effect until the application has been determined.

(10) On the hearing of an application for a DVPO, section 97 of the Magistrates' Courts Act 1980 (summons to witness and warrant for his arrest) does not apply in relation to a person for whose protection the DVPO would be made, except where the person has given oral or written evidence at the hearing.

28 CONDITIONS FOR AND CONTENTS OF A DOMESTIC VIOLENCE PROTECTION ORDER

(1) The court may make a DVPO if two conditions are met.

(2) The first condition is that the court is satisfied on the balance of probabilities that P has been violent towards, or has threatened violence towards, an associated person.

(3) The second condition is that the court thinks that making the DVPO is necessary to protect that person from violence or a threat of violence by P.

(4) Before making a DVPO, the court must, in particular, consider—
(a) the welfare of any person under the age of 18 whose interests the court considers relevant to the making of the DVPO (whether or not that person is an associated person), and
(b) any opinion of which the court is made aware—
(i) of the person for whose protection the DVPO would be made, and
(ii) in the case of provision included by virtue of subsection (8), of any other associated person who lives in the premises to which the provision would relate.

(5) But the court may make a DVPO in circumstances where the person for whose protection it is made does not consent to the making of the DVPO.

(6) A DVPO must contain provision to prohibit P from molesting the person for whose protection it is made.

(7) Provision required to be included by virtue of subsection (6) may be expressed so as to refer to molestation in general, to particular acts of molestation, or to both.

(8) If P lives in premises which are also lived in by a person for whose protection the DVPO is made, the DVPO may also contain provision—
(a) to prohibit P from evicting or excluding from the premises the person for whose protection the DVPO is made,
(b) to prohibit P from entering the premises,
(c) to require P to leave the premises, or
(d) to prohibit P from coming within such distance of the premises as may be specified in the DVPO.

(9) A DVPO must state that a constable may arrest P without warrant if the constable has reasonable grounds for believing that P is in breach of the DVPO.

(10) A DVPO may be in force for—
(a) no fewer than 14 days beginning with the day on which it is made, and
(b) no more than 28 days beginning with that day.

(11) A DVPO must state the period for which it is to be in force.

29 BREACH OF A DOMESTIC VIOLENCE PROTECTION ORDER

(1) A person arrested by virtue of section 28(9) for a breach of a DVPO must be held in custody and brought before a magistrates' court within the period of 24 hours beginning with the time of the arrest.

(2) If the matter is not disposed of when the person is brought before the court, the court may remand the person.

(3) In calculating when the period of 24 hours mentioned in subsection (1) ends, Christmas Day, Good Friday, any Sunday and any day which is a bank holiday in England and Wales under the Banking and Financial Dealings Act 1971 are to be disregarded.

. . .

33 PILOT SCHEMES

(1) The Secretary of State may by order made by statutory instrument provide for any provision of sections 24 to 32 to come into force for a period of time to be specified in or under the order for the purpose of assessing the effectiveness of the provision.

(2) Such an order may make different provision for different areas.

(3) More than one order may be made under this section.

(4) Provision included in an order under this section does not affect the provision that may be included in relation to sections 24 to 32 in an order under section 59 (commencement).

NB – The above provisions of the Crime and Security Act 2010 have been implemented for the purpose of regional pilots from 30 June 2011 for a period of 12 months.

International Instruments

United Nations Convention on the Rights of the Child
(2 September 1990)

Part I

Article 1
For the purposes of the present Convention, a child means every human being below the age of eighteen years unless under the law applicable to the child, majority is attained earlier.

Article 2
1. States Parties shall respect and ensure the rights set forth in the present Convention to each child within their jurisdiction without discrimination of any kind, irrespective of the child's or his or her parent's or legal guardian's race, colour, sex, language, religion, political or other opinion, national, ethnic or social origin, property, disability, birth or other status.
2. States Parties shall take all appropriate measures to ensure that the child is protected against all forms of discrimination or punishment on the basis of the status, activities, expressed opinions, or beliefs of the child's parents, legal guardians, or family members.

Article 3
1. In all actions concerning children, whether undertaken by public or private social welfare institutions, courts of law, administrative authorities or legislative bodies, the best interests of the child shall be a primary consideration.
2. States Parties undertake to ensure the child such protection and care as is necessary for his or her well-being, taking into account the rights and duties of his or her parents, legal guardians, or other individuals legally responsible for him or her, and, to this end, shall take all appropriate legislative and administrative measures.
3. States Parties shall ensure that the institutions, services and facilities responsible for the care or protection of children shall conform with the standards established by competent authorities, particularly in the areas of safety, health, in the number and suitability of their staff, as well as competent supervision.

Article 4
States Parties shall undertake all appropriate legislative, administrative, and other measures for the implementation of the rights recognized in the present Convention. With regard to economic, social and cultural rights, States Parties shall undertake such measures to the

maximum extent of their available resources and, where needed, within the framework of international co-operation.

Article 5

States Parties shall respect the responsibilities, rights and duties of parents or, where applicable, the members of the extended family or community as provided for by local custom, legal guardians or other persons legally responsible for the child, to provide, in a manner consistent with the evolving capacities of the child, appropriate direction and guidance in the exercise by the child of the rights recognized in the present Convention.

Article 6

1. States Parties recognize that every child has the inherent right to life.
2. States Parties shall ensure to the maximum extent possible the survival and development of the child.

Article 7

1. The child shall be registered immediately after birth and shall have the right from birth to a name, the right to acquire a nationality and. as far as possible, the right to know and be cared for by his or her parents.
2. States Parties shall ensure the implementation of these rights in accordance with their national law and their obligations under the relevant international instruments in this field, in particular where the child would otherwise be stateless.

Article 8

1. States Parties undertake to respect the right of the child to preserve his or her identity, including nationality, name and family relations as recognized by law without unlawful interference.
2. Where a child is illegally deprived of some or all of the elements of his or her identity, States Parties shall provide appropriate assistance and protection, with a view to re-establishing speedily his or her identity.

Article 9

1. States Parties shall ensure that a child shall not be separated from his or her parents against their will, except when competent authorities subject to judicial review determine, in accordance with applicable law and procedures, that such separation is necessary for the best interests of the child. Such determination may be necessary in a particular case such as one involving abuse or neglect of the child by the parents, or one where the parents are living separately and a decision must be made as to the child's place of residence.
2. In any proceedings pursuant to paragraph 1 of the present article, all interested parties shall be given an opportunity to participate in the proceedings and make their views known.
3. States Parties shall respect the right of the child who is separated from one or both parents to maintain personal relations and direct contact with both parents on a regular basis, except if it is contrary to the child's best interests.
4. Where such separation results from any action initiated by a State Party, such as the detention, imprisonment, exile, deportation or death (including death arising from any cause while the person is in the custody of the State) of one or both parents or of the child, that State Party shall, upon request, provide the parents, the child or, if appropriate,

another member of the family with the essential information concerning the whereabouts of the absent member(s) of the family unless the provision of the information would be detrimental to the well-being of the child. States Parties shall further ensure that the submission of such a request shall of itself entail no adverse consequences for the person(s) concerned.

Article 10

1. In accordance with the obligation of States Parties under article 9, paragraph 1, applications by a child or his or her parents to enter or leave a State Party for the purpose of family reunification shall be dealt with by States Parties in a positive, humane and expeditious manner. States Parties shall further ensure that the submission of such a request shall entail no adverse consequences for the applicants and for the members of their family.

2. A child whose parents reside in different States shall have the right to maintain on a regular basis, save in exceptional circumstances personal relations and direct contacts with both parents. Towards that end and in accordance with the obligation of States Parties under article 9, paragraph 1, States Parties shall respect the right of the child and his or her parents to leave any country, including their own, and to enter their own country. The right to leave any country shall be subject only to such restrictions as are prescribed by law and which are necessary to protect the national security, public order (ordre public), public health or morals or the rights and freedoms of others and are consistent with the other rights recognized in the present Convention.

Article 11

1. States Parties shall take measures to combat the illicit transfer and non-return of children abroad.

2. To this end, States Parties shall promote the conclusion of bilateral or multilateral agreements or accession to existing agreements.

Article 12

1. States Parties shall assure to the child who is capable of forming his or her own views the right to express those views freely in all matters affecting the child, the views of the child being given due weight in accordance with the age and maturity of the child.

2. For this purpose, the child shall in particular be provided the opportunity to be heard in any judicial and administrative proceedings affecting the child, either directly, or through a representative or an appropriate body, in a manner consistent with the procedural rules of national law.

Article 13

1. The child shall have the right to freedom of expression; this right shall include freedom to seek, receive and impart information and ideas of all kinds, regardless of frontiers, either orally, in writing or in print, in the form of art, or through any other media of the child's choice.

2. The exercise of this right may be subject to certain restrictions, but these shall only be such as are provided by law and are necessary:
   (a) for respect of the rights or reputations of others; or
   (b) for the protection of national security or of public order (ordre public), or of public health or morals.

Article 14

1. States Parties shall respect the right of the child to freedom of thought, conscience and religion.

2. States Parties shall respect the rights and duties of the parents and, when applicable, legal guardians, to provide direction to the child in the exercise of his or her right in a manner consistent with the evolving capacities of the child.

3. Freedom to manifest one's religion or beliefs may be subject only to such limitations as are prescribed by law and are necessary to protect public safety, order, health or morals, or the fundamental rights and freedoms of others.

Article 15

1. States Parties recognize the rights of the child to freedom of association and to freedom of peaceful assembly.

2. No restrictions may be placed on the exercise of these rights other than those imposed in conformity with the law and which are necessary in a democratic society in the interests of national security or public safety, public order (ordre public), the protection of public health or morals or the protection of the rights and freedoms of others.

Article 16

1. No child shall be subjected to arbitrary or unlawful interference with his or her privacy, family, or correspondence, nor to unlawful attacks on his or her honour and reputation.

2. The child has the right to the protection of the law against such interference or attacks.

Article 17

States Parties recognize the important function performed by the mass media and shall ensure that the child has access to information and material from a diversity of national and international sources, especially those aimed at the promotion of his or her social, spiritual and moral well-being and physical and mental health.

To this end, States Parties shall:

(a) encourage the mass media to disseminate information and material of social and cultural benefit to the child and in accordance with the spirit of article 29;

(b) encourage international co-operation in the production, exchange and dissemination of such information and material from a diversity of cultural, national and international sources;

(c) encourage the production and dissemination of children's books;

(d) encourage the mass media to have particular regard to the linguistic needs of the child who belongs to a minority group or who is indigenous;

(e) encourage the development of appropriate guidelines for the protection of the child from information and material injurious to his or her well-being, bearing in mind the provisions of articles 13 and 18.

Article 18

1. States Parties shall use their best efforts to ensure recognition of the principle that both parents have common responsibilities for the upbringing and development of the child. Parents or, as the case may be, legal guardians, have the primary responsibility for the upbringing and development of the child. The best interests of the child will be their basic concern.

2. For the purpose of guaranteeing and promoting the rights set forth in the present Convention, States Parties shall render appropriate assistance to parents and legal guardians in the performance of their child-rearing responsibilities and shall ensure the development of institutions, facilities and services for the care of children.

3. States Parties shall take all appropriate measures to ensure that children of working parents have the right to benefit from child-care services and facilities for which they are eligible.

Article 19

1. States Parties shall take all appropriate legislative, administrative, social and educational measures to protect the child from all forms of physical or mental violence, injury or abuse, neglect or negligent treatment, maltreatment or exploitation, including sexual abuse, while in the care of parent(s), legal guardian(s) or any other person who has the care of the child.

2. Such protective measures should, as appropriate, include effective procedures for the establishment of social programmes to provide necessary support for the child and for those who have the care of the child, as well as for other forms of prevention and for identification, reporting, referral, investigation, treatment and follow-up of instances of child maltreatment described heretofore, and, as appropriate, for judicial involvement.

Article 20

1. A child temporarily or permanently deprived of his or her family environment, or in whose own best interests cannot be allowed to remain in that environment, shall be entitled to special protection and assistance provided by the State.

2. States Parties shall in accordance with their national laws ensure alternative care for such a child.

3. Such care could include, inter alia, foster placement, kafalah of Islamic law, adoption or if necessary placement in suitable institutions for the care of children. When considering solutions, due regard shall be paid to the desirability of continuity in a child's upbringing and to the child's ethnic, religious, cultural and linguistic background.

Article 21

States Parties that recognize and/or permit the system of adoption shall ensure that the best interests of the child shall be the paramount consideration and they shall:

(a) ensure that the adoption of a child is authorized only by competent authorities who determine, in accordance with applicable law and procedures and on the basis of all pertinent and reliable information, that the adoption is permissible in view of the child's status concerning parents, relatives and legal guardians and that, if required, the persons concerned have given their informed consent to the adoption on the basis of such counselling as may be necessary;

(b) recognize that inter-country adoption may be considered as an alternative means of child's care, if the child cannot be placed in a foster or an adoptive family or cannot in any suitable manner be cared for in the child's country of origin;

(c) ensure that the child concerned by inter-country adoption enjoys safeguards and standards equivalent to those existing in the case of national adoption;

(d) take all appropriate measures to ensure that, in inter-country adoption, the placement does not result in improper financial gain for those involved in it;

(e) promote, where appropriate, the objectives of the present article by concluding bilateral or multilateral arrangements or agreements, and endeavour, within this framework, to ensure that the placement of the child in another country is carried out by competent authorities or organs.

Article 22

1. States Parties shall take appropriate measures to ensure that a child who is seeking refugee status or who is considered a refugee in accordance with applicable international or domestic law and procedures shall, whether unaccompanied or accompanied by his or her parents or by any other person, receive appropriate protection and humanitarian assistance in the enjoyment of applicable rights set forth in the present Convention and in other international human rights or humanitarian instruments to which the said States are Parties.

2. For this purpose, States Parties shall provide, as they consider appropriate, co-operation in any efforts by the United Nations and other competent intergovernmental organizations or non-governmental organizations co-operating with the United Nations to protect and assist such a child and to trace the parents or other members of the family of any refugee child in order to obtain information necessary for reunification with his or her family. In cases where no parents or other members of the family can be found, the child shall be accorded the same protection as any other child permanently or temporarily deprived of his or her family environment for any reason, as set forth in the present Convention.

Article 23

1. States Parties recognize that a mentally or physically disabled child should enjoy a full and decent life, in conditions which ensure dignity, promote self-reliance and facilitate the child's active participation in the community.

2. States Parties recognize the right of the disabled child to special care and shall encourage and ensure the extension, subject to available resources, to the eligible child and those responsible for his or her care, of assistance for which application is made and which is appropriate to the child's condition and to the circumstances of the parents or others caring for the child.

3. Recognizing the special needs of a disabled child, assistance extended in accordance with paragraph 2 of the present article shall be provided free of charge, whenever possible, taking into account the financial resources of the parents or others caring for the child, and shall be designed to ensure that the disabled child has effective access to and receives education, training, health care services, rehabilitation services, preparation for employment and recreation opportunities in a manner conducive to the child's achieving the fullest possible social integration and individual development, including his or her cultural and spiritual development.

4. States Parties shall promote, in the spirit of international cooperation, the exchange of appropriate information in the field of preventive health care and of medical, psychological and functional treatment of disabled children, including dissemination of and access to information concerning methods of rehabilitation, education and vocational services, with the aim of enabling States Parties to improve their capabilities and skills and to widen their experience in these areas. In this regard, particular account shall be taken of the needs of developing countries.

Article 24

1. States Parties recognize the right of the child to the enjoyment of the highest attainable standard of health and to facilities for the treatment of illness and rehabilitation of health.

States Parties shall strive to ensure that no child is deprived of his or her right of access to such health care services.

2. States Parties shall pursue full implementation of this right and, in particular, shall take appropriate measures:
   (a) to diminish infant and child mortality;
   (b) to ensure the provision of necessary medical assistance and health care to all children with emphasis on the development of primary health care;
   (c) to combat disease and malnutrition, including within the framework of primary health care, through, inter alia, the application of readily available technology and through the provision of adequate nutritious foods and clean drinking-water, taking into consideration the dangers and risks of environmental pollution;
   (d) to ensure appropriate pre-natal and post-natal health care for mothers;
   (e) to ensure that all segments of society, in particular parents and children, are informed, have access to education and are supported in the use of basic knowledge of child health and nutrition, the advantages of breastfeeding, hygiene and environmental sanitation and the prevention of accidents;
   (f) to develop preventive health care, guidance for parents and family planning education and services.

3. States Parties shall take all effective and appropriate measures with a view to abolishing traditional practices prejudicial to the health of children.

4. States Parties undertake to promote and encourage international co-operation with a view to achieving progressively the full realization of the right recognized in the present article. In this regard, particular account shall be taken of the needs of developing countries.

Article 25

States Parties recognize the right of a child who has been placed by the competent authorities for the purposes of care, protection or treatment of his or her physical or mental health, to a periodic review of the treatment provided to the child and all other circumstances relevant to his or her placement.

Article 26

1. States Parties shall recognize for every child the right to benefit from social security, including social insurance, and shall take the necessary measures to achieve the full realization of this right in accordance with their national law.

2. The benefits should, where appropriate, be granted, taking into account the resources and the circumstances of the child and persons having responsibility for the maintenance of the child, as well as any other consideration relevant to an application for benefits made by or on behalf of the child.

Article 27

1. States Parties recognize the right of every child to a standard of living adequate for the child's physical, mental, spiritual, moral and social development.

2. The parent(s) or others responsible for the child have the primary responsibility to secure, within their abilities and financial capacities, the conditions of living necessary for the child's development.

3. States Parties, in accordance with national conditions and within their means, shall take appropriate measures to assist parents and others responsible for the child to implement this right and shall in case of need provide material assistance and support programmes, particularly with regard to nutrition, clothing and housing.

4. States Parties shall take all appropriate measures to secure the recovery of maintenance for the child from the parents or other persons having financial responsibility for the child, both within the State Party and from abroad. In particular, where the person having financial responsibility for the child lives in a State different from that of the child, States Parties shall promote the accession to international agreements or the conclusion of such agreements, as well as the making of other appropriate arrangements.

Article 28

1. States Parties recognize the right of the child to education, and with a view to achieving this right progressively and on the basis of equal opportunity, they shall, in particular:
   (a) make primary education compulsory and available free to all;
   (b) encourage the development of different forms of secondary education, including general and vocational education, make them available and accessible to every child, and take appropriate measures such as the introduction of free education and offering financial assistance in case of need;
   (c) make higher education accessible to all on the basis of capacity by every appropriate means;
   (d) make educational and vocational information and guidance available and accessible to all children;
   (e) take measures to encourage regular attendance at schools and the reduction of drop-out rates.

2. States Parties shall take all appropriate measures to ensure that school discipline is administered in a manner consistent with the child's human dignity and in conformity with the present Convention.

3. States Parties shall promote and encourage international cooperation in matters relating to education, in particular with a view to contributing to the elimination of ignorance and illiteracy throughout the world and facilitating access to scientific and technical knowledge and modern teaching methods. In this regard, particular account shall be taken of the needs of developing countries.

Article 29

1. States Parties agree that the education of the child shall be directed to:
   (a) the development of the child's personality, talents and mental and physical abilities to their fullest potential;
   (b) the development of respect for human rights and fundamental freedoms, and for the principles enshrined in the Charter of the United Nations;
   (c) the development of respect for the child's parents, his or her own cultural identity, language and values, for the national values of the country in which the child is living, the country from which he or she may originate, and for civilizations different from his or her own;
   (d) the preparation of the child for responsible life in a free society, in the spirit of understanding, peace, tolerance, equality of sexes, and friendship among all peoples, ethnic, national and religious groups and persons of indigenous origin;
   (e) the development of respect for the natural environment.

2. No part of the present article or article 28 shall be construed so as to interfere with the liberty of individuals and bodies to establish and direct educational institutions, subject always to the observance of the principle set forth in paragraph 1 of the present article and to the requirements that the education given in such institutions shall conform to such minimum standards as may be laid down by the State.

Article 30

In those States in which ethnic, religious or linguistic minorities or persons of indigenous origin exist, a child belonging to such a minority or who is indigenous shall not be denied the right, in community with other members of his or her group, to enjoy his or her own culture, to profess and practise his or her own religion, or to use his or her own language.

Article 31

1. States Parties recognize the right of the child to rest and leisure, to engage in play and recreational activities appropriate to the age of the child and to participate freely in cultural life and the arts.
2. States Parties shall respect and promote the right of the child to participate fully in cultural and artistic life and shall encourage the provision of appropriate and equal opportunities for cultural, artistic, recreational and leisure activity.

Article 32

1. States Parties recognize the right of the child to be protected from economic exploitation and from performing any work that is likely to be hazardous or to interfere with the child's education, or to be harmful to the child's health or physical, mental, spiritual, moral or social development.
2. States Parties shall take legislative, administrative, social and educational measures to ensure the implementation of the present article. To this end, and having regard to the relevant provisions of other international instruments, States Parties shall in particular:
   (a) provide for a minimum age or minimum ages for admission to employment;
   (b) provide for appropriate regulation of the hours and conditions of employment;
   (c) provide for appropriate penalties or other sanctions to ensure the effective enforcement of the present article.

Article 33

States Parties shall take all appropriate measures, including legislative, administrative, social and educational measures, to protect children from the illicit use of narcotic drugs and psychotropic substances as defined in the relevant international treaties, and to prevent the use of children in the illicit production and trafficking of such substances.

Article 34

States Parties undertake to protect the child from all forms of sexual exploitation and sexual abuse. For these purposes, States Parties shall in particular take all appropriate national, bilateral and multilateral measures to prevent:

(a) the inducement or coercion of a child to engage in any unlawful sexual activity;

(b) the exploitative use of children in prostitution or other unlawful sexual practices;

(c) the exploitative use of children in pornographic performances and materials.

Article 35

States Parties shall take all appropriate national, bilateral and multilateral measures to prevent the abduction of, the sale of or traffic in children for any purpose or in any form.

Article 36

States Parties shall protect the child against all other forms of exploitation prejudicial to any aspects of the child's welfare.

Article 37

States Parties shall ensure that:

(a) No child shall be subjected to torture or other cruel, inhuman or degrading treatment or punishment. Neither capital punishment nor life imprisonment without possibility of release shall be imposed for offences committed by persons below eighteen years of age.

(b) No child shall be deprived of his or her liberty unlawfully or arbitrarily. The arrest, detention or imprisonment of a child shall be in conformity with the law and shall be used only as a measure of last resort and for the shortest appropriate period of time.

(c) Every child deprived of liberty shall be treated with humanity and respect for the inherent dignity of the human person, and in a manner which takes into account the needs of persons of his or her age. In particular, every child deprived of liberty shall be separated from adults unless it is considered in the child's best interest not to do so and shall have the right to maintain contact with his or her family through correspondence and visits, save in exceptional circumstances.

(d) Every child deprived of his or her liberty shall have the right to prompt access to legal and other appropriate assistance, as well as the right to challenge the legality of the deprivation of his or her liberty before a court or other competent, independent and impartial authority, and to a prompt decision on any such action.

Appendix

These provisions of the Family Law Act 1996 are *not* in force.

Family Law Act 1996
(1996 c 27)

PART II DIVORCE AND SEPARATION

Court orders

2 DIVORCE AND SEPARATION

(1) The court may—
  (a) by making an order (to be known as a divorce order), dissolve a marriage; or
  (b) by making an order (to be known as a separation order), provide for the separation of the parties to a marriage.

(2) Any such order comes into force on being made.

(3) A separation order remains in force—
  (a) while the marriage continues; or
  (b) until cancelled by the court on the joint application of the parties.

3 CIRCUMSTANCES IN WHICH ORDERS ARE MADE

(1) If an application for a divorce order or for a separation order is made to the court under this section by one or both of the parties to a marriage, the court shall make the order applied for if (but only if)—
  (a) the marriage has broken down irretrievably;
  (b) the requirements of section 8 about information meetings are satisfied;
  (c) the requirements of section 9 about the parties' arrangements for the future are satisfied; and
  (d) the application has not been withdrawn.

(2) A divorce order may not be made if an order preventing divorce is in force under section 10.

(3) If the court is considering an application for a divorce order and an application for a separation order in respect of the same marriage it shall proceed as if it were considering only the application for a divorce order unless—
  (a) an order preventing divorce is in force with respect to the marriage;
  (b) the court makes an order preventing divorce; or
  (c) section 7(6) or (13) applies.

4 CONVERSION OF SEPARATION ORDER INTO DIVORCE ORDER

(1) A separation order which is made before the second anniversary of the marriage may not be converted into a divorce order under this section until after that anniversary.

(2) A separation order may not be converted into a divorce order under this section at any time while—
(a) an order preventing divorce is in force under section 10; or
(b) subsection (4) applies.

(3) Otherwise, if a separation order is in force and an application for a divorce order—
(a) is made under this section by either or both of the parties to the marriage, and
(b) is not withdrawn, the court shall grant the application once the requirements of section 11 have been satisfied.

(4) Subject to subsection (5), this subsection applies if—
(a) there is a child of the family who is under the age of sixteen when the application under this section is made; or
(b) the application under this section is made by one party and the other party applies to the court, before the end of such period as may be prescribed by rules of court, for time for further reflection.

(5) Subsection (4)—
(a) does not apply if, at the time when the application under this section is made, there is an occupation order or a non-molestation order in force in favour of the applicant, or of a child of the family, made against the other party;
(b) does not apply if the court is satisfied that delaying the making of a divorce order would be significantly detrimental to the welfare of any child of the family;
(c) ceases to apply—
(i) at the end of the period of six months beginning with the end of the period for reflection and consideration by reference to which the separation order was made; or
(ii) if earlier, on there ceasing to be any children of the family to whom subsection (4)(a) applied.

Marital breakdown

5 MARITAL BREAKDOWN

(1) A marriage is to be taken to have broken down irretrievably if (but only if)—
(a) a statement has been made by one (or both) of the parties that the maker of the statement (or each of them) believes that the marriage has broken down;
(b) the statement complies with the requirements of section 6;
(c) the period for reflection and consideration fixed by section 7 has ended; and
(d) the application under section 3 is accompanied by a declaration by the party making the application that—
(i) having reflected on the breakdown, and
(ii) having considered the requirements of this Part as to the parties' arrangements for the future,
the applicant believes that the marriage cannot be saved.

(2) The statement and the application under section 3 do not have to be made by the same party.

(3) An application may not be made under section 3 by reference to a particular statement if—

(a) the parties have jointly given notice (in accordance with rules of court) withdrawing the statement; or
(b) a period of one year ("the specified period") has passed since the end of the period for reflection and consideration.

(4) Any period during which an order preventing divorce is in force is not to count towards the specified period mentioned in subsection (3)(b).

(5) Subsection (6) applies if, before the end of the specified period, the parties jointly give notice to the court that they are attempting reconciliation but require additional time.

(6) The specified period—
(a) stops running on the day on which the notice is received by the court; but
(b) resumes running on the day on which either of the parties gives notice to the court that the attempted reconciliation has been unsuccessful.

(7) If the specified period is interrupted by a continuous period of more than 18 months, any application by either of the parties for a divorce order or for a separation order must be by reference to a new statement received by the court at any time after the end of the 18 months.

(8) The Lord Chancellor may by order amend subsection (3)(b) by varying the specified period.

6 STATEMENT OF MARITAL BREAKDOWN

(1) A statement under section 5(1)(a) is to be known as a statement of marital breakdown;

but in this Part it is generally referred to as "a statement".

(2) If a statement is made by one party it must also state that that party—
(a) is aware of the purpose of the period for reflection and consideration as described in section 7; and
(b) wishes to make arrangements for the future.

(3) If a statement is made by both parties it must also state that each of them—
(a) is aware of the purpose of the period for reflection and consideration as described in section 7; and
(b) wishes to make arrangements for the future.

(4) A statement must be given to the court in accordance with the requirements of rules made under section 12.

(5) A statement must also satisfy any other requirements imposed by rules made under that section.

(6) A statement made at a time when the circumstances of the case include any of those mentioned in subsection (7) is ineffective for the purposes of this Part.

(7) The circumstances are—
(a) that a statement has previously been made with respect to the marriage and it is, or will become, possible—
(i) for an application for a divorce order, or
(ii) for an application for a separation order,
to be made by reference to the previous statement;
(b) that such an application has been made in relation to the marriage and has not been withdrawn;
(c) that a separation order is in force.

Reflection and consideration

7 PERIOD FOR REFLECTION AND CONSIDERATION

(1) Where a statement has been made, a period for the parties—
(a) to reflect on whether the marriage can be saved and to have an opportunity to effect a reconciliation, and
(b) to consider what arrangements should be made for the future,
must pass before an application for a divorce order or for a separation order may be made by reference to that statement.

(2) That period is to be known as the period for reflection and consideration.

(3) The period for reflection and consideration is nine months beginning with the fourteenth day after the day on which the statement is received by the court.

(4) Where—
(a) the statement has been made by one party,
(b) rules made under section 12 require the court to serve a copy of the statement on the other party, and
(c) failure to comply with the rules causes inordinate delay in service,
the court may, on the application of that other party, extend the period for reflection and consideration.

(5) An extension under subsection (4) may be for any period not exceeding the time between—
(a) the beginning of the period for reflection and consideration; and
(b) the time when service is effected.

(6) A statement which is made before the first anniversary of the marriage to which it relates is ineffective for the purposes of any application for a divorce order.

(7) Subsection (8) applies if, at any time during the period for reflection and consideration, the parties jointly give notice to the court that they are attempting a reconciliation but require additional time.

(8) The period for reflection and consideration—
(a) stops running on the day on which the notice is received by the court; but
(b) resumes running on the day on which either of the parties gives notice to the court that the attempted reconciliation has been unsuccessful.

(9) If the period for reflection and consideration is interrupted under subsection (8) by a continuous period of more than 18 months, any application by either of the parties for a divorce order or for a separation order must be by reference to a new statement received by the court at any time after the end of the 18 months.

(10) Where an application for a divorce order is made by one party, subsection (13) applies if—
(a) the other party applies to the court, within the prescribed period, for time for further reflection; and
(b) the requirements of section 9 (except any imposed under section 9(3)) are satisfied.

(11) Where any application for a divorce order is made, subsection (13) also applies if there is a child of the family who is under the age of sixteen when the application is made.

(12) Subsection (13) does not apply if—
(a) at the time when the application for a divorce order is made, there is an occupation order or a non-molestation order in force in favour of the applicant, or of a child of the family, made against the other party; or

(b) the court is satisfied that delaying the making of a divorce order would be significantly detrimental to the welfare of any child of the family.

(13) If this subsection applies, the period for reflection and consideration is extended by a period of six months, but—
(a) only in relation to the application for a divorce order in respect of which the application under subsection (10) was made; and
(b) without invalidating that application for a divorce order.

(14) A period for reflection and consideration which is extended under subsection (13), and which has not otherwise come to an end, comes to an end on there ceasing to be any children of the family to whom subsection (11) applied.

8 ATTENDANCE AT INFORMATION MEETINGS

(1) The requirements about information meetings are as follows.

(2) A party making a statement must (except in prescribed circumstances) have attended an information meeting not less than three months before making the statement.

(3) Different information meetings must be arranged with respect to different marriages.

(4) In the case of a statement made by both parties, the parties may attend separate meetings or the same meeting.

(5) Where one party has made a statement, the other party must (except in prescribed circumstances) attend an information meeting before—
(a) making any application to the court—
(i) with respect to a child of the family; or
(ii) of a prescribed description relating to property or financial matters; or
(b) contesting any such application.

(6) In this section "information meeting" means a meeting organised, in accordance with prescribed provisions for the purpose—
(a) of providing, in accordance with prescribed provisions, relevant information to the party or parties attending about matters which may arise in connection with the provisions of, or made under, this Part or Part III; and
(b) of giving the party or parties attending the information meeting the opportunity of having a meeting with a marriage counsellor and of encouraging that party or those parties to attend that meeting.

(7) An information meeting must be conducted by a person who—
(a) is qualified and appointed in accordance with prescribed provisions; and
(b) will have no financial or other interest in any marital proceedings between the parties.

(8) Regulations made under this section may, in particular, make provision—
(a) about the places and times at which information meetings are to be held;
(b) for written information to be given to persons attending them;
(c) for the giving of information to parties (otherwise than at information meetings) in cases in which the requirement to attend such meetings does not apply;
(d) for information of a prescribed kind to be given only with the approval of the Lord Chancellor or only by a person or by persons approved by him; and
(e) for information to be given, in prescribed circumstances, only with the approval of the Lord Chancellor or only by a person, or by persons, approved by him.

(9) Regulations made under subsection (6) must, in particular, make provision with respect to the giving of information about—

(a) marriage counselling and other marriage support services;
(b) the importance to be attached to the welfare, wishes and feelings of children;
(c) how the parties may acquire a better understanding of the ways in which children can be helped to cope with the breakdown of a marriage;
(d) the nature of the financial questions that may arise on divorce or separation, and services which are available to help the parties;
(e) protection available against violence, and how to obtain support and assistance;
(f) mediation;
(g) the availability to each of the parties of independent legal advice and representation;
(h) the availability of services funded by the Legal Services Commission as part of the Community Legal Service, and where parties can get advice about obtaining such services;
(i) the divorce and separation process.

(10) Before making any regulations under subsection (6), the Lord Chancellor must consult such persons concerned with the provision of relevant information as he considers appropriate.

(11) A meeting with a marriage counsellor arranged under this section—
(a) must be held in accordance with prescribed provisions; and
(b) must be with a person qualified and appointed in accordance with prescribed provisions.

(12) A person who would not be required to make any contribution towards mediation funded for him by the Legal Services Commission as part of the Community Legal Service shall not be required to make any contribution towards the cost of a meeting with a marriage counsellor arranged for him under this section.

(13) In this section "prescribed" means prescribed by regulations made by the Lord Chancellor.

9 ARRANGEMENTS FOR THE FUTURE

(1) The requirements as to the parties' arrangements for the future are as follows.

(2) One of the following must be produced to the court—
(a) a court order (made by consent or otherwise) dealing with their financial arrangements;
(b) a negotiated agreement as to their financial arrangements;
(c) a declaration by both parties that they have made their financial arrangements;
(d) a declaration by one of the parties (to which no objection has been notified to the court by the other party) that—
(i) he has no significant assets and does not intend to make an application for financial provision;
(ii) he believes that the other party has no significant assets and does not intend to make an application for financial provision; and
(iii) there are therefore no financial arrangements to be made.

(5) The requirements of section 11 must have been satisfied.

(6) Schedule 1 supplements the provisions of this section.

(7) If the court is satisfied, on an application made by one of the parties after the end of the period for reflection and consideration, that the circumstances of the case are—
(a) those set out in paragraph 1 of Schedule 1,
(b) those set out in paragraph 2 of that Schedule,
(c) those set out in paragraph 3 of that Schedule, or

(d) those set out in paragraph 4 of that Schedule,
it may make a divorce order or a separation order even though the requirements of subsection (2) have not been satisfied.

Orders preventing divorce

10 HARDSHIP: ORDERS PREVENTING DIVORCE

(1) If an application for a divorce order has been made by one of the parties to a marriage, the court may, on the application of the other party, order that the marriage is not to be dissolved.

(2) Such an order (an "order preventing divorce") may be made only if the court is satisfied—
(a) that dissolution of the marriage would result in substantial financial or other hardship to the other party or to a child of the family; and
(b) that it would be wrong, in all the circumstances (including the conduct of the parties and the interests of any child of the family), for the marriage to be dissolved.

(3) If an application for the cancellation of an order preventing divorce is made by one or both of the parties, the court shall cancel the order unless it is still satisfied—
(a) that dissolution of the marriage would result in substantial financial or other hardship to the party in whose favour the order was made or to a child of the family; and
(b) that it would be wrong, in all the circumstances (including the conduct of the parties and the interests of any child of the family), for the marriage to be dissolved.

(4) If an order preventing a divorce is cancelled, the court may make a divorce order in respect of the marriage only if an application is made under section 3 or 4(3) after the cancellation.

(5) An order preventing divorce may include conditions which must be satisfied before an application for cancellation may be made under subsection (3).

(6) In this section "hardship" includes the loss of a chance to obtain a future benefit (as well as the loss of an existing benefit).

Welfare of children

11 WELFARE OF CHILDREN

(1) In any proceedings for a divorce order or a separation order, the court shall consider—
(a) whether there are any children of the family to whom this section applies; and
(b) where there are any such children, whether (in the light of the arrangements which have been, or are proposed to be, made for their upbringing and welfare) it should exercise any of its powers under the Children Act 1989 with respect to any of them.

(2) Where, in any case to which this section applies, it appears to the court that—
(a) the circumstances of the case require it, or are likely to require it, to exercise any of its powers under the Children Act 1989 with respect to any such child,
(b) it is not in a position to exercise the power, or (as the case may be) those powers, without giving further consideration to the case, and
(c) there are exceptional circumstances which make it desirable in the interests of the child that the court should give a direction under this section,
it may direct that the divorce order or separation order is not to be made until the court orders otherwise.

(3) In deciding whether the circumstances are as mentioned in subsection (2)(a), the court shall treat the welfare of the child as paramount.

(4) In making that decision, the court shall also have particular regard, on the evidence before it, to—
 (a) the wishes and feelings of the child considered in the light of his age and understanding and the circumstances in which those wishes were expressed;
 (b) the conduct of the parties in relation to the upbringing of the child;
 (c) the general principle that, in the absence of evidence to the contrary, the welfare of the child will be best served by—
  (i) his having regular contact with those who have parental responsibility for him and with other members of his family; and
  (ii) the maintenance of as good a continuing relationship with his parents as is possible; and
 (d) any risk to the child attributable to—
  (i) where the person with whom the child will reside is living or proposes to live;
  (ii) any person with whom that person is living or with whom he proposes to live; or
  (iii) any other arrangements for his care and upbringing.

(5) This section applies to—
 (a) any child of the family who has not reached the age of sixteen at the date when the court considers the case in accordance with the requirements of this section; and
 (b) any child of the family who has reached that age at that date and in relation to whom the court directs that this section shall apply.

Resolution of disputes

13 DIRECTIONS WITH RESPECT TO MEDIATION

(1) After the court has received a statement, it may give a direction requiring each party to attend a meeting arranged in accordance with the direction for the purpose—
 (a) of enabling an explanation to be given of the facilities available to the parties for mediation in relation to disputes between them; and
 (b) of providing an opportunity for each party to agree to take advantage of those facilities.

(2) A direction may be given at any time, including in the course of proceedings connected with the breakdown of the marriage (as to which see section 25).

(3) A direction may be given on the application of either of the parties or on the initiative of the court.

(4) The parties are to be required to attend the same meeting unless—
 (a) one of them asks, or both of them ask, for separate meetings; or
 (b) the court considers separate meetings to be more appropriate.

(5) A direction shall—
 (a) specify a person chosen by the court (with that person's agreement) to arrange and conduct the meeting or meetings; and
 (b) require such person as may be specified in the direction to produce to the court, at such time as the court may direct, a report stating—
  (i) whether the parties have complied with the direction; and
  (ii) if they have, whether they have agreed to take part in any mediation.

SCHEDULE 1 ARRANGEMENTS FOR THE FUTURE

The first exemption

1 The circumstances referred to in section 9(7)(a) are that—
(a) the requirements of section 11 have been satisfied;
(b) the applicant has, during the period for reflection and consideration, taken such steps as are reasonably practicable to try to reach agreement about the parties' financial arrangements; and
(c) the applicant has made an application to the court for financial relief and has complied with all requirements of the court in relation to proceedings for financial relief but—
(i) the other party has delayed in complying with requirements of the court or has otherwise been obstructive; or
(ii) for reasons which are beyond the control of the applicant, or of the other party, the court has been prevented from obtaining the information
which it requires to determine the financial position of the parties.

The second exemption

2 The circumstances referred to in section 9(7)(b) are that—
(a) the requirements of section 11 have been satisfied;
(b) the applicant has, during the period for reflection and consideration, taken such steps as are reasonably practicable to try to reach agreement about the parties' financial arrangements;
(c) because of—
(i) the ill health or disability of the applicant, the other party or a child of the family (whether physical or mental), or
(ii) an injury suffered by the applicant, the other party or a child of the family,
the applicant has not been able to reach agreement with the other party about those arrangements and is unlikely to be able to do so in the foreseeable future; and
(d) a delay in making the order applied for under section 3—
(i) would be significantly detrimental to the welfare of any child of the family; or
(ii) would be seriously prejudicial to the applicant.

The third exemption

3 The circumstances referred to in section 9(7)(c) are that—
(a) the requirements of section 11 have been satisfied;
(b) the applicant has found it impossible to contact the other party; and
(c) as a result, it has been impossible for the applicant to reach agreement with the other party about their financial arrangements.

The fourth exemption

4 The circumstances referred to in section 9(7)(d) are that—
(a) the requirements of section 11 have been satisfied;
(b) an occupation order or a non-molestation order is in force in favour of the applicant or a child of the family, made against the other party;
(c) the applicant has, during the period for reflection and consideration, taken such steps as are reasonably practicable to try to reach agreement about the parties' financial arrangements;
(d) the applicant has not been able to reach agreement with the other party about those arrangements and is unlikely to be able to do so in the foreseeable future; and
(e) a delay in making the order applied for under section 3—
(i) would be significantly detrimental to the welfare of any child of the family; or
(ii) would be seriously prejudicial to the applicant.

Thematic Index